1 MONTH OF FREE READING

at

www.ForgottenBooks.com

By purchasing this book you are eligible for one month membership to ForgottenBooks.com, giving you unlimited access to our entire collection of over 1,000,000 titles via our web site and mobile apps.

To claim your free month visit:
www.forgottenbooks.com/free846899

* Offer is valid for 45 days from date of purchase. Terms and conditions apply.

ISBN 978-0-266-52543-1
PIBN 10846899

This book is a reproduction of an important historical work. Forgotten Books uses
state-of-the-art technology to digitally reconstruct the work, preserving the original format
whilst repairing imperfections present in the aged copy. In rare cases, an imperfection in
the original, such as a blemish or missing page, may be replicated in our edition. We do,
however, repair the vast majority of imperfections successfully; any imperfections that
remain are intentionally left to preserve the state of such historical works.

Forgotten Books is a registered trademark of FB &c Ltd.
Copyright © 2018 FB &c Ltd.
FB &c Ltd, Dalton House, 60 Windsor Avenue, London, SW19 2RR.
Company number 08720141. Registered in England and Wales.

For support please visit www.forgottenbooks.com

ANNALS OF ULSTER,

OTHERWISE,

αηηαλα seηαιτ,

ANNALS OF SENAT;

A CHRONICLE OF IRISH AFFAIRS

A.D. 431–1131 : 1155–1541.

VOL. II.
A.D. 1057–1131: 1155–1378.

EDITED, WITH TRANSLATION AND NOTES,

By

B. MAC CARTHY, D.D., M.R.I.A.

PUBLISHED BY THE AUTHORITY OF THE LORDS COMMISSIONERS OF HER MAJESTY'S
TREASURY, UNDER THE DIRECTION OF THE COUNCIL OF THE
ROYAL IRISH ACADEMY.

DUBLIN:

PRINTED FOR HER MAJESTY'S STATIONERY OFFICE,
BY ALEX. THOM & CO. (Limited), 87, 88 & 89, ABBEY-STREET.
THE QUEEN'S PRINTING OFFICE.

And to be purchased, either directly or through any Bookseller, from
HODGES, FIGGIS & Co., 104, Grafton Street, Dublin ; or
EYRE & SPOTTISWOODE, East Harding Street, Fleet Street, E.C.; or
ADAM and CHARLES BLACK, 6, North Bridge, Edinburgh.

1893.

Price 10s.

CONTENTS.

Pages

CORRIGENDA AND ADDENDA.

P. 27, note 2, l. 4, *for* period *read* or period.
,, 28, l. 14, ,, Cenann ṗa *read* Cenannṗa.
,, 32, n. 3, l. 1, ,, *Chiarains* ,, *Chiarain.*
,, 37, l. 10, ,, out of ,, for.
,, 40, ,, ,, Fiaċn aUa ,, Fiaċna Ua.
,, 90, l. 26 ,, oċ ,, oe.
,, 102, ,, 27, ,, xxx. ,, xx.
,, 108, n. 1, l. 6, ,, *uii. mogha* ,, *uiii. mogha.*
,, 116, l. 17, ,, aċuicim ,, a ċuicim.
,, n. 2, ll. 3-6, the error is corrected in Vol. II. of the *A.L.C.*
,, 127, l. 4, *dele* ².
,, 128, ,, 10, *for* ṗoėimleḋ *read* ṗoėimleḋ.
,, 129, ,, 32, ,, nnaebli ,, lainn the.
,, 132, ,, 1, ,, pangaṫup ,, pangaṫup.
,, 133, ,, ,, reach ,, reached.
,, 138, l. 23, ,, bpeġ ,, bpeġ.
,, 140, ,, 17, ,, ḋaiḃ impaiḃ *read* ḋaiḃᵈ impaiḃᵈ.
,, 158, ,, 27, ,, of a ,, of ı.
,, 170, ,, 23, ,, Ḋomnall ,, Ḋomnallⁿ.
,, 172, ,, 2, ,, roon ,, roonᵇ.
,, 175, ,, 7, ,, rested ,, rested [peaceful]ly.
,, 230, ,, 25, ,, ṫáinic³ ,, ṫáinic⁹.
,, 232, ,, 6, ,, cpeiċhi pın ,, cpeiċ bıpın.
,, 234, ,, 20, ,, Ṫuaıpċepṫ ,, Ṫuaıpċepṫ.
,, 243, ,, 1, ,, encolsure ,, enclosure.
,, 259, col. 2, l. 11, *dele* seems to have.
,, 265, ll. 7, 8, *for* Muircertagh *read* Muircertach.
,, 273, l. 10, *after* in *insert* the land of.
,, 279, ,, 15, *for* foreign countries *read* neighbouring territories.
,, 290, ,, 16, *dele* B 61a.
,, 298, ,, 12, *for* Loċlann *read* Laċlann.
,, 305, ,, 12, } *for* raised *read* elected.
,, ,, n. 4, l. 1,}
,, 306, l. 18, *for* hUa² *read* hUa¹.
,, 308, ,, 3, *add* ¹ *to* Ruaıġpı.
,, 312, ,, 20, *for* Ḋonċaḋ *read* Ḋonnċaḋ.
,, 322, col. 2, l. 6, *dele* the ref. no.
,, 332, l. 7, *for* Cıapaıḋe *read* Cıapaıḋe.
,, ,, 25, *prefix* ᴄᴄ *to* In.
,, 353, ,, 4,} *for* driving *read* pursuing.
,, 387, ,, 29,}
,, 377, ,, 26, ,, the direction *read* an attack.
,, ,, ,, assumed ,, undertaken.
,, 380, l. 12, ,, beċ ,, beċ ı.
,, 383, ,, 5, *dele* a.
,, ,, 6, *for* foray *read* forays.

CORRIGENDA AND ADDENDA.

P. 387, l. 23, *for* forces *read* moveables.
,, 388, ,, 3, ,, Iaɼ ,, Iɼa.
,, 392, ,, 20, ,, muinnceɼ *read* muin[n]ceɼ.
,, 414, ,, 19, ,, Cliono— ,, Cloino—.
,, 418, ,, 17, ,, tabaiɼ taɼ ,, tabaiɼt aɼ.
,, 428, ,, 10, ,, aili ,, ailib.
,, 432, ,, 3, ,, Catalim ,, Catal im.
,, 443, ,, 25, ,, Gaidhel ,, Foreigner.
,, 445, n. 6, l. 2, *for* *timpanist* *read* *timpanists*.
,, 453, ,, 3, *insert* by — Mandeville *after* do Burgh.
,, 456, l. 18, *for* Cancobuɼ *read* Concobuɼ.
,, 458, ,, 24, ,, Uɼóɼ ,, Uɼóiɼ.
,, 461, ,, 12, ,, Foreigner ,, Gaidhel.
,, 466, ,, 25, ,, Uɼóiɼ ,, Uɼóɼ.
,, 479, ,, 11, ,, pledge of ,, prize over (*lit.* of).
,, 480, ,, 18, ,, Ocuc ,, Ocuɼ.
,, 483, ,, 3, ,, passed ,, reached [his end].
,, 485, ,, 16, ,, dispersing ,, despoiling.
     Add Note: Lit. *relative to moveables*; i.e. a defeat in which what the vanquished were driving off fell to the victors.
,, 486, l. 9, *for*, mac *read* Mac.
,, ,, 22, ,, Muinnciɼ *read* Muin[n]ciɼ.
,, 487, ,, 8, *dele*, son of.
,, 507, ,, 14, *for* apple *read* wild apple.
,, 508, ,, 22, ,, Ƅɼiain, mic, *read* Ƅɼiain Mic.
,, ,, 36, *dele* Iom., B.
,, 509, ,, 25, *for* son—Tawny *read* Mac-Ui Neill-buidhe.
,, 516, ,, 13, *dele* ref. no. ².
,, 518, n. 4, l. 2, *for* from *read* form.
,, 522, l. 14, ,, ɔo ,, ɔoa.
,, ,, 25, ,, ɼɼ ,, ɼ.
,, ,, 27, ,, —Ɛaɼaić *read* —eaɼaić.
,, 525, ,, 28, ,, him ,, them.
,, 526, ,, 10, ,, Clainn— ,, Clainn—.
,, 527, ,, 1, *after* slain *insert* and [other] persons were slain.
,, 529, ,, 15, *for* with *read* by.
,, ,, 21, ,, movement *read* jeopardy.
,, 546, ,, 3, ,, maɼb ,, maɼb ɔo.
,, 548, ,, ,, Ɗalacuin ,, Ɗalacun.
,, 552, ,, 10, ,, ɔo oman ,, o ɔoman.
,, 554, ,, 12, ,, Ƅaile-ata-na-ɼiġ *read* baile Ⱥta-na-ɼiġ.
,, 555, ,, 16, ,, prowess ,, championship.
,, ,, 17, ,, benevolence ,, prowess.
,, 561, ,, 16, ,, Eerghal ,, Ferghal.
,, 562, ,, 30, ,, —uile ,, —Ⱦauile.
,, 564, ,, 6, ,, moɼtuuɼ ,, moɼtua.

annala uladh.

ANNALS OF ULSTER;

OTHERWISE,

annala senait,

ANNALS OF SENAT.

annala uladh.

(A 44d; B 41c)

Kal. Ian. iiii. f., l. xxi., Anno Domini M.° L.° uiii.° Niall hUa hEicneca[i]n, ri Ceniuil-Endai, a ruir occ|*irur¹ ert.—Dungal hUa Donncada, ri Eoganacta Cairil, do tuitim la Murcad, mac m-briain, cum multir.—Finnguine hUa Finnguine, ridomna Muman, do tuitim la Mael-Seclainn hUaᵃ m-bric.—Ecmarcac, mac Cernaig, aircinnec Duin-Let-glairre, do dul dia ailieri.—Maidm ria Ruaidri hUa Ruadaca[i]n co n-Airrferaid, for Gilla-Crirt hUa Faelcon 7 for Uib-Eacac.—Mael-ruanaid hUa Focarta, ri Deirce[i]rt Eile, do tuitim la Donncad, mac briain.—Muirceartac hUaᵇ Tregaic, ri hUa-m-barce, mortuur² ert.—Dubdalete hUa Cinaeda, aircinnec Corcaige 7 Robartac, mac Fer-domnaig, comarba Coluim-cille, in Domino dormi-erunt.—Domnall hUa Ruairc do marbad la Domnall, mac Maelruanaig, ri Fer-Manac.

* | denotes commencement of MS. column.

[Contractions: t. m., top margin; f. m., foot margin; r. m., right margin; l. m., left margin; c. m., centre margin; itl., interlined; t. h. (written by) text hand; n. t. h., not (written by) text hand.]

A.D. 1057. ¹ Occirrur, B. ² mortur, B.—ᵃ mac—*son*, B. ᵇ m[ac], but a dot is placed underneath, to signify deletion and h[Ua] placed on c. m., B.

1057. ¹ [*Donnchadh*].—All the MSS., followed by the *Annals of Loch Ce* (ad an.), have *Murchadh*. To correspond therewith, *son* must be changed into *grandson*; as Murchadh was slain in the battle of Clontarf, but Donchadh had a son named Murchadh. As this was apparently a general engagement, it seems more probable that the mistake of the transcription took place in the proper name. The *Four Masters* solve the difficulty by omitting this portion of the entry. O'Conor saw nothing that required correction.

² *Royal-heir.*—Literally *royal material* (*regia materies*), signifying heir apparent.

ANNALS OF ULSTER.

KALENDS of Jan. on 4th feria, 21st of the moon, A.D. 1057. Niall Ua hEicnechain, King of Cenel-Endai, was slain by his own [kinsmen].—Dungal Ua Donnchadha, King of the Eoganacht of Cashel, fell by Murchadh [Donnchadh][1], son of Brian [Boruma], along with many others.—Finnguine Ua Finnguine, royal heir[2] of Munster, fell by Mael-Sechlainn[3] Ua[4] Bric.—Echmarcach, son of Cernach, herenagh[5] of Dun-leth-glais, went on his pilgrimage[6].—A defeat [was inflicted] by Ruaidhri Ua Ruadhacain with the Airrthir upon Gilla-Crist Ua Faelchon and upon the Ui-Eachach.—Maelruanaidh Ua Focarta, king of the South of Eili, fell by Donnchad, son of Brian [Boruma].—Muircertach Ua Tresaich, king of Ui-Barrce, died.—Dubdalethe Ua Cinaedha, herenagh of Cork and Robartach[7], son of Ferdomnach, successor of [St.] Colum-cille, slept in the Lord.—Domnall Ua Ruairc was killed by Domnall, son of Maelruanaigh, king of Fir-Manach.

[1057]

---

[3] *Mael-Sechlainn. Devotee (lit. tonsured) of (St.) Sechlann* (or Sechnall), disciple of St. Patrick. By omission of the infected *s*, the name was Maelechlainn (Melaghlin); which, in turn, in disregard of the origin, became Malachias and Malachy. See Vol. I., p. 8.

[4] *Ua.*—The reading of B (*son*) is also found in the *Annals of Loch Ce* (*ad an.*) But *Ua* (*grandson*), the lection of A, is given in both of them at the year 1059, where the killing of Mael-Sechlainn is entered. C follows A.

[5] *Herenagh.*—For the explanation of this term, see O'Donovan, *Four Masters,* iii., p. 47 sq.

[6] *Went on his pilgrimage.*—That is, either over sea; or, more probably, to another native establishment (perhaps Armagh; cf. 1003[=1004], 1037, *supra*, 1063, *infra*), to end his life in penitential exercises.

[7] *Robartach.*—Abbot of Kells, which at that time (*Adamnan*, p. 399) was apparently the official seat of the successor of St. Columba. He succeeded Mael-Muire, A.D. 1040 (*supra*). Dr. Reeves suggests (*loc. cit.*) that he was son of Ferdomnach, who died 1007 (=1008), *supra*.

4 annala ulaoh.

Kal. Ian. u. p., l. 11., Anno Domini M.° L.° uiii.
Imbleaċ-ibair do lorcaḋ co leir, iter daimliac 7 cloicteċ.—Lulaċ, mac Gilla-Comgain, airdriġ Alban, do marbaḋ la Mael-Coluim, mac Donnċaḋa, i caṫ.—Maidm Sleiḃe-Crot ria n-Diarmait, mac Mail-na-mbó, for Donncaḋ, mac Briain, i torċair Cairbri hUa Ligdai, aircinneċ Imleċa-ibair, 7 Rigbardan, mac Concoirne, ri Ele et alii multi.—Gallbrat hUa Cerbaill, ridomna Teṁraċ, mortuur[1] ert.—Colman hUa hAireċtaiġ, comarba Comgaill; hUa Flanncua, aircinneċ Imleaċa-ibair, in pace quieuerunt.—Mac-beaṫaḋ, mac Finnlaiċ, airdriġ Alban, do marbaḋ la Mael-Coluim,[2] mac Donnċaḋa, i caṫ.

Kal. Ian. 111. p., l. x. 111., Anno Domini M.° L.° ix.° Creċ la Mael-Seċlainn hUa Motaḋa[i]n i n-Airteraiḃ, co ruc tri cet[a] bo, uel paulo plur 7 co romarḃ Gilla-Muire Mac Aireċtaiġ, muire
B 42a Clainne-Sinaiġ.—Mael-Seċlainn | hUa Buic do muċaḋ i n-uaim la Mael-Seċlainn hUa Faelain.—Aeḋ hUa Dubdai, ri hUa-n-Amalgaḋa, a ruir occirur[b] ert.—
A 45a Creċ la | hArdgar Mac Loċlainn co Ceniul-Eogain i n-Dal-Araiḋe, co tucrat boroma mor 7 da cet[a] duine

A.D. 1058. 1 Mortur, B. 2 Mael-Seċlainn, A. This is erroneous. It was probably an oversight.

A.D. 1059. a .c., A, B. The Roman notation is regularly employed in the MSS. b occirrur, B.

1058. 1 *Both.*—Literally *between*.
2 *Gilla-Comgain.*—"Gillie" (*servant*; employed in the secondary sense of *devotee* as a proper name) of St. Comgan of Kilchoan, in Scotland (Reeves, *Adamnan*, p. 420). This is, perhaps, the Comgan, whose commemoration in the Martyrology of Tallaght adds another to the instances of the designation *Cele-De: III. Id.* [Oct. Oct. 13]. *Comgani, Cele De* (L.L. [Book of Leinster], Lith. ed., p. 363 h).
3 *Successor of* [*St.*] *Comgall.*—That is, abbot of Bangor, co. Down.
4 *Mac-Beathadh.*—The sequence of

Kalends of Jan. on 5th feria, 2nd of the moon, A.D. [1058] 1058. Imblech-ibair was burned entirely, both[1] stone church and steeple.—Lulach, son of Gilla-Comgain,[2] arch-king of Scotland, was killed by Mael-Coluim, son of Donn-chadh, in battle.—The defeat of Sliabh-Crot [was inflicted] by Diarmait, son of Mail-na-mbo, upon Donn-chadh, son of Brian [Boruma], wherein fell Cairbri Ua Ligdai, herenagh of Imblech-ibair, and Righbardan, son of Cucoirne, king of Eili, and many others.— Gallbrat Ua Cerbaill, royal heir of Tara, died.—Colman Ua hAirechtaigh, successor of [St.] Comgall[3]; Ua Flanncua, herenagh of Imblech-ibair, slept in peace.—Mac-Beathadh,[4] son of Finnlaech, arch-king of Scotland, was killed by Mael-Coluim, son of Donnchadh, in battle.

Kalends of Jan. on 6th feria, 13th of the moon, A.D. [1059] 1059. A foray by Mael-Sechlainn Ua Motadhain into the Airthir, so that he took away 300 cows, or a little more, and killed Gilla-Muire Mac Airechtaigh, steward of Clann-Sinaigh.—Mael-Sechlaimn Ua Bric was smothered in a cave by Mael-Sechlainn Ua Faelain.—Aedh Ua Dubdai, king of Ui-Amalgadha, was slain by his own [kinsmen].—A foray by Ardgar Mac Lochlainn along with[1] the Cenel-Eogain into Dal-Araidhe, so that they took away great cattle-spoil, and 200 persons were either killed or

---

the items respecting Lulach and Mac-Beathadh (the Macbeth of Shakespeare) should be reversed. Marianus Scotus, who had his information from a pilgrim that came straight from Scotland, writes in two autograph notes in his Chronicle (*ad an.* 1070 [=1058]): *Macfinlaeg occiditur in Augusto. Lulag successit et occiditur in Martio: cui Moel-Colmim successit . . . Macfinlaeg regnavit annis xvii., ad missam Sanctae Mariae. Lulach a nativitate Sanctae Mariae ad missam Sancti Patricii in mense Martio regnavit. Inde Moelcoluim regnavit annis xx., usque ad missam Sancti Patricii.*

1059. [1] *Along with.*—The original is *co* (with), which the *Four Masters* changed into *do* (of). O'Donovan, accordingly, has "[one] of the Cinel-Eoghain;" which a native annalist would deem it superfluous to apply to a king of that clan.

6 αnnαlα ulαδh.

eτep mαpbαδ 7 epξαbαil.—Cαtαl, mαc Tiξepnαin, pí Ιαptαιp Con[n]αct; Congαlαč hUα Rιαcαιn, pιδomnα Tempαč; Dυαpcαn hUα hEξpα[ι], pí Luιξne; ξillα-Coem-ξιn, mαc ξillα-Comξαιll, pιδomnα Lαιξen, occιpι[b] punτ.—ξillα-Domαngα[ι]pτ hUα Cončαιlle, pí hUα-Nιαllα[ι]n; Muιpeδαč hUα flαιnn, pι hUα-Tυιpτpe; Tomαlταč hUα Mαel-Ôpenαιnn, muιpe Sιl-Muιpeδαιč, mopτuι punτ.—Domnαll Mαc Eoδogα, αιpcιnneč Mαιnιpτpeč [Ôuιčι]; Eočαιδ hUα Cιnαeδα, αιpcιnneč Ατα-τpuιm; αneplιp Mαc Uιδιp, αιpcιnneč Lupcα; Conαιng hUα fαιpčeαllαιξ, αιpcιnneč Dpomα-leαčαn [mopτuι punτ].

Ôιp.[a] Kαl. Ιαn. uιι. f.,[b] L. xx. ιιιι., Αnno Domιnι M.° Lx.cc Cocαδ mop ι n-Αpδ-Mαčα eτep Cυmupcαč hUα n-Epoδα[ι]n 7 Dυbδαleιčι, comαpbα Pατpαιc, ιmon[1] αbδαιne.—Cenαnnup[2] δο lopcαδ δο leιp, co n-α δαιmlιαc.—Leιčξleαnn δο lopcαδ δο leιp, cenmoτα ιn [δ]epταč.—Domnαll Deιpeč, ppιm αnmcαpα Epenn 7 Conn nα m-boč Cluαnα-mαc-Noιp αδ Chpιpτum uocατι punτ:

Dα[d] blιαδαιn δec 'n-α τepcαιδ,
Coιc mιle cen δen epbαιδ—

[a] pιαδomnα, but with deletion mark under the first α, B. [b] occιppι, B.

A.D. 1060. [1] mon (i.e., aphæresis of ι), B. [2] Ceαnαnnup, B. [a] om., B. [b] f. is placed overhead, having been omitted at first, B. [c] Mιllιppιmo αc Lx. αnno Domιnιcαe Incαpnατιonιp inserted, t. h., B. [d-d] f. m., t. h., the place of insertion being indicated by marks prefixed, corresponding with marks placed on margin opposite the entry, A; om., B.

[2] *Either killed or captured.*—Literally: [took] 200 *persons, between killing and capturing.*

[3] *Gilla-Domangairt.*—Devotee of *(St.)* *Domangart*, of Rath-Muirbuilg (Murlough), Co. Antrim, brother of St. Muru of Fahan, Co. Donegal. A gloss in the L. B. copy of the Calendar of Oengus suggests a line containing the name of Domangart as the true reading in the quatrain for March 24 (the feast day), where the text commemorates St. Mochta of Louth.

[4] *Tomaltagh Ua Mael-Brenainn.*—The only member of the O'Mulrenin family, according to O'Donovan (*F. M.* p. 876), that ever became chief of all the Ui-Mureadhaigh. This is based on the reading of the *Four Masters*, who give, here and elsewhere, *tigherna* (lord) for *muire* (steward). The equation is, of course quite groundless.

captured.²—Cathal, son of Tigernan, king of the West of Connacht; Congalach Ua Riacain, royal heir of Tara; Duarcan Ua hEghrai, king of Luighne; Gilla-Coemgin, son of Gilla-Comhgaill, royal heir of Leinster, were slain.—Gilla-Domangairt³ Ua Conchaille, king of Ui-Niallain; Muiredach Ua Flainn, king of Ui-Tuirtre; Tomaltach Ua Mael-Brenainn,⁴ steward of Sil-Muiredaich, died.—Domnall Mac Eodosa, herenagh of Mainister-[Buithi]; Eochaidh Ua Cinaedha, herenagh of Ath-truim; Aneslis Mac Uidhir, herenagh of Lusca; Conaing Ua Fairchellaigh, herenagh of Druim-leathan [died].

[1059]

Kalends of Jan. on 7th feria, 24th of the moon, A.D. 1060. Great war in Ard-Macha between Cumuscach¹ Ua Erodhain and Dubdaleithi, successor of [St.] Patrick, respecting the abbacy.—Cenannus was burned entirely, with its stone church.—Lethglenn was burned entirely, except the oratory.—Domnall Deisech [i.e., of the Desi], chief soul-friend of Ireland and Conn-na-mbocht² of Cluain-mac-Nois, were called to Christ:

[1060] Bis.

Two years [and] ten ended,³
Five thousand without any defect—

They further add that this individual was smothered in the cave along with Ua Bric. The improbability of a Roscommon chief taking part in a South Waterford clan feud doubtless never occurred to them.

1060. ¹ *Cumascach.*—In the list of the successors of Patrick (L. L. p. 42, and L. B. [Lebar Brec], Litho. ed. p. 220), he is given next after Dubdaleithi. The *Annals of Innisfallen* (ad an.) say the latter was deposed in favour of the former. See *infra*, A.D. 1064.

² *Conn-na-mbocht—Conn of the poor.* —Best known as the grandfather of Mael-Muire the compiler of Lebar na hUidri (*Book of the Dun* [*cow*]), an 11th cent. MS. in the Royal Irish Academy, and published in facsimile.

For his epitaph (*Oroit do Chunn—a prayer for Conn*) and a notice of his family, see *Christian Inscriptions* (fig. 147, p. 65 sq.).

³ *Ended.*—Lit., *in their excision*. The preposition *i* with the possessive forms a native idiom, expressing state or condition. (See O'Donovan, *Irish Grammar*, p. 291; Windisch, *Wörterbuch*, p. 608-9). The computation (5012), including the current year, gives the Hebrew reckoning, A.M. 3952.

Fuair hUa Forreid co ruilid,
Do reir rodeid, robuilid—
O ċur domain dognaing tic
Co heitreċt Domnaill Ueiric.⁴—

Mael-Ciara[i]n hUa Roboca[i]n, aircinneċ 8uird, mortu[u]r erc.—Muircertaċ, mac Gilla-Fhulartaig,⁵ ridomna na n-Dere, occirur⁶ erc.—Maidm ria Feraib Breg (idon,⁶ ria n-Gairbeid hUa Caturaig⁷) ror Gailengaib (idon⁶ Leoċan, mac mic Maela[i]n⁷) 7 ror Cairpri.—Flannacan hUa Ceallaig, ri Breg, do éc i n-a ailitre.

Kal. Ian. 11. f., l. u., Anno Domini M.° lx.° 1.°
B 42b Muiredaċ | hUa Mael-Coluim, aircinneċ Daire; Ciaran, rui-ecnaid Erenn; Ocan hUa Cormaca[i]n, aircinneċ Innri-Cu[m]rcraid; Tigernaċ bairrceċ, comarba Finnen, 7 ard anmċara Erenn; Conaing, mac ind abad, roraircinneċ Ard[a]-Maċa, in penitentia¹ quieuerunt.—Domnall hUa Maeldoraid do marbad la Ruaidri hUa Cananna[i]n i caċ.—Gairbeid hUa Caturaig, ri Breg; Cu-Ulad, mac Congalaig, ri Uaċtair-tire, in penitentia² mortui runt.—Niall, mac Mail-8eċlainn, ri Ailig, mortuur³ erc.—
8luagad la hAed hUa Conċobair co Cenn-corad,
A 45b |co robrir in caċraig 7 co romuċ in tirrait.—Gleann-da-loċa⁴ do lorcad do leir.⁵

³ Gilla ualartaig (f, being silent, was om. by scribe), B. ⁴ occirrur, B.
** l. m., t. h., A, B. ⁵⁵ itl., t. h., A, B.
A.D.1061. ¹ peneteneia, B. ² peneteneia, B. ³ morcur, B.—ᵃ⁻ᵃ om., C.

---

⁴ Ua Forreidh.—Most probably, the one whose obit is given at 1088. Living in Emly, he must have heard of the fame of Domnall, who belonged to a neighbouring county (Waterford).

⁵ Come.—Literally, comes. The numerals, according to native usage, are nom. abs. Collectively (= period), they form the subject of tic (sg.)

⁶ Ghilla-Fhulartaigh.—Devotee of (St.) Fulartach, who died A.D. 778 (=779), supra. The Mart. of Tallaght (L. L., p. 358a) has: iiii. Kal. Ap. Fularta[i]ch, mic Bric (son of Brec). The occurrence of Fulartach's name in the present entry may be taken as proof that his father was eponymous head of the Ui Bric.

Ua Forreidh[4] acutely found, [1060]
According to very established, very decisive rule—
From beginning of the evil hoary world come[5]
To decease of Domnall Deisech.—

Mael-Ciarain Ua Robocain, herenagh of Sord, died.—Muircertach, son of Gilla-Fhulartaigh[6] [Ua Bric], royal heir of the Desi, was slain.—A defeat [was inflicted] by the men of Bregha (namely, by Gairbeid Ua Catusaigh) upon the Gailenga (that is, [upon] Leochan, grandson of Maelan) and upon the Cairpri.—Flannacan Ua Ceallaigh, king of Bregha, died in his pilgrimage.[7]

Kalends of Jan. on 2nd feria, 5th of the moon, A.D. [1061] 1061. Muiredhach Ua Mael-Coluim, herenagh of Daire; Ciaran, most eminent sage of Ireland; Ocan Ua Cormacain, herenagh of Inis-Cumscraigh; Tigernach of Bairrce,[1] successor of [St.] Finnian and archsoul-friend of Ireland; Conaing, son of the abbot, deputy-herenagh[2] of Ard-Macha, rested in penance.[3]—Domnall Ua Maeldoraidh[4] was killed by Ruaidhri Ua Canannain in battle.—Gairbheidh Ua Cathusaigh, king of Bregha; Cu-Uladh, son of Conghalach, king of Uachtar-tire, died in penance.[3]—Niall, son of Mael-Sechlainn, king of Ailech, died.—A hosting by Aedh Ua Conchobair to Cenn-coradh, so that he broke down[5] the city and choked up the [holy?] well.—Gleann-da-locha was burned entirely.

---

[7] *Died in his pilgrimage.*—That is, probably, in a religious house situated outside his own territory.

A.D. 1061. [1] *Tigernach of Bairce.*—The abbot under whom Marianus Scotus says he lived before his departure for the Continent (*Chron. ad an.* 1065=1043). He presided over the monastery of St. Finnian of Magh-bile (Moville), County Down.

Deputy-herenagh.—Literally, *servant-herenagh*; one acting under (and doubtless nominated by) the herenagh.

[3] *In penance.*—Signifying, apparently, that official functions had been laid aside, the better to prepare for death. Herein it differed from *dying in pilgrimage*, that monks remained in their own, and clerics and laics entered local establishments.

[4] *Domnall Ua Maeldoraidh.*—The *Annals of Loch Cé*, which have this entry under the present year, give Domnall under the following year as killed by Aedh Ua Conchobhair!

[5] *Broke down.*—Meaning, very probably, that he razed the royal residence and the fortifications.

[Cal. Ian. 111. p., l. x. ui., Anno Domini M.° lx.° ii.°
Ruaidri hUa Flaitbertaig, ri Iartair Connact, do
marbad la hAed¹ hUa Concobair ı cat.—Gılla-Crıst
hUa Maeldoraıd, comarba Colaım-cılle eter Erınn
7 Albaın; Maelruanaıg hUa Daıgrı, prım anmcara
Tuaırce[ı]rt Erenn, ın Chrırto dormıerunt.—Tadg,
mac Aeda hUı Concobaır, do marbad la Claınn-
Corcraıd (7ª la hIartar Connact, per dolum°).—Cret
la hArdgar Mac Loclaınn ı Coıced Connact, co
tuctat re^b mıle do buaıb, mıle ımorro° do daınıb.—
Donncuan hUa Macaınen do marbad do Gılla-
Cıaraın hUı Macaınen, rı Mugdorn.—Eocaıd, mac
Neıll, mıc Eocada, rıdomna Coıcıd Erenn 7 Eocaıd
hUa Laıtein, rı Sıl-Duıbtıre, ın penıtentıa² mortuı
runt.—Ruaıdrı, mac Concaırrgı, rıdomna Fern-muıgı,
do marbad do mac Neıll hUı Ruaırc.

[Cal. Ian. iiii. p., l. xx. uii., Anno Domini M.° lx.° iii.°
Gormlaıt, ıngen Catail, mıc Ruaıdrı, ın perıgrına-
tıone ı n-Ard-Maca dormıuıt.—Motodan hUa Celeca[ı]n, recnar Ard[a]-Maca, mortuur¹ ert.—Catal
hUa Donncada, aırdrı hUa-n-Ecat Muman; Cudurlıg
hUa Taıdg, rı Fern-Lı; | Mael-Seclaınn hUa Moto-
da[ı]n, rıdomna Aılıg, a ruır ınımıcır (idon,ª o
Cenel-Conaıllª), occırı runt.—Coınnmed mor la Mac
Loclaınn o ta Glenn-Suılıde rıar co hIartur Luıgne 7
co Muaıd Ou-n-Amalgaıd, du ı tangatur² rıg Connact

A.D. 1062. ¹ hAed, B. ² pene—, B. ᵃ⁻ᵃ itl., t. h., A; om., B. ᵇ.ui.,
A, B. ᶜ uero (the Latin equivalent), B.

A.D. 1063. ¹ mortur, B. ²—dur, B. ᵃ⁻ᵃ itl., t. h., A; l. m., t. h., B.

1062. ¹ *Both in.*—Lit., *between.*
For Gilla-Crist (who succeeded
Robartach in 1057) see Reeves,
Adamnan, p. 400.

² *Fifth.*—That is *fifth* division; Ireland having been anciently divided
into *five* provinces: Meath, Ulster,
Leinster, Munster, and Connaught.
See Vol. 1, p. 386.

³ *Eochaidh.*—The *Four Masters* at
the present year say he died on
Thursday, Nov. 13. But the 13th
fell on Wednesday in this year.

ANNALS OF ULSTER. 11

Kalends of Jan. on 3rd feria, 16th of the moon, A.D. 1062. [1062]
Ruaidhri Ua Flaithbertaigh, king of the West of Connacht, was killed by Aedh Ua Conchobhair in battle.—Gilla-Crist Ua Maeldoraidh, successor of [St.] Colum-cille, both in[1] Ireland and Scotland; Maelruanaigh Ua Daighri, chief soul-friend of the North of Ireland, slept in Christ.—Tadhg, son of Aedh Ua Concobair, was killed by the Clann-Coscraidh (and by the West of Connacht in treachery).—A foray by Ardgar Mac Lochlainn into the Fifth[2] of Connacht, so that they took away six thousand cows, also a thousand persons.—Donncuan Ua Machainen was killed by Gilla-Ciarain Ua Machainen, king of Mughdoirn.—Eochaidh,[3] son of Niall, son of Eochaidh, royal heir of the Fifth of Ireland,[4] and Eochaidh Ua Laithein, king of Sil-Duibtire, died in penance.—Ruaidhri, son of Cucairrgi, royal heir of Fern-magh, was killed by the son of Niall Ua Ruairc.

Kalends of Jan. on 4th feria, 27th of the moon, A.D. 1063. [1063]
Gormlaith, daughter of Cathal, son of Ruaidhri [Ua Flaithbertaigh], slept in pilgrimage in Ard-Macha.—Motadan Ua Celecain, vice-abbot of Ard-Macha, died.—Cathal[1] Ua Donnchadha, arch-king of the Ui-Echach of Munster; Cuduiligh Ua Taidhg, king of Fir-Li; Mael-Sechlainn Ua Motodain, royal heir of Ailech, by his enemies (namely, by Cenel-Conaill), were slain.—Great coigny[2] [was levied] by Mac Lochlainn from Glenn-Suilidhe[3] westwards to the western part of Luighne and to [the river] Muaidh of Ui-Amalgadha, where all the kings of Connacht came

---

[4] *Fifth of Ireland.*—That is, Ulster; the Fifth, or Province, *par excellence.*

1063. [1] *Cathal.*—Slain, according to the *F. M.*, by his own son. The items of this entry are too discrepant to be included in one formula. Cuduiligh is said (in the *F. M.*) to have died a natural death. *Suis inimicis* can mean *their enemies*, with reference to all three. I have followed the gloss in restricting it to Mael-Sechlainn.

[2] *Coigny.*—Or *coigne* (anglicized form of the *coinnmedh* of the text), cess levied in lieu of billeting. The *F. M.* make it a *hosting* (*sluighedh*); O'Conor, *an army.*

[3] *From Glenn-Suilidhe.*—Literally, *from [where] is Glenn Suilidhe.*

uile 1 n-a teč, im Œeð hUa Concoḃaıṗ 7 ım Œeð, mac mıc Neıll Uı Ruaıṗc 7 ım mac Œıṗt hUı Ruaıṗc.— hUaım Œlla ı Ceaṗa do ġabaıl o Chonnactaıð ṗoṗ muınteṗ Œeða hUı Concoḃaıṗ, ın ṗo mucta ṗeṗca[b] aṗ cet.[b]—Niall, mac Eoċaða, aıṗdṗı Ulað, a ec ı n-1d Nouembıṗ, 7 1 n-Daṗdaın, 7 1° n-octmad [uaṫad] dec [eṗcı].[c]—Cinaeð, mac Œıċıṗ, aıṗcınneċ Lıṗṁoıṗ-Moċutu; Eoċaıð hUa Dalla[ı]n, aıṗcınneċ Coınneıṗe', ın pace doṗmıeṗunt.

A45c|Ḃıṗ.[a] Kal. Ian. u. ṗ., L ıx., Œnno Domını M.° Lx.° 1111.° Dolġen hUa 8onaı, aıṗcınneċ Œıṗd-ṗṗata; ın Dall hUa Lona[ı]n, ṗṗım eıceṗ ṗeṗ Muman; Ġılla-aṗṗaı hUa Maelmıċıġ,[1] ın penıtentıa moṗtuı ṗunt.—Coṗmac, aıṗcınneċ Œıṗd-ḃṗeca[ı]n; Eoċaıð hUa Doıṗeıd, aıṗcınneċ Domnaıġ-moıṗ Muıġı-lča, ın Domıno doṗmıeṗunt.—Muıṗċeṗtac hUa Neıll, ṗı Teloa-o[ı]ġ, o Uıḃ-Cṗemtaınn occıṗuṗ eṗt.—Donnċað, mac Ḃṗıaın, aıṗdṗı Muman, (do[b] aṫṗıġað 7[b]) do ec ı Roım ı n-a aılıṫṗı.—Duḃdaleıṫı (mac[b] Mael-Muıṗe[b]), comaṗba Ṗatṗaıc, ı Kalaınn 8eptımbıṗ ın bona penetentıa moṗtuuṗ eṗt. Mael-Iṗu,[2] mac Œmalgaða, do ġabaıl na haḃdaıne.—Dıaṗmaıt hUa Loṗca[ı]n, ṗıdomna Laıġen, do maṗbað la Cınel-Eoġaın ı n-Ulltaıḃ.—

[b-b] Lx. aṗ .c., A, B. [c-c] ın .xuııı., A, B. [3] Coınneṗe, B.

A.D. 1064. [1] Maeıl—, B. [2]-Iṗa, A.—[a] om., B.; [b-b] ıtl, t. h., A; om., B.

[a] *Into his house.*—An idiomatic expression, signifying to make formal submission.

[b] *With.*—Literally, *around*.

[c] *On the Ides.*—The *Four Masters* say that Niall and his son, Eochaidh, died on Thursday, Nov. 13, 1062. But Tigernach agrees with these Annals in placing the obit of Eochaidh at 1062, and that of his father at this year. Furthermore, what is decisive on the subject, in 1062, Nov. 13 fell on Wednesday; but in 1063, as the text states, on Thursday.

With regard to the lunar reckoning, it is worthy of note that its accuracy is confirmed by the *old rule* in Bede (*De rat. temp.* xxii.) "November in the Ides, 317." Deduct the current day and add the January epact (as given above), $27 = 343$. Divide by 59 (two consecutive lunations) and from the remainder, 48, subtract 30. This gives the 18 of the text. New Moon accordingly fell on Oct. 27.

into his house[4] with[5] Aedh Ua Concobhair, and with[6] [1063] Aedh, grandson of Niall Ua Ruairc, and with[6] the son of Art Ua Ruairc.—The cave of Alla in Cera was captured by the Connachtmen against the people of Aedh Ua Concobhair, wherein were smothered sixty above one hundred [persons].—Niall, son of Eochaidh, arch-king of Ulidia, died on the Ides[4] of November [Nov. 13] and on Thursday and on the 18th [of the moon].—Cinaedh Mac Aichir, herenagh of Lis-mor of [St.] Mochutu; Eochaidh Ua Dallain, herenagh of Coindere, slept in peace.

Kalends of Jan. on 5th feria, 9th of the moon, A.D. [1064]Bis 1064. Dolghen Ua Sonai, herenagh of Ard-sratha; the Blind Ua Lonain, chief poet of the Men of Munster; Gilla-arrai Ua Maelmithigh, died in penance.—Cormac, herenagh of Ard-Brecain; Eochaidh Ua Doireid, herenagh of Domnach-mor of Magh-Itha, slept in the Lord.— Muircertach Ua Neill, king of Telach-og, was slain by the Ui-Cremtainn.—Donnchadh, son of Brian [Boruma], arch-king of Munster, (was deposed and) died in Rome in his pilgrimage.—Dubdaleithi (son of Mael-Muire), successor of Patrick, died on the Kalends of September [Sep. 1] in good penance.[1] Mael-Isu, son of Amalgaidh, took the abbacy.—Diarmait Ua Lorcain, royal heir of Leinster, was killed by the Cenel-Eogain in Ulster.—Airdgar Mac

---

Hereby are to be corrected the Calendars (*e.g.* Nicolas, *Chron. of Hist.*; Hampson, *Med. Aevi Kal.*) that place the Golden Number XIX. (1063 was the last year of the Cycle.) at October 26. It is accurately indicated in the Calendar, Embolismal Computus and Decemnovennal Tables appended to the printed editions of the above-named work of Bede.

O'Donovan queries whether "the 18th" refers to the reign of Niall. But at 1016 he had given the slaying of Niall's predecessor from these Annals. In the list of Kings of Ulidia in L. L. (p. 41 d) "42 or 50" years are assigned to Niall.

Marianus Scotus has: A.D. 1087 [=1065], *Nial mac Eochada*, rex *Ulad*, obiit Id. Nov. This postdates the obit by two years.

1064. [1] *In good penance.*—This perhaps signifies that Dubdaleithe acquiesced in his deposition (A.D. 1060), and devoted his remaining years exclusively to religious exercises.

14 *annala ulaoh.*

Airgdar Mac Lochlainn, rí Ailig, do ec i Telach-óg et sepultur est i n-Ard-Maca, in mausolio regum.— Mac Leobelem,³ rí Bretan, do marbad la mac Iacoib.— Ecmarcach,⁴ rí Gall, do ecaib.

Hic⁵ est primus annus undecimi Cicli magni Parchalis a constitucione mundi; principium uero tercii Cicli magni Parchalis ab Incarnacione Domini et habet quatuor Concurrenter bissextiles et est secundus annus Indiccionis.⁶

Kl. Ian. uii. f., l. xx., Anno Domini M.° lx.° u°. Dubtach Albanach, primh anmcara Erenn 7 Albann, i n-Ard-Maca quieuit:

Dubtach, duini oligtec, dur,
Ronbia in forad rigtec roen,
Nemh fuair in t-anmcara, adcio,
Aratir claptana coem.—

B 42d   Donnchad hUa Matgamna, rí Ulad, do marbad | a m-bennchar a fuir.—Domnall, aircinnech Lugbaid 7 aircinnech Droma, a n-ec.—Aed hUa Ualgairg do

³ Leo belem, A; mac (son), having been omitted at first, is placed overhead with reference mark, B. ⁴ Eacmarcac, B.—c-c om., B; given in C.

A.D. 1065. ᵃ⁻ᵃ t. m., t. h., with corresponding reference marks, A; om., B.

---

² *Mausoleum of the kings.*—Called the *cemetery of the kings*, supra, A.D. 934 (=935). See Reeves, *Ancient Churches of Armagh*, p. 18.

³ *The son of Llywelyn.*—Called Grufud in the Brut y Tywysogion (A.D. 1061), and Grifin in the *Annales Cambriæ* (A.D. 1063). In both he is stated to have fallen by the treachery of his own men.

⁴ *Echmarcach.*—See Vol. I., p. 591, note 12. According to Marianus Scotus, he died in Rome. *Donnchad, filius Briain, de Hibernia atque Echmarcach, rex innarenn* (? perhaps, in *Manenn*, of Manann), *viri inter suos non ignobiles, Romam venientes obierunt* (1087=1065).

⁵ *Eleventh.*—This Cycle has been discussed in the Introduction.

⁶ *Third.*—The second so-called Dionysian Great Cycle commenced A.D. 532 (531 of text), *supra*.

⁷ *Four.*—The reading in A is *uii. Concurrentes*. The scribe, namely, not understanding the text, mistook the two first letters of *iiii.* for *u.* O'Donovan (*F. M.*, p. 887) gives Kal. 4 as the lection of C: meaning that New Year's Day fell on Wednes-

Lochlainn, king of Ailech, died in Telach-og and was [1064] buried in Ard-Macha, in the mausoleum of the kings.'—The son of Llywelyn,² king of the Britons, was killed by the son of James.—Echmarcach⁴, king of the Foreigners [of Dublin], died.

This is the first year of the eleventh⁵ great Paschal Cycle from the formation of the world; but the commencement of the third⁶ great Paschal Cycle from the Incarnation of the Lord. And it hath four⁷ bissextile Concurrents and is the second year of the Indiction.

Kalends of Jan. on 7th feria, 20th of the moon, A.D. [1065] 1065. Dubtach, the Scotsman, chief soul-friend of Ireland and Scotland, rested in Ard-Macha:

> Dubthach,¹ person righteous, dour,
> For him there will be a dwelling roomy, noble,
> Heaven the soul-friend found, it is seen,

Donnchadh Ua Mathgamna, king of Ulidia, was killed² in Bennchar by his own [subjects].—Domnall, herenagh of Lughbadh and the Herenagh of Druim, their death³ [took place].—Aedh Ua Ualghairg took the kingship of

---

day in 1064. But, as shown in the text, it fell on Thursday. *Habet* (not *Kal.*) is the word in the C. MS.

The Calendar use of Concurrents is explained in text-books of Chronology.

Bissextile also distinguishes this (the 9th) year from the 4th, 15th and 26th years of the Solar Cycle of 28. These three years (in the Old Style) have four Concurrents, but are not bissextile. The Indiction is correct.

1065. ¹ *Dubhtach*.—His connexion with Ireland is told in the Breviary of Aberdeen: *In qua utriusque Veteris et Novi Testamenti precepta et leges accuratissime didicit* (quoted in *Adamnan*, p. 401). He probably died on a pilgrimage to Armagh.

The last line of the quatrain I am unable to translate. *Thir* may be for *th[ȧ]ir, continued, constant.* O'Donovan renders it: "[In exchange] for his fair, thin-boarded domicile." His text is: *ar a thir clár tana coemh* (p. 886-7).

² *Was killed.*—Marianus Scotus, A.D. 1088 [=1066], says: *in templo Bennchuir, verno tempore, occiditur.* His slayer is given by name in the third next entry.

³ *Their death.*—O'Conor reads *Droma-Anec* and gives the equivalent as *Dromanecensis*; taking *a n-ec* (their death) to be a factor in a local name. He adds (*obierunt*), to find a verb to complete the imaginary sense. *Domnall* and *Herenagh*, according to native idiom, are nominatives absolute.

ξabaıl ριξe. Ceneoıl-Eogaın.—Оροοuρ, naṁa Comξaıll, quı occıoıt ρegem ı m-ḃennċoρ, oo maρbaδ la ρıξ Oal-n-Αραιοe.—Mac Ταιδξ hUı Ceallaıξ, ρı hUa-Maıne 7 hUa flaıtḃeρtaıξ, ρı ıaρtaıρ Con[n]aċt, occıρı ρunt la hΑeδ hUa Conċobaıρ.—Oomnall hUa Loınξρıξ, ρı. Oal-n-Αραιοe 7 Muıρceρtaċ hUa Maelfabaıll, ρí Caıρce-ḃρaċaıδe, oo maρbaδ o hUıb-Meıċ Menna-Τıρe.—Leocan, mac Laıδξnen, ρí Ʒaılenξ, oo maρbaδ la Conċobuρ hUa Mael-Seċlaınn.—Eċṁıleδ hUa Αιτeιδ, ρí Ua-n-Eċaċ, oo maρbaδ oo Chenıul-Eoξaın.¹

(No⁵ ξumao aρ ın ḳallaınn ρı buo coıρ Oonnċaδ, mac Ḃρıaın ḃoρuma, oo beċ, ρecunoum alıum lıḃρum ; quı tamen uıoetuρ moρı anno ρρeteρıto, ρecunoum hunc lıḃρum.ᵇ)

ḳal. Ιan. 1. ρ., l. 1., Αnno Oomını M.º Lx.º uı.º Αeδ hUa Ruaıρc, ρı hUa-m-Ḃρıuın,¹ moρtuuρ eρt ρtatım ıaρ n-oρcaın ρeρıne Ρatρaıc.—Ceallaċ, mac Muıρceρtaıξ hUı Ceallaıξ; Ʒılla-Ḃρaıtı, ρı hUa-m-Ḃρıuın ; Mac Sena[ı]n, ρı Ʒaılenξ ; Ʒılla-Monınne, mac Αeδa mıc uı Ualξaıρξ, | occıρı ρunt.—Cnoṁeρ

A.D. 1065. ¹ Chenel, B.— ᵇᵇ l. m., n. t. h., A ; om., B.

A.D. 1066. ¹ m-Ḃρuın, A. ᵃ —tuρ, B.

---

⁴ *Enemy of* [*St.*] *Comgall.*—The murder within the church was regarded as a personal affront to the patron, St. Comgall.

⁵ *Domnall Ua Loingsigh.* — Marianus Scotus (*ubi sup.*) writes: *i fel Tigernaeg Cluana eius occisus*—*slain on the feast of Tigernach of Cluaineois* (Clones, co. Monaghan). That is, (Monday) April 4. This corresponds with the *rerno tempore* (p. 15, note 2, *supra*) of Donnchad's assassination. Strange, that no local chronicle noted the date.

⁶ *Another book.*—This other book is probably the Annals of Boyle, which state that Donnchadh went to Rome on a pilgrimage in this year. Marianus Scotus (p. 14, note 4, *supra*) also says that he went to Rome in 1087 [=1065].

1066.—¹ *Shrine of Patrick.*—Apparently, in Armagh; but the Four Masters say it was after plundering Clonmacnoise and Clonfert.

² *Gilla-Moninne.*—*Devotee of* (*St.*) *Moninne* (Virgin), of Slieve Gallion, co. Londonderry. Her obit is given *supra*,

Cenel-Eogain.—Brodur, the enemy of [St.] Comgall, who [1065] slew the king [Donnchadh] in Bennchor, was killed by the king of Dal-Araidhe.—The son of Tadhg Ua Ceallaigh, king of Ui-Maine and Ua Flaithbertaigh, king of the West of Connacht, were slain by Aedh Ua Conchobair. —Domnall Ua Loingsigh, king of Dal-Araidhe and Muircertach Ua Maelfhabaill, king of Carraic-Brachaidhe were killed by the Ui-Meith of Menna-Tire.—Leocan, son of Laidgnen, king of Gailenga, was killed by Conchobur Ua Mael-Sechlainn.—Echmhiledh Ua Ateidh, king of Ui-Echach, was killed by the Cenel-Eogain.

(Or it may be [that it is] on this Kalend [i.e. year] it were right for Donnchadh, son of Brian Boruma, to be, according to another book. He seems, however, to have died in the past year, according to this book.)

Kalends of Jan. on 1st feria, 1st of the moon, A.D. [1066] 1066. Aed Ua Ruairc, king of Ui-Briuin, died straightway after rifling the Shrine of Patrick.[1]—Ceallach, son of Muircertach Ua Ceallaigh; Gilla-Braiti [Ua Ruairc], king of Ui-Briuin, the son of Senan [Ua Leochain], king of Gailenga; Gilla-Moninne,[2] son of Aedh great grandson of Ualgarg [Ua Ruairc], were slain.—Great nutcrop in all Ireland, so[3] that it impedes the rivers.—The successor

---

A D. 519 (=520): Quies Darercae, quae Mouinne nominata est. The Saint's name possesses a literary interest. In the so-called *Chronicon Scotorum*, Mac Firbis gives his original thus: Quies Darerca .... quae Moninne, Aninne sanatho postea nominata est (Marginal A.D. 514). The reading is: quae Moninne a Ninne sanato, etc. The explanation is given in the Book of Leinster (p. 271 c): "fili balb rathroise aicce, ar cotissed a erlabra dó. Ocus issed toesech rolabair, idon : *Nin, Nin*. Unde dicebatur *Moninne*. Ocus Ninnine éices ainm in fhiled—A dumb poet fasted with her, in order that his speech might come to him. And what he first said is this, namely: *Nin, Nin*. Whence she was called *Moninne* (*My Ninne*). And Ninnine the sage (was) the name of the poet." He was the author of a beautiful poetical invocation of St. Patrick in the native tongue, preserved in the *Book of Hymns*.

[3] *So, etc.*—The Latin portion is omitted in C.

mor i n-Erinn uile, ut rebellet' fluminibur.—Comarba
Daire (ioon, Donncaḋ hUa Duimein) 7 Cinaeḋ, mac
mic Oḋormaic, ri Conaille, in penitencia mortui runt.

|Cal. Ian. 11. f., l. x.11., Anno Domini M.° lx.° uiii.°
Scolaiġ, mac Inḋractaiġ, aircinneċ Muc[r]noma; Aircinneċ Duin-leṫ-glaire; Aeḋ, mac mic Ualgairg, muire
hUa-n-Duibinnreċt; Ectigern, mac Flainn Mainirtreċ, ioon, aircinneċ Mainirtreċ, in pace dormierunt.
—Sloigeḋ la Tairrdelbaċ hUa m-Briain co Loċ Cime, co
romarbaḋ d'on t-sluagaḋ hUa Concobuir, ri Ciaraiḋe-
Luaċra.—Ceall-dara co n-a tempall do lorcaḋ.—Aeḋ
hUa Concobuir (ioon, Aeḋ in ga bearnaiġ), airdri
Coiciḋ Connaċt, luam gaisciḋ Leiṫi Cuinn, do marbaḋ
la Conmacne i caṫ, i torcradar ile (7 Aeḋ hUa
Concenaind, ri hUa-n-Diarmata, et alii multi cum eis),
ioon, le hAeḋ, mac Airt uallaiġ hUi Ruairc, a caṫ
Thurlaiġ-Aċonaiḋ :

Seċt m-bliaḋna fercat, ni ruaill,
Ocuy mile, mor in buaiḋ,
O gein Crirt, ni roeḋ in rmaċt,
Co torċair Aeḋ, ri Connaċt.

B 43 a b ir | Kl. Ian. iii. f., l. xx. iii., Anno Domini M.° lx.° uiii.°
Domnall hUa Caṫuraiġ, aircinneċ Duin; Colman hUa
Criċa[i]n, ferleiġinn Arda-Maċa; Mac in Becanaiġ,
comarba Comġaill; Cinaeḋ, comarba Coemġin, ad
Chrirtum migrauerunt.—Mael-Iru, comarba Patraic,

⁷ rebellat, A, B; but a was underdotted and e placed overhead, B.
⁴ penetenti, B.—ᵇ ᵇ itl., t. h., A, B.

A.D. 1067. ¹—glairi, B.—ᵃ ᵃ itl., t. h., A; om., B. ᵇ ᵇ f. m., t. h., with
relative signs of reference, A; om., B. Seċt and fercat are respectively .uii.
and .lx. in the (A) MS.

A.D. 1068. ¹ Repeated by oversight, B. ² Airdmaċa, A. ³ Beccananaiġ,
B. ᵃ om., B. ᵇ ᵇ om., A.

1067. ¹ *Flann.*—Lector of Monas- | ² *Half of Conn.*—"Id est, the
terboice, who died in 1056, *supra*. | north half of Ireland," C.

[of Colum-cille in the monastery] of Daire (namely, Donnchad Ua Duimein) and Cinaedh, grandson of Odhormac, king of Conaille, died in penance. [1066]

Kalends of Jan. on 2nd feria, 12th of the moon, A.D. 1067. Scolaighi, son of Innrachtach, herenagh of Mucnom; the Herenagh of Dun-lethglaise; Aedh, grandson of Ualgarg, steward of Ui-Duibinnrecht; Ecthigern, son of Flann[1] of Mainister[-Buithi], namely, the herenagh of Mainister[-Buithi], slept in peace.—A hosting by Tairrdelbach Ua Briain to Loch-Cime, so that Ua Concobuir, king of Ciaraidhe-Luachra, was killed on that hosting.—Cell-dara, with its church, was burned.—Aedh Ua Concobuir (namely, Aedh "of the gapped spear"), arch-king of the Fifth of Connacht, helmsman of the championship of the Half of Conn,[2] was killed by the Conmacni, in a battle in which fell many (and Aedh Ua Concenaind, king of Ui-Diarmata and many others with them), namely, by Aedh, son of Art Ua Ruairc the haughty, in the battle of Turlach-Adhnaich: [1067]

> Seven years [and] sixty, not trifling,
> And a thousand, great the triumph,
> From Birth of Christ, not vain the sway,
> Until fell Aedh, king of Connacht.

Kalends of Jan. on 3rd feria, 23rd of the moon, A.D. 1068. Domnall Ua Cathusaigh, herenagh of Dun; Colman Ua Crichain, lector of Ard-Macha; Mac-in-Becanaigh, successor of [St.] Comgall[1]; Cinaedh, successor of [St.] Coemghen,[2] departed to Christ.—Mael-Isu, successor of Patrick, [went] upon circuit of Munster [1860 Bis].

A.D. 1068. [1] *Successor of [St.] Comgall.*—Namely, abbot of Bangor, co. Down. The entry in the Four Masters states that he was also successor of St. Mocholmog; that is, bishop of Dromore.

[2] *Successor of [St.] Coemghen.*—That is, abbot of Glendalough, co. Wicklow.

B 2

for cuairt Muman cetna fect, co tuc a lancuairt, eter rperal 7 eoburta.—Murcað hUa Briain, riðomna Muman, do marbað la firu Tebta.¹—Flaiτ-bertac hUa Fergail, rí Telca-ó[i]cc, do ξuin do Cheniul-m-binniξ.⁵—Domnall, mac Neill, mic Mael-Seclainn (idon,ᶜ Domnall na m-bocτᶜ), rí Ailiξ, do marbað (idon,ᵈ maidm Sitbeᵈ) d'Aeð hUa Mael-Seclainn, idon, a derbratair.

|Cal. Ian. u. f., l. IIII., Anno Domini M.° Lx.° ix.₀ Cobcac, rasart Cille-dara, in Chrirto quieuit.—Dun-da-letglar 7 Ard-rrata 7 Lurca 7 Sord¹ Coluim-cille ab igne dif[r]irata[e] funt.—hUa Aeða, rí hUa-Fiasrac Arda-rrata; Aeð, mac Dubξaill, recnar Cluana-Fiacna; Flannacan, mac Aeða, foraircinneac Arda-Maca, in penitentia² mortui funt.

| Cal. Ian. ui. f., l. x.u., Anno Domini m.° Lxx.° Caturac, mac Cairpri, aircinneac Mungarte,¹ do éc.—Murcað, mac Diarmata, rí Laigen 7 Gall, do ec et refultur ert i n-Aτ-cliaτ.—hOa hEocaiden, rí Dal-n-Araiðe, occifur ert a fuif.—Fergal hUa Laiðgnen, aircinneac [Fh]ocna, do ec.—Gilla-patraic hUa Mael-cocaiξ fefuit morte immatura.—Abbar la, idon, mac

⁴—tbaB. ⁵Cinel-b—, B. ᵉ⁻ᶜitl., t. h., A, B. ᵈ⁻ᵈitl., t. h., A; l. m., t. h., B.
A.D. 1069. ¹Sort, B. ²penitencia, A.
A.D. 1070. ¹—te, B.

---

[3] *Both cess and donations.*—Literally, *between scruple and offerings.* That the *Screpal* (from the Latin *Scripulum*) was coined money, can hardly be inferred from the distinction here made between itself and the offerings in kind. Compare the passage in the Confession of St. Patrick: Forte autem, quando baptizavi tot milia hominum, speraverim ab aliquo illorum vel dimedio [*lege*—ium] scriptule? Dicite mihi et reddam vobis. Also the expression in the sixth Canon of the Irish Synod published by Wasserschleben (*Die Buss-ordnungen der abendlländische Kirche*, p. 141): duodecim discipuli [*lege* scripuli] usque viginti.

More likely, to judge from the Brehon Laws, the word represented a standard of value. The meaning, accordingly, would be that the sum was made up of the proceeds of a rate, supplemented by voluntary contri-

the first time, so that he took away his full circuit [1068]Bis. [amount], both cess and donations².—Murchadh Ua Briain,⁴ royal heir of Munster, was killed by the Men of Tebtha.—Flaithbertach Ua Fergail, king of Telach-oc, was wounded [mortally] by the Cenel-Binnigh.—Domnall, son of Niall, son of Mael-Sechlainn (namely, Domnall "of the poor"), king of Ailech, was killed (that is, [in] the Defeat of Sithbe) by Aedh, grandson of Mael-Sechlainn, namely, his brother.

Kalends of Jan. on 5th feria, 4th of the moon, A.D. [1069] 1069. Cobthach, priest of Cell-dara,¹ rested in Christ.—Dun-da-lethglas and Ard-sratha and Lusca and Sord of [St.] Colum-cille were wasted by fire.—Ua Aedha, king of Ui-Fiachrach of Ard-sratha; Aedh, son of Dubghall, vice-abbot of Cluain-Fiachna; Flannacan, son of Aedh, deputy-herenagh² of Ard-Macha, died in penance.

Kalends of Jan. on 6th feria, 15th of the moon, A.D. [1070] 1070. Cathusach, son of Cairpre, herenagh¹ of Mungarit, died.—Murchadh, son of Diarmait,² king of Leinster and of the Foreigners, died³ and was buried in Ath-cliath.—Ua hEochaiden, king of Dal-Araidhe, was slain by his own [tribesmen].—Fergal Ua Laidhgnen, herenagh of [F]othan, died.—Gilla-Patraic Ua Maelchothaigh perished by a premature death.—The abbot of Ia, namely,

---

butions. This is confirmed by the entry under 1106 (*infra*), in which the apportionment of the levy is set forth.

⁴ *Murchad Ua Briain.*—Murchad, *sciathgerr, oa Briaen* [Murchad short-shield, grandson of Brian (Boruma)] *occiditur mense Septembris* (Marianus Scotus, A.D. 1090=1068).

1069. ¹ *Priest of Cell-dara.*—That is, Chaplain of the monastery of the nuns of St. Brigit, Kildare.

² *Deputy-herenagh.* — See p. 9, note 2, *supra*.

1070. ¹ *Herenagh.*—But the Annals of Innisfallen, which in Munster affairs are far more reliable than the Annals of Ulster, state that Cathusach was *successor of Deacon Nessan;* that is, abbot of Mungret, co Limerick.

² *Diarmait.*—Slain in 1072, *infra*.

³ *Died.*—The Four Masters say his death took place "precisely on Sunday, the festival of Mary in winter." But in this year Dec. 8 fell on Wednesday.

Marianus Scotus (A.D. 1091 [=

mic baeżen, do maṗbaḋ do mac ind abaḋ hUi Maeldoṗaiḋ.—Caṫbaṗṗ hUa Maelċoṫaiḋ do maṗbaḋ do mac hUi[a] Induiṗge ṫṗia meabail.—Muiṗceṗtaċ hUa Loingṗiġ decollatuṗ eṗt a ṗuiṗ.—Eilill hUa hCairetiġ, comaṗba Ciaṗa[i]n, quieuit.—Mac Ġoṗma[i]n, ṗeṗleiġinn Cenannṡa 7 ṡui ecna Eṗenn [quieuit].—Teṗmonn Dabeo[i]c[a] d'aṗġain[3] do Ruaiḋṗi hUa Cananna[i]n et uindicauit Dominuṗ et Dabeocc ante plenum annum. | Ġluniaiṗn, mac Diaṗmata, do maṗbaḋ do Ṫuaṫaib Luiġne la ṫaeb cṗeiċe allaiġniḋ.—Ri Ṫebṫa 7 ṗi Caiṗṗṗi occiṗi[b] ṡunt.—Mael-Bṗiġte, mac Caṫuṗaiġ mic ind abaḋ, ṡoṡaiṗcinneċ Aṗd[a]-Maċa, occiṡuṡ eṗt.

|Cal. Ian. uii. ṡ., L. xx. iii., Anno Domini m.° lxx.° i.° Ri Ulaḋ, idon, Ua[1] Flaṫṡai,[1] do aṡṗiġaḋ la hUa Maelṗuanaiġ 7 la hUltu; aċt ṡomaṗbad in t-Ua Maelṗu[a]naiġ ṡin ṗo ceṫoiṗ in bello la Donnṡleiḃe hUa n-Eoċaḋa.—Ġilla-Cṗiṡt hUa Cloṫoca[i]n, ṡeṗleiġinn Aṗda-Maċa,[2] in Chṡiṡto quieuit.—Ceall-daṗa 7 Ġlenn-da-loċa 7 Cluain-dolca[i]n cṗemaṫ[a]e ṡunt.

|Cal. Ian. i. ṡ., L. uii., Anno Domini m.° lxx.° ii.° Mael-Muiṗe hUa Muiṗiġa[i]n, aiṡcinneċ Ṫuiḋniġa,[2] quieuit.—Ġilla-Cṗiṡt hUa Longa[i]n, maeṗ Muman, do éc.—Dubdil, comaṗba Bṗiġte, in Chṡiṡto quieuit.—Diaṗmait, mac Mail-na-mbo, ṗi Laiġen 7 Ġall, do

A.D. 1070. [2]—óġ, B. [3] do aṗġain, B. [a] om., B. [b] occiṡṗi, B.
A.D. 1071. [1-1] hUa Flaṫṡṗi, A. [2] Aiṗd—, A.
A.D. 1072. [1] om., B. [2] Ṫuiġniḋa, B.

1069]) has: "*Murchad, oa Maelnambo, oa Briaen*, obiit verno tempore. Murchad, grandson of Mael-na-mbo, [and] descendant of Brian [Boruma] died in spring time." Note the double use of *oa* (*grandson* and *descendant*). Murchad was grandson of Mael-nambo and great grandson of Brian, whose grand-daughter was Diarmait's wife (A.D. 1080 *infra*).

[2] *Son of the abbot.*—See *Adamnan*, p. 402, note b.

[3] *Ciaran.*—That is, the founder of Clonmacnoise. According to the obit in the Four Masters, Ua hAiretigh died as a pilgrim at Clonard, co. Meath.

[4] *Eminent learned man.*—Literally, *sage of wisdom*. The Annals of Innisfallen state that Mac Gormain was also lector of Clonmacnoise.

the grandson of Baethen, was killed by the son of the [1070] abbot[2] Ua Maeldoraidh.—Cathbarr Ua Maelchothaidh was killed by the son of Ua Indirge through treachery.—Muircertach Ua Loingsigh was beheaded by his own [tribesmen].—Eilill Ua hAiretigh, successor of [St.] Ciaran,[2] rested.—Mac Gormain, lector of Cenannus and eminent learned man[4] of Ireland [rested].—The Termonn of [St.] Dabeoc was pillaged by Ruaidri Ua Canannain. And God and Dabeoc avenged[5] before the completion of a year.—Iron-knee, son of Diarmait,[6] was killed by the Tuatha-Luighne, in addition to a foray[7] [made by them] in Leinster.—The king of Tebtha and the king of Cairpri were slain.—Mael-Brighte, son of Cathusach son of the abbot, deputy-herenagh of Ard-Macha, was slain.

Kalends of Jan. on 7th feria, 26th of the moon, A.D. [1071] 1071. The king of Ulidia, namely, Ua Flathrai,[1] was deposed by Ua Maelruanaigh[2] and by the Ulidians; but that [same] Ua Maelruanaigh was killed immediately in battle by Donnsleibhe Ua Eochadha.—Gilla-Crist Ua Clothocain, lector of Ard-Macha, rested in Christ.—Celldara and Glenn-da-locha and Cluain-dolcain were burned.

Kalends of Jan. on 1st feria, 7th of the moon, A.D. [1072]Bis. 1072. Mael-Muire Ua Muiregain, herenagh of Tuidhnigha, rested.—Gilla-Crist Ua Longain, steward of Munster, died.—Dubdil, successor of Brigit [i.e., abbess of Kildare],

---

[5] *Avenged.*—*Vindicavit;* the singular is employed by the Irish idiom, whereby the number of the verb is determined by that of the next following subject.

[6] *Diarmait.*—See A.D. 1070, note 2, *supra.*

[7] *Foray.*—*Creich* in the original, which O'Conor characteristically takes for a local designation: *prope Creich in Lagenia.*

1071. [1] *Ua Flathrai.*—His proper name, as given in the following year, was *Cu-Uladh*—Hound of Ulidia. His predecessor, Ua Mathgamna, was slain in 1065, *supra.* This agrees with the regnal list in L.L. (p. 41), which assigns six years to Ua Flathrai.

[2] *Ua Maelruanaigh.*—There is a Lochlaind Mac Maelruanaigh, to whom one month is assigned in the L.L. list, between Aed Meranach and Donnsleibhe Ua Eochadha. But this is at variance with the Annals. See 1080, note 4; 1083, note 2, *infra.*

24 annala ulaʋh.

tuitim i cat (cat" Oʋʋa") la Concobup hUa Mael-Seclainn, la pig Tempac 7 áp gall 7 Laigen ime (ιʋon,[b] i Maipt 7[1] pept[c] 1ʋ pebpa[b]).—Cu-Ulaʋ hUa platpai 7 Mac Cpriʋa, pi hUa-gobla, ʋo mapbaʋ la ʋepcept m-bpeg.—hUa pocapta, pi Eile, ʋo mapbaʋ la hUa m-bpiain.—Ruaiʋpi hUa Cananna[i]n, pi Ceniuil-Conaill, ʋo mapbaʋ la hUa Maelʋopaiʋ (ιʋon,[b] Oen-gup.[b])—ppaingc ʋo ʋul i n-Albain, co tucpat mac pig Alban Leo i n-eitipect.

A 46b

| Kal Ian. iii.[a] p., L x. uiii., Anno Domini m.° Lxx.° iii.° bebinn, ingen bpiain, in pepigpinatione i n-Apo-Maca moptua ept.—Concoʋap hUa Mael-Seclainn, pi Tempac, ʋo mapbaʋ ʋo mac plainʋ hUi Mael-Seclainn ʋap aiptec baclu Ipu, baculo ppepente.—Domnall, mac mic Ualgaipg, toipec hUa-n-Duibinnpact; Cucaille hUa pinn, pi pep-Roip; Copmac hUa Clotaga[i]n. moep Muman, in penitencia[b] moptui punt.—Slogaʋ la Taipp-ʋelbac illeit Cuinn, co n-ʋepna cpeic n-ʋiaipmiʋe pop

B 43c

gailengaiʋ 7 | co pomapb Maelmopʋa hUa Catupaig, pi bpeag.—Sitpiuc, mac Amlaim 7 ʋa hUa m-bpiain ʋo mapbaʋ i Manainn.

[a]—I.m., n. t. h., A; om., B. [b] itl., t. h., A, B; om., B. [c] .uiii., A, B. A.D. 1073. [a] .iiii., B. Incorrectly. [b] penitencia, A.

1072. [1] *Tuesday.*—Marianus Scotus says he was slain on Monday, the 6th. *Diarmait, rex Lagen,* viii. Idus Februarii, feria secunda, occissus (A.D. 1094=1072).

[2] *Cu-Uladh Ua Flathrai.* — *Cú-Ulad ua Flaithrae,* feria sexta, iiii. Idus Februarii, occiditur (Marianus Scotus, A.D. 1094=1072). February 10 fell on Friday in that year.

[3] *The Franks.*—That is, William the Conqueror and his forces. The Anglo-Saxon Chronicle (A.D. 1072) says that when William crossed the Tweed, Malcolm gave him hostages. Amongst these, we learn from a subsequent entry, A D. 1093, was Donnchad (called Duncan in the Chronicle). He lived for twenty-one years at the English Court.

1073. [1] *Bebinn.* "Bevin ny [=*ingen* (*daughter*), a form retained in the present language] Brien in her pilgrimage died, in Rome, id est, Ardmagh," C.

[2] *Conchobar Ua-Mael-Seclainn.*— *Conchobor ua Mael-Sechnaell,* rex *Midi,* ix. Kalendas Aprilis, Dominico die Palmarum, occiditur (Marianus Scotus, A.D. 1095=1073). In 1073, Easter Sunday fell on March 31, and Palm Sunday consequently on March 24.

rested in Christ.—Diarmait, son of Mail-na-mbo, king of Leinster and of the Foreigners, fell in battle (the battle of Odhbha) by Conchobur Ua Mael-Sechlainn, king of Tara, and slaughter of Foreigners and of Leinstermen [was inflicted] around him (namely, on Tuesday[1] and on the 7th of the Ides [7th] of February).—Cu-Uladh Ua Flathrai[2] and Mac Assidha, king of Ui-Gobla, were killed by the [people of the] South of Bregha.—Ua Focarta, king of Eili, was killed by Ua Briain.—Ruaidhri Ua Canannain, king of Cenel-Conaill, was killed by Ua Maeldoraidh (namely, Oenghus).—The Franks' went into Scotland, so that they took away the son of the king of Scotland with them in hostageship. [1072] Bis.

Kalends of Jan. on 3rd feria, 18th of the moon, A.D. 1073. Bebinn,[1] daughter of Brian [Boruma], died in pilgrimage in Ard-Macha.—Concobhar Ua Mael-Sechlainn,[2] king of Tara, was killed by the son of Fland Ua Mael-Sechlainn in violation of the honour of the Staff of Jesus,[2] in presence of the Staff.[3]—Domnall, grandson of Ualgarg, chief of Ui-Duibhinnracht; Cuchaille Ua Finn, king of Fir-Rois; Cormac Ua Clothagain, steward of Munster, died in penance.—A hosting by Tairrdelbach [Ua Briain] into the Half of Conn, so that he carried off[4] countless spoil from[5] the Gailenga and killed Maelmordha Ua Cathusaigh, king of Bregha.—Sitriuc, son of Amhlam, [King of Dublin] and two grandsons of Brian [Boruma] were killed in [the Isle of] Manann. [1073

---

[2] *Staff of Jesus.*—A crozier traditionally believed to have been given by our Lord to St. Patrick. At first preserved in Armagh, it was brought to Dublin at the end of the twelfth century, where it was destroyed by the Reformers in 1538. See O'Curry, *MS. Materials*, p. 606.

[3] *In presence of the Staff.*—From this expression it may be inferred that the assassination took place during Divine Service. The *Annals of Innisfallen* state that the son of Fland wrested the Staff from Conchobar and struck him with it, thereby causing his death. Being a relic, it was probably being borne at the time by the king in the procession of the Palms.

[4] *Carried off.*—Literally, committed.

[5] *From.*—Literally, upon

Kal. 1an. 1111. p., L. xx.ix., Anno Domini m.° lxx.° 1111.°
Mac Mael-brenainn (idon,ª Diarmait'), comarba
brenainn; plaitem hUa Caro[i]c aircinnec Roir-cre;
Dunan, ardeprcop 5all; Cormac hUa Maelduin, rui
ind ecnai 7 i¹ crabad, ruam uitam feliciter finierunt.
—Maelmorda,ᵇ comarba Ailbe, in pace quieuit.—Cu-
cairce hUa Ceallaig, comarba Muru, quieuit.ᵇ—Ard-
Maca do lorcad Dia-Mairt iar m-belltaine, co n-a
uilib templaib 7 cloccaib, eter Raic 7 Trian.—Cum-
urcac hUa hErodu[i]n,² cenn boct Erenn, port peniten-
tiam³ optimam in pace quieuit.—Ragnall hUa
Madada[i]n,⁴ ridomna Ailig, occisus est a suis.

Kal. 1an. u. p., L. x., Anno Domini m.° lxx.° u.° 5or-
raig, macª Amlaim, mic Ragnaill,ᵇ ri Ata-cliat;
Cinaet hUa Conbeatad, toiriuc Ceniu[i]l-binnig, mortui
sunt.—Slogad la Tairrdelbac 7 la Let Moga illeit
Cuinn, co torriactur co hAt-firdead, co tarrat
Airgialla maidmᵇ Arda-monannᵇ for Muircertac

A.D. 1074. ¹ In (of the), B. ² hErodu[i]n, B. ³ penetenciam, B.
⁴ Madada[i]n, B. ᵃ⁻ᵃ itl, t. h., A, B. ᵇ r. m., t. h., A. The omission of
the items from the text was doubtless an oversight on the part of the copyist.
Ceallaig, with the exception of Ce, was cut away in trimming the edges.
The entries are omitted in C.

A.D. 1075. ¹ Occisus, B. ᵃ⁻ᵃ Mac Amlaim—*son of Amhlam*—in text,
with no mac Ragnaill—*or, son of Raghnall*—itl., t. h., A; mac mic
Ragnaill—*son of the son (grandson) of Raghnall*—in text, B. This last is
likewise the reading of C. It is also, what is more decisive, given in the Annals
of Innisfallen. Amhlam is mentioned at 1073, *supra*; Raghnall was slain in
the battle of Tara, 979 (=980), *supra*. Hereby is removed the "uncertainty"
(arising from the A—MS.) which caused Dr. Todd (*War of the Gaidhill, etc.*,
p. 290) to omit Godfrey's name from the Genealogical Table (p. 278). ᵇ r. m.
t. h., A; text, B.

1074. ¹ *Successor of* [*St.*] *Brenainn.*—That is, according to the Annals of Innisfallen, bishop of Ardfert,
co. Kerry.

² *Herenagh.*—He is called abbot
in the Annals of Innisfallen.

³ *Successor of* [*St.*] *Ailbe.*—Bishop
of Emly, co. Tipperary.

⁴ *Successor of* [*St.*] *Muru.*—Abbot
of Fahan, co. Donegal.

⁵ *Both Close and Third.*—(Literally,
between Close and Third.) That is, the

Kalends of Jan. on 4th feria, 29th of the moon, A.D. [1074] 1074. The son of Mael-Brenainn (namely, Diarmait), successor of [St.] Brenainn[1]; Flaithemh Ua Caroic, herenagh[2] of Ros-cre; Dunan, archbishop of the Foreigners [of Dublin]; Cormac Ua Maelduin, master of learning and in piety, felicitously finished their life.—Maelmordha, successor of [St.] Ailbe,[3] rested in peace.—Cucarrce Ua Ceallaigh, successor of [St.] Muru,[4] rested.—Ard-Macha was burned on Tuesday after May-Day [May 6], with all its churches and bells, both Close and Third.[5]—Cumuscach Ua hEroduin,[6] head of the poor of Ireland, after most excellent penance rested in peace.—Ragnall Ua Madadhain, royal heir of Ailech, was slain by his own [tribesmen].

Kalends of Jan. on 5th feria, 10th of the moon, A.D. [1075] 1075. Godfrey, son of Amhlam, son of Raghnall, king of Ath-cliath; Cinaeth Ua Conbeathad, chief of Cenel-Binnigh, died.—A hosting by Tairrdelbach and by the Half of Mogh[1] into the Half of Conn, till they reached Ath-fhirdeadh, so that the Airgialla inflicted the defeat of Ard-Monain upon Muircertach Ua Briain, a place where

---

whole of the city. Armagh consisted of the *Fort*, or *Close* (*locum in alto positum*, Book of Armagh, fol. 20 d), and suburbs (*suburbana ejus*, ib.) The latter were called *Thirds* from their number. See Reeves, *Ancient Churches of Armagh*, p. 14.

[6] *Ua hEroduin*.—Another obit, evidently from a different source, is given by the Four Masters at 1075. In it Ua hEroduin is called Abbot of Armagh.

1075. [1] *Half of Mogh.*—The Southern half of Ireland. So called from Mogh Nuadat (whose first name was Eogan Taidlech), father of Ailill Olum, the father of Eogan Mor (named from the grandfather), eponymous head of the Eoganachts. (L.L. p. 319 b).

[2] *Nights.*—Night, the context shows, in these Annals and elsewhere, sometimes signifies by synecdoche the νυχθήμερον, period, from nightfall to nightfall (cf. *se'n-night, fortnight*). Festiva sancti Columbae nox et solemnis dies nos invenit valde tristificatos (Adamnan, *Vita Col.*, iii. 45). Here the singular shows that *nox* and *dies* are taken collectively. The Tripartite Life of St. Patrick mentions the *forty nights of Lent* (Part ii). The same expression glosses *forty nights* in the Senchas Mor (i. 196). The Book of Armagh (folio 18 c) has *three nights* (that is, nights and days). See Ideler, *Handbuch der math. u. tech. Chronologie*, Berlin, 1825, vol. i. p. 79 sq.

28 annala ulaoh.

hUa m-Ḃriain, ou i torcratur ile.—Donnc̄aḃ hUa Cananna[i]n, ri [Ceniuil-]Conaill, occirur¹ ert.—Domnall, mac Murc̄aḋa, ri Aea-cliaẗ, oo ec oo galur tri n-oiḋce.—Domnall hUa Cainoelba[i]n oo marbaḋ oo Airgiallaib.

bir.ᵃ {Cal. Ian. uii. r., l. xx. 1., Anno Domini m.° lxx.° uii.° Ḡairbeiṫ hUa Innrec̄taiġ, ri hUa-Meiṫ, o Ferait
A 16c Miḋe; Gilla-Crirt hUa | Duiboara, ri Fer-Manac̄, i n-Daim-inir la Firu-Manac̄, occiri runt.—Domnall hUa Crica[i]n, ri hUa-Fiac̄rac Aroa-grata, 7 ar ime oo marbaḋ o'Uib-Tuirtri 7 oo Ceniul-m-Ḃinniġ Ġlinni.—Murc̄aḋ, mac Flainn hUi Mail-Sec̄lainn, ri Temrac̄ fri re tri n-oiḋci, oo marbaḋ i cloiccc̄iuc̄
B 43d Cenjann ra oo mac mic Maela[i]n, ri Ġaileng.—Sloiġeḋ la Tairroelbac̄ i Connactu, co tainicᶠ ri Connac̄t i n-a ṫec̄, ioon, Ruaiḋri hUa Concobair.—Maiom belat ria n-Aeḋ hUa Mael-Sec̄lainn 7 ria Ferait Muiġi-Iṫa for Ciannac̄t[a], co rolaḋ a n-oerġár.—Cele, mac Donnaca[i]n, cenn craḃaḋ Erenn, in Chrirto quieuit.—Gormlaiṫ, ingen Ui Fhocarta,² benᵇ Tairroelbaiġ hUi Ḃriain, oo ec.

{Cal. Ian. i. r., l. ii., Anno Domini M.° lxx.° uiii.° Sloiġeḋ la Tairroealbac̄ hUa m-Ḃriain i n-hUib-Ceinnrelaiġ, gurrocuibriġ mac Domnaill remair, ioon, ri hUa-Ceinnrelaiġ.—Mac mic Maela[i]n, ioon¹, ri Ġaileng, oo marbaḋ la Mael-Sec̄lainn, la riġ Temrac̄.—hUa Loingriġ, ri Dal-Araiḋe, a ruir occirur ert.—Murc̄aḋ

A.D. 1076. ¹tainig, A. ²ócarta (f om., not being pronounced), B. ³bean, B.—ᵃ om., B.
A.D. 1077. ¹om., A.

1076. ¹ *Nights.*—See note 2 under the preceding year.
² *Grandson of Maelan.* — Tigerrach says (A.D. 1076) his name was Amlaim. The patronymic was Ua Leochain.
³ *Stark slaughter.*—Literally, red slaughter.

⁴ *Cele.*—Bishop of Leinster (Kildare), according to the Four Masters. They add that he died [probably, as pilgrim] in Glendalough.
⁵ *Died.*—In Killaloe (Annals of Innisfallen).

fell many.—Donnchadh Ua Canannain, king of Cenel- [1075]
Conaill, was slain.—Domnall, son of Murchadh, king of
Ath-cliath, died of an illness of three nights.[2]—Domnall
Ua Caindelbain was killed by the Airgialla.

Kalends of Jan. on 6th feria, 21st of the moon, A.D. [1076] Bis.
1076. Gairbeith Ua Innrechtaigh, king of Ui-Meith, by
the Men of Meath; Gilla-Crist Ua Duibdara, king of
Fir-Manach, in Daim-inis by the Fir-Manach, were slain.
—Domnall Ua Oricain, king of Ui-Fiacrach of Ard-sratha,
—and slaughter [took place] around him—was killed by
the Ui-Tuirtri and by the Cenel-Binnigh of the Glen.—
Murchadh, son of Flann Ua Mail-Sechlainn, king of Tara
for the space of three nights,[1] was killed in the steeple of
Cenannus by the grandson of Maelan,[2] king of Gailenga.—
A hosting by Tairrdelbach into Connacht, so that the
king of Connacht, namely, Ruaidhri Ua Conchobair, came
into his house.—The defeat of Belat [was inflicted] by
Aedh Ua Mael-Sechlainn and by the Men of Magh-Itha
upon the Ciannachta, so that stark slaughter[3] of them
was inflicted.—Cele,[4] son of Donnacan, head of the piety
of Ireland, rested in Christ.—Gormlaith, daughter of Ua
Focarta [King of Eili], wife of Tairrdelbach Ua Briain, died.[5]

Kalends of Jan. on 1st feria, 2nd of the moon, A.D. [1077]
1077. A hosting by Tairrdelbach Ua Briain into Ui-
Ceinnselaigh, so that he fettered the son of Domnall the
Fat, namely, the king of Ui-Ceinnselaigh.—The grandson
of Maelan,[1] namely, king of Gailenga, was killed by Mael-
Sechlainn, [that is] by the king of Tara.—Ua Loingsigh,
king of Dal-Araidhe, was slain by his own [tribesmen].
—Murchadh [son of Conchobar] Ua Mael-Sechlainn was

1077. [1] *Grandson of Maelan.*— adds that it took place immediately
Tigernach and the Innisfallen Annals after the assassination; the latter,
agree in placing the slaying of Mur- before the end of two months.
chad's slayer at 1076. The former

30 annala ulaoh.

hUa Mael-Seciainn do marbad o Feraib Cebta.—
Maidm Maile-dergi for Feru-Manac ria Cenel-
Eogain Celca-o[i]g,² dú i torcradur ile.—Colcu hUa
Eroda[i]n,⁴ cenn boct Airde-Maca, in pace quieuit.—
Ailbe, ingen ind abad, ben⁵ rig Airter 7 comarba
Moninne 7 Gilla-Patraic, ri Cairpri-hUa-Ciardai, in
penitentia mortui runt.—hUa Celeca[i]n, ridomna
Airter⁶ 7 Ruarc hUa Caduraig, occisi runt.

Kal. Ian. ii. f., L. x.iii., Anno Domini M.º lxx.º iiii.º
Lorcan, hUa Briain, do ecaib.—Letlobur¹ hUa Laidgnen, idon,¹ airdri Airgiall,² do marbad la Ruaidri
hUa Ruadaca[i]n.—Concobar hUa Briain, ri Celca-
ó[i]c 7 ridamna Erenn, do marbad (id^b ert, cum rua
uxore^b) do Cenel-Binnig Glinni.—Dubera, ingen
Athalgada, comarba Patraic, ben rig Airter, do ecaib.
—Domnall, mac mic Tigernain, ri Conmacne; Catal,
mac Domnaill, ri Ceniuil³-Ennai, o Ceniul-Eogain na
hInnri (idon,^b im madmum Muigi-leine^1b); Concubur
hUa Donncada, ridomna Cairl, occisi runt.—Maidm
for Uib-Cremtainn ria Feraib Fernmuigi i Sleib-
[F]uait, i torcair Goll-claraig et alii multi.⁵ Ar
for Conailib ria n-Uib-Meit, i torcair mac hUi
Treoda[i]n⁶, ri Conaille.

²Celca-oc, B. ³—dar, B. ⁴Eru—, B. ⁵bean, A. ⁶—tear, A.
A.D. 1078. ¹ om., A. ²Airgialla, A, B. ³Cenel, B. ⁴Maigi-Leane,
B. ⁵multi, B. ⁶Therodan, B.—ª airdri Airgiall in Letlobur—
arc*King of Airgialla (was) Lethlobur*, l. m., t. h., A.; om., B.   ᵇ l. m., t. h.,
A; r. m., t. h., B.

ª *Daughter of the abbot.*—O'Donovan (p. 910) equates Ailbe and the
successor of St. Moninne (of Newry),
and infers that this is an instance of
a married woman being an abbess.
But the text of the *Four Masters* does
not necessarily mean this. It can
signify that Colcu, Aillbe and the
abbess died. This is put beyond doubt
by the present entry, where the
meaning is clearly that Aillbe and
the abbess and Gilla-Patraic, all

killed by the Men of Tebtha.—The defeat of Mail- [1077]
derg [was inflicted] upon the Fir-Manach by the Cenel-
Eogain of Telach-oc, a place where fell many.—Colcu
Ua Erodhain, head of the poor of Ard-Macha, rested in
peace.—Aillbe, daughter of the abbot,² wife of the king
of the Airthir; and the successor of [St.] Moninne; and
Gilla-Patraic, king of Cairpri-Ua-Ciardai, died in penance.
—Ua Celecain, royal heir of the Airthir, and Ruairc Ua
Cadusaigh were slain.

Kalends of Jan. on 2nd feria, 13th of the moon, A.D. [1078]
1078. Lorcan, grandson of Brian [Boruma] died.—Leth-
lobur Ua Laidhgnen, namely, archking of Airgialla,
was killed by Ruaidhri Ua Ruadhacain.—Concobar Ua
Briain, king of Telach-oc and royal heir of Ireland, was
killed (together, namely, with his wife) by the Cenel-
Binnigh of the Glen.¹—Dubesa, daughter of Amhalgaidh
successor of Patrick, wife of the king of the Airthir, died.
—Domnall, son of Mac Tigernain, king of Conmacni;
Cathal, son of Domnall, king of Cenel-Ennai, by Cenel-
Eogain of the Island (namely, in the defeat of Magh-
Leine); Concobur Ua Donnchadha, royal heir of Cashel,
were slain.—A defeat [was inflicted] upon the Ui-
Cremtainn by the Men of Fern-magh on Sliab-[F]uait,²
wherein fell Goll-claraigh and others many. Slaughter
[was inflicted] upon the Conaille by the Ui-Meith,
wherein fell the son of Ua Treodain, king of Conaille.

---

three, died in penance: very probably at Armagh. Colcu was perhaps the brother of Cumusach Ua hEroduin, who died in 1074, *supra*.

1078. ¹ *Cenel-Binnigh of the Glen.*—How it happened that O'Brien was slain by this Tyrone sept appears from the Annals of Innisfallen, which state that he had received the kingship in Cenel-Eogain (was crowned in Tullaghoge). They add (without mention of the wife) that the slayer was slain straightway, and that Kennedy O'Brien received the kingship.

² *Sliab-[F]uait.—Mount [F]uat.*—The infected *f* (*fh*) was omitted in pronunciation.—" Slevfuaid." C.

32 αnnala ulαoh.

A 46d
B 44a.

|Cal. 1an. 111. p., L xx. 1111., Anno Domini M.° lxx.° ix.° Ceallaċ hUa Ruanaḋa, apollam Erenn; Cu-Miḋe, mac mic Lorca[i]n, ri Fernmuiġi; mac Gillai'-Oiġḋe hUi Lorca[i]n, tecnap Arḋa-Maċa; mac Cuinn, cenn boċt Cluana-mac-Noir, quieuerunt in pace.ª

|Cal. 1an. [i]u. p., L. u., Anno Domini M.° lxxx.° Donn hUa Leṫlobu[i]r¹, ri Fern-muiġi, do marbaḋ do hUiḃ-Laċen i 8leiḃ-[f]uait.—hUa Ciarḋa[i], ri Cairbre, mortu[u]r ert.—Ceallaċ, comarba Patraic, natur ert.—Derbforgaill,² inġen mic Briain, ben Diarmata, mic Mail-na-mbo, do écaib i n-Imliġ.—Eoċaiḋ hUa Merliġ, ri Fern-muiġi, do marbaḋ rer volum.—Donnrleiḃe hUa Eoċaḋa do ḋul irin Mumain co maiṫib Ulaḋ lair, ar cenn tuarurtail.—Maiḋm Aṫa-Erġail i taeḃ Cloċair for Feru'-Manaċ ria n-Domnall hUa Loċlainn 7 ria Feraiḃ Muiġi-Iṫa, i torcraḋur' inġrimtiḋe Arḋa-Maċa,⁵ iḋon, 8itriuc hUa Coema[i]n 7 mac Neill hUi 8herraiġ⁶ et alii:

(Aṫ-Erġa[i]l,ª
i n-ḋionġnat laeiċ a terḃaiḋ;
8oċaiḋe ber cen inṁain
D'iomġuin Aṫa-Erġail.ª)

A.D. 1079. ¹ Ġilla—, A.—²-ª moriuntur, C.
A.D. 1080. ¹—bair, B. ²Derborġaill (f om.), B. ³Feraiḃ—, B. ⁴—ḋar, B. ⁵Maċa om., B. ⁶ferraiġ. A.—ª-ª on text space, n. t. h., A; om., B.

1079. ¹ *Ceallach Ua Ruanadha; Cu-Midhe.*—"Cellach O'Ruanaa, arch-poet of Ireland. Cumie," etc., C. The infected *d* (*dh*) in *Ruanadha* and *Cu-Midhe* (*Hound of Meath*) was not pronounced. For Ua Ruanadha (O'Rooney) see *Todd Lectures*, Ser. iii, Lect. ii.

² *Gilla-Digde.*—*Devotee of* (*St.*) *Digde* (Virgin). One of the name is given in the Martyrology of Tallaght at Jan. 6; another, at Apr. 25.

³ [*Mael-Chiarains, Devotee of* (*St.*) *Ciaran*].—Supplied from the Four Masters. See *Christian Inscriptions*, pp. 66-7.

1080. ¹*Sliab* [*F*]*uat.*—"Slevuaid, *id est*, Mountaine," C.

² *Through treachery.*—"By sleight," C.

³ *Nobles.*—Literally, *worthies*.

⁴ *For the sake of stipend.*—The translator of C. correctly renders: "to bring wages." They were *condottieri*, in fact.

Kalends of Jan. on 3rd feria, 24th of the moon, A.D. [1079] 1079. Ceallach[1] Ua Ruanadha, chief bardic professor of Ireland; Cu-Midhe,[1] grandson of Lorcan, king of Fernmagh; the son of Gilla-Digde[2] Ua Lorcain, vice-abbot of Ard-Macha; [Mael-Chiarain][3] the son of Conn, head of the poor of Cluain-mac-Nois, rested in peace.

Kalends of Jan. on 4th feria, 5th of moon, A.D. 1080. [1080 Bis.] Donn Ua Lethlobuir, king of Fern-magh, was killed by the Ui Lathen on Sliab-[F]uait.[1]—Ua Ciardai, king of Cairbri, died.—Ceallach [Celsus], successor of Patrick, was born.—Derbfhorgaill, daughter of the son of Brian [Boruma], wife of Diarmait, son of Mail-na-mbo, died in Imlech.—Eochaidh Ua Merligh, king of Fern-magh, was killed through treachery.[2]—Donnsleibhe Ua Eochada went into Munster with the nobles[3] of Ulidia along with him for the sake of stipend.[4]—The defeat of the Ford of Ergal by the side of Clochar [was inflicted] upon the Fir-Manach by Domnall Ua Lochlainn and by the Men of Magh-Itha, wherein fell the persecutors[5] of Ard-Macha, namely, Sitriuc Ua Coemain and the son of Niall Ua Serraigh and others:

(The Ford of Ergal [it is],
Wherein heroes cause[6] the dispersing;
A multitude shall be without delight
From the conflict of the Ford of Ergal.)

The Annals of Innisfallen, at 1078, state that Donnsleibhe was dethroned and went to O'Brien, his place being taken by (Aed) Meranach Ua Eochadha.

[5] *The persecutors* (*ingrinntide*[-*i*]).—O'Conor, to whom nothing apparently presented any difficulty, reads *in grainntide Ard*, and translates by *Granarii custos Armachanus!* The translator of C. taking his text to be = *i n-glinntib*, renders it: "in the valleys."

[6] *Wherein heroes cause.*—In the original, *i n-diongnat laeich*; which the Four Masters, according to O'Donovan, transcribe *in drong naittlaic*. The editor, however, renders the words [?] by "people shall hereafter be there (dispersed)"! Furthermore (to judge from the printed text), they give the verse in two lines, ending respectively in *aterbhaid* and *Erghail*. But it is a quatrain in *Rannaihacht bec gairet*,—heptasyllabic lines ending in dissyllables. The metre is called *gairet* (*short*),

C

}Cal. Ian. ui. f., l. x.ui., Anno Domini M.° lxxx.° i.°
Mac Ingeippce, pi Conaille, do mapbaḋ o Fepaiḋ-
Fepn-muiġi.—Ma[c] Craiṫ hUa Oca[i]n, muipe Ceniuil-
Fepẓupa¹; Maelmiṫiġ hUa Maelpuanaiġ, pi hUa-
Tuipcpi, o Cenel-Ḃinniġ Ẓlinni; hUa Uaṫmupa[i]n,²
pi Fep-li, occipi punc.—hUa Maṫgamna, pi Ulaḋ do
mapbaḋ la hUa n-Eoċaḋa i n-Ḃun-da-leṫẓlap.—Ẓilla-
Crone, uapalyacapc Apda-Maċa; hUa Robapcaiġ,
aipcinneċ Condepe³; Flann hUa Lopca[i]n, uapalyacapc
Luẓbaiḋ, in penicencia dopmiepunc.—Copcaċ co n-a
cemplaiḋ 7 Ceall-da-lua ab iẓne dir[p]pacu[e] punc.

}Cal. Ian. uii. f., l. xx. uii., Anno Domini M.° lxxx.° ii.°
Ẓilla-Cpipc hUa Maelpabaill, pi Caippce-Ḃpacaiḋe;
| Finnċaḋ, mac Aṁalẓaḋa, coipeċ Cloinne-Ḃpepail;
Domnall, mac Concobuip hUi Ḃpiain; Caṫal, mac Aeḋa
hUi Conċobaip¹; Flaiṫbepcaċ hUa Maeladuin, pi
Luipẓ; Uiḋpin, mac Mael-Muipe, coipeċ Ceniuil-
Fepaḋaiġ,² omnep occipi punc.

(Domnall,ª Mac Taiḋẓ hUi Concobaip, pidamna
Connaċc, do mapbaḋ la Caṫal hUa Concobaip cpia
Fell.—Caṫal hUa Concobuip do ṫuicim hi caṫ la
Ruaiḋpi hUa Concobaip, co poċaiḋe moip uimeª.)

| }Cal. Ian. i. f., l. ix., Anno Domini M.° lxxx.° iii.°
Domnall hUa Cananna[i]n, pi Ceniu[i]l-Conaill,¹ a
puip occipup epc.—Aeḋ hUa Mael-Seċlainn, pi Ailiġ;

A.D. 1081. ¹ Ceniul—, A. ²—mapan, B. ³ Connepe, B.
A.D. 1082. ¹—buip, B. ² Cenel—, B.—ª f. m., n. t. h., A; om., B;
given in C.
A.D. 1083. ¹ Cenel—, B.

---

because the opening line is (four syllables) *short* of the normal number. See *Todd. Lect., ubi sup.*
1081. ¹ *Steward.*—Here again, the *Four Masters* change *maire* of the Ulster Annals into *tigherna* (lord).

² *Ua Mathgamna.*—This entry is at variance with the Ulidian regnal list (L.L., p. 41), in making Ua Mathgamna king. The correct version is probably that of the Annals of Inisfallen, in which it is stated

Kalends of Jan. on 6th feria, 16th of the moon, A.D. [1081] 1081. Mac Ingerrce, king of Conaille, was killed by the Men of Fern-magh.—Ma[c] Oraith Ua Ocain, steward[1] of Cenel-Fergusa; Maelmithigh Ua Maelruanaigh, king of Ui-Tuirtri, by the Cenel-Binnigh of the Glen; Ua Uathmarain, king of Fir-Li, were slain.—Ua Mathgamna,[2] king of Ulidia, was killed by Ua Eochadha in Dun-da-lethglas.—Gilla-Crone,[3] eminent priest of Ard-Macha; Ua Robartaigh, herenagh of Condere; Flann Ua Lorcain, eminent priest of Lughbaid,[4] slept in penance.—Cork with its churches and Cell-da-lua were wasted by fire.

Kalends of Jan. on 1st feria, 9th of the moon, A.D. [1082] 1082. Gilla-Crist Ua Maelfhabaill, king of Carraic-Bracaidhe; Finnchadh, son of Amhalgaidh, chief of Clann-Bresail; Domnall, son of Conchobur Ua Briain; Cathal, son of Aedh Ua Conchobair; Flaithbertach Ua Maeladuin, king of Lurg; Uidhrin, son of Mael-Muire, chief of Cenel-Feradhaigh, were all slain.

(Domnall,[1] son of Tadhg Ua Concobair, royal heir of Connacht, was killed by Cathal Ua Concobair through treachery.—Cathal[1] Ua Concobair fell in battle[2] by Ruaidhri Ua Concobair, with a great multitude around him.)

Kalends of Jan. on 1st feria, 9th of the moon, A.D. [1083] 1083. Domnall Ua Canannain, king of Cenel-Conaill, was slain by his own [tribesmen].—Aedh Ua Mael-

---

that Gall-na-gorta Ua Mathgamna was slain in Downpatrick by Donn-sleibhe Ua Eochadha.

[3] *Gilla-Crone.*—*Devotee of (St.) Crone (Virgin).* Seventeen of the name are given in the Homonymous Lists of Saints in the Book of Leinster (p. 369 a).

[4] *Priest of Lughbaid.*—The Annals of Inisfallen say he was lector of Emly.

The Four Masters reverse the order of this and the preceding obit, and state (doubtless by an error of transcription) that Ua Robartaigh (O'Roarty) was herenagh of Louth.

1082. [1] *Domnall; Cathall.*—These two bracketted items are found in Tigernach and the Annals of Boyle.

[2] *Fell in battle.*—The so-called Annals of Loch Ce (*ad an.*) state that O'Conor died a natural death (*mortuus est*).

Muircertach hUa Cairill, aircinnech Duin, ʀui brethem-
nacta 7 geanchair; Tadg² hUa Taidg, aircinnech Cille-
da-lua, in pace quieuerunt.—Gilla-Moninne, aircinnech
Lugbaid, occisus³ est.—Aed Meranach do batud ac
Luimniuch.—Ri Ceniuil-Ennai⁴ do marbad la Donnchad
hUa Mael-Sechlainn, la rig n-Ailig.—Domnall hUa
Lochlainn do gabail rigi Ceniuil-Eogain. Creʃ rig
lair ron Conaillib, co tuc boroma mor 7 co tarait
tuarurtal d'on creich sin do feraib Fern-muigi.

[b.r.] |Cal. Ian. 11. f., l. xx., Anno Domini M.º lxxx.º iiii.º
Donnchad hUa Maelruanaig, perrecutor aec[c]leria-
rum, do marbad eter corp 7 anmain o feraib-Luirg.—
Glenn-da-locha, cum suis templis, do lorcad.—Muiredach
hUa Cethnen, aircinnech Cluana-Eoir, do ecc.—Slogad
la Donnsleibe, ri Ulad, co Drochat-n-Atha, co tarat
tuarurtal do mac Cailig hUi Ruairc. Creʃ la Domnall hUa Lochlainn tar a eir i¹ n-Ulltaib, co tucsat
boroma mor.—Slogad la feru Muman i Mide 7 ir
ron an fluagad sin adbat Concobur hUa Cetfada.
Docuatur² Conmacne i Tuath-Mumain tar a n-eiʀi,
co roloircret duine³ 7 cella⁴ 7 co pucsat creich.—Maidm⁵
Mona-Cruinneoice⁶ ria Leth Moga for Donnchad hUa
Ruairc, i torchair hUa Ruairc (idon,ᵇ Donnchad, mac

² Taidg, B.   ³ —ʀʀuʃ, B.   ⁴ Ceniul—, B.
A.D. 1084. ¹ a, B.   ² —dar, B.   ³ dúne, B.   ⁴ cealla, B.   ⁵ batud, B.
—ᵃ⁻ᵃ Cat mona-cruinneogi—Battle of Moin-cruinneogi—is placed on left
margin, n. t. h., opposite these words, A.   ᵇ⁻ᵇ itl., t. h., A ; om., B.

1083.   ¹ Herenagh. — Tigernach
and the Innisfallen Annals call
him, probably with justice, Comarba
(=bishop).

² Aedh Meranach. — Aed the
furious. Tigernach calls him Ua
Eochadha, King of Ulidia. (See
1080, note 4, supra; from which,
taken with present entry, is to be
corrected the list of Kings in L.L. (p.

41 d), in which two years are assigned to his reign. The scribe mistook u for ii.)

His being drowned at Limerick
shows that Aed, like Donnsleibhe,
was in the service of O'Brien.

³ Royal foray.—An idiomatic expression, signifying the first expedition
made by a king after his inaugura-
tion.

Sechlainn, king of Ailech; Muircertach Ua Cairill, [1083] herenagh of Dun, doctor of jurisprudence and of history; Tadhg Ua Taidhg, herenagh[1] of Cell-da-lua, rested in peace.—Gilla-Moninne, herenagh of Lughbaidh, was slain. —Aedh Meranach[2] was drowned at Limerick.—The king of Cenel-Ennai was killed by Donnchadh Ua Mael-Sechlainn, [that is] by the king of Ailech.—Domnall Ua Lochlainn took the kingship of Cenel-Eogain. A royal foray[3] [was made] by him upon Conaille, so that he took away great cattle-spoil and gave stipend out of that foray to the Men of Fern-magh.

Kalends of Jan. on 2nd feria, 20th of the moon, A.D. [1084 Bis. 1084. Donnchadh Ua Maelruanaigh, persecutor of churches, was killed, both body and soul,[1] by the Men of Lurg.—Glenn-da-locha, with its churches, was burned.— Muiredhach Ua Cethnen, herenagh of Cluain-eois, died.— A hosting by Donnsleibhe, king of Ulidia,[2] to Drochat-atha, so that he gave stipend to the son of Cailech Ua Ruairc. A foray [was made] by Domnall Ua Lochlainn after him[3] into Ulidia, so that they took away great cattle-spoil.—A hosting by the Men of Munster into Meath, and it is upon that hosting died Concobur Ua Cetfatha. The Conmacni went into Thomond after them,[4] so that they burned forts and churches and took away spoil.—The defeat of Moin-cruinneoice [was inflicted] by the Half of Mogh upon Donnchadh Ua Ruairc, wherein fell Ua Ruairc (namely, Donnchadh, son of Cailech Ua Ruairc) and Cennetigh Ua Briain and others most

---

1084. [1] *Both body and soul.*— Literally, *between body and soul.* That is, that he was either captured and put to death without benefit of clergy; or killed in the act of desecration.

[2] *Donnsleibhe, King of Ulidia.*—

That is, Ua Eochadha. See A.D. 1080, note 4, *supra.*

[3] *After him.*—That is, whilst Donnsleibhe was absent on the expedition.

[4] *After them.*—When, namely, the Munstermen were gone to Meath.

38 annala ulaḋh.

Cailiġ hUi Ruairc⁽ᵇ⁾) 7 Cenneitiġ hUa Ḃriain et alii plurimi (hi° quartoecim⁽ᵈ⁾ Kalann Nouimbrir⁽ᶜ⁾).—Domnall hUa Ġailmreḋaiġ do marbaḋ do Domnall hUa Loċlainn.—Ġilla-Patraic, errroc Aṫa-cliaṫ, do baṫaḋ.⁽ᵉ⁾

(hoc° anno ecclesia Sanct[a]e Puince de Rororrḃir funoata est°.)

Kal. Ian. 1111.ᵃ f., L. 1., Anno Domini M.° lxxx.° u.°
Mac Soilliġ, airċinneċ Innri-cain-Deġa; Uġaire hUa
Laiḋġnen, airċinneċ | Ferna; Ġormġal Loiġreċ, comarba reclera Ḃriġte i n-Ard-Maċa, rui⁽ᵇ⁾ i n-ecna 7 i crabaḋ⁽ᵇ⁾;
Mael-rneċtai, mac Lulaiġ, ri Muireḃ; Cleireċ hUa
Selbaiḋ, airċinneċ Corcaiġi¹, suam uitam feliciter finierunt.—Murċaḋ hUa Maeldoraiḋ, ri Ceniu[i]l-Conaill; Domnall, mac Mael-Coluim, ri Alban; Muireḋaċ, mac Ruaiḋri hUi Ruaḋaca[i]n; hUalġarc hUa Ruairc, rioḋomna Connaċt; Oenġur hUa Cainoel-ba[i]n, ri Loeġuiri,² suam uitam infeliciter finierunt.

| Kal. Ian. u. f., L. xii., Anno Domini M.° lxxx.° ui.°
Mael-Iru hUa Ḃrolca[i]n, rui in ecnai 7 in crabaḋ 7¹

ᵃ⁻ᵃ l. m., t. h., A; om., B, C. ᵈ.x.1111., MS. ᶜ⁻ᶜ l. m., n. t. h., A; om., B.
A.D. 1085. ¹—aiḋe, B. ²—aire, B ᵃ.uii., B. The scribe took the first two ii. of 1111. for u., a mistake of frequent recurrence. ᵇ⁻ᵇ rui ino ecnai 7 in crabaḋ —*master of wisdom and of piety*, B.

---

⁵ *The 14th.*—The Four Masters (*ad an.*) say *the 4th* of the Kalends [Oct. 29]. They overlooked x. in the xiiii. of their original (MS. A).

⁶ *Gilla-Patraic.*—*Devotee of* [*St.*] *Patrick.* He was consecrated in London in 1073 by Lanfranc, Archbishop of Canterbury, in accordance with the request of the Dublin clergy. He made a profession to Lanfranc, from whom he received letters *dignas valde memoriae* (Appendix to Anglo-Saxon Chronicle), to be delivered to the kings of Ireland.

⁷ *This year, etc.*—Given in Irish in the Four Masters.

⁸ *At.*—Literally, *of.* Of the twelve given in the Homonymous Lists (L.L. p. 369b), the Saint intended was most probably Fainche of Lough Ree, whose feast was Jan. 1 (Mart. Tal., L.L. p. 355 c).

1085. ¹ *Superior.*—Literally, *successor;* but employed here and elsewhere in the secondary sense of superior (abbot, or bishop, or both). Gormgal was an abbot.

² *Mael-snechtai.*—His name occurs,

numerous (on the 14th' of the Kalends of November [Oct. 19].—Domnall Ua Gailmredhaigh was killed by Domnall Ua Lochlainn.—Gilla-Patraic,⁶ bishop of Ath-cliath, was drowned.

(This⁷ year the church of Saint Fuinche [Fainche] at⁸ Rosoirrther was founded.)

Kalends of Jan. on 4th feria, 1st of the moon, A.D. 1085. Mac Soillig, herenagh of Inis-cain of [St.] Daig; Ughaire Ua Laidhgnen, herenagh of Ferns; Gormgal Loigsech, superior¹ of the establishment of Brigit in Ard-Macha, eminent in wisdom and in piety; Mael-snechtai,² son of Lulach, king of Moray; Cleirech Ua Selbaidh, herenagh³ of Cork, felicitously finished their life.—Murchadh Ua Maeldoraidh, king of Cenel-Conaill; Domnall, son of Mael-Coluim, king of Scotland; Muiredach, son of Ruaidhri Ua Ruadacain; Ualgarc Ua Ruairc, royal heir of Connacht; Oengus Ua Caindelbain, king of Loeghaire, infelicitously⁴ finished their life. [1085]

Kalends of Jan. on 5th feria, 12th of the moon, A.D. 1086. Mael-Isu Ua Brolcain,¹ master of wisdom and of [1086]

as grantor of land to [St.] Drostan, in the second Gaelic charter in the *Book of Déar* (a ninth cent. Evangelistarium in the Public Library, Cambridge). His obit was thus doubtless recorded in the Columban Annals; whence it passed into the present Chronicle.

³ *Herenagh*—The Annals of Innisfallen call him *Comorba*, i.e., successor of [Finn-]barr; that is, bishop of Cork.

⁴ *Infelicitously.*—That is, suddenly or by violence.

1086. ¹ *Mael-Isu Ua Brolcain.*—Of Mael-Isu's poems in the native tongue, that in the *Book of Hymns*, with the rubric *Mael-Isu dixit*, may perhaps be reckoned as one. It consists of three quatrains, praying to the Holy Ghost through Christ. The final distich embodies well the *Filioque* clause of the Nicene Creed:

A Isu, ronnoeba,
Rensoera do Spirut.

"O Jesus! may Thy Spirit us sanctify, us save."

Another is contained in the *Yellow Book of Lecan* (a MS. in the Library of Trinity College, Dublin, classed H. 2, 16), col. 336, with the heading *Mael-Isu* [MS. form is *Ihu.*]*h Ua Brolchain cecinit*. It is an invocation of the Archangel Michael in nine stanzas.

A third is given in *Lebar Brec* (Lith. ed., p. 101), with the inscrip-

40 ανναλα υλαδη.

1 ꞃιlιδεčτ¹ ι² m-beꞃlaı³ ceččaꞃδaι, ꞃuum⁴ ꞃꞃıꞃıτum emıꞃıτ:

Sepτıcım⁵ Kalann Febꞃa,
Aıδcı ꞃeıle Fuꞃꞃa ꞃınn,
Aobaτ Mael-Iꞃꞃu hUa Oꞃolca[ı]n,
Ač! cıa ꝺanaċ τꞃom τam τınn?—

Mael-Seċlaınn hUa Faəla[ı]n, aτloeċ τoȝaıδı; Macbeaταꝺ hUa Concobuıꞃ, ꞃı Cıaꞃaıδe; Eꞃċaδ hUa Mael-Ḟoȝamaıꞃ, aꞃꝺeꞃꞃcop Connaτ; Mael-Coemȝın, uaꞃaleꞃꞃcop Ulaδ; ꞃıaċn a U ı Rona[ı]n, aıꞃcınneċ Cluana-ꝺolca[ı]n, ın pace ꝺoꞃmıeꞃunτ.—Aṁalȝaıδ, mac Ruaıδꞃı hUı Ruaδaca[ı]n, ꝺo maꞃbaδ ꝺo Feꞃaıδ Feꞃn-muıȝı.— Taıꞃꞃꝺelbaċ⁵ hUa Oꞃıaın, ꞃı Eꞃenn, ꝺo ec ı Cınn-ċoꞃaδ, ıaꞃ moꞃ maꞃτꞃa 7 ıaꞃ n-aıτꞃıȝı Ḟoτa 7 ıaꞃ τomaılτ Cuıꞃp Cꞃıꞃτ 7 a Ḟhola, ı ꞃꞃıꝺ Iꝺ Iuıl, ıꞃın ꞃeċτmaꝺ⁶ blıaδaın ꞃeċτmoȝmaꝺ⁶ a aıꞃı:

Aıδċı⁵ Maıꞃτ, ı ꞃꞃıꝺ Iτ Iuıl,
1 ꞃeıl Iacoıb co n-ȝlanꞃuın,
1 nomaꝺ⁴ ꞃıċeτ, aoδaτ
In τ-aıꞃꝺꞃıȝ τenn, Taıꞃꞃꝺelbaċ.⁵

A.D. 1086. ¹,¹ 7 ꞃılıδeccτa—*and of poetry*, B. ²,³ ın beꞃlaı—*of the language* B. ³ꞃuam, A. ⁴—ꝺeal—, A. ⁵,⁵ t. m., with relative marks, t. h., A; om B.—ᵇ,ᵇ.uıı. maꝺ blıaδaın .lxx. maꝺ, A, B. ᶜ om., B. ᵈ .ıx., MS. (A).

---

tion *Moel-Isu hUa Brochcha[i]n cecinit.* This is a bilingual rhymed prayer of seven stanzas to God the Son. The opening quatrain will best show the structure. Its singularity, no doubt, caused the chronicler to class the author as an adept "in poetry in either language."

Deus meus, adjuva me,
Tucc dam do sherc, a mic mo De,
Tucc dam do sherc, a mic mo De,
Deus meus, adjuva me.

(The second line means: Give to me Thy love (=love of Thee), O Son of my God).

From the foregoing it is evident why Ua Brolcain took the name of Mael-Isu—*Devotee of Jesus.*

² *Night.*—See 1075, note 2, *supra.*
³ *Fursa.*—XVII. Kal. [Feb.] *Dormitatio[nis] Fursei* (Mart. Tal., L.L. 356 b). For his *Vision* (Vol. I. p. 97; where he is erroneously styled bishop), see Bede, H. E. iii. 19. His death (Vol. I. pp. 109, 117) took place probably in 650.

⁴ *Alas!* etc.—The original of this line is thus given by the *Four Masters*: *Acht cidheadh nir trom tamh tinn* (rendered by O'Donovan: "But,

piety and in poetry in either language, sent forth his [1086]
spirit:

    The seventeenth of the Kalends of February [Jan. 16],
    The night[3] of the feast of Fursa[3] fair,
    Died Mael-Isu Ua Brolchain,

Alas[4]! who [is there] to whom it is not grievous plague sore!—Mael-Sechlainn Ua Foelain, lay-brother[5] select; Macbeathad Ua Concobuir, king of Ciaraidhe; Erchadh Ua Mael-fhoghamair, archbishop of Connacht [Tuam]; Mael-Coemghin, archbishop of Ulidia [Down]; Fiachna Ua Ronain, herenagh of Cluain-dolcain, slept in peace.—Amhalgaidh, son of Ruaidhri Ua Ruadhacain, was killed by the Men of Fern-magh.—Tairrdelbach Ua Briain, king of Ireland, died in Cenn-coradh, after much suffering and after long penance and after partaking of the Body of Christ and of His Blood, on the 2nd of the Ides [14th] of July, in the seventh year [and] seventieth of his age:

    The night of Tuesday,[6] on the foreday of the Ides of July,
    On the feast of James[7] of pure mind,
    On the ninth [and] twentieth[8] [of the moon], died
    The stout archking, Tairrdelbach.

---

however, not of a heavy severe fit"). Thus misled, Colgan perpetuated the error: *Nulla tamen infirmitate correptus* (*AA. SS.*, p. 108). His version has been adopted by O'Conor (note at A.D. 1086 in his edition of the *Annals of Ulster*).

[5] *Lay-brother.*—Literally, *ex-laic*. The *athloech* was the *laicus*, or *frater conversus*, of the Latin Monastic Rules: a monk who was neither in Holy Orders, nor bound to recitation of the Office.

The (*Penitential*) *Commutations* (in Rawlinson B. 512, a MS. in the Bodleian Library, Oxford) have: *Arra na n-athlaech ocus na n-athlae-* *ces cetumus*—The commutation of lay-brothers and lay-sisters (is to be set forth) first (folio 42 d). As Ua Foelain (O'Phelan) was member of a ruling family, his humility appeared remarkable in the selection of the lowest grade in the monastery.

[6] *Tuesday.*—July 14 fell on that day in 1086. For *night*, see 1075, note 2, *supra*. *La* (day) being monosyllabic, *aidchi* was employed here and in the preceding quatrain to produce a line of seven syllables.

[7] *On the feast of James.*—The incidence of the festival is taken perhaps from the Calendar of Oengus (where the saint is called a bishop).

D

Ταιδc° ιmoρρo,' α mac, oo éc a cιnn ṁíρ.°—Maιom
na Cρinča ρoρ Mael-Seaclainn ρια Laιξniδ 7 ρια
ξallaιδ, 1 τoρčaιρ Mael-Cιaρa[ι]n hUa Caδuρaιξ, ρι
Uρeξ eτ alιι mulτι.—Maιom ρια n-Ccιρτeρaιδ ρoρ
Uιδ-Ečač,⁵ 1 τoρčaιρ Oomnall hUa Ccτειδ.—Maιom
Eočaille ρια n-Ulltaιδ ρoρ Ccιρξιallu 7 ρoρ Ua-Ruaδ-
aca[ι]n, δύ 1 τoρčaιρ Cumuρcač hUa Laιčειn, ρι Sιl-
Oυιδτιρe 7 ξιlla-Monιnne hUa Eočaδa, muιρe Cloιnnι-
Sιnaιξ eτ alιι mulτι.⁶

ḳal. 1an. uι. ρ., L. xx.ιιι., Ccnno Oomιnι M.° lxxx.°
uιι.° Oomnall, mac ξιlla-ρaτραιc, ρι Oρραιξι, oo ec.—
Caτal hUa Ceτρaδa oo maρbaδ oo Laιξniδ.—Cu-ρleιbe
hUa Cιaρδa[ι], ρι Caιρbρe, α ρuιρ occιρuρ eρτ.—Mael-
Sečlainn, mac Concobuιρ, ρι Τeamρač, oo maρbaδ la
ρiρu Τeτba¹ | 1 mebaιl (ιoon° 1 n-Ccρo-ačaιδ Eρρcoιρ
Mel°).—Oomnall hUa Laιčen oo maρbaδ la Oomnall,
mac Mιc Loclainn.—Caτ (ι⁵ Coρunn⁶) eτeρ Ruaιδρι
hUa Concobaιρ, ρι Connačτ 7 Ccεδ hUa Ruaιρc, ρι
Conmaιcne, 1 τoρčaιρ Ccεδ, ρι Conmaιcne° 7 maιčι Con-
maιcne.—Lonξuρ la macu mιc Raξnaιll 7 la mac ριξ
Ulaδ 1 Manaιnn, δύ 1 τoρcρaτoυρ² maιc³ mιc Raξnaιll.—
Meρ⁴ móρ ιn hoc anno.

ᵃ⁻ᵃ om., A. ᶠueρo, the Latin equivalent, B. ᵇ—Eačač, B. ⁶om., B.

A.D. 1087. ¹Τετρα, A. ²-cρaταρ, B. ³mac, A. The omission of
ι was doubtless an oversight. ⁴meaρρ, B. ᵃ⁻ᵃ itl., t.h., A; om., B. ᵇ⁻ᵇ itl.,
t. h., A; ιoon, 1 Coρunn—*that is, in Corann,* r. m., t. h., B. ᶜ⁻ᶜιoon,
Ccεδ—*namely, Aedh,* itl., t. h. over ρι Conmaιcne, B.

But it is not so found in the Hieronymian Martyrologies (*Acta SS., Jun. t. vi., p.* 1), some of which give St. James of Nisibis and St. James of Alexandria at July 15.

⁵ *On the ninth* [*and*] *twentieth.*—The Four Masters read *Iar ndó fichet adbath* " after two (and) twenty died." But the change can be detected with certainty. The metre is *Debide* (consisting, namely, of heptasyllabic lines). The syllable short in the reading of the Four Masters accordingly betrays the line in question. The 29th of the July moon coincided in 1086 with the 14th of the solar month ; new moon having occurred on June 16. Not understanding to

ANNALS OF ULSTER. 43

Taidhc, his son, also died at the end of a month.—[1086] The defeat of Crinach [was inflicted] upon Mael-Sechlainn by the Leinstermen and by the Foreigners, wherein fell Mael-Ciarain Ua Cadhusaigh, king of Bregha and others many.—A defeat [was inflicted] by the Airthir upon the Ui-Echach, wherein fell Domnall Ua Atteidh.—The defeat of Eochaill [was inflicted] by the Ulidians upon the Airgialla and upon Ua Ruadhacain, a place wherein fell Cumuscach Ua Laithen, king of Sil-Duibhtire and Gilla-Moninne Ua Eochadha, steward[9] of Clann-Sinaigh and many others.

Kalends of Jan. on 6th feria, 23rd of the moon, A.D. [1087] 1087. Domnall, son of Gilla-Patraic,[1] king of Ossory, died. Cathal Ua Cetfada was killed by the Leinstermen.—Cu-sleibe Ua Ciardhai, king of Cairpri, was slain by his own [kinsmen].—Mael-Sechlainn, son of Concobur, king of Tara, was killed by the men of Tebtha in treachery (namely, in Ard-achaidh of Bishop Mel).—Domnall Ua Laithen was killed by Domnall, son of Mac Lochlainn.—A battle [was fought] (namely, in Corann) between Ruidhri Ua Concobair, king of Connacht and Aedh Ua Ruairc, king of Conmaicni, wherein fell Aedh, king of Conmaicni and the nobles[2] of Conmaicni.—A fleet [was led] by the grandsons of Ragnall and by the son of the king of Ulidia into Manann,[3] a place where fell the grandsons of Ragnall.—A great crop this year.

---

what the numerals had reference, the Four Masters changed them to signify the regnal years (22) of the deceased. Herein, needless to add, they have been followed by O'Conor. O'Donovan renders the phrase "on the twenty-second" and makes no remark.

[9] *Steward (muire).*—*Lord (tigherna),* Four Masters.

1087. [1] *Gilla-Patraic.*—Died A.D. 1055 (*supra*).

[2] *Nobles.*—Literally, *good* (men).

[3] *Mannan.*—" Id est, Ile of Man." C. The *grandsons,* there can be little doubt, were the sons of the Amhlam (Olaf) mentioned at 1075 (*supra*).

D 2

44 annala ulaoh.

(Τranrlacio⁴ reliquiarum Sancti Nicholaui hoc anno, reptimo Idur Maii.ᵈ)

bir.ᵃ Kal. Ian. uii. r., L, 1111., Anno Domini M° lxxx.° uiii.°
Catalan hUa Forreib, rui ino ecnai 7 in crabab, 1 ter[t] Non Marta, 1 n-Imlig-ibair, Dia-Domnaig Init[e], in pace quieuit:

   Catalanᵇ, in crabaib coir,
   ba rruig ramaib¹, ba renoir,
   ror nem, 1 n-a n-grianan n-gle,
   Luib 1 reil Ciarain Saigre.ᵇ—

Slogab la Domnall, mac Mic Loclainn, la rig n-Ailig, 1 Connactu, co tarb Ruaibri | giallu Connact do 7 co n-deocarur diblinaib irin Mumain, co roloircet Luimnec 7 in macaire co Dun-aceb, co tucrat leo cenn mic Cailig 7 co rotocglairet Cenn-corab 7 araile.—Tigernac hUa broein, aircinnec Cluana-mac-Noir, in Chrirto quieuit.
—Ar mor ror gallu Ata-cliat 7 Loca-Carman 7 Puirt-lairgi ria n-Uib-Eacac Muman irind lo romiberatur Corgaig do arcain.—Mael-Iru hUa Mael-Ghiric, aroriLe Erenn, do ec.

(hocᶜ anno natus ert Toirrdelbac hUa Concobair ri Erenn.ᶜ)

ᵈ⁻ᵈ n. t. h., A; om., B; given in C.
A.D. 1088. ¹ ramta is the genitive employed elsewhere in the Annals.—ᵃ om., B. ᵇ⁻ᵇ f. m., t. h., with corresponding reference marks, A; om., B. ᶜ⁻ᶜ n. t. h., A; om., B; given in C.

ᵃ *Translation, etc.*—The relics of St. Nicholas of Myra were carried off from the church of Myra by some merchants of Bari, in Italy and placed in the church of St. Stephen at Bari, on the 9th of May, in this year.

1088. ¹ *Sunday of the beginning* [of Lent].—O'Conor, by an inexcusable blunder, renders this by *Dominica in Quinquagesima*. In 1088, Easter fell upon April 16. *Quinquagesima* was, accordingly, Feb. 26. The first Sunday of Lent, as the text correctly states, coincided with the feast of St. Ciaran, March 5th. O'Donovan's *Shrovetide Sunday* (*F. M.* p. 931), which is the same as O'Conor's *Quinquagesima*, was doubtless taken from C.

²⁻² *Elder—senior.*—This bilingual (Hiberno-Latin) hendiadys is em-

ANNALS OF ULSTER. 45

(Translation[4] of the relics of Saint Nicholas [took place] [1087]
this year, on the seventh of the Ides [9th] of May.)

Kalends of Jan. on 7th feria, 4th of the moon, A.D. [1088] Bis.
1088.—Cathalan Ua Forreidh, master of wisdom and of
piety, on the third of the Nones [5th] of March rested
in peace, in Imlech-ibhair, the Sunday of the beginning [of
Lent] :[1]

> Cathalan, the devotee just,
> He was a community elder[2], he was a senior ;[2]
> To heaven, into its sunny mansion bright,
> He went on the feast [March 5] of Ciaran of Saighir.—

A hosting [was made] by Domnall, son of Mac Lochlainn,
[namely] by the king of Ailech, into Connacht, so that
Ruaidhri gave the pledges of Connacht to him and they went,
both of them, into Munster, until they burned Limerick
and the plain as far as Dun-ached [and] carried away with
them the head of the son of Cailech[3] [Ua Ruairc] and
razed Cenn-coradh and so on[4].—Tighernach Ua Broein,[5]
herenagh of Cluain-mac-Nois, rested in Christ.—Great
slaughter [was inflicted] upon the Foreigners of Ath-cliath
and of Loch Carman and of Port-lairgi by the Ui-Eachach
of Munster, on the day they designed to pillage Cork.—
Mael-Isu Ua Mael-Ghiric,[6] archpoet of Ireland died.

(This year[7] was born Toirrdelbach Ua Concobair, king
of Ireland.)

---

ployed to eke out the line. The *sruth* was the *senior* of the Latin Rule: a monk who acted as counsellor to the abbot and spiritual director to the brethren.

[3] *Son of Cailech.*—That is, Donchad, son of Cailech O'Rourke, who was slain in the battle of Monecronock, co. Kildare (*supra*, A.D. 1084). Tigernach (*sub eod. an.*) states that his head was carried to Limerick.

[4] *And so on.*—This expression signifies that the account which the compiler had before him was more diffuse.

[5] *Tighernach Ua Broein.*—The well-known compiler of the *Annals of Tigernach*. It seems strange that a curt obit like this is all that was devoted to him in the present Chronicle.

[6] *Mael-Ghiric.*—Devotee of *Quiricus* (or *Gricus*), martyr, of Antioch: commemorated in the Calendar of Oengus, at June 16).

[7] *This year, etc.*—Given in the *Annals of Boyle* under 1088.

46 annala ulaoh.

Kal. Ian. 11. f., L., x. u., Anno Domini M., lxxx., ix. Lurca do Lorcab 7 noi⁴ ficit⁴ duine do Lorcad i n-a daimliac o Fheraib Muman.—Ceall-dara do Lorcab ter in hoc anno.—Donncad, mac Domnaill remair, ri Laigen, a ruir occifur ert.—Muircertac hUa Laitein, ri Sil-Duibtire, do éc.—Cuit [ti]gernaide fer fern-muigi 7 rocaide¹ arcena do marbad la hUib-Ecac² 7 la hUlltu i Sleib-[f]uait.—Donncad, hua⁵ Gilla-Patraic, ri Orraigi, a ruir occifur ert.—Gill[a]-Patraic hUa Celeca[i]n, recnar Arda-Maca, do ec aidce Notlaic mo[i]r.

B 45a Kal. Ian. 111. f., L. xx. ui., Anno Domini M.° xc.° Idon, bliadain deirid¹ Ogdata 7 ind nocadmad bliadain ar mili o Gein Crirt. Maelduin hUa Rebaca[i]n, comarba Mocutu; Cian hUa Duacalla, comarba Cainnig i Ciannact[aib], in Chrirto raufauerunt.—Maelruanaig hUa Cairella[i]n, muire Clainni-Diarmata; Gilla-Crirt hUa Luing, muire Ceniuil-Maine, do marbad i n-aen lo fer dolum o Domnall hUa Loclainn.—

A.D. 1089. ¹ rocaidi, B. ²—Eacac, A.—ᵃ·ᵇ ix. xx., A, B. ᵇ mac—son, B.
A.D. 1090. ¹ deifeid, B.

1089. ¹ *Were burned.*—They had probably fled to the church for protection.
² *Some of the nobility.*—Literally, *a lordly portion.* The Four Masters state that twelve tanists of noble tribes fell. (For the *noble* and *free* tribes, see O'Donovan, *Book of Rights*, pp. 174-5.)
O'Conor misreads the text *Cuit Gernaide for Fernmuighe* and translates: *Praelium Gernadiense contra Fernmoyenses.* C. has "the battle of Gernaide"; but the battle was fought at Sliab-Fuait (the Fews mountains, co. Armagh).
³ *Grandson.*—He was son of Domnall, who died 1087 (*supra*).

1090. ¹ *Ogdoad.*—O Conor translates *Oydata* by *novae numerationis*, with a reference to A.D. 963 (=964), *supra.* At the place referred to, he renders *lan tadchoir* by *plenaria numeratio poetica*; because, according to him, the Irish poets numbered 500 years from St. Patrick's advent in 432 down to the year 963! This is scarcely worth refutation. *Tadchoir* is a well-authenticated word, meaning *reversion*, return (*ni fil taidchur*—there is not return: *na bid taidchur*—let there not be return. Würzburg *Codex Paulinus*, fol. 3a). Hence, in a secondary sense, it signifies *Cycle.* The *full Cycle* means the great Paschal Cycle of

Kalends of Jan. on 2nd feria, 15th of the moon, A.D. 1089.—Lusk was burned and nine score persons were burned[1] in its stone church by the men of Munster.—Cell-dara was burned thrice in this year.—Donnchadh, son of Domnall the Fat, king of Leinster, was slain by his own [kinsmen].—Muircertach Ua Laithen, king of Sil-Duibthire, died.—Some of the nobility[2] of the men of Fern-magh and a multitude besides were killed by the Ui-Echach and by the Ulidians on Sliab-[F]uait.—Donnchadh, grandson[3] of Gilla-Patraic, king of Ossory, was slain by his own [kinsmen].—Gilla-Patraic Ua Celecain, vice-abbot of Ard-Macha, died on the night of great Christmas. [1089]

Kalends of Jan. on 3rd feria, 26th of moon, A.D. 1090: namely, the final year of the Ogdoad[1] and the ninetieth year above a thousand from the birth of Christ. Maelduin Ua Rebacain, successor of [St.] Mochutu[2]; Cian Ua Buachalla, successor of [St.] Cainnech in Ciannachta,[3] reposed in Christ.—Maelruanaigh Ua Cairellain, steward[4] of Clan-Diarmata; Gilla-Crist Ua Lunigh, steward[4] of Cenel-Maine, were killed on one day in treachery by Domnall Ua Lochlainn.—The stone church of the Relics[5] [1090]

---

632 years, as distinct from the solar and lunar cycles of 28 and 19 respectively. It is fancifully employed A.D. 963 (=964), *supra*, to denote that a period equal thereto elapsed from the coming of St. Patrick, in 432, down to that year.

Ogdoad (ὀγδοάς) signifies the eight first years of the Cycle of Nineteen. (The remaining eleven were called *Hendecad*, ἐνδεκάς.) The last year thereof being sufficiently designated by the epact, *xxvi.*, this formal identification was superfluous. It was taken apparently from the margin of a Paschal Table. (See

Bede: *De temp. rat., cap. xlvi.*: *De Ogdoade et Hendecade.*)

[2] *Successor of* [St.] *Mochutu.*—That is, bishop of Lismore, co. Waterford.

[3] *Successor of* [St.] *Cainnech in Cianachta.*—"I.e. abbot of Drumachose, in the barony of Keenacht and co. Londonderry." (O'Donovan, *Four Masters,* p. 938.)

[4] *Steward.—Muire*; lord (*tigherna*), *Four Masters*.

[5] *Relics.*—Literally, *graves.* From the Book of Armagh we learn that a procession took place thereto

Damliac na Ferta do lorcad co cet taiξi[b] ime.—Comdal eter Domnall, mac Mic Loclainn 7 Muircertac hUa Driain, ri Cairil 7 mac Flainn hUi Mael-Seclainn, ri Temrach, co tartrat a² n-giallu* uili³ do riξ Ailiξ. (Taitlec^b hUa hEξra do erξabail^b)

Kal. Ian. iiii. f., L uii., Anno Domini M.° xc.° i.° Murcad, mac mic Domnaill remair, do marbad i medail la Enna, mac Diarmata.— | In let iartarac do Rait Arda-Maca¹ do lorcad.—Donnrleibe hUa Eocada, ri Ulad, do marbad la mac Mic Loclainn, la riξ Oiliξ, i m-belac goirt-in-ibair i cat.—Mac Aeda, mic Ruaidri, ri Iartair Con[n]act, do éc.—Mael-Iru, comarba Patraic, i quindecim² Kalann Enair, in renitentia² quieuit. Domnall, mac Amalgada, do oironed irin abdaine i n-a inad ro cetoir.—Bliadain tra rucac co n-deξrin in bliadain ri.

Kal. Ian. u. f., L x. uiii., Anno Domini M.° xc.° ii.° In craibdec hUa Follamain¹ do Con[n]actaib do batud.— Cluain-mac-Noir do milliud la firu Muman.—Ruaidri hUa Concobuir, airdri Con[n]act, do dallud la hUa

²⁻²giallu (that is, the pers. pron. om.), A. ³uile, A.—ᵃc., A, B. ᵇ⁻ᵇn. t. h., A; om., B. Given in C.

A.D. 1091. ¹ Airdmacha, A. —cia, A.—ᵃ x.u., A, B. 9 Kal. Januarii (Dec. 24), C.

A.D. 1092. ¹ Follorhain, B.

every Sunday from the church in the Close. The prescribed Psalms are also given. Fundamentum orationis in unaquaque die Dominica in Alto Machae ad Sargifagum Martyrum (glossed on centre margin, *du ferti martur*—to grave of relics) adeundum ab eoque revertendum: id est: *Domine, clamavi ad te* [Ps. cxl.], usque in finem; *Ut quid, Deus, repulisti in finem* [Ps. lxxiii. (usque in finem)] et *Beati inmaculati* [Ps. cxviii.], usque in finem; Benedictionis [-es, Dan. iii. 57-88] et xv. Psalmi Graduum [Ps. cxix.-cxxxiii.].

⁶ *They.*—Namely, Muircertach and the son of Flann.

⁷ *King of Ailech.*—That is, Domnall, son of Mac Lochlainn.

⁸ *Ua Eghra.*—O'Hara, king of the Connaught Luighni; slain in 1095 by the Conmaicni of Dunmore, co. Galway.

[in Ard-Macha] was burned, with one hundred houses [1090] therearound.—A meeting between Domnall, son of Mac Lochlainn, and Muircertach Ua Briain, king of Cashel and the son of Flann Ua Mael-Sechlainn, king of Tara, so that they[6] gave all their pledges to the king of Ailech.[7]
(Taitlech Ua Eghra[8] was taken prisoner.)

Kalends of Jan. on 4th feria, 7th of the moon, A.D. [1091] 1091.—Murchadh, grandson of Domnall the Fat, was killed in treachery by Enna, son of Diarmait.—The western half of the Close of Ard-Macha was burned.—Donnsleibe Ua Eochadha,[1] king of Ulidia, was killed by the son of Mac Lochlainn, [namely] by the king of Ailech, in the "Pass of the Field of the Yew," in battle.—The son of Aedh, son of Ruaidhri, king of the West of Connacht, died.—Mael-Isu, successor of [St.] Patrick, on the fifteenth of the Kalends of January [Dec. 18][2] rested in penance. Domnall, son of Ambalgaidh, was immediately instituted [*recte,* intruded] into the abbacy in his stead.—A sappy year in sooth with good weather [was] this year.

Kalends of Jan. on 5th feria, 18th of the moon, A.D. [1092]Bis. 1092.—The Devotee Ua Follamhaim of Connacht was drowned.[1]—Cluain-mac-Nois was laid waste by the men of Munster.—Ruaidhri Ua Conchobuir, archking of Connacht, was blinded by Ua Flaithbertaigh (namely, Flaithbertach) in treachery.—Muiredach Mac Cartaigh,

---

1091. [1] *Donnsleibe Ua Eochadha.*—He slew his predecessor, Ua Mathgamna, in 1081, *supra*. The regnal list in L.L. (p. 41c) gives him a reign of 30 years!

[2] [Dec. 18].—Dec. 28, according to the Annals of Loch Ce; Dec. 20, according to the *Four Masters*, who have been followed by Colgan (*Tr. Th.*, p. 229). The true date cannot be determined in the absence of the lunation.

1092. [1] *Drowned.*—In Loch Carrgin ("Cargin's Lough, near Tulsk, co. Roscommon," O'Donovan, *F.M.*, Vol. ii. p. 942), according to the Annals of Boyle.

[2] *The close of Ard-Macha, etc.*—

Flaitbertaiʃ (idon,ᵇ Flaitbertaċᵇ) 1 mebail.—Muiredaċ Mac Carṫaiʃ, ri Eoganaċta Cairil, mortu[i]r ert.—Flaitbertaċ, mac Ruaiḋri hUi Ruaḋaca[i]n, o Uiḃ-Eċaċ occirur ert.—Domnall, macᶜ Amalgaḋa, comarba Patraic, for cuairt Ceniuil-Eogain, co tuc a reir.—Raiṫ Aird-Maċa co n-a tempull do lorcaḋ 1 quartᵗ Kalann Septemher 7 rreċ do Tṙuin Mor 7 | rreċ do Tṙiun Saxan.—Enna, mac Diarmata,ᵃ ri hUa-Ceinnrelaiʃ, a ruir occirur ert.—Connmaċ hUa Cairill, uaral errcop Con[n]aċt, quieuit.—Mael-Iru hUa hAṙṙaċta[i]n, comarba Ailbe, in pace quieuit.

Kal. Ian. uii. f., l. xx. ix., Anno Domini M.ᵒ xc.ᵒ iii.ᵒ Donnċaḋ Mac Carṗtaiʃ, ri Eoganaċta Cairil; Trenair hUa Ceallaiʃ, ri Ḃreʃ; Aeḋ hUa Daiʃella[i]n, ri Ferṅ-muiʒi; Aeḋ, mac Cataill hUi Conċobair, riḋomna Connaċt, omnes occiri sunt.—Aeḋ, aircinneċ Daimliac-Cianna[i]n; Ailill hUa Nialla[i]n, comarba Ciara[i]n 7 Crona[i]n 7 Mic Duaċ; Foċuḋ, ardersgop Alban, in Christo quieuerunt.—Sil-Muiredaiʃ do innarba[ḋ] a Con[n]aċtaiḃ do Muirceṙtaċ hUa Ḃriain.—Aeḋ hUa Cananna[i]n, ri Ceniuil-Conaill, do valluḋ la Domnall hUa Loċlainn, la riʒ n-Ailiʒ.—Mael-Coluim,¹ mac

A.D. 1092.² iiii., A; Karṫ, B. ³—matai, B. ᵃ om., B. ᵇ⁻ᵇ itl., t. h., A; om., B. ᵉ mac Mic—*son of Mac*, B.
A.D. 1093. ¹—Colaim, B.

The remaining Third, that of Massan, was left intact.

³ [*Kinsmen*].—That is, according to the Leinster regnal List (L.L. 39 d), Donchad, son of Murchad (1091, *supra*) and the sons of Domnall (1087, *supra*).

⁴ *Successor of* [*St.*] *Ailbe*.—That is, bishop of Emly.

1093. ¹ *Donchadh Mac Carthaigh, etc.*—This entry is a typical instance of the method in which these Annals were compiled. By omission of the respective means and of the persons whereby death was inflicted, four independent items, given as such in the *Four Masters*, are included in one formula. It also well illustrates the liability of such summaries to serious error. For the *Annals of Innisfallen*, an authority beyond question in Munster affairs, state that Mac Carthy was killed in the preceding year.

king of the Eoganacht of Cashel, died.—Flaithbertach, [1092] son of Ruaidhri Ua Ruadhacain, was slain by the Ui-Echach.—Domnall, son of Amhalghaidh, successor of Patrick, [went] upon circuit of Cenel-Eoga in, so that he took away his due.—The Close of Ard-Macha[2] with its church was burned on the 4th of the Kalends of September [Aug. 29] and a street of the Great Third and a street of the Third of the Saxons.—Enna, son of Diarmait, king of Ui-Ceinnselaigh, was slain by his own [kiusmen[3]].—Connmac Ua Cairill, archbishop of Connacht, rested.—Mael-Isu Ua hArrachtain, successor of [St.] Ailbe,[4] rested in peace.

Kalends of Jan. on 7th feria, 29th of the moon, A.D. [1093] 1093.—Donnchadh Mac Carthaigh,[1] king of the Eoganacht of Cashel; Trenair Ua Ceallaigh, king of Bregha; Aedh Ua Baighellain, king of Fern-mhagh; Aedh, son of Cathal Ua Conchobair, royal heir of Connacht, all were slain.— Aedh, herenagh of Daimliac-Ciannain; Ailill Ua Niallain, successor of [St.] Ciaran[2] and of [St.] Cronan and of [St.] Mac Duach; Fothud,[3] archbishop of Scotland, rested in Christ.—The Sil-Muiredaigh were expelled from Connacht by Muircertach Ua Briain.—Aedh Ua Canannain, king of Cenel-Conaill, was blinded by Domnall Ua Lochlainn, [that is] by the king of Ailech.—Mael-Coluim, son of

---

Of the four persons here mentioned, the two *Aedhs* are given in the *Annals of Loch Cé*. Ua Baighellain, they say, died a natural death. To Ua Conchobair is appended *omnes occisi sunt !* This affords strong presumption that their compiler had the *Annals of Ulster* before him. If so, it is a clear proof that he did not understand his original.

[2]*Of [St.] Ciaran and of [St.] Cronan and of [St.] Mac Duach.*—That is, Abbot-bishop of Clonmacnoise, Tomgraney and Kilmacduagh. O'Donovan (p. 945) erroneously takes the *F. M.* to mean three different persons.

[3] *Fothud.*—See Reeves, *Adamnan*, p. 402. The learned writer's proposed identification of Fothud with Modach, Bishop of St. Andrew's (*Culdees*, Trans. R.I.A., Antiq. XXIV. 246), seems improbable.

52 annala ulaoh.

Donncaḋa, airori Alban 7 Etharo, a mac, do marbaḋ
do Francaiḃ (idon,ᵃ i n-Inber-Alda i Saxanaiḃᵃ). A
rigan, imorro,ᵇ Margareta, do éc dia cumaiḋ ria cenn
nomaiḋe.—Sil-Muiredaiġ dorí[ḃ]iri i Connactu cen
cetugaḋ.—Merᵃ mor in hoc anno.

A 48a   Kal. Ian. 1. f., l. x., Anno Domini M.º xc.º iiii.ᵃ
Flaiṫbertac hUa Ateiḋ, ri hUa-n-Eaċaċ, do dalluḋ
la Donncaḋ hUa n-Eoċaḋa, la riġ Ulaḋ.—Slogaḋ la
Muirceartac hUa m-Briain co hAt-cliat, co roinnarḃ
Goffraiġ Méranac a riġe Gall 7 co romarḃ Domnall
hUa Mael-Seclainn, ri Teṁrac.—Ar Airter do
ḋeġdainiḃ (idon,ᵃ im Ua Fedeca[i]n 7 im Donn, mac
Oengura*) do cor la hUlltaiḃ.—Ruaiḋri hUa Donnaca[i]n, ri Araḋ; Concobur hUa Conċoḋair, ri Cianaċta, in
penitentiaⁱ mortui sunt.—Maidmᵇ ria Sil-Muiredaiġ
for Tuad-Mumain i torcradurᵉ tri cet,ᶜ uel paulo
plur.ᵇ—Domnall, comarba Patraic, for cuairt
Muman cetna cur, co tuc a lanċuairt feribuil la
taeb n-eodarta.—Donncaḋ, mac Mael-Choluim, ri
Alban, do marbaḋ o [a] braitriḃ féin (idon,ᵉ o Domnall 7 o Etmondᶜ) per dolum.—Doinenn mor i n-Erinn
uile, dia rofar domatu.

(Catʰ Fiḋnaċa, du hi drocair leṫ Iartair Connaċt 7

ᵃ mear, B.—ᵃᵃ r. m., t. h., A, B. ᵇ uero (the Latin equivalent), B.
A.D. 1094. ¹—cia, A. ² torcrad (i.e., the contraction for ur was not
placed above d), B.—ᶜᶜ l. m., t. h., A ; om., B. ᵇᵇ l. m., t. h., A; r. m.
t. h., B. ᵉ c. (contraction for *centum*, the Latin equivalent), A, B. ᵈᵈ
itl., t. h., A, B. ᵉᵉ om., C. ᶠᶠ n. t. h., A ; om., B; given in C.

---

⁴ *Novena.*—*Nomaidhe* is, perhaps, from *noi*, nine. According to the *Anglo Saxon Chronicle*, A.D. 1093, when the queen heard of the death of her husband and son, she went with her priest to the church, received the last rites and prayed God that she might give up the ghost.

In the *Brut y Tywysogion* (A.D. 1091), it is stated she prayed that she might not survive and God heard her prayer, for by the seventh day she was dead.

⁵ *Into Connacht.*—Their expulsion by O'Brien forms the second entry of this year.

Donnchadh, archking of Scotland and Edward, his son, [1093] were killed by the Franks (namely, in Inber-Alda, in Saxonland). His queen, moreover, Margaret, died of grief therefor before the end of a novena.⁴—The Sil-Muiredaigh again [came] into Connacht⁵ without permission [of Ua Briain].—Great crop in this year.

Kalends of Jan. on 1st feria, 10th of the moon, A.D. [1094] 1094.—Flaithbertach Ua Ateidh, king of Ui-Eachach, was blinded by Donnchadh Ua Eochadha, [namely] by the king of Ulidia.—A hosting by Muircertach Ua Briain to Ath-cliath, so that he expelled Geoffrey Meranach from the kingship of the Foreigners and killed Domnall Ua Mael-Sechlainn, king of Tara.—Slaughter of good persons of the Airthir (that is, including Ua Fedecain and including Donn, son of Oengus) was committed by Ulidians.— Ruaidhri Ua Donnacain, king of Aradh; Concobur Ua Conchobhair, king of Ciannachta, died in penance.—A defeat [was inflicted] by the Sil-Muiredaigh upon Thomond, wherein fell three hundred, or a little more.—Domnall,¹ successor of [St.] Patrick, [went] upon circuit of Munster for the first time, so that he took away his full circuit[-dues] of cess, along with donations.—Donnchadh,² son of Mael-Coluim, king of Scotland, was killed by his own brothers (namely, by Domnall and by Edmond) in treachery.— Great severity of weather in all Ireland, whereof arose dearth.

(The battle³ of Fidhnach, wherein fell one-half of the

1094. ¹ *Domnall, etc.*—This visitation is not mentioned in the *Annals of Innisfallen.*

² *Donchadh, etc.*—He had, according to the Anglo-Saxon Chronicle, taken forcible possession of the throne, on the death of his uncle, in the preceding year. The same Chronicle says (A.D. 1095) that he was slain at the instigation of his uncle, Dufenal [Domnall], who (A.D. 1094) thus succeeded him. As this agrees with the Innisfallen Annals, which omit mention of the brothers, it is more likely to be correct.

³ *The battle, etc.*—Given in the *Annals of Boyle* (ad an.), with the

leiṫ Corcumruaḋ la Taḋg, mac Ruaiḋri hUi Concobair'.)

Kal. Ian. 11. f., L xx. 1., Anno Domini M.° xc.° u.° Sneċta mór do ferṫain in Cetain iar Kalainn, co romarb ár doene 7 én 7 ceṫra.¹—Cenannus co n-a templaiḃ; Dermaċ co n-|a lebraiḃ; Ard-sraṫa co n-a templall 7 ilcella aile arċena cremaṫ[a]e runt.—Senoir² Mac Mael-Molua, ard fenoir Erenn, in pace dormiuit.—Ouḃṫaċ hUa Soċuind, uarafsacart na Ferta; Donngus, eprcop Aṫa-cliaṫ; Aeḋ, mac Mail-Iru,³ idon,ᵃ mac comarba Patraic [mortui]ᵇ runtᵇ.—Gilla-Ciara[i]n, mac Mic Ualgairg, muire hUa-n-Ouiḃinnraċt, a fuir occifur ert°.—hUa Eicnig, rí fer-Manaċ, do marbaḋ a fuir.—Maidm Arda-aċaḋ ria n-Dail-Araide for Ultu, dú i torċair Gilla-Comgaill hUa Cairill.—Teidm mór i n-Erinn, co romarb ár doene, o Kalainn Augu[i]rt co Ḃelltaine iar cinn (idon,ᵈ bliaḋain na mortlaᵈ).—Muirċertaċ hUa Cairre, muire Cenuil-Oenġura 7 rídomna Ailig, moritur.—Cairpri hUa Ceiṫernaig, idon, uasal epscop hUa-Ceinnfelaig, in penitencia moritur.—Gorfraig Meranaċ, ri Gall, mortu[u]r ert.

Kal. Ian. III. f., L 11., Anno Domini M.° xc.° ui.° plann hUa Anbeiṫ, ri Deirce[i]rt Airgiall; Mael-Patraic, mac Ermedaig, eprcop Ard[a]-Maċa; Coluim hUa

A.D. 1095. ¹ ceatra, B. ² Sean—, A. ³ Mael—, A. ᵃ om., A. ᵇ⁻ᵇ om., A, B; "died," C. ᶜ om., C. ᵈ⁻ᵈ l. m., t. h., A, B; om., C.

---

variant *in quo ceciderunt multi* for *du hi drochair leth* ("wherein fell one half").

1095. ¹ *Wrought havoc.*—Literally, *slew a slaughter.*

² *Mael-Molua.*— Devotee of [St.] Molua (of Clonfert—Mulloe, King's Co.). A Latin gloss, having no reference to the text, in the L.B. Calendar of Oengus, at April 16, states that: *The archbishop of Ireland, the Senior Mac Maildalua, died on the 3rd of the Ides* [11th] *of April. As some* [poet] *said* [in a native Debide quatrain which is quoted]. *Archbishop* was probably a Latin rendering of *uasalepscop,* eminent bishop.

³ *Donngus.*—For Donngus, or Donatus, see Lanigan, *Ec. Hist.*, iii. 482.

West of Connacht and half of Corcomruadh, [was gained] [1094] by Tadhg, son of Ruaidhri Ua Concobair.)

Kalends of Jan. on 2nd feria, 21st of the moon, A.D. [1095] 1095.—Great snow fell on the Wednesday after New-Year's Day [Jan. 3], so that it wrought havoc[1] of people and of birds and of cattle.—Cenannus with its churches, Dermagh with its books, Ard-sratha with its church, and many other churches besides were burned.—Senior Mac Mael-Molua,[2] chief religious counsellor of Ireland, slept in peace.—Dubhtbach Ua Sochuind, archpriest of the [church of the] Relics [in Ard-Macha]; Donngus,[3] bishop of Ath-cliath; Aedh,[4] son of Mail-Isu, namely, the son of the successor of [St.] Patrick [died].—Gilla-Ciarain, son of Mac Ualgarig, steward[5] of Ui-Duibhhinnrecht, was slain by his own [tribesmen].—Ua Eicnigh, king of Fir-Manach, was killed by his own [kinsmen.]—The defeat of Ard-achad [was inflicted] by the Dal-Araidhe upon the Ulidians, wherein fell Gilla-Comghaill Ua[6] Cairill.—Great plague in Ireland, so that it wrought havoc[1] of people, from the Kalend [1st] of August to May-day thereafter (namely, the Year of the Mortality).—Muircertach Ua Cairre, steward of Cenel-Oenghusa and royal heir of Ailech, dies.—Cairpri Ua Ceithernaigh, eminent bishop of Ui-Ceinnselaigh [Ferns],[7] dies in penance.—Geoffrey Meranach, king of the Foreigners [of Dublin], died.

Kalends of Jan. on 3rd feria, 2nd of the moon, A.D. [1096] Bis. 1096.—Flann Ua Anbcidh, king of the South of Airghialla; Mael-Patraic, son of Ermedhach, bishop of Ard-Macha[1];

---

[4] *Aedh, etc.*—"Hugh mac Maelisa, Coarb of Patrike, died," C. But the "Coarb" at the time was Domnall, son of Amalghaidh. The Mail-Isu in question died 1091 (*supra.*)

[5] *Steward.—Muire;* lord (tigherna), *Four Masters.*

[6] *Ua, etc.*—From *Ua* to *people* (in the following entry), both inclusive,

is omitted by O'Conor, who remarks *quaedam desunt*. But there is no lacuna in his MS. (B).

[7] [*Ferns*].—The Annals of Innisfallen (*ad an.*) call him bishop-abbot of Ferns.

1096. [1] *Bishop of Ard-Macha.*—Domnall was titular Primate at the time. Mael-Patraic was consecrated

56 αnnαlα ulαoh.

Ωnpαbα[i]n¹, αipcinneč Ruip-αiliείp; Flαnn hUα Muipe-
cά[i]n, αipcinneč Ωcenτpuiṁ, in Chpiτο ορμιερunc.—
Maξgαmαin hUα 8egoαι, pi Copcouione; Cončοbup
hUα Ωnníαραι, | pi Ciαnnαčτ 7 hUα Cein, pi hUα-mic-
Cαipεinn, do comείιcim i cliατai.—Uαmon mόρ ρορ
Feραί Epenn piα feil' Eoin nα bliαonα rα, co ροčεταιρε
Όiατρια τροιρcτί comαρbα Patραic 7 cleipeč n-Epenn
αρčenα.—Mαc Oubgαill hUα Maelčοταιξ do mαρbαο
do U Innεipξι.—Muipceρταč hUα Όubοαι, pi hUα-n-
Ωṁαlgαοα, do mαρbαο α ρuip.—Moττaṫαn hUα Mot-
τaοα[i]n, pi 8il-Ωnmčαοα, mopτu[u]ρ eρτ.'—Cu-Ulαο
hUα Ceilecα[i]n (ioon,ᵇ puoαmnα Ωipgiαllᵇ) do mαρbαο
lα Coiceo n-Epenn (ioon,ᵇ lα³ hUlτuᵃᵇ).—Żillα-Oρρen, mαc
Mic Copτen, pí Όealbnα, occipus eρτ.—hUα Cαčαil,
αipcinneč Tuαmα-gρene, in Chpiτο quieuiτ.—Eοgαn
hUα Ceρnαιξ, αιρcinneč Ὀαιρε, in no[i]oecim Kαllαnn
Enαιρ quieuiτ.

Kαl. Ιαn. u. f., L τ. ιιι., Ωnno Όomini m.° τc.° uιι.°
Leρξur hUα Cρuimείρ, comαρbα Comξαιll, pοσε peni-
τenciαm opτimαm¹ obιιτ.—Tαὸξ, mαc Ruαiοpi hUi Con-
cοhαιρ, puoαmnα Con[n]αčτ, α ρuis occipus eρτ.—Flαn-
nαcαn puαο, αipcinneč Ruip-Comαιn, in pαce quieuiτ.—

A.D. 1096. ¹ Ωnρu—, B. ² fel, B. ³·³ le hUllτcio, B. ⁴ om., B.
ᵇ·ᵇ itl., t.h., A, B.

A.D. 1097. ¹ obτimαm, A, B.

---

for the exercise of episcopal functions; as Domnall was, in all probability, a layman, perhaps a monk. His place apparently remained vacant until 1109 (*infra*), when it was assumed by Caincomrach O'Boyle.

² *Great fear.*—See 771 (=772), 798 (=799), *supra*. The *Four Masters* state that the fear arose because the Feast (Decollation) of John the Baptist (August 29) fell on Friday in 1096. But this is puerile; every festival must fall four times on the same day within the solar Cycle of 28 years. According to the so-called *Vision of Adamnan* (L.B., p. 258b-259b), great havoc of the men of Ireland was to be wrought by a fiery ploughshare, when the anniversary in question should fall on Friday, in a Bissextile and Embolismal year, at the end of a Cycle. The three first-named conditions were literally verified in the present year. The year was also to-

Colum Ua Anradhain, herenagh of Ros-ailithir; Flann Ua [1096] Muirecain, herenagh of Aentruim, slept in Christ.—Mathgamain Ua Segdhai, king of Corcoduibhne; Conchobur Ua Anniaraidh, king of Ciannachta and Ua Cein, king of Ui-mic-Cairthinn, mutually fell in combats.—Great fear [fell] [2]upon the men of Ireland before the feast of John of this year, until God spared [them] through the fastings of the successor of Patrick and of the clergy of Ireland besides.—Ua Maelchothaigh, son of Dubhgall, was killed by Ua Inneirghi.[3]—Muircertach Ua Dubhdai, king of Ui-Amhalghadha, was killed by his own [kinsmen].—Mottadhan Ua Mottadhain, king of Sil-Anmchada, died.—Cu-Uladh Ua Celecain (namely, royal heir of Airgialla) was killed by the Fifth of Ireland (that is, by Ulster).—Gilla-Ossen,[4] son of Mac Corten, king of Delbna, was slain.—Ua Cathail, herenagh of Tuaimgrene, rested in Christ.—Eogan Ua Cernaigh, herenagh of Daire, rested on the nineteenth[5] of the Kalends of January [Dec. 14].

Kalends of Jan. on 5th feria, 13th of the moon, A.D. [1097] 1097.—Lerghus Ua Cruimthir, successor of [St.] Comgall,[1] died after most excellent penance.—Tadhg, son of Ruaidhri Ua Concobair, royal heir of Connacht, was slain by his own [kinsmen].—Flannacan the Red, herenagh of Ros-Comain, rested in peace.—The belfry of Mainister

---

wards the end, being the fourteenth, of the Cycle of Nineteen. Assuming that the prophecy was well-known, these coincidences were sufficiently striking to account for the popular terror.

[3] *Ua Inneirghi.*—"O'Hindry" in C; not "his [own people]," as O'Donovan misread (*Four Masters*, Vol. ii., p. 954).

[4] *Gilla-Ossen.* — *Derotee of* [*St.*] *Ossan* (of Rath Ossain, *Fort of Ossan*, west of Trim. *Mart. Don.*, Feb.

17). Ossan is given in the List of Deacons in L. L. (p. 366e).

[5] *Nineteenth.*—The *F.M.* say the eighteenth. But against them are to be placed A, B, C (which last has 19 *Kal. Jan.*; not, as O'Donovan, *loc. cit.*, says, 9 *Kal. Jan.*) and the Annals of Loch Ce (*ad an.*).

1097. [1] *Successor of* [St.] *Comgall.* —That is, Abbot of Bangor, co. Down.

[2] *The wright Ua Brolcain.*—His obit is given at 1029 (*supra*).

E

58 annala ulaoh.

B 45d Cloicéeč Maimirtreč[-buiti] co n-a lebraib | 7 tair-cedaid imdaid do lorcad.—Mael-brigte, mac in t-rair hUi brolca[i]n, uaral erscop Cille-dara 7 Coicid Laigen, port penitenciam optimam quieuit.—Slogad la Muir-certač hUa m-briain 7 la Leč Moga co Mag Muir-temne. Slogad dano la Domnall hUa Ločlainn co Tuaircert Erenn co fid Conaille do čabairt cača doib co rurtairmerc Domnall, comarba patraic, ro gne rič[a].—Loclann hUa Duidara, ri fern-muigi, do marbad do Ui[b]-briuin breifne.—Cnomer mor irin bliadain ri: trica² bliadan² on čnomer aile ª guran cnome[r]ra ᵇ (idon ᶜ, bliadain na cnó rinn; idon, co ragaibči reredač² cnó ar aen pinginn ᶜ).

Kal. Ian. ui. f., l. xx. iiii., Anno Domini M.° xc.° uiii.° flaičbertač hUa flaičbertaig, ri Iartair Connačt, do marbad do Sil-Muiredaig.—Tri longa do longaib gall na n-Innri do flat do Ulltaib 7 a fairenn do marbad, idon, riče¹ ar cet¹, uel paulo plur.—Mael-Iru Ua Stuir, reriba filorofiae Mumunenrium, immo omnium Scotorum, in Chrirto quieuit.— | Diarmait, mac Enna, mic Diarmata, ri Laigen, do marbad do clainn Mur-cada, mic Diarmata (idon ª, ror lar Cille-dara ª).—

A 48c

A.D. 1097. ²⁻² xxx. bliadain, A, B.—³. ui.edač, A, B.—ª ra-*this*, B. —ᵇ cnomer aile romainn—(*to the*) *other nut-crop* (*that happened next*) *before us*, B ; C. follows the order of A. ᶜ⁻ᶜ r. m., t.h., A, B ; given in C.

A.D. 1098. ¹⁻¹ .xx. ar .c., A, B. ª⁻ª l.m., t. h., A ; r.m., t. h., B.

³ *Half of Mogh.* — Namely, the southern moiety of Ireland.

⁴ *Thirty years.*—The nut-crop next preceding is entered at 1066 (*supra*).

⁵ *Sixth.*—" Id est, the sixth parte of the barrell," C. " *Sesedach* is cognate with the Latin Sextarius and the French *Sesterot* and *Sextier*, a measure both of fluids and of corn, being about a pint and a half, but varying in magnitude in different times and countries." (O'Donovan, *Four Masters*, Vol. ii. p. 822.)

⁶ *Penny.* — In the *Senchus Mor* (Vol. ii. p. 220), the *pinguin* is one-third of the *screpal.* In another Brehon law tract (O'Donovan, *F.M.* ii. 822) the silver *pinginn* is said to

ANNALS OF ULSTER. 59

[-Buithi] with its books and many treasures was burned.— [1097] Mael-Brighte, son of the wright Ua Brolcain,[2] eminent bishop of Cell-dara and of the Fifth of Leinster, rested after most excellent penance.—A hosting by Muircertach Ua Briain and by the half of Mogh[3] to the Plain of Muirtembne. A hosting also by Domnall Ua Lochlainn, together with the North of Ireland, to the Wood of Conaille, to give battle to them, until Domnall, successor of Patrick, prevented them under guise of peace.—Lochlann Ua Duibhdara, king of Fern-magh, was killed by the Ui-Briuin of Breifne.—Great nut-crop in this year: thirty years[3] from the other nut-crop to this nut-crop (namely, the year of the Fair Nuts; so that, namely, [the measure called] the Sixth[4] of nuts used to be got for one penny[5]).

Kalends of Jan. on 6th feria, 24th of the moon, A.D. [1098] 1098.—Flaithbertach Ua Flaithbertaigh, king of the West of Connacht, was killed by the Sil-Muiredhaigh.—Three ships of the ships of the Foreigners of the Islands were wrecked by the Ulidians and their crews[1] killed, namely, twenty over a hundred, or a little more.—Mael-Isu Ua Stuir, master of philosophy[2] of the Momonians, nay, of all the Scots, rested in Christ.—Diarmait, son of Enna, son of Diarmait, king of Leinster, was killed by the sons of Murcad, son of Diarmait (namely, in the centre of Cell-dara).—Eochaidh, successor of [St.] Ciannan,[3] died

---

weigh seven grains of wheat. This corresponds pretty closely with the Roman weight (24 grains = 1 scruple).

1098. [1] *Crews.* — Literally, *folk* (*fairenn*), a collective substantive.

Master of philosophy. — Literally, *scribe of philosophy*. Scribe is here employed in the sense of 1 Esdr. vii. (scribae erudito, 11; scriba legis,

21). Portion of the Commentary of St. Columbanus on Ps. xliv. 2 (Lingua mea calamus scribae, etc.) is: tamquam cuidam scribae docto calamus aptus obsequitur (Ml. fol. 64d). The *Four Masters* make it *scribe and philosopher.*

[3] *Successor of [St.] Ciannan.*—That is, Abbot of Duleek, co. Meath.

E 2

Eocaiḋ, comarba Ciannain, porc penicenciam' obiic.—
Rónan hUa Ḋaimin, comarba Ḟobuir prius ec religiorus
opcimus porc 7 Mael-Marcain hUa Cellaiġ, comarba
Mhura [ḟh]ocna, larguṡ ec ṡapienṡ, in una die in pace
quieuerunc.—Ḟlaicberraċ, mac Ciġernaiġ Ḃairrciḋ,
comarba Ḟinnia[i]n, in perigrinacione quieuic.—
Ḋomnall Oa Enna, uaral erscop Iarcair Eorpa 7 tobur
conuersli in domain (ruí in úird cecarḋa[i], idon, Roman 7 na n-Ġaiḋel'), porc penicenciam' opcimam, ruam
uicam ḟelicicer hi deci[m] Kalann Decimber ṡiniuic.
—Mac Mara[i]ṡ Cairbreċ, anmcara toġaiḋe; Ḋomnall
Mac Robarcaiġ, comarba Coluim-cille ṡri ṡé, in pace
dormierunc.—Maidm Ḟercri-ruiliḋe ṡor Ceniul-
Conaill ria Cenel-n-Eoġain, i torċair Eiṡerraċ hUa
Coirce[i]rc ec alii mulci.

(In hoc anno Aed hUa Maeil-Eoin, comarba Ciarain
Cluana-mac-Noir, nacur erc.)

Kal. Ian. uii. ṡ., l. u., Anno Ḋomini M.° xc.° ix.°
Arṡalc mor ṡo Erinn uile.—Cenannus ab igne
uir[ṡ]ipara erc.—Diarmaic hUa Maelaṫġen, airċinneċ
Ḋuin, | in nocre Parṡ[ha]e' quieuic.—Ceall-dara [de]
demedia parce cremaca' erc.—Caencompac hUa
Ḃaiġill do ġabail erscoboici' Arda-Maċa Dia-Ḋomnaiġ
Cenġciġir.—Ḋonnċad, mac Mic Maenaiġ, abb Ia;

³—ciam, A. ³ n-Ġoei—, A.—ᵃ⁻ᵃ l.m., t.h., A; r. m., t.h., B. ᵇ⁻ᵇ n.t.h., A.; om., B; given in C.
A.D. 1099. ¹—ṡca, B. ²—mace, B. ³—iḋe, B.

---

⁴ *Superior.*—Literally, *successor* (of St. Fechin of Fore, co. Westmeath). The *Four Masters* render *religiosus* by *riaghloir* ("moderator," O'Donovan, ii. 959)! The meaning is that Ronan laid aside the abbacy and became a simple monk (presumably in the same monastery).

⁵ *Liberal and wise.* — *Largus et sapiens* is translated by the F.M.

Learghas eccnaidh—Learghas, the sage! Furthermore, they state that Domnall Ua Robartaigh, Mael-Isu, Eochaidh, Ronan, Mael-Martain and "Learghas," all six, died the same day.

⁶ *Successor of [St.] Finnian.*—Abbot of Moville, co. Down.

⁷ [*Nov.* 22].—Dec. 1, F.M. A, B and C are against them. For Ua Enna (O'Heney), who was archbishop

after penance.—Ronan Ua Daimin, superior[4] of Fobur [1098] first and a most excellent religious afterwards and Mael-Martain Ua Cellaigh, successor of [St.] Muru of [F]othan, [a] liberal and wise [man],[5] rested in peace on the same day.—Flaithbertach, son of Tighernach of Bairrche, successor of [St.] Finnian,[6] rested in pilgrimage.—Domnall Ua Enna, eminent bishop of the West of Europe and fount of the generosity of the world, (doctor of either Law, namely, of the Romans and of the Gaidil) after most excellent penance, finished his life felicitously, on the tenth of the Kalends of December [Nov. 22].[7]—Mac Marais[8] of Cairbre, select soul-friend; Domnall Mac Robartaigh,[9] successor of [St.] Colum-cille for a [long] space, slept in peace.—The defeat of Fersad-Suilidhe [was inflicted] upon the Cenel-Conaill by the Cenel-Eogain, wherein fell Eicertach Ua Toirceirt and many others.

(In this year Aed Ua Mail-Eoin,[10] successor of [St.] Ciaran of Cluain-mac-Nois, was born.)

Kalends of Jan. on 7th feria, 5th of the moon, A.D. [1099] 1099.— Great destitution throughout all Ireland.—Cenannus was wasted by fire.—Diarmait Ua Maelathgen herenagh of Dun, rested on the night of Easter [April 10].—Cell-dara was burned from the half.—Caincomrac Ua Baighill assumed the episcopacy of Ard-Macha on the Sunday of Pentecost [May 29].—Donnchad, son of Mac

---

of Cashel, see Lanigan, *Eccl. Hist. of Ireland*, Vol. iii., p. 455, sq.

[8] *Mac Marais.*—Very probably, he who wrote the second charter of the Book of Kells; *Oraid do Mac Maras trog ro scrib*, etc.; "A Prayer for Mac Maras, the wretched, who wrote," etc.

[9] *Domnall Mac Robartaigh.*—Abbot of Kells since 1062; hence the "[long] space" of the text. He appears as one of the grantors in the charter mentioned in the previous

note. See Reeves, *Adamnan*, p. 400.

The Annals of Loch Ce (*ad an.*) omit the obit of Mac Marais and retain *obierunt*.

[10] *Aedh Ua Mail-Eoin.*—Mail-Eoin signifies devotee of John (the Evangelist). The obit of this abbot is given at 1153 by the *F.M.* (perhaps from the present Annals, which may have contained the missing portion when the *F M.* had them in their possession).

Ua hÍnaȧan Ua Meictıpe, comapba Mic Leinin[e]; Annuv
hUa Lonȝapca[ı]n, comapba Coluım mic Cpemȟainn,
ın pace pauȯauepunc.—Sloȝaḃ la Muıpcepcaȭ hUa
m-Ḃpiain 7 la Leṫ Moȝa co 8liaḃ-[Ḟh]uaıc, co n-ṗepna
'Ȯomnall, comapba Ṗacpaıo, pıȷ m-bliaḋna eteppu 7
Tuaıpcepc Epenn.⁴—Sloȝaḃ la 'Ȯomnall hUa Loċlainn
7 la Tuaıpcepc n-Epenn tap Tuaım ı n-Ullcaıḃ. Ula[ı]ḋ
ṗono ı Cpaıḃ-teleȧ ılonȝpopc. Coıṅpaıcıc⁵ a n-ṗí
mapcploiȝ: maıḃep ȯop mapcpluaȝ Ulaḃ 7 mapḃṫaıp
hUa Aṁpaın ann. Facaıṗ Ula[ı]ḃ ıap pın allonȝpopc⁺
7 loıpcıt Cenel-Eoȝain é 7 tepcaıt Cpaıḃ-tealȧa.
'Ȯobepap ṗoıḃ ıap pın ṗa etepı 7 comapba Comȝaıll
ıllaım ȯpıa ṗa etepı aıle:

Tuctȧᵇ ȝeıll Ulaḃ ap eıcın,
Innıȯc ȯiaḃaın co ȯeıȝ,
Ia 'Ȯomnall coᶜ loınne leoṁaınᶜ,
Ocup la Sıl Eoȝaın (noᵈ, Claınıı[-Eoȝaın]ᵈ) ȯeıl.

'Ȯa etıpe tpena tuctȧ
'Ȯo loeċpaıḃ Ulaḃ o ċeın,
In tpeȯ cen ṗıbaḃ, abb Comȝaıll,
'Ȯo pıȝaḃ 'Ȯomnaıll hUı Neıll.

In nomaıṗ bliaḃaın ap noȧc,
Ap mıle bliaḃan[-ḋaın, MS.] co m-blaıḃ,
O ȝeın Cpıȯc, cıınnti cen cpınaḃ,
Iȯ ınntı ȯopıleṗ ȯeın.ᵇ—

A.D. 1099. ᵃ n. E—, A. ᵇ—ȝıc, B. ᵃ a lonȝpopc—*their stronghold*,
A. ᵇ⁻ᵇ t.m., with corresponding marks, t.h., A; om., B. ᶜ⁻ᶜ Reading of *Four
Masters*; hUa Flaınn mup leoṁaın, MS. (which I do not understand).
ᵈ⁻ᵈ ıtl., t. h., MS.

1099. ¹ *Successor of [St. Colman].*
—That is, bishop of Cloyne. Anmchadh and Mac-tire (wolf), eponymous
heads of Ui Anmchadha and Ui Mectire, the two chief families of Ui.
Liathain (Barrymore, co. Cork), were
respectively descended (in the ninth
degree) from Brocc and Ailill, sons
of Echu Liathain, from whom the
territory was named. Echu, like his
contemporary, Nathfraech, King of
Cashel in the first half of the fifth
century, was of the race of Eoghan
Mor. (From Mac Caille, son of Brocc,
descended the neighbouring sept of
Ui-Mic-Caille, Imokilly.) Ua Mectire was thus bishop of his native
diocese. Benefaction to the cathedral

Maenaigh, abbot of Ia; Uamnachan Ua Meictire, successor [1099] of [St. Colman][1] son of Leinin[2]; Annud Ua Longarcain, successor of [St.] Colum, son of Cremhthann,[3] reposed in peace.—A hosting by Muircertach Ua Briain and by Half of Mogh to Sliabh-[F]uait, until Domnall, successor of [St.] Patrick, made peace of a year between them and the North of Ireland.—A hosting by Domnall Ua Lochlainn and by the North of Ireland past Tuaim into Ulidia. The Ulidians, howbeit, [were] at Craibh-telcha[4] in camp. Their two horse-hosts encounter: defeat is inflicted upon the horse-host of the Ulidians and Ua Amrain is killed there. Thereafter the Ulidians abandon the camp and the Cenel-Eogain burn it and uproot Craibh-telcha. After that, there are given to them two hostages and the successsor of [St.] Comgall in pledge [*lit.*, in hand] for two other hostages:

Taken were the pledges of the Ulidians by force—
Witnesses tell it accurately—
By Domnall of [*lit.*, with] the fury of the lion,
And by generous Sil-Eogain (or, Clann[-Eogain]).

Two strong hostages were given
Of the heroes of the Ulidians formerly;
The third without fail [was] the abbot [*i.e.*, successor] of Comgall,
To the royal power of Domnall Ua Neill.

The ninth year above ninety,
Above a thousand blooming years,
From birth of Christ [who was] formed without decay,
It is in it occurred that.—

---

church, in all likelihood, caused the insertion of his name in the Annals.

[2] *Son of Leinin.*—So called in native documents, to distinguish him from the numerous other Colmans. *Cellmic-Lenine* (Church of the Son of Lenin)

is a prebend in the diocese of Cloyne. The father's name lives likewise in Killiney—*Cell-inghen-Lenine*, Church of the Daughters of Lenin. They were six virgins. The seventh sister, Aglenn, was the first wife of Echaidh,

Daṁliac Arda-grata do lorcut do peraiḃ na Craibe
ror Uiḃ-Fiacraċ.—Ruaiḋri hUa Ruaḋaca[i]n, ri Eirtir
Airxiall, 7 maccaim | riġ⁶ Erenn, in quadrageṡimo
quinto⁵ anno regni ṡui, in decimo Kalendarum Decim-
briṡ, ṡuam uitam finiuit.

Kal. Ian. 1. f., L x. ui., Anno Domini M.° c.° Flann
hUa Cinaeḋa, airċinneċ Aċa-truim, ard ollam Miḋe
[in pace quieuit].—Donnċaḋ Mac Eoċaḋa, ri Ulaḋ 7
drem¹ do maiṫiḃ Ulaḋ ime, do xaḃail la Domnall hUa
Loċlainn, la riġ n-Ailiġ, i quint Kalann Iuin.—Creċ la
Domnall hUa Loċlainn, co roort feru-ḃreġ 7 Fine-Ġall.
—Sloxaḋ la Muirċertaċ hUa m-Ḃriain co hErr-ruaiḋ².
—Longur Aċa-cliaṫ co hInir-n-Eogain, co rolaḋ a n-ár,
eter baṫaḋ 7 marbaḋ.—Mac mic Ġilla-Coluim Ui Doṁ-
naill, ri Ceniuil-Luxdaċ³, a fuir occisur ert.—Arrid hUa
Aṁraḋain⁴, muire Dal-Fiataċ; Ġilla-Ḃrixdi hUa
Cuirc, ri Muscraiḋe-Ḃregain; Ġilla-na-noeḃ hUa
hEiḋinn, ri hUa-Fiacraċ, mortui runt.—Eċri hUa
Mael-muire, ri Ciannaċt, do marbaḋ d'ó Chonċobair
Ciannaċt.

A.D. 1099. ⁶ ri (nom. sg.), B. ᶜ⁻ᶜ xl. u., A.B.
A.D. 110). ¹ dream, B. ² h Ear—, A. ³ Ceniul—, B. ⁴ hAṁraḋan,
B. ⁵ om., B.

---

sixth in descent from Niall of the Nine Hostages. One of her sons is mentioned in Adamnan's Life of St. Columba (ii. 43) as *Columbanus, filius Echudi.* O'Clery (*Mart. of Donegal*, March 6, Nov. 24) erroneously states they were of the race of Aenghus, son (instead of Aenghus, brother) of Mogh Nuadhat.

Colman belonged to the bardic order. The Lives of SS. Senan and Brendan (of Ardfert) and Cormac's *Glossary* respectively contain one of his poetical compositions. Each of the three is in a different metre.

³ *Successor of* [St.] *Colum, son of Cremthann.*—Namely, Abbot of Terryglas, co. Tipperary.

⁴ *Craibh-telcha.*—The wide-branching tree (lit. *branch*) *of the hill*; under which the kings of Ulidia (cos. Down and Antrim) were inaugurated.

⁵ *Royal scion.*—That is, par excellence. Literally, *fair son of the kings of Ireland.*

1100. ¹ *With.*—Literally, *and. Party* is nom. abs. in the original.

² *Nobles.*—See A.D. 1087, note 1 They had probably gone to celebrate Pentecost at Armagh (for the

The stone church of Ard-sratha was burned by the [1099] men of Craib against the Ui-Fiachrach.—Ruaidhri Ua Ruadhacain, king of the East of Airghialla and royal scion[5] of Ireland, finished his life in the 45th year of his reign, on the 10th of the Kalends of December [Nov. 22].

Kalends of Jan. on 1st feria, 16th of the moon, A.D. [1100] Bis. 1100. Flann Ua Cinaedha, herenagh of Ath-truim, chief bardic professor of Meath [rested in peace].—Donnchadh Mac [*recte*, Ua] Eochadha, king of Ulidia, with[1] a party of the nobles[2] of Ulidia about him, was captured by Domnall Ua Lochlainn, [namely] by the king of Ailech, on the 5th of the Kalends of June [Monday, May 28].—A foray by Domnall Ua Lochlainn, so that he laid waste Fir-Bregh and Fine-Gall.—A hosting by Muircertach Ua Briain to Ess-ruadh.—The fleet of Ath-cliath [sailed] to Inis-Eogain, whereof ensued their destruction, both by drowning and killing.—The grandson of Gilla-Coluim Ua Domnaill, king of Cenel-Lughdach, was slain by his own [kinsmen]. —Assid Ua Ambradhain, steward[3] of Dal-Fiatach; Gilla-Brighte Ua Cuirc, king of Muscraidh-Bregain[4]; Gilla-na-noebh[5] Ua Eidhinn, king of Ui-Fiachrach, died.— Echri Ua Mael-Muire, king of Ciannachta, was killed by O'Conchobair[6] of the Ciannachta [of Glenn-Geimhin].

---

solemnity with which the feast was there held, see 980[-1], 818[-9], 892[-3] *supra*) and were captured, as they were returning, on the Monday after the Octave. This will explain what is stated under next year, that their liberation took place in a church of that city.

[3] *Steward (muire).*—Lord (*tigherna*), Four Masters.

[4] *Bregain.*—O'Connor prints *b. guin* and leaves a blank in his translation. He overlooked the mark of contraction (=*re*) attached to *b* in his MS. (B). The Annals of Innisfallen state that the person in question was son of Domnall Ua Cuirc.

[5] *Gilla-na-noebh.*—That is, Devotee of the Saints.

[6] *O'Conchobair.*—"The O'Conors are still numerous in Glengiven, which was the ancient name of the vale of the river Roa (Roe), near Dungiven, which flows through the very centre of this Cianachta." (O'Donovan, *Book of Rights*, p. 123).

66 annala ulaoh.

(hoc[b] anno ecclesia sancti Sinelli de Clain-inis fundata est[b].)

Kal. Ian. iii. f., l. xx. uii., Anno Domini M.° c.° i.°
Donnchad, | mac Aedha Ui Ruairc, do marbad do Feraid-Manach; Riagán, epscop Droma-moir 7 Coicid[a] Ulad, in pace quieuit.—Inis-Cathaig do orcain do Ghallaib.—Slogad la Muircertach hUa m-Briain 7 la Leth Moga i Con[n]achtaib dar Es[r]-ruaid i Tir-n-Eogain, co rorsailset Aileach[1] 7 co roloirsret 7 co rosaraigret illcella archena[b] im Fachain Mura[c] 7 im Ard-srata. Dollotur iar sin sor Fertais-Champsa, co roloirsret Cuil-ratain 7 co n-dernairt duinebad ann. Zabair siallu Ulad iar sin. Doluid dar Slighid Midluachra dia thig.—Cres la Donnchad hUa Mael-Sechlainn i Fern-mhuig, conursaraid hUa Cerbaill 7 co romarb da cét dib, uel paulo plus.—Ferdomnach, epscop Cille-dara, in pace quieuit.—Cathal hUa Muirica[i]n, ri Tethba[2], decollatus est.—Donnchad hUa Eochada, ri Ulad, do suarlucud a cuibrich la Domnall, mac Mic[b] Lochlainn, la rig n-Ailig, dar cenn a mic 7 a comaltai, idon, i n-Domliac Arda-Macha, tre impide comarba Patraic 7 samtha Patraic archena, iar comluga fo bachaill Isu 7 fo minnaib archena, i[d] n-undecim Kalann[d] Ianair[3]. |

Kal. Ian. iiii. f., l. ix., Anno Domini M.° c.° ii.° Sort

A.D. 1100. b-b r.m., n.t.h., A; om., B.
A.D. 1101. [1]—leach, A. [2] Tethra, A. [3] enair, B.—[a] .u.id, A, B. [b] om., B. [c] moir—great, B, C. [d-d] in .xi. Kl., A, B.
[Chasm in A, up to A.D. 1109 (exclusive).]

---

[7] *This year, etc.*—I have not found this item elsewhere. The festival of St. Sinell was held on Nov. 12.

1101. [1] *Fifth of Ulidia.*—O'Conor here commits an error which is redeemed by some originality. The MS. forms, *.u.idh Ul.* (with mark of contraction attached to *l*), he reads as *v. id Jul.*; making the bishop die on July 11.

[2] *Including.*—Literally, *around*.
[3] *Over the road of Midhluachair.*— "Over at Sligo;" which, by the omission of *Midhluachra* and by mistaking *slighe*, a road, for Sligo town, shows the translator of C. disregarded and misunderstood his text.

As the Road of Midhluachair led from Tara to Ulster, the meaning is

(This year[7] the church of Saint Sinell of Clain-inis was founded.) [1100]

Kalends of Jan. on 3rd feria, 27th of the moon, A.D. 1101. Donnchadh, son of Aedh Ua Ruairc, was killed by the Fir-Manach.—Riagan, bishop of Druim-mor and of the Fifth of Ulidia,[1] rested in peace.—Inis-Cathaigh was pillaged by the Foreigners.—A hosting by Muircertach Ua Briain and by the Half of Mogh into Connacht, past Ess-ruadh into Tir-Eogain, so that they demolished Ailech and burned and profaned many churches also, including[2] Fathan of [St.] Mura and Ard-sratha. They went after that over Fertas-Camsa, until they burned Cuil-rathain and committed massacre therein. He [Ua Briain] takes the hostages of Ulidia after that [and] went over the Road of Midhluachair[3] to his house.—A foray by Donnchadh Ua Mael-Sechlainn into Fern-mhagh, until Ua Cerbaill overtook them and killed two hundred of them, or a little more.—Ferdomnach, bishop of Cell-dara, rested in peace.—Cathal[4] Ua Muiricain, king of Tebtha, was beheaded.—Donnchadh Ua Eochadha, king of Ulidia, was freed from fetters by Domnall, son of Mac Lochlainn, [that is] by the king of Ailech, in return for his son and his foster-brother: namely, in the stone church of Ard-Macha, through the intercession of the successor of [St.] Patrick and of the community of [St.] Patrick besides, after co-swearing[5] by the Staff of Jesus and by the Relics as well, on the 11th of the Kalends of January [Dec. 22]. [1101]

---

that O'Brien entered Tara as King of Ireland, on the march home to Kinkora (near Killaloe).

[4] *Cathal, etc.*—Over this item the text hand wrote: Sug na caelan 7 ıꞅ e ꞃomaꞃb Mael-Sectainn— "Juice ... and it is he that killed Mael-Sechlainn;" meaning that *sug na caelan* was a nick-name of Ua Muirecain and that he was the slayer of Mael-Sechlainn, King of Tara (1087, *supra*).

[5] *Co-swearing.*—Namely, by the son of Mac Lochlainn and Ua Eochadha. See 1100, note 2.

68 annala ulaḋh.

Coluim-cille do lorcaḋ.—Donnċaḋ, mac Eċrí hUi Aitiḋ-ridomna hUa-n-Eaċaċ, do marbaḋ do Ulltaib (don[a] irin coiced[1] mir iar raruxuḋ Patraic do[a]).—Domnall, mac Tigernain hUi Ruairc, ri Conmaicne, do marbaḋ do Conmaicniḃ fein.—Cú-ṁaiġi hUa Cairill, aircinneċ Duin, mortuur ert.—Flaitbertaċ Mac Fotaiẋ, ri hUa-Fiacraċ Arda-rrata, do marbaḋ do Feraiḃ-Luirg. 8loxaḋ la Cinel-n-Eogain co Maġ-Coba. Dolotur Ulaiḋ irin aiḋċi irin longport, co romarbrat Ṡitriuc hUa Mael-faḋaill (don[b], ri Cairrce-Ḃraċaide[b]) 7 Sitriuc, mac Conraiẋ, mic Eogain 7 alii.—Maẋnur, ri Loċlainni, co longair moir do ċuiḋeċt i Manainn 7 rí m-bliaḋna do denum doiḃ 7 do Feraiḃ Erenn.— Eitereḋa Fer n-Erenn illaim Domnaill, comarba Patraic, re rí m-bliaḋna eter hUa m-Briain (don[b], Muirċertaċ[b]) 7 hUa Loċlainn (don[b], Domnall[b]) 7 araile.—Muireḋaċ hUa Cirduba[i]n, aircinneċ Luẋbaiḋ, do ṁarbaḋ do Feraiḃ Miḋe beur.—Rorr-ailiṫir (do[c] ert, cum patre ruo[c]) do arcain do Uiḃ-Eċaċ i n-diẋail marbṫa Ui Donnċaḋa (don,[a] Mic na hefluimme[a]).—Cairil do lorcaḋ do Eiliḃ.—Muẋron hUa Morẋair, airoferleiġind Arda-Maċa 7 iarṫair Eorpa uile, | corum multir tertibur, i ter[t] Non Octimber, ruam uitam feliciter finiuit (don,[a] i Maugarit[a]).

kal. Ian. u. f., l. xx., Anno Domini M.º c.º iii.º 8cannep croḋa eter Feru-Luirg 7 Tuaiṫ-Raṫa, i

A.D. 1102. [1].u.ed, MS. (B)—[a-a] itl., t.h., MS.; om., C. [b-b] itl., t. h., MS. Given in text of C. [c-c] itl., t.h., MS.; "with yᵉ fryers," C.

B 46c

1102. [1] *Namely, etc.*—The portion within brackets is omitted by the *F.M.* and by O'Conor. The offence is stated in the *Annals of Loch Cé* to have been committed against the community of St. Patrick. The *Annals of Innisfallen*, with more precision, state that the Ui-Echach made a great raid upon the community of Armagh and slew four-and-twenty of the church-folk.

[2] *In custody of Domnall.*—As O'Brien and O'Loghlinn each claimed to be paramount, the hostages were deposited with a superior acknowledged by both.

[3] *And so on.*—That is, the com-

Kalends of Jan. on 4th feria, 9th of the moon, A.D. [1102] 1102. Sort of Colum-cille was burned.—Donnchadh, son of Echri Ua Aitidh, royal heir of the Ui-Eachach, was killed by the Ulidians (namely,[1] in the fifth month after the profaning of Patrick by him).—Domnall, son of Tigernan Ua Ruairc, king of Conmaicni, was killed by the Conmaicni themselves. — Cu-mhaighi Ua Cairill, herenagh of Dun, died.—Flaithbertach Mac Fothaigh, king of Ui-Fiacrach of Ard-sratha, was killed by the men of Lurg.—A hosting by the Cenel-Eogain to Magh-Coba. The Ulidians went in the night into the camp, so that they killed Sitriuc Ua Mael-fhabhaill (namely, king of Carraic-Brachaide) and Sitriuc, son of Conrach, son of Eogan and others.—Maghnus, king of Lochlann, went with a large fleet into Manann and peace of a year was made by them and by the Men of Ireland.—The hostages of the Men of Ireland [were placed] in custody of Domnall,[2] successor of [St.] Patrick, for [securing] peace of a year between Ua Briain (that is, Muircertach) and Ua Lochlainn (namely, Domnall) and so on.[3]—Muiredhach Ua Cirdubain, herenagh of Lughbadh, was killed by the Men of Meath also.—Ross-ailithir (namely, with its superior[4]) was pillaged by the Ui-Echach [of Munster], in revenge of the killing of Ua Donnchadha, namely, of Mac-na-her-luime[5].—Cashel was burned by the Eili.—Mughron Ua Morghair, archlector of Ard-Macha and of all the West of Europe, felicitously finished his life (namely, in Mungarit[6]) before many witnesses, on [Sunday] the 3rd of the Nones [5th] of October.

Kalends of Jan. on 5th feria, 20th of the moon, A.D. [1103] 1103. A courageous skirmish [was fought] between the

---

piler omitted details contained in the authority he worked from.

Though this portion of the MS. is missing, to judge from the F. M., who give this entry with equal brevity, the expression was contained in A.

The items passed over were perhaps the names of the hostages.

[4] *Superior.* — "With ye fryers," C. The reading of the translator's original was thus apparently *cum fratribus suis.*

τοrċair ar ceċtarδe.—Ua Cananna[i]n δo innarba[δ] a riξi Thire-Conaill la Domnall hUa Loċlainn.—Muirċaδ δonn (iδon,[a] Ua Ruaδaca[i]n[a]) δo marbaδ (ri[b] uerum erċ[b]) ror creiċ i Maξ-Coba 7 in ċreċ hirin δo marbaδ in Gilla guit hUi Cormaic irinδ lo ceċna.—Raξnall hUa Oca[i]n, reċcaire Telċa-ó[i]g, δo marbaδ δo feraiδ Maiξi-lċa.—Coċaδ mor eċer Cenel-n-Eogain 7 Ulltu, co ċainig Muirċerċaċ hUa briain co feraib Muman 7 Laiξen 7 Orraiξi 7 co maiċiδ Connaċt 7 co feraiδ Miδe im a riξaiδ co Maξ-Coba i roirriċin Ulaδ. Dolloċur δiblinaiδ co Macaire Airδ-Maċa (iδon,[c] co Cill na Conraire[c]), co m-baċur reċcmain a forδairi for Airδ-Maċa Domnall hUa Loċlainn co Tuairċerċ Erenn firin re rin i n-Uib-breraiL-Maċa, aξaiδ i ċ'aξaiδ friu. O robaċur ċoirrriξ imorro fir Muman, δoluiδ Muirċerċaċ co hAenaċ-Maċa 7 co hEriuin 7 ċimceall δo Airδ-Maċa. co farġaiδ oċt n-unga oir forrin alċoir 7 co roġeall oċt fiċċe[e] bo. Ocur imrair i Maξ-Coba δori[ċ]iri (iδ[b] erċ, non imreċraċor[b]) 7 facbair Coiċeδ Laiξen anδ 7 roċaiδi δo feraiδ Muman. Aċnaiξ feiu imorro for creaċuδ i n-Dal-Araiδe, co farcaiδ Donnċaδ, mac Toirrδelbaiξ, ann 7 mac hUi Concobuir, ri Ciaraiδe 7 hUa beoain eċ alii orċimi. Dolluiδ Domnall· hUa Loċlainn co Tuairċerċ Erenn i Maξ-Coba for amur Laiξen. Teċaiċ imorro Laiξin 7 Orraiξi 7 Fir Muman 7 Gaill, amal robaċur, i n-a n-aξaiδ 7 feraiċ caċ (iδon,[f] in-

A.D. 1103. [a-a] itl., t.h., MS. Given in text of C. [b-b] itl., t.h., MS.; om., C. [c-c] itl., t.h., MS. "To Kill—Cornajre" (by metathesis of *n* and *r*), C. [d] un. main, MS. [e] xx., MS.

[5] *Mac-na-herluime.—Son of the patron-church.* He had probably, in accordance with the decree in the *Collectio Canonum Hibernensis* (XLII. 14: *De alumnis ecclesiae*), been dedicated from his youth to the church of Roscarbery.

[6] *In Mungarit.—*From this it can be inferred that he had gone *on pilgrimage* to the monastery of Mungret (co. Limerick), to prepare for death.

1103. [1] *Raiding-force.—*Literally, *raid: crech* being employed in a secondary sense, as a collective, signifying the agents (whence the Anglo-Irish *creaght*).

Men of Lurg and the Tuath-ratha, wherein fell a large [1103] number on both sides.—Ua-Canannain was expelled from the kingship of Tir-Conaill by Domnall Ua Lochlainn.— Murcad the Brown (namely, Ua Ruadacain) was killed (if it is true) on a raid in Magh-Cobha and that raiding-force[1] slew the Stammerer, Gilla Ua Cormaic, on the same day. —Raghnall Ua Ocain, lawgiver of Telach-og, was killed by the Men of Magh-Itha.—Great war between the Cenel-Eogain and Ulidians, so that Muircertach Ua Briain came with the Men of Munster and of Leinster and of Ossory and with the nobles of Connacht and with the Men of Meath, including their kings, to Magh-Cobha, in aid of the Ulidians. Both [forces] went to the Plain of Ard-Macha (namely, to Cell-na-Conraire), so that they were a week in leaguer against Ard-Macha. Domnall Ua Lochlainn with the North of Ireland [was] during that space in Ui-Bresail-Macha, face to face[2] against them. Howbeit, when the Men of Munster were tired out, Muircertach went to Aenach-Macha and to Emhain and around to Ard-Macha, so that he left eight ounces of gold upon the altar and promised eight score cows. And he turns into Magh-Cobha again (namely, not having obtained [his request[3]]) and leaves the Fifth of Leinster and a detachment of the Men of Munster therein. But he applied himself to pillaging in Dal-Araidhe, so that he lost[4] there Donnchadh, son of Toirrdelbach and the son of Ua Conchobuir, King of Ciaraidhe and Ua Beoain and others most excellent[5]. Domnall Ua Lochlainn went with the North of Ireland into Magh-Cobha to attack Leinster. Howbeit, Leinster and Ossory and the Men of Munster and the Foreigners, as they were, come against them and they fight a battle (that is, on the Nones [5th] of August

---

[2] *Face to face.*—Literally, *face to thy face.* The narrator, as it were, addresses the auditor.

[3] *Request.*—Perhaps that the archbishop of Armagh would deliver up the hostages mentioned under the preceding year.

72 ccmiala ulaoh.

Noin Ccuzu[i]rt 7 1 Cetain 7 1 nomao⸢ [uacao] ficec⸢ [ercai] 7 irin octmao ló iap tecc oo [Cpo-]Macai'). Maioir tpa pop Lee Moza 7 latep a n-ap: eoon, ap Laizen, im Muipcertac, mac Zilla-Mocolmo[i]c 7 im oa Ua Lopca[i]n 7 im Muipcertac, mac Mic Zopma[i]n et alii; ap hUa-Ceinnpealaiz, im oa mac Mael-Mhopba 7 im hU[a] Ria[i]n (ioon,ᵃ pi hUa-n-Opona*) et alii; ap Orpaizi, im Zilla-patpaic puao, ioon, pi Orpaiz 7 im pizpaio Orpaizi apceana; ap Zall Cca-cliac, im Toprtain, mac Eric 7 im pol, mac Ccmaino 7 im beollan Cpmunn et alii; ap Fer Muman, im oa hUa bric, ioon, oa pioomna na n-Oerpe 7 im hUa Failbe, ioon, pioomna Copcoduibne 7 erri Laizen 7¹ im hUa Muire-daiz, pí Ciaraibe, co n-a mac; et alii | multi optimi quor caura breuitatir reribere² pretermirimur. Tepnatur Cenel-n-Eogain co Tuairrept Erenn co corcar mor 7 co petaib imbaib, imon pupoll pizoa 7 im camlinne 7 im fetaib imoaib arceana.—Maznur, pi Loclainni, oo marbao for creic i n-Ulltaib.—Catalan mac Sena[i]n oo marbao oo Chairpri[b].—Murcao hUa Flaiteca[i]n, aircinnec Ccroa-bo, pui ecnai 7 éanaiz 7 airciuil, in reripinatione rua¹ (ioon,ᵃ i n-Ccro-Maca²) feliciter obiit.

B 46d

[bip.] Kal. Ian. iii. f., L 1., Cnno Oomini M.° c.° iiii.° Feiblimib, mac Flaino Mainirtrec, miler optimur Chrirti, in pace quie[uit].—Maiom fia n-Ulltaib for Oal-n-Ccraide, i torcair Dubcenn hUa Oama[i]n i fri-

---

¹ ioon—namely, MS.; "and," C. ² reribi, MS. (B).
ᵃ Ⅱ. m., t.h., MS.; om., C. ᵍ⸍ⁱˣ. xx., MS. ᵇ uiii, MS. ¹ ruam, MS.; om., C.

⁴ *Lost.*—Literally, *left* (on the field of battle).

⁵ *Others most excellent.*—In giving the nominative, the compiler overlooked the fact that the context requires the accusative.

⁶ *The 29th.*—The lunation, which is correct, has been omitted by the Four Masters (Vol. ii. p. 974).

O'Donovan's *Tuesday* (*ib.*, p. 975) is to be corrected to *Wednesday*, in accordance with his text.

⁷ *Others.*—Cf. note 5 (*supra*).

⁸ *Sub-king.*—The name is not given in the *Annals of Innisfallen*.

⁹ *And many, etc.*—"And many more, which for brevity of wry-tinge we omit," C.

and on Wednesday and on the 29th[6] [day of the moon] [1103] and on the eighth day after [his, Ua Briain's] coming to Ard-Macha). But defeat is inflicted upon the Half of Mogh and slaughter o them ensues,—namely, slaughter of Leinster, around Muircertach, son of Gilla-Mocholmoic and around the two Ui Lorcain and around Muircertach, son of Mac Gormain and others[7]; slaughter of the Ui-Ceinnselaigh, around the two sons of Mael-Mhordha and around Ua Riain (namely, king of Ui-Drona) and others[7]; slaughter of Ossory, around Gilla-Patraic the Red, that is, king of Ossory and around the royal family of Ossory also; slaughter of the Foreigners of Ath-cliath, around Torstan, son of Eric and around Paul, son of Amand and around Beollan Armunn and others[7]; slaughter of the Men of Munster, around the two Ui Bric, that is, the two royal heirs of the Dessi and around Ua Failbhe, namely, royal heir of Corcoduibhne and the sub-king[8] of Leinster and around Ua Muiredaigh, king of Ciaraidhe, with his son and many other[9] most excellent persons, whom for brevity sake we pass over writing. Cenel-Eogain with the North of Ireland returned with great triumph and with many treasures, including the royal pavilion [of Ua Briain] and including the [royal] banner [of the same] and including many treasures [of his] besides.—Magbnus, king of Lochlann, was killed upon a foray in Ulidia.—Cathalan Mac Senian, was killed by the Cairpri.—Murchadh Ua Flaithecain, herenagh of Ard-bo, master of learning, liberality and poetry, died felicitously on his pilgrimage (namely, in Ard-Macha).

Kalends of Jan. on 6th feria, 1st of the moon, A.D. [1104 Bis.] 1104. Feidhlimidh, son of Flann[1] of Mainister[-Buithi], most worthy soldier of Christ, rested in peace.[2]—A defeat

---

1104. [1]*Flann.*—Died 1056 (*supra*). For his Synchronisms, see *Todd Lectures*, Series III., No. II.

[2] *Rested in peace.*—As *Soldier of Christ* signified a monk it may be inferred that Feidhlimidh belonged to the community of Monasterboice (co. Louth).

ξuin.—Concobuṗ (iḋon,ᵃ hUa Concobaiṗᵃ), mac Mael-
Seċlainn, ṗí Coṗcombṗuaḋ, moṗtu[u]ṗ [eṗṫ].—Mac na
haiḋċe hUa Ruaiṗc a ṗuiṗ ḟṗaṫṗibuṗ occiṗuṗ eṗṫ.—
8loẋaḋ la Muiṗceṗṫaċ hUa m-Ḃṗiain co Maġ
Muiṗṫeṁne, co ṗomillṡeṫ ṫṗebaiṗe in ṁaiġi 7 iṗin
ṫ-ḟluaẋaḋ ṡin ṗoheṗcṗaḋ Cú-Ulaḋ hUa Cainḋelba[i]n,
ṗí Loeġaiṗe, co n-ḋeṗbailṫ ḋe.—8loẋaḋ la Ḋomnall
hUa Loċlainn, co Maġ-Coḃa, co ṫuc ġiallu Ulaḋ 7 co
n-ḋeoċaiḋ co Ṫeṁṗaiġ, co ṗoloiṗc bloiḋ moiṗ ḋo Loeġaiṗi
7 co ṫaṗaiṫ ṫeṗmonn ḋoiḃ aṗċena.—Coṗmac hUa Coṗ-
maic, ṫoiṡeċ Monaċᵇ ḋo éc.—Ḋunċaḋ hUa Concobuiṗ,
ṗí Ciannaċṫᶜ, ḋo maṗbaḋ ḋia ḋoiniḃ ḟein.

Kal. Ian. 1; ḟ., L.x. ii., Anno Ḋomini M.° c.° u.° Muiṗeḋaċ
Mac Cana; Maelṗuanaiḋ hUa Ḃilṗin (iḋon,ᵃ ṗi hUa-
Caiṗḃṗeᵃ); Mael-Seċlainn hUa Conainġ (iḋon,ᵇ ḋo Ḋal-
Caiṡᵇ) in peniṫenṫia moṗṫui ṡunṫ.—Concobuṗ, mac
Mael-Seċlainn, ṗiḋomna Ṫeṁṗaċ, occiṡuṡ eṗṫᶜ.—Ḋom-
nall, comaṗba Paṫṗaic, ḋo ṫeċṫ co hAṫ-cliaṫ ḋo
ḋenum ṡiṫa eṫeṗ Muiṗceṗṫaċ hUa m-Ḃṗiain 7 mac Mic
Loċlainn (iḋon,ᵃ Ḋomnallᵃ), conoṗoġaiḃ ġaluṗ ann 7 co
ṫucaḋ inḋ-a ġaluṗ co Ḋomnaċ Aiṗṫeṗ-Eṁna, coṗohonġaḋ
ann 7 co ṫucaḋ iaṗ ṡin co Ḋamliac, co n-ḋeṗbailṫ ann.
Ocuṡ ṫucaḋ a ċoṗṗ co hAṗḋ-Maċa, iḋon, i ṗṗiḋ Io
Aġu[i]ṗṫ 7 i Saṫuṗn 7 i ḟeil Laṡṗein Innṡi-Muṗen 7
iᵈ n-oċṫmaḋ [uaṫaḋ] ṗiċeoᵈ [eṗcai]. Ceallaċ, mac Aeḋa,

A.D. 1104. ᵃ⁻ᵃ iṫl., t.h., MS.; given in text, C. ᵇ Maonaċ, C.
ᶜ "Connaught," C.

A.D. 1105. ᵃ⁻ᵃ iṫl., t.h., MS.; given in text, C. ᵇ,ᵇ iṫl., t.h., MS.;
om., C. ᶜ⁻ᶜ occiṗi ṡunṫ, MS., C. ᵈ⁻ᵈ in. uiii.maḋ. xx.iṫ, MS. From
iḋon (inclusive) to end of sentence om., C.

³ *Encounter.*—Literally, *counter-
wounding.*

⁴ *Spared the inhabitants.*—Literally, *gave them termonn besides.*
Termonn = Latin *terminus*, land
bounded off for a church or monastery; then, right of asylum;
hence, as here, to spare life. Cf.
the *Collectio Canonum Hibernensis*:
De locis consecratis (XLV.), *De civitatibus refugii* (XXVIII.).

1105. ¹ *Damliae* (Duleek, co.
Meath) — *Ard-Macha.* — Taking
damliac literally, the Four Masters

ANNALS OF ULSTER.

[was inflicted] by the Ulidians upon the Dal-Araidhe, [1104] wherein fell Dubcenn Ua Damain in the encounter.³—Concobur (that is, Ua Concobair), son of Mael-Sechlainn, king of Corcombruadh, died.—"Son of the Night" Ua Ruairc was slain by his kinsmen.—A hosting by Muircertach Ua Briain to the Plain of Muirthemhne, so that they destroyed the tillage of the Plain. And in that hosting Cu-Uladh Ua Caindelbain, king of Loeghaire, was thrown [off a horse], so that he died thereof.—A hosting by Domnall Ua Lochlainn to Magh-Cobha, so that he took away the pledges of Ulidia and went to Tara and burned large portion of Loeghaire and spared the inhabitants.⁴—Cormac Ua Cormaic, chief of Monaigh, died.—Dunchadh Ua Concobuir, king of the Cianuachta [of Glenn-Gemhin], was killed by his own people.

Kalends of Jan. on 1st feria, 12th of the moon, A.D. [1105] 1105. Muiredhach Mac Cana; Maelruanaidh Ua Bilrin (namely, king of Cairbri); Mael-Sechlainn Ua Consing (that is, of the Dal-Cais) died in penance.—Conchobur, son of Mael-Sechlainn, royal heir of Tara, was slain.—Domnall, successor of Patrick, went to Ath-cliath to make peace between Muircertach Ua Briain and the son of Mac Lochlainn (namely, Domnall), so that he took illness there and he was carried in his illness to Domnach of Airthir-Emhna. There he was anointed and he was carried after that to Damliac¹ and he died there. And his body was carried to Ard-Macha,¹ that is, on the 2nd of the Ides [12th] of August and on Saturday and on the feast of [St.] Lasrian of Inis-Muren [*recte*, Inis-Muredaigh] and on the 28th² [of the moon]. Ceallach, son of Aedh, son of

---

state that Domnall was carried to the *stone-church of Armagh* and died there!

² *On the* 28*th*.—O'Conor gives *in xxviii.*, leaving a blank after, as

if the scribe had omitted some necessary words. There is no hiatus in the MS.

In the *Annals of Loch Cé* (*ad an.*), all the criteria of the day are

76 αннαlα ulατoh.

mic Mail-Іѕа, ᴅo oiᴘᴅneᵬ i n-a inaᵬ i comaᴘbuᴘ Paτ-
ᴘаiс, а τoxа ꜰeᴘ | n-Єᴘеnn 7 ᴅoсuaiᵬ ꜰо xᴘaᴅаiᵬ illоu
ꜰeili αᴅomnain.—Niаll oᵬoᴘ hUа Cоncobuiᴘ ᴅо mаᴘ-
bаᵬ.—Muiᴘxiᴘ hUа Conсenainᴅ ᴅо éс.—8luаxаᵬ lа
Muiᴘсeᴘτаċ hUа m-bᴘiаin, со ᴘоinnаᴘb ᴅоnnċаᵬ hUа
Маel-8eċlаinn а ᴘixi iаᴘτаiᴘ Miᵬe.

Kal. 1an. 11. ꜰ., L. xx. 111., Ꮯnnо ᴅоmini M.° c.° ui.° Cᴘeċ-
ꜰluаixeᵬ lа ᴅоmnаll hUа Loċlainn i ꜰоiᴘiᵬin ᴅоnn-
ċаᴅа hUi Маel-8eċlainn, со ꜰoоᴘτaᴅuᴘ iаᴘτаᴘ Miᵬe 7
со τáᴘuᴘ ᴅоnnċаᵬ аnn ꜰoᴘ ᴘсeṁleᵬ 7 со ᴘоmаᴘbаᵬ é.—
ᴅiᴘiᴘτ-ᴅiаᴘmаτа со n-a ᴅeᴘτаix ᴅо lоᴘсаᵬ.—Тuаċаl,
соmаᴘbа Соeṁxin, in ᴘасе quieuiτ.—Ceаllaċ, соmаᴘbа
Раτᴘаiс, ꜰoᴘ сuаiᴘτ Ceniuil-Єоxаin сeτnа ċuᴘ, со τuс
a óx-ᴘeiᴘ: iᴅоn, bó сeċ ᴘeṁᴘ,ᵃ no аx n-ᴅáᴘа сeċ τᴘiᴘ,
no leċ-unxа сeċ сeτ[ᴘ]аiᴘ, lа τаeᵬ n-eᴅᵬаᴘτ n-imᴅа
olċenа.—Cаτbаᴘᴘ hUа ᴅоmnаill, ᴘi Ceneо[i]l-Luxᴅаċ
[moᴘτuuᴘᵇ eᴘτᵇ].—Ceаllaċ ꜰoᴘ сuаiᴘτ Muman сeτnа
ċuᴘ be[u]ᴘ, со τuс а lаn-ċuаiᴘτ: iᴅon ᴘeċτᶜ m-bае 7
ᴘeċτᶜ саiᴘix 7 leċ-unxа сeċ ꜰuinᴅ τᴘiċа-сeτᵈ i Múmа[i]n,
lа τаeᵬ ᴘéτ n-imᴅа olċenа. Осuᴘ аᴘᴘоeτ imoᴘᴘо Ceаllaċ xᴘаᴅа uаꜰаleᴘꜰсоiᴘ ᴅо'n ċuᴘ ᴘin, а ꜰоᴘсоnxᴘа ꜰeᴘ

A.D. 1106. ᵃ .ui.eᴘ, MS. ᵇ⁻ᵇ "Dyed," C. ᶜ .uii., MS. ᵈ—.c., MS.

omitted. The Four Masters pass over the lunation.

³*Received Holy Orders.*—Literally, *went under degrees.* Cellach (usually called by the meaningless Latin alias, Celsus) was, it thus appears, one of the eight intruded laymen mentioned in St. Bernard's Life of St. Malachy. In addition, he was ordained *per saltum* and, being but 26 years old, under the canonical age, which in the Irish Church, according to the *Collectio Canonum Hibernensis* (III. 11), was 30 years for the priesthood. As a set-off, perhaps, to those irregularities, the Orders were not conferred until Quarter-Tense Saturday, which fell on September 23 in 1105. By *Men of Ireland* are accordingly to be understood the immediate adherents of the person thrust into the succession.

⁴ *Fiach, etc.*—Thus given in C.; also in the *Annals of Boyle* (ad an.), with the variant *Fiachra*.

1106. ¹ *Successor of [St.] Coemghen.*—Abbot of Glendalough, co. Wicklow.

Mail-Isu, was instituted in his place in the succession of Patrick, by choice of the Men of Ireland. And he received Holy Orders on the day of the feast of Adomnan [Sep. 23].—Niall Ua Concobuir the Swarthy was killed.—Muirghis Ua Concheanaind [king of Ui-Diarmada] died.—A hosting by Muircertach Ua Briain, so that he expelled Donnchadh Ua Mael-Sechlainn from the kingship of the West of Meath.

("Fiach[3] O'Flain was killed.")

Kalends of Jan. on 2nd feria, 23rd of the moon, A.D. 1106. A foray-hosting by Domnall Ua Lochlainn in aid of Donnchadh Ua Mael-Sechlainn, so that they wasted the West of Meath and Donnchadh was overtaken on a surprise-party and he was killed.—Disirt-Diarmata with its oratory was burned.—Tuathal, successor of [St.] Coemhghen,[1] rested in peace.—Ceallach, successor of Patrick, [went] upon circuit of Cenel-Eogain [for] the first turn, so that he took away his full demand: namely, a cow for every six, or an in-calf heifer for every three, or a half ounce [of silver] for every four, besides many donations also.—Cathbarr Ua Domnaill,[2] king of Cenel-Lughdach, died.—Ceallach [successor of Patrick went] upon circuit[3] of Munster also [for] the first turn, so that he took away his full circuit[-sum]: namely, seven cows and seven sheep and a half ounce for every cantred[4] of land in Munster, besides many valuable gifts as well. And Ceallach also received the orders of archbishop[5] on that occasion, by direction of the Men of

---

[2] *Cathbarr Ua Domnaill.*—His name occurs on the reliquary called the *Cathach*, a silver case, enclosing the Psalter. See Reeves, *Adamnan*, p. 319, sq.

[3] *Circuit.*—This visitation of Munster, it is significant, was not mentioned in the *Annals of Innisfallen.*

[4] *Cantred.*—Literally, *thirty hundred*. About twice the size of a barony, according to Dr. Reeves (*Townland Distribution of Ireland*, Proc. R.I.A., vii., p. 475).

[5] *Orders of archbishop.*—As the non-consecration of Cellach in the preceding year, we may assume, was owing to the suffragan being

78 ANNALA ULAÓH.

n-Epenn.—Caincompuc hUa Oaigill, uaral epscop Aipo-
Maca, in pace quieuit.—Etzaip, pi Alban, moptuup est.

Kal. 1an. 111. p., L 1111., Anno Domini M.° c.° u11.° Snec-
tai lai co n-aiōce vo septain in Cetain^a pia peil Patpaic, co pola áp cetpa 1 n-Epinn—Cenn-copaò vo
lopcaò (vo^b ait^b) etep va Caipc, co perccait vabac etep
miò 7 bpogoiv.—Concobup, mac Duinnsleiōe, pivomna
Ulaò, vo mapbaò vo sepaiò sepn-muigi.—Maiom pia
n-Ui[b]-Ópepail sop Ui[b]-Meiē, 1 toscaip a n-áp, im a
pig, ivon,.Aeò hUa Innpeactaig.—Catupac hUa Cuam-
ma[i]n, pi hUa-m-Ópiuin Apcaille, vo guin vo Uib-Cpe-
meainn, co n-vepbailt ve. Eogan, mac Mic Riahaig, vo
mapbaò 'n-a òigail—sliuc ōoinenn mop ipin bliaòain
pi, co pomill na happanna.—Mael-Patpaic hUa
B 47b Opuca[i]n vo | gabail sepupaleiginn Aipve-Maca
illoo peile Ailbe 7 Molaipi Daim-innpi. Mael-Colaim
hUa Opolca[i]n vo gabail epscopoite iap n-amapac.—
Sic m-bliaòna vo ōenam vo Chellaē, comapba Patpaic,
itep Mupcaò hUa m-Ópiain 7 Domnall, mac Mic
Loclainn.

[b_{ir}.] Kal. 1an. 1111. p., L x. u., Anno Domini M.° c.° u11.°
Luimnec vo lopcaò vo aitt.—Domnall hUa Anbeit, pi
hUa-Meit; Domnall hUa Ruaipc, pi hUa m-Ópiuin,
occipi runt.—Ceallaē, comapba Patpaic, sop cuaipt

A.D. 1107. ^a .c.ain, MS. ^{b-b} itl., t.h., MS.; om., C.

---

alive, it will follow that the present event, though recorded in connexion with the Munster visitation, took place after the death of O'Boyle.

In addition, Ceilach's assumption of the primacy had, according to the present Annals, been acquiesced in by the southern moiety of Ireland.

[6] *Bishop of Ard-Macha.*—That is, without territorial jurisdiction. He had been consecrated as suffragan of Domnall on Whitsunday, 1099 (*supra*).

[7] *Donnell, etc.*—Given thus in C. The original is in *Annals of Boyle* (*ad an.*).

1107. [1] *Fell.*—Literally, *to fall.*

[2] *Wednesday.*—The date is thus fixed, because the feast of St. Patrick fell on Sunday in this year.

Ireland.—Caincomruc Ua Baighill, eminent bishop of [1106] Ard-Macha,[6] rested in peace.—Etgair, king of Scotland, died.

("Donell[7] Mac Rory O'Conor deposed by Murtagh O'Bryan and put Tirlagh, his cossen, in his place to be king.")

Kalends of Jan. on 3rd feria, 4th of the moon, A.D. [1107] 1107. Snow of a day and a night fell[1] [on] the Wednesday[2] [March 13] before the feast of Patrick, so that there ensued destruction of cattle in Ireland.—Cenn-coradh was burned (by lightning) between the two Easters[3] [April 14-April 21], together with sixty vats of mead and bragget.—Conchobur, son of Donnsleibhe [Ua Eochadha], royal heir of Ulidia, was killed by the Men of Fern-Magh.—A defeat [was inflicted] by the Ui-Bresail upon the Ui-Meith, wherein fell a slaughter of them, including their king, namely, Aedh Ua Innreachtaigh.—Cathusach Ua Tuammain, king of the Ui-Briuin of Archaille, was wounded by the Ui-Cremhthainn, so that he died thereof. Eogan, son of Mac Riabaigh, was killed in revenge of him.—Excessive wet bad weather in this year, so that it destroyed the crops.—Mael-Patraic Ua Drucain took the lectorship of Ard-Macha on the day of the feast of [St.] Ailbe and of [St.] Molaisse of Daimh-inis [Sep. 12]. Mael-Coluim Ua Brolchain received episcopal consecration[4] after the morrow.—Peace of a year was made by Cellach, successor of Patrick, between Murchadh Ua Briain and Domnall, son of Mac Lochlainn.

Kalends of Jan. on 4th feria, 15th of the moon, A.D. [1108 Bis.] 1108. Limerick was burned by lightning.—Domnall Ua Anbeith, king of Ui-Meith; Domnall Ua Ruairc, king of Ui-Briuin, were slain.[1]—Ceallach, successor of Patrick,

---

[3] *Two Easters.*—That is, Easter Sunday and Low Sunday. The latter was called in Irish *Minchaisc, little Easter* (1109 *infra*).

[4] *Episcopal consecration.*—Literally, *episcopacy*. He succeeded Ua Baighill, who died in 1106, *supra*.

1108. [1] *Were slain.*—The plural

Connacht cetna* cur, co tuc a óg-reir.—Oengur hUa Cleircen, moer Dhail-Cair; Ceallac hUa Coemora[i]n, comarba Cainnig [obierunt*].—Atac gaiti do tiactain hi ter[t] Non Septimbir.—Tec do gabail do U° Matgamna 7 do U° Maelruanaig ror goll n-garbraide (idon,*d* Eocaid, mac Duinnfleide hUi Eotada*d*), idon, ror rig n-Ulad 7 a dicennad leo.—Aed, mac Duiddaleiti (idon,*e* forairrcinnech Airda-Maca*c*), adbur comarba Patraic, do éc.—Dairmer mór ro Erinn uile.—Bliadain rutac co n-degrin 7 commad arda 7 meara in bliadain ri.—Inir-hUa-Labrada do togail la Firumanac.

Kal. Ian. ui. f., l. xx. ui., Anno Domini M.° c.° ix.° Acur in Chairc ror rert[1] Kalann Mai 7 Mincairc [ror] ala laitiu do Shamrad 7 feil Mocoemó[i]c* Léit ror Satarn Initi. Gilla-Ailde hUa Ciarmaic, ri Aine-Cliac, mortuur[2] ert.—Mael-Iru hUa Cuilen, uaralerroc Tuairceirt Erenn; Aengur hUa Domnalla[i]n, primanmcara Samta Coluim-cille [obierunt].—Ar hUa-m-Brerail im a rig, idon, im Dartin 7 hUi-n-Ecac

A.D. 1108. *a* .c. na, MS. *b* Also om. in C. *c* Accented, MS. *d-d* partly itl., partly r.m., t.h., MS.; om., C. *e-e* itl., t.h., MS.; given in text, C.

A.D. 1109. [1] uiii., A, B. [2]—tur. B. *a* Mocolmóc, A, B, C.

formula is retained with only one of the two names in the *Annals of Loch Cé*; proving that the compiler did not understand the original.

[2] *Successor of* [*St.*] *Cainnech.*—Abbot of Aghaboe, co. Kilkenny.

[3] *Came.*—Literally, *to come.*

[4] *Ua Maelruanaigh.*—He is not mentioned in the list in L. L. (p. 41d), which states that the king was killed by Eochaid Ua Mathgamna. Herewith the *Annals of Innisfallen* (*ad an.*) agree.

[5] *Eligible to be successor.*—Literally, *material of a successor.*

Adbur with the genitive signifies idiomatically one qualified by descent, or otherwise, for an office. After the death of his father, Dubdaleithe, in 1064 (*supra*), Aedh's claim was successively set aside in favour of Mail-Isu and Domnall, sons of Amalgaid. He was too old for election when Domnall died.

1109. [1] *Second day.*—In *diebus*. O'Conor. Little Easter he translates by *Pentecostes*. But this was an oversight, as at 1107 he gives *Dominica in Albis*. The same criteria are noted at 918 (=919), *supra*.

ANNALS OF ULSTER. 81

[went] upon circuit of Connacht the first time, so that he took away his full demand.—Oengus Ua Cleirchen, steward of Dal-Cais; Ceallach Ua Coemorain, successor of [St.] Cainnech,[2] died.—A gust of wind came[3] on the 3rd of the Nones [3rd] of September.—A house was seized by Ua Mathgamna and by Ua Maelruanaigh[4] upon Goll Garbhraidhe (namely, Eochaidh, son of Donnsleibhe Ua Eochadha), that is, the king of Ulidia and he was beheaded by them.—Aedh, son of Dubdaleithi (namely, deputy-herenagh of Ard-Macha), one eligible to be successor[5] of Patrick, died.—Great oak-crop throughout all Ireland.—A sappy year with good weather and abundance of corn and of fruit [was] this year.—Inis-Ua-Labradha was razed by the Fir-Manach. [1108]

Kalends of Jan. on 6th feria, 26th of the moon, A.D. 1109. And Easter [fell] upon the 7th of the Kalends of May [April 25] and little Easter [upon] the 2nd day[1] of Summer [May 2] and the feast of Mochoemoc of Liath upon the Saturday of the Beginning [of Lent,[2] March 13]. [1109]

Gilla-Ailbe Ua Ciarmaic, king of Aine-Oliach, died.—Mael-Isu Ua Cuilen, eminent bishop of the North of Ireland; Oengus Ua Domnallain, chief soul-friend of the Community of Colum-cille, died.—Slaughter of the Ui-Bresail [took place] around their king, that is, around

---

[3] *Beginning [of Lent].*—It was the Saturday before the first Sunday in Lent. All these data, which are so valuable for determining the year, have been omitted by the Four Masters.

The equivalence of *Init* (gen. *initi*, —*e*), *Initium* and *Lent* is shown in the following excerpts from Calendars:

Viii. Id. [Feb.]—*Primus dies forsa m-bi prim [uathad] esc[a]i Initi*—[Feb.] 6. First day on which is the first [day] of the moon of Lent (L. B. *Cal. of Oengus*, p. 80).

Vi. Id. [Feb.]—*Primus dies forsa m-bi Init*—[Feb.] 8. First day on which is Lent (*ib.*)

Vi. Id. [Feb.]—*Initii principium* (Cal. appended to Bede's works).

Vi. Id. [Feb.]—*Primitus incepit iciunandi tempus adortum* (Metrical Cal. *Galba*, Brit. Mus., Hampson: *Med. Aevi Kal.*, p. 399).

Vi. Id. [Feb.]—*Prima Quadragesima[e] Dominica* (Cal. *Vitellius*, *ib.*, p. 423).

In the Calendar, the Golden Number XVI. stands opposite Feb.

82 annala ulaḋh.

do ṫuitim la hUa-Meiṫ 7 la Ceru Cern-muiġi.—Sloġaḋ la Muircertaċ hUa m-Briain i roiriḋin Murċaḋa hUi Mail-Seċlainn, co roairg dréim do Ui[b]-Briuin. Sloġaḋ dano la Domnall hUa Loċlainn co Tuaircert Erenn co Sliaḃ-n-[Ph]uait, co n-derna Cellaċ, comarba Patraic, riṫ m-bliaḋna eter hUa m-Briain 7 hUa Loċlainn, co n-deċadur Tuaircert n-Erenn iar rin co Maġ hUa-m-Brerail, ror ammur Ulaḋ batur i Maġ-Coḃa, co tardrat Ula[i]ḋ na teora ġiallu roṫoġrat rein doiḃ.—Cocriċ, comarba Samṫainne Cluana-Bronaiġ, quieuit.—Aeḋ hUa Ruairc do ṫeċt illongport Murċaḋa hUi Mael-Seċlainn ro dó, | co rolla ár tria ercaine Samṫa Patraic.—Ar hUa-Meiṫ im a riġ ıdon, Goll Bairċe 7 dreim d'Ferraiḃ Cern-muiġi do ṫuitim la hUi-Brerail 7 la hUiḃ-Eċaċ.—Domnall ruaḋ Mac Gilla-Patraic, rí Orraiġi, do marbaḋ do mac-caeb aile ic cor cloċe.—Donnċad hUa Duibdirma mortu[u]r ert

(Gilla-Patraic hUa Selbaiġ, airċinneċ Corcaiġi morıtur.)

Kal. Ian. un. f., l. un., Anno Domini M.° c.° x.°
Eċtigern hUa Ferġail, rrimaċlaeċ toġaide, in pace quieuit.—Gilla-Coluim hUa Maelmuaiḋ, rí Fer-ceall iugulatur ert.—Cernaċ, mac Mic Ulċa, airċinneċ Cula-raṫain, in penitentia mortuur ert.—(hUla[i]ḋ do arcain Mucnuma dia lar.) Flann hUa Aeḋa, comarba EineaCrann, mortuur ert.—Maelruanaiġ hUa Maċanen,

[3] dono, B. [4] Cea—, B. [5] ṫuinne, B. [6] rolá, B. [7] dream, A. [8] caiḋe, A. [b-b] l. m., t.h., A, B.; om., C.
A.D. 1110. [1]—loeċ, B. [a] repeated in B by mistake. [b] l.m. t. h., A.; om., B, C.

6, and Feb. 8 is the first Sunday of Lent, when Easter (XVI. D) falls on March 22 (the earliest date).
The omission of Ash-Wednesday is noteworthy.
[3] *To attack.* — Literally, *upon attack.*

[4] *Superioress.*—Literally, *successor.*
[5] *Malediction.*—According to an entry in the F.M., Murchad had pillaged Fir-Rois and killed the king, in violation of the Staff of Jesus and the successor of Patrick the same year.

Dartin and the Ui-Echach were overthrown by the Ui-Meith and by the Men of Fern-magh.—A hosting by Muircertach Ua Briain in aid of Murchadh Ua Mael-Sechlainn, so that he harried some of Ui-Briuin.—A hosting also by Domnall Ua Lochlainn with the North of Ireland to Sliab-[F]uait, until Cellach, successor of Patrick, made peace of a year between Ua Briain and Ua Lochlainn: so that the North of Ireland went after that to the Plain of Ui-Bresail, to attack[3] the Ulidians who were in Magh-Cobha, until the Ulidians gave up to them the three pledges they themselves chose.—Cocrich, superioress[4] [of the Community] of [St.] Samhthainn of Cluain-Bronaigh, rested.—Aedh Ua Ruairc went twice into the camp of Murchadh Ua Mael-Sechlainn, so that he inflicted slaughter through the malediction[5] of the Community of Patrick.—Slaughter of the Ui-Meith [took place] around their king, namely, Goll Bairche and some of the Men of Fern-Magh fell by the Ui-Bresail and by the Ui-Echach.—Domnall Mac Gilla-Patraic the Red, king of Ossory, was killed by another youth in playing a game.—Donnchadh Ua Duibdirma died. [1109]

(Gilla-Patraic[6] Ua Selbaigh, herenagh of Cork, dies.)

Kalends of Jan. on 7th feria, 7th of the moon, A.D. 1110. Echtigern Ua Ferghail, a very select laybrother,[1] rested in peace.—Gilla-Coluim Ua Maelmuaidh, king of Fir-Ceall, was strangled.—Cormac, son of Mac Ulcha, herenagh of Cuil-rathain, died in penance.—(The Ulidians pillaged Mucnom to its centre.—)Flann Ua Aedha, successor of [St.] Eine of Ara, died.—Maelruanaigh Ua Mochainen, king of Mughdoirn, was slain.[2]—Murchadh, [1110]

---

[6] *Gilla-Patraic*, etc.—Given in C.; also in the *Annals of Innisfallen* (*ad an.*; where he is called successor of Barr, that is, bishop of Cork).

1110. [1] *Lay-brother.*—See 1086, note 5. C. renders the word *athlaech* "old champion"!

[2] *Was slain.*—The Four Masters erroneously state that he died a natural death.

[3] *Three.*—In the *Chronicon Scotorum* the names of only two are given.

ní Muġḋoṙn, occiṙuṙ eṙt.—Muṙċaḋ, mac Taıḋg hUı Ḃṙıaın, ṙıḋoṁna Muṁan, moṙtuuṙ eṙt.—Ḃeḃınn, ınġen Cenneıṫġ hUı Ḃṙıaın, ben Ḋoṁnaıll hUı Loċlaınn, ṙıġ Aılıġ, moṙtua eṙt.—Cṙeċ la Ḋoṁnall hUa Loċlaınn ı Connaċtaıḋ, co tuc mıle ḋo ḃṙaıt 7 ılmıle ḋo ḃuaıḃ[c] (no[d], ḋo ċeṫṙaıḃ[d]).—Maıḋm Rōıṙ (no[e], na Rōṙ[e]) aṙ ḃelaıḃ Cṙuaċna ṙıa Sıl-Muıṙeḋaıġ aṙ Conmaıcnıḃ, ı toṙcṙatuṙ tṙı hOe [Ḟh]eṙġaıle 7 maıṫı ımḋa aṙċena.— Ḃṙan hUa Ḃṙıċ, ṙenoıṙ Iaṙ-Muṁan ; Ġılla-Ṗatṙaıc hUa Ḋuıḃṙaċa, ṙeṙleıġınn Cılle-ḋa-lūa 7 ṙuı Muṁan ; Ṡeṙḋoṁnaċ ḋall, ṙeṙleıġınn Cılle-ḋaṙa, (ıḋon[f], ṙuı cṙuıtıṙeċta[f]) [moṙtuı ṙunt].—Cellaċ, comaṙḃa Ṗatṙaıc, cetna cuṙ ṙoṙ cuaıṙt Mıḋe, co tuc a ṙeıṙ.

(Maıḋm[g] ṙıa Conmaıcnıḃ ṙoṙ Sıl-Muıṙeḋaıġ, ıḋon, maıḋm Muıġı-Ḃṙenġaıṙ[c].)

A 49

Kal. Ian. 1. ṗ., L x. uıııı., Anno Ḋomını M.° c.° x.° ı.° Ḋoıṅenn ḋeṙmaıṙ ṙeoıḋ 7 ṡneċtaı, co ṙolaı aṙ cenntaı 7 altaı.—Saṫuṙaċ hUa Leaḋaı ḋo Shamaḋ Ṗatṙaıc, uaṡal ṙenoıṙ Eṙenn, ın pace quıeuıt.—Luġmaġ ḋo loṙcaḋ. —Poṙt-laıṙġı ḋo loṙcaḋ.—Ceanannuṙ ḋo loṙcaḋ.— Sloġaḋ la hUıllıu co Tealaċ-n-ōc, co ṙoṫeṙcṙat a ḃıleḋa. Cṙeċ la Nıall hUa Loċlaınn, co tuc mıle (no[a] tṙı mıle[a]) ḋo ḃuaıḃ ı n-a n-ḋıġaıl.—Tene ḋı[1] aıtt[1] ḋo loṙcaḋ Ḋuın-ḋa-leṫġlaṡ, eteṙ Raıṫ 7 Tṙıan.—Senaḋ ḋo tınol ı Ṡıaḋmıc-Aenġuṡa la maıṫıḃ Eṙenn ım Chellaċ, comaṙḃa Ṗatṙaıc 7 ım Mael-Muıṙe hUa n-Ḋuna[ı]n, ım

---

A.D. 1110. [c] ċeṫṙaıḃ—*cattle,* B. [d-d] itl., t.h., A.; om., B. C. gives text and gloss—"of cowes and chattle." [e-e] itl., t.h., A.; om., B, C. [f-f] itl., t.h., A ; ıḋon, ṙuı ṙṙuıċı ṙeċta—*namely, very distinguished master of law,* B ; followed by C: "Chief lerned in lawe." [g-g] n.t.h., A ; om., B. Given in C.

A.D. 1111. [1-1] ḋaıtt (= ḋı aıtt), B. [2] coecaıt, A ; .Laıt, B. [3] Nıall— [aın], A. The omission of the bracketted portion was, no doubt, a mis-

[4] *Senior.*—See A.D. 1088, note[2-3].
[5] *Harping.*—The F.M. improve upon B and read *sruithe rechta.* But the unaspirated *t* of their original shows that *sruiti rechta* arose from misreading *cruitirechta.*
[6] *Defeat.*—Given in C. ; also in the *Annals of Boyle.*

son of Tadhg Ua Briain, royal heir of Munster, died.— [1110] Bebinn, daughter of Cennetigh Ua Briain, wife of Domnall Ua Lochlainn, king of Ailech, died.—A foray by Domnall Ua Lochlainn into Connacht, so that he took away a thousand captives and many thousands of cows (or of cattle).—The defeat of Ros (or of the Rossa) in front of Cruachan [was inflicted] by the Sil-Muiredhaigh on the Conmaicni, wherein fell three[3] Ui [F]ergaile and many nobles besides.—Bran Ua Bruic, senior[4] of West Munster; Gilla-Patraic Ua Duibratha, lector of Cell-da-lua and doctor of Munster; Ferdomnach the Blind, lector of Cell-dara (namely, a master of harping[5]), died.—Cellach, successor of Patrick, [went] the first time upon circuit of Meath, so that he took away his demand.

(Defeat[6] [was inflicted] by the Conmaicni upon the Sil-Muiredaig, namely, the Defeat of Magh-Brengair.)

Kalends of Jan. on 1st feria, 18th of the moon, A.D. [1111] 1111. Very great bad weather of frost and snow, so that it caused destruction of tame and wild animals.—Cathusach Ua Leadai of the Community of Patrick, eminent senior[1] of Ireland, rested in peace.—Lugmagh was burned.—Port-lairgi was burned.—Cenannus was burned.—A hosting by the Ulidians to Telach-oc, so that they uprooted its trees.[2] A foray [was made] by Niall Ua Lochlainn, so that he took away a thousand (or three thousand) cows, in revenge thereof.—Fire of lightning burned Dun-da-lethglas, both Close and Third.[3]—A Synod was assembled at Fiadh-Mic-Oenghusa[4] by the nobles of Ireland around Cellach, successor of Patrick and around Mael-Muire Ua

---

1111. [1] *Senior.*—See note [4] of preceding year. C. took *samadh* (*community*) to signify "reliques."

[2] *Trees.*—See A.D. 1099, note [3].

[3] *Close and Third.*— From this it may be inferred that Down-patrick was built on the plan of Armagh.

[4] *Fiadh-Mic-Oenghusa.*— *The wood of the son of Oengus.* See Lanigan, iv. 37, and O'Donovan's note, Four Masters, ii. 991-2.

huaṛal-ḟenoiṛ Eṛenn, co coicaiṫ² n-eṛṛcop, uel paulo pluṛ, co tṛi cetaiḃ ṛacaṛt 7 co tṛi miliḃ mac n-ecalṛa, im Muiṛceṛtaċ, im hUa Ḃṛiain (Muiṛceṛtaċᵇ moṛ O Ḃṛiainᵇ), co maiṫiḃ Leṫe Moġa, im eṛail ṛiaġla 7 roḃeṛa | ṛoṛ caċ, eteṛ tuaṫ 7 eclaiṛ.—Donnċaḋ hUa hAnluain, ṛi hUa-Niallain,² do maṛḃaḋ ḋia ḃṛaiṫṛiḃ i meḃail. Na ḃṛaiṫṛi hiṛin ṛein do maṛḃaḋ do Uiḃ-Niallain⁰ i n-a ḋiġail ṛia cenn ṛiċeṫ aiḋċe.—Coṁḃal iteṛ Domnall hUa Loċlainn 7 Donnċaḋ hUa n-Eoċaḋa econ Cuan, co n-deṛnṛat lanṛiṫ 7 co taṛdṛat Ula[i]ḋ eteṛeḃa a ṛiaṛa ṛein do Domnall hUa Loċlainn.

[biṛ.] Kal. Ian. ii. ḟ., L xx. ix., Anno Domini M.º c.º x.º ii.º Raiṫ Aṛda-Maċa co n-a tempull do loṛcaḋ i² n-decim Kallannª Aṗṛil 7 da ṛṛeiṫ Tṛiun Maṛṛain¹ 7 in tṛeṛ ṛṛeiṫ do Tṛiun moṛ.—Conġalaċ, mac Mic Conċaille, aiṛċinneċ Daiṛe, iṛin ceṫṛamaḋᶜ ḃliaḋain noċaṫᶜ aetatiṛ ṛu[a]e, in penitentia² optima quieuit.—Creċ la Domnall hUa Loċlainn taṛ Ḟine-n-Ġall, co tuc ḃoṛoma moṛ 7 ḃṛaitt imḋa.—Ġoṛmlaḋ, inġen Muṛċaḋa Mic Diaṛmata, iḋon, coṁaṛba Ḃṛiġte, in bona penitencia moṛtua eṛt.

Kal. Ian. iiii. ḟ., L x., Anno Domini M.º c. x.º iii.º Connla hUa Ḟlainn, coṁaṛba Molaiṛe Leṫġlinne, quieuit.—Caeṛ-ceineḋ do ċiaċtain aiḋċe ḟeili¹ Ṗatṛaic ṛoṛ Cṛuaċan-Aiġle, co ṛoṁill tṛiċit² do'nd oeṛ

take.—ᵃ⁻ᵃ itl., t.h., A, B. Adopted into text, C, ᵇ⁻ᵇ r.m., n.t.h., A; om., B, C. ᶜ xx., A, B.

A.D. 1112. ¹ Maṛan, A. ²penitencia, A.—ᵃ⁻ᵃ in .x. kl., A, B. ᵇ om., B. ᶜ⁻ᵉ iiii.maḋ ḃliaḋain xc., A, B.

A.D. 1113. ¹ ḟeil, A. ₐ xxx., A, B.

1112. ¹ *Great Third.*—The Saxon Third was uninjured. ² *Successor of [St.] Brigit.*—That is, abbess of Kildare. 1113. ¹ *Of the fasting folk.*—O'Conor reads *don does troscthi-de*	*tuguriis jejunantium.* But *oes* with the genitive is a living idiom, denoting a class, or description of persons. According to the Tripartite Life (Part II.) and the Book of Armagh (fol. 13 c, d), St. Patrick

Dunain, eminent senior of Ireland, with 50 bishops, or a [1111] little more, together with 300 priests and with 3000 ecclesiastics, around Muircertach Ua Briain (Muircertach O'Briain the Great), together with the nobles of the Half of Mogh, to enjoin rule and good conduct upon every one, both laic and cleric.—Donnchadh Ua Anluain, king of Ui-Niallain, was killed by his kinsmen in treachery. These same kinsmen were killed by the Ui-Niallain in revenge thereof, before the end of twenty nights.—A meeting [took place] between Domnall Ua Lochlainn and Donnchadh Ua Ua Eochadha at the Cuan, so they made plenary peace and the Ulidians gave hostages of his own choice to Domnall Ua Lochlainn.

Kalends of Jan. on 2nd feria, 29th of the moon, A.D. [1112 Bis.] 1112. The Close of Ard-Macha, with its church, was burned on the 10th of the Kalends of April [March 23] and two streets of Massan-Third and the third street of the Great Third.[1]—Congalach, son of Mac Conchaille, herenagh of Daire, rested in most excellent penance, in the 94th year of his age.—A foray by Domnall Ua Lochlainn over Fine-Gall, so that he took away great cattle-spoil and many captives.—Gormlaith, daughter of Murchadh Mac Diarmata, namely, successor of [St.] Brigit,[2] died in good penance.

Kalends of Jan. on 4th feria, 10th of the moon, A.D. [1113] 1113. Connla Ua Flainn, successor of [St.] Molaise of Leithglenn, rested.—A thunderbolt come on [Monday, March 17] the night of the feast of Patrick upon Cruachan-Aighle, so that it destroyed thirty of the fasting folk[1].—

---

fasted during a Lent on Cruachan-Aighle (Croagh-Patrick, co. Mayo). The observance of the fast by pilgrims, it appears from the present entry, had become customary there at this time.

[2] *The [two Saints] Ui Suanaigh.*— There were two grandsons of Sua-nach, who were likewise abbots of Rahen, King's Co.,—Fidmuine, whose obit is given *supra*, A.D. 756 (=757) and who is commemorated in the Calendar of Oengus at May 16 and Fidairle (not given in the Calendar), whose festival was Oct. 1.

[3] *Steward.* — Of the Armagh,

88 ⁊ΠΝΝ⁊Ι⁊ ΠΙ⁊ΟΗ.

τροιϝc[ϫ]ι.—Διαρμαιτ hUa Cellaiʒ, | comarba hU[a] Suanaiʒ; Diarmaiṫᵇ hUa Lonʒa[ı]n, maer Muman, ı n-aıởi ϝeıleραòραıϝᵇ; Mael-8eaclaınn hUaConcobaır, ρι Corcomruaϝ; Fınởαıρe hUa Loınϝρıʒ, ρí Daıl-Αραιde, ın penıτentıa morτuı ϝunτ.—Flannacanᵇ, mac Mael-Iϝu, aòbur abbaò Αιρò-Maca, ıar n-a onʒaò ⁊ ıar n-aıṫριʒe ṫoʒaıde, ın pace obııτ.ᵇ—Donncaò hUa Τaır-ceırτ òo marbaò la Níall hUa Loclaınn, la ρıʒ Cenıu[ı]l-Conaıll.—Domnall, mac Donncaòa huıᶜ ʒıllaı-Patραıc, òo marbaò òo ʒull ʒabraın.—8loʒaò la Domnall hUa Loclaınn co Ceneol-Eoʒaın ⁊ Conaıll ⁊ Αırʒıalluᵃ (co ʒlenn-Rıʒʒᵈ), co ροınnarbraταρ Donncaò a ρıʒe Ulaò ⁊ co ρορannʒατ Ulltu eτeρ hUa Matʒamna ⁊ macu Duınnρleıòe. Dal-n-Αραιde ımorροᵉ ⁊ hUı-Eacac aıce ϝeın. 8loʒaò la Muır-certac hUa m-bρıaın co ϝeραıò Muman ⁊ co Laıʒnıò ⁊ Connactaıò co Maʒ-Coòa, ı ϝoıριṫın Donncaòa. 8loʒaò òano la Domnall | hUa Loclaınn cur na ϝloʒaıò ρeṁραιτıò co Maʒ-Coòa beur, ı ϝoıριṫın Ulaò, co ρaıòe ımeρeᵃ caτa eτeρρu, co ρoneτarrcar Cellac, comarba Ρατραıc, ϝo ʒne ρıṫ[a]. Donncaò ımorρo hUa Eocaòa òo ṫallaò la hEocaıò hUa Matʒaṁna ⁊ la hUlltu.—8loʒaò la Muırcertac hUa m-bρıaın ⁊ la Leıṫ Moʒa, eτer Loec ⁊ cleırıuc, co ʒrenoıc. Domnall, ımorρo, mac Mıc Loclaınn, co maıṫıò Tuaırce[ı]ρτ Erenn co Cluaın-caın ϝer-ροır, co m-baòar ϝρı ρe mıϝ cınò comar, co n-òeρnaı Ceallac, comarba Ρατραıc ⁊ baċall Iϝu beoϝ ρıṫ m-blıaòna eτarru.—8caınnear croòa eter

² —ʒıall, A. ³ ımeırı, A.— ᵇ⁻ᵇ om., B.; given in C. ᶜ mıc—*of the son*, B. C. agrees with A. ᵈ⁻ᵈ ıτl, t.h., A, B. ᵉ om., A.

---

or primatial, cess (1106, *supra*). In explanation of the term, it is to be noted that in the *Annals of Innisfallen* (ad an.) O'Longan is called superior (*comarba*) of Ard-Patrick (co. Limerick). This church is mentioned in the Tripartite as founded by St. Patrick. In the *Chronicon Scotorum* he is called herenagh of Ard-Patrick. It is added that he was killed by lightning on Croagh-Patrick, a statement that hardly agrees with the *quievit in Christo* of the provincial Chronicle.

Diarmait Ua Cellaigh, successor of the [two Saints] Ui [1113] Suanaigh[2]; Diarmait Ua Longain, steward[3] of Munster, on the night of the feast of Patrick; Mael-Sechlainn Ua Conchobair, king of Corcomruadh; Findchaise Ua Loingsigh, king of Dal-Araidhe, died in penance.—Flannacan, son of Mael-Isu, one eligible to be abbot[4] of Ard-Macha, after his being anointed and after select penance, died in peace.— Donnchadh Ua Taircheirt was killed by Niall Ua Lochlainn, [namely] by the king of Cenel-Conaill.—Domnall, son of Donnchadh grandson of Gilla-Patraic [king of Ossory], was killed by [his brother] Goll Gabrain.—A hosting by Domnall Ua Lochlainn together with the Cenel-Eogain and [Cenel-]Cona[i]ll and the Airgialla (to Glenn-Righe), so that they expelled Donnchadh from the kingship of Ulidia and divided Ulidia between Ua Mathgamna and the sons of Donnsleibhe [Ua Eochadha]. Dal-Araidhe, however, and Ui-Echach [were reserved] to himself. A hosting by Muircertach Ua Briain with the men of Munster and with the Leinstermen and Connacht to Magh-Cobha, in aid of Donnchadh. A hosting also by Domnall Ua Lochlainn with the hosts aforesaid to Magh-Cobha too, in aid of the Ulidians: so that there was imminence of battle between them, until Ceallach, successor of Patrick, separated them under guise of peace. Nevertheless, Donnchadh Ua Eochadha was blinded[5] by Eochaidh Ua Mathgamna and by the Ulidians.—A hosting by Muircertach Ua Briain and by the Half of Mogh, both laic and cleric, to Grenoc. But Domnall, son of Mac Lochlainn, [came] with the nobles of the North of Ireland to Cluain-cain of Fir-Rois, so that they were for the space of a month facing each other, until Ceallach, successor of Patrick and the Staff of Jesus also made peace of a year between them.— A courageous skirmish [was fought] between the men of

---

[4] *Eligible to be abbot.*—Literally, *material of an abbot, materies abbatis.* | —(See 1108, note 5.) Flannacan was uncle of Cellach. It was

Fhiru Fern-muiġi raḋein ı torcraḋar ḋa riḋomna Fern-muiġi, iḋon, hUa Cricá[i]n 7 hUa Ḋonnaca[i]n.

Kal. Ian. u. f., L. xx. 1., Anno Ḋomini M.° c.° x.° 1111.° Flann, mac Mic* [Fh]lannċaḋa, comarba Molaıġı Ḋaiminnri; Mael-Coluım hUa Cormaca[i]n, comarba Einne Arann; Ḋiarmaic hUa Flainnċua, comarba Ailbe Imleċa-iḋair, huaral-errcop 7 ferleiġinḋ¹, errneḋaċ reoit 7 biıḋ, einiġ 7 ḋeirce; Ferḋomnaċ hUa Clucain, comarba Cenannra, in pace quieuerunt.—Teiḋm ġalair moir ḋo ġabail Muircercaiġ hUi Ḃriain, riġ Erenn, co n-ḋernai anfabracta² ḋe 7 co rorcar fri a riġe. Ḋiarmaic imorro ḋo ġabail riġi Muman i n-a riaḋnuire, cen ċecuġuḋ.—Sluaġaḋ la Ḋomnall hUa Loċlainn co Raıt-Cennaiġ, co táiniġ Eoċaiḋ hUa Maṫġamna co n-Ulltaiḋ i n-a ceċ 7 Ḋonnċaḋ hUa Loingriġ co n-Ḋal-Araiḋe 7 Aeḋ hUa Ruairc co feraiḋ Ḃreifne 7 Murċaḋ hUa Mael-Seċlainn co feraiḋ Miḋe. Ḋollocar iar rin, ḋiblinaiḋ, ḋar Aṫ-luain co Ḋun-Leoḋa, co táiniġ Tairrḋelbaċ hUa Conċobair co Connaċtaiḋ 7 Niall hUa Loċlainn, aᵇ mac faḋeinᵇ, co Cenel-Conaill i³ n-a airiuċt.³ Ḋoċocar immurro uile iar rin co Celaiġ-hUa-n-Ḋeḋaiġ⁴ i n-Ḋail-Cair, co n-ḋernracar orraḋ m-bliaḋna 7 Fır Muman. Ḋoḋeoċaiḋ ḋono Ḋomnall hUa Loċlainn ar fuc Connaċc ḋia tiġ.—Aeḋ, mac Ḋonnċaḋa hUi Eoċaḋa, riḋomna Ulaḋ; Ḋonnċaḋ hUa Loingriġ, ri Ḋail-

A.D. 1114. ¹ ferleiġinn, A. ² anfabracta(ḋṫ om.), B. ᵃ·ᵃ inn-a aeriċt, A. ⁴ —eġaiġ, B.—ᵃ om., B ; given in C. ᵇᵇ iḋon, mac Ḋomnaill faḋéin—*namely, the son of Domnall himself,* itl., t.h., B. C. agrees with A.

---

owing perhaps to old age that he had been passed over in favour of his nephew.

⁵ *Blinded.*—Thereby he became incapacitated to reign. Accordingly, in the regnal List (L. L. p. 41d), his successors, Aed and Eochaid (sons of Donnsleibe) are set down after mention of his blinding, when he had reigned three years.

1114. ¹ *Ferdomnach Ua Clucaain.*— He is called successor (comarba) of Colum-cille in the third charter of the Book of Kells, in which he appears amongst the guarantors. See Reeves' *Adamnan*, p. 402.

³ *A skeleton.*—For co n-dernai anfh-

Fern-magh themselves, wherein fell two royal heirs of [1113] Fern-magh, namely, Ua Cricain and Ua Donnacain.

Kalends of Jan. on 5th feria, 21st of the moon, A.D. [1114] 1114. Flann, son of Mac Flannchadha, successor of [St.] Molaise of Daim-inis; Mael-Coluim Ua Cormacain, successor of [St.] Eine of Ara; Diarmait Ua Flannchua, successor of [St.] Ailbe of Imlech-ibhair, archbishop and lector, bestower of treasure and of food, of hospitality and of charity; Ferdomnach Ua Clucain,[1] successor [of St. Columba in the monastery] of Cenannus, rested in peace. —A fit of heavy illness seized Muircertach Ua Briain, king of Ireland, so that he became a skeleton[2] and parted with his kingship. But Diarmait took the kingship of Munster in his presence, without permission.—A hosting by Domnall Ua Lochlainn to Rath-Cennaigh, so that there came into his house Eochaidh Ua Mathgamna with the Ulidians and Donnchadh Ua Loingsigh with the Dal-Araidhe and Aedh Ua Ruairc with the men of Breifne and Murchadh Ua Mael-Sechlainn with the men of Meath. They went after that, both [hosts], past Ath-Luain to Dun-Leodha, so that Tairrdelbach Ua Concobhair with the Connacht-men and Niall Ua Lochlainn, his own son, with the Cenel Conaill, came into his assembly. They all moreover went after that to Telach-Ua-Dedhaigh in Dal-Cais, so that they and the men of Munster made a truce of a year. Thereupon Domnall Ua Lochlainn went throughout Connacht to his house.—Aedh,[3] son of Donnchadh[4] Ua Eochadha, royal heir of Ulidia; Donnchadh Ua Loingsigh, king of Dal-Araidhe; Ua Canannain (namely, Ruaidhri),

---

abrachta, O'Conor (by overlooking the contraction-marks, and misreading and dividing the last word) has *condna on bhabrasa*—ita ut surdesceret! But O'Donovan, who was not *bothered* by the term, aptly quotes (*F. M.*, ii. 997-8) from *Cormac's Glossary* to prove that *anfabrachtai* meant a person wasted by disease.

[3] *Aedh, etc.*—Of the four mentioned in this entry, the Four Masters state that all but Ua Canannain died natural deaths.

Αραιδε; hUα Cananna[ɪ]n (ɪdon,ᶜ Ruaɪdp1ᶜ), pɪdom|ɴα Ceníuɪl-Concaɪll (oᵈ Cenel-Εoʒαɪnᵈ) ; Muɪpcepταč hUα Ločlαɪnn, pɪdomnα Œɪlɪʒ, ɪnɪupτe ɪnτeppecτɪ punτ.

Kαl. Ιαn. uɪ. p., L. ɪɪ., Œnno Domɪnɪ M.° c.° x.° u.° Doɪnenn depmαɪp peoɪd 7 pnečτα[ɪ] o'nᵃ coɪcɪd dec Kαlαnn Εnαɪpᵃ co coɪcɪdᵇ dec Kαlαnn Mαpταɪ,ᵇ uel paulo pluρ, co polaɪ áp en 7 ceτpαɪ 7 dαɪne: dɪα² pοṗαɪρ τepcαɪ moρ po Επɪnn uɪle 7 ɪllαɪʒnɪŭ peoč cač.—Dɪαp- mαɪτ hUα bpɪαɪn, pɪ Mumαn, do epʒαbαɪl lα Muɪp- cepταč hUα m-bpɪαɪn.—Εpce do ċαbαɪpτ do macαɪb mɪc Œedα, mɪc Ruαɪdpɪ, ɪm Τhαɪppdelbαč hUα Concobαɪp, ɪm pɪʒ Connαčτ (ɪdon, ɪ n-Œτ-boᶜ), co poloɪτpeτ 7 cop'[b]o³ ċpolɪʒɪ dó.—Mαɪdm pɪα n-Domnαll hUα m-bpɪαɪn 7 pɪα ʒallαɪb Œτα-clɪaτ pop Lαɪʒnɪb, ɪ τopcαɪp Donnčαd, hua Mαɪl-nα-mbo, pɪ hUα-Ceɪnnpelαɪʒ | 7 Concobup hUα Concobuɪp, pɪ hUα-pαɪlʒɪ, co n-α macαɪb 7 poċαɪdɪ αpčenα.—Domnαll, mac Ταɪdʒ hUɪ bpɪαɪn, pɪdomnα Mumαn, do mαpbαd do Connαčταɪb.—Muɪpcepταč hUα bpɪαɪn do ʒαbαɪl α pɪʒɪ dopɪ[ṫ]ɪpɪ 7 do čɪαčταɪn, pluαɪʒed, ɪllαɪʒnɪb 7 ɪ m-bpeʒαɪb.—Dαṁlɪacc Œpdα-bpecα[ɪ]n, co n-α lán do doɪnɪb, do lopcαd do pepαɪb, Mumαn 7 ceαllα ɪmdα αpčenα ɪ pepαɪb-bpeαʒ.—Cpeαč mop lα Ταɪppdeαl- bαč hUα Concobuɪp 7 lα Connαčταɪb, co poαɪpʒpeτ co Luɪmnneč (ɪdon,ᵈ Τuαṫ-Mumα[n]ᵈ), co pucpατ boppomα dɪαɪpṁɪde 7 bpαɪτ ɪmdα.—Mαel-Seċlαɪnn hUα Mαel- Seċlαɪnn, pɪdomnα Τeṁpαč, occɪpuρ epτ.

ᶜ⁻ᶜ itl., t.h., A, B ; given in C. ᵈ⁻ᵈ itl., t.h., B ; om., A, C.

A.D. 1115. ¹ polαc, A. The *c* is meaningless. ²7—*and*, prefixed, B.
³ ʒup'bo, B.—ᵃ⁻ᵃ o'n .u.ɪd dec Kl. Εnαɪp, A; o .xu. Kl. Ιαnαɪp, B.
ᵇ u.ɪd .x. Kl. Mαpτα, A; .xu. Kle. Mαpταn, B. ᶜ⁻ᶜ itl., t.h., A.; om., B.,; given in C.

[Chasm in A up to A.D. 1162.]

ᵈ⁻ᵈ itl., t.h., MS. (B) ; given in C.

---

⁴ *Donnchadh.*—He was deposed and blinded in the preceeding year.

⁴ *Were unjustly slain.*—The phrase, as here given, is applied to one of the individuals in the *Annals of Loch Cé* (ad an.).

1115. ¹ *Dangerous illness.*—Literally, *gory lying-down.*

² *Murtagh, etc: Mahon, etc.; Murtagh, etc.; Maolmai, etc.*—Given in C. The entries here and elsewhere found in C. and omitted in B may

royal heir of Cenel-Conaill (by the Cenel-Eogain); Muircertach Ua Lochlainn royal heir of Ailech, were unjustly slain.[4]

Kalends of Jan. on 6th feria, 2nd of the moon, A.D. 1115. Very hard weather of frost and snow from the 15th of the Kalends of January [Dec. 18] to the 15th of the Kalends of March [Feb. 15], or a little longer; so that it caused destruction of birds and cattle and people: whereof grew great dearth throughout all Ireland and in Leinster beyond every [place].—Diarmait Ua Briain, king of Munster, was taken prisoner by Muircertach Ua Briain. —An attack was made by the sons of Aedh, son of Ruaidhri, upon Tairrdelbach Ua Conchobair, [that is,] upon the king of Connacht (namely, in Ath-bo), so that they injured him and dangerous illness[1] resulted to him. —A defeat [was inflicted] by Domnall Ua Briain and by the Foreigners of Ath-cliath upon the Leinstermen, wherein fell Donnchadh, grandson of Mail-na-mbo, king of Ui-Ceinnselaigh and Conchobur Ua Conchobuir, king of Ui-Failghi, with their sons and a multitude besides ("and Murtagh[2] O'Teg, king of Ferlii, [was] killed").— Domnall, son of Tadhg Ua Briain, royal heir of Munster, was killed by the Connachtmen.—("Mahon[2] Mac Maoilmaii, King of O'Neachaii in Munster; Maoilsechlain O'Fogartai, king of Eli [died]."—)Muircertach Ua Briain took his kingship again[3] and went on a hosting into Leinster and into Bregha.—("Murtagh[2] O'Ciarmaic, king of O'Hane; O'Conor Kyerry; Donell [Mac?] Murcha O'Flainn; Mac Flanchaa, king of Muskrai, all killed."—)The stone church of Ard-Brecain, with its complement of people, was burned by the Men of Munster and many churches besides in Fir-Bregh.—Great foray[4] by Tairrdelbach Ua Conchobuir and

[1114]

[1115]

have been contained in A. (See textual note a, 1117 infra.) Most of them relate to Munster, and of these the Annals of Innisfallen pass over the greater part. It thus follows that there existed a chornicle of Momonian affairs, of which nothing is known at present.

[3] *Took his kingdom again.*—See the second entry under the preceeding year.

Kal. Ian. uii. f., L. x. iii., Anno Domini M.° c.° x.° ui.°
Ceallac, comarba Patraic, for cuairt Connact do'nd
ara cur, co tuc a lancuairt.—Ceall-da-lua co n-a
tempoll do lorcad.—Corcac mor Muman; 7 Imlec-
ibair; Dairtec Mael-Iru Ui Brolca[i]n; 7 blod do
Lismor; Acad-mbo Cainnig; Cluain-Iraird crematae
funt.—Tec n-abbad mor Arda-Maca, co ficit taxi[b]
ime, do lorcad i torc Corxair na bliadna ra.—
Magna pestilentia famis adhuc ardet | illeit Moga,
eter Laixnicu 7 Muimnecu, co rofaraig cealla 7 duine
7 tuata 7 co roe[r]rraid¹ ro Erinn 7 dar muir 7 co
rola ar inna mete mactata.—Ladmunn, mac Domnaill,
hua rig Alban, do marbad do Feraib Moruab.—Derbail, ingen Toirrdelbaig hUi Briain, mortua est.

Kal. Ian. ii. f., L, xx. iiii., Anno Domini M.° c.° x.° uii.°
Concobur hUa Carilla[i]n do marbad do Feraib-Manac.
—Caturac hUa Cnaill, uasal-ercor Connact, in
Chrirto dormiuit.ᵃ—Mael-Brixte Mac Rona[i]n,
comarba Cenannra, 7 ar Muinntiri Cenannra ime, do
marbad do Aed hUa Ruairc 7 do Ui[b]-Briuin i n-Aine

A.D. 1116. ¹—raig, MS. ᵃ⁻ᵃ cremata ert, MS. ᵇ xx.it, MS.
A.D. 1117. ᵃ dormierunt, MS.; in Chrirto dormierunt, C.:
which proves that the "Owen" and "Conor" items were contained in A.

---

³ *Fvray.*—Made when O'Brien was absent in Leinster.

1116. ¹*Hugh, etc.; Congalach, etc.*—Given in C.

²*The Oratory, etc.*—O Donovan (F. M. ii., p. 1002) says it was at Lismore. Dr. Reeves (*Adamnan*, p. 406), with more caution, says it was seemingly there. According to the *Annals of Innisfallen,* Ua Brolchain died at Lismore. But, it is safe to infer that he retired to that establishment to prepare for his end; whilst the present entry cannot be construed to signify that he erected any building in Lismore. The oratory, it is most probable, was in Armagh;

Mael-Isu having belonged to that community.

³ *Lisaigy.*—*Lis aigedh—fort of the guests,* i. e., guest-house. "Gil-kyaran" (*devotee of [St.] Ciaran*) shows that it belonged to Clonmacnoise. A similar establishment existed in Armagh (1003=4, 1016, *supra.*)

⁴ *Roaveai.*—*Ruadh beith — Red birch.* O'Donovan (*F. M.,* ii. 1003) strangely took *rolddh a n-dr* of his text to signify that O'Brien *slaughtered the inhabitants* of Roevehagh (co. Galway). The expression means that the Thomond invading forces were annihilated.

by the Connachtmen, so that they harried as far as [1115] Limerick (namely, Thomond), until they took away cattle-spoil innumerable and captives many.—("Maolmai[2] O'Ciardai, king of Carbrei [was slain]."—)Mael-Sechlainn Ua Mael-Sechlainn, royal heir of Tara, was slain.

Kalends of Jan. on 7th feria, 13th of the moon, A.D. [1116 Bis.] 1116. Ceallach, successor of Patrick, [went] upon circuit of Connacht for the second turn, so that he took away his full circuit [demand].—("Hugh[1] O'Kinelvan, king of Laoire; Ecbry Lochan, King of Mallon?, died."—)Ceall da-lua with its church was burned.—Great Cork of Munster; and Imlech-ibhair; the Oratory[2] of Mael-Isu Ua Brolchain; and part of Lismor; Achadh-bo of [St.] Cainnech; [and] Cluain-iraird were burned.—The great house of the abbots of Ard-Macha with twenty houses around it was burned in the beginning of the Lent of this year.—Great famine-pestilence still rages in the Half of Mogh, amongst both Leinstermen and Munstermen; so that it desolated churches and forts and districts and spread throughout Ireland and over sea and caused destruction to an [in]conceivable degree.—Ladhmunn, son of Domnall, grandson of [Donnchadh] the king of Scotland, was killed by the men of Moray.—Derbail, daughter of Toirrdelbach Ua Briain, died.

("Congalach[1] Mac Gilkyaran, airchinnech of Lisaigy,[3] in bona penitentia quievit.—The slaughter of Roaveai[4] upon Diermad O'Bryan.")

Kalends of Jan. on 2nd feria, 24th of the moon, A.D. [1117] 1117. Conchobur Ua Cairillain was killed by the Fir-Manach.—("Diermatt[1] Mac Enna, king of Leinster, died in Dublin.—Owen Mac Echtiern, Coarb of [St.] Buti; Conor O'Follovan, Coarb of Clon-Iraird;") Cathusach Ua Cnaill, archbishop of Connacht, slept in Christ.—Mael-Brighte

---

1117. [1] *Diermatt, etc.*—Given in C. The first item is found in the *Annals of Boyle*, where, for *died in Dublin*, the reading is: *and of Ath-claith*, died (*ad an.*). The F. M. have the two other entries; taken, apparently, from A.

Domnaig Cruim-Duba[i]n. Faciep Domini ruper facientep haec[b] rcelera, ut perdat de terra memoriam eorum [Cf. Ps. xxxiii. 17].—Cat (idon[c], Cat Leca[i]n[c]) do denam do brian, mac Murcada 7 do macaib mic Catail hUi Concobair co Connactaib impu fri Tairrdealbac, mac n-Diarmata 7 fri Dal-Cair, co remaid for Dal-Cair 7 co polad a n-ár.—Ar Ceniuil-n-Eogain na hInnri do cor la Cenel-Conaill 7 maiti imdai do tuitim ann.—Caturac hUa Cnaaill, uaral-erscop Connact; Flann hUa Sculu, erscop Connere; Mael-Muire, erscop Duin-da-letglar; Gilla-Mocua Mac Camcuarta, erscop Daimliacc; Ceallac hUa Colma[i]n, erscop Ferna; Anmcad hUa Anmcada, erscop Arda-rerta Brenaind; Muiredac hUa hEnlainge, erscop Cluanarerta Brenaind; Maelruanaig[d] hUa Ciflica[i]n, comarba Robair fri ré ciana, omner in Chriscto dormierunt —Mael-Muire hUa Dúna[i]n, rui erscoir Goidel 7 cenn cleirec n-Erenn 7 muire derce in domain, in reptuagerimo rertimo anno aetatir ruae, in nono[e] Kalendar[e] Ianuarii, relegionir ruae magnae optimum currum conrum[m]auit.

Kal. Ian. iii. f., L u., Anno Domini M.° c.° x.° uiii.

A.D. 1117. [b] om., MS.; given in C. [c-c] itl., t.h., MS.; given in C. [d] Owing to a stain, it is impossible to discern the mark of contraction = aig; but the reading here given is certain from C. [e-e] nonir Kllanoir, MS.; *Non. Kal.*, C.

² *Mael-Brighte Mac Ronain.*—See Reeves' *Adamnan*, p. 403.

³ *Friday.*—For *Aine* the F. M. read *oidhche* (night). The Sunday of Crom Duban was the last of Summer, according to O'Flaherty, who adds that it was so called to commemorate the destruction of the idol Cenn-(Crom-)cruaich by St. Patrick, as narrated in the Second Part of the Tripartite. In hujus vero memorabilis idolomachiae memoriam arbitror Dominicam proximam ante Kal. Aug. solenni ritu per Hiberniam dedicatam, quam vulgo *Domnach Cromduibh*, i. e., Dominicam Crom Nigri nuncupant; nigri sc. ob horrendum et deformem visibilis spectri speciem: alii rectius in victoris gratiam Dominicam S. Patricii nominant (*Ogygia*, Pars III., c. xxii. p. 198-9).

But for all this he gives no authority. "Colgan (Tr. Th. p. 508), in translating the text of the Four Masters, fell into a ludicrous error by making that day the festival of St. Cromdubh. But there was no such saint." (Lanigan, *E. H*, iv. 56).

Mac Ronain,[2] superior of Cenannus—and slaughter of the [1117] Community of Cenannus [took place] along with him— was killed by Aedh Ua Ruairc and by the Ui-Briuin on the Friday[3] before the Sunday of Crom-duban. The countenance[4] of the Lord is against those who do these evil things, to cut off the remembrance of them from the earth [Cf. Ps. xxxiii. 17].—A battle (namely, the battle of Lecan) was fought by Brian, son of Murchadh and by the grandsons of Cathal Ua Conchobair and the Connacht-men along with them against Tairrdelbach, son of Diarmait and against the Dal-Cais, so that defeat was inflicted upon the Dal-Cais and slaughter of them ensued.—Slaughter of the Cenel-Eogain of the Island was inflicted by the Cenel-Conaill and many nobles fell there.—Cathusach[5] Ua Cnaill, archbishop of Connacht; Flann Ua Sculu, bishop of Connere; Mael-Muire, bishop of Dun-da-lethglas; Gilla-Mochua Mac Camchuarta, bishop of Daimliacc; Ceallach Ua Colmain, bishop of Ferna; Anmchadh Ua Anmchadha, bishop of Ard-ferta of [St.] Brenann; Muiredhach Ua hEnlainge, bishop of Cluain-ferta of [St.] Brenann; Maelruanaigh Ua Ciflichain, successor [of St. Fechin] of Fobar for a long time, all slept in Christ.—Mael-Muire Ua Dunain, learned bishop of the Goidhil and head of the clergy of Ireland and steward of the almsdeeds of the world, consummated the most excellent course of his great religious life in the 77th year of his age, on the 9th of the Kalends of January [Dec. 24].

("Mael-Muire[6] O'Dunan, archbishop of Munster, quievit.—The battle of Lettracs [Lettracha-Odhrain].")

Kalends of Jan. on 3rd feria, 5th of the moon, A.D. 1118. [1118]

---

[4] *The countenance, etc.*—The Vulgate is: Vultus autem Domini super facientes mala, ut perdat de terra memoriam e *um.

[5] *Cathusach*—A repetition of an obit in the second entry under this year.

[6] *Mael-Muire, etc.*—Given in C. Taken, doubtless, from the *Annals of Boyle*.

annala ulaτoh.

Laiδgnen hua Ouiboapa, pi ꝑeꞃ-manač, oo marbaδ oo Uiδ-ꝓ|ačꞃač 7 o'ꝑeꞃaiδ na Cꞃaiδe.—Oiaꞃmaiτ hua bꞃiain, ꞃi muman 7 Leiτi moxa aꞃčeana, moꞃτuuꞃ eꞃτ i Coꞃcaiʒ moꞃ muman, iaꞃ n-onʒaδ 7 aiθꞃiʒi.—meꞃꞃ ceτ· n-unʒa oo aiδmiδ aiꞃꝑꞃinn Ceallaiʒ, comaꞃba ꝑaτꞃaic, oo baδuδ i n-Oaball 7 biδʒaδ oóꞃéin.—ꝑaꞃchaliꞃ, comaꞃba ꝑeτaiꞃ, ꞃeꞃuuꞃ ꞃeleʒioꞃuꞃ cum oilexione Oei eτ ꝓꞃoximi, ao Chꞃiꞃτum miʒꞃauiτ.—maꞃia, inʒen mail-Coluim, inʒen ꞃiʒ Alban, ben ꞃiʒ Saxan, moꞃτua eꞃτ.—8loxaδ la Τaiꞃꞃoelbač hua Concoδaiꞃ, la ꞃiʒ Connačτ 7 la muꞃčaδ hua mael-8ečlainn, ꞃi Τemꞃač, imailli ꝑꞃiꞃ 7 la hAeδ hua Ruaiꞃc iꞃin mumain, conꝓčτaoup, ʒlenn-maxaiꞃ 7 co τaꞃo Oeꞃ-mumain oo mac Caꞃꝑτaiʒ 7 Τuaδ-mumain oo macaiδ Oiaꞃmaoa 7 co τuc a n-ʒiallu oiblinaiδ. 8loxaδ aileᵇ leiꞃ co hAτ-cliaδ, co τuc mac ꞃiʒ Τhemꞃač boi illaim ʒall 7 ʒiallu ʒall ꞃaδéin 7 ʒiallu Laiʒen 7 Oꞃꞃaiʒi.—8cel inʒnaδ inoiꞃτ na hailiτꞃiʒ: 1oon, τalamcumꞃcuxuδ móꞃ i 8leib-Elꞃa, co ꞃomoδaiʒ ilcaτꞃača 7 áꞃ n-oaine inntiδ.—8ʒel inʒnaδ aileᵇ a n-Eꞃinn: 1oon, muiꞃꞃouδón oo xabail o'iaꞃʒaiꞃiδ Coꞃaδ-liꞃaꞃʒlinn i n-Oꞃꞃaiʒiδ 7 aꞃaile ic ꝑoꞃτ-laiꞃʒe.—maioun Cinn-oaiꞃe ꞃoꞃ Uiδ-ečač Ulaδ ꞃia muꞃčaδ hua Ruaδaca[i]n, co ꞃolaδ a n-áꞃ.—Ruaiδꞃi hua Concobuiꞃ,

A.D. 1118.   ᵃ .c., MS.   ᵇ .ꝓ., MS.

1118. ¹ *Himself was endangered.*—Literally, *fright (happened) to himself.* The carrying of so much church plate shows that Cellach was engaged on a Visitation of the diocese.

² *Paschalis.*—Died Jan. 2, 1118.

³ *Maria.*—Married in Westminster, 1100; died and was buried there this year, according to the Anglo Saxon Chronicle.

Bryan, etc.; Donell, etc.—Given in C.; also in the *Annals of Innisfallen* and the *Four Masters*.

⁵ *Earthquake.*—At 1117, the Anglo-Saxon Chronicle states that an earthquake occurred in Lombardy on the Octave of St. John the Evangelist (Jan. 3). As the next preceding event of the same chronicle is said to have taken place on the 17th of the Kalends of January (Dec. 17), the entry in question probably belongs (as in the text) to 1118

Laidbgnen Ua Duibdara, king of Fir-Manach, was killed [1118] by the Ui-Fiachrach and by the Men of Craibh.—Diarmait Ua Briain, king of Munster and of the Half of Mogh besides, died in great Cork of Munster after unction and penance.—The value of one hundred ounces of the Mass-requisites of Cellach, successor of Patrick, was drowned in the Daball and himself[1] was in danger.—Paschalis,[2] successor of Peter, a religious servant with love of God and of the neighbour, passed to Christ.—Maria,[3] daughter of Mael-Coluim, [i.e.] daughter of the king of Scotland, wife of [Henry] the king of the Saxons, died.—("Bryan[4] Mac Murough O'Bryan, heyr of Munster, killed by Teig Mac Carthai and by Desmond.")—A hosting by Tairrdelbach Ua Concobhair [that is], by the king of Connacht and by Murchadh Ua Mael-Sechlainn, king of Tara, along with him and by Aed Ua Ruairc into Munster, until they reached Glenn-Maghair and he gave Desmond to Mac Carthaigh and Thomond to the sons of Diarmait [Ua Briain] and took their pledges from them both. Another hosting by him to Ath-cliath, so that he took away the son of the king of Tara, who was in custody of the Foreigners and the pledges of the Foreigners themselves and the pledges of Leinster and of Ossory.—A wonderful tale the pilgrims tell: namely, a great earthquake[5] at Mount-Elpha shook many cities and killed many persons therein.—Another wonderful tale in Ireland: a mermaid was taken by fishermen of the Weir[6] of Lisarglinn, in Ossory and another at Port-Lairge.—("Donell[4] Mac Roary O'Conor, heyre of Connaght, died.")—)The defeat of Cenn-daire [was inflicted] upon the Ui-Echach of Ulidia by Murchadh Ua Ruadhacain, so that slaughter of them was inflicted.—Ruaidhri Ua Conchobuir, king of Connacht for a long time, died [in

---

[6] *Of the Weir, etc.*—O'Conor's transcript and translation are perhaps worth quotation: *cor adh lis ar glinn in Osraighibh, ocus ar aile ic Puirt-lairge*—cujus longitudo talis, ut extremitas una esset in Ossoria, altera Waterfordiae (quae Surio disterminabantur)!

100 ⁊ ɑnnɑlɑ ulɑƈoh.

ɼi Connaċṫ ꝼɼi ꝛe ciana, ꝺo éc inꝺ ailiṫɼiꞇ iɼin ṫ-ꝼeiɼiṫ bliaḋain ꝛċeṫᵈ iaɼ n-a ḋalluḋ.

|Cal. 1an. 1111. ꝛ., l. x. ui., Ɑnno Ꝺomini Ⅿ.° c.° x.° ix.ᵉ Cenn-coɼaḃ ꝺo ꝛcaileḋ ꝺo Connaċṫaiḃ.—Muiɼceɼtaċ hUa bɼiain, ɼi Eɼenn ⁊ tuiɼ oɼꝺain ⁊ aiɼeċaiɼ iaɼṫaiɼ in ꝺomain, iaɼ m-buaiḋ ɼiʒi ⁊ aiṫɼiʒi i ꝼéil Ⅿoċoemó[i]c leiṫ ⁊ i² ṫeɼṫᵈ 1ꝺ Ⅿaɼṫa, in quinta ꝼeɼia, in uiʒeɼima octaua luna, moɼtu[u]ɼ eɼṫ.—Cú-collċaille hUa ḋaiʒella[i]n, aꝛꝺollaṁ Eɼenn aɼ ḋan ⁊ aɼ ꝺeiɼc, aɼ aineċ, aɼ coinꝺeɼcle coitċinn ꝼɼi tɼuaʒu ⁊ tɼiunu, ꝺo maɼbaḋ ꝺo ꝼeɼɼaiḃ-Luiɼʒ ⁊ ꝺo Ṫhuaiḋ-Raṫa cum ꝛua uxoɼe et ꝺuobuꝛ ꝼiliiꝛ | ɼaṫiɼ boniꝛ et cum tɼiʒinta quinque ali[i]ꝛ, eteɼ ṁuinntiɼ ⁊ oeʒeḃu, in una ꝺomu, hi Saṫuɼn Minċaꝛc ⁊ hi ꝼeil ḋeca[i]n, maic Cula.—Ruaiḋɼi hUa Ṫompaiɼ, aiɼcinneċ [ꝛh]aṫna-móɼe, quieuiṫ.— ꝼlaiṫbeɼtaċ hUa laiḋʒnen, ɼi ꝼeɼn-ṁuiʒi ꝼɼi ɼé, ꝺo éc.— ꝼeɼʒail Innɼi Loċa-Cɼé, ɼenóiɼ aiɼmiṫneċ, miliḋ toʒaiḋe 'Óé, aꝺ Chɼiꝛtum miʒɼauiṫ.—Conċoḃuɼ hUa ʒailmɼeḋaiʒ,

ᵉᶜ A later hand wrote *in perigrinatione* (the Latin equivalent) overhead.
ᵈ xx., MS.

A.D. 1119. ᵃ⁻ᵃ i.ui., MS. ; "6 Ides" (10 *Martii* was written on the margin by another hand), C.

---

⁷ *26th year.*—See 1092, *supra.* The bracketed words are from the C. translation.

1119. ¹ *The 3rd.*—This is a typical instance, showing the value of the ferial and lunation. The Dominical Letter was E and the Golden Number XVIII. March 10 of the text would accordingly be Monday, moon 25. On the other hand, Thursday, moon 25, are a double proof that the date was March 13. Consequently, the scribe, by the most frequently recurring of all errors, mistook *ii.* for *u.*, thereby changing 3 (*iii.*) into 6 (*vi.*).

From C. it may be inferred that *ui.* was likewise the reading of A.

The Four Masters followed the *ui.* of the MS. and omitted, as in most of the similar instances, the week-day and lunation. Whereupon, O'Donovan corrects *sixth* into *fourth*, noting that O'Clery's Irish Calendar gives March 12 as the feast of Mochoemoc. This is, however, a mistake. All the native authorities, including O'Clery's *Marytrology of Donegal*, assign the festival to the 13th. The same error of *sixth* for *third* occurs in the *Annals of Loch Cé* (*ad an.*)

² *Donell*, etc.; *Hugh*, etc.—Given in C.; also in *F. M.*

³ *Both.*—Literally, *between.*

⁴ *Little Easter.*—Low Sunday.

Clon-Mac-Nois] in pilgrimage, in the 26th year[7] after his blinding. [1118]

Kalends of Jan. on 4th feria, 16th of the moon, A.D. 1119. Cenn-coradh was razed by the Connachtmen.—Muircertach Ua Briain, king of Ireland and tower of the splendour and principality of the West of the world, died, after victory of kingship and penance, on the feast of Mochoemoc of Liath and on the 3rd[1] of the Ides [13th] of March, on the 5th feria, on the 28th of the moon.—(" Donell[2] O'Hadeth, king of O'Neachay, killed by Echry Mac Laithvertay O'Hadith, king of O'Neachai after."—) Cucolichaille Ua Baighellain, arch-ollam of Ireland for science and for almsdeeds, for hospitality, for general benevolence towards weak and strong, was killed by the men of Lurg and and by Tuath-Ratha, with his wife and two very good sons and with thirty-five others, both[3] domestics and guests, in the same house, on the Saturday of Little Easter[4] [April 5] and on the feast of [St.] Becan, son of Cula.[5]—Ruaidhri Ua Tomrair, herenagh of [F]athan-mor, rested.—Flaithbertach Ua Laidhgnen, king of Fern-magh for a [long] time, died.—(" Hugh[2] Mac Branan's sonn, king of East Leinster, killed.—Donagh Mac Gillpatrick's sonn, heyr of Ossory, killed by Ossorij themselves."—) Ferghail[6] of the Island of Loch-Cre, venerable religious counsellor, soldier select of God, passed to Christ.—Conchobur Ua Gailm- [1119]

---

[5] *Becan, Son of Cula.*—According to the gloss in the L. B. Calendar of Oengus, he was patron of Imlech-fia (near Kells, co. Meath). Cula, the Martyrology of Tallaght states (L. L. p. 358d), was the name of his mother.

[6] *Ferghail.*—The *Annals of Innisfallen* give the obit under the year 1120; which, more probably, is the correct date.

The Ruaidhri item is placed immediately before this in C., which omits the two final entries.

[7] *Three Innocent Children.*—The week-day and moon's age are correct; but I have not found the feast in native authorities. According to the *Annals of Innisfallen*, Niall was killed in the year following. But the data here given are too precise and too much in accord to be erroneous.

102 ᴀɴɴᴀʟᴀ ᴜʟᴀᴅʜ.

toiṗuc̄ Ceniuil-Moeóin, do marḃaḋ do [U]iḃ-Duḃdai 7 do Clainn [Ṗh]laic̄ḃerṫaiġ.—Niall, mac Domnaill hUi Loc̄lainn, ridomna Ailiġ 7 Erenn 7 tetra Erenn ar cruṫ 7 ar ceill, ar ainec̄ 7 ar ergna, do ṫuitim la Cenel-Moen, irin oc̄tmaḋ[b] bliaḋain ric̄eṫ[c] a aiṙi, i Luan 7 i n-dec̄maḋ[c] [uaṫaḋ ercai] 7 i ṙeil na tri mac n-ennac, in decimo[d] octauo[d] Kalendar Ianuarii.

[ḃ.ṙ.] Kal. Ian. u. ṙ., l. [xx.uii.,[a]] Anno Domini M.° c.° xx.° 8loiġeḋ la Domnall hUa Loc̄lainn i ṙoiridin Murc̄aḋa hUi Mael-Sec̄lainn co hAṫ-luain, i n-aiġiḋ Connac̄t, co tarat Toirrdelbac̄ hUa Conc̄oḃuir ḃreġiṙḋ uṁpo.— Maidm Mac̄airi Chille-more hUa Nialla[i]n ria Raġ-nall, mac Mic Riaḃaiġ, ṙor Uiḃ-Eac̄ac̄, co polaḋ a n-ár. —Conc̄oḃur, mac Ṗlaiṅdaca[i]n, mic Duinnc̄ua[i]n, toiṙec̄ Muinntiṙe-Ḃiṙn, do ġuin i 8leiḃ-[Ṗh]uait do [U]iḃ-Creṁtaind 7 a éc de.—Ceallac̄, comarḃa Patraic, ṙor cuairt Muman, co tuc a óġreiṙ 7 co ṙarġaiḋ bennac̄tain. —Ḃranan, mac Ġilla-Criṙt, ri Corco-Ac̄lann, do éc.— Ec̄marc̄ac̄ Mac Uiḋrein, toiṙec̄ Cheniuil-Ṙeraḋaiġ, do ṁarḃaḋ do Ṙeraiḃ-Manac̄.

Kal. Ian. iii. ṙ., l. ix., Anno Domini M.° c.° xx.° i.° Domnall, mac Arḋġair Mic Loc̄lainn, arori Erenn, derrṙcaic̄ec̄ Ġoeiḋel ar cruṫ 7 cenel, ar ceill 7 ġairceḋ, ar ṙonuṙ 7 roḃartain, ar ṫionacal ṙeoit 7 ḃiḋ, do éc a n-Daiṙi Coluim-cille, irin oc̄tmaḋ[a] bliaḋain triċat ṙeġni ṙui, irin treṙ[b] bliaḋain imorro reċtmoġat[b] aetatir

[b-b] .uiii. ḃliaḋain. xxx.MS. [c] .x.mad, MS. [d-d] decimar octauar, MS.
A.D. 1120. [a] Left blank in MS.

A.D.1121. [a-a] .uiii. ḃliaḋain .xxx.. MS. [b] .iii. ḃliaḋain imorro.lxx., MS.; "76th yeare," O. (taking *iii.* to be *ui.*)

1120. [1] *False peace.*—One which events proved he did not intend to observe.

[2] *Circuit.*—The *Annals of Inisfallen* state that this was part of a visitation of all Ireland made by Cellach. The second part of the entry is rendered in C.: "was there much reverenced, that they deserved his benediction"!

1121. [1] *The 4th.*—The F. M. copy

redhaigh, chief of Cenel-Moain, was killed by the [1119]
Ui-Dubhdai and by the Clann-[Fh]laithbertaigh.—
Niall, son of Domnall Ua Lochlainn, royal heir of
Ailech and of Ireland and paragon of Ireland for
form and for sense, for generosity and for erudition,
fell by the Cenel-Moain, in the 28th year of his age, on
Monday and on the 10th [of the moon] and on the feast
of the Three Innocent Children,[6] the 18th of the Kalends
of January [Dec. 15].

Kalends of Jan. on 5th feria, 27th of the moon, A.D. [1120 Bis.]
1120. A hosting by Domnall Ua Lochlainn, in aid of Murchadh Ua Mael-Sechlainn, to Ath-luain against Connacht,
so that Toirrdelbach Ua Conchobuir gave a false peace[1] in
regard to them.—The defeat of the Plain of Cell-mor of Ui-
Niallain [was inflicted] by Raghnall, son of Mac Riabaigh,
upon the Ui-Eachach, so that their slaughter ensued.—
Conchobur, son of Flandacan, son of Donnchuan, chief of
Muinnter-Birn, was wounded at Slaibh-[Fh]uait by the
Ui-Cremhtaind and he died thereof.—Cellach, successor of
Patrick, [went] upon circuit[2] of Munster, so that he took
away his full demand and left a benediction.—Branan, son
of Gilla-Crist, king of Corco-Achlann, died.—Echmarchach
Mac Uidhrein, chief of Cenel-Feradhaigh, was killed by
the Fir-Manach.

Kalends of Jan. on 7th feria, 9th of the moon, A.D.
1121. Domnall, son of Ardghar Mac Lochlainn, archking [1121]
of Ireland, the [most] distinguished of the Goedhil for
form and for birth, for sense and for prowess, for happiness and prosperity, for bestowal of treasure and of food,
died in Daire of Colum-cille, in the 38th year of his reign
and in the 73rd year of his age and on the night of
Wednesday and on the 4th[1] [*recte*, 5th] of the Ides [10th,

---

the mistake of the MS., omitting, as elsewhere, the moon's age, the means whereby the error could be readily rectified.

B 49b ꞃuaᴅ 7 ı n-aıᴆċᴅ Ceᴛaıneᶜ 7 ı quaꞃᴛ | ᴛᴅ ꝼebꞃe 7 ı n-oċᴛmaᴆᵈ ᴅéc [eꞃcaı] 7 ı ꞃeıl Moċuaꞃó[ı]c ınᴅ ecnaı.—Cu-Maıꞃı, mac ꞌDeoꞃaıᴆ hUı ꝼhlaınᴅ, ꞃı ꞌDeꞃlaıꞃ, ᴅo baᴆuᴆ ıllōċ-eċaċ, ıaꞃ n-ɡabaıl 1nnꞃı-ꞌDaꞃcaꞃcꞃenn ꞃaıꞃ ᴅ'Uıᴆ-Eċaċ, ᴅu ı ᴛoꞃcaıꞃ coıceꞃ' aꞃ ceᴛoꞃċaıᴛ'.—ɢılla-eꞃꞃcoıꞃ-Eoɡaın hUa Cnᴅıaꞃaıᴆ, ꞃı Cıanaċᴛa, ᴅo maꞃbaᴆ ᴅıa bꞃaᴛꞃıᴆ ꞃoꞃ laꞃ ꞃeılɡı ᴆennċaıꞃ.—Sluaꞃaᴆ la ᴛaıꞃꞃᴅelbaċ hUa Conċobuıꞃ 7 la Coıceᴆ' Con[n]aċᴛ ı n-ꞌDeꞃ-Mumaın, co ꞃoınnꞃeꞃeᴛaꞃ o ᴛá Maꞃ-ꝼeımín co ᴛꞃaıꞃ-lı, eᴛeꞃ ᴛuaᴛa 7 ċealla, ıᴅon, ꞃeċᴛmoɡaˢ ceall, uel paulo pluꞃ.—Cꞃeaċꞃluaꞃaᴆ la ᴛaıꞃꞃᴅelbaċ hUa Conċo-baıꞃ ᴆeꞃ ı n-ꞌDeꞃ-Mumaın, co ꞃoaċᴛ ᴛeꞃmonn lıꞃmoıꞃ 7 co ᴛaꞃaıᴆ boꞃoma ᴅıaꞃꞁe 7 co ꞃaꞃɡaıb Muıꞃeᴆac hUa ꝼlaıċbeꞃᴛaıɡ, ꞃı ıaꞃᴛaıꞃ Con[n]aċᴛ, 7 Ceᴆ hUa n-Eıᴆın, ꞃı hUa-ꝼıaċꞃaċ.—Cloıċᴛeċ ᴛelċa-ınnmuınn ı n-Oꞃꞃaıɡıᴆ

ᵃ .c.aıne,MS. ᵈ .um., MS. ᶜᵉ .u.eꞃ aꞃ .xl., MS. ᶠ.u.eᴆ, MS. ᵍ .lxx MS.

---

² *Mochuaroc of the Wisdom.*—He is thus designated in the Calendar of Oengus also. Mochuaroc signifies *my little* (literally, *young*) *Cuar.* In a Würzburg Latin MS. of the 8th century in Irish character, he is said to have committed to writing, lest it should lapse from memory, a Paschal Computus which his master, Mosinu (or Sillan, third abbot of Bangor: *ob.* 609=610, *supra*), had learned by rote from an erudite Greek (Schepss : *Die ältesten Evangelienhandschriften der Würzburger Universitätsbibliothek,* p. 27). The introduction of the Decemnovennal Cycle into his monastery would thus account for the epithet "of the Wisdom."

Another appellation of affection is *Cuaran (little Cuar),* under which title he is patron of Kilcoran (*Cell Cuarain,* Church of Cuaran—*perierunt etiam ruinae*), about a mile west of Youghal. He is locally remembered in a native couplet as *Cuaran of the None.* The reason is given in a bilingual and partially corrupt gloss in the L. B. Calendar of Oengus. *Is aire atberar* ' *Mochuaroc na Nona* ' *friss, ar is e toisech rodelig ceilebrad Nóna : quia cum media vel ora* [*pro* vel ora *lege* Hora] *apud antiquos celebra*[*ba*]*tur* —"It is for this *Mochuaroc of the None* is applied (lit. *said*) to him, because he is the first that separated the celebration of None: for by the ancient [monks] it used to be celebrated along with the Middle (Canonical) Hour [Sext]."

This is explained by the *Rule of the*

recte, 9th] of February and on the 18th [of the moon] and on the feast of [St.] Mochuaroc of the Wisdom.[2]—Cu-Maighi, son of Deoradh Ua Flainn, king of Derlas, was drowned[3] in Loch-Echach, after Inis-Darcarcrenn had been taken from[4] him by the Ui-Echach, wherein fell five and forty persons.—Gilla-Epscoip-Eogain[5] Ua Andiaraidh, king of Ciannachta, was killed by his own kinsmen in the centre of the cemetery of Bennchar.—A hosting by Tairrdelbach Ua Conchobuir and by the Fifth of Connacht into Desmond, so that they laid waste from Magh-Feimen to Tragh-Li, both lands and churches, namely, seventy churches, or a little more.—A foray-hosting by Tairrdelbach Ua Conchobair and by the Fifth of Connacht again into Desmond, until he reached the Termon of Lis-mor and obtained cattle-spoil innumerable and he lost[6] Muiredach Ua Flaithbertaigh, king of the West of Connacht and Aedh Ua Eidhin, king of Ui-Fiachrach.—The steeple [*lit.*, bell-house] of Telach-Innmuinn in Ossory

[1121]

---

[38] *Abbots*: *A prima hora usque ad horam tertiam Deo vacent fratres; a tertia vero usque ad nonam quidquid iniunctum fuerit . . . faciant* (Cap. x.). Sext was thus deferred from the *sixth* hour (12 noon) until the *ninth* (3 p.m.) and joined to None. In the Benedictine Rule, this deviation was followed from Sep. 15 to Lent: *Hora secunda agatur Tertia et usque ad Nonam omnes in opus suum laborent*. The change effected by St. Cuaran consisted in replacing the celebration of Sext at the proper Canonical hour, thus leaving None to be recited *separately*.

Colgan (*AA. SS.* p. 302) gives the purport of the L. B. gloss as follows: *Vocatur Mochuarocus de Nona, ideo quod sit primus qui curavit celebrationem Missae fieri seorsim, quia cum media Nona apud antiquos celebrabatur*. This is typical of Colgan's work of the kind. The original, needless to say, makes no mention of Mass; *cum media Nona* is meaningless; whilst the *ancient* monks celebrated Mass after Prime, Tierce, Sext and None respectively, according to the different seasons of the liturgical year.

[3] *Drowned*.—The Annals of Inisfallen add that the act was done by himself.

[4] *From*.—Literally, *upon*.

[5] *Gilla-Epscoip-Eogain*—*Devotee of Bishop Eugene* (founder of Ard sratha, Ard-straw, co. Tyrone).

[6] *Lost*.—Literally. *left* (*dead*) on the battle-field.

do dluiġi do ċairṫéineḋ : cloċ do rġeinm ar, co romarḃ macleiġind irin ċill—Samual hUa Anġli, erscop Ata-cliaṫ, in pace quieuit. Ceallaċ, comarba Patraic, do ġaḃail erscoroiti Ata-cliaṫ a toġa Ġall 7 Ġaeiḋel.—Da rrreiṫ Trin-Mhara[i]n, o ḋorur Raṫa co sroir m-Ḃriġte, do lorcaḋ.—Ataċ ġoiṫi do ṫiaċtain inHon Decimbir, co rola a benncoror do ċloicṫiuċ Aird-Maċa 7 co n-derna riḋar mor ro Erinn uile.

|Cal. Ian. 1. r., L, xx., Anno Domini M.* c.° xx.° 11.° Aeḋ hUa Ruairc, ri Conmaicne, do ṫuitim la Feru Miḋe ic ḃreiṫ creiċe uaṫiḃ.—Scrin Cholmain, mic Luaċain, d'roġḃail i n-ailaiḋ Lainne, rerċubat i talṁain, Dia-Cetain* in Ḃraiṫ.—Sluaiġeḋ la Tairrḋelbaċ hUa Conċobuir co Loċ-Saileċ i Miḋe, co táiniġ Mac Murċaḋa, ri Laiġen 7 Ġall, i n-a teċ.—Mor, inġen Domnaill hUi Loċlainn, ben Ta[i]rrḋealbaiġ hUi Concobuir, do éc.—Creċ mor la Conċobur hUa Loċlainn, 7 la Cenel n-Eoġain, co ranġadur Cill-ruaiḋ i n-Ulltaiḃ, co tucradur boroma diarṁiḋe.—Mael-Coluim hUa Ḃrolċa[i]n, erscop Aird-Maċa, do éc i n-a ailiṫri i n-Dirurt Daire ro buaiḋ martra 7 haiṫriġi.—Aeḋ hUa Duiḃdirma, toireċ na Ḃreḋa 7 cenn einiġ tuairce[i]rt Erenn 7 Domnall, a braṫair, mortui runt.

A.D. 1122. * dia .c.ain, MS.

---

[7] *Samuel Ua Angli.*—See Lanigan, *E. H.* iii. 12, sq.

[8] *Ceallach, etc.*—See Lanigan, *E. H.* iii. 45-6.

[9] *Two streets.*—C. gives *Dasreith*, taking the two native words as one, signifying the proper name of a place.

[10] *Door of the Close.*—" The mote doore," C.

[11] *Pinnacle-cover.*—" Brasen topp," C.

[12] *And caused, etc.*—" And maine prodigies were shewn over all Ireland " ! C.

1122. [1] *A man's grave [deep] in earth.* —" A cubite deep in the ground," C. The original expression occurs in the *Feast of Bricriu* (L. U. 103a, lines 15-6 ; 108b, lines 28-9). The meaning is shown in the Book of Armagh (fol. 8c): Et dixit [angelus] ei: *Ne reliquiae a terra reducuntur[-antur] corporis tui et cubitus de terra super corpus fiat.* Quod . . factum . . demonstratum est; quia . . . fodientes humum antropi

was split by a thunderbolt: a stone leaped thereout, so [1121] that it killed a student in the church.—Samuel Ua Angli,[7] bishop of Ath-cliath, rested in peace. Ceallach,[8] successor of Patrick, took the episcopacy of Ath-cliath by choice of the Foreigners and of the Gaidhil.—Two streets[9] of Masan-Third, from the door of the Close[10] to the Cross of [St.] Brigit, were burned.—A gust of wind came on the Nones [5th] of December, so that it took off the pinnacle-cover[11] of the steeple [*lit.*, bell-house] of Ard-Macha and caused[12] great destruction of woods throughout all Ireland.

Kalends of Jan. on 1st feria, 20th of the moon, A.D. [1122] 1122. Aedh Ua Ruairc, king of Conmaicni, fell by the Men of Meath, in carrying off spoil from them.—The Shrine of [St.] Colman, son of Luachan, was found in the tomb of Lann, a man's grave [deep] in earth,[1] the Wednesday of the Betrayal[2] [March 22].—A hosting by Tairrdelbach Ua Conchobuir to Loch-Sailech in Meath, so that Mac Murchadha, king of Leinster and of the Foreigners, came into his house.—Mor, daughter of Domnall Ua Lochlainn, wife of Tairrdealbhach Ua Conchobuir, died.—Great foray by Conchobur Ua Lochlainn and by the Cenel-Eogain, until they reached Cell-ruadh in Ulidia, so that they took away countless cattle-spoil.—Mael-Coluim Ua Brolchain, [suffragan] bishop of Ard-Macha, died on his pilgrimage in the Hermitage[3] of Daire, with victory of suffering and of penance.—Aedh Ua Duibdirma, chief of the Bredach and head of the hospitality of the North of Ireland and Domnall, his brother, died.

[ἄνθρωποι] ignem a sepulchro inrumpere viderunt.

For St. Colman, of Lynally, King's County, see Vol. I., p. 87; O'Donovan, Four Masters, I., p. 235-6; *Adamnan*, i. 5, ii. 16 and the notes thereon.

[2] *The Wednesday of the Betrayal.*—"The Wednesday before Easter," C. This is correct.

[3] *Hermitage.*—See *Adamnan*, p. 366. As Cellach was a real archbishop, O'Brolchain was enabled to retire to Derry.

[Cal. Ian. 11. f., l. 1., Anno Domini M.° c.° xx.° 111.° Gailenga do ġabail tiġ 1 n-Daimliac—Cianna[i]n ror
Murċaḋ hUa Mael-Seċlainn, ror riġ Temraċ, co colo-
irċret in teċ 7 oċtmoġa[a] taiġi ime 7 co romarbrat
roċaidi dia muinnter. Ternai imorro Murċaḋ, do
aiṁeċ Cianna[i]n, cen marbaḋ, cen lorcaḋ.—Ammus
anaitmiġ do ċabairt ror Comarba Ailbe (idon,[b] Mael-
morḋa, mac Mic Cloċna[b]) : idon, teċ do ġabail rair ror
lar Imleċa rein 7 ror mac Cerbaill hUi Ciarmaic
(idon,[c] in Aine[c]), co romarbaḋ morṡerer[d] ann. Ternatur imorro na doene maiti arr, tria raċ Ailbe 7
na hecailri. Roloirceḋ imorro ann Bernan Ailbe.
Romarbaḋ imorro ria cind mir inti roġaḋ in teċ, idon,
in gilla caeċ hUa Ciarmaic—7 deoċain eiriḋe iar n-
aimmniuġuḋ—7 ro beanaḋ a cenn de i raruġuḋ Ailbe 7
in Coimdeġ.—Oenġur hUa Gorma[i]n, comarba Comġaill,
do éc i n-ailitri illirmor Moċutu.—Flann hUa Duib-
innri, airċinneċ Luġmaiġ; Cú-Cairil hUa Cerbaill, ri
Fern-ṁuiġi; Mael-Muire hUa Condubá[i]n, airċinneċ
Daire-Luṫrain; Donnṡleiḃe Mac Caṫala[i]n, ronus 7

A.D 1123. [a] uiii.moġa, MS. [b-b] itl., t. h., MS.; given in C., with
omission of *Mic-Mac.* [c-c] itl., t. h., MS.; given in C. [d] mor.ui., MS.

1123. [1] *Eighty houses.*—"Eight of his household servants"! C.

The reading in B affords a natural explanation of this apparently inexplicable error. The translator took *uii.mogha* to be two words (*uiii.=ocht--eight*; *mogha*, pl. of *mogh—servant*) and *taighi* to be gen. sing. of *tech—house*. Whence "eight [of his] household servants."

[2] *Attack.*—Not mentioned, strange to say, in the *Annals of Innisfallen.*

[3] *Successor of [St.] Ailbe.*—Bishop of Emly, co. Tipperary.

[4] *Seven.*—Literally, *great six.*

[5] *Gapped* [*Bell*]. — Erroneously rendered *mitre* in C. For the *Bernan Ailbhe*, see Petrie's *Round Towers*, p. 335-6.

[6] *Cilla-caech.* — *Purblind gillie.* The soubriquet supplies a probable motive for the outrage. Owing to the visual defect, the bishop had refused to confer the Order of priesthood. Thereby Ua Ciarmhaic (O'Kirby) was effectually debarred from the preferment which lay open to him as a member of the reigning family.

Kalends of Jan. on 2nd feria, 1st of the moon, A.D. 1123. [1123] The Gailenga captured a house in Daimliac of [St.] Ciannan upon Murchadh Ua Mael-Sechlainn, king of Tara, so that they burned the house and eighty houses[1] around it and killed a number of his people. Murchadh, however, escaped by protection of [St.] Ciannan, without being killed or burned.—An unprecedented attack[2] was made upon the successor of [St.] Ailbe[3] (namely, Mael-Mordha, son of Mac Clothna): to wit, a house was seized upon him and upon the son of Cerball Ua Ciarmhaic (that is, the king of Aine), in the centre of Imlech itself, so that seven[4] were killed therein. Howbeit, the noble persons escaped therefrom, through favour of [St.] Ailbe and of the church. There was likewise burned the Gapped [Bell][5] of [St.] Ailbe. Now, he who seized the house was killed before the end of a novena, namely, the Gilla-caech[5] Ua Ciarmhaic—and the same person was a deacon[6] by profession[7]—and his head was cut off, because of[8] the profanation of [St.] Ailbe and of the Lord.—Oenghus Ua Gormain, successor of [St.] Comgall of Bangor, died in pilgrimage in Lis-mor of [St.] Mochutu.—Flann[9] Ua Duibhinnsi, herenagh of Lughmagh; Cu-Caisil Ua Cerbaill, king of Fernmagh; Mael-Muire Ua Condubhain, herenagh of Daire-Luhrain; Donnsleibhe Mac Cathalain, the prosperity and happiness of all Ulidia, died.—Donnchadh Mac

---

[7] *By profession.*—Literally, *according to nomination.*

[8] *Because of.*—Literally, *in.* The offence was homicide (punishable by death), according to Canon XXXI. of the First Patrician Synod: Si quis conduxerit e duobus clericis, quos discordare convenit per discordiam aliquam, prolatum uni e duobus hostem ad interficiendum, homicidam congruum est nominari: qui clericus ab omnibus rectis [recte] habeatur alienus.

This enactment was incorporated into the *Collectio Canonum Hibernensis* (x. *De multimodis causis clericorum*: 23).

[9] *Flann, etc.*—Of the four names in this entry, the last alone is given in the *Annals of Loch Cé.* But the compiler placed after it the *mortui sunt* of the Ulster Annals.

roḃarṫu Ulaḋ uile, mortui sunt.—Donnċaḋ Mac Gill[a]-Patraic ruaḋ, ri Osraiġi, a suis occisus est.—Congalaċ hUa [Fh]laiṫbertaiġ, ridomna Ailiġ., occisus est.

[bis.] Kal. Ian. iii. f., l. x.ii., Anno Domini M.° c.° xx.° iiii.°[a] Torfind, mac Turcaill, priṁoigṫigern[a] Gall n-Erenn, subita morte periit.—Tadg, mac Mic Carrṫaiġ, ri Des-Mumain[-an], in penitentia mortuus est.—Biḋgaḋ mor do riġ Teṁraċ Dia-Domnaiġ Casc[a]: idon, a teċ Casca do ṫuitim fair 7 for a teġlaċ.—Luimneċ do loscaḋ uile, aċtmaḋ beac.—Alaxandair, mac Mael-Choluim, ri Alban, in bona penitentia mortuus est.—Gaill Des-Muman do marbaḋ la Tairrdelbaċ hUa
B 49d Concobair: | idon, Mael-Seċlainn, mac Cormaic, mic Mic Carrṫaiġ, ri Caisil 7 hUa Ciarmeic a hAne 7 hUa Cobṫaiġ do [U]ib-Cuanaċ-Cnamċaille.—Ardgar, mac mic Aeḋa hUi Mael-Seċlainn, ridomna Ailiġ, do marbaḋ la Muinnter Daire i n-aineċ Coluim-cille.

Kal. Ian. u. f., l. xx. iii., Anno Domini M.° c.° xx.° u.° Quint Id Ianair imorro for Oen-diden 7 prim [uaṫad escai] firrsi. Ocus is innti tuargbaḋ a buinde diden for in damliac mor Aird-Maċa, iar n-a lanecor do ṡlinntiuċ la Cellaċ, comarba Patraic, isin triċadmaḋ

A.D. 1124. [a] The iiii. were at first uii.; but u was altered into ii, by the text hand.

1124. [1] *Easter house.*—From this expression, taken in connection with the house-seizures mentioned in the Annals, it may be concluded that it was customary for kings to spend the week before Easter or Pentecost at a church, where houses were set apart for themselves and their retinues.

[2] *Died.*—On April 23, according to the Anglo Saxon Chronicle.

[3] *Of Ane.*—Literally, *from Aine* (the district around Knockany, co. Limerick). In the Annals of Loch Ce (*ad an.*), the original, *a hAne*, is read *Achaine* and applied as the personal name of Ua Cobthaigh (O'Coffey).

Gilla-Patraic the Red, king of Ossory, was slain by his own [kinsmen].—Conghalach Ua [F]laithbertaigh, royal heir of Ailech, was slain.

Kalends of Jan. on 3rd feria, 12th of the moon, A.D. 1124. Torfind, son of Turcall, chief young lord of the Foreigners of Ireland, perished by sudden death.—Tadhg, son of Mac Carthaigh, king of Desmond, died in penance. —Great peril [happened] to the king of Tara, on Easter Sunday [April 6]: namely, his Easter house[1] to fall upon him and upon his [*lit.*, the] household.—Limerick was burned, all but a little.—Alexander, son of Mael-Coluim, king of Scotland, died[2] in good penance.—The hostages of Desmond were killed by Tairrdelbach Ua Conchobair: namely, Mael-Sechlainn, son of Cormac, son of Mac Carthaigh, king of Cashel and Ua Ciarmaic of Ane,[3] and Ua Cobthaigh of Ui-Cuanach-Cnamchaille.—Ardghar, grandson of Aedh Ua-Mael-Sechlainn, royal heir of Ailech, was killed by the Community of Daire, in reparation[4] to [St.] Columcille.

Kalends of Jan. on 5th feria, 23rd of the moon, A.D. 1125. The 5th of the Ides[1] [9th] of January [was] upon Friday and the 1st [day of the moon fell] thereon. And it is on that [day] its protecting ridge was raised[2] upon the great stone church of Ard-Macha, after its being fully covered with shingle by Cellach, successor of Patrick, in the

---

[4] *In reparation.*—"Within the libertie"! C. I do not know what was the offence.

1125. [1] *The 5th of the Ides, etc.*—The translator of C. mistook the meaning of this entry. "The fift of the Ides of January was the church of Ardmagh broken in the roofe, which was covered by Ceallagh, the Corbe of St. Patrick; being unrooffed in an hundred and thirtie years before." The week-day is given, but the lunation omitted, by the Four Masters.

[2] *Ridge was raised.*—That is, the work was formally completed.

112   annala ulaoh.

bliaðain ar ċet⁰ o n-a raḃai rlinnciuč rair co comlan.—
Ʒilla-braici hUa Ruaire do baċuð iLLoċ-Ccillinne.—
Sluaʒað la Cairrdelbač hUa Concobuir i Miðe, co
roinnarb Murċað hUa Mael-Seċlainn ar a riʒi 7 co
carac cri riʒa ror Feru Miðe. Marbio cra⁰ Domnall
Mac Murċaða in crer riʒ ria cion nomaiðe. idon,
Mael-Seċlainn, mac Donnċaða.—Creċ doċuaið Mur-
ċerċaċ hUa Cerḃaill, rí Deirċe[i]rc Fern-muiʒi, i
Ferais-Breʒ, conurcaraið Diarmaid hUa Mael-
Seċlainn co Ferais Miðe 7 co Ferais Breʒ, co romar-
bað Muircerċaċ ann 7 ár a creiče ime.

Kal. Ian. ui. r., l. iiii., Œnno Domini M. c.⁰ xx.⁰ ui.⁰
Ennai, mac Mic Murċaða, ri Laiʒen, morcuur erc—
Sluaʒað la Cairrdelbač hUa Concobuir iLLaiʒniḃ, co
roʒaið a n-ʒiallu.—hUa Maelruanaiʒ, rí Fer-Manaċ,
a ruir occirur erc.—Mael-Iru hUa Conne, rui Ʒoeiðil
i renčur 7 i m-briceṁnaċt 7 i n-Urd Racraic, iar n-
a[i]ċriʒe ċoʒaiðe in Chrirto quieuic.—Corcaċ mor Muman co n-a cempull do lorcað.—Domnall hUa Duḃdai
do baðuð, iar n-denam creiċi i Cir-Conaill.—Riʒðerur
Coirrdelbaiʒ hUi Concobuir co hŒċ-cliaċ, co caro riʒi
Œċa-cliaċ 7 Laiʒen dia mac, idon, do Concobuir.—Œnrud

A.D. 1125. ᵃ .c., MS. ᵇ h[autem] (the Latin equivalent), MS.

---

³ *Thirtieth year above one hundred.*
—At 995 (=996), *supra* (995 according to a quatrain in the *F. M.*),
Armagh, including the stone church,
was destroyed by lightning. The
meaning is, that the restoration of the
roof had been carried out at intervals
during the period.

⁴ *Before the end of a norena.*—
"Within three dayes and three
nights after"! C. The *F. M.* omit the
expression.

1126. ¹ *Died.*—In Wexford, according to the List of Leinster kings
in L. L. (p. 39d).

² *A Goedhel eminent.*—Literally,
a master of a Goedhel. By an em-
phatic native idiom, which is still
operative, instead of a sb. qualified
by an adj., the corresponding sb.
of the adj. (or the adj. used as sb.)
is employed with the genitive of
the sb.

thirtieth year above one hundred[3] since there was a com- [1125]
plete shingle roof upon it before.—Gilla-braiti Ua Ruairc
was drowned in Loch-Aillinne.—A hosting by Tairrdelbach Ua Conchobair into Meath, so that he expelled
Murchadh Ua Mael-Sechlainn from the kingship and
placed three kings over the men of Meath. But Domnall,
son of Murchadh, kills the third king, namely, Mael-
Sechlainn, son of Donnchadh, before the end of a novena[4].
—Muircertach Ua Cerbaill, king of the South of Fern-
magh, went on a foray into Fir-Bregh, until Diarmaid Ua
Mael-Sechlainn with the Men of Meath and the Men of
Bregha overtook them, so that Muircertach was killed
there and slaughter of the foraying force [took place]
around him.

Kalends of Jan. on 6th feria, 4th of the moon, A.D. [1126]
1126. Ennai, son of Mac Murchadha, king of Leinster,
died.[1]—A hosting by Tairrdelbach Ua Conchobuir into
Leinster, so that he took away their pledges.—Ua Maelruanaigh, king of Fir-Manach, was slain by his own
[kinsmen].—Mael-Isu Ua Conne, a Goedhel eminent
in history and in jurisprudence[2] and in the Order of
Patrick, rested in Christ after select penance.—Great
Cork of Munster with its church was burned.—
Domnall Ua Dubhdai was drowned, after making a foray
in Tir-Conaill.—Royal progress of Toirrdelbach Ua Conchobuir to Ath-cliath, so that he gave the kingship of

The *Order of Patrick* may have embodied the primatial rights and privileges, as formulated and claimed with such prominence in the Tripartite Life and the Book of Armagh. The following from Tirechan (Book of Armagh, fol. 11b) is characteristic of the spirit pervading the Patrician Documents in their present form. Si quaereret heres [=*comarba*] Patricii paruchiam [i.e., diocesim] illius, potest pene totam insolam sibi reddere in paruchiam. (Cf. *The Tripartite Life of St. Patrick*, etc., Trans. R. I. A., xxix. 184.)

[3] *Both laic and cleric.*—Literally, *between land and church.*

[4] *Treacherous foray.*—"A stealing army," C. It signifies that the foray was made when Ua Tuachair was nominally at peace with the Airthir.

114 ⱭNNⱭLⱭ ULⱭƊh.

cocaiḋ ṁoip ı n-Epınn, cop'bo ecen ꝺo ċomapba Paꞇpaıc biḗ mí pop blıaḋaın ppı hⱭpꝺ-Maċa ı n-eċꞇaıp, oc pıċuxuḋ Pep n-Epenn 7 oc ꞇabaıpꞇ pıaxla 7 poḃepa pop caċ, eꞇep ꞇuaıċ 7 eacluıp.—Cpec meaḃla la Ruaıḋpı hUa Tuaċaıp ı n-Ɑıpċepaıḃ, conaꞇcapċaꝺap Ɑıpċıp, co polaḋ a n-ap 7 co poꝺıċennaḋ paḋem.—Muıpeḋaċ hUa Cuıllen, aıpcınneċ Cloċaıp, ꝺo mapbaḋ ꝺ'Pepaıḃ-Manaċ.—Ꝺaṁlıac peıxlepa Poıl 7 Peꝺaıp, ꝺopoṅaḋ la hImap hUa n-Ⱥeḋaca[ı]n, ꝺo ċoıpecpaḋ ꝺo Cheallaċ, comapba Paꞇpaıc, ı[c] n-ꝺoꝺecım Kallaınn[c] Nouımbıp.—Cpeċpluaxaḋ la Taıppꝺelḃaċ hUa Conċoḃaıp a n-Ꝺep-Mumaın, cḃ poaċꞇ Xlenn-Maxaıp 7 co ꞇuc bopoma ꝺıaıpṁıḋe.

Kal. Ian. uıı., p., l. x. u., Ⱥnno Ꝺomını M.° c.° xx.° uıı.° Sluaxaḋ la Toıppꝺelḃaċ hUa Concoḃuıp ı n-Ꝺep-Mumaın, co poaċꞇ Copcaıx moıp Muman, co ꞇuc xıallu Muman co leıp.—Ⱥıpċıp ꝺo xaḃaıl ꞇaıxı Plaınn Mıc Sınaıx ı Tpıun Saxan pop Raxnall, mac Mıc Rıaḃaıx, aıḋcı Luaın Inıꞇe 7 a ꝺıċennaḋ leó.—Caꞇ eꞇep Ulꞇu paḋem, ı ꞇopcpaꝺuıp ꝺa pıx Ulaḋ, ıꝺon, Iıall Mac Ꝺuınnꞇleıḃe 7 áp Ulaḋ ıme 7 Eoċaıḋ hUa Maꞇxamna ı pruexuıṅ.—Xılla-Cpıpꞇ hUa heıcníx, pí Pep-Manaċ 7 aıpꝺpıx Ⱥıpxıall, ꝺo úc ı Cloċap-mac-n-Ꝺaımın ıap n-aıꞇpıxı ꞇoxaıḋe.—Pıp Muṁan 7 Laıxın ꝺo ımpoḋ ꝺopu[ċ]ıpı pop Taıppḋelḃaċ hUa Concoḃuıp 7 a n-xeıll

A.D. 1126. ᵃ⁻ᵃ ın .xıı. KL. MS.

---

[5] *The stone church.*—Colgan evades the difficulty of distinguishing between *Damliac* and *Recles* (monastery) by employing the term *Basilica* (*Triad. Thaum.*, p. 300).

[6] *Imar.*—The tutor of St Malachy; *vir sanctissimae vitae*, according to St. Bernard. His name is in the Carthusian Martyrology at Nov. 12 (Lanigan, *E. II.* iv. 99). The Martyrology of Donegal has it (I know not why) at Aug. 13. He died on a pilgrimage at Rome in 1134.

[7] *He reached.* — " He wasted," C. The same error is repeated in the first entry of next year. It arose probably from mistaking the contraction mark over *s* for the grave accent of *a*; thus reading *roacht* as *ro*[*fh*]*ds*.

Ath-cliath to his son, namely, to Conchobur.—A storm of [1126] great war in Ireland, so that it was necessary for the successor of Patrick to be a month above a year abroad from Ard-Macha, pacifying the men of Ireland and imposing rule and good conduct upon every one, both laic and cleric[3].—A treacherous foray[4] [was made] by Ruaidhri Ua Tuachair into the Airthir, until the Airthir overtook them, so that slaughter of them was inflicted and he was beheaded himself.—Muiredhach Ua Cuillen, herenagh of Clochar, was killed by the Fir-Manach.—The stone church[5] of the Monastery of [SS.] Paul and Peter, that was built by Imar[6] Ua Aedhacain, was consecrated by Ceallach, successor of Patrick, on [Thursday] the 12th of the Kalends of November [Oct. 21].—A foray-hosting by Tairrdelbach Ua Conchobhair into Desmond, until he reached[7] Glenn-Maghair and took away countless cattle-spoil.

Kalends of Jan. on 7th feria, 15th of the moon, A.D. [1127] 1127. A hosting by Tairrdelbach Ua Conchobair into Desmond, until he reached great Cork of Munster, so that he took away the pledges of all Munster.—The Airthir seized the house of Flann Mac Sinaigh in the Third of the Saxons upon Raghnall, son of Mac Riabaigh, on the night of Monday of the Beginning [of Lent,[1] Feb. 21] ; and he was beheaded by them.—A battle between the Ulidians themselves, wherein fell two kings of Ulidia in combat, namely Niall[2] Mac Duinnshleibhe [Ua Eochada], with slaughter of the Ulidians around him and Eochaidh Ua Mathgamna.—Gilla-Crist Ua hEicnigh, king of Fir-Manach and arch-king of Airgialla, died in Clochar-mac-Daimin after choice penance.—The Men of Munster and the Lagenians turned again upon Tairrdelbach Ua Con-

---

1127. [1] *Beginning [of Lent].*—See 1109, note 2, *supra.*

[3]*Niall.*—Not given in the Ulidian regnal list (L. L. 41d).

[2] *He placed.* — Very gross is the error of the scribe, or compiler, of the (so-called) *Annals of Loch Cé*, who took the *rat sum* of the MS. to

116 ccnnala ulaoh.

do ḃilriuxuḃ doiḃ 7 a mac d'aṫrixuḃ do Laixniḃ 7 do Ghallaiḃ. Araide, dorat rum rí aile* rorro, idon, Domnall, mac Mic Phaelain.—Cearball, mac Mic Phaelain—7 ár hUa-Paelain ime—do ċuitim la hUiḃ-Pailxi ror lar Cille-dara, i cornum comurbu[i]r Briẋte. —Tailltiu, ingen Murċada hUi Mael-Seċlainn, ben Tairrdelbaix hUi Concobuir, d'éc.—Mael-Briẋte hUa Poranna[i]n, airċinneċ Arda-rrata ; Mael-Briẋte hUa Cinaeta, airċinneċ Airde-Trea, in bona penetencia mortui runt.—Gilla-Crirt hUa Mael-Eoin, comarba Ciarain Cluana-mac-Noir, ronur 7 robarḋu airċinneċ ċell n-Erenn, in Chrirto quieuit.

[Bir.] Kal. 1an. 1. r., l. xx.ui., Anno Domini m.° c.° xx.° uiii.°
B 50b | Birrextilir* 7 embolerm[atic]ur annur. Pir Mhaix-Iṫa (idon,[b] Domnall hUa Gailmredaix 7 Cenel-Maein[b]) do gabail taixi ror rix Per-Manaċ, idon, ror Paelan hUa n-Duibdara 7 aṫuitim leó 7 roṡaide do ṁaiċiḃ Per-Manaċ ime. — Gill[a]-Patraic, mac Tuaṫail, comarba Coemgin, do marbad d'Uib-Muiredaix ror lar Glinne-da-loċa.—Maidm ria marerluaẋ Concobair, mic Mic Loċlainn, ror marerluaẋ Tigernain Ua [Ui] Ruairc, i torċair hUa Ciardai,

A.D. 1127. ª .ii., MS.
A.D. 1128. ª Birextur, MS. b-b itl., t. h., MS.; om., C.

be plural and read *radsat* (they gave). The editor accepts this and improves upon it by taking *eli* (another) to be the local name, *Eli!* (He omits to say whether the territory of the name in Tipperary, or that in the King's Co., is intended.) He ought to have known that the legitimate successor of Enna was Diarmait Mac Murchadha, who brought over the English. But he was probably misled by the translator of C., who has: "his (O Conor's sonn) deposed by Leinster and Galls, through misdemeanours of Danyell O'Eylan, king of Ely." O'Donovan (p. 1027) also took the verb as plural, signifying that the Leinstermen and Foreigners "elected another king over them " !

[3] *Contending.*—That is, which of two nuns belonging respectively to the two tribes mentioned should be the new abbess. The F. M. mention the fray, but omit the cause.

1128. [1] *Embolismal.* — That is, having a lunar month *thrown in*

chobuir and their pledges were forfeited by them, and his [1127] son was deposed by the Lagenians and by the Foreigners. Howbeit, he placed[2] another king over them, namely, Domnall, son of Mac Faelain.—Cearball, son of Mac Faelain— and slaughter of the Ui-Faelain [took place] around him— fell by the Ui-Failghi in the centre of Cell-dara, in contending[3] for the succession of [St.] Brigit.—Tailltiu, daughter of Murchadh Ua Mael-Sechlainn, wife of Tairrdelbach Ua Conchobhuir, died.—Mael-Brighte Ua Forannain, herenagh of Ard-sratha; Mael-Brighte Ua Cinaetha, herenagh of Ard-Trea, died in good penance.—Gilla-Crist Ua Mael-Eoin, successor of Ciaran of Cluain-mac-Nois, happiness and prosperity of the herenaghs of the churches of Ireland, rested in Christ.

Kalends of Jan. on 1st feria, 26th of the moon, A.D. 1128. [1128 Bis] A Bissextile and Embolismal[1] year. The Men of Magh-Itha (namely, Domnall Ua Gailmredaigh and the Cenel-Maien) seized a house upon the king of Fir-Manach, that is, upon Faelan Ua Duibhdhara; and he fell by them, and a number of the nobles of Fir-Manach around him.—Gilla-Patraic, son of Tuathal [Ua Tuathail], successor of [St.] Coemhgen, was killed by the Ui-Muiredaigh in the centre of Glenn-da-locha.—A defeat [was inflicted] by the horse-host of Conchobar, son of Mac Lochlainn, upon the horse-host of Tigernan Ua Ruairc, wherein fell Ua Ciardhai, king of Cairpri

---

[μῆν ἐμβόλιμος]; thus giving thirteen moons to the year in the luni-solar reckoning. The present is the third Embolism of the Decemnovennal Cycle: Epact 26, Golden Number VIII. (See *Todd Lectures*, Series III, No. IV.)

Its place in the Calendar is indicated in a marginal gloss in the L. B. Cal. of Oengus, opposite March 6: Tertius Embolismus cicli decinnovenalis hic incipit et conturbat regulum [-am]. For the *disturbance*, see Bede, *De temp. rat.*, c. xx.

This Embolism is of historical interest. It was the proof assigned in his reply to Pope Leo the Great by Paschasinus, bishop of Lilybaeum, why the Easter of 444 should be celebrated on the Alexan-

rí Cairpri ⁊ Catal hUa Rogeallaig ⁊ Sitriuc hUa Mael-brigte ⁊ mac Aeda hUi Ohucoai, rí hUa-n-Amalgada ⁊ alii multi.—Muirgir hUa Nio[i]c, aircinnec Tuama-da-gualann rri re, do éc i n-Inir-in-gaill.—Grim granna, anaicnig, aimarmartac, rotoill earcoine fer n-Erenn, eter loec ⁊ cleirec, do nac rrue macramla i n-Erinn riam, do denam do Thigernan hUa Ruairc ⁊ do hUi[b]-Briuin : idon, comarba Patraic do noctjaruged i n-a riadiu[i]re : idon, a cuideca do flat ⁊ dream dib do marbad ⁊ maccleirec dia muinntir féin, dobí ro Chulebad, do marbad ann. Is e morro an iarmuirt dofarr do'n mignim ra, co nac ruil i n-Erinn comuirce ir tairiri do duine rodefta, no currodigailter o 'Ohia ⁊ o doeinib in t-olc ra. In dinrem ra tra tucad for comarba Patraic, irr amal ⁊ dinrim in Coimdeg ; uair adrubairt in Coimdeo fein irin t-Shoircéla: Qui^c uor rrermit, me rrermit; qui me rrermit, rrermit eum qui me mirit^e.—Creac-rluagad la Tairrdelbac hUa Concobuir illaignib, co roact Loc-Carman; airreig, timcell Laigen co hAt-cliat ⁊ doroine bo-didad mór in conair rin ; o At-cliat, d'a cig dori[c]iri. Ata tra miclu an t-fluaigaid rin for Tigernan hUa Ruairc.—Creac la Magnur ⁊ la Briu fern-muigi hi Tir-Briuin, co tucrad gabala mora.

^{c-c} qui uor. etc., et qui me, etc., C.

---

drine date, April 23, in preference to the Roman, March 26.

²*In charge of the sacred requisites and relics*—Literally, *under a Culebadh*. This expression, according to the Irish idiom, implies an office. In the Carlsruhe (Irish) Codex of St. Augustine (No. cxcv. fol. 19c), *culebath* glosses *flabellum*. But the context (*quo etiam muscas abigentes acrem commovemus*) shows that here the word is taken literally, *gnat-destroyer*. The employment of the *flabellum*, or fan, at Mass, as in the Greek Church, was too striking a ceremony to escape incidental mention in native hagiography. A *Culebadh* was among the Columban relics at Kells. According to the *Seafaring of Snedgus and Mac Ringail*(*Adamnan*, p. 323), it consisted of a leaf as large as the hide of a great ox. It was to be placed upon the altar. This description appears to identify it with the veil, or *Coopertorium quo altare tegitur cum oblationibus*, of Gregory of Tours

and Cathal Ua Rogheallaigh, and Sitriuc Ua Mael-Brighte, [1128] the son of Aedh Ua Dubhdai, king of Ui-Amalghadha, and many others.—Muirghis Ua Nioic, herenagh of Tuaim-da-ghualann for [a long] space, died in Inis-in-Ghaill.— A deed ugly, unprecedented, ill-issuing, that deserved the curse of the Men of Ireland, both laic and cleric, whereof the like was not found in Ireland before, was done by Tigernan Ua Ruairc and by the Ui-Briuin: namely, the successor of [St.] Patrick was stark dishonoured in his own presence: that is, his retinue was waylaid, and some of them were killed; and a student of his own household, who was in charge of the sacred requisites and relics[2] was killed there.—Now the result that grew out of this ill deed is this, that there is no protection which is secure for a person henceforth, until this evil is avenged by God and by men. For this disrespect that was put upon the successor of Patrick, it is the same as disrespect of the Lord; since the Lord himself said in the Gospel: "He that despiseth you, despiseth Me; he that despiseth Me, despiseth Him who sent Me" [Luke x. 14].—A foray-hosting by Tairrdelbach Ua Concobhuir into Leinster, until he reached Loch Carman: herefrom, around Leinster to Ath-cliath, and he wrought great destruction of cattle on that route; from Ath-cliath, to his house again. But the ill-fame of that hosting is upon Tigernan Ua Ruairc.—A foray by Maghnus and by the men of Fern-magh into Tir-Briuin, so that

---

(De Vitis Patr., viii.. Cf. *The Stowe Missal*, Trans. R. I. A., vol. xxvii. p. 169). That veil had enough in common with the *muscifugium* to have the Irish equivalent of *flabellum* applied thereto. Thence, in a secondary sense, *culebadh* would come to signify the requisites for Mass and for administration of the Sacraments; *fo culebadh* designating the custodian thereof.

The circumstances of the present outrage suggest a more comprehensive meaning. When engaged upon a visitation, the primate always had the *insignia* (=Irish *minna*; for which see the *Stowe Missal*, ubi sup., p. 174) of St. Patrick carried about with him. These are divided into *consecrated* (insignia consecrata) and *other* (aliorum insignium) in the *Liber Angeli* (Book of Armagh, fol. 21c). The former are intended in a passage of

beirið Tigernan co n-Ui[b]-Briuin 7 co ροčaιοι moir aili^d ρορρο ιс Ατ-Φhιρσeað. Ρeρταιρ τρα cat eτeρρu 7 meabaið ρορ Tigernan 7 ρορ Ui[b]-Briuin 7 marbτuρ τρι˙ čeτ no ceτρι čeτ˙ oib, ı τοριč eıniξ Ρατραιс.— |

Sluaξað la Concoburι hUa Locλainn 7 la Cenel-n-Eogain 7 la Dal-n-Αραιδε 7 la hEiρgialλαιb ı Maξ-Coba, co τισραc gιalλu hUa-n-Εταč. 1mροιτ ιαρ ριν ρορ a laım cli ı Ρeραιð-Uρeξ, co ρargaιbρeτ δρeιm dιa muιnnτeρ ann 7 co n-δeρηραc col móρ ριαð Dhιa 7 ριa[ð] ðαιniδ : ιδon, loρcað Ατα-τρuım co n-a τempluıð 7 ροčaιδe δο ðul marτρa ιηnτιð. Non' ımρeτρατa ρace Dei uel [h]omι- num, ρeτρο ambulaueρunτ'.—Siτ m-bliaðna co leτ, uel ραulo plur, δο ðenum δο comορbα Ρατραιс eτeρ Connačτι 7 Ρeρu Mumaın.

Kal. 1an. 111. ρ., l., uıı., Anno Domιnı M.˚ c.˚ xx.˚ ıx.˚ Mac Mara[ı]ρ hUa Reboča[ı]n, αιρcınneč Lır-móιρ Močuτu [δο ec].—Gilla-Močonna hUa Duιboιρma δο marbað δο Ulltaιð ı n-1nır-Tαιτι.—Ceallač, comarba Ρατραιс, mac oξe 7 αιρδeρρcορ larčair Eορρα 7 oeın čenn ροριαραιξρeτur gοιðιl 7 Gaιll, laıč 7 cleριč, ιaρ n-οιρδneð δono eρρcορ 7 ρacaρτ 7 αιρ[ı] gača gραιð arčena 7 ιaρ coιρecρað τempall 7 reιlgeð n-ιmða, ιaρ τιδnacal ρeoτ 7 moeine, ιaρ n-aραιl ριaξla 7 ροðera ρορ cač, eτeρ τuaιč 7 eclaιρ, ιaρ m-beτaιξ ceιlebuρταιξ- αιρρρennaıξ, oénτιξ, eapnaıgτιð, ιaρ n-οιngað 7 αιčριξι čogaıðe, ροčaιð a anmaın a n-uč τ αιngel 7 αrčaιngel, ı n-Αρδ-Ρατραιс, ιρın Mumaın, ı Kalaınn Αρρıl, ın

^d .ıı, MS. ^e .ccc. ^f .cccc . MS. ^{f.f} non ımρeτρατ[a], etc., C.

Tirechan, which connects them with a veil. Et ordinavit ibi [Dunseverick, co. Antrim] Olcanum sanctum episcopum, quem nutrivit, Patricius et dedit illi partem de reliquiis Petri et Pauli et aliorum et velum quod custodivit reliquias (Book of Armagh, fol. 15b). The veil here mentioned, it can be inferred, signified the cover, or reliquary. The phrase in the text will thus include a person in charge of relics.

The expression is not translated in C. The whole entry is omitted ("perhaps intentionally," O Donovan, ii. 1029) by the Four Masters.

they took great captures. Tigernan [Ua Ruairc], with [1128] the Ui-Briuin and with another large force, comes up with them at Ath-Fhirdeadh. Battle is then fought between them, and defeat inflicted upon Tigernan and upon the Ui-Briuin ; and three hundred, or four hundred of them are killed, as a first reparation [3] to Patrick.—A hosting by Conchobur Ua Lochlainn and by the Cenel-Eogain and by the Dal-Araidhe and by the Airgialla into Magh-Cobha, so that they took away the pledges of the Ui-Echach. They turn after that on their left hand into Fir-Bregh, until they lost a party of their people there and did a great crime before God and before men : namely, the burning of Ath-truim with its churches and a multitude underwent violent death in them. They marched back, without having obtained the peace of God, or of men.—Peace of a year and a half, or a little longer, was made by the successor of Patrick between the Connachtmen and the Men of Munster.

Kalends of Jan. on 3rd feria, 7th of the moon, A.D. [1129] 1129. Mac Marais Ua Rebochain, herenagh of Lis-mor of Mochutu [died].—Gilla-Mochonna,[1] Ua Duibdirma was killed by the Ulidians in Inis-Taiti.—Ceallach, successor of Patrick, son of purity and eminent bishop of the West of Europe and the one head to whom served the Goidhil and the Foreigners, laics and clerics, after ordaining bishops and priests and persons of every [church] grade besides and after the consecration of many churches and cemeteries ; after bestowing of treasures and of wealth ; after enjoining of rule and good conduct upon every one, both laic and cleric ; after a Mass-celebrating, fasting, prayerful life ; after Unction and choice penance, he sent forth his spirit into the bosom of

---

[3] *First reparation.*—Meaning that other punishments were inflicted subsequently.

1129. [1] *Gilla-Mochonna.*—Devotee *of (St.) Mochonna.* As Inis-Taiti was an island in Lough Beg, co.

rocunoa ᚱepιa ⁊ ιᚱιn ceṫpamaö* bliaöaιn ᚱíceṫ* a aboaιne ⁊ ιᚱιn cóιcaᴛmaö^b bliaöaιn a aιᚱι. Rυcaö ᴛᚱa a ċopp hι ᴛeᚱᴛ^c Hon Ccpᚱιl co leᚱ·móᚱ mocυᴛυ, oo ᚱeιᚱ a ᴛιmna ᚱaöéιn ⁊ ᚱoᚱᚱιċaιᚱeö co ᚱalmaιö ⁊ ymnaιö ⁊ cannᴛaιcιö. Ocυᚱ ᚱohaönaιceö co honóᚱaċ ι n-aιlaιö ιn[n]a n-eᚱᚱcop ι ᚱᚱιo Hon Ccpᚱιl, ιn qυιnᴛa ᚱepιa. Mυιᚱceᚱᴛaċ, mac Oomnaιll, o'oιᚱoneö ι com-υᚱbυᚱ Paᴛᚱaιc ιnHon CcpᚱιL.—Ṫeaċ Colυιm-cιlle ι

A.D. 1129. ᵃ⁻ᵃ .ιιιι.maö —.xx.ιc, MS. ᵇ.l.maö, MS. ᶜ.ιιι., MS.

Londonderry, the saint here intended was one of the two SS. Mochonna venerated in Derry on March 8 and May 13, respectively.

² *Ard-Patraic.*—The obit of O'Longan (1113, *supra*), the authorities cited in the note there given and two entries of a similar kind in these Annals explain the presence of Cellach at Ard-patrick. O'Longan belonged to one of the tribes (mentioned in note 4, *infra*) that, by a perversion of the principle regulating succession in endowed churches (*Senchas Mor*, Brehon Laws, i. 73 sq.; Book of Armagh, fol. 16d, 17a), temporarily diverted the primacy into lay hands. The head of the name, Gilla-Crist (Book of Leinster p. 334a, l. 39; Book of Ballymote, p. 115 b, l. 34) and Ua Sinachain of the kindred sept, the Ui-Sinaich, who died respectively in 1072 and 1052 (*supra*), are called *stewards of Munster*. Whence it can be inferred that they were likewise incumbents of Ardpatrick. That church consequently was immediately subject to Armagh: its superiors were the stewards, or custodians, of the primatial cess in Munster and were selected from the families in question.

Cellach had accordingly arrived there, either to visit, whether officially, or through courtesy; or, it may be, in connection with the truce between Munster and Connaught mentioned under the preceding year.

³ *Tomb of the bishops.*—Colgan, who was advised by the F. M., translates: *in sanctuario episcoporum vulgo appellato!* (Tr. Th., p. 301). The error, as was to be expected, has been copied by O'Conor.

"His [Latin] name [Celsus] is in the Roman Martyrology at the 6th of April. . . Its being placed at 6 April is owing to another mistake of Baronius [the first mistake, Note to *Rom. Mart.*, Ap. 6, was assigning the death to 1128], who was the first to insert it in the Roman Martyrology, which he revised by order of Gregory XIII. It was already in Molanus' Additions to Usuard, published in the year 1568. . . . As his interment was marked iv. April, this notation was probably mistaken

angels and archangels, in Ard-Patraic[2] in Munster, on the Kalends [1st] of April, on the 2nd feria, and in the 24th year of his abbacy and in the 50th year of his age. His body was then carried on the 3rd of the Nones [3rd] of April to Lis-mor of Mochutu, according to his own will and it was waked with psalms and hymns and canticles. And it was buried with honour in the tomb of the bishops, on the 2nd of the Nones [4th] of April, on the 5th feria. Muircertach, son of Domnall, was instituted[4] [*recte*, intruded] into the succession of Patrick on the Nones [5th] of April. —The house of Colum-cille in Cell-mic-nEnain[5] was seized

[1129]

for VI. April., and thus adding a confusion of said day with that of his death, this error seems to have originated" (Lanigan, *E. H.* iv. 89-91).

[4] *Instituted.*—As the time was too short for the news to reach Armagh, much less for a canonical election to take place, between Monday and Thursday, the "institution," there can be little doubt, was performed in Lismore. The chief members of the family to which Cellach belonged thus accompanied him to Munster. In the *Liber Angeli*, or Book of primatial privileges, the ordinary retinue is set down as fifty. Receptio archiepiscopi, heredis cathedrae meae urbis, cum comitibus suis, numero quinquaginta (Book of Armagh, fol. 206).

Feidlimid, who belonged to the sixth generation from Conn of the Hundred Battles (2nd cent. A.D.), had amongst his five sons two named Bresal and Echaid : eponymous heads of the Ui-Bresail and the Ui-Echach, whose respective territories were the baronies of Oneilland East and Armagh (co. Armagh).

Sixteenth in descent from Bresal was Cumuscach, great grandson of Erudan, who held forcible possession of the primatial see from 1060 to 1064 and died in 1074 (*supra*).

In the fourth degree from Echaid was Sinach, eponymous head of the Ui-Sinaich. This was the sept that supplied almost all the lay succession in Armagh, as appears from the following table (Book of Leinster, pp. 334b, 338c; Book of Ballymote, pp. 113-4). The genealogy appears defective by comparison with that of the Ui-Bresail ; but, for the present purpose, this is immaterial.

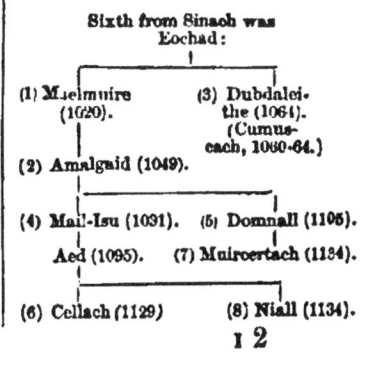

Sixth from Sinach was Eochad :

(1) Maelmuire (1020).

(2) Amalgaid (1049).

(3) Dubdalethe (1064). (Cumuscach, 1060-64.)

(4) Mail-Isu (1031). (5) Domnall (1105).

Aed (1095). (7) Muircertach (1134).

(6) Cellach (1129). (8) Niall (1134).

Cill-mic-n-Enain do ẋabail d'O Chaircerc ꝼor Aeḋ, mac
Caṫba[i]ꞃꞃ 11 Domnaill | 7 a loꞃcaḋ dó.—Cairtel
Aṫa-luain do ḋenaṁ la Tairrdelbaċ hUa Conċobair.
—Ƿilla-Criꞃt, mac 1lic Uiḋꞃin, toiꞃeċ Cenuil-Ƿeraḋ-
aiꞃ, do loꞃcaḋ a tiṡ a altꞃann hi Tiꞃ-Manaċ, 1 meḃail.
—Niall hUa Criċa[i]n, ꞃi hUa-Ƿiaċꞃaċ Aꞃda-ꞃrata,
do maꞃbaḋ d'Uib-Cennetiꞃ.

Kal. 1an. 1111. ꝼ., L x. uiii., Anno Domini M.º c.º xxx.º
8oꞃd Coluim-cille, co n-a ṫempall 7 co n-a minnaiḃ
imdaiḃ do loꞃcaḋ.—Cú-Aiꝼꞃne hUa Concobair, ꞃi hUa-
Ƿailṡi, do éc.—Aṁlaim, mac 1ic 8hena[i]n, ꞃi Ƿaileng
(1don,[b] coċoll ꝼliuċ[b]); Oenṡur hUa Cainnelba[i]n, ꞃi
Loeṡaire 7 ꞃoċaide aile do maiċiḃ do ċuitim la Ƿiꞃu
Ḃꞃeiꝼne 1 Sleiḃ-Ƿuaire.—bellum eter Ƿhiꞃu Alban 7
Ƿeru Moꞃeb 1 torcꞃadaꞃ ceiṫri[c] mile d'Ƿheraiḃ Moꞃeb,
im a ꞃi, idon, Oenṡur, mac ingine Luluiꞃ; mile imoꞃro
(uel[d] centum, quod erc uerius[d]) d'Ƿheraiḃ Alban 1 ꝼriṫ-
ṡuin.—8luaṡaḋ la Conċobuꞃ hUa Loċlainn 7 la Tuair-
ceꞃt n-Eꞃenn 1 n-Ulltaib, go ꞃoċinolꞃatur Ulaiḋ do
ċabairt cata doiḃ. Meḃair imoꞃro ꝼor Ulltaib, co
ꞃoláḋ a n-ár, im Aeḋ hUa Loingriꞃ, ꞃi Dal-Araide 7
im Ƿilla-Ƿatraic hUa Seꞃꞃaiꞃ, ꞃi Dal-buinde 7 im

A.D. 1130. [a] om., C. [b] r. m., t. h., MS.; om., C. [c] .iiii., MS. [d-d] itl.,
t. h., MS.; om., C. The two first words are written l.c., which should perhaps be read as no, cet—or, *a hundred*, to correspond with the native text.

Cellach was a layman on his accession. Niall died in 1139.

From the foregoing and the notices in the Annals we see that the *plebilis progenies* (the tribe in whose territory Armagh stood) usurped the position and discharged by deputy the sacred functions of the *ecclesiastica progenies* (Book of Armagh, fol. 16d).

Cell-mic-n-Enain.—Church of the Son of Enan. Now (by substitution of *r* for *n*), Kilmacrenan (county Donegal).

[5] *By O'Tairchert.*—The editor of the Annals of Loch Cè says (in a note ad an.) that "the F. M. have *Ua Tairchert*, which is likely to be correct, although the form *Tairchert* occurs also in the Annals of Ulster." But he mistook the form *dó = do O* for the preposition *do* (by).

by O'Tairchert[6] upon Aedh, son of Cathbarr Ua Domnaill and he was burned by him.—The castle of Ath-luain was built by Tairrdelbach Ua Conchobair.—Gilla-Crist, son of Mac Uidhrin, chief of Cenel-Feradhaigh, was burned in the house of his fosterer in Tir-Manach, in treachery.— Niall[7] Ua Crichain, king of the Ui-Fiachrach of Ard-sratha, was killed by the Ui-Cennetigh.

Kalends of Jan. on 4th feria, 18th of the moon, A.D. 1130. Sord of Colum-cille with its church and with its many relics was burned.—Cu-Aiffne Ua Conchobair, king of Ui-Failghi, died.—Amhlaim, son of Mac Senain, king of Gailenga (namely, "Wet Cowl"); Oenghus Ua Caindelhain, king of Loegaire and a number of nobles besides fell by the Men of Breifni at Sliabh-Guaire.—War[1] between the Men of Scotland and the Men of Moray, wherein fell four thousand of the Men of Moray, around their king, namely, Oenghus, son of the daughter of Lulach[2]; one thousand also (or one hundred, which is truer) of the Men of Scotland [fell] in the contest.—A hosting by Conchobur Ua Lochlainn and by the North of Ireland into Ulidia, so that the Ulidians assembled to give battle to them. Defeat, however, is inflicted upon the Ulidians and a slaughter of them ensued, around Aedh Ua Loingsigh, king of Dal-Araidhe and around Gilla-Patraic Ua Serraigh, king of

[1129]

[1130]

---

[7] *Niall.*—His name terminates the genealogy in the Books of Leinster (p. 338e) and Ballymote (p. 113e), proving that the compilation was made during his life-time. He was tenth from Crichan, who was likewise the tenth from Colla Uais (4th century A.D.)

1130. [1] *War.* — Eodem anno (septimo); Comes Moraviensis, Angusius, apud Strucathrow cum gente sua peremptus est. (Fordun, *Chron. Gent. Scot.,* v. 33.) In the *Gesta Annalia* (cap. 1), the place is called *Strucathroch.* It was in Forfarshire. In the *Anglo Saxon Chronicle* (Cot. Tib. B IV.), the slaying of *Anagus* is given at this year.

[2] *Lulach.*—Slain in 1058 (*supra*).

Dubpailbe Mac Caiptin 7 im focaive apcena. Innpic imoppo in tip co haiptep na hCCpva, etep tuaib 7 cill, co tucpat mile vo bpait, uel° paulo plup° 7 ilmile imoppo vo buaib 7 vo eacaib. Maiti imoppo Ulab im a pig iap pein co hCCpv-Maca, i comvail Concobaip, co n-vepnpat pit 7 comluigi 7 co papgpat giallu.—Mear mop cet topaib co° coitcenn i n-Epinn uile° ipin bliabain pi.

Kal. Ian. u. p., L. xx. ix., CCnno Domini m.° c.° xxx.° 1.° Crecfluagab la Tairpvelbac hUa Concobuip 7 la Coicib° Chonnact i Mumain, co poaipgret hUi-Conaill-ghabpa.—Sluagab la Concobap hUa m-Opiain 7 la firu Muman illaignib, co pogab a n-giallu 7 iap pein i Mibe, co poaipgreat Inip Loca-Seimvive 7 co pocompuc a mapcfluag 7 mapcfluag Connact, co pemaib pop mapcfluag Connact.

[B 50d ends.b]

* * *
* *

[B 51 a.1]

Rucab ap Loc-Siglen 7 pobói coictigir ap mir ano, no ní ir uilliu 7 pofuarluic in eclur naem 7 pat Patpaic he 7 pomapbaiv na coimévaigi pobavup ic a coimev.—Dopur tempaill Daipe vo benam la comapba Coluim-

---
⁎ om., C.
A.D. 1131. ᵃ .u. ɪo̅, MS.
ᵇ A chasm occurs in the MS. (B), up to end of A.D. 1155.
[1] On the upper margin, a modern (17th century) hand wrote: "Fower leaves are wanting before this." That is the number of the lost folios.

1131. [1] *Connacht.*—The missing years up to and including portion of 1138 are in great part the same, it is safe to conclude, as those in the *Annals of Loch Ce.* Thenceforward (the Annals of Loch Ce being blank to 1169 inclusive) the entries, though unrecognisable at present, were, there can be no doubt, embodied in the main by the *Four Masters.*

[2] *Mael-Isu.*—Given in C and (in almost the same words) in the *Annals of Loch Ce.*

1132. [1] *The house.*—This imperfect

Dál-Buinde and around Dubhrailbhe Mac Cairtin and around a multitude besides. Moreover, they pillage the country as far as the East of the Ard, both secular and church land,[2] so that they took away a thousand captives, or a little more, and likewise many thousands of cows and of horses. The nobles of Ulidia also [went] after that with their king to Ard-Macha, into the assembly of Conchobhar, so that they made peace and co-swearing and left pledges.—Great crop of every produce generally in all Ireland in this year. [1130]

Kalends of Jan. on 5th feria, 29th of the moon, A.D. 1131. A foray-hosting by Tairrdelbach Ua Concobuir and by the Fifth of Connacht into Munster, so that they harried Ui-Conaill-Ghabra.—A hosting by Conchobhar Ua Briain and by the Men of Munster into Leinster, so that he received their pledges and after that [he went] into Meath, so that they harried the Island of Loch-Semhdide and their horse-host and the horse-host of Connacht met and defeat was inflicted upon the horse-host of Connacht.[1] [1131]

(Mael-Isu[2] O'Foglada, episcopus Cassil, in senectute bona quievit.)

(Kalends of Jan. on 6th feria, 10th of the moon, A.D. 1132. The house[1] [of the abbess] of Kildare was made (*recte*, seized) by the Kenselaghs . . .) [1132 Bis.]

* * * * *

[Kalends of Jan. on 7th feria, 24th of the moon, A.D. 1155.] [1155]

[Tigernan[1] Ua Ruairc took Donnchadh Ua Cerbaill, lord of Oirghialla, prisoner, after Donnchadh had gone

---

entry is given in C. (The luni-solar notation is in Latin.) The remainder which is contained in the *Annals of Loch Cé*, states that the church was | burned, that a large number were slain and that the abbess was violated.
1155. [1] *Tigernan - Cenannus.* — Taken from the Four Masters.

cille, ιδοη, la ꜰlaιtbertaċ hUa bρolċa[ι]n.—αmlaιm Mac Canaι (muιre Ceniuιl-[O]enguρa), tuιρ gaιρceb 7 beoδaċta Cenιuιl-Eogaιn uιle, mortu[u]ρ erτ.

[bιρ.] Kal. Ian. 1. ρ., l u., αnno Domιnι M° c.° L° uι.°
Taιrrδelbaċ hUa Concobuιρ, aιρδρί Connaċt, tuιρ orδaιn 7 oιρeċu[ι]ρ Erenn uιle aρ gaιρceδ 7 cιδnacul ρét 7 maιne δo laeċaιδ 7 δo cleιρcιδ, ιn pace quιeuιt.—Sluagaδ la Muιρceρtaċ hUa Loċlaιnn ι n-Ulltaιδ, co tuc bραιgδι fρι a ρeιρ. Ocuρ ιρ ρορ an ρluagaδ ριn δαno ρomarbaδ hUa hIn[n]eιρgι ρoρ ρceιmleδ.—αeδ hUa Cananna[ι]n, ρί Ceniuιl-Conaιll, δo marbaδ la hUa Caċa[ι]n 7 la ꜰeραιδ na Cρaιbe.—Sluagaδ aιle δano la hUa Laċlaιnδ co n-δeιρceρt m-bρeg, co tuc braιgδe Laιgen o Mac Muρċaδa tar cenn a Coιcιδ uιle. δocuaδuρ ιαρ ρeιn Cenel-n-Eogaιn 7 αιρgιallu ι n-Orraιgιb, co ριaċtaδuρ Clar δhaιρe-mόιρ, co tangaδuρ maιċι Orraιgι hι teċ hUι Laċlaιnn.—Meaρρ moρ ιριn bliaδaιn ρι ρο Erιnn uιle. Hoι m-bliaδna o'n meρ moρ aιlι guρan bliaδaιn ρι.

Kal. Ian. III. ρ., l x. uι., αnno Domιnι M.° c.° L° uιι.°
Gιlla-Patρaιc Mac Carρtaιg, aιρcιnneċ Corcaιgι, ιn Chριρto quιeuιt.—Cu-Ulaδ hUa Caιnδelba[ι]n δo marbaδ ι mebaιl la δonnċaδ, mac δomnaιll ρuςαιδ hUι Mael-Seċlaιnn, taρ ραρugaδ comarba Patρaιc 7 baċlu

A.D. 1155. ᵃᵃ l. m., t. h., MS. This year om., C.
A.D. 1156. ᵃ .п., MS. ᵇ .u.ιŏ., MS.

---

² *Ua Brolchain.*—See the exhaustive note, *Adamnan*, p. 405-6.

³ *Steward.*—(*muire*).—Lord (*tigherna*), F. M.

1156. ¹ *Tower* (*tuir*).—The F. M. change *tuir* into *tuile* (flood).

² *Nine years.*—At 1147 the F. M. record, very likely from the missing portion of these Annals, a great crop throughout Ireland.

1157. ¹ *Who thereby dishonoured.*—Literally (lit., *beyond*) *profanation of* (the successor, etc.). "In spight of," C.

Ua Caindelbain (O'Quinlan) was chief of the Ui-Laeghaire (so called from Laeghaire, the contemporary of St. Patrick), whose territory comprised the baronies of Upper and Lower Navan, co. Meath. According to Mageoghegan,

to meet him with a small force to Cenannus.] He was [1155] carried upon [an island of] Loch-Sighlen and was a fortnight above a month therein, or something more and holy church and the favour of Patrick freed him and the guards that were guarding him were killed.—The door of the church of Daire was made by the successor of Colum-cille, namely, by Flaithbertach Ua Brolchain.[2]—Amlaim Mac Canai (steward[3] of Cenel-[O]engusa), tower of the championship and activity of all Cenel-Eogain, died.

Kalends of Jan. on 1st feria, 5th of the moon, A.D. 1156. [1156 Bis.] Tairrdelbach Ua Conchobuir, archking of Connacht, tower[1] of the splendour and of the principality of all Ireland for prowess and bestowal of treasures and of wealth to laics and to clerics, rested in peace.—A hosting by Muircertach Ua Lochlainn into Ulidia, so that he took away pledges to his choice. And it is upon that hosting also Ua Inneirghi was killed on a surprise party.—Aedh Ua Canannain, king of Cenel-Conaill, was killed by Ua Cathain and by the Men of the Craibh.—Another hosting also by Muircertach Ua Lachlainn to the South of Bregha, so that he took away the hostages of Leinster from [Diarmait] Mac Murchadha in return for [giving to Diarmait] the whole province. After that the Cenel-Eogain and the Airghialla went into Ossory, until they reached the Plain of Daire-mor, so that the nobles of Ossory came into the house of Ua Lachlainn.—Great crop in this year throughout all Ireland. Nine[2] years from the other great crop to this year.

Kalends of Jan. on 3rd feria, 16th of the moon, A.D. [1157] 1157. Gilla-Patraic Mac Carrthaigh, herenagh of Cork, rested in Christ.—Cu-Uladh Ua Caindelbain was killed in treachery by Donnchadh, son of Domnall Ua Mael-Sechnaehli Merry, who thereby dishonoured[1] the successor

---

he "was unhappilly and treacherously killed by Donogh mac Don- | nell [son of Domnall] O'Melaughlyn, King of Meath: having

Irru 7 Mic Lachlaind co maiṫiḃ in Tuairce[i]rt.—
Daiṁ-inir co n-a templuiḃ do Lorcud.—Comarba
Patraic (idon,ᵃ airdeprcop Erennᵃ) do ċoirecraḋ
tempaill na manaċ i riaḋnu[i]ri cleireċ n-Erenn, idon,
in Leżlaic 7 U[i] Orein 7 Ḃrenne 7 na n-eprcop arcena
7 i riaḋnu[i]re laeċ n-imda, im hUa Lachlaind, idon, im
riż Erenn 7 Donnċaḋ hUa Cerbaill 7 Tigernan¹ hUa
Ruairc. Dorad dano Muircertaċ hUa Lochlainn oċtᵇ
ficciu bo 7 tri ficteᶜ ungai d'ór do'n Coimḋiġ 7 do na
cleirċiḃ. Dorat dano baile ic Drochat-aṫa do na
cleirċiḃ, idon, Finnaḃair-na-n-ingean. Ocur tri ficitᶜ
ungai d'ór o hUa Cerbaill 7 tri ficitᶜ unga[i] ailiᵈ o
ingin hUi Mail-Seċlainn, o ṁnai Tigernain hUi Ruairc.
Rohercoiccennaiżeḋ dano do'n ċur rin o ċuaiṫ 7 o
eclair in t-ingrinnctiḋ[e] mallaċtaċ roraraiżertar
comarba Patraic 7 baċall Iru 7 cleirċiu Erenn
arcena: idon, Donnċaḃ hUa Mael-Seclainn.—Sluażaḋ
la Muircertaċ hUa Lachlainn co Tuaircert Erenn i

A.D. 1157. ¹ Tigernain, MS. ᵃ⁻ᵃ itl., t. h., B.; given in C. ᵇ .uni., MS.
ᶜ .xx., MS. ᵈ .ii., MS.

---

sworne to each other before by the ensewing oathes to be true to one another, without effusion of blood (for performance of which oathes the primatt of Ardmach was bound, the Pope's Legatt, Grenon, archbushopp of Dublyn, the abbot of the monkes of Ireland [Ua Brolchain]): the coworb [successor] of St. Queran [of Clonmacnoise] with his oaths [=*minna*, relics], the Staff, or Bachall, of Jesus, the cowarb of St. Feichyn [of Fore, co. Westmeath] with his oaths, the oaths [relics] of St. Columb-kill. These oaths and sureties were taken before King Mortagh [Mac Lochlainn], Donnogh O'Kervall king of Uriell, Tyernan O'Royrck, king of the Brenie and Dermott Mac Morrogh, king of Lynster and the principallest of Meath and Teaffa also. And if there were no such oaths or securities, it was a wicked act to kill such a noblehearted man without cause."

² *In presence of.*—The F. M. may be pardoned for calling this a Synodal Assembly; but the same excuse cannot be pleaded for Colgan, who gravely sets it down as a Synodal Convention (*Conventus Synodalis*) for consecrating the Basilica of the Monastery (AA. SS., p. 655)! (*To conse-*

of Patrick and the Staff of Jesus and Mac Lachlainn, along [1157] with the nobles of the North.—Daimh-inis with its churches was burned.—The successor of Patrick (namely, the archbishop of Ireland) consecrated the church of the Monks [of Mellifont, near Drogheda], in presence of[2] the clergy of Ireland, that is, of the Legate[3] and of Ua Osein and of Grenne and of the other bishops and in presence of many of the laity, around Ua Lachlainn, that is, around the king of Ireland and Donnchadh Ua Cerbaill and Tigernan Ua Ruairc. Moreover, Muircertach Ua Lochlainn gave eight[4] score cows and three score ounces of gold to the Lord and to the clergy. He gave also a townland at Drochait-atha to the clergy, namely, Finnabhair-na-ningen. And three score ounces of gold [were given] by Ua Cerbaill and three score ounces more by the daughter of Ua Mael-Sechlainn, [namely] by the wife of Tigernan Ua Ruairc. On that occasion also was excommunicated by laity and by clergy the persecutor accursed, that dishonoured the successor of Patrick and the Staff of Jesus and the clergy of Ireland besides, namely, Donnchadh[5] Ua Mael-Sechlainn.—A hosting by Muircertach Ua Lachlainn along with the North of Ireland into

---

crate is omitted in O'Donovan's translation.)

The wonder is to find Lanigan (*E. H.* iv. 164) led astray thereby. He adds however: " This synod, or assembly, was held for the mere object of consecrating a church ; and in fact very little more seems to have been done by it" (p. 167).

[3] *The Legate.*—Christian Ua Condoirche, bishop of Lismore. The F. M. omit his name, and also those of Ua Osein (archbishop of Tuam) and of Grenne (archbishop of Dublin).

The omission is accordingly repeated in the hitherto published accounts of the transaction.

O'Donovan (p. 1126) gives the reading of C. as "the Legat Ui Conorchi and the bishops also." But it is : " the Legat, U Osen, Grene and the bishops also."

[4] *Eight.*—The F. M. give seven (score) : whence Colgan has *centum et quadraginta* (*loc. cit.*).

[5] *Donnchadh.*—His offence is stated in the second entry of this year. According to Mageoghegan, "the

Mumain, co ṙanġaḋur ṙaicẽi Luimniġ 7 co tanġaḋur maicẽi Muman im a piġaiḃ i teac hUi Laclainḋ 7 co ṙarġaiḃret a m-braiġti aicce.

Kal. Ian. iiii. ṙ., L. xx. uiii., Anno Domini M.° c.° L.° uiii.° Domnall hUa Lonġarġa[i]n, aroerrcop Muman, in Chriṡto quieuit.—Sluaġaḋ ḋanoLa hUa Laclainḋ hi Tir-Conaill, co romill ṡanait do leir.—Senoḋ ḋo tinol La comarba ṡatraic 7 la cleirciḃ Erenn irin Bri-mic-Thaiḋġ, ḋú i rabaḋur coic· errcoir ṙicet, ḋo erail riaġla 7 roḃera ar cac i coitcenn. Ir ḋo'n cur rin roorḋaiġret cleiriġ Erenn, im Chomarba ṡatraic 7 im [in] Leġait, cataiṙ ḋo comarba Coluim-cille, iḋon, ḋo Fhlaitḃertac hUa Brolca[i]n, amal ġac n-errcop 7 aro-aḃḋaine cell Coluim-cille ṙo Erinn uile co coitcenn.

Kal. Ian. u. ṙ., L ix., Anno Domini M.° c.° L.° ix.° Diarmait, mac Taiḋġ hUi Mailruanaiġ, mortuur ert. —Sluaġaḋ· La Muircertac hUa Loclainn a Miḋe, co ṙarġaiḃ Donncaḋ hUa Mail-Seclainn i lanriġe Miḋe, o Shinainn co ṙairrġi.·—Sloġaḋ la Muircertac hUa Loclainn co maicẽiḃ Cheineil-Eoġain i ṙoiṙiḋn Airġall co hAt-Fhirḋeaḋ. Tanġaḋur | imorro Connacta 7 Conṁaicne 7 U[i]-Briuin ḋo leir 7 cac mor ḋo Muim-necaiḃ conicce At-na-Cairberna, ḋo taḃairt cata ḋoiḃ. Atractaḋur imorro Cenel-n-Eoġain 7 Airġallu im hUa

A.D. 1158. ᵃ⁻ᵃ .u. eṙr.xx., MS.
A.D. 1159. ᵃ⁻ᵃ om., C.

---

whole kingdome and government [were] given to his brother Dermott, as more worthy thereof.' See 1159, note 1 (*infra*).

1158. ¹ *Also*.—That is, as well as into Munster, the incursion into which is the last item of the preceding year.

² *The Legate*.—Not mentioned by the *Four Masters*.

³ *Chair*.—That is, he was made either a mitred abbot, or a bishop with-

Munster, until they reach the Green of Limerick and the [1157] nobles of Munster around their kings came into the house of Ua Lachlainn and left their pledges with him.

Kalends of Jan. on 4th feria, 27th of the moon, A.D. [1158] 1158. Domnall Ua Longargain, archbishop of Munster, rested in Christ.—A hosting by Ua Lachlainn into Tir-Conaill also,[1] so that he wasted Fanat entirely.—A Synod was assembled by the successor of Patrick and by the clergy of Ireland at the Hill of Mac Taidhg, wherein were five [and] twenty bishops, to enjoin rule and good conduct upon every one in common. It is on that occasion the clergy of Ireland, along with the successor of Patrick and along with the Legate,[2] appointed a Chair[3] for the successor of Colum-cille, that is, for Flaithbertach Ua Brolchain, the same as [for] every bishop and the arch-abbacy in general of the churches of Colum-cille throughout all Ireland.

Kalends of Jan. on 5th feria, 9th of the moon, A.D. 1159. [1159] Diarmait, son of Tadhg Ua Maelruanaigh, died.—A hosting by Muircertach Ua Lachlainn[1] into Meath, so that he left Donnchadh Ua Mael-Sechlainn in full kingship of Meath, from [the river] Shannon to sea.—A hosting by Muircertach Ua Lachlainn along with the nobles of Cenel-Eogain to Ath-Fhirdeadh in aid of the Airghialla. Howbeit, the Connachtmen and the Conmaicni and all the Ui-Briuin and a large battalion of Munstermen came as far as Ath-na-caisberna to give battle to them. On the other side, the Cenel-Eogain and Airgialla under Ua

---

out jurisdiction (more probably the former). See 1173, note 1; 1247, note 2 (*infra*).

1159. [1] *Ua Lachlainn.*—He was the principal of those by whom

Donnchadh had been deposed in favour of his brother, Dermot, after the excommunication pronounced in 1157!

Loclainn for amuſ in Ata cetna. Maiḋiſ tra for
Connactaiḃ 7 for Conmaicne 7 for Ua-Ḃriuin, amal
robatur uile, iḋon, ré[b] cata mora ḋoiḃ 7 lait na ḋá cat
aile[a] a n-derʒár: iḋon, áſ Connact, im Ʒilla-Criſt, mac
Diarmaḋa, mic Taiḋʒ 7 im Muirceſtaċ, mac Taiḋʒ 7
mac Ḋomnaill hUi Ḟhlaiṫberταiʒ, iḋon, mac ríʒ
iarṫair Chonnact 7 Ḃrian Mainec, mac Concoḃair, mic
Thoirrḋelbaiʒ 7 hUi Manḋaca[i]n (iḋon,[d] Muireḃac[d]),
ri hUa-Ḃriuin na Sinna 7 Ḃranan, mac Ʒilla-Criſt
Mic Ḃrana[i]n, iḋon, rí Corco-Aclann 7 mac Ḟhinna[i]n
hUi Siḃlen, ri hUa-n-Ecac Muaiḋe 7 alii multi nobiler;
7 áſ hUa-m-Ḃriuin, im mac Tiʒerna[i]n hUi
Cumra[i]n 7 im mac Ʒilla-Ḟhinnen U[i] Rotaiʒ 7 mac
Suiḃne hUi Ʒhala[i]n 7 Mac Conbuiḋe hUi Thorma-
ḋa[i]n 7 mac Aeḋa na n-amur, airri Conmaicne, 7 U[a]
Ḋonncaḋa 7 Finnbarr, mac Finnḋairr O[i] Ʒheruḃuḋ,
toiſec Muinnteri-Ʒeruḃa[i]n. Ocur[e] ḋrem mor ḋo Muim-
necaiḃ, im mac Ʒilla-Ciara[i]n hUi Cennetiʒ. ·Ocur[e]
Mac na haiḋci hUa Cernaca[i]n do marbaḋ ar
naṁaraċ for creic. Ocur tucratur Cenel-n-Eoʒain
boroma n-ḋiairmiḋe ḋo'n creic rin 7 ternatur imorro
Cenel-n-Eoʒain co corcar mór ḋia tiʒiḃ iar réin.—
Sluaʒaḋ la Muirceſtac hUa Laclainn co Ceniul-n-

[b].ui., MS. [c].ii., MS. [d-d] itl., t. h., B. ; om., C. [e] Et (the Latin equivalent used as a contraction), MS.

---

[2] *Ford.*—That is, *Ath-na-caisberna*;
in the neighbourhood of Ardee
(Ath-Fhirdeadh), co. Louth.
[3] *The two other battalions.*—Namely, of the Cenel-Eogain and of the
Airghialla.
[4] *Upon them.*—Literally, *their
(stark slaughter)*; the possessive
being used objectively. O'Donovan
(*F. M.* ii. 1135) translates *lait na
dd cath aile a n-dergdr* by "the two
other battalions were dreadfully
slaughtered." But the list of the
slain, which does not include a
single Ulster name, places the
meaning beyond doubt.
[5] *Brian Mainech.*—So called from
having been fostered in Ui-Maine
(the O'Kellys' country in cos. Galway
and Roscommon).
[6] *Many other nobles.*—The compiler overlooked the fact that the
context required the accusative,
not the nominative.

Lachlainn advanced to attack the same Ford.² But defeat [1159] is inflicted upon the Connachtmen and upon the Conmaicni and upon the Ui-Briuin, as they were [in] all, namely, six large battalions of them and the two other battalions³ inflict stark slaughter upon them⁴: to wit, slaughter of Connachtmen, around Gilla-Crist, son of Diarmaid, son of Tadhg [Mac Diarmata] and around Muircertach, son of Tadhg [Mac Diarmata] and the son of Domnall Ua Flaithbertaigh, that is, the son of the king of the west of Connacht, and Brian Mainech,⁵ son of Conchobhar, son of Toirrdhelbach [Ua Conchobair] and Ua Mandachain (namely, Muiredhach), king of Ui-Briuin-na-Sinna and Branan, son of Gilla-Crist Mac Branain, that is, king of Corco-Achlann and the son of Finnan Ua Sibhlen, king of the Ui-Echach of Muaidh; and many other nobles⁶ [were slain]; and slaughter of the Ui-Briuin, around the son of Tigernan Ua Cumrain and around the son of Gilla-Finnen⁷ Ua Rothaigh and the son of Suibne Ua Galain and the son of Cu-buidhe⁸ Ua Tormadain and the son of Aedh "of the onsets," sub-king [?] of Conmaicni and Ua Donnchadha and Finnbharr, son of Finnbharr Ua Gerudhain,⁹ chief of Muinnter-Gerudhain. And a large force of Munstermen [was slain], around the son of Gilla-Ciarain Ua Cennetigh. And "Son of the Night"¹⁰ Ua Cernachain was killed on the morrow on a foray. And the Cenel-Eogain took away countless cattle-spoil on that foray. And the Cenel-Eogain returned indeed with great triumph to their homes after that.—A hosting by Muircertach Ua Lachlainn with the Cenel-Eogain and with the Airgialla and the Ulidians and Cenel-Conaill into Connacht, so that

---

⁷ *Gilla-Finnen.*—*Devotee of* [*St.*] *Finnian* (of Clonard, co. Meath).
⁸ *Cu-buidhe.*—Literally, *canis flavus*.
⁹ *Gerudhain.*—Gerudan, C.; Gerudhud, B.

¹⁰ "*Son of the Night.*"—So called, perhaps, from the many nocturnal raids in which he took part.

Eogain 7 co n-Cipgiallaib 7 Ulltaib 7 Ceniul-Conaill 1 Connactaib, co poloipcet Dún-mór 7 Dún-Ciaraibi 7 Dún-na-n-Gall 7 co pomillpet mor do'n tír apcena, co popoipet iar rin dia tír, cen rit, cen giallu. Ocur ir do'n cur rin tucrat leo hUa Gailmpedaig 7 Cenel-Maien.—Mael-Muire hUa Loingrig, epscop Luirmoir, ruam uitam feliciter finiuit.—Murcad hUa Ruadaca[i]n, rí Cirter, mortuur ert.—Tri hUi Maeldoraid do marbad la hUa Cananna[i]n hi meabail.

[br.] Kal. Ian. ui. f., l. xx., Anno Domini M.° c.° lx.° Donncad hUa Mael-Seclainn, ri Mide, do marbad do macaib hUi Findalla[i]n i mebail.—hUa Cananna[i]n, rí Ceniul-Conaill, do marbad la Cenel-Conaill radéin, idon, tec do lorcud | d'Ua baigill rair.—Flaitbertac hUa Caturaig, ri Saitne [do éc].—Finn hUa Gorma[i]n, epscop Cille-dara, abb manac Ibair-Cinntracta fri ré, ad Chriytum migrauit.—Drodur, mac Torcaill, ri Ata-cliat, do marbad do Deircert brex.—Maidm Maigi-Lugad ria Cenel-n-Eogain Tolca-oac for hUa n-Gailmpedaig 7 for Domnall hUa Cruca[i]n 7 for Ua Fiacrac, co romarbad drem mór dib. Ocur ir do'n cur rin dorocair co neimcintac Muircertac hUa Neill la Loclann hUa Laclainn, cotorcair iar rin Loclann i n-a digail la mac hUi Neill.—Sluagad la Muircertac hUa Loclainn co Ceniul-Eogain 7 co n-Cirgiallaib, co

A.D. 1160. ᵃ Cinntracta om., C. ᵇ The order of this and of the following sentence is improperly reversed in C.

---

¹¹ *Gained over to them.*—Literally, *took with them.* "Won," C. That is, succeeded in getting O'Gormley and his clan to become their allies. How short-lived was the alliance, is shown in the two concluding entries of the following year.

¹² *Mael-Muire.*—*Devotee of Mary.*

1160. ¹ *South of Bregha.*—The entry in the Four Masters states that he was slain by Maelcron Mac Gilla-Seachnaill (who was probably the brother of Domnall, lord of Bregia).

² *Dishonouring.*—The specific act is not stated.

they burned Dun-mor and Dun-Ciaraidhi and Dun-na- [1159]
nGall and wasted much of the land besides, until they
returned to their own country after that, without peace,
without pledges. And it is on that occasion they gained
over to them[11] Ua Gailmredhaigh and the Cenel-Maien.—
Mael-Muire[12] Ua Loingsigh, bishop of Lis-mor, felicitously
finished his life.—Murchadh Ua Ruadhacain, king of the
Airthir, died.—Three Ui-Maeldoraidh were killed by Ua
Canannain in treachery.

Kalends of Jan. on 6th feria, 20th of the moon, A.D. [1160 Bis.]
1160. Donnchadh Ua Mael-Sechlainn, king of Meath,
was killed by the sons of Ua Findallain [lord of
Delbna-mor] in treachery.—Ua Canannain, king of
Cenel-Conaill, was killed by the Cenel-Conaill themselves,—namely, a house was burned by Ua Baighill
upon him.—Flaithbertach Ua Cathusaigh, king of
Saitni, died.—Finn Ua Gormain, bishop of Cell-dara,
abbot of the monks of Ibhar-Cinntrachta for a [long] time,
passed to Christ.—Brodur, son of Torcall, king of Ath-
cliath, was killed by the South of Bregha.[1]—The defeat of
Magh-Lughad [was inflicted] by the Cenel-Eogain of
Telach-oc upon Ua Gailmredhaigh and upon Domnall Ua
Cricain and upon the Ui-Fiacrach, so that a large party of
them were killed. And it is on that occasion Muircertach
Ua Neill fell innocently [i.e., undesignedly] by Lochlann Ua
Lachlainn, [but] so that in revenge of him Lochlann fell
afterwards by the son of Ua Neill.—A hosting by Muir-
certach Ua Lachlainn along with the Cenel-Eogain and the
Airgialla, until they came to Magh-dula, to expel Ua

---

[3] *Oaths.*—Literally, *relics.* From being employed to swear upon relics, evangelisteria, missals, rituals, croziers, and similar objects of veneration came to have the secondary meaning of oaths. (Cf. *The Stowe Missal*, Tr. R, I. A., xxvii, 174-5.)

ranṡaḋur Maġ-n-ḋula ḋo innarbuḋ hui Ṡairmleẋaiḋ. Aṫroċair ṫra hUa Ṡairmleẋaiḋ 1 mebail la Ḋomnall hUa Maelruanaiġ, ar erail hUi Loċlainn, iar rarużuḋ cleireċ n-Erenn 7 a ṁinḋ ḋó. Ocur rucaḋ a cenn co hArḋ-Maċa 1 n-éineċ Patraic 7 Coluim-cille.

|Kal. Ian. 1. r., L. 1., Anno Domini M.° c.° lx.° 1.° Ua hOirréin, arḋ-errcop Connaċt, aḋ Chrirtum miġrauit—Cuairt Orraiżi ḋo ḋenam la comarba Coluim-cille, iḋon, la Flaiṫberṫaċ hUa Ḃrolċa[i]n : iḋon, reċt* rċit[b] ḋam; aċt ar e a riaċ rotaiḋbeḋ ann,—iḋon, rċe[b] 7 ceṫri[c] ceṫ uinże ḋ'arżut żil : iḋon, ṫri huinże 1 n-żaċ ḋam.—Ṡorrraiż hUa Raġallaiġ ḋo marbaḋ,—Sluaġaḋ la Muirċertaċ hUa Loċlainn hi Ṫir-m-Ḃriuin : irreḋ ḋocuaḋur ḋar Comur Cluana-Eoir, ar rut an tire, co rarżaib Tiżernan a Longrort ḋoib. Arrein co Tirrait-Merra[i]n. Airżiallu 7 Ulaiḋ conice rein cucai, 7 Mac Murċaḋa co Laiżniḃ 7 caṫ ḋo Ġallaiḃ, co n-ḋeoċaḋur uile 1 Maż-Teṫḃa.[1] Tainiż ḋano hUa Concobuir tar Sinainḋ aniar 7 ḋorat braiżḋe ḋ'U[a] Loċlainn 7 ḋano tuc hUa Loċlainn a ċoiżeḋ coṁlan ḋórom.—Teṫ ḋo żabail ḋo Chaṫal[2] hUa Raġallaiż ror Mael-Seċlainn hUa Ruairc ror Lar Sláine, co romarbaḋ ann Muirċertaċ hUa Ceallaiż, ri Ḃreż, co n-ḋreim ḋo ṁaiṫiḃ ime. | Terrai imorro Mael-Seċlainn arr.—Iṁar hUa hInnreċtaiż, airċinneċ Mucnoma 7 ri hUa-Meiṫ rri ré, ḋo éc.—Sluaġaḋ aile la hUa Loċlainn hi Miḋe, 1 com-

A.D. 1161. ¹ Terra, MS. ² Ġċatal, MS. ᵃ .uii., M.S. ᵇ .xx., MS. ᶜ .cccc., MS.

ᵃ *In reparation to.*—Literally, *in reparation of.*

1161. ¹ *Ua hOisein.*—Called *Aed* (Hugh) in the *Annals of Innisfallen;* in which his death is entered under the previous year.

² *Pure.*—Literally, *white.*

³ *For.*—Literally, *in.*

⁴ *Killed.*—At Kells, by Mael. Sechlainn O'Ruairc according to the Four Masters. The reprisal made by

Gairmleghaidh [from Cenel-Moain]. But Ua Gairmleghaidh fell in treachery by Domnall Ua Maelruanaigh, by direction of Ua Lochlainn, after the dishonouring² of the clergy of Ireland and of his oaths³ by him. And his [lit., the] head was carried to Ard-Macha, in reparation to⁴ [SS.] Patrick and Colum-cille. [1160]

Kalends of Jan. on 1st feria, 1st of the moon, A.D. 1161. Ua hOissein,¹ archbishop of Connacht, passed to Christ.— The circuit of Ossory was made by the successor of Colum-cille, namely, by Flaithbertach Ua Brolcha[i]n: that is, seven score oxen [were given]: but it is their value that was presented there,—namely, four hundred and twenty ounces of pure² silver: to wit, three ounces for³ every ox. —Goeffrey Ua Raghallaigh [lord of Breifni] was killed.⁴—A hosting by Muircertach Ua Lochlainn into Tir-Briuin: the way⁵ they went [was] past the Confluence of Cluain-Eois, through the length of the country, until Tigernan [Ua Ruairc] abandoned his camp to them. From that to the Well of Messan. The Airgialla and Ulidians [came] to that place to him and Mac Murchadha with the Leinstermen and a battalion of Foreigners [came], so that they all went into the Plain of Tethbha. Then Ua Conchobuir came from the west, across the Shannon and gave pledges to Ua Lochlainn and thereupon Ua Lochlainn gave his entire Fifth [i.e. Province] to him.—A house was seized by Cathal Ua Raghallaigh upon Mael-Sechlainn Ua Ruairc in the centre of Slane, so that Muircertach Ua Ceallaigh, king of Bregha, was killed there, with a party of nobles around him. Mael-Sechlainn, however, escaped therefrom.—Imhar Ua Innrechtaigh, herenagh of Mucnom and king of Ui-Meith for a [long] time, died.—Another hosting⁶ by Ua Lochlainn [1161]

Cathal, son of Geoffrey, is told in the next entry but one.

⁵ *The way.*—Literally, *It is [the way]*. The object was to emphasize the openness of the route; no opposition being dreaded.

⁶ *Another hosting.*—The first is mentioned in the third item of this

140 annala ulaoh.

ɒail ꝼeꞃ n-Eꞃenn eceꞃ loeċu 7 cleiꞃċiu, co hƆƆc-na-ɒaiꞃbꞃiξe, co ꞃoξaɓ a m-bꞃaiξɒe uili. Iꞃ ɒo'n ċuꞃ ꞃin ꞃoꞃaeꞃaic cealla Coluim-cille 1 Miɓe 7 1 Laiξniu la comaꞃba Coluim-cille, iɒon, la ꝼlaicbeꞃcaċ hUa Ɓꞃol-ċa[i]n 7 cucaɓ ɒó a cain 7 a ꞃmaċc, uaiꞃ ꞃoɒɒaꞃ ɒoeꞃa ꞃeimeꞃin.

Kal. Ian. 11. ꝼ., l. xii., Anno Domini M.° c.° lx.° 11.° Eꞃꞃꞃcaꞃɒuξ na caiξi o ċempluiɓ Daiꞃe ɒo ɒenum la comaꞃba Coluim-cille (iɒon,ᵃ ꝼlaicbeꞃcaċ) 7 la ꞃiξ Eꞃenn, iɒon, la Muiꞃceꞃcaċ hUa Loċlainn; ɒú in ꞃocóξbaɓ oċcmoξaᵇ caiξi, no ni iꞃ uilliu. Ocuꞃ ɒenam caiꞃil in eꞃlaiꞃ la comaꞃba Coluim-cille beoꞃ 7 mallaċc aꞃ inci cicꞃa caiꞃiꞃ ɒoξꞃeꞃ.—Imbleċ-iɓaiꞃ co n-a cempall ɒo loꞃcuɓ.—Senaɓ cleiꞃeċ n-Eꞃenn, im comaꞃba Pacꞃaic, iɒon, im Ƶilla Mac Liaċ, | mac Ruaiɒꞃi, ic Cloenaɒ,¹ iꞃꞃabacuꞃ² ꞃéᶜ eꞃꞃuic ꞃiċec,ᵉ co n-ab[b]aɓaiɓ imɒaiɓ, ic eꞃail ꞃiaξla 7 ꞃobeꞃa. Ocuꞃ iꞃᵉ ɒo'n cuꞃ ꞃinᶠ ꞃocinnꞃec cleiꞃiċ Eꞃenn ξꞃaɓa aꞃɒeꞃꞃuic Eꞃenn ɒo ċomaꞃba Pacꞃaic, amail ꞃoboi ꞃiam 7 na baɓ ꝼeꞃleiξinɒ³ 1 cill 1 n-Eꞃinn neċᶜ aċcᶜ ɒalca Aꞃɒ-Maċa.—Sloξaɓ la Muiꞃceꞃcaċ hUa Loċlainn co n-eꞃṁóꞃ Leiċi Cuinn co Maξ-Ꝼicaꞃca,⁴ co ꞃabacuꞃ² ꞃecc-

A 50a

A.D. 1162. ¹ Clae-, A. ²—ɒuꞃ, B. ³—ξinn, B. ⁴—Ꝼiɒaꞃɒa, B. ᵃ⁻ᵃ L m. t. h., MS.; om., C. ᵇ .lxxx., MS. ᶜ⁻ᶜ .uii.—.xx., A, B. ᵈ⁻ᵈ co na n-abaɓaiɓ —*with their abbots*, A. ᵉ om., A. ᶠ ċuꞃ, B. ᵍ⁻ᵍ in neċ na bu—*the one who should not be*, B.

---

year. As the result of these two expeditions, O'Conor called himself king of Ireland.

⁷ *Subject.*—That is, to assessment by the respective temporal lords.

1162. ¹ *Centre.*—From this account it can be inferred that the churches of Derry stood in proximity. On the removal of the adjacent houses, a circular wall was built, to mark off the space thus acquired as one to which the right of asylum attached. (Cf. the *Collectio Canonum Hibernensis*, xxviii. De civitatibus refugii; xliv. 2: De debito termino circa omnem locum sanctum.) The *Four Masters* change *churches* into *church*, being followed in the error by Colgan (*Tr. Th.*, p. 505).

⁵ *Come over it.*—That is, violate the

into Meath, into an assembly of the Men of Ireland, both [1161] laics and clerics, at Ath-na-Dairbrighe, so that he received the pledges of them all. It is on that occasion the churches of Colum-cille in Meath and Leinster were freed by the successor of Colum-cille, namely, by Flaithbertach Ua Brolcha[i]n, and their tribute and jurisdiction were given to him, for they were subject[7] before that.

Kalends of Jan. on 2nd feria, 12th of the moon, A.D. 1162. [1162] Total separation of the houses from the churches of Daire was made by the successor of Colum-cille (namely, Flaithbertach) and by the king of Ireland, that is, by Muircertach Ua Lochlainn; where were demolished eighty houses, or something more. And the stone wall of the Centre[1] was likewise built by the successor of Colum-cille and malediction [pronounced] upon him who should come over it[2] for ever.—Imblech-ibhair with its church was burned. —A Synod of the clergy of Ireland [was held] around the successor of Patrick, to wit, around Gilla Mac Liach, son of Ruaidhri, at Cloenad, wherein were six [and] twenty bishops, with many abbots, enjoining rule and good conduct. And it is on that occasion the clergy of Ireland assigned[3] the Orders of archbishop of Ireland to the successor of Patrick, as it was before[3] and that no one should be lector in a church in Ireland, except an alumnus of Ard-Macha.—A hosting by Muircertach Ua Lochlainn along with very large portion of the Half of Conn to Magh-Fitharta, so that they were a week therein, burning the

---

place by forcibly entering to carry off a refugee. (Cf. the *Col. Can. Hib.* XLIV. 7: De violatione templi Dei cum septis punienda. *Templum cum septis* signifies a church surrounded by enclosures.)

[3-3] *Assigned—before.*—That is, it was enacted that henceforth no layman be intruded into the Armagh succession. (Cf. A.D. 1129, note 4, *supra*.) The deep-rooted abuse connected with the primacy was thereby formally eliminated. It is characteristic of the Four Masters

142 annala ulaoh.

nain ann ic lorcað arða 7 baileð Ᵹall· Cucracur²
imorro na Ᵹaill maiom ror a marerluaᵹ, co romarð-
rac rerer,⁵ no morferer,⁵ oið 7 ni fuaracur² a peir
oo'n⁶ čur rin.—Argain Ᵹall· Aca-cliač la Oiarmaic
Mac Murčaða 7 nerc mór oo ᵹabail rorro, amail na
roᵹaðað reiihe o cein móir.—Cuairð Ceneoil-Eoᵹain
la comarba ratraic, ioon, la Ᵹilla Mic Liac, mac
Ruaiðri, oanað rriɬ inncramail reimpi⁵.—Ᵹrene,
erscop Aca-cliač 7 aroerpos⁷ Laiᵹen, in Chrirco
quieuic. Comarba ratraic oo oironeð⁸ Lorca[i]n hUi
Cuačail, comarba Coemᵹin,⁹ i n-a inað.

(Mael-Sečnaill¹ hUa Ruaire occirur erc.—Abbacia
Duelliae hoc anno runoaca erc.—An cornomaið, hUa
Ouðoa, occirrur erc.¹)

Kal. Ian. iii. r., l. xx. iii., Anno Domini M.° c.° lx.° iii,*
Mael-Iru hUa Laiᵹena[i]n, erscop 7 ab[b] Imbleča¹-
ibair 7 abb² Dealaiᵹ-conᵹlair rri ré, in Chrirco
quieuic.—Cerball· hUa Ᵹilla-ratraic, ri Oeirce[i]rc
Orraiᵹi, morcu[u]r erc.*—Mael-Irru hUa Corc[r]a[i]n,
comarba | Comᵹaill, cenn crabaio Ulað uile, ao

B 52b

A.D. 1162. ⁵⁻⁵ .ui.ur, no morferiur, A.; .ui.ur, no mor.ui.ur, B.
⁶ oo, A. Scribe forgot to place the contraction mark of n over o. ⁷ airo—,B.
⁸ oirneð, A. ⁹ Caiin—, A. ᵇ ᵇ om., B, C.   ᵢᵢ n. t. h., A.; om., B, C.

A.D. 1163. ¹ Imleča—, B. ² ab, A.—ᵃ ᵃ om., B, C.

---

that they should have passed over a National Synodal Decree of such importance.

³ *Grene.* — Called Gregory by Ware (*Bishops*, at Dublin), followed by most writers. Lanigan's correction of the native annalists (*E. H.* iv.173) is noteworthy: "In divers Irish Annals Gregory's death is placed in 1162. But this is a mistake, owing to their having confounded the year of it with that of the accession of his successor, St. Laurence O'Toole, which was in 1162"!

⁴ *Lorcan Ua Tuathail.*—That is, St. Laurence O'Toole. For the family and territories, see O'Donovan's valuable note(*F. M.* iii. 515sq.) Tuathal, mentioned at 1014 (*supra*) as father of Dunlang, king of Leinster, was the eponymous head.

corn and towns of the Foreigners. The foreigners, however, [1162] inflicted defeat upon their horse-host, so that they killed six or seven of them and [the Ultonians] got not their demand on that occasion.—Pillaging of the Foreigners of Ath-cliath by Diarmait Mac Murchadha and great sway was obtained [by him] over them, such as was not obtained before for a long time.—The circuit of Cenel-Eogain [was made] by the successor of Patrick, namely, by Gilla Mac Liach, son of Ruaidri, to which nothing similar [in the amount of donations] was found before it.— Grene,³ bishop of Ath-cliath and archbishop of Leinster, rested in Christ. The successor of Patrick ordained Lorcan Ua Tuathail,⁴ successor of [St.] Coemghen, in his stead.

(Mael-Sechnaill⁵ Ua Ruairc was slain.—The abbey of Boyle was founded this year.—The Defender Ua Dubhda was slain.)

Kalends of Jan. on 3rd feria, 23rd of the moon, A.D. [1163] 1163. Mael-Isu Ua Laighena[i]n, bishop and abbot of Imblech-ibair and abbot of Belach-conglais for a [long] time, rested in Christ.¹—Cerball Ua [*recte*, Mac] Gilla-Patraic, king of the South of Ossory, died.—Mael-Issu Ua Corc[r]ain, successor of [St.] Comgall,² head of the piety of all Ulster, passed to Christ.—A lime-kiln,³ wherein

---

Seventh in descent from Tuathal was Muirchertach, king of the Ui-Muridaigh. He had seven sons, Lorcan being apparently the eldest. His only daughter, Mor, became the wife of Dermot Mac Murrogh, King of Leinster (L. L. 337d; where the words missing by erasure from the heading of the genealogy are *Ua-Muridaigh*).

⁵ *Mael-Sechnaill.*—This entry is given in the *Four Masters*. The remaining two entries are found in the *Annals of Boyle*, at 1161 and 1162 respectively.

1163. ¹ *Rested in Christ.*—In Emly, according to the *Annals of Innisfallen*, which omit mention of his having been abbot of Baltinglas.

² *Successor of [St.] Comgall.* — That is, abbot of Bangor, co. Down.

³ *Lime-kiln.*—Literally, *fire of lime*: the contained, by metonymy, for the container. Similarly, *Cenel* (sept),

Chpirtum migrauit.—Tene-aeil i faeil ferca⁵ traixeo
ap cac³ lec oo oenam la Comapba Coluim-cille, ioon,
la flaicbeptac, mac in epcuip hUi Opolca[i]n 7 la
famao Coluim-cille, fpi pé ficec laa.

(Niall,⁴ mac Muipceptaig, mic Mic Loclainn, oo
gabail la hU-Maine.ᵈ)

[bip.] Kal. Ian. iiii. f., L. iiii., Anno Domini m.° c.° lx.° iiii.°
Donncao hUa Opiain, epfcop Cille-oa-lua, in Chpirto
quieuic.—Maici* muinntepi la,ᵇ ioon, in facapc mop,
A 50b Augurtin 7 in fepleigin (ioon,ᶜ Oubpioeᶜ) | 7 in oipep-
tac, ioon Mac Gilla-ouib 7 cenn na Ceile-n-De, ioon,
Mac fopcellaig 7 maici muinntepi la apcena oo
ciactain ap cenn comapba Coluim-cille, ioon, [fh]laic-
beptaic hUi Opolcain, oo gabail aboaine la a comaipli
Somaplib 7 fep Aep[t]ep-gaioel¹ 7 Innpi-gall, co
pofajapcaei comapba fatpaic 7 pi Epenn, ioon, Ua Loclainn 7 maici Cene[oi]l-Eogain e.—Gilla-fatpaic hUa
Mael-Mena oo éc.*—Somaplib² Mac Gille-Aoamnain
7 a mac oo mapbao 7 ap fep Aep[t]ep-ghaeoel³ 7
Cinntipe 7 fep Innpi-gall 7 Gall Aca-cliac ime.—Blob
o'Apo-Maca oo lopcao.—Tempull⁴ mop Oaipi⁵ oo

ᵃ guc, B. ᵇ lx , A, B. *.xx., A, B. ᵈ⁻ᵈ n. t. h., A; om., B, C.

A.D. 1164. ¹ Eupep—(the first e is *caudata*), MS. (A) ² lig. B. ³ n-
gaeioel, B. ⁴ pall, B. ⁵ pe, B. ** om., B, C. ᵇ Oaipe was first written;
subsequently, each letter was dotted above and below, to signify deletion, MS.

Clann (clan), *Fir* (men), *Muinnter* (tribe), *Pobul* (people), *Sil* (progeny), *Ui* (descendants), used with the patronymic, sometimes signify the territories, not the inhabitants thereof (prout utrumlibet usus accommodarit, *Ogygia*, III. lxxvi. 361). Compare Blackfriars, Whitefriars.

The *Four Masters* (followed by Colgan, *loc. cit.*) against A, B and C, say the kiln was 70 feet square. Colgan adds that it was built in connection with repairing the church of Derry. On the same page, unconscious apparently of the contradiction, he records the building of the new church of that city.

⁴ *Niall.*—Given in the *Annals of Boyle*.

1164. ¹ *Select, etc.*—This incident,

are sixty feet on every side, was made by the successor of [1163] Colum-cille, that is, by Flaithbertach, son of the bishop Ua Brolchain and by the Community of Colum-cille in the space of twenty days.

(Niall,[4] son of Muircertach, son of Mac Lochlainn, was taken prisoner by the Ui-Maine.)

Kalends of Jan. on 4th feria, 4th of the moon, A.D. 1164. [1164 Bis.] Donnchadh Ua Briain, bishop of Cell-da-lua, rested in Christ.—Select[1] members of the Community of Ia, namely, the arch-priest, Augustin and the lector (that is, Dubsidhe) and the Eremite, Mac Gilla-duib and the Head of the Celi-De, namely, Mac Forcellaigh and select members of the Community of Ia besides came on behalf of the successor of Colum-cille. namely, Flaithbertach Ua Brolchain's acceptance of the abbacy of Ia, by advice of Somharlidh and of the Men of Airthir-Gaedhel and of Insi-Gall; but the successor of Patrick and the king of Ireland, that is, Ua Lochlainn and the nobles of Cenel-Eogain prevented him.—Gilla-Patraic Ua Mael-Mena died.—Somharlidh[2] Mac Gilla-Adhamhnain[3] and his son were killed and slaughter of the Men of Airthir-Gaedhel and of Cenn-tire and of the men of Insi-Gall and of the Foreigners of Ath-cliath [took place] around

---

so honourable to Ua Brolchain and without which an allusion in his obituary notice (*infra*, 1175) could not be understood, is passed over by the *Four Masters*. See the note in *Adamnan* (p. 407) and the references there given.

[2] *Somharlidh.*—Somerledus itaque, rex Ergadine . . ., copioso exercitu et maxima classe de Hibernia et aliis diversis locis contracto, apud Reinfrieu [on the Clyde] praedaturus applicuit; sed . . a paucis provincialibus ibidem est occisus. For-

dun, *Gest. Annal.*, iv. (*ad. an.*) See also the extract from the *Chronicle of Man*, quoted in *Adamnan*, p. 408.

[3] *Gilla-Adhamhnain.*—Devotee of [St.] *Adamnan*; (ninth) abbot of Iona from 679 to 704. Adamnan's chief work, the *Life of St. Columba*, has been edited with a wealth of illustration by Dr. Reeves.

[4] *Great church.* — *Tempul mor;* "from which the city of Derry receives its parochial name of Templemore" (*Adamnan*, p. 408).

ꝺenum la comarba Coluim-cille, ꝓon, la Flaiṫbertaċ, mac in erpuic hUi Ḃrolcain 7 ra ramuṫ Coluim[-cille] 7 la Muirceartaċ hUa Loċlainn, la[d] hairꝺriġ n-Erenn. Ocur[a] tairrnic cloċ in tempaill moir rein Daire, ꝺ raelet noċa[e] traiẋeꝺ, rri ré ceṫorċat[f] laa.[e]

(Aṁlaim,[r] mac Gilla-Caimġin U Cheinneiꝺig, ꝺo ṫallaṫ.[s])

Kal. Ian. ui. r., l. x. u., Anno Domini m.º c.º lx.º u.º
Tairrꝺelbaċ hUa Ḃriain ꝺo innarba[ṫ] a riġ[1] Muman la a[a] mac, ꝓon, la Muirceartaċ 7 ré rein ꝺo ġabail riġ[1] ꝺ'eir a aṫar.—Doṁnall[b] hUa Gilla-Patraic, ri Tuairce[i]rt Orraiẋi, 7 Concobur hUa Ḃroiġte, ri Cinn-caille 7 Paitin hUa hAeꝺa, cainneal hUa-Ceinnrelaiġ uile, ꝺo ṁarbaṫ ꝺo Ma[c] Craiṫ hUa Morṫai 7 ꝺo Laiċir tria ꝺroċṙata.—Cocaṫ eter Fhiru Miṫe 7 hUiḃ-Ḃriuin 7 irin ċocaṫ rin romarbaṫ Gitriuc hUa Ruairc la hUa Ciarṫai 7 la Cairpri.[b]—Impuꝺ Ulaṫ ꝺano[a] ror Ua[2] Loċlainn[3] 7 creċ leo ror hUiḃ-Meiṫ, co[e] ruċrat bú imꝺa 7 co romarbrat roċaiꝺe[d] ꝺo ꝺainiḃ. Creċ ꝺono leo ror Ui[b]-Ḃrerail oirrter 7 creċ aile ror Dail-riatai.—Sluaẋaꝺ la Muirceartaċ hUa Loċlainn, eter Conall 7 Eoġan 7 Airġiallu, i n-Ulltaiḃ, co roairgret in tir uile, cenmoṫat primċella Ulaṫ 7

(A) ᶜᶜitl, t. h., MS. (A)   ᵈ om., B.   ᵉ .lxxxx., MS. (A)   ᶠ .xl., MS. (A)
ᵍ n. t. h., A ; om., B, C.

A.D. 1165. ¹ riġe, B.   ²hUa, A.   ³laċ—, B.   ᵃ om., A. The la is probably=la a—*with his.*   ᵇ⋅ᵇ om., B, C.   ᶜ ocur co—*and so that,* B.   ᵈ ar n-ꝺiairmiꝺe—*slaughter hard to number,* B.   C. follows A.

---

⁵ *Ninety.*—Mistaking the original, the *Four Masters* (followed by Colgan) say *eighty*.

⁶ *Amhlaim.*—Given (the verb is omitted in O'Conor's text) in the *Annals of Boyle*. The *Four Masters* add that the deed was done by Toirrdelbach Ua Briain (Turlough O'Brien). The entry is not given (perhaps intentionally) in the *Annals of Innisfallen*.

⁷ *Gilla-Caimʝhin.* — Devotee of [*St.*] *Kerin* (of Glendalough).

1165. ¹ [*Mac*] *Gilla-Patraic.*—

him.—Portion of Ard-Macha was burned.—The great church [1164] of[4] Daire was built by the successor of Colum-cille, that is, by Flaithbertach, son of the bishop Ua Brolchain and by the Community of Colum-cille and by Muircertach Ua Lochlainn, arch-king of Ireland. And the [top] stone of that great church,' wherein there are ninety[5] feet [in length], was completed within the space of forty days.

(Amhlaim,[6] son of Gilla-Caimghin[7] Ua Ceinnedig, was blinded.)

Kalends of Jan. on 6th feria, 15th of the moon, A.D. [1165] 1165. Tairrdelbach Ua Briain was expelled from the kingship of Munster by his son, that is, by Muircertach and he [Muircertach] himself took the kingship after his father.— Domnall Ua [recte, Mac[1]] Gilla-Patraic, king of the North of Ossory, and Conchobar Ua Broighte, king of Cenn-caille and Paitin Ua Aedha, the candle of all Ui-Ceinnselaigh, were killed by Ma[c] Craith Ua Mordhai and by the Laichsi for evil causes.—War [took place] between the Men of Meath and the Ui-Briuin and it is in that war Sitriuc[1] Ua Ruairc was killed by Ua Ciardhai and by the Cairpri.—The turning of the Ulidians upon Ua Lochlainn [took place] and a foray [was made] by them upon the Ui-Meith, so that they took away many cows and killed a multitude of persons. A foray also [was made] by them upon the eastern Ui-Bresail and another foray upon Dal-riatai.—A hosting by Muircertach Ua Lochlainn, [along with] both [Cenel-]Cona[i]ll and [Cenel-]Eoga[i]n and the Airgialla, into Ulidia, so that they harried all the country, except the chief churches of the Ulidians and killed a countless

---

So called in the Ossorian list of kings (L. L. 41a), which agrees with the text in stating that he was slain by the Laichsi (the sept that inhabited and gave the name to Leix, Queen's Co.)

[2] *Sitriuc.*—The *Four Masters* make this portion a distinct item, and omit the connection between the war and the death of Sitriuc.

148 annala ulaḋ.

co romarbrat ár n-ṽiairṁiṫe⁴ ṽib, im Eċmarcaċ, mac
Mic Ḟilla-erpuic 7 im hUa⁰ | Lomanaiḟ 7 co róinnarbrat Eoċaiṫ Mac Ṽuinnrleiṫe a hUllταiṫ 7 co⁵ n-ṽarait⁵
hUa Loċlainn riḟe ṽo Ṽun[n]rleiṫe 7 co n-ṽartrat⁶
Ula[i]ṫ uile a n-ḟeill ṽ'Ul[a] Loċlainn τria nert riḟe.—
Ṽiarmait Mac Arta[i]n, toireċ Clainne-Roḟartaiḟ,
eneċ 7 eḟnuṁ hUa-n-Eċaċ uile, mortuur ert.—Toċurtal
Saxan 7 Ḟall Aτa-cliaċ la mac na Rerir ṽo ḟaṫail
forṫairi for Ṽretnaiṫ 7 robatar uile re ré leiṫbliaṫna
ic⁷ a⁷ τoḟail 7 nír'ḟetrat. Et reuerri runt rine pace
retro.—Mael-Coluim Cennmor, mac Eanric, arṽri
Alban, in crirταiṫe ar rerr ṽo bai ṽo Ḟaiṫelaiṫ⁸ re
muir anair, ar ṽeirc 7' aineċ 7' crabuṫ, ṽo éc.—
Triallaiṫ⁴ Eoċaiṫ ṽo riṽiri riḟi Ulaṫ ṽo ḟaṫail, co
roṽiċuirret Ula[i]ṫ he, ar huaṁon hUi Loċlainn 7 co
roḟeirṁliḟeṫ he la Ṽonnċaṫ hUa Cerḃaill, la harṽriḟ
Airḟiall, tre forċonḟra hUi Loċlainn.—Sluaḟaṫ aile
la Muircertaċ hUa Loċlainn co Ceniul-Eoḟain co hInirLaċain, | co roloirret in inṽri 7 co rurmúrrat 7 co tucrat Ula[i]ṫ uile a m-braiḟτi ṽ'Ul[a]⁵ Loċlainn. Tecait iarrin^h Cenel-n-Eoḟain ini hUa⁹ Loċlainn ṽia τiḟiṫ, co corcur mor 7 co lonḟaiṫ imṽaiṫ leo 7 co retaiṫ imṽaiṫ arċena. Arreiṫe hUa Loċlainn ṽ'Arṽ-Maċa. Tιcc iar rein
Ṽonnċaṫ hUa Cerḃaill, airṽri Airḟiall 7 Eoċaiṫ Mac

---

¹⁻ṁ, B. ¹⁻³ co n-ṽorat, A. ⁶tarṽrat, B. ⁷⁻⁷ ca (aphaeresis of ι), A.
⁸ Ḟhoeṽeal—, B. ⁹ O, A.—* om., A; given in C. ᶠ ar—for, B. ᵍ ṽu
hUa, B. ʰ iarum—afterwards, B.

---

³ *Mac Duinnsleibhe.*—(Mac Dunlevy.) The Donnsleibhe from whom the family name took its origin was slain in 1091, *supra.* Eochaid mentioned in the text according to the Ulidian regnal list (L. L. 41d), was son of Conchobur, son of Cu-Ulad Ua Flathrai (killed 1072, *supra*).

⁴ *Donnsleibhe.*—There can be little doubt that he was the same as the Donnsleibhe mentioned in the second entry of the following year. The *Four Masters* omit this portion.

⁵ *For the space of half a year.*—
"Half a yeare bickering and battering and yet could not prevayle,"
C. *Brut y Tywysogion* states (*ad an*). that the king remained many days in camp at Caerleon, until ships from

number of them, including Echmarcach, son of Mac Gilla-espuic and including Ua Lomanaigh and they expelled Eochaidh Mac Duinnsleibhe[5] [Ua Eochadha] from Ulidia. And Ua Lochlainn gave the kingship to Donnsleibhe [Mac Duinnsleibhe Ua Eochadha] and all the Ulidians gave their pledges to Ua Lochlainn, through the might of his regal power.—Diarmait Mac Artain, chief of Clann-Fogartaigh, hospitality and benefaction of all Ui-Echach, died.—An expedition of the Saxons and of the Foreigners of Ath-cliath [set out] with the son of the Empress, to subjugate the Britons and they were all for the space of half a year[5] attacking them and they availed not. And they returned without peace backwards.—Mael-Coluim Great-head, son of Henry, arch-king of Scotland, the best Christian that was of the Gaidhil [who dwell] by the sea on the east for almsdeeds, hospitality and piety, died.—Eochaidh [Mac Duinnsleibhe Ua Eochadha] again attempts to obtain the kingship of Ulidia; but the Ulidians expelled him through fear of Ua Lochlainn and he was fettered by Donnchadh Ua Cerbaill, arch-king of Airgialla, by order of Ua Lochlainn.—Another hosting by Muircertach Ua Lochlainn along with the Cenel-Eogain to Inis-lachain,[6] so that they burned the Island [Inis-lachain] and razed it. And all Ulidia gave their pledges to Ua Lochlainn. After that, the Cenel-Eogain around Ua Lochlainn come to their houses with great triumph and with many ships and numerous treasures beside. From here Ua Lochlainn [goes] to Ard-Macha. After that, Donnchadh Ua Cerbaill, arch-king of Airgialla and Eochaidh Mac Duinnsleibhe

[1165]

Dublin and other cities in Ireland came to him. Finding these forces insufficient, he gave them presents and dismissed them; himself and his army returning to England.

[6] *Inis-lachain.—Duck-island*: Inis-loughan, co. Antrim. See the description by Fynes Moryson, quoted in O'Donovan (*F. M.*, ii. 1154).

Duinnsleibe 7 compail hUi Loclainn, do čuinncid ri͠gi
do Mac Duinnsleibe, co n-daraic¹⁰ hUa Loclainn uile do
Mac Duinnsleibe tar¹¹ cenn¹¹ giall Ulad uile: co n-
daraic¹² Mac Duinnsleibe mac cec toirig d'Ulltaib¹³ 7
a ingin fein i¹⁴ m-braigtečur d'O Loclainn. Ocur tucta
seoit imda dó, im claidiub mic ind Iarla 7 co n-dorat
bairce do¹⁵ hUa¹⁵ Loclainn; co¹⁶ n-daraic¹⁶ hUa Loclainn do¹⁵ hUa¹⁵ Cerbaill é. Ocur tucad dono baile do
cleirčib Sobaill, tria rag rigi hUi Loclainn.

(Domnall' Mac Gilli-Patraic, ri Osraigi; Magnur
hUa Canannan, ri Ceineoil-Conaill; 7 Gilla-Crird hUa
Mail-Brenaind, tairec Clainni-Concobuir, 7 Ma[c]-
Craič hUa Concobuir, ri Ciarraide-Luacra, mortui
runt.')

Kal. Ian. uii. f., l. xx. ui., Anno Domini M.° c.° lx.° ui.°
Domnall' Mac Gille-Močolmo[i]c do marbad do
A 50d Laignib | fein.—Cucuač Mac Gilli-érfuic do marbad
do Dun[n]sleibe, mac mic Eočada.ᵃ—Aed hUa Mael-
fadaill, ri Cairrce-brasaide, do marbad la Muircertač hUa Loclainn fer dolum.—Ard-Mača do lorcad

¹⁰ n-dorat, B. ¹¹⁻¹¹ dar g-cenn, A. ¹²—tartait, A. ¹³ do U—, B. ¹⁴ a, A.
¹⁵⁻¹⁵ dO=do O, A. ¹⁶⁻¹⁶ co tarait, B. ¹¹ n. t. h., A; om., B, C.
A.D. 1166. ᵃ⁻ᵃ om., B, C.

---

⁷ *Sword.*—O'Donovan (p. 1155) says this was evidently won by Mac Duinnsleibe from the Danes of the Hebrides. But he gives no authority for the statement.

⁸ *Domnall, etc.*—Given in the *Annals of Boyle*. The first is a replica of the initial item in the second entry of this year. The *Annals of Boyle*, in agreement with the original text, state that he was slain.

⁹ *King of Ciarraidhe Luachra.*—Lord (*tigherna*) of Ciarraighe-Luachra, *Four Masters*. O'Donovan, by an oversight, has "lord of Conchobbair" (ii. p. 1156).

The *Annals of Boyle*, according to O'Conor's text, have: Gilla-Crist U[a] Mail-Brenaind and M[ac] Craith Ua Conchubur Chiarraigi (O'Conor Kerry) die.

Mail-Brenaind signifies *devotee of*

[Ua Eochadha] come into the presence of Ua Lochlainn, to ask for the kingship for [Eochaidh] Mac Duinnsleibhe, so that Ua Lochlainn gave the entire [kingship] to Mac Duinnsleibhe, in return for the pledges of all Ulidia. So that Mac Duinnsleibhe gave the son of every chief of Ulidia and his own daughter in pledge to O'Lochlainn. And there were given to him [Ua Lochlainn] many treasures, including the sword[7] of the son of the Earl and he [Mac Duinnsleibhe] gave Bairche to Ua Lochlainn [and] Ua Lochlainn gave it to [Donnchadh] Ua Cerbaill. And, moreover, there was given a townland to the clergy of Saball, by reason of the prosperity of the reign of Ua Lochlainn.

(Domnall[8] Mac Gilla-Patraic, king of Ossory; Maghnus Ua Canannain, king of Cenel-Conaill and Gilla-Crisd Ua Mael-Brenaind, chief of Clann-Conchobuir and Ma[c] Craith Ua Concobuir, king of Ciarraide-Luachra,[9] died.)

[1166]

Kalends of Jan. on 7th feria, 26th of the moon, A.D. 1166. Domnall[1] Mac Gilla-Mocholmoic was killed by the Lagenians themselves.—Cucuach Mac Gilla-espuic was killed by Donnsleibhe, grandson of Eochaidh[2] [Ua Eochadha].—Aedh Ua Maelfabhaill, king of Carraic-Bracaidhe, was killed by Muircertach Ua Lochlainn in treachery.—Ard-Macha was burned the day of the feast of [St.] Senan[3] and Wednesday in the incidence[4] of the day of

---

(St.) Brenann (of Clonfert, county Galway).

1166. [1] Domnall.—His name is the last in the genealogy (L. L. 337d) of the kings of the Ui-Dunchadha (a sept that inhabited the portion of Dublin county through which flows the Dodder). He was fourth in descent from the eponymous head, Gilla-Mocholmoic (devotee of St. Mocholmoc—my young Colum— of Terryglas, co. Tipperary, whose feast was Dec. 13). In the pedigree given by O'Donovan (F. M. ii. 816), insert "son of Cellach" (L. L. loc. cit.) before "son of Dunchadh."

[2] Eochaidh.—Died 1051, supra.

[3] Senan.—Of any of the known saints of this name, no feast fell on Wednesday, May 11, in this year. Senan may perhaps be a scribal

la feile Sena[i]n 7ᵃ Cetain ap ai laiti pectmaine 7 octmaḋᵇ uataḋ ap ai aeppa epci*: ιοοn, o cpoip Choluim-cille, na ɔi ppeiṫ co cpoip eppuic Eoʒain 7 o cpoip eppuic Eoʒain in ɔ-apa ppeiṫ co cpoip ɔopuip Rata 7 in Raiṫ uile co n-a templaiḃ,— cenmoṫa pecler poil 7 petaip 7 uaiti ɔo taiʒiḃ apḋena— 7 ppeiṫ ppi Raiṫ aniap,—ιοοn, o ta cpoip Secnaill co cpopa ḃpiʒti, aċtmaḋ becc.—Cenannup 7 Luʒmaʒ¹ 7 Inip-cain-Deʒa 7 cella imɔa aile cpemata[e] punt.— Et Daipe Coluim-cille ex maiope papte cpemata ept 7 in ɔubpeicler ɔo lopcaḋ: quoɔ non auɔitum ept ab antiquip tempopibup.—Ocup Appɔ-mbó ɔo lopcaḋ o Ruaiḋpi, mac Mic² Canai 7 o mac Ʒille-Muipe hUi Monpai³ 7 o Cpotpaiʒiḃ.—Eoċaiḋ Mac Duinnpleiḃe ɔo ḃallaḋ la Muipceptaċ hUa Loclainn, tap planacup Comapba patpaic 7 ḃacla Ippu 7 Donnċaḋa hUi Cepḃaill, ιοοn, aipɔpi Aipʒiall.—Sluaʒaḋ la Ruaiḋpi hUa Concoḃaip i Miḋe, co poʒaiḋ ḃpaiʒti pep Miḋe. Appiḃe co bAt-cliaṫ, co poʒaiḋ ḃpaiʒti Ʒall 7 Mic Mupċaḋa 7 Laiʒen uile. Appiḃe co Dpocat-ata ɔoċum Aipʒiall, co tainiʒ Donnċaḋ hUa Cepḃaill, pi Aipʒiall, i n-a ṫeċ 7 co tap|at ḃpaiʒti ɔó 7 co n-ɔecaiḋ plan iap pin ɔia ṫiʒ, iap n-innapba[ḋ] Diapmata Mic Mupċaḋa, piʒ Laiʒen, ɔap muip.—Sluaʒaḋ la Donnċaḋ hUa

B 52d

---

¹—buṫ, A.   ²ic, A.   ³ Mopnai (by metathesis) B.   ᵇ .uiii., MS. (A)

---

error for *Senach* (of Loch Erne), whose festival corresponded with the textual solar and lunar criteria. The saint's name and the data relative to the day are all omitted by the Four Masters.

⁴ *In the incidence.*—Literally, *on the unit* (particular day).

⁵ *Bishop Eogan.*—Patron of Ardstraw (*Ard-sratha*), co. Tyrone. He is probably the *son of Erc* whom Tirechan mentions as consecrated by St. Patrick. Et venit in Arddsratho et Macc Ercae episcopum ordinavit (Book of Armagh, fol. 15b).

⁶ *Sechnall.*—See A. D. 419, note 1; A.D. 447, note 3, *supra*.

⁷ *Blinded.*—The same is stated in the Ulidian regnal list (L. L. 41d);

the week and the 8th lunar day in the incidence[4] of the age [1166] of the moon : that is, from the Cross of Colum-cille, the two streets to the Cross of Bishop Eogan[5] and from the Cross of Bishop Eogan one of the two streets, up to the Cross of the door of the Close and all the Close with its churches—except the monastery of [SS.] Paul and Peter and a few of the houses besides—and a street towards the Close to the west,—namely, from the Cross of [St.] Sechnall[6] to the Crosses of [St.] Brigit [was burned], except a little.— Cenannus and Lughmagh and Inis-cain of [St.] Daig and many other churches were burned.—Daire of Colum-cille was burned for the greater part and the Penitentiary was burned,—a thing unheard of from ancient times.—And Ard-bo was burned by Ruaidhri, son of Mac Canai and by the son of Gilla-Muire Ua Monrai and by the Crotraighi. —Eochaidh Mac Duinnsleibhe [Ua Eochadha] was blinded[7] by Muircertach Ua Lochlainn, in violation of the protection of the successor of Patrick and of the Staff of Jesus and of Donnchadh Ua Cerbaill, namely, the arch-king of Airgialla.—A hosting by Ruaidhri Ua Concobair into Meath, so that he received the pledges of the Men of Meath. From this, [he marches] to Ath-cliath, so that he received the pledges of the Foreigners and of Mac Murchadha and of all Leinster. From this, to Drochait-atha, to the Airgialla, so that Donnchadh Ua Cerbaill, king of Airgialla, came into his house and gave pledges to him. And he went safe to his house after that, after expelling[8] Diarmait Mac Murchadha, king of Leinster, over sea.— A hosting by Donnchadh Ua Cerbaill, with the Airghialla

---

according to which Eochaidh (having become incapacitated to reign) was succeeded by his brother, Maghnus.

[8] *Expelling*.—The date of Mac Murrough's expulsion is fixed by a contemporaneous marginal note in the Book of Leinster (275, marg. sup.

[CC] Muiri, ir mor in gnim doriṅgned 1 n-hErinn indiu (indon, [1] kalainn Auguist) :

Cerball co n-Cirgiallaib 7 co n-Ui[b]-briuin 7 Connaicnib hi Tir-n-Eogain d'innraigib hUi Loclainn tria erail Ceniuil-Eogain⁵ fein, ar trecab doib hUi⁶ Loclainn, airdrig Erenn. Co tainic rim co dreim uataib do Ceneol-Eogain Tailca-o[i]g do tabairt ammuis forru i fid-O-n-Ectac. Ocur cid iatribe, dotreicrit eirim. Co torcair ann Muirceartac (mac⁵ Neill⁵) hUa Laclainn, airdrig Erenn, 7 rob' é Augurt iartair Tuairce[i]rt Eorpa uile, ar egnaim 7 gairceb. Ocur romarbab uatab do Cenel-Eogain ann, idon, tri fir déc. Mirbail mor 7 firt aibra dorigneb annrin: idon, ri Erenn do tuitim cen cat, cen cliatab, iar rarugub dó Comarba patraic 7 baclu Iru 7 Comarba Coluim-cille 7 Sorcela[i] Martain 7 cléirec imda aile. Rucab tra a corp co hArd-Maca 7 rohabnact and, tar rarugub Comarba | Coluim-cille co n-a famub 7 rotrairc budéin Colum-cille ime 7 toirec macleigind⁷ Daire im a breit d'a[d] reilic.—Diarmait Mac Murcada, toirec Muinnteri-birn, a fuir fratribur interfectur [ert].—Sluagab la Ruaidri hUa Concobair 7 la Tigernan hUa Ruairc co her-ruaib, co tangatur Cenel-Conaill i' n-a tec,' co tardrat a m-braigti do hUa' Concobair, co tarat⁸ det rictiu bó doib, i n-ecmair oir 7 etaig.

⁵Cenel-n-Eo—.A. ⁶O, A. ⁷—inn, A. ⁸tard, B.—ᶜitl., t. h., A; om.' B, C. ᵈdi—to, B; with which C agrees. ᵉi tec hUi Chončobair,—into the house of Ua Conchobair, B. C is in agreement. ᶠom., B, C. The do which precedes hUa in the text is consequently, according to B and C, to be translated to him (Ua Conchobair); not, to (Ua Conchobair).

---

idon, Diarmait, mac Dondc[ad]a Mic Murcada, ri Lagen 7 Gall, do innarba[d] do Fheraib hErenn dar muir. Uc! Uc! a Choimdiu, cid dogen?

[O] Mary, great is the deed that has been done in Ireland to-day

(namely, [on Monday] the Kalends [1st] of August): to wit, Diarmait, son of Dondchadh Mac Murchadha, king of the Lagenians and Foreigners, to be expelled by the Men of Ireland. Alas! alas! O God, what shall I do?

and with the Ui-Briuin and the Conmaicni, into Tir-Eogain, [1166] to attack Ua Lochlainn, by direction of the Cenel-Eogain themselves, in consequence of Ua Lochlainn, arch-king of Ireland, being abandoned by them. So that [Ua Lochlainn] came, with a small party of the Cenel-Eogain of Telach-og, to deliver an assault upon them at Fidh-O-n-Echtach. And even those very men, they abandoned him. So there fell in that place Muircertach (son of Niall) Ua Lachlainn, arch-king of Ireland. And he was the Augustus of all the North-West of Europe for valour and championship. And a few of Cenel-Eogain were killed there, namely, thirteen men. A great marvel and wonderful deed was done then: to wit, the king of Ireland to fall without battle, without contest, after his dishonouring the successor of Patrick and the Staff of Jesus and the successor of Colum-cille and the Gospel[9] of Martin and many clergy besides [by blinding Mac Duinnsleibhe Ua Eochadha]. Howbeit, his body was carried to Ard-Macha and buried there, in dishonour of the successor of Colum-cille with his Community and Colum-cille himself[10] and the head of the students of Daire fasted[10] regarding it,—for his being carried to [Christian] burial.[11]—Diarmait Mac Murchadha, chief of Muinnter-Birn, was slain by his kinsmen.—A hosting by Ruaidhri Ua Conchobair and by Tigernan Ua Ruairc to Essruadh, so that the Cenel-Conaill came into his house [and] gave their pledges to Ua Conchobair [and] he gave them eight score cows, besides gold and clothing.

---

[9] *Gospel of Martin.*—Traditionally believed to have belonged to St. Martin of Tours. (*Adamnan,* p. 324, sq.)

[10] *Himself fasted.*—That is, in the person of his successor, the abbot of Derry. C. has: " Kolum Kille himself fasted;" not, "the Coarb of Colum Kille," etc., as O'Donovan (F. M. ii. 1161) reads.

[11] *To burial.*—Literally, *to his burial.*

(Sluaixeð⁵ la Ruaiðri hUa Conćobair 7 la Diarmait hUa Mail-[Sh]eclainn 7 la Tiʒernan hUa Ruairc illaiʒniḃ, i n-Orraiʒiḃ, hi Mumain, co tanʒaḋur riʒraiḋ Leti Moʒa uile hi teć Ruaiḋri hUi Conćobair, co rorisʒrat he.—Ʒilla Mac Aiblen, comarba Ḃrenainð Cluana-ḟearta, quieuit.⁵—Toirrḋelbaċʰ hUa Ḃriain reʒnauit iterum, Anno Domini 1166.ʰ—No,ⁱ comaḋ ar in kalainn ri tir tic marḃaḋ Muircertaiʒ.¹)

kal. Ian. 1. f., l. uii., Anno Domini M.° c.° lx.° uii.° Muircertać, mac Laʒmainð¹ hUi Duiḃðirma, ri ḟorðroma, tuir airećair Tuairce[i]rt Erenn uile,² ðo marḃaḋ i meḃail la Donnćaḋ hUa Duiḃðirma 7 larin³ Ḃretaiʒ⁴ for lar Muiʒi-bile 7 ða mac tó ðo marḃaḋ ar namaraċ 7 mac ðo ḋalluḋ.—Sluaʒaḋ la Ruaiðri hUa Conćobair co maiṫiḃ Erenn uime co hArð-Mać. Arriḋe co ḃelaċ-ʒrene 7 ariḋe co ḟernaċ-na-meḃla 7 co roṫinolrat Cenel-n-Eoʒain im Niall Mac Loċlainn | ʒrinne caṫa, ðo taḃairt ammair lonʒruirt for ḟeraiḃ Erenn. Rotairmerc tria Dia réin, tria ḃennactain ratraic 7 tria raṫ Ruaiðri hUi Conćobair 7 ḟer n-Erenn arcena, co roiaḋrat Cenel-n-Eoʒain im muine failec irriet na rluaʒ, co n-ḋećaiḋ caċ i n-aʒ a ćeile annrin, tenmoṫat ðoine ðo marḃaḋ. Co rorṁallrað na rluaiʒ iar rin im hUa⁵ Conćobair⁵ ðul⁶ ðo innreḋ 7 lorcuḋ Tire-Eoʒain, co tanʒaður ðrem ðo Chenel-

ᶠᶠ n. t. h., A; m., B, C.   ʰʰ 50d, f. m., n. t. h., A; om., B, C.   ⁱⁱ 50d, r. m., opposite the Sluaʒaḋ entry, t. h., A; om., B, C.

A.D. 1167. ¹Laðmuinn, B. ²--li, B. ³laran, B. ⁴m-ḃ—, B. ⁵⁵ O C- —buir, A. ⁶ðol, B.

---

¹² *A hosting, etc.*—Found in substance in the *Annals of Boyle*.

¹³ *Gilla Mac Aiblen, etc.*—Given also in the *Four Masters*. The *Annals of Innisfallen* add the surname, *Ua Anmchadha* and omit the place. The patronymic (see 1099, note 1, *supra*) leaves little doubt that the see in question was Ardfert, not Clonfert.

¹⁴ *Toirrdelbach, etc.*—This item is contained in the *Annals of Boyle*.

(A hosting[13] by Ruaidhri Ua Conchobair and by Diarmait Ua Mail[-Sh]echlainn and by Tigernan Ua Ruairc into Leinster, [and] into Ossory [and] into Munster, so that the kings of all the Half of Mogh came into the house of Ruaidhri Ua Conchobair [and] made him [arch-]king.—Gilla Ma[i]c Aiblen[13] successor of [St.] Brenand of Cluain-fearta, rested.—Toirrdelbach[14] [Ua Briain] reigned again, A.D. 1166.—Or it may be on this year below [next year] the killing of Muircertach [Ua Lochlainn] occurs.)

[1166]

Kalends of Jan. on 1st feria, 7th of the moon, A.D. 1167. Muircertach, son of Lagmand Ua Duibhdirma, king of Fordruim, tower of principality of all the North of Ireland, was killed in treachery by Donnchadh Ua Duibdirma and by the Bretach in the centre of Maghbile and two sons of his were killed on the morrow and a son was blinded.—A hosting by Ruaidhri Ua Concobair with the nobles of Ireland about him to Ard-Macha. From this [they marched] to Belach-grene and from this to Fernach-na-mebhla, until the Cenel-Eogain collected a fighting force around Niall Mac Lochlainn, to deliver a camp attack upon the men of Ireland. Howbeit, God prevented that, through the benediction of Patrick and through the felicity of Ruaidhri Ua Concobair and of the Men of Ireland likewise. For [*lit.*, so that] the Cenel-Eogain closed around a sallow brake that appeared like[1] the [opposing] forces, so that each [of them] proceeded to slaughter the other there, except that persons were not killed. So the hosts after that proceeded under Ua Conchobair to go to pillage and burn Tir-Eogain, until some

[1167]

1167. [1] *That appeared like.*—Literally, *in the appearance* (of). The translator of C. mistook the meaning: "For Kindred Owen strayed into a grove of willowes and, thinking it was the camp, fell upon it and killed some of themselves."

Eogain 1 n-a ceċ 7 co n-vaporac bpaiṡci vo 7ª co n-veċacap 1ap pin, ap puc Pep-Manaé 7 vo Epp-puaiḃ, implan via ciṡ.—Mael-Miċel⁰ Mac Doiteċa[1]n uapalpacapc 7 pepleiṡinn 1 n-Apv-Maċa, puam uicam peliciceр piniuic.ᵇ—Muipeḃaċ Mac Canai vo mapbaḋ vo macaiḃ Meic Loċlainn 1 n-éineċ Pacpaic 7 Baċlu Ipu, 1ap n-a epail via bpaiṫpiḃ pein.

(Uacu hUa Conċenainv, pi hUa-n-Diapmaca, in clep[1]cacu mopicup.—Diapmaic Mac Mupċaḋa vo ċuivecc cap muip in bliaḋain pi.—Coippvelḃaċ hUa Opiain vo eg in bliaḋain pi.ᶜ)

Kal. 1an. 11. p., L x. uiii., Anno Domini M.° c.° lx.° uiii.° Muipcepcaċ, mac Coippvelbaiṡ hUi Opiain, pi Dail-Caip, vo mapbaḋ ic Oun-na- | pciaḋ vo mac Mupċaḋa Mic Capċaiṡ, pi Oep-Muman. Romapbaḋ po ċecoip mac mic Concoḃaip 1² n-a² viṡail la Diapmaic pino 7 la hUa Paela[i]n 7 peċcª meic piṡ co n-a muinncepaiḋ.—Plannacan hUa Duḃcaiċ, eppcop na Cuac (8il-ᵇ Muipevaiṡᵇ), pui ecnai 7 pencaip lapcaip Epenn uile, 1 Cungu ic ailiṫpi mopcu[u]p epc.—8luaṡaḋ la Ruaiḋpi hUa Concobuip co hAċ-luain, co cainic Ua 5illa-Pacpaic, pi Oppaiṡi 1 n-a ceċ³ 7 co capaic ceiṫpi⁴ bpaiṡci vo annpein⁴ 7 popleic a pluaṡu peime vap Aċ-cpoċa ipin Mumain 7 pe pein vap Aċ-luain 1 Maṡ-Léna 1 conne Pep n-Epenn: co panṡavup

ᵃom., B.   C follows A.   ᵇᵇom., B, C.   ᶜⁿn. t. h., A; om., B, C.

A.D. 1168. ¹ Oal, B. ²²na (aphaeresis of a), B. ³ ceṡ, A. ⁴ ainn—, A.
ᵃ .iiii., A, B. ᵇᵇ itl., t. h., A; om., B, C. ᶜ .iiii., A, B.

---

² *In reparation, etc.*—This portion is omitted by the Four Masters. The offence is not stated in any authority accessible to me. For the vendetta, see the first item of 1170.

³ *A cleric.*—In Clonmacnoise according to the *Four Masters*, who give the three items. The second is found in the *Annals of Innisfallen*; the third, in the *Annals of Boyle*.

⁴ *From over sea.*—According to

of the Cenel-Eogain came into his house and gave hostages to him. And they went after that, through the length of Fir-Manach and to Ess-ruadh, safe to their home[s].—Mael-Michel Mac Doithechain, eminent priest and lector in Ard-Macha, felicitously finished his life.—Muiredhach Mac Canai was killed by the sons of Mac Lochlainn in reparation[2] to Patrick and the Staff of Jesus, by direction of his own kinsmen.

[1167]

(Uatu Ua Conchenaind, king of Ui-Diarmata, dies a cleric.[3]—Diarmait Mac Murchadha came from over sea[4] this year.—Toirrdelbach[5] Ua Briain died this year.)

Kalends of Jan. on 2nd feria, 18th of the moon, A.D. 1168. Muircertach, son of Toirrdelbach Ua Briain, king of Dal-Cais, was killed at Dun-na-sciath by the son[1] of Murchadh Mac Carthaigh, king of Desmond. The grandson of Conchobar [Ua Briain] was killed immediately in revenge of him by Diarmait the Fair and by Ua Faelain and seven sons of kings with their retinues [were killed].—Flannacan Ua Dubhtaich, bishop of the Tuatha (Sil-Muiredaigh) [Elphin], the master of wisdom and history in [*lit.*, of] all the West of Ireland, died in pilgrimage at Cunga.—A hosting by Ruaidhri Ua Concobuir to Ath-luain, so that Ua [*recte*, Mac] Gilla-Patraic, king of Ossory, came into his house and gave four hostages to him on the occasion. And he sent his hosts forward, past Ath-crodha, into Munster and himself [went] past Ath-luain into Magh-

[1168 Bis.]

Giraldus Cambrensis (*Exp. Hib.* I. 2), he had gone to Henry II. (who was in Aquitane) and procured letters patent in his favour. He then returned to England, obtained promises of aid from Robert Fitz Stephen and Maurice Fitz Gerald, sailed from Bristol about August 1, and spent the winter in concealment at Ferns.

[5] *Toirrdelbach.*—In the *Annals of Boyle* he is called king of the *Half of Mogh* (the southern moiety of Ireland).

1168. [1] *Son of Murchadh Mac Carthaigh.*—This (which is likewise the reading of C.) must be an error. The *Annals of Innisfallen*, an authority not likely to err on a matter of the kind, state that the

co Ṡpein-cliaċ, co táinic Mac Captaiġ ı n-a ṫeċ 7 co ṫapaıc noı[d] m-bpaıġtı ṅó annrein[*] 7 co popoinneṅ ın Muma ı n-ṅó etep mac Copmaıc 7 Ḋoṁnall hUa Ḃpıaın 7 co pucaṅ ṅa pıċıṫ[ꞇ] ṅec bó po tpı, ı n-aıneċlann Muıpceptaıċ hUı Ḃpıaın, pop Ḋep-Mumaın. Co poimpaí hUa Concobaıp ṅıa tıġ.—Ḋonnċaṅ hUa Cepbaıll, aıpṅpı[5] Aıpġıall, ṅo letpaṅ ṅo ṫuaıġ ġıllaı [p]pıṫoliṁa ṅó péın, ıṅon, Ua Ḋuıbne ṅo Ceniul[6]-Eoġaın 7 ın pí pop mépca 7 a éc ṅé.

(Maıṅm[e] Aṫa-ın-ċomaıp pop Apt hUa Maıl-Sheċlaınn 7 pop Aıpṫıup Mıṅe. Ḋıapmaıt U Maıl-Seċlaınn 7 la[p]ṫap Mıṅe uıctopes puepunt.—In ġılla Leıṫṅepġ, ıṅon, hUa Concobaıp Copcumpuaṅ, occıpup eꞅt.[ꞇ])

B 53b |Cal. 1an. 1111.[a] p., L xx. ıx[*], Anno Ḋomını M.[o] c.[o] lx.[o] ıx.[*] Ḋaṁlıac Cıanna[ı]n ṅo lopcaṅ.—Ḋıapmaıt hUa Mael-Seċlaınn, pí Mıṅe, ṅo mapbaṅ ṅo mac a bpaṫap, ıṅon, ṅo Ḋomnall Ḃpeġaċ 7 ṅo Ḋonnċaṅ Ceınnpelaċ hUa Ceallaıġ.—Ipın blıaṅaın cétna ṅopat Ruaıṅpı hUa Concobaıp, pí Epenn, ṅeıċ m-bú ceċa[1] blıaṅna uaṅ péın 7 o caċ[2] pıġ ı n-a ṅeġaıṅ co bpaṫ ṅo peplleıġınn Aıpṅ-Maċa, ı n-onoıp Patpaıc, ap leıġınn ṅo ṅenaṁ ṅo macaıḃleıġınnEpenn 7 Alban.

A. [5]—pıġ, A. [6]—neol, A. [d].ıx., A, B. [e] om., A, C. [f].xx.ıt., A, B. [g-g] n. t. b., A; om., B, C.

A.D. 1169. [1] ġaċa, A. [2] ġaċ, B.—[a-a] n. t. b., A; a blank was left by the original scribe. [b] om., A.

---

slayer was Conchobar, grandson of Conchobar Ua Briain. This agrees also with the next assertion of the present entry.

[2] *Whilst.*—Literally, *and.* The altercation was provoked by the king when intoxicated.

[3] *Died.*—Not immediately. According to the entry in the Four Masters, O'Carroll died "after victory of Unction and penance and after granting three hundred ounces of gold for love of the Lord to clerics and to churches." His death is given in the *Annals of Innisfallen* under the following year.

This, most likely, is the true date. For according to a eulogistic obit in the *Antiphonary of Armagh*, he

Lena, to meet the Men of Ireland, until they reached [1168] Grian-cliach, so that Mac Carthaigh came into his house and gave nine hostages to him on the occasion. And Munster was divided in two, between the sons of Cormac [Mac Carthaigh] and Domnall Ua Briain and thrice twelve score cows were levied upon Munster in honour fine [of the killing] of Muircertach Ua Briain. So Ua Conchobair returned to his house.—Donnchadh Ua Cerbaill, arch-king of Airgialla, was mangled with the [battle-]axe of a serving gillie of his own, namely, Ua Duibhne of Cenel-Eogain, whilst [*lit.*, and] the king [was] drunk and he died[3] thereof.

(The defeat[4] of Ath-in-chomair [was inflicted] upon Art Ua Mail-Sechlainn and the West of Meath were victors. —"The Half-red[-faced][5] Gillie," namely, Ua Concobair of Corcumruadh, was slain.)

Kalends of Jan. on 4th feria, 29th of the moon, A.D. 1169. Damhliac of [St.] Ciannan was burned.—Diarmait Ua Mael-Sechlainn, king of Meath, was killed by the son of his brother, namely, by Domnall of Bregha[1] and by Donnchadh Ceinnselach Ua Ceallaigh.—In the same year, Ruaidhri Ua Concobair, king of Ireland, gave[2] ten cows

---

died in 1170, B. 1. 1., T.C.D.: the—left-hand—page opposite the opening of the Calendar; the luni-solar criteria of the year are given. See Petrie, *Round Towers*, p. 391, where for conuenꞃ the MS. has conueꞃꞃ—*lay-brothers* (not, "*conventuals*").

[4] *The defeat, etc.*—This item is given in substance in the *Annals of Boyle*, and more circumstantially in the *Four Masters*. The other entry is given in both and in the *Annals of Innisfallen*.

[5] *Half-red[-faced]*.—Cf. the *Feast of Bricriu* (L. U. 106a, ll. 34-5): *Drech lethderg, lethgabur laiss*—countenance half-red, half white had he [*lit.*, with him].

1169. [1] *Domnall of Bregha.*—"Donell Bregagh (id est, liar)"! C. But *Bregach* here is not from *breg*, a lie, but from *Breg*, (the plain of) Bregia, the eastern portion of Meath; from having been fostered in which Domnall was so called.

[2] *Gave.*—This endowment shows that O'Conor claimed to be supreme king of Ireland.

(ꝼerċaiꞃ° hUa Niallain, ταiꞃeċ Clainni-Uαtαċ, moꞃtuuꞃ eꞃt.—Loinʒeꞃ Roбeꞃꞅ mic Stemin ꝺo ꞅiαċταin i n-Eꞃinn, hi ꞅoꞃiʒin Mic Muꞃċαꝺα.—Raʒnall hUa Mαilmiαꝺαiʒ, τaiꞃeċ Muinnτiꞃi-hΘolaiꞃ, moꞃτuuꞃ eꞃτ. —Conʒαlaċ hUa Tomalταiʒ, ꞅeꞃleiʒinꝺ Cluana-mac-Noiꞅ 7 uaꞃalꝼaccaꞃτ, quieuiτ.ᵃ)

Kal. Ian. uᵃ. ꝼ., L xᵃ., Œnno Domini M.° c.° Lxx.° Concoбaꞃ, mac Muiꞃceꞃτaiʒ hUi Loċlainn, ꞃi Ceneoil-Eoʒain 7 ꞃiꝺomna Eꞃenn uile, ꝺo maꞃбaꝺ ꝺo Œeꝺ bic Mac Canaeˡ 7 ꝺoˀ Uibˀ-Caꞃaca[i]n, Dia-8aταiꞃn Caꞃc, A 51c aꞃ laꞃ Tꞃin moiꞃ i n-Œꞃꝺ-Maċa.— | Donnċaꝺ Ceinn-ꞃealaċ hUa Ceallaiʒ ꝺo maꞃбaꝺ ꝺo Laiʒniб.

(8luaiʒeꝺᵇ la Ruaiꝺꞃi hUa Conċoбaiꞃ 7 la Mail-8eaċlainn 7 la Tiʒeꞃnan hUa Ruaiꞃc 7 la Muꞃċaꝺ hUa Ceꞃбuill cu hŒτ-cliaτ i n-aiꞃiꞃ caτα ꝺo Mac Muꞃċαꝺα 7 ꝺo'nꝺ Iaꞃla. In τan τꞃα ꞃoбαꝺαꞃ aꞃ i n-aiʒτi ic [ꝼ]iꞃnaiꝺi in ċαtα, nuċuꞃꞃατꞃeiʒꞃeτ nucuꝼaccaꝺaꞃ in ꝺun τꞃe ċeiniꝺ, iꝺon, τeni ꝺi aiτt. Roꝼoi ꝺono iaꞃ ꞅen hUa Conċuбαiꞃ, iαꞃ ꞅemiꝺ ċατα ꝺo τaбαiꞃτ ꝺo. Roċuaiꝺ iαꞃ ꞅein Mac Muꞃċαꝺα inn-Œτ-cliατ, iaꞃ τaбαiꞃτ бꞃeiτꞃi ꝺo Ʒhallaiб Œτα-cliατ ꝺo. Ocuꞅ ꞃoꝼeall ꞅoꞃ a бꞃeiτiꞃ 7 ꞃomaꞃбaꝺ ꝺaine imꝺα ann 7 ꞃoinnaꞃb na Ʒalla.—бꞃaiʒꝺe. Mic Muꞃċαꝺα, iꝺon, a m[h]ac ꞃein 7 mac a m[h]ic, iꝺon, mac Domnaill Chaemanaiʒ 7 mac a

ᵃᵃ n. t. b., A; om., B, C.
A.D. 1170. ¹ Cana, B. ²⁻² ꝺUib=ꝺo Uib, B. ᵃ⁻ᵃ n. t. h., a blank was left by the first scribe, A. ᵇᵇ 51c, f. m.; 51d, t. m., n. t. h., with corresponding marks on the margin at end of the Œτh-cliατh item and prefixed to the added entry, A; om., B, C.

³ *Students.*—"Scollers," C. ; not, "strollers [i.e. poor scholars]," as in O'Donovan (F. M. ii. 1174).

⁴ *Ferchair, etc.*—All these entries are given by the *Four Masters*. The two first are found in the *Annals of Boyle*.

⁵ *Fitz Stephen.* — See Gilbert's *Viceroys of Ireland*, p. 12 sq. Cambrensis (*Exp. Hib.* i. 3), states that he arrived with 390 men in three ships, landing at Bannow about May 1.

1170. ¹ *Was killed.*—See the last

every year from himself and from every king after him [1169] to doom to the lector of Ard-Macha, in honour of [St.] Patrick, to give lectures to students[3] of Ireland and Scotland.

(Ferchair[4] Ua Niallain, chief of the Clann-Uatach, died.—The fleet of Robert Fitz Stephen[5] came to Ireland in aid of Mac Murchadha.—Ragnall Ua Mailmiadhaigh, chief of Muinnter-Eolais, died.—Conghalach Ua Tomaltaigh, lector of Cluain-mac-Nois and eminent priest, died.)

Kalends of Jan. on 5th feria, 10th of the moon, A.D. [1170] 1170. Concobhar, son of Muircertach Ua Lochlainn, king of Cenel-Eogain, royal heir of all Ireland, was killed[1] by Aedh Mac Cana the Little and by the Ui-Caraca[i]n, Easter [Holy] Saturday [April 4], in the centre of the Great Third in Ard-Macha.—Donnchadh Ceinnselach Ua Cellaigh was killed by the Leinstermen.

(A hosting[2] by Ruaidhri Ua Conchobair and by Mael-Sechlainn and by Tigernan Ua Ruairc and by Murchadh Ua Cerbuill to Ath-cliath to give battle to Mac Murchadha and to the Earl.[3] When, however, they were face to face preparing for the battle, they noticed no[thing] until they saw the fort on fire, that is, [by] fire of lightning. Howbeit, after that Ua Conchubair turned back, after refusal of battle was offered to him. Thereafter, Mac Murchadha went into Ath-cliath, after giving his word to the Foreigners of Ath-cliath. And he failed upon his word and many persons were killed there and he expelled the Foreigners. The hostages of Mac Murchadha, namely, his own son[4] and his grandson, that is, the son of

---

(original) entry under 1167 (*supra*).

[2] *A hosting, etc.*—This hosting occurred prior to the second capture of Dublin, the chief item in the following entry. The sequence intended (textual note b-b) by the interpolator is consequently erroneous.

[3] *The Earl.*—Strongbow. See Gilbert, *loc. cit.*

[4] *Son.*—Conchobar (Conor), the

c[h]omalta, ıdon, mac hUı Chaellaıðe, do marbað la Ruaıðrı hUa Conchubaır, cre arlach Tıgernaın hUı Ruaırc.[b])

Ath-cliath do milleð do Dhıarmaıt Mac Murchaða 7 do Allmurchaıð[3] tuc leır anaır do mıllıuð na hErenn ı[4] n-dıgaıl a ınnarb[th]a dar muır ar a ferunn fein 7 a mhıc do marbað. Tucrat dono ar for Gallaıb Ath-cliath 7 Puırt-laırgı 7 tucta tra aır ımda forrurum. Do milltea dono Laıgın 7 Fır-Miðe, eter cella 7 tuata, leó 7 rogabrat At-cliath 7 Purt-Laırgı.

Gnım mór aınrıal do ðenum do'n manach, ıdon, do Amlaım, mac Comarba Fınnéın Muıgı-bıle 7 do Magnur Mac Duınnrleıðe, do ríg Ulað, co toırıgıð Ulað 7 co n-Ultaıð archena, cenamota Mael-Iru, erруc 7 Gılla-Domangaırt Mac Cormaıc, comarba Comgaıll 7 Mael-Martaın, comarba Fınnéın co n-a muınnteraıð: ıdon, Coımtınol Canonach Rıagulla co n-a n-abaıð, roорdaıg Mael-Moedoıc hUa Morgaır, Legaıt Comarba Petaır, ı Saball Patraıc, do ınnarba[ð] arın Maınırtır rocumdaıgretar féın 7 do° arcaın[e] co leır, eter Libru 7 aıðmí, bu 7 daınıu, eochu 7 caırchıu 7 na huıle rotınoılat ann o aımrır ın Legaıt rempaıtı

[3] Allmar—, B. [4] a, A. [e-o] a n-argaın—*they were despoiled* (lit., *their despoiling*), B; followed by C.

---

only legitimate son of Mac Murrough. The phonetic form is accurately given by Cambrensis (*Cnuchurum. Exp. Hib.* i. 10).

[5] *Dumnall Carmanach.* — Anglicized Kavanagh. He was so called, according to Keating (O'Donovan, *F. M.* ii. 1143), from having been fostered at Cell-Caemhain (church of St. Caemhan; Kilcavan, near Gorey, co. Wexford). He was the illegitimate son of Dermot and eponymous head of the Mac Morrough Kavanaghs. (See O'Donovan, *F. M.* iii., 20.)

[6] *Ath-cliath.*—Opposite this word, on the right margin, in A, there is a Latin note which is partly cut away, in consequence of trimming the edges. The remainder is, except a few isolated words, wholly illegible. Iste [Mac] [Mur]chad . . filius . . uxorem . . Hiberniae . . . ab Hibernia ex[pulsus] in sui subsidium ad Hiberniam . . .

Domnall Caemanach[5] and the son of his foster-brother, to [1170] wit, the son of Ua Caellaidhe, were killed by Ruaidhri Ua Conchubhair, through suggestion of Tigernan Ua Ruairc.)

Ath-cliath[5] was destroyed by Diarmait Mac Murchadha and by the transmarine men he brought with him from the east to destroy Ireland, in revenge for his expulsion over sea out of his own land and of the killing of his son. Howbeit, they inflicted slaughter upon the Foreigners of Athcliath and Port-lairgi and, on the other hand, many slaughters were inflicted upon themselves. Moreover, Leinster and the country of Meath, both churches and territories, were destroyed by them and they took Ath-cliath and Port-lairgi.

A great, unbecoming deed was done by the monk, namely, by Amlaimh, son of the successor of [St.] Finnian of Magh-bile and by Magbnus Mac Duinnsleibhe [Ua Eochadha], king of Ulidia, along with the chiefs of Ulidia and with the Ulidians besides, except the bishop, Mael-Isu and Gilla-Domanghairt[7] Mac Cormaic, successor of [St.] Comgall and Mael-Martain, successor of [St.] Finnian, with their communities: that is, the Congregation of Canons Regular, with their abbot, whom Mael-Moedoic Ua Morgair, Legate of the successor of [St.] Peter, instituted in Saball of [St.] Patrick, were expelled out of the

---

tum primum . . . Maricium . . . atque . .

The meaning was probably in substance that Mac Murrough was expelled from Ireland for the abduction of O'Rourke's wife and engaged Fitz Gerald and Fitz Stephen to aid him in recovering his kingdom.

The textual entry displays considerable confusion. The order of the events is as follows: (1) East Leinster laid waste; (2) Dublin submits to Mac Murrough; (3) Waterford taken with great loss of life; (4) Dublin taken, followed by slaughter of the citizens; (5) Meath laid waste; (6) Mac Murrough's son (and the other hostages) slain by O'Conor.

[7] *Gilla-Domanghairt.*—See 1058, note 2, *supra.*

conice ṛéin, cenmotát na ínaıp 7 na capaı ṛobatap[5] ímpu ıṛınd uaıṛ ṛéin, tṛıa ṛoṛmat 7 baıṫ collaıṫe 7 ṛaınt onóıṛı dó ṛéin. Uaıṛ ṛodıċuıṛṛetaṛ manaıẋ. Oṛoċaıt-ata é aṛan abdaıne, tṛıa ċuıṛıd dlıẋteċaıṫ. Uċ! Uċ! Uċ! tṛa. Maıṛẋ doṛóne 7 maıṛẋ ċıṛ[d] ı n-deṛnaṫ[d] ın ẋnım. Aċt ní deċaıṫ[6] cen ınneċaṫ[7] o'n Coımdıẋ; uaıṛ ṛomaṛbaıt ı n-oınṛeċt[8] o uaıtıṫ naıṁat na toıṛıẋ doṛone 7 ṛoẋonaṫ ın ṛí 7 ṛomaṛbaṫ ẋaṛ bıc ıaṛtaın co haınṛeċtnaċ[9] ıṛın baıle ı n-deṛnaṫ ın coṁaıṛle aınṛıṛen ṛın, ıdon, ı n-Oun. Oıa-Maıṛt tṛa ṛodıċuıṛeṫ ın Coımtínol. Oıa-Maıṛt tṛa,[e] ı cınn blıadna, ṛomaṛbaıt maıtı Ulaṫ 7 ṛoẋonaṫ a ṛıẋ. Oıa-Maıṛt, ẋaıṛıt ıaṛtaın, ṛomaṛbaṫ é ṛein o [a] deṛbṛataıṛ ı n-Oun.—Oıaṛmaıt hUa Aınbṛeıt,[10] ṛí hUa-Meıt 7 coıṛeċ maṛcṛluaıẋı ṛıẋ Aı Lıẋ, do maṛbaṫ do Lonẋaıṛ táıṁe a hInnṛıṫ-Oṛcc ıṛın ınnṛı ṛocumtaıẋeṫ aca ṛéın ṛoṛ Loċ-Ruıṫe,[f] ıdon, ṛoṛ Inıṛ-Lacaın.[f]

A 61d |Cal. Ian. uı.[a] ṛ., L. xx. ı.,[a] Anno Domini M.° c.° lxx.° ı.° Oıaṛmaıt Mac Muṛċada, ṛí Coıcıḋ Laıẋen, ıaṛ mılleṫ ceall n-ımḋa 7 tuat, do éc ı ṛeṛna, cen onẋaṫ, cen Coṛp Cṛıṛt, cen aıṫṛıẋı, cen tımna, ı n-eıneċ Coluım-cılle 7 Ṛınneın 7 na naem aṛċena, ı-ṛa cella ṛoṁıll.—Aṛcall, mac Toṛcaıll, ṛı Aṫa-

[5] baṫaṛ B. [6] deo—, A. [7] ınnea—, A. [8] oın[ṛ]eċt (ṛ om.), A. [9] hanṛeċtna, B. [10] Aınṛeıt, A.—[d-d] repeated without being deleted, B. [e] om., A. [f] n. t. h. (from Ruıṫe inclusive), A. Omitted by oversight, most likely.
A.D. 1171. [a-a] n. t. h., on blank left by first scribe, A.

---

[8] *Drochait-atha*—The monastery of Mellifont, near Drogheda (*Drochait-atha—Bridge of the Ford*), is intended. The charges against Anlaimh, abbot of Saul (Sabhall), co. Down, were investigated in that community, with the result stated in the text.

[9] *For, etc.*—See the fifth entry under the following year.

[10] *He himself.*—That is, the king. The monk, Amlaimh, became bishop (1175, *infra*).

1171. [1] *Without Unction, etc.*—. In the List in L.L. (p. 39d), on the other hand, he is said to have died

monastery they themselves built and were despoiled com- [1170]
pletely, both of books and furniture, cows and persons,
horses and sheep and all things they had collected therein
from the time of the Legate aforesaid to then, save the
tunics and the capes which were upon them at that hour,—
through carnal jealousy and self-love and desire of honour
for himself. For the monks of Drochait-atha[8] deposed him
from the abbacy [of Saball] for just causes. Alas! alas! alas!
in sooth. Woe who did and woe the country wherein was
done the deed. But it went not without vengeance from
the Lord; for[9] the chiefs who did it were killed at one and
the same time by a few enemies and the king was wounded
and killed unhappily a little while after, in the place
wherein that unrighteous counsel was decided upon, namely,
in Dun. Now, on Tuesday the Congregation was expelled;
on Tuesday, at the end of a year, the nobles of Ulidia were
killed and the king was wounded; on Tuesday, a little
after, he himself[10] was killed by his brother in Dun.—
Diarmait Ua Ainbfheith, king of Ui-Meith and leader of the
horse-host of the king of Ailech, was killed by a fleet that
came from the Islands of Orcc to the Island that was
built by himself upon Loch-Ruidhe, namely, upon Inis-
Lachain.

Kalends of Jan. on 6th feria, 21st of the moon, A.D. [1171]
1171. Diarmait Mac Murchadha, king of the Fifth of
Leinster, after destroying many churches and territories,
died in Ferna without Unction,[1] without Body of Christ,
without penance, without a will, in reparation to Colum-
cille and Finnian and to the saints besides, whose churches
he destroyed.—Ascall,[2] son of Torcall, king of Ath-cliath

---

in the 61st year of his age and the | *iar sin* (The Saxons after that)
46th of his reign, after victory of | miserabiliter regnant. Amen,
Unction and penance. The com- | Amen.
piler of the List adds: *Saxain* | [2] *Ascall—John.*—See the account

cliaṫ 7 Eoan (mearʙ) a hInnriḃ-Orc (ṫainic, a forṫaċṫ Arcaill 7 Ghall Aṫa-cliaṫʙ) do marbaḋ do na Gallaiḃ ceṫna.—Domnallꞌ hUa Focarṫa, ri Eile-deir-cirṫ, do marbaḋ la Orraiġiḃ.ᶜ—Saḋḃ, inġen Gluin-iairnn Mic Murċaḋa, comarba Briġṫe, do ec i n-aiṫriġe. —Creċ mór la Maġnur Mac Duinnrleiḃe co n-Ullṫaiḃ uile i Cuil-in-ṫuairce[i]rṫ, co roairgreṫ Cuil-raṫain 7 cealla aile, co rucraṫ uaṫaḋ bec do Chenel-Eoġain forroᵈ, im Conċobur Ua Caṫa[i]n 7 co ṫucraṫ cliaṫaḋ 7 co romarbṫaṫ fer ar ficiṫ², eṫer ṫoireċu 7 macu ṫoireċ¹ 7 roċaiḋe aile maille friu 7 roġonaḋ Maġnur féin.ᵈ Ocur in Maġnur rin dono, | domarbaḋ ġairiṫ iarṫainᵉ do Dunnrleiḃe, idonᵈ, d'a derbraṫair féin 7 do Gilla-Oenġura Mac Gilla-errruic, idon, do reṫṫaire Monaċ, i n-Dun, iar n-olcaiḃ moraiḃ imḋaiḃ do ḋenum dó : idon, iar lecuḋ a ṁná forṫa féin 7 iar m-breiṫ a ṁná o [a] aiṫi, idon, o Choin-maiġi hUa³ Fhlainn 7 ri ac a derbraṫair féin ar ṫúr, idon, ic Aeḋ ; iar ṫabairṫ eisin doᵈ dono for mnai a derbraṫar aile, idon, Eoċaḋa ; iar faruġuḋ cloc 7 baċall, cleireċ 7 cell. Donnrleiḃe do ġabail riġi i' n-aꞌ deġaiḋ.—Ane, inġen Mic Duinnrleiḃe, riġan Oirġiall, do éc.—Maidm (idon,ᶠ maidm in Luaiṫredᵍ) for Tiġernan hUa Ruaireʰ 7 for Feraib Miḋe 7 ar Feraib Fern-muiġi imal[l]eᵈ ar faiċṫi Aṫa-cliaṫ ria Milo de Cocan⁵ co n-a muinnṫer, dú i ṫorċair roċaiḋe

A.D. 1171. ¹ ṫoirniċ, A. ²xx. iṫ, A, B. ³O, A. ⁴ male (aphaeresis of i), A. ⁵Gogan, B. ᵇ iṫl., n. t. h., A; om., B, C. ᵇᵇ iil., n. t. h., A; om., B, C. ᶜ⁻ᶜ om., B, C. ᵈ om., A. ᵉ iar féin—*after that*, B. ᶠ n-a (aphaeresis of i), A. ᶠᵍ c. m., n. t. h., A, C; Maidm an Luaṫfriġ, fecundum quordam.— *Defeat of the Ashes, according to some*, r. m., n. t. h., B. ʰ ar—*on*, B.

of their deaths in Giraldus Cambrensis (*Exp. Hib.*), or Gilbert (*ubi sup.* p. 19 sq.).

³ *Mad.* — Duce Johanne agnomine *the Wode*, quod Latine sonat Insano, vel Vehementi (*Exp. Hib.* i. 21).

⁴ *Cuil-in-tuaiscirt.*—*Corner of the North* (or co. Antrim); in which *Cuil-rathain*,—*Corner of the fern*,— Coleraine, is situated.

and John³ (the Mad) from the Islands of Orc (who came [1171] in aid of Torcall and of the Foreigners of Ath-cliath) were killed by the same Foreigners.—Domnall Ua Focarta, king of the South of Eili, was killed by the Ossorians.—Sadhbb, daughter of Iron-knee Mac Murchadha, successor of [St.] Brigit [i.e. abbess of Kildare] died in penance.—Great foraying force [was led] by Maghnus Mac Duinnsleibhe [Ua Eochadha] with all Ulidia into Cuil-in-tuaisceirt⁴, so that they plundered Cuil-rathain and other churches, until a small number of the Cenel-Eogain under Conchobur Ua Cathain overtook them and gave battle and killed one and twenty men, both chiefs and sons of chiefs, and a multitude of others along with them. And Maghnus himself was wounded. And moreover that Maghnus was killed shortly after in Dun by Donnsleibhe, that is, by his own brother and by Gilla-Oenghusa Mac Gilla-espuic, namely, by the lawgiver of Monaigh,⁵ after great evils had been done by him,—namely, after leaving his own wedded wife and after taking his wife from his fosterer, that is, from Cu-maighi Ua Flainn and she [had been] the wife of his own brother at first, namely, of Aedh; after inflicting violence upon the wife of his other brother also, that is, of Eochaidh; after profanation of bells and croziers, clerics and churches. Donnsleibhe took the kingship in his stead.—Ane, daughter of the Mac Duinnsleibhe [Ua Eochadha] queen of Airghialla,⁶ died.—Defeat (namely, the Defeat of the Ashes⁷) [was inflicted] upon Tigernan Ua Ruairc and upon the Men of Meath and upon the Men of Fern-magh, all together, on the Green of Ath-cliath

---

³ *Lawgiver of Monaigh.*—" The monks heard, or servant!" C. The translator took Monaigh, a local name, to be genitive of *manach* a monk.

⁶ *Queen of Airghialla.*—According to the entry in the Four Masters, she was wife of Murrough O'Carroll, king of that territory.

⁷ *Defeat of the Ashes.*—So called perhaps from having been inflicted on Ash-Wednesday. But Cam-

M

mór,ım Ceð hUa Ruaıpc,pí Macaıpe-ʒaıleṅʒ 7 pıoomna hUa-bpıuın 7 Cconmaıcne. Romapbṫa oono ann cóıc toıpıʒe oo fepaıð fepn-ṁuıʒe, ıoon, Mael-Moċta Mac Confebla 7 Concoḃuıp, a oepḃpaṫaıp, oa ṫoıpeċ Cheneoıl-fepaoaıʒ.—féníð hUa Conʒaıle, caınnel ʒaıpcıð 7 eínıʒ Oıpʒıall,⁶ moptuuıʳ eʳτ.ˡ—Raʒnall͡c hUa Cuaτċaıp, toıpeċ Claınnı-Ruaoṗaċ ; ʒılla-ʒeímpıð Ṁac-ın-ʒabano, toıpeċ fep-Oapcaċa 7 pocaıðe aıle maılle ppıu, non longe popτ puppaoıcτa, oecımo pexτo Kalenoap Nouem-bpıpᵉ [moptuı puṅt].— | Uenıτ ın hıbepnıam henpıcuṡ (macᵇ na Peıpıpıᵇ), potentıppımuṡ pex Cngliae et ıoem Oux Noṙmannı[a]e et Ccquıτanı[a]e et Comep Cnoe-ʒauu[a]e et alıapum multaṙum teṙṙapum oomınuṡ, cum oucentıṡ quaoṙaʒıntıa nauıbuṡ. (Comaðᵋ eṙıṅ ppımuṡ aouentuṡ Shaxanaċ ın hıbepnıamˡ.) Ocuṡ taınıc hı tıṙ oc Puṙt-laṙʒı 7 poʒaɒ ʒıallu Muman. Tanıc ıap peın co hCC-clıaṫ 7 poʒaɒ ʒıallu Laıʒen 7 fep Mıðe 7 hUa-m-bpıuın 7 Cıṙʒıall 7 Ulaɒ.—Petpuṡ (hUaᵃ Moṙðaᵇ), epıscopus hUa-Maıne 7 Connaċt (no,ᵏ epṡuc Cluana-fepta-bpenaınoᵏ), manaċ cṙaıɒðeċ 7 fep auxtoṙɒa, oo baɒuɒ ıṙın t-Sınaıno (ıoon,ᵇ ıc Puṙt-oa-Chaıneʒᵇ), ıoᴵ epṫ, pexto Kalenoap Ianuaṙıı.ˡ

(Tomaṡᵐ Cantuapenpıṡ maṙtıpıʒatuṡ.ⁿ—Oomnall hUa Maıl-muaıo, pı fep-Cell, occıpuṡ [eṙṫ].—Mael-cṙon Mac ʒıllı-Seċnaıll, pı Oeıṙce[ı]ṙt ɒṙeʒ, moṙıcuṡ.ⁿ)

⁶Oep—, A. ¹¹om., A. ᴶᴶl. m., t. h., A; om., B, C. ᵏ⁻ᵏ l. m., n. t. b., A; om., B, C. ᴵ⁻ᴵ .ı. uı. kl. Ienaıp (the native rendering of the Latin of A), B. ᵐ⁻ᵐ 5ld, r. m., n. t. h., A; om., B, C. ⁿ⁻ⁿ 5ᴸ d, f. m., n. t. h., A; om., B, C.

brensis states that it took place about Sept. 1 (*Exp. Hib.* i. 29).

⁸ *Son of the Empress*.—Opposite *Mac na Peirisi*, on the right margin, in B, by another hand is : *Alias, na hImpera*[*si*], *quia fuit, Impe*[*atricis*] *filius*—Otherwise, [son] of the *Empress* [Matilda], etc. (The bracketted letters were cut off in trimming the edge.) The meaning is that *hImperasi* was the true reading, being derived from *Imperatrix*. Also, on the centre margin, is written: *Rex Angliae venit in*

by Milo De Cogan with his people, wherein fell a large [1171] number around Aedh Ua Ruairc, king of Machaire-Gaileng and royal heir of the Ui-Briuin and Conmaicni. There were also killed there five chiefs of the Men of Fern-magh [and two others], namely, Mael-Mochta Mac Confhebla and Conchobhur, his brother,—two chiefs of Cenel-Feradhaigh.—Fenidh Ua Conghaile, candle of the championship and hospitality of Oirghialla, died.—Raghnall Ua Tuathchair, chief of Clann-Ruadhrach; Gilla-geimridh Mac-in-Ghaband, chief of Fir-Darcacha and a number of others along with them died not long after the aforesaid events, on the 16th of the Kalends of November [Oct. 17].—There came into Ireland Henry (son of the Empress[8]), most puissant king of England and also Duke of Normandy and Aquitaine and Count of Anjou and Lord of many other lands, with 240 ships. (So that that was the first advent of the Saxons into Ireland.) And he came to land at Port-lairgi and received the pledges of Munster. He came after that to Ath-cliath and received the pledges of Leinster and of the Men of Meath and of the Ui-Briuin and Airgialla and Ulidia.—Peter (Ua Mordha), bishop of Ui-Maine of Connacht (otherwise,[9] bishop of Cluain-ferta of [St.] Brenann), a devout monk and authoritative man, was drowned in the Sinand (namely, at Port-da-Chaineg), namely, on the 6th of the Kalends of January [Dec. 27].

(Thomas of Canterbury is martyred.[10]—Domnall Ua Mail-muaid, king of Fir-cell, was slain.[11]—Mael-cron[12] Mac Gilli-Sechnaill, king of the South of Bregha, dies.)

Hiberniam hoc anno. For Henry's doings in Ireland, see Benedict of Peterborough and Hoveden (A.D. 1171-2).

[9] *Otherwise.*—The Ui-Maine of Connaught included the diocese of Clonfert. The alternative reading is that given in the *Annals of Innisfallen* and of *Boyle*.

[10] *Martyred.*—On December 29 of the preceding year, in the Cathedral of Canterbury. See the account in Benedict of Peterborough (*ad an*).

[11] *Slain.*—By the people of Monaghan, according to the F.M.

[12] *Mael-cron.*—Given in the Four Masters.

[ḃıṗ.] Kal. Ian. uıı.ᵃ ṗ.ᵃ L, ıı., Anno Domini M. c.° lxx.° ıı.ᵃ
Ri Saxan (iḋon, henricc, mac na peiriṗᵇ) do ṫul a herinn
Dıa-Domnaıġ Carc, ıar ceılebraḋ Aıffrinn.—Tiġernan
hUa Ruaırc, rı Breıfne 7 Conmaıcne, ferı cumaċta
more fri ré fota, do marbaḋ do Shaxanaiḃ cetna 7 do
Domnall, mac Annaıḃ, via cenıul féın ımaılle² friu. A
diċennaḋ dono doıḃ 7 a cenn 7 a corp do breıṫ co docraıḋ
B 54a co hAṫ-clıaṫ. In cenn | do toġbaıl for dorur in duıne
ı n-a rgaṫ derg truaġ do Ġhaıḋelaıḃ. In corp dono do
croċaḋ ı n-ınud aıle 7 a corra rúar.—Tıġernaċᶜ hUa
Mael-Eoın, comarba Cıarain (Cluanaᵈ-mac-Noırᵈ),
quıeuıt ın Chrırto.—Inır-Eoġaın do [f]aruġuḋ la Cenel-
Conaıll 7 ar do ċor for a doeniḃ.ᵉ—Maıdm for Cenel-n-
Eoġaın la Flaiṫbertaċ hUa Maeldoraıḋ 7 la Cenel-
Conaıll 7 ár lanmor do ċor forru. Mirbuıl tra do
noeṁaıḃ ın Coımdeḋ³ ın⁴ ní rın,⁴ iḋon, do Patraıc 7 do
Colum-cılle 7 do na naemaıḃ arċena, ıra cella romıllret.
—Mael-Mıʜre° Mac Murċaḋa, toıreċ Muınnterı-Bırn
7 to[ı]re[ċ] 7 rı hUa-n-Eċaċ, do marbaḋ la hAeḋ Mac
Oenġura 7 la Claınn-Aeḋaᵃ hUaᵃ-n-Eċdaċ Ulaḋ.ᵉ—Lan-
cuaırt Coıcıḋ Connaċt ın ceṫramaḋ reċt la Ġılla Mac
Lıac, comarba Patraıc, ıḋon, la Prımaıtᵇ Erenn, co
hArd-Maċa.—Domnall hUa Ferġaıl, ard toıreċ Conmaıcne, do marbaḋ la muınnter rıġ Saxan.—Ġılla-
Aeḋa, errric Corcaıġi, fer lan do raṫ Dé, ın bona
renectute quıeuıt.

A.D. 1172. ¹ fear, A. ² male (aphaeresis of ı). A. ³—deġ, B.
⁴⁻⁴ mırin, A. ⁵—ımraıt (*chief prophet !*), B.—ᵃ⁻ᵃ n. t. h., on blank left by
scribe, A. ᵇ⁻ᵇ itl., n. t. h., A ; om., B, C. ᶜ⁻ᶜ om., B, C. ᵈ⁻ᵈ partly on c. m.,
partly on l. m., n. t. h., MS. (A). ᵉ⁻ᵉ Eaḋa hUı—, MS. (A).

1172. ¹*The king.*—Opposite these words, on the centre margin in B, is: *Rediit in Angliam.* According to Benedict, the royal retinue sailed on Easter Sunday and the king on the following day.

² *With.*—Literally, *and*.
³ *Mael-Eoin.*—*Devotee of* [St.] *John* (the Evangelist). This may be the *Maeliohain episcop* (*Mael-Iohain, bishop*) of the Clonmacnoise tombstone (O'D., F.M. iii. 4).

Kalends of Jan. on 7th feria, 2nd of the moon, A.D. [1172 Bis.] 1172. The king[1] of the Saxons (namely, Henry, son of the Empress) went from Ireland on Easter Sunday [April 16], after celebration of Mass.—Tigernan Ua Ruairc, king of Breifni and Conmaicni, a man of great power for a long time, was killed by the same Saxons and by Domnall, son of Annadh [Ua Ruairc] of his own clan along with them. He was beheaded also by them and his head and his body were carried ignominiously to Ath-cliath. The head was raised over the door of the fortress,—a sore, miserable sight for the Gaidhil. The body was hung in another place, with[2] its feet upwards.—Tigernach Ua Mael-Eoin,[3] successor of Ciaran (of Cluain-mac-Nois), rested in peace. —Inis-Eogain was wasted by the Cenel-Conaill and slaughter inflicted upon its inhabitants.—Defeat [was inflicted] upon the Cenel-Eogain by Flaithbertach Ua Maeldoraidh and by the Cenel-Conaill and great slaughter was put upon them. A marvel [wrought] by the saints of God [was] that thing: namely, by Patrick and by Colum-cille and by the saints besides, whose churches they destroyed.—Mael-Muire Mac Murchadha, chief of Muinnter-Birn and chief and king of the Ui-Echach, was killed by Aedh Mac Oenghusa and by the Clann-Aedha of the Ui-Echach of Ulidia.—The full circuit [cess] of the Fifth of Connacht [was carried] for the fourth time by Gilla Mac Liac, successor of Patrick, namely, by the Primate of Ireland, to Ard-Macha.—Domnall Ua Fergail, arch-chief of Conmaicni, was killed by the people of the king of the Saxons.—Gilla-Aedha,[4] bishop of Cork, a man full of the grace of God, rested in good old age.

---

[4] *Gilla-Aedha.*—Devotee of (St.) Aed (perhaps of Rahugh, co. Westmeath). According to the obit in the Four Masters (where the surname is O'Muidhin—O'Muigin, *Annals of Boyle*,— which was unknown to O'Donovan, iii. 3), he had been a monk of Errew in Lough Con, co. Mayo. In the *Annals of Innisfallen*, he is called *bishop* (the compiler

174 annala ulaoh.

(Murċaḋ' mac Murċaḋa 7 Murċaḋ hUa Br[i]ain occiri sunt.—Gilla-Crist, mac comarba Ciarain Cluana-mac-Nois, quieuit.—Diarmoit hUa Caellaiḋe occisur [ert.]¹)

A 52b   Kal. Ian. 11.ᵃ f.,ᵃ l. x. 111., Anno Domini M.° c.° lxx.° 111.ᵃ Cinaeṫ hUa Rona[i]n, ersus Glinne-da-loċa,¹ do cum- ranad co [rteaṁail].—Muireḋaċ hUa Coḃṫaiġ,³ ersoc Cene[oi]l-Eogain 7 Tuairce[i]rt Erenn uile, in mac óge 7 in lec loġmur 7 in gem gloine 7 in petlu solusta 7 cirti tairceḋa ind³ ecnai³ 7 croeḃ cnuaraiġ na Canoine 7° torur na derce 7 na cennsa 7 na hailgeine 7 in coluim ar gloine craiḋe 7 in tuirtuir ar ennga 7 in noeṁ De etur doiniḃ, iar n-orones do sacart 7 deo- caine 7 oer[a] ceṫa grai[ḋ] arḋena,—idon, reċtnoġaᵈ sacart, 7 iar n-aenuġaḋ eclus n-imḋa 7 iar coisecrad tempall 7 reilec 7 iar n-denum mainirtreċ 7 reicles n- imḋa 7 ceċ[a] luḋrai eclustactai arḋena 7ᶜ iar tiḋnucul buiḋ 7 etaiġ do boċtaiḃ, iar m-buaiḋ craḃaḋ 7 oiliṫri 7 aiṫriġe,⁴ rosaiḃ⁵ a sririt docum nime i n-duḃreicles Coluim-cille i n-Daire, i quart Io Febrai, in serta [septima] feria. Doronaḋ dono mirbuil mor irin aiḋċe adbaṫ,—in aḋaiġ⁶ do solustuġuḋ o ta Iarmeirġi co gairm in coiliġ 7 in doman uile for lasaḋ 7 coer mor

ᵃ⁻ᵃ f. m., n. t. h., A ; om., B, C.

A.D. 1173. ¹—laċa, A. ²Cort—, B.³·³ na hecna (i.e. the scribe took the word to be feminine), B. ⁴—gi, A. ⁵roeiḋ, B. ⁶aġaiḋ, B. ᵃ⁻ᵃ n. t. h., on space left blank, A. ᵇ·ᵇ in pace quieuit (the Latin equivalent of the A—text), B, C. ᶜ⁻ᶜ om., B, C. ᵈ .lxx., MS. (A).

---

evidently deemed it superfluous to add the place) and *head of the piety of Ireland*. In the *Annals of Boyle* he is called bishop of Cork.

⁵ *Murchadh*, etc.— The first and third of these entries are found in the *Annals of Boyle* and the *F.M.*, respectively.

⁶ *Were slain.*—Insimul occisi sunt, *Annals of Boyle*.

⁷ *Gilla-Crist.*— *Devotee of Christ*. He may have been the son of O'Malone, who died this year.

1173. ¹ *Bishop of Cenel-Eogain.*— That is, of Derry (*North of Ireland* may signify Raphoe). This proves

(Murchadh[5] Mac Murchadha and Murchadh Ua Briain were slain.[6]—Gilla-Crist,[7] son of the successor of Ciaran of Cluain-mac-Nois, rested.—Diarmod Ua Caellaidhe was slain.)

Kalends of Jan. on 2nd feria, 13th of the moon, A.D. 1173. Cinaeth Ua Rona[i]n, bishop of Glenn-da-locha, rested.—Muiredhach Ua Cobhthaigh, bishop of Cenel-Eogain[1] and of all the North of Ireland, the son of chastity and the precious stone and the gem of purity and the shining star and the preserving casket of wisdom and the fruitful branch of the Canon and the fount of charity and meekness and kindliness and the dove for purity of heart and the turtle for innocence and the saint of God among men, after ordaining priests and deacons and persons of every [church-]grade besides,—namely, seventy priests and after renovating many churches and after consecrating churches and cemeteries and after building many monasteries and regular churches and [performing] every ecclesiastical work besides and after bestowal of food and clothing to the poor, after victory and piety and penance and pilgrimage, he sent forth his spirit unto heaven in the Penitentiary of Colum-cille in Daire, on the 4th of the Ides [10th] of February, on the 6th [*recte*, 7th] feria.[2] Now, a great marvel was wrought on the night he died,—the night was illuminated from Nocturn[3] to the call of the

---

that O'Brolchain was not made bishop of the first-named see in 1158 (*supra*).

[2] *6th feria.*—*Sixth feria* is the reading of the *Annals of Loch Ce* also. From this it is evident that the compiler did not understand these criteria, but copied what he found in the MS. The Four Masters omit the week-day.

In 1173, February 10 fell on the seventh feria, or Saturday.

[3] *Nocturn.*—Literally, *afterrising;* here employed to denote midnight. The time and rationale are given in the *Vita Columbae* and *Navigatio Brandani*. Media nocte, pulsata personante clocca, festinus surgens, ad ecclesiam pergit (*Vita Col*. iii. 23). Vir Dei et qui cum illo erant

ceineŏ d'eiphi op in baile 7 a toét poipber 7 eiphi do
čač uile, indap leo pob' é in laa. Ocup poboi amlaiŏ pein
pe muip anaip.—Etpú hUa Miaŏačain, eppuc Cluana, in
bona penectute quieuit.—Cpeč mop la Aeŏ Mac
Oenzupa 7 la Clainn-Aeŏa, co poaipcpet Tpian mop
(i° n-Apd-Mača°). Ocup pomapbaŏ in pep pin i cind tpi
mip, iap n-apcain Apd-Mača do.

(Domnall¹ Bpezač hUa Mail-[Sh]eclainn, pi Miŏe,
obiit.—Mael-Močta hUa Piadbpa (no°, hUa Mail-
[Sh]eclainn°), abb Cluana-mac-Noip, quieuit.—Mael-Ipu
Mac in daipd, eppcop Cluana-pepta Bpenaind, quieuit.
—Imap, mac [Mic] Capzamna¹ [toipeč Muintipe-Mail-
pinna mopitup].)

Kal. Ian. iii.° p., l. xx. iiii., Anno Domini M.°c.° lxx.° iiii.°
Flann¹ hUa Zopma[i]n, apdpepleizinn Apd-Mača 7
Epenn | uile, pep eolač, comaptamail i n-ecna diaŏa 7
domunda, iap m-beiŏ bliaŏain ap picit⁵ i Francaiŏ 7 i
Saxanaiŏ ic poglaim 7 picé⁵ bliaŏain ic pollamnuzaŏ
pcol n-Epenn, atbat co pitamuil i tpedecim° Kallann°
Appilip, Dia-Cetain pia Caipc, peptuazepimo aetatip
pu[a]e anno.—Mael-Patpaic O Vana[i]n, eppuc Condeipe
7 Dail-Apaiŏe, pep eipmitneč, lán do noeime | 7 do
čennpa 7 do zlaine cpiŏe, do éc co lanpectnač i n-hi

B 54b

A 52o

** itl., n. t. h., A.; om., B, C. ᵇᵇ n. t. h., A; om., B, C. ᶜᶜ itl., MS. (A).

A.D. 1174. ¹ Flopinnt (=Florentius), A. ² Coimŏe, B. ³ n. t. h.,
on blank space, A. ᵇ .xx., A, B. ᶜᵈ .xiii. kl., A, B.

dederunt corpora quieti, usque ad
tertiam noctis vigiliam [i.e. mediam
noctem]. Evigilans vero vir Dei,
suscitavit fratres ad vigilias noctis
(*Nav. Bran.* c. v).

⁴ *Call of the cock.*—The *Gallici-
nium* (3 a.m.) is meant.

⁵ *By the sea on the east* (re muir
anair).—That is, in Scotland. The
expression is employed in this
sense in the obit of Malcolm Cenn-

mor, 1165 (*supra*). The meaningless reading of B is: *co romhuir in
aair*—so that it overcame the [*night*]
air. Following this, C renders it
"untill the ayer was cleered."

⁶ *Cluain[-a(i)rard].*—The square
bracketted portion is given in C.

⁷ *Great Third.*—See *supra*, A.D.
1074, note 5.

⁸ *Domnall, etc.*— Domnall of

cock⁴ and the whole world [was] a-blaze and a large mass of fire arose over the place and went south-east and every one arose, it seemed to them it was the day. And it was like that by the sea on the east.⁵—Etru Ua Miadhachain, bishop of Cluain[-a(i)rard],⁶ rested in good old age.—Great foray by Aedh Mac Oenghusa and by the Clann-Aedha, so that they pillaged the Great Third⁷ (in Ard-Macha). And that man was killed before three months, after the pillaging of Ard-Macha by him.

(Domnall⁸ Ua Mael-[Sh]echlainn the Bregian, king of Meath, died.—Mael-Mochta⁹ Ua Fiadbra (or¹⁰ Ua Mael-[Sh]echlainn), abbot of Cluain-mac-Nois, rested.—Mael-Isu Mac-in-Baird,¹¹ bishop of Cluain-ferta of [St.] Brenann, rested.—Imar¹² son [of Mac] Cargamna [chief of Muinnter-Mail-Shinna, dies].)

[1173]

Kalends of Jan. on 3rd feria, 24th of the moon, A.D. 1174. Flann Ua Gorma[i]n, arch-lector of Ard-Macha and of all Ireland, a man learned, observant in divine and human wisdom, after having been a year and twenty learning amongst the Franks and Saxons and twenty years directing the schools of Ireland, died peacefully on the 13th of the Kalends of April [March 20], the Wednesday before Easter, in the 70th year of his age.—Mael-Patraic O'Banain,¹ bishop of Condeiri and Dal-Araidhe, a venerable man, full of holiness and of meekness and of purity of heart, died full piously in I[ona] of Colum-cille, after

[1174]

Bregha was slain. Annals of Boyle. He was fostered in Bregia.

⁹ *Mochta.*—The patron saint of Louth.

¹⁰ *Or, etc.*—This is the surname given in the *F.M.* The remaining items are found in the *Annals of Boyle.*

¹¹ *Mac-in-Baird.*—Son of the Bard.

Anglicized Mac Ward. The family were hereditary poets of O'Kelly of Hy-many (O'Donovan, F. M. iii. 11.)

¹² *Imar, etc.*—Given in the *Annals of Boyle.*

1174. ¹ *O'Banain.*—See Reeves, *Adamnan* p. 408, and the works there referred to.

178   αnnαlα ulαδh.

Coluim-cille ιαρ ρentαtαιδ toξαιδe.—ξilla-mac-Liac, mac Ruαιδρι, comαρba Ρατραιc, αρδερρuc 7 ρριmαιδ Αιρδ-Mαčα 7 Ερenn uile, mac όξe lάn δo ξlαιne cριδe 7 δo ριδαṁla, δo éc co ρeččnαč ιαρ[g] ρentαtαιδ toξαιδe[d], ι[e] ρexc Kαlαnn Αρριl,[ee] Οια-Cetαιn ιαρ Cαιρc, octoξerιmo ρeptιmo αetατιρ ρuαe αnno, epιρcopαtuρ hautem tριξerιmo ρeptιmo. Roboí ιn ρeρ uαραl ριn ρé bliαδnα δec[f] co lαnonoραč ι n-αδδαιne Coluim-cille ι n-Οαιρe ρια comuρbuρ Ρατραιc.—ξilla-Moča̓δbeo, abb Mαιnιρtρeč Ρetαιρ 7 Ροιl ι n-Αρδ-Mαčα, moξ tρebαιρ, tαιριρι δo'n Coιmδιξ, δo éc ρριδιe[g] Καlenδαρ[g] Αρριlιρ, ρeptuαξerιmo [α]etατιρ ρu[α]e αnno.

(Cαδ Ουρluιρ lα Οomnαll hUα m-Ορναιn 7 lα Cončobuρ Mαenṁαιξι ρορ muιnntιρ mιc nα Ρεριρι (ιδοn, ριξ 8αxαn[i]).—Maelρuαnαιξ hUα Cιαρδα, ρι Cαιρρρι, occιρuρ eρt.—8enoδ bιρρα[h].—Α.Ο. 1174. Mαel-Iρu hUα Connαčtα[ι]n, epιρcopuρ 8hιl-Muιρeδαιξ, quιeuιt.— Αmlαιm hUα Cuιnδ, tαιρeαč Muιnntιρι-ξιllξα[ι]n, moρtuuρ eρt.—Muιρξιuρ hUα Ουδčαιξ, ceč abb nα buιlle,

[d-d] om., B, C. [ee] 1 .uι. kl. Αρριl, B; .ι. .uι. kl. Αρριlιρ, A. [f] .x.uι. bl., A, B. [gg] .ιι. kl., A, B. [h-h] n. t. h., A; om., B, C. [i] itl., MS. (A). [j] 52b, f.m., n. t. h., A; om., B, C.

---

[2] *Son of Ruaidhri.*—In the colophon to the exquisite Evangelisterium of Mael-Brigte in the British Museum (Harleian, 1802, fol. 166b). Cf. *Appendix to Report on Rymer's Foedera, Supplement*, Pl. XVI.; Reeves, *Proc. R.I.A.* v. 62-3), he is called *grandson of Ruaidhri*. According to an interlinear gloss in the original hand he was *son of the poet of the Ui-Birn*—mac ιnδ [ḟ]ιρ δανα δο [U]ıb-bιρn (a Tyrone sept whose territory bounded part of Monaghan). In the list of *Successors of Patrick* (L. L. 42d), he is likewise styled *son of the poet*.

[3] *March 27th, the Wednesday after Easter.*—The F.M. copy these data and, nevertheless, place the obit under 1173,—a year in which the Wednesday in Easter week fell on April 11! O'Donovan left th error uncorrected (iii. 13).

Gelasius is given in the Martyrology of Donegal at March 27.

[4] *87th of his age.*—He was consequently born in 1087. Yet O'Conor

choice old age.—Gilla Mac Liac [Gelasius], son of [1174] Ruaidhri,[2] successor of Patrick, archbishop and primate of Ard-Macha and of all Ireland, son of chastity, full of purity of heart and of peace, died piously after choice old age, on the 6th of the Kalends of April [March 27], the Wednesday after Easter,[3] in the 87th year of his age,[4] the 37th of his episcopacy.[5] That noble man was sixteen years full honourably in the abbacy of Colum-cille in Daire before [receiving] the succession of Patrick.—Gilla-Mochaidbeo,[6] abbot of the Monastery of Peter and Paul in Ard-Macha, a diligent, steadfast servant to the Lord, died on [Sunday] the 2nd of the Kalends of April [March 31], in the 70th year of his age.

(The battle[7] of Durlus [was gained] by Domnall Ua Briain and by Conchobur Maenmhaighi upon the people of the son of the Empress (namely, of the king of the Saxons).—Maelruanaigh[8] Ua Ciarda, king of Cairpri, was slain.—The Synod[7] of Birr [was celebrated].—A.D. 1174. Mael-Isu[7] Ua Connachtain, bishop of Sil-Muirethaigh [Elphin], rested.—Amlaim Ua Cuind, chief of Muinnter-Gillga[i]n, died.—Muirguis[7] Ua Dubhthaigh, first abbot

---

(*R. H. S.* ii. *Annals of Boyle,* p. 17) confidently states that Mac Liag, who died in 1016 (*supra*), was his father!

[3] *37th of his episcopacy.* — He became archbishop on the resignation of St. Malachy in 1137. There is independent evidence that he was primate in 1138. According to the colophon, he was in the *succession of Patrick,* when the Mael-Brigte Codex was written: namely, *in the year of the sixteenth Epact* [*falling*] *upon Jan.* 1—ɪroın, ɪ m-bliaoain oano ꝑeꞃꞇoe oeac ꝛoꞃ Kalann Enaıꞃ.

[6] *Mochaidbeo.*—His name is in the Martyrology of Donegal at October 11.

[7] *The battle, etc.; The Synod, etc.; Mael-Isu, etc.; Muirgius, etc.*—Given in the *Annals of Boyle.*

For the battle of Thurles (which is also found in the *Annals of Innisfallen*), see the masterly note of O'Donovan (F. M. iii. 16 sq).

To the Synod of Birr is perhaps to be referred the transfer of Westmeath to the See of Clonmacnoise, recorded by the F.M. at this year.

[8] *Maelruanaigh, etc.* — A more detailed account is in the F.M.

quieuit.—Imap, mac Mic Capgamna hUi Ʒilla-Ulta[i]n, toipeč Muinntepi [Mail-Sinna,ᵏ mopitup ᵏ].)

|Cal. Ian. 1111.ᵃ p., L u., Anno Domini M.ᶜ c.° lxx.° u.°
Mael-Ipu (ioon,ᵇ mac in čleipiʒ cuippᵇ), eppuc Ulað, puí ecna[i] 7 cpaba[i]ð, plenup dierum in Chpipto quieuit.
—Flaicbeptačᶦ hUa Ɓpolča[i]n, comapba Coluim-cille, tuip ecna[i] 7 einiʒ, pep via tucaðup cleipiʒ Epenn sačaip eppuic apᵒ ecna[i] 7 apᵒ febup 7 via tapcupˣ comuppup hIa, do éc co pečtnač iap tpeblait toʒaiðe i n-dubpeclepᵌ Coluim-cille. Ʒilla Mac Liac hUa Ɓpana[i]n do oipðneð i n-a inað i comuppup Coluim-cille.—Mac comapba Finnein (ioon,ᵇ Amlaimᵇ), abb Saƀaill, do éc i n-eppcopoiti Ulað.—Mac Copmaic eppuc Ulað, do éc.—Concobup,ᵈ mac Mic Končaille (peʒánaiʒᵉ), abb peiclepa Poil 7 Petaip 7 comapba Patpaic iaptain, do éc i Roim, iap točt d'acallaim comapba Petaip.ᵈ—Maiom ap Cenel-n-Enna pia n-Ečmapčač hUa Cača[i]n 7 pe Niall hUa n-Ʒailmpeðaiʒ 7 áp mór do čup poppu.

ᵏ⋅ᵏ Cut away in binding; Mael-Sinna is certain.

A.D. 1175. ¹laič—(p om.), A. ²—ʒup, B. ³peič—, A. ᵃ⋅ᵃ n. t. h., on blank space, A. ᵇ⋅ᵇ itl., n. t. h., A; om., B, C. ᶜ ap a—*for his*, B, C. ᵈ⋅ᵈ om., B, C. ᵉ itl., n. t. h., MS. (A).

⁹ *Boyle*.—Respecting the history of the foundation of this abbey given by O'Donovan (F. M. iii. 14) from the *Annals of Boyle*, it may be well to quote the original entries.

Abbatia de Buellio hoc anno fundata est, anno Dominic[a]e Incarnationis MCXLVIII.

Abbatia Buellensis hoc anno fundata est iuxta Buellium MCLXI; ab initio vero mundi VICCCLX. Primo incepit esse apud Grellech-dinach; secundo, apud Druimconaind; tertio, apud Bunfinni; quarto, apud Buellium.

In primo loco, primus abbas Petrus Ua Morda fuit; in secundo, Aed Ua Maccain per duos annos. Post eum Mauricius in eodem loco per vi. annos ("nearly three years," O'Donovan, *loc. cit.*), et apud Bunfinni duos et dimidium. In Buellio vero abbatizavit xiii. et dimidium.

[A.D. MCLXXIV.] Murgius Ua Dubtaich, primus abbas Buellii et

of Boyle,[9] rested.—Imar[10] son of Mac Cargamna Ua Gilla-Ultain,[11] chief of Muinnter-Mail-Sinna, dies.) [1174]

Kalends of Jan. on 4th feria, 5th of the moon, A.D. 1175. Mael-Isu (namely, son of "the Stooped Cleric"), bishop of Ulidia [Down], master of wisdom and piety, rested full of days in Christ.—Flaithbertach Ua Brolcha[i]n, successor of Colum-cille, tower of wisdom and hospitality, a man to whom the clergy of Ireland gave the chair[1] of a bishop for wisdom and for his excellence and to whom was offered[2] the succession of Ia, died piously, after choice tribulation, in the Penitentiary of Colum-cille. Gilla Mac Liac Ua Brana[i]n[3] was instituted in his stead in the succession of Colum-cille.—The son of the successor of [St.] Finnian (namely, Amlaimh[4]) [deposed] abbot of Saball, died in the episcopacy of Ulidia.—Mac Cormaic, bishop of Ulidia, died.—Conchobur,[5] son of Mac Conchaille (the wild-deer hunter), abbot of the Regular abbey of [SS.] Paul and Peter and successor of Patrick afterwards, died in Rome, after arriving to confer with the successor of Peter.—Defeat [was inflicted] on the Cenel-Enna by Echmarcach Ua Catha[i]n and by Niall Ua Gailmredhaigh and great slaughter was put upon them. [1175]

---

tertius secundum antiquitatem domus, quievit.

[10] *Imar, etc.*—Compare the final (additional) item of the preceding year.

[11] *Gilla-Ultain.*—Devotee of [St.] *Ultan* (probably of Ardbraccan, co. Meath).

1175. [1] *Chair of bishop.*—Supra, 1158.

[2] *Was offered.*—In 1164 (*supra*).

[3] *Ua Brana[i]n.*—See *Adamnan*, p. 408.

[4] *Amlaimh.*—The same who pro-

cured the expulsion of the Canons Regular from Saball (Saul) in 1170. The *F. M.* omit the obit.

[5] *Conchobur.*—He was the immediate successor of Gelasius. *Segdnach* (for which compare *ség, a wild-deer*, in Cormac's *Glossary*) forms part of the text in the *Annals of Boyle*.

[6] *Was slain.*—By the son of Mac Coghlan (lord of Delvin Eathra, the barony of Garrycastle, King's Co.), according to the entry in the Four Masters.

(ᵹilla-Coluim' hUa Maelṁuaiḋ, ri ḟer-Ceall, occiruṛ erṫ.—Maᵹnur hUa Mael-Sheacnaill do croċaḋ la ᵹallaiḃ.—Miḋe d'ḟarruᵹuḋ o Œṫ-luain ᵹu Oroċeṫ-aṫa.—Domnall Caemanaċ, mac Diarmoda Mic Murċaḋa, ri Laiᵹean [occiruṛ erṫ].—Sluaᵹaḋ la ᵹallaiḃ ᵹu Luimneaċ, ᵹu n-deaċadair rair.')

[bir]
B 54c
A 52d

Kal. Ian. u., ṗ., l. x. ui., Œnno Domini M.º c.º lxx.º ui.ᵗ Saxain do innarba[ḋ] do Domnall hUa Briain a Luimniuċ | tre ḟorbairi¹ do denum forṛu.—Bean-Miḋe, inᵹen Donnċaḋa hUi Cerbaill, ben Con-maiᵹi² hUi Ḟhlainn,³ riᵹan hUa-Tuirtri 7 Fer-li, do éc.—Inᵹen Ruaiḋri hUi Conċoḃair, ben [Ḟh]laithbertaiᵹ hUi Maeldoraiḋ, do marbaḋ do macaiḃ hUi Cairella[i]n.—Ḟabor 7 Cenannur do ḟaruᵹaḋ⁴ do Ghallaiḃ 7 do hUib-Briuin.—Niall,* mac Mic loċlainn, do marbaḋ do Muintear-Branain.ᵃ—Luᵹmaḋ do ḟaruᵹaḋ do na Saxaiḃ.—Cairtel ᵹall 'ᵹa ḋenaṁ i Cenannur.—In t-

⁽⁽n. t. h., A; om., B, C.
A.D. 1176. ¹orbairi (ḟ om.), A.   ²—ḋe, B.   ³lainn (ḟ om.), B.   ⁴ar—(ḟ om.), A.   ⁵ra (aphaeresis of i), A.   ᵃ⁻ᵃ om., B, C.

---

⁷ *Maghnus.*—He was lord of East Meath. The Four Masters state he was hanged by the Foreigners (English), after they had acted treacherously towards him (most likely, by seizing him at a conference) at Trim.

⁸ *Wasted.*—This was probably the incursion described by Cambrensis: Rothericus vero Connactensis, Sinnenensis fluvii fluenta transcurrens, in manu valida Mediam invasit, cunctaque ejusdem castra vacua reperiens atque deserta, usque ad ipsos Dubliniæ fines igne combusta soloque confracta redegit (*Exp. Hib.*, ii. 2).

⁹ *Domnall.*—Given in the *Annals of Boyle.*

In the Four Masters it is stated that he was treacherously slain by O'Foran and O'Nolan.

¹⁰ *A hosting.*—Given in the *Annals of Innisfallen* and in the *Annals of Boyle.* For a characteristic description of the capture by Cambrensis, see the chapter *Nobilis Limerici expugnatio* (*Exp. Hib.* ii. 7).

1176. ¹ *The Saxons.*—On the right hand margin, a 17th-century hand wrote in B: *Anglici* [*expul*]*si ex Limerice a Domnalldo*. Cambrensis, however, states (*Exp. Hib.* ii. 14) that, on hearing of the death of

(Gilla-Coluim Ua Maelmhuaidh, king of Fir-cell, was slain.⁶—Maghnus⁷ Ua Mael-Seachnaill was banged by the Foreigners.—Meath was wasted⁸ from Ath-luain to Drochait-atha.—Domnall⁹ Caemanach, [illegitimate] son of Diarmaid Mac Murchadha, king of Leinster [was slain].—A hosting¹⁰ by the Foreigners to Limerick, so that they overcame it.)

Kalends of Jan. on 5th feria, 16th of the moon, A.D. 1176. The Saxons¹ were expelled by Domnall Ua Briain from Limerick, by a leaguer being made against them.— Bean-Midhe², daughter of Donnchadh Ua Cerbaill, wife of Cu-maighi³ Ua Flainn, queen of Ui-Tuirtri and Fir-Li, died.—The daughter of Ruaidbri Ua Conchobair, wife of [F]laithbertach Ua Maeldoraidh, was killed by the sons of Ua Cairella[i]n.—Fabor and Cenannus were wasted⁴ by the Foreigners and by the Ui-Briuin.—Niall, son of Mac Lochlainn, was killed by Muinnter-Branain.—Lughmadh was wasted by the Saxons.—A castle⁵ of the Foreigners

---

Strongbow, Raymond Le Gros set out for Dublin, having committed Limerick to Donald (O'Brien), as baron of the king and received hostages and multiplied oaths respecting its safe custody and restitution and the preservation of peace. But, no sooner had the English left than Donald, with the characteristic infidelity of his nation, set the city on fire in four places! Giraldus took no trouble to enquire what motive could have prompted O'Brien to burn a place that thus peaceably reverted to his possession.

² *Bean—Midhe.—Woman of Meath.* "It was very common as the proper name of a woman among the ancient Irish, as was also Bean-Muman, meaning *woman, or lady, of Munster*" (O'Donovan, F.M. iii. 24).

³ *Cu-Maighi,—Hound of the plain*; *Cu-Midhe,—Hound of Meath.*—Both these names were employed amongst the family of O'Flynn (O.'D. F.M. iii. 25).

⁴ *Wasted.*—That is, in consequence of the battles fought thereat between the opposing forces.

⁵ *A castle.*—The compiler of the *Annals of Loch C̣* makes this into "The castles of the Foreigners and of Cenannus were a-building" (*Caislen Gall ocus Cenantus ag a n-denum*)! The editor takes *Gall* for a local name and gravely says that

Iarla Saxanac do éc i n-Aĉ-cliaĉ do bainne aillri
rogab ar a ĉoir tria mirbuiliḃ Briġti 7 Coluim-cille
7 na noeṁ arĉena, ira⁵ cella romill.—Cairtel Slaine i
raibe Ricard Fléimenn⁶ co n-a rluaġ, ar a raḃur ic
milliuḋ Airġiall 7 hUa-m-Briuin 7 Fer-Miḋe, do
milliuḋ la Mael-Seĉlainn, mac Mic Loĉlainn, la riġ
Ceneoil-Eogain 7 la Cenel-n-Eogain buḋein 7 la hAir-
ġiallaib, dú in romarbaḋ cet, no ní ir moo, do Ghallaiḃ,
re taeḃ ban 7 lenum 7 eĉ in ĉairteoil do marbaḋ, co na
térna duine i m-beĉaiḋ arin cairtel. Ocur roraraiġti
tri cairteoil i Miḋe iar⁶ nabaraĉ⁶ ar uaṁan Cenuil⁷-
Eogain, idon, cairtel Cenannra 7 cairtel Calatruma 7
cairtel⁸ Daire-Phatraic.—Cu-maiġe hUa Flainn, rí
hUa-Turtri 7 Fer-Li 7 Dal-Araide, do marbaḋ do
Coin-Miḋe, d'a braḋair rein 7 do Feraiḃ-Li.

(Diarmoid,ᵉ mac Cormaic Mheġ Carrĉaiġ, ri Dear-
ṁuġan, do gabail la a mac rein, idon, la Cormac
liaĉan.ᵉ)

Kal. Ian. uii.ᵃr.,ᵃ L.xx. uii., Anno Domini M.° c.° lxx.° uii.°
Dun-daleṫglar do milleḋ do hEoan¹ do-Chuirt 7 do na
ruterib tangadur imaille rir 7 cairtel do ḋenaṁ doiḃ
ann, ara tucrat maidm ra ḋó ror Ulltaiḃ 7 maidm ror
Cenel-n-Eogain 7 ror Airġiallaiḃ, dú in romarbaḋ Concobur hUa Cairell-a[i]n (idon,ᵇ toireĉ Clainni-

---

ᵉ rlem,—B. ⁷ cenel, A. ⁸ cairlen, B. ᵇ ar nabaraĉ—*on the morrow*,
B ; followed by C. ᵈ⁻ᵈ n. t. h., A ; om., B, C.

A.D. 1177. ¹ reon, B. ᵃ⁻ᵃ blank in A. ᵇ⁻ᵇ itl., t. h., A, B ; given in C.

there is no trace of any " castle of Gall " (p. 152).

⁶ *Saxon Earl.*—See O'Donovan (*loc. cit.*) and Gilbert (*Viceroys*, p. 40, sq.).

⁷ *Alive.*—Literally, *in life*.

⁸ *Diarmoid.*—Abridged apparently from the *Annals of Innisfallen* (*ad an.*); which add that Cormac was treacherously slain and his father again reigned in the same year.

1177. ¹ *John De Courcy.*—According to Cambrensis (*Exp. Hib.* ii. 17), he marched, with 22 knights and 300 men, in three days through Meath and Oriel and, on the morning of the fourth day, about Feb. 1, entered Down : the king,

was a-building at Cenannus.—The Saxon Earl[6][Strongbow] [1176] died in Ath-cliath of an ulcer he got on his foot, through the miracles of Brigit and Colum-cille and the saints besides, whose churches he destroyed.—The castle of Slane, wherein was Ricard Fleming with his host, wherefrom the Airgialla and Ui-Briuin and Fir-Midhe were being pillaged, was destroyed by Mael-Sechlainn, son of Mac Lochlainn, king of Cenel-Eogain and by the Cenel-Eogain themselves and by the Airgialla; where were killed one hundred or more of the Foreigners, besides women and children and the horses of the castle that were killed, so that no person escaped alive[7] out of the castle. And three castles in Meath were razed on the morrow for fear of the Cenel-Eogain, namely, the castle of Cenannus and the castle of Calatruim and the castle of Daire of [St.] Patrick.—Cu-maighi[2] Ua Flainn, king of Ui-Tuirtri and Fir-Li and Dal-Araidhe, was killed by Cu-Midhe[3], his own brother and by the Fir-Li.

(Diarmoid,[8] son of Cormac Mac Carrthaigh, king of Desmond, was taken prisoner by his own son, that is, by Cormac the Gray.)

Kalends of Jan. on 7th feria, 27th of the moon, A.D. [1177] 1177. Dun-da-lethglas was destroyed by John De Courcy[1] and by the knights that came with him, and a castle[2] was made by them there, wherefrom they twice[3] inflicted defeat upon Ulidia and defeat upon Cenel-Eogain and upon Airgialla; where was killed Conchobur Ua Cairella[i]n

---

Dunlevy (who succeeded his brother, Roderick in the kingdom of Ulidia in 1171, *supra*), having taken to flight.

[2] *Castle.*—Exili municipio, quod in urbis angulo tenuiter crexerat (*Exp. Hib.* ii. 17).

[3] *Twice.*—Giraldus states (*loc. cit.*) that the first defeat was inflicted after the Purification (Feb. 2), upon a force of 10,000; the second, on the Nativity of St John (June 24), upon 15,000.

Diarmata^b), 7 Gilla Mac Liac hUa Donngaile, toiseč fer-droma 7 in sosonad do raigtid Domnall hUa [Fh]laithertaig—7 mard é do na gonaid rin i peicler Phoil i n-Ard-Maca, iar caitim Cuirp Crist 7 iar n-a ongad—7 in pomarbait² maiti imda aili. Dorat dono Cončobur hUa Cairpella[i]n reimerin (idon,^c irin n-erraċ^c) maidm for hUa Maeldoraid 7 for Cenel-Conaill, dú in pomarbad ár Ceneoil-hEnna[i] 'ma³ mac hUi Sherraig 7 ima³ maitib imdaib arčena.—Milid Gogan co n-a risirib do breit do mac Ruaidri (idon,^d Murčad^d) hUi Concobuir co Ros-Comain do milliud Connaċt | ar ulcaid ris [a] atair. Roloisčret imurra Connačta ra cetoir Tuaim-da-gualann 7 cealla arčena in tire^e ar ulcaid rirna Gallaib 7 tugrat maidm forrna Gallu 7 rodicuirset ar eisin ar a tir iat. Robail dono Ruaidri hUa Concobuir in mac rin (idon,^f Murčad^f) iar rin, i n-digail in turuir rain.—Aed hUa Neill (idon,^g in macam toinlerc^g), ri Cene[oi]l-Eogain re heḋ 7 risomna Erenn uile, do marbad la Mael-Sečlainn, mac Mic Loċlainn 7 la hArogal, mac Mic Loclainn (idon,^r mac do'n Mael-Sečlainn rin^f). Arogal dono rein do marbad do hUa Neill ic a marbad annrein.—In tirranac, hUa Coinnecen, ardollam Tuairce[i]rt Erenn

^a pomarbad, A. ³im, B. ᶜᶜ itl., t. h., A ; irin erraċ, c. m., t. b., B; "in the Lent," C. ᵈᵈ itl., t. h., A ; Muirčertač, itl. t. h., B; "Murtagh," C. ᵉ (cealla arčena in tire) do milliud—(*moreover, the churches of the territory*) were (lit., *to be*) *despoiled*, added, B ; followed by C. The fatal objection to this reading is the introduction of an Infinitive between two Indicatives. ᶠᶠ itl., n. t. h., A; om., B, C. ᵍ·ᵍ l. m., t. h., A ; om., B, C.

---

⁴ *Milo Cogan, etc.*—In the *Exp. Hib.* (ii. 19) no mention is made of Murchadh O'Conor. De Cogan is said to have had 40 knights and 500 men. The Connaughtmen burned cities, towns, churches and such provisions as they were unable to conceal. They likewise cast down crucifixes and images of Saints in presence of the enemy. The invading force advanced as far as Tuam. There it remained

(namely, chief of Clann-Diarmata) and Gilla Mac Liac Ua
Donngaille, chief of Fir-Droma, and wherein was wounded
with arrows Domnall Ua [F]laithbertaigh—and he died
of those wounds in the monastery [of Canons Regular]
of Paul [and Peter] in Ard-Macha, after partaking of the
Body of Christ and after his anointing—and wherein
were killed many other nobles. Now, Conchobur Ua
Cairella[i]n before that (namely, in the Spring) inflicted
defeat upon the Cenel-Eogain and upon Ua Maeldoraidh;
where a great number of the Cenel-Eogain were killed,
around the son of Mac Sherraigh and around many nobles
besides.—Milo Cogan[4] with his knights was taken by the
son of Ruaidhri (namely, Murchadh) Ua Conchobhuir to
Ros-Comain to destroy Connacht, for evil[5] towards his
father. The Connachtmen, however, immediately burned
Tuaim-da-gualann and the churches of the country besides,
for evil[5] towards the Foreigners and they inflicted defeat
upon the Foreigners and drove them by force out of the
country. Moreover, Ruaidhri Ua Conchobuir blinded that
son (namely, Murchadh) afterwards, in revenge of that
expedition.—Aedh Ua Neill (namely, "The lazy youth"[6]),
king of Cenel-Eogain for a time and royal heir of all Ireland, was killed by Mael-Sechlainn, son of Mac Lochlainn
and by Ardgal, son of Mac Lochlainn (that is, son to that
Mael-Sechlainn). But Ardgal himself was killed by Ua
Neill at his [Ua Neill] being killed there.—The Timpanist[7]
Ua Coinnecen, arch-ollam of the North of Ireland, was

---

eight days; but, finding the land void of sustenance, returned to the Shannon. In a wood close by the river, King Roderick was encountered at the head of three large armies. A fierce conflict ensued. The English lost three, slew many of the enemy and escaped safe to Dublin! Credat Judaeus.

[5] *Evil.*—Plural in the original.

[6] *Lazy youth.*—So called, doubtless, by antiphrasis.

[7] *Timpanist.*—For the Timpanist, see O'Curry (*Manners and Customs*, etc., iii. 364 sq.) For the stringed instrument, the Timpan, see *ib.*, 359 sq., and i dxxviii—ix.

do marbaḋ do Chenel-Conaill co n-a mnai 7 co n-a muinnter.—Sluaxaḋ la hEoan[1] do-Cuirt 7 larna ricriḃ i n-Dal-Araiḋe, (7' xu Dun-da-leṫxlar'), d'ar'marbrat Domnall, mac mic Caturaix, ri Dal-Araiḋe. Tainic dono hEoan[1] do'n turur cetna i n-hUib-Tuirtri 7 i Feraiḋ-Li, co roloirc Cú-Miḋe hUa Flaind Airṫear-Maixi reime 7 co roloircet Cuil-rataim 7 ċealla imḋa eile. Niall hUa Xailmreḋaix, ri Fer-Maxi-Iṫa 7 Cheneoil-Enna[i], do marbaḋ do Donnċaḋ hUa Chairella[i]n 7 do Clainn-Diarmata, ar lar Daire Colum-cille 7 teċ[4] do lorcaḋ air ann, co tainix ar amaċ, co romarbaḋ i n-dorur in taixi. Doroine dono Donnċaḋ hUa Cairella[i]n,[5] toireċ Clainni-Diarmata, rit re Colum-cille 7 re Muinnter Daire annrein tar a cenn rein 7 a mic 7 a oa: idon,[b] [a] mainċene rein tria biṫu 7 a meic 7 a oa 7 a iarmoa co braṫ do[h] Colum-cille 7 do Mhuinnter Daire 7 baile-biataix i[6] farraḋ Domnaix-moir. Ocur Mac-riaḃaċ, idon, corn ir ferr do[7] boi i n-Erinn, do tabairt do Mhuinnter Daire i[6] n-xill re tri fictiḃ bó. Ocur teċ ḋo denum do'n cleiriuċ, ira teċ roloircetḋ for Ua n-Xairmleḋaix[8] 7 a croḋ uile do ic frir donsoḋ ro loircret imi. Clann-Diarmata imurra arċena do ḋenum fritha tar a cenn rein.

(Uimanur' Cardinalir uenit in Hiberniam. Senuḋ ċlereaċ Erind i nd-Aṫ-ċliaṫ cum Uiuiano.—Conċuḃar

[4] teaċ, A. [5] illan, B. [6] a, A. [7] om., B. [8] n-Xailm—, B. [h-h] 7 a iarmoa 7 a mainċeine rein tria biṫu do—*and of his posterity and his own monastic service for ever to*, B; which C follows. [14] n. t. h., A; om., B, C.

---

[8] This expedition is not mentioned by Cambrensis.

[9] *Monastic service.*—For the *mainchine*, or Monastic Service, see the *Senchas Mor* (*Brehon Laws*, iii. 36, 68).

[10] *Ballybetagh.*—That is, *townland* of a *Biatach* (one who held his land on condition of supplying food (*biad*) to those billeted upon him by the chief). "A Ballybetagh was the thirtieth part of a *triocha cead*, or barony. It contained four quarters, or *seisreaghs*, each sies-

killed by the Cenel-Conaill with his wife and with his people. [1177] —A hosting[8] by John De Courcy and by the knights into Dal-Araidhe (and to [*recte*, from] Dun-da-lethlas), on which they killed Domnall, grandson of Cathusach [Mac Duinnsleibhe Ua Eochadha], king of Dal-Araidhe. Moreover, John went during the same expedition into Ui-Tuirtri and into Fir-Li, until Cu-Midhe Ua Flainn burned Airthir-Maighi before him and they [John's forces] burned Cuil-rathain and many other churches.—Niall Ua Gailmredhaigh, king of the Men of Magh-Itha and of Cenel-Ennai, was killed by Donnchadh Ua Cairella[i]n and by the Clann-Diarmata, in the centre of Daire of Colum-cille: and [it happened thus:] a house was burned upon him there, so that he came out from it [and] was killed at the door of the house. However, Donnchadh Ua Cairella[i]n, chief of Clann-Diarmata, made peace with Colum-cille and with the Community of Daire then, on behalf of himself and his son and his grand sons,—to wit, the monastic service[9] of himself for ever and of his son and of his grandsons and of his posterity to doom unto Colum-cille and unto the Community of Daire and [to give] a bally-betagh[10] in the neighbourhood of Domnach-mor. And "The Gray Son," that is, the best goblet that was in Ireland, was given to the Community of Daire, in pledge for three score cows. And [he agreed] to make a house for the cleric whose house was burned upon Ua Gairmledhaigh and to pay him all the chattel that they burned about him. The Clann-Diarmata also made peace on their own behalf.

(Cardinal[11] Vivianus[12] came into Ireland. A Synod[13] of the clergy of Ireland along with Vivianus.—Conchubar[11]

---

reagh containing 120 acres of the *large* Irish measure" (O'Donovan, *F.M.* iii. 27).

[11] *Cardinal; Conchubar.*—Given in the *Annals of Boyle*, with the father's name omitted from the second entry.

[12] *Vivianus.*—Cardinal priest of

Maenmaiʙe do ɣaɓail la aṫaiɼ, ɪdon, la Ruaiɣɼi hUa Conċoɓaiɼ.¹)

|Cal. 1an. 1.ᵃ ꝼ.,ᵃ l. ix., Anno Domini M.° c.° lxx.° uiii.ᵃ ɪdon, cet bliaḋain noɪdecta[ɪ]. Concobuɼ, mac Conallaiɣ hUi Luiniɣ, do ɣaɓail toiɼiɣecta Ceniuil-Maien¹ 7 Domnall, mac Domnaill hUi Ɣailpɼedaiɣ, do innaɼba[ḋ] a Muiɣ-hIta ɪ² n-Iniɼ-n-Eoɣain docum Donnċaḋa hUi Duiɓdiɼma. Cenel-Maien imuɼɼo iɼin bliaḋain cetna, ɪdon, ɪ cinn oen ɼaiṫi, do ḋenam aṫtoiɼiɣ do mac Conallaiɣ 7 do tabaiɼt toiɼiɣecta do Domnall, mac Domnaill.—Muinnteɼ Domnaill hUi Ɣailm-ɼedaiɣ, ɪdon, mac Ɣille-caiċ hUa n-Eɪdeɼla 7 hUa [ꝼh]lannaca[ɪ]n, do maɼbaḋ mic Conallaiɣ hUi Luiniɣ, aɼ laɼ tiɣi Domnaill hUi Ɣailpɼedaiċ, ɪ meḋail 7 haiɼċinneċ na hEɼnaiḋe³ maɼoen ɼiɼ ic a ċomaiɼce. Aṫtoiɼeċ dono do ḋenum do Domnall hUa Ɣailpɼedaiɣ 7 Cenel-Maien do tabaiɼt toiɼiɣecta do Ruaiḋɼi hUa [ꝼh]laiṫbeɼtaiɣ. Mebol imuɼɼo do ḋenum do tɼu macaiḋ hUi [ꝼh]laiṫbeɼtaiɣ ꝼoɼ Cenel-Moen 7 do Clainn Domnaill aɼċena. Domnall dono, mac Dom-naill hUi Ɣailpɼedaiɣ, do maɼbaḋ inntiɼiḋeᵇ 7 Tiɣeɼnan, mac Raɣnaill mic Domnaill 7 oċtuɼ lanbiataċ do maiṫiḃ Cene[oi]l-Moen maɼoen⁴ ɼiu.—Raɣ-

A.D. 1178. ¹ Ceneol-Maiean, A. ² α, A. ³—naiɣi, B. ⁴ aɼoen, B. ᵃ⁻ᵃ blank space, A. ᵇ iɼin meḋoil ɼin—*in that treachery*, B; "in that murther," C (following B).

St. Stephen on the Coelian Mount and Papal Legate. Hoveden (in agreement with Benedict of Peterborough) states that he spent the Christmas of 1176 in Man with Guthred, the king. After the Epiphany he set sail for Ireland and landed at Down. On his way thence, along the coast, to Dublin, he was arrested by the army of De Courcy (and apparently brought back to Down). John, however, allowed him to proceed and, at his request, liberated the bishop of Down, who had been taken prisoner in the first battle of Down.

Maenmhaidhe was taken prisoner by his father, namely [1177] by Ruaighri Ua Conchobhair.)

Kalends of Jan. on 1st feria, 9th of the moon, A.D. [1178] 1178. Namely, the 1st year[1] of the Decemnovennal [Cycle]. Conchobur, son of Conallach Ua Luinigh, took the chieftaincy of Cenel-Maien and Domnall, son of Domnall Ua Gailmredhaigh, was expelled from Magh-Itha into Inis-Eogain, to Donnchadh Ua Duibdirma. The Cenel-Maien, however, in the same year, namely, before the end of one quarter, deposed the son of Conallach and gave the chieftaincy to Domnall, son of Domnall.—The people of Domnall Ua Gailmredhaigh, that is, the son of "the blind gillie" Ua Eiderla and Ua [F]lannacain, killed the son of Conallach Ua Luinigh in the centre of the house of Domnall Ua Gailmredhaigh, in treachery and the herenagh of the Ernaidhe [was] with him, protecting him. However, Domnall Ua Gailmredhaigh was deposed and Cenel-Maien gave the chieftainship to Ruaidhri Ua [F]laithbertaigh. Nevertheless, a treacherous attack was made by the three sons of Ua [F]laithbertagh and the Clann-Domnall also upon the Cenel-Moien. Howbeit, Domnall, son of Domnall Ua Gailmredhaigh, was killed in that same [attack] and Tighernan, son of Raghnall, son of Domnall [was killed] and eight full biatachs of the nobles of Cenel-Moien along with them [were killed].—

---

[13] *A Synod.*—Of bishops, held in Dublin, according to Cambrensis (*Exp. Hib.* ii. 11). The Legate (*ib.*) proclaimed the right of the English king over Ireland and the papal confirmation thereof, and commanded clergy and laity to submit, under threat of anathema. And, it being customary (in time of war) for the Irish to carry provisions for safety to churches, he empowered an English expeditionary force, when victuals were not otherwise obtainable, to extract those found in churches, on payment of a fair price!

1178. [1] *1st year.*—The Epact, ix., sufficiently denoted the initial year of the Decemnovennal Cycle.

nall, mac Etmarcaiġ hUi Chaḟa[i]n, do maṙbaḋ do Cenel-
Maia[i]n i toraċ in t-ramhraiḋ rin. Conaḋ i n-a diẛail
riḋe dorocair Ṡalaċ hUa Luinniẛ 7 Muircertaċ hUa
Peata[i]n 7 ir 'n-a diẛail doronaḋ mebol Clainni-Ḋoṁ-
naill, ror Cenel-Moen.—Irin⁵ bliaḋain rin dono tainic
morẛaċ aḋbuil, co rotrarcair bloḋ⁶ dermair do
ċailltiḃ 7 do rṙobaḋaiḃ 7 do railẛiḃ diṁórraiḃ ror⁷ Lár
7 ror⁷ lantalmain. Rotrarcair dono re⁸ riċiċ⁸ ralaċ,
uel paulo plur, i n-Ḋaire Coluim-cil[l]e.—Ir^d inntirin^d
dono táinic hEoan co n-a ritirū ó Ḋhun ar creċaḋ co-
Machaire-Conaille, co n-dernrat^e airẛċi ann^e 7 co rab-
B 55b   atur aidċi illongrort⁹ i n-Ṡlind-Iriẛi. Táinic imurro¹⁰
Murċaḋ hUa Cerḃaill, rí Airẛiall 7 Mac Ḋuinnrleiḃe,
ri Ulaḋ, cu' n-Ulltaiḃ' cucu¹¹ in aidċe rin 7 tucrat
taelcaċ doiḃ. Romebaiḋ dono ror Ṡallaiḃ 7 rocuireḋ
derẛár rorru. Táinic dono in t-Seoan cetna ar creċaiḃ
i n-Ḋal-n-Araiḋe 7 i n-hUiḃ-Tuirtri. Tuc dano
Cu-Miḋe hUa Flaind, ri hUa-Tuirtri 7 Fer-Li
tailcaċ doiḃ. Romaiḋ dono in cat rin ror Ṡallaiḃ 7
rocuireḋ a n-ár.

(Ammus^g Cualẛní la hUlta 7 la Ṡalla ror Sean do-
Cuirti.^f—Ṡilla-Crirt^h hUa hEoḋaiẛ, erircorur Con-
ṁaicne, quieuit.—Aṁlaiḃ hUa Ḋomnalla[i]n, ollam
Connaċt, quieuit.^h)

⁵ir (in om.), A. ⁶brodd, A. ⁷rri—*against,* B. ⁸.ui. xx.it., A, B.
⁹The it is om., probably from oversight, A. ¹⁰dono, B. ¹¹cuq, B; i.e.
q=cu, by an absurd scribal affectation of Latin. ᵉ Co (rotrarcair)—
So that (it prostrated), B. ^d-d irin bliaḋain rin—*in that year,* B; "in that
same yeare," C. ^e-e co roairẛret muinntera iṁda—"that they spoyled
many people [territories]," B and C respectively. ^f-f om., B, C. ^g-g n. t. h.,
A; om., B, C. ^h-h f. m., n. t. h., A; om., B, C.

² *Made an onset upon them.*—Literally, *gave an onset to them.*

³ *Defeat was inflicted.*—This is
the fourth battle of Cambrensis.
Quartum apud Uriel (Oirghialla),
ubi multi quoque suorum interempti et alii in fugam conversi
(*Exp. Hib.* ii. 17).

⁴ *Fir-Li.*—Cambrensis erroneo-
ously makes this the third battle.
Tertium erat apud Ferli, praedæ
captione, ubi, ob arctum viæ

Raghnall, son of Echmarcach Ua Catha[i]n, was killed by [1178] the Cenel-Maien in the beginning of that summer. So, in revenge of that, fell Galach Ua Luinigh and Muircertach Ua Peatain and it is in revenge of it the treacherous attack of the sons of Domnall was made upon the Cenel-Moien.—It is in that year also there came a wonderful, violent wind which prostrated a very large portion of woods and forests and very great oaks full flat on the ground. It prostrated also six score oaks, or a little more, in Daire of Colum-cille.—It is in that year likewise went John [De Courcy], with his knights, pillaging from Dun to the Plain of Conaille, so that they took many preys therein and were a night in camp in Glenn-righi. Howbeit, Murchadh Ua Cerbaill, king of Airgialla, and Mac Duinnsleibhe [Ua Eochadha], king of Ulidia, with the Ulidians came up with them that night and made an onset upon them.[2] Thereupon defeat was inflicted[3] upon the Foreigners and stark slaughter was put upon them. The same John, notwithstanding, went for preys into Dal-Araidhe and into Ui-Tuirtri. But Cu-Midhe Ua Flainn, king of Ui-Tuirtri and Fir-Li[4], made an onset upon them[2]. That battle also went against the Foreigners and slaughter of them was inflicted.

(The attack of Cualnge[5] [was gained] by Ulidians and by Foreigners over John De Courcy.—Gilla-Crist[6] Ua hEodhaigh, bishop of Conmaicni [Ardagh], rested.—Amhlaibh[6] Ua Domnalla[i]n, ollam of Connacht, rested.)

---

transitum, . . . sic pars Johannis victa succubuit, aliis interemptis, aliis per nemorosa dispersis, ut vix Johanni undecim milites superstites adhaesissent. Ipse vero . . . per triginta stadia se ab hostili multitudine continue defendendo, equis amissis, usque ad castrum suum, duobus diebus et noctibus jejuni, armati, pedites, miro conatu memoriaque dignissimo, evaserunt.

[5] *Attack of Cualgne.*—This is the first defeat mentioned in the final original entry of the present year.

[6] *Gilla-Crist; Amlaibh.*—Given in *Annals of Boyle*; the second is in the Four Masters also.

annala ulaoh.

Kal. Ian. 11.² f.¹ L. xx., Anno Domini M.° c.° lxx.° ix.⁹ d'aois, [in] d-apa bliadain do Noidecda, in⁶ cper bliadain pop direx.⁶ Sid do denum do Dhonncad hUa Caipella[i]n 7 do Clainn-Diapmata uile pe Cenel-Moien¹ 7 pi hUa n-Gailmpedaig, doon, pi hAmlaim, mac Menma[i]n,² doon, depbpatain mna Donncada hUi Caipella[i]n, ap lap tempaill Apda-ppata, ima minnaid Domnaig-mop 7 na hepnaidi 7 Apda-ppata. hUa Gailmpedaig dono do taidect ipin loo³ ap nabapat do gabail tuillid plan⁴ co tet Donncada hUi Caipella[i]n. Mebol áinpial do denum pop⁵ lap in aipecta i n-dopup taigi hUi Caipilla[i]n, i piadnu[i]pe a depbpetap pein,ᵈ doon, mna Donncada: doon, tpiap d'a muinnten do mapbad mapoen pip pein, doon, Cinaet, mac Apt (doon, Lanbiatat) hUi Dpaca[i]n 7 mac Gilla-Cpipt mic Copmaic, mic Reoda[i]n, doon, depbcomalta do Donncad hUa Caipella[i]n.—Apd-Mata do lopcad ex maiopi⁶ papte: doon, na huile peiclepa 7 in[n]a huile tempaill pobatap⁷ ann, uile do lopcad,⁷ cenmota peiclep Dpigti 7 tempoll na pepta.—hUa Ruadaca[i]n, pí hUa-n-Etat, do ec do galap tpi n-aidte iap n-a innapba[d] 7 iap papugud Canoine Patpaic do gap poime.—Cealla Thpe-hEogain o Shleib pader do polmugud tpia tocad 7 tpia dotmataid ipin bliadain pin.—Gilla-Domnaig hUa Papanna[i]n,⁷ aipcinnet Apda-ppata 7 Mael-Muipe,

A.D. 1179. ¹—Maian, A. ²Menmaien, B. ³loa, A. ⁴lan (p om.), A. ⁵ap—on, B. ⁶maiope, B. ⁷pop—, B. ᵃ⁻ᵃ blank space, A. ᵇ⁻ᵇ om., A. ᶜ dono—*indeed*—added, B. ᵈ om., A; C follows B. ᵉ⁻ᵉ om., B, C.

1179. ¹ *Inhospitable.—assembly.—* "A filthy murther committed in midest of the congregacion," C.

² *Three.*—Himself, perhaps, and the two here mentioned.

³ *Church of the relics.* — This church is twice mentioned in the Book of Armagh. First, in connexion with the donation of the place by Daire to St. Patrick. Dedit [Daire] illi [Patricio] locum alium in inferiori terra, ubi nunc est *Fertae Martyrum* [shrine of the relics] iuxta *Ardd-Machae* (Fol. 6d). Secondly, in connexion with the Sunday procession: in Alto-*Machae*

Kalends of Jan. on 2nd feria, 20th of the moon, A.D. [1179] 1179. Namely, the 2nd of the Decemnovennal [Cycle], the 3rd year above a Bissextile. Peace was made by Donnchadh Ua Cairella[i]n and by all Clann-Diarmata with the Cenel-Moien and Ua Galmredhaigh: namely, with Amlaim, son of Menman, that is the brother of the wife of Donnchadh Ua Cairilla[i]n, in the centre of the church of Ard-sratha, upon the relics of Domnach-mor and of the Ernaidhe and of Ard-sratha. Thereupon Ua Gailmredhaigh came on the morrow, to receive additional sureties, to the house of Donnchadh Ua Cairilla[i]n. Inhospitable treachery[1] was committed in the midst of the assembly,[1] at the door of the house of Ua Cairilla[i]n, in the presence of his [Amlaim's] own sister, namely, the wife of Donnchadh: that is, three[2] of his [Amlaim's] people were killed along with himself, namely, Cinaeth (that is, a full Biatach), son of Art Ua Braca[i]n and the son of Gilla-Crist, son of Cormac Mac Reodain, to wit, the very foster-brother to Donnchadh Ua Cairella[i]n.—Ard-Macha was burned for the greater part: that is, all the houses of Canons Regular and all the churches that were in it, all were burned, save the house of the Canons Regular of Brigit and the church of the Relics.[3]—Ua Ruadhacain, king of Ui-Ecbach, died after three nights' illness, after his expulsion and after his profanation[4] of the Canon of Patrick a short time before. —The churches of Tir-Eogain from the mountain southwards were desolated through war and through dearth in that year.—Gilla-Domnaigh[5] Ua Faranna[i]n, herenagh of

---

ad Sargifagum Martyrum (glossed on the margin *du ferti martur*—to the shrine [*lit.* grave] of the relics) adeundum ab eoque revertendum (Fol. 21d).

[4] *Profanation.*—This took place, probably, by breaking an engagement ratified by oath on the Book of Armagh, anciently called the *Canon of Patrick.*

[5] *Gilla-Domnaigh.* — *Devotee of Sunday*; i.e., one zealous for the observance of that day.

mac Gilla-Cumain, recnap in baile cetna[i], in Chrirto quieuerunt.—Colman[a] hUa Scannla[i]n, aircinneac Cluane, moptu[u]r erc.[b]—Cluane[s] 7 Apd-rrata 7 Domnac-mór 7 in[d] Airnaibe do folmuzud do[b] feraib Muizi-Ita.—Noenenac,[c] mac in firleizinn, Ua Touaid, toirec Clainne-Finzin 7 a n-aircinneé arcena 7 a comurplec, moptu[u]r erc.[c]

(Ragnall,[f] mac Mic Ragnaill, toirec Maintiri-hEolair, occirur erc.—Tuatal hUa Connactaiz, epircopur Thiri-Opuin, quieuit.—Sneacta na mure hoc anno.[f])

B55c[Bis.] |Kal. 1an. iii.[a] f.,[a] L 1., Anno Domini M.[o] c.[o] lxxx.[o] Gilla-in-Coimded[1] hUa[2] Cara[i]n, comarba patraic, do éc.—Mac Neill hUa Coema[i]n do marbad do Dhonncad Mac Catmail 7 a marbad fein ann.—Ragnall hUa Cairella[i]n do marbad do Cenel-Moen i[3] n-einec Coluim-cille ar[b] lar Daire.[b]—Mac Aindilir

A 53d hUi Docurtaiz do m|arbad do mac Magnur[a] hUi Cellaca[i]n.[c]—Mac-Craic hUa Daizri, aircinnec Daire, do éc.—Donncad hUa Cairella[i]n do marbad do Ceneol-Conaill tria mirbuil Coluim-cille.—Aindiler hUa Docurtaiz do ec i n-Daire Coluim-cille.

(Cat[d] na Concubar, ison, Concubar Maenmuide, mac

[a]—no, B. [b]o—by, B. [c-c] n. t. h., A; om., B, C.
A.D. 1180. [1] Coimdeg, B. [2] O, A. [3] a, A. [a-a] blank space, A [b-b] om., A; "in the middest of Dyry," C. [c-c] om., B, C.

---

[e] *Magh-Itha.*— C adds: "and O'Moltoray [Ua Maeldoraidh] at Dramchey [Drumcliabh, Drumcliff]. They burnt Esdara throughly and turned againe to Conaght; they went into their houldings. Conaght and Mounstermen sett uppon them and killed most of them and the Galls [Foreigners, i.e. English] left the country forcibly with some bickering.—And O'Cuin's daughter, queen of Mounster, pylgrimaging at Dyry [Derry], dyed, with overcoming the divell and the world."

The original of the foregoing is the conclusion of 1188. *Magh-Itha* is the last word on B 55b. The

Ard-sratha and Mael-Muire, son of Gilla-Cumain, vice-abbot of the same place, rested in Christ.—Colman Ua Scanla[i]n, herenagh of Cluain [-Umha], died.—Cluane and Ard-sratha and Domnach-mor and the Ernaidhe were desolated by the Men of Magh-Itha.[6]—Noenenach Ua Touaid, son of the Lector, chief of the Clann-Finghin and their herenagh besides and their counsellor, died.

(Raghnall, son of Mac Raghnaill, chief of Muinnter-Eolais, was slain.—Tuathal[7] Ua Connachtaigh, bishop of Tir-Briuin [Enaghdune], rested.—"The snow of the destruction"[8] [fell] this year).

Kalends of Jan. on 3rd feria, 1st of the moon, A.D. 1180. Gilla-in-Coimdedh[1] Ua Cara[i]n, successor of Patrick, died.—The son of Niall Ua Coema[i]n was killed by Donnchadh Mac Cathmail and [Donnchadh] himself was killed therein.[2]—Raghnall Ua Cairella[i]n was killed by the Cenel-Maien in the centre of Daire, in reparation to Colum-cille.[3]—The son of Aindiles Ua Dochurtaigh was killed by the son of Maghnus Ua Cellaca[i]n.—Mac-Craith Ua Daighri, herenagh[4] of Daire, died.—Donnchadh Ua Cairella[i]n was killed by the Cenel-Eogain through miracle of Colum-cille.—Aindiles Ua Dochartaigh died in Daire of Colum-cille.

(The battle[5] of the Conchubhars: namely, Conchubhar

[1179]

[1180 Bis.]

---

translator turned over two folios and began with 56c. "Houldings" arose from mistaking the local name *Segdais* for *tegdais*. "Some bickering" is also wrong.

[7] *Tuathal.*—Given in the *Four Masters*.

[8] *Of the destruction.*—Cf. perdidisti—*ro muris* (L. B. 43b). The reading in the *Annals of Boyle* is *na nemi* (O'Conor's *n anemi*)—*of the venom.* The snow was doubtless so called from the great loss of life and property caused thereby.

1180. [1] *Gilla-in-Coimdedh.* — Devotee of the Lord.

[2] *Therein.*—That is, in the act of slaying.

[3] *In reparation to Colum-cille.*—"Being uppon Columkill's proteccion!" C.

[4] *Herenagh, etc.*—"Archdeane of Dyry, kylled," C.

[5] *The battle.*—Abridged apparently from the *Annals of Boyle*.

Ruaiḋri hUi Choncubair 7 Concobur hUa Ceallaiġ, ou i torcair Concobur hUa Ceallaiġ 7 a mac, ioon, Taoġ 7 a ḋerbrataiṙ, ioon, Oiarmuio 7 mac Oiarmooa, ioon, Mael-Seaclainn 7 mac Taiḋġ hUi Concobuir, ioon, cliamuin.—Ġilla-Crirt, mac Mic Carroamna, tairec Muinntiri Mail-Shinna, occirur ert.ᵈ)

|Cal. Ian. u.ᵃ r.,ᵃ L. xii., Anno Domini M.° c.° Lxxx.° 1.° Aeḋ Mac Murcaḋa, riġtoireć Muinnteri-Birn 7 Airter 7 in Tricha-cet, oo marbaḋ oo Mac Matġamna i mebail airecta.—Irinᵇ bliaḋain ri oonoᵇ robrir Plaitbertać hUa Maeloorai̇ḋ, ioon, rí Ceneoil-Conaill,¹ caḃ for macaiḃ riġ Connact, ioon, Oia-Sataiṙn Ceṅṫciġir 7ᵈ romarbaḋ imorro⁰ ré² meic riġ éc oo macaiḃ riġ Connact ann⁰ 7 oerġár Connact arcena.—Sloġaḋ la Oomnall, mac Aeḋa hUi Loclainn 7 la Cenel-n-Eogain Tolca-óac i n-Ultaiḃ 7 oobrireoṫur caḋ ar Ultaiḃ 7 ar hUib-Tuirtri 7 ar Peraiḃ-Li um³ Ruaiḋri Mac Ouinnrleiḃe 7 im Coin-Miḋe hUa Phlainn.—Creacᵇ mor la Peraiḃ Maiġi-hItą im O Catą[i]n ioon, Ectmarcać 7 Cenel-m-Binniġ Glinne, co n-oecatur tar Tuaim 7 corainġretar Phiru-Li 7 hUa-Tuirtri 7 ġu riġratur ilmile oo buaiḃ.ᵇ—Tomaltać hUa Concobair oo ġabail comurbu[i]r Patraic 7 co n-oernaḋᵈ cuairt Ceneoil-Eogain leir,ᵇ co rue cuairt moirᵇ 7 co tuc bennactain rariḃ.ᶠ

ᵈ⁻ᵈ n. t. h., A.; om., B, C.
A.D. 1181. ¹ Cenel—, A. ² .ui., A, B. ³ im, B. ⁴ n-oernaḋ— he made, B. ᵃ⁻ᵃ blank space, A. ᵇ⁻ᵇ om., B, C. ᶜ oono—indeed—added, B. ᵈ oú in—a place in which, B; followed by C. ᵉ om. (being unnecessary, in consequence of the reading in the preceding note), B, C. ᶠ om., B, C.

---

⁶ Gilla-Crist.—Given in the Annals of Boyle. The two additional entries are reproduced in the Four Masters.
1181. ¹ Cantred.—In the original, Tricha-cet: for which see 1106, note 4; 1177, note 10.
² Battle.—For a fuller account, see the Annals of Loch Ce (ad. an.).

Maenmbuidhe, son of Ruaighri Ua Conchubair and Conchobur Ua Ceallaigh, wherein fell Conchobuir Ua Ceallaigh and his son, that is, Tadg and his brother, namely, Diarmuid and the son of Diarmuid, namely, Mael-Sechlainn and the son of Tadg Ua Chonchobuir, that is, the son-in-law.—Gilla-Crist,[6] son of Mac Carrdamna, chief of Muinnter-Mail-Sinna, was slain.) [1180]

Kalends of Jan. on 5th feria, 12th of the moon, A.D. 1181. Aedh Mac Murchadha, royal chief of Muinnter-Birn and the Airthir and the Cantred,[1] was killed by Mac Mathgamna in treachery, at a meeting.—In this year also Flaithbertach Ua Maeldoraidh, namely, king of Cenel-Conaill, gained a battle[2] upon the sons of the kings of Connacht, that is, on the Saturday of Pentecost [May 23] and there were killed indeed sixteen sons of kings of the sons of kings of Connacht and [there was] stark slaughter of Connacht besides.—A hosting by Domnall, son of Aedh Ua Lochlainn and by the Cenel-Eogain of Telach-oc into Ulidia and they gained a battle over the Ulidians and over Ui-Tuirtri and over Fir-Li, around Ruaidbri Mac Duinnsleibhe [Ua Eochadha] and around Cu-Midhe Ua Flainn.— A great foray by the Men of Magh-Itha around O'Cathain, namely, Echmarcach and by the Cenel-Binnigh of the Glenn, until they went past Tuaim [on the Bann] and harried Fir-Li and Ui-Tuirtri and took away many thousands of cows.—Tomaltach Ua Conchobair assumed the succession of Patrick[3] and the circuit of Cenel-Eogain was made by him, so that he took away large circuit [cess] and gave a blessing to them. [1181]

The *Annals of Innisfallen* merely say: "A battle between the Connachtmen and Cenel-Eogain;" the *Annals of Boyle*, with still greater brevity: "the battle of the royal-heirs."

[3] *Succession of Patrick*.—That is, he was made archbishop of Armagh,

200

(Domnall᙮ hUa Ceinneuig, ri Ur-Muman, occirur [ert].—Donnsleibe O Gabra, ri Sleibe-Lugu, occirur [ert].—Domnall hUa Concenainn, ri hUa-n-Diarmata, occirur [ert].—Ccan hUa pallamain, tairec Clainni-Uadac, moritur.—Cat na rigdomna, du i torcradar da mac Toirrdelbaig hUi Concobair, idon, Brian Luigneč 7 Magnur 7 tri meic Ceda, mic Toirrdelbaig U[i] Concobuir, idon, Mael-Secnaill 7 Muirctač 7 Muirčertač et ceteri.᙮)

Kal. Ian. ui᙮. f᙮., L xx. iii., Cnno Domini M.° c.° lxxx.° ii.° Sluagad la Domnall hUa Loclainn co Dun-mbó i n-Dal Riatai 7 cat do tabairt dó[b] do Ghallaib annsein 7 maidm for[c] Cenel-n-Eogain 7 Ragnall O Breirlen do marbad ann 7 Gilla-Crirt O Cača[i]n do[d] marbad ann[d] et alii multi. Ocur Sorcela Martain do br[e]it do Ghallaib leó.

(Domnall᙮ hUa hUallača[i]n, ardercor Muman, quieuit.—Milid Goccan 7 Remonn 7 Cenn-cuilind 7 da mac Steimin et alii multi occiri runt.—Maidm reim

[a-a] n. t. h., A; om., B, C.

A.D. 1182. [a-a] blank space, A. [b] doib—*to them*, B, C. [c] ar—*on*, B. [d-d] om., B, C. [e-e] n. t. h., A; om., B, C.

in succession to Ua Carain, who died in the previous year.

[4] *Domnall; Donnsleibhe.*—Given in the *Annals of Boyle* (ad an.).

[5] *The battle, etc.*—This refers to the second original entry of the present year. The names agree with those in the *Annals of Loch Ce.*

1182. [1] *Gospel of Martin.*—See under 1166, note 2. On the present occasion, it was most probably borne in battle as a *Cathach*, or *præliator*, to ensure victory to the native forces.

[2] *Domnall; Milo; A defeat.*—The three entries are in the *Annals of Boyle.*

[3] *Milo Cogan.*—Mac Geoghegan in his *Annals*, at 1181, says: "Miles Cogan, Reymond Delagrosa, Keann-koylean and the two sons of Fitz Stephens were killed by Mac Tyer, prince of Imokoylle" [recte, Ui-Liathain].

Cambrensis writes: Milo, Milonisque gener nuper effectus, Radulphus, Stephanidae fiilius, versus Lismoriae partes profecti, cum in campis sedentes colloquium cum Waterfordensibus expectassent; a

(Domnall[4] Ua Ceinneidig, king of Ormond, was slain.— [1181]
Donnsleibe[4] O'Gadhra, king of Sliab-Lughu, was slain.—
Domnall Ua Concenainn, king of Ui-Diarmata, was slain.
—Acan Ua Fallamhain, chief of the Clann-Uadach, dies.—
The battle[5] of the royal-heirs, wherein fell two sons of
Toirrdelbach Ua Concobair, namely, Briain of Luighni
and Magnus and three sons of Aedh, son of Toirrdelbach
Ua Conchobuir, that is, Mael-Secnaill and Muirethach and
Muircertach and others.)

Kalends of Jan. on 6th feria, 23rd of the moon, A.D [1182]
1182. A hosting by Domnall Ua Lochlainn to Dun-mbo
in Dal-riatai and battle was there given by him to the
Foreigners and defeat [was inflicted] upon Cenel-Eogain
and Raghnall Ua Breislein was killed there and Gilla-
Crist Ua Catha[i]n was killed there and many others
[were killed]. And the Gospel[1] of [St] Martin was carried
off with them by the Foreigners.

(Domnall[2] Ua hUallachain, archbishop of Munster, rested.
—Milo[2] Cogan[3] and Remonn[4] and Cenn-cuilind[5] and the
two[6] Fitz Stephens and many others were slain.—A defeat[2]

---

proditore Machtiro, qui eos ea nocte hospitari debuerat, cum aliis quinque militibus, improvisis a tergo securium ictibus sunt interempti (*Exp. Hib.* ii. 20).

For the family of Mectire, see 1199, note 1, *supra*; for his alleged treachery, O'Donovan (*F. M.* iii. 61, note *e*).

[4] *Remonn.*—Giraldus (*Exp. Hib.* ii. 35) mentions the death *Reimundi Hugonidae* [Fitz Hugh] *apud Olethan* [Ui-Liathain, the baronies of Barrymore and Kinnatalloon, co. Cork. The name lives in *Caislean Ua-Liathain*, Castlelyons]. He places it after the arrival of prince John. But, as his dates are unreliable and the place accords, *Reimundus*, we may conclude, is the *Remonn* of the text.

[5] *Cenn-Cuilind.*—*Holly-head.* This can hardly be the *Reimundus Cantitunensis* of Cambrensis, whose death is said to have occurred in Ossory, *apud Ossiriam* [*Exp. Hib.* ii. 35], after 1185.

[6] *Two.*—Cambrensis names but one, Radulph (*Exp. Hib.* ii. 20).

Ruaiḋri hUa Concobuir 7 reim Concobuir Maenmuiġi ror Ḋonnċaḋ, mac Ḋomnaill Miḋiġ 7 ror hUa Maeloraiḋ, ubi multi ceciderunt.ᶜ)

Kal. 1an. uiii.ᵃ r.,ᵃ L. iiii., Anno Ḋomini M.º c.º lxxx.º iii.º Taċur itir in¹ Ġilla-riabaċ hUa Flaiṫbertaiġ² 7 mac hUi Ġhaḟlmpeḋaiġ | 7 O [Fh]laiṫbertaiċ do marbaḋ ann 7 drem do Ceniul-Moen³ do marbaḋ ann.

(Orḋoᵇ Templariorum 7 horritalariorum conrirmatur.ᵇ—Ḋonnċaḋ,ᶜ mac Ḋomnaill Miḋig, occirur [ert.]— Gilla-Ira hUa Mailin, erruc Maiġ-Eó, moritur.—Coġaḋ mor eter Ruaiḋri hUa Concobuir 7 a mac, iḋon, Concobur Maenmuiġi.ᶜ)

[bir.] Kal. 1an. i. r., L. x.u., Anno Ḋomini M.º c., lxxx. iiii.. Ḋeiċ taiġi risiṫ¹ do maiṫiḃ Muinnterir Arḋa-Maċa² do argain do Ġhallaiḃ na Miḋe.—Mael-Iru hUa Cerbaill do ġabail comurbuir rarais iar n-a faġbail do Tomaltaċ hUa Concobuir.—Art hUa Mael-[Sh]eċlainn,ᵇ rí Iartair Miḋe, do marbaḋ i meḋail ar erail Ġall. MaelSeċlainn bec do ġabail riġi i n-a inaḋ.—Cairtel ḋ'[f]atuġuḋ la Ġallaiḃ i Cill-rair.—Cairtel aile do milliuḋ la Mael-Seċlainn 7 la Concobur Maenmaiġi hUa Concobair co rosaiḋe moir do Ġhallaiḃ anḋ.

A.D. 1183. ¹ an, A. ² lant-(ṫ om.), B. ³ Cheneol-Moean, A.—⁴ blank space, A. ᵇ⁻ᵇ 53d r. m., t. h., A; om., B, C. ᶜ⁻ᶜ n. t. h., A; om., B, C.
A.D. 1184. ¹ xx., A, B. ² Airdmaċa, A.

1183. ¹ *Gilla-riabhach.* — The *swarthy gillie.*

² *The Order, etc.* — This entry (which likewise occurs in Clyn's Annals, *ad. an.*) is a strange jumble of errors. The Order of Templars was confirmed by the Council of Troyes in 1128. Arnaud de Toroge, the eighth Grand Master, ruled from 1179 to 1184.

The Order of the Hospitallers of St. John (the Baptist) of Jerusalem was confirmed by Pope Paschal II. in 1113. Roger des Moulins, the seventh Grand Master, governed from 1177 to 1187.

The earliest notices of the Orders in Anglo-Irish documents are perhaps the grant by King John (July, 1199) of possessions in Ireland to

[was inflicted] by Ruaidhri Ua Conchobuir and by Conco- [1182]
bur Maenmuighi upon Donnchadh, son of Domnall the
Midian and upon Ua Maeldoraidh, where many fell.)

Kalends of Jan. on 7th feria, 4th of the moon, A.D. [1183]
1183. A contest [took place] between the Gilla-riabhach[1]
Ua Flaithbertaigh and the son of Ua Gailmredhaigh and
O[F]laithbertaigh was killed there and a party of the
Cenel-Moien was killed there.

(The Order[2] of Templars and Hospitallers is confirmed.
—Donnchadh,[3] son of Domnall the Midian, was slain.—
Gilla-Isu[3] Ua Mailin, bishop of Magh-Eo, dies.—Great
war[3] between Ruaidhri Ua Concobuir and his son, namely,
Concobur Maenmuighi.)

Kalends of Jan. on 1st feria, 15th of the moon, A.D. [1184 Bis.]
1184. Thirty houses of the principal members[1] of the
Community of Ard-Macha were pillaged by the Foreigners
of Meath.—Mael-Isu Ua Cerbaill [bishop of Clogher] took
the succession of Patrick, after it was laid aside by Tomaltach Ua Conchobair.—Art Ua Mael-Sechlainn, king of the
West of Meath, was killed by direction of the Foreigners.
Mael-Sechlainn the Little took the kingship in his
stead.—A castle[2] was built by the Foreigners in Cell-fair.
—Another castle was destroyed by Mael-Sechlainn and by
Conchobur Maenmaighi Ua Conchobair, with a large
number of Foreigners therein.

---

the Knights Templars and a grant by the same (June, 1200) of a charter of liberties to the Knights Hospitallers (*Calendar of Documents relating to Ireland*, Vol. I. Nos. 85, 123).

Donnchadh ; Gilla-Isu ; Great war.—These three items are erroneously inserted in this place. See them under next year.

1184. [1] *Principal members.*—Lite-rally, *good* (*men*). For *maithibh* the Four Masters have *roighnibh cumhdaighthi*, which seems meaningless. O'Donovan translates it "of the best houses," which is not the sense of the original.

[2] *Castle.*—This, most probably, is the *castellum de Kilair*, which Cambrensis states was built by De Lacy (in 1182). (*Exp. Hib.* ii. 23.)

(Donnchad,ᵃ mac Domnaill Midig, occirur [erc].—
Gilla-Iru hUa Mailin, erpuc Muigi-eo, moritur.—
Cogad mor eter Ruaidri hUa Concobair 7 a mac, idon,
Concobur Maenmuigi.—Brian Breifnec, mac Toirr-
delbaig hUi Concobair, moritur.—Flann hUa Finnachta,
tairec Clainni-Murchada, moritur.)

Kal. Ian. iii. f., L. ui., Anno Domini M.° c.° lxxx.° u.°
Merr mor (idon,ᶜ dairmer) irin bliadain ri co coitcenn.
—Pilip Uinferra¹ co n-Gallaib Erenn ime i n-Ard-
Maca co cenn ré² la 7 ré n-oidce i ceptmedon in
Chorgair.—Amlaim hUa Muiretaig, errcop Ard[a]-
Maca 7 Ceniuil-Feradaig,³ lochrann rolurta noroillrigid
tuait 7 eclair, in Chrirto quieuit, i⁴ n-Dun⁴-Cruchnai 7
a tabairt co honorac co Dairi Coluim-cille 7 a adnucal
fo coraib a atar, idon, in⁵ erruic hUi Cobtaig (idon,ᵇ
i toeb in tempaillᵇ biccᶜ), octogerimoᵈ rexto [a]etatir
ru[a]e anno.ᵈ Fogurtac hUa Cerballa[i]n do Ceniul-
Ellanna do oirdned i n-a inad.—Gilla-Crirt Mac
Catmail, rigtoirec Ceneoil-Feradaig 7 na Clann, (idonᵉ
Clann-Oengura 7 Clann-Duibinnrect 7 Clann-Fhogur-
taig) 7 hUa-Cenn[f]ataᵉ 7 Clainni-Colla⁷ do feraib-

ᵃ⁻ᵉ n. t. h., A; om., B, C.

A.D. 1185. ¹ Un—B. ² ui, A, B. ³—eradaig (f om.), A. ⁴⁻⁴ inn[d]un (eclipsed d om.), A. ⁵ an, A. ⁶—Cennfoda, B. ⁷ Congail, A. ᵃ⁻ᵃ itl., t. h., A; om., B, C. ᵇ⁻ᵇ itl., t. h., A, B; given in C. ᶜ itl., t. h., A; om., B, C. ᵈ⁻ᵈ itl., t. h., A; om., B, C. ᵉ⁻ᵉ itl., t. h., A; part of text, B, C.

---

³ *Donnchadh, etc.*—These items (with the exception of the third and *son-Concobair* of the fourth) are given in the *Annals of Boyle* under this year. Observe the capricious variants in the transcription of the three entries that are also placed under the preceding year: *Midigh-Midig, Isu-Isa, Muighi-Maighi, Concobhair-Conchobair.*

⁴ *Great war.*—According to the *Annals of Boyle*, Ruaidhri gave up the kingship to his son in 1183 and "reigned again" in 1184. The present entry (if it be not misplaced; Cf. the first additional item of 1185) will thus signify that he re-took possession by force.

1185. ¹ *Philip of Worcester.*—This agrees with Cambrensis, who calls

(Donnchadh,[3] son of Domnall the Midian, was slain.— Gilla-Isu Ua Mailin, bishop of Magh-Eo, dies.—Great war[4] between Ruaidhri Ua Conchobair and his son, namely, Concobur Maenmuighi.—Brian of Breifni, son of Toirrdelbach Ua Concobair, dies.—Flann Ua Finnachta, chief of Clann-Murchadha, dies.)

[1184]

Kalends of Jan. on 3rd feria, 26th of the moon, A.D. 1185. Great crop (namely, oak-crop) generally in this year.—Philip[1] of Worcester, with the Foreigners of Ireland along with him, [stayed] in Ard-Macha for six days and six nights in the very middle of the Lent.—Amhlaim Ua Muirethaigh, bishop of Ard-Macha and Cenel-Feradhaigh, the shining lamp that used to illuminate laity and clergy, rested in Christ in Dun-Cruthnai. And he was carried honourably to Daire of Colum-cille and buried at the feet of his father, namely, the bishop Ua Cobhthaigh[2] (that is, beside the small church), in the 86th year of his age. Fogartach Ua Cerballa[i]n of Cenel-Ellanna was instituted in his stead.—Gilla-Crist Mac Cathmail, royal chief of Cenel-Feradhaigh and of the Clanns, namely, Clann-Oengusa and Clann-Duibhinnrecht and Clann-Fhogur-

[1185]

---

him *Philippus Wigorniensis* and gives an account of what he did in Armagh on that occasion :

Revocato Hugone de Laci, Philippus Wigorniensis, . . . cum militibus quadraginta, procurator in insulam est transmissus [anno 1184]. . . . Elapsa vero hieme, convocato exercitu magno, circa Kalendas Martii Archmatiam profectus sacro quadragesimali tempore, a clero sacro auri tributum execrabile tam exigens quam extorquens, cum sius per urbem Lugdunensem [Louth] Dubliniam indemnis est reversus (*Exp. Hib.* ii. 25). The same is given in substance in the *Top. Hib. dist.* ii. c. 50.

[2] *Ua Cobthaigh.*—" It looks very odd," O'Donovan observes, (Four Masters, *iii.* p. 69) " that a bishop O'Murray (Ua Muirethaigh) should be the son of a bishop O'Coffey." His mother, the editor of the *Annals of Loch Cé* suggests, may have been of the family of O'Murray and he may have adopted her name. He succeeded Ua Cerbaill (O'Carroll),

Manach, cenn comairle Tuairc[e]irt Erenn, do marbad, idon, i prid Noin Mai, la hUa n-Eignig 7 la Muinnter-Coema[i]n 7 a cenn do breit leo, co fuit uaidib i cinn mís iartain.—hEoan Sinter (idon, rine terra), mac rig Saxan, do tect i n-Erinn, lucht tri fichet long, no ní ir móa, re taeb iraide reime do Gallaib i n-Erind.—Mael-Isu hUa Muiredaig, ferleiginn Daire Coluim-cille, do éc i n-a fenoir togaide 7 Mael-Cainnig hUa Fercomair do gabail a inaid.— Mael-Seclainn, mac Muircertaic hUi Loclainn, do marbad do Gallaib.

(Cogad eter Ruaidri hUa Concobuir 7 Concobur Maenmuigi, a mac. Domnall hUa Briain i foiridin Ruaidri, gur'mill 7 gur'loirc 7 gur'airg cella iartair Connact, gur'marb a n-daine.—Catal Carrac, mac Concobair Maenmuigi, d'argain 7 do lorcad Cilli-da-lua i n-digail na n-olc sin.—[Diarmait, mac Toirdelbaig U[i] Briain, do dalluod la] Domnall hUa Briain.—Rigi Connact do gabail do Concobur Maenmaigi.)

Kal. Ian. iiii. f., L. uii., Anno Domini M.° c.° lxxx.° ui.° Tachair mor i Tuaircert Erenn irin bliadain si.— Atrigad Domnaill, mic Aeda hUi Loclainn 7 rigad Ruaidri hUi [Fh]laithbertaic is dreim do Cheniul-Eogain Talca-óac.—Gilla-patraic mac mic in gilla

8.8 rinetra (=rine terra), A. 9 tractain, B. 10 xx., A, B. 1-4 itl. t. h.. A, B; "John sine terra," C. 5-6 om., B, C. b-b n. t. h., A: om., B, C. 14 t. m., n. t. h. (first entry is imperfect, owing to excision of margin), A; om., B, C.
A.D. 1186. 1 Laclainn, B. a-a blank space, A. b-b om., B, C.

² *Sixty ships strong.*—Literally, the folk of three score ships
For the date of John's arrival, see Cambrensis, *Exp. Hib.* ii. 32; for his doings in Ireland, *ib.* 36 (Rolls' ed.).

taigh and the Ui-Cenn[fh]ata and the Clann-Colla of Fir- [1185]
Manach, head of counsel of the North of Ireland, was
killed, namely, on [Sunday] the 2nd of the Nones [6th] of
May, by Ua Eignigh and by Muinnter-Coema[i]n. And his
head was carried away by them, but was gotten from them
at the end of a month after.—John Lack-land, son of the
king of the Saxons, came into Ireland, sixty[3] ships strong,
or something more, besides what was before him of
Foreigners in Ireland.—Mael-Isu Ua Muiredhaigh, lector
of Daire of Colum-cille, died a choice elder.[4] And Mael-
Cainnigh Ua Fercomais took his place.—Mael-Sechlainn,
son of Muircertach Ua Lochlainn, was killed by the
Foreigners.

(War[5] between Ruaidhri Ua Conchobuir and his son,
Concobur Maenmuighi. Domnall Ua Briain [went] in
aid of Ruaidhri, so that he destroyed and burned
and pillaged the churches of the West of Connacht
[and] killed the inhabitants. Cathal Carrach, son of
Conchobar Maenmuighi, plundered and burned Cell-da-lua
in revenge of those evils.—[Diarmait, son of Tordelbach
Ua Briain, was blinded by] Domnall Ua Briain.—The
kingship of Connacht was assumed by Concobur Maenmaighi.)

Kalends of Jan. on 4th feria, 7th of the moon, A.D. [1186]
1186. Great disturbance in the North of Ireland in this
year.—Deposition of Domnall, son of Aedh Ua Lochlainn
and crowning of Ruaidhri Ua [F]laithbertach by a party
of the Cenel-Eogain of Telach-oc.—Gilla-Patraic, grand-

---

[4] *A choice elder.*—Literally, *in his choice elder*; a native idiom expressing state, or condition.

War, etc.—These items, in- cluding the portion within square brackets), are given (the first at great length) in the *Annals of Boyle.*

cuipp, τοιρες hUa-Όpana[ι]n, το mapβaτ la Όomnall hUa Loclainn, τρια epail Muinnτepi-Όpana[ι]n ρειn.ᵇ

(A)

Uga Όe-laci το mapβaτ τ'O Miατaιξ το τebτa (ιτon,ᶜ malapτaς 7 τιρcailτeς neimeτ 7 cell Epenn, α mapβaτ ι n-eineς Col[uim-cille ιc cumτaς] capτeoil, ιτon, α n-Όep[maιξ]ᶜ).

(B)

huξaᵈ Όe-laci, malapτaς, τιρcailτeς ceall 7 neimeτ Epenn, το mapβaτ τ'U Miατaιξ το βpeξmunaιτ, lapιn 8ιnnaς Ua Caτapnaιξ, ι n-eineς Coluim-cille, ιc cumτaς caιpτeoιl ι n-α ςill, ιτon, ι n-Όupmuιξ, ρexcenτepιmo quατpaξepιmo anno ex quo ρunτaτa eρτ Όapιa eccleρια.ᵈ

Innapβa[τ] Ruaιτρι hUι Conςoβaιp la Conςoβuρ Maenmuιξe,¹ l'a mac ρειn 7 milliuτ Connaςτ eτappu.² —Conn hUa βpeιρlen, coιnnel eιnιξ 7 ξaιρcιτ Tuaιpce[ι]ρτ Epenn, το mapβaτ το τpeιm το Chenel-Eoξaιn 7 Iniρ-Eoξaιn uile το apcaιn τpιτρειn, cen³ co ρaιβe cin τοιτ ann.

(Conςuβap⁰ hUa Plaιςβepτaιξ το mapβaτ la Ruaιτρι hUa Plaιςβepτaιξ, la a τepβρaτaιp ρειn, ι nτ-Αpaιnτ.—Ruaιτρι hUa Conςuβaιp τ'innapβa[τ] τ'α mac ρειn, ιτon, το Conςuβap Mhaenmuιτe.—Όepβopξall, ιnξen

² eτoppa, B. ³ cιn, A. ᶜ⁻ᶜ Partly itl., partly r. m., t. h. [parts within square brackets are wanting, owing to excision of edge of folio], A; om., C. For the reading of B, see parallel entry. ᵈ⁻ᵈ Given in B and C after the Innapβa[τ] item. ᵉ⁻ᵉ n., t. h., A; om., B, C.

1186. ¹ *O'Miadhaigh.*—"A workman," C.

² *Ua Miadhaigh of Breghmuna.*—"Killed as aforesaid, by one of Brewny, by the Fox O'Catharny." C. This translator, it thus appears, had before him the entries as given in A and B. O'Donovan has taken needless pains (p. 72 *sq.*) to confirm the accuracy of the native accounts of De Lacy's death.

³ *640th year.*—O'Donovan inserts "[540 f]." This would date the foundation half a century after the

son of "the stooping gillie," chief of Ui-Brana[i]n, was [1186] killed by Domnall Ua Lochlainn, by direction of the Muinnter-Brana[i]n themselves.

(A)	(B)
Ugo De Lacy was killed by O'Miadhaigh[1] of Tebtha (that is, the destroyer and the dissolver of the sanctuaries and churches of Ireland—he was killed in reparation to Colum-cille, whilst building a castle namely, in Dermagh).	Hugo De Lacy, destroyer [and] dissolver of the churches and sanctuaries of Ireland, was killed by Ua Miadhaigh of Breghmuna,[2] by [direction] of the "Fox" Ua Catharnaigh, in reparation to Colum-cille, whilst building a castle in his church, namely, in Durmagh, in the 640th[3] year since the church of Dairmagh was founded.

Expulsion of Ruaidhri Ua Conchobair by Conchobur Maenmaige, his own son and destruction of Connacht [ensued] between them.—Conn Ua Breislen, candle of hospitality and championship of the North of Ireland, was killed by a party of the Cenel-Eogain and Inis-Eogain was all ravaged through that, although they had no guilt[y part] therein.

(Conchubhar[4] Ua Flaithbertaigh was killed by Ruaidhri Ua Flaithbertaigh, by his own brother, in Ara.—Ruaidhri[4] Ua Conchubair was expelled by his own son, namely, by Conchobhar Maenmhuidhe.—Derbhorgall,[5] daughter of

---

death of St. Columba,—a conclusion quite untenable. The *Daria* intended, the context shows, was Durrow (King's County). It was thus, if the entry can be relied upon, founded in the same year as Derry (545=546, *supra*).

[4] *Conchubhar ; Ruaidhri.*—Given in *Annals of Boyle*, with omission of *by his own brother*, *by his own son* respectively.

[5] *Derbhorgall.*—Whose elopement with Diarmait Mac Murchadha

m uṗċaıṫ hUı Maeıl-Sheċlaınn, ꝺo ḋul ꝩo Ꞃoıċeꞇ-Aꞇa ꝺ'a hoılıċꞇꞃı.'—Opꝺo' Caꞃ[ꞇhuꞃanoꞃum] conꝼıꞃmaꞇuꞃ.')

[Cal. 1an. u.² ꝼ., 'L. x.uııı., Anno Domını M° c.° Lxxx° uııı.' Ruaıḋꞃı hUa [Ꝼh]laıṫbeꞃꞇaıċ, ꞃı Cene[oı]l-Eoꝩaın, ꝺo maꞃbaṫ aꞃ cꞃeıċ ı Ꞇıꞃ-Conaıll.—Caꞃꞃac Laċa-Ce ꝺo loꞃcaꝺ ı meṫon laa, ꝺú ın ꞃobaıṫeṫ 7 ın ꞃoloıꞃceṫ ınꝩen hUı Eꞃḋın, ben Conċobaıꞃ Mıc Dıaꞃmaꞇa, ꞃı[ꝩ] Moıꝩı-Luıꞃꝩ 7 ꞃeċꞇ,¹ no ní ıꞃ moo, eꞇeꞃ ꝼıꞃu ıꞃ mna, ꝺo loꞃcaṫ 7 baꝺuṫ ꞃı² ꞃé oen uaıꞃe ınnꞇı.—Dꞃuım-clıaṫ ꝺo aꞃcaın ꝺo mac Mael-Sheċlaınn hUı Ruaıꞃc (ıꝺon,ᵇ ꝺo Aeṫᵇ), ꝺo ꞃıꝩ hUa-m-Bꞃıuın 7 Conmaıcne 7 ꝺo mac Caċaıl hUı Ruaıꞃc 7 ꝺo Ghallaıṫ na Mıṫe ımaılle ꞃıu.³ Aċꞇ ꝺoꞃoıne Dıa ꝼıꞃꞇ amꞃa aꞃ Colum-cılle ann, ıꝺon, ꞃomaꞃbaṫ mac Mael-Seċlaınn hUı Ruaıꞃc (ıꝺon,ᵇ Aeṫᵇ) ꞃıa cınn caıcıṫıꞃı⁴ ıaꞃ ꞃeın (ı^c Conmaıcne^e) 7 ꞃoꝺallaṫ mac Caċaıl hUı Ru|aıꞃc, ꞃıꞃı ꞇanꝩaꞃ ın ꝼluaıꝩeṫ ı ꞇaıꝩ hUı Maelꝺoꞃaıṫ, ı n-eıneċ Coluım-cılle 7 ꞃomaꞃbaıꞇ⁵ ꞃe⁶ ꝼıċıꞇ⁶ ꝺo aeꞃ ꝩꞃaṫa meıc Mael-Seċlaınn aꞃ ꝼuꞇ Conmaıcne 7 Caıꞃꞃꞃı Dꞃoma-clıaṫ ꞇꞃıa mıꞃbuıl Coluım-cılle.

(Mael-Iꞃuꝺ hUa Ceaꞃḃuıll, eꞃꞃcop Oıꞃꝩıall, quıeuıꞇ.—Muıꞃꝩıuꞃ, mac Ꞇaıꝺꝩ hUı Mhaılꞃuaınıꝩ,⁷ ꞃı Mhuıꝩe-Luıꞃꝩ, obııꞇ.ᵈ)

^{f,f}r. m., n. t. h., A; om., B, C.
A.D. 1187. ¹ uıı, A, B. ² ꝼꞃí, B. ³ ꝼꞃıu, B. ⁴ caeıccıꝩꞃ, A. ⁵⁻baṫ, B. ⁴⁻⁶.uı.xx:, A, B. ⁷-ꞃuaꞃıꝩ, MS. (A). ᵃ,ᵃ blank space, A. ᵇ,ᵇ itl., n. t. h., A; om., B, C. ᶜ,ᶜ itl, t. h., A, B; om., C. ᵈ,ᵈ n. t. h., A; om., B, C.

---

was the alleged cause of the introduction of the English into Ireland.

The Order, etc.—The bracketted portion is from Clyn's Annals. The item is post-dated by more than a century.

1187. ¹ *The Rock.*—By metonymy for the castle and dwellings built on the Rock.

² *Burned.*—By lightning, according to the *Annals of Loch Cé* (which give the occurrence under 1185 and, more briefly, at 1187).

³ *Mid-day.*—The *Annals of Loch Cé* (1185) state the burning took place: ıꞃın Aoıne ıaꞃ n-Inıꞇ ċoꞃꝩuıꞃ —*on the Friday after the Beginning* [of the second and more strictly

Murchadh Ua Mael-Sechlainn, went to Drochait-atha on her pilgrimage.—The Order[6] of Car[thusians] is confirmed.) [1186]

Kalends of Jan. on 5th feria, 18th of the moon, A.D. 1187. Ruaidhri Ua [F]laithbertaigh, king of Cenel-Eogain, was killed on a foray in Tir-Conaill.—The Rock[1] of Loch Ce was burned[2] at mid-day,[3] where was drowned and burned[4] the daughter of Ua Eidhin, wife of Conchobair Mac Diarmata, king of Magh-Luirg. And seven hundred, or something more, both men and women, were burned and drowned in the space of one hour therein.—Druim-cliabh was pillaged by the son of Mael-Sechlainn Ua Ruairc (namely, by Aedh), king of Ui-Briuin and Conmaicni and by the son of Cathal Ua Ruairc and by the Foreigners of Meath along with them. But God wrought a wonderful deed for Colum-cille therein,—that is, the son of Mael-Sechlainn Ua Ruairc (namely, Aedh) was killed (in Conmaicni) before the end of a fortnight thereafter. And the son of Cathal Ua Ruairc, with whom came the hosting into the house of Ua Maeldoraidh, was blinded in reparation to Colum-cille. And six score of the minions of the son of Mael-Sechlainn were killed throughout the length of Conmaicni and Cairpri of Druim-cliabh, through miracle of Colum-cille. [1187]

(Mael-Isu[5] Ua Cearbhuill, bishop of Oirghialla, rested.—Muirghius,[5] son of Tadhg Ua Mailruanaigh, king of Magh-Luirg, died.)

---

observed moiety] *of Lent*; i.e., the Friday after the fourth Sunday of Lent. (See *Todd Lectures*, Ser. III. No. IV.) This will account for the otherwise incredible loss of life. The people had assembled from the mainland for divine service.

[4] *Drowned and burned.*—A hysteron proteron. Her dress having become ignited, the queen rushed into the lake to extinguish the flame and was drowned.

[5] *Mael-Isu; Muirghius.* — Given under the preceding year in the

B 56b[b₁ŗ] Kal. Ian. ui.ᵃ ꝑ.,ᵃ L. xx.ıx., Anno Domini M.°c.°lxxx.° uııı.
Ruaıdrı hUa Cananna[ı]n, rí Ceneoıl-Conaıll rı hed
7 rídomna Erenn, do marbad do [ꝑh]laıtbertać hUa
Maeldoraıd trıa mebaıl ıc Drocat Slıcıẓı,¹ ıarᵇ n-a
brecad do lar Droma-clıad ımać 7 bratair dó do
marbad ımaılle rır 7 drem d'a muınntır. hUa
Ẓaırb (ıdon,ᵃ Maẓnurᶜ), toıreć Fer-Droma, roımír
lama ar hUa Cananna[ı]n, do marbad do muınntır
Ećmarcaıẓ hUı Dočartaıẓ ı n-díẓaıl hUı Chananna[ı]n.
—Domnall hUa Cananna[ı]n do letrad a čoırı dıa
tuaıẓ féın ı n-Daıre ıẓ² ẓaıt arclaınne connaıd 7 a éc
de trıa mírbaıl Coluım-cılle.—Martaın hUa brolaıẓ,
ardecnaıd Ẓoeıdel uıle 7 aroferleıẓınn Aırd-Mača,
do éc.—Amlaım hUa Daıẓrı do tőćt co hI d'a aılıtrı
7 a éc ı n-hI ıar n-aıtrıẓı toẓaıdı.—Ẓaıll Caırteoıl
Maıẓı-Coba 7 drem d'Uıb-Ećać Ulad do čaıbdećt ar
creıć hı Tır-n-Eoẓaın, co torrastadar co Léım-mıc-
Neıll 7 co roẓabrat bú andrın 7ᵈ co n-dečaıd Domnall
hUaLočlaınn 'n-a n-deẓaıd 7 lućt a componna féın, co
ruc forra ı Cabán-na-crann-ard, co tardrat debaıd 7
co romaıd ar na Ẓallaıb 7 co rocuıred* a n-ár and 7
co tardad ẓadad do ẓallẓaı ırın ríẓ a aenor, co
torčaır annrın ı frıtẓuın, ıdon, Domnall, mac Aeda
hUıLočlaınn, rí Aılıẓ³ 7 rídamna Erenn ar cruč 7 ar
čeıll 7 ar taıẓedur 7 ar trebaıre.⁴ Ocur rucad ín la
rın féın co hArd-Mača 7 rohadnaıced ann co honorać.
—Sluaẓad la hEoan Do-Chúırt 7 la Ẓallaıb Erenn uıle
ı Connaċtaıb ımaılle³ ꝛe Concobur hUa n-Dıarmata.

A.D. 1188. ¹ ꝛıẓó, B. ²ı, A. ³O₁—, B. ⁴—baır, A. ᵃ⁻ᵃ blank space, A. ᵇ ıdon, ıaꝛ—*namely, after*, B. ᶜ⁻ᶜ itl, t. h., A, B; given in C. ᵈ om., B; given in C. ᵉ romarbad—*was killed*, B.

Annals of Boyle. Ua Cerbaill (O'Carroll) was elected archbishop of Armagh in 1184. He died, according to Ware (vol. i. p. 180), on his journey to Rome.

Kalends of Jan. on 6th feria, 29th of the moon, A.D. 1188. Ruaidhri Ua Cananna[i]n, king of Cenel-Conaill for a time and royal heir of Ireland, was killed by Flaithbertach Ua Maeldoraidh through treachery, at the Bridge of Slicech, after decoying him out from the centre of Druim-cliabh. And a brother of his was killed along with him and a party of his people. Ua Gairb (namely, Maghnus), chief of Fir-Droma, who laid [violent] hands on Ua Cananna[i]n, was killed by the people of Echmarcach Ua Dochartaigh in revenge of Ua Cananna[i]n.—Domnall Ua Cananna[i]n laid open his foot with his own axe, whilst cutting a faggot of firewood in Daire and he died thereof, by miracle of Coluim-cille.—Martin Ua Brolaigh, arch-sage of all the Goeidhil and arch-lector of Ard-Macha, died.—Amhlaim Ua Daighri came to I[ona] on his pilgrimage and he died in I[ona] after choice penance.—The Foreigners of the castle of Magh-Coba and a party of the Ui-Echach of Ulidia came on a foray into Tir-Eogain, until they reached to Leim-mic-Neill[1] and seized cows there. And Domnall Ua Lochlainn went against them with a force of his own party, until he overtook them at Cabhan of the High Trees. They gave them battle and it went against the Foreigners and slaughter of them was inflicted. And a thrust of a foreign spear was given to the king alone, so that he fell there in the conflict: that is, Domnall, son of Aedh Ua Lochlainn, king of Ailech and [worthy to be] royal heir of Ireland for form and for sense and for excellence and for prudence. And he was carried that very day to Ard-Macha and buried there honourably.—A hosting by John De-Courcy and by the Foreigners of all Ireland into Connacht, along with Con-

---

1188. [1] *Leim-mic-Neill.*—Leap of the son of *Niall* (grandson, according to O'Donovan, *F. M.* iii. 81, of Aedh, king of Ireland, who died 818=819, *supra*). The place was near Dungannon, co. Tyrone (*ib.*)

A 54d Tinoilib Con|cobap Maenmaiʒi (ɪron,ᵃ ɲi Connacͮͭ)
Connacta 7 τιc Domnall hUa Opiain, ɲí Muman, co
opéim o'ɼepaɪƃ Muman ɪ ɼoċpaiτi ɲiʒ Connacͭ. Ⱥcuɼ
loiɼciτ ní oo ċellaɪƃ ɪn τɪɲe ɲempu 7 ní ɲoleicɼeτ
ɼcoilɪuƃᵇ ooɪƃ. Imċloeɪτ ɪmuɲɲo na ʒaɪll aniaɲ co
héɼ-oaɲa oo ċuɪƃecͭͭ ɪ' Τɪɲ-Conaɪll. O'τcualaτuɲ
B 66c ɪmuɲɲo na ʒaɪll Cenel-Conaɪll | 7 hUa Maeloopaɪƃ oo
bɪƃ ɪc Opúɪm-clɪaƃ, ɲoloɪɼcɼeτ Eaɼ-oaɲa oo leɪɲ 7
imcloɪτ aɲ[ɪɕ]ɪɲ[i] ɪ Connaċτaɪƃ 7 τecaiτ ɪɲɪn Seʒoaɪɼ
7 aτnaʒaiτ Connacτaᶠ 7 Ɣɪɲ Muman ammuɼ ɼoɲɲuᵍ 7
maɲbaiτ a n-áɲ 7 ɼacbaiτ na ʒaɪll ɪn τɪɲ aɲ eɪcɪn can
a becc oo ʒleuƃ.—Eτaín, ɪnʒen hUi Cuɪnn, ɲíʒan
Muman, oo báɪ 'ca haɪlɪɕɲɪ ɪc Daɪɲe, oo éc ɪaɲ m-buaɪƃ
o oomon 7 o ƃeṁan.

(Muɪɲċeɼτaċ,ʰ mac Uaɕu, hUa Chonċeanaino, ɲɪ hUa-
n-Ohɪaɲmaτa, moɼτuuɼ eɼτ.—Domnall, mac Loċlaino
hU Mhaeɪlɼuanaɪƃ 7 Ɣeaɲʒal hUa Τaɪɖʒ ɪn τeʒlaɪʒ 7
Ɣlaɪɕbeɼτaċ, mac Rɪucca, hUa Ɣhinnaċτa, occɪɲɪ ɼunτ.ʰ
—Muɪɲċeɼτaċⁱ hUa Oɲaɪn, ɲɪ Oɲeʒṁuɪne, occiɼuɼ eɼτ.ᵢ
—hUaʲ Maɪlɼuanaɪƃ occɪɼuɼ eɼτ Ⱥnno Domɪnɪ 1188.ʲ)

Kal. Ian. 1. ɼ., l. x., Ⱥnno Domɪnɪ m.° c.° lxxx.° ix.°
Domnall, macᵃ Muɪɲċeɼτaɪʒ hUɪ Loċlaɪnn, oo maɲbaƃ
oo ʒhallaɪƃ Dhal-Ⱥɲaɪƃe acu ɼeɪn.—Muɲċaƃ hUa
Ceɼbaɪll, aɪɼoɼɪʒ Ⱥiɼʒɪall, oo éc ɪɲɪn Maínɪɼτɪɲ-moɪɲ

ᵇ maɪlle (aphaeresis of ɪ), A. ᶜ ɼcoeɪlso, B. ⁷ ɼoɲɲa, B. ᶠ co—το, B;
with which agrees C. ᵍ om. (manifestly by oversight), A. ʰ⁻ʰ n. t. h., A;
om., B, C. ⁱ⁻ⁱ 54c, l.m., n. t. h., A; om., B, C. ʲ 54d, t. m., n. t. h.
(overhead, another item was cut away in trimming the edge), A; om., B, C.

A.D. 1189. ᵃ mac mic—*grandson* (mic was added by mistake), B.

---

² *On their march.*—Literally, *before them*.

³ *Ua Maeldoraidh, etc.*—The author of C., having forgotten apparently that he had translated from this to the end of the year under 1179, renders it thus in this place: "and O'Moyldoray were at Drumkliew, they burnt Esdara all and turned to Connaght againe and into camp [" their houldings," 1179 : *recte* the Seghdais]. And Connaght

cobur Ua Diarmata. Concobar Maenmhaighi (namely, [1188]
king of Connacht) musters the Connachtmen and Domnall
Ua Briain, king of Munster, comes with a party of the
Men of Munster into the force of the king of Connacht.
And they burn some of the churches of the country on
their march[2] and some they allowed to escape them [intact].
Howbeit, the Foreigners turn back to Ess-dara to come
into Tir-Conaill. But, when they heard that the Cenel-
Conaill and Ua Maeldoraidh[3] were at Druim-cliabh, they
burned Ess-dara completely and turn again into Connacht
and come into the Seghdais. And the Connachtmen and
Men of Munster deliver an attack upon them and the
Foreigners are killed with slaughter and leave the country
by force without a whit of triumph.—Etain, daughter of
Ua Cuinn, queen of Munster, who was on her pilgrimage
at Daire, died after victory over[4] the world and over[4] the
demon.

(Muircertach[5] Ua Concheanainn, son of Uathu, king of
Ui-Diarmata, died.—Domnall, son of Lochlann Ua Maeil-
ruanaidh and Fearghal Ua Taidhg "of the [hospitable]
household" and Flaithbertach, Ua Finnachta, son of Riucc,
were slain.—Muircertach Ua Brain, king of Breghmhuine,
was slain.—Ua Mailruanaidh[6] was slain, A.D. 1188.)

Kalends of Jan. on 1st feria, 10th of the moon, A.D. [1189]
1189. Domnall, son of Muircertach Ua Lochlainn, was
killed by the Foreigners of Dal-Araidhe, [whilst] amongst
themselves.—Murchadh Ua Cerbaill, arch-king of Air-

---

and Munster came uppon them and slaughtered them and left the country by force, without much fight ["with some bickering," 1179].—Edyn, O'Cuyn's daughter that was pilgrim at Dyry, died."

[4] *Over.*—Literally, *from.*

[5] *Muircertach, etc.*—These four items are given in the *Annals of Loch Ce* under this year.

[6] *Ua Mailruanaidh.*—"Taithleoh, son of Conchobar, son of Diarmaid, son of Tadhg Ua Maelruanaidh, was slain," *Annals of Loch Ce.*

216 ANNALA ULADH.

ap n-aiċriġi ċoġaiḋ.—Apo-Maċa do lorcaḋ o ċpora[iḋ] ḃpiġci co peicler ḃpiġci, eċep Raiċ 7 Cpian 7 ċempul. —Eċmileḋ, mac Mic Canai, ronup 7 robapċain Chipe-hEoġain uile, do éc.—Mac na haiḋċe hUa Mailpuanaiḋ, pí Fep-Manaċ, do aḋpiġaḋ 7 a dul doċum hUi Cepḃaill Acur creċ Ġall do ċuiḋeċċ ipin¹ ċip 7 compaiciḋ hUa Cepḃaill 7 hUa Maelpuanaiḋ rpiú 7 maiḋip rop Ua Cepḃaill 7 mapbċa[i]p hUa Maelpuanaiḋ ann.ᵇ—Conċoḃup Maenmaiġi, mac Ruaiḋpi, aipopi Connaċċ 7 pioamna Epenn uile, do mapbaḋ d'a luċċ ġpaḋa rein, ċpia epail a ḃpaċap, idon, Concoḃaip hUi n-Diapmaċa (mac Copmaicᶜ; aliap,ᵈ mac Ruaiḋpiᵈ)- Conċoḃup hUa n-Diapmaċa dono do mapbaḋ la Caċal cappaċ, mac Concoḃaip Mhaenmaiġi,¹² n-diġail a aċap.— Apo-Maċa do apcain la hEoan Do-Chuipċ 7 la Ġallaiḃ Epenn.—Mac na Pepepi, pí Saxan, do éc.—Mael-Cainniġ hUa Fepcomaip, repleiġinn Daipe, do baċuḋ eċep Aipd 7 Inip-Eoġain.

(Muipcepċaċᶜ hUa Flannaca[i]n, ċoirečh Chlainne-Caċail, mopċuur erċ.ᶜ)

A 55a |Cal. 1an. (11.ᵃ r.,ᵃ) L. xx. 1., Anno Domini M.ᵒ c.ᵒ lxxxx.ᵃ [Lonġᵇ Caċail Cpoiḃḋepġ hi Conċoḃaip, pí Connaċċ, do baċaḋ ap Loċ-Riḃ 7 robaiḋed .xxxui. uipi, im Aipeċċaċ hUa Raḋuiḋ, dux Clainni-Comalċaiġᵇ] 7° im

¹ ir, B. ²a, A. ᵇ om., B, C. ᶜ⁻ᶜ itl, t. h., A; om., B, C. ᵈ⁻ᵈ r. m., n. t. h. A; om., B, C. ᵉ⁻ᵉ n. t. h., A; om., B, C.

A.D. 1190. ᵃ⁻ᵃ blank space, A. The year is blank in A, B, C. ᵇ Supplied from *Annals of Loch Cé,* A.D. 1190. ᶜ⁻ᶜ On text space, n. t. h., A; om., B, C.

1189. ¹ *Mellifont.*—For the Irish Cistercian monasteries, see the erudite Introduction to the *Triumphalia Monasterii S. Crucis,* ed. Rev. D. Murphy, S.J., Dublin, 1891.

² *Close and Third.*—See 1074, note 5, *supra.*

³ *Echmiledh.* — *Horse - soldier;* knight.

⁴ *Son of Ruaidhri.*—The alterna-

gialla, died in the Great Monastery [of Mellifont[1]] after choice penance.—Ard-Macha was burned from the Crosses of Brigit to the Regular church of Brigit, both Close and Third[2] and church.—Echmiledh,[3] son of Mac Canai, happiness and prosperity of all Tir-Eogain, died.—"Son of the night" Ua Mailruanaigh, king of Fir-Manach, was deposed and went to Ua Cerbaill. And a foray[-party] of the Foreigners came into the country and Ua Cerbaill and Ua Maelruanaigh encounter them and defeat is inflicted upon Ua Cerbaill and Ua Maelruanaidh is killed there.— Conchobur Maenmaighi, son of Ruaidhri [Ua Conchobair], arch-king of Connacht and royal heir of all Ireland, was killed by his own minions, by direction of his kinsman, namely, Conchobar Ua Diarmata (son of Cormac; otherwise, son of Ruaidhri[4]). Conchobar Ua Diarmata, however, was killed by Cathal Carrach, son of Conchobar Maenmaighi, in revenge of his father.—Ard-Macha was pillaged by John De-Courcy and by the Foreigners of Ireland.— The son of the Empress,[5] king of the Saxons, died.—Mael-Cainnigh Ua Fercomais, lector of Daire, was drowned between Ard and Inis-Eogain.

(Muircertach[2] Ua Flannaca[i]n, chief of Clann-Cathail, died.)

[1190] Kalends of Jan. on 2nd feria, 21st of the moon, A.D. 1190.

[A ship[1] of Cathal Red-hand Ua Conchobhair, king of Connacht, foundered on Loch-Ribh and there were drowned thirty-six men, including Airechtach Ua Radhuibh, chief of Clann Tomaltaigh] (and including

---

tive is correct, according to the *Annals of Loch Cé*.

[5] *Son of the Empress.*—Henry II. died at Chinon in Touraine, July 6, 1189.

[2] *Muircertach.* — Given (with *Murchad* for *Muircertach* and *dux* for *toiseach*) in the *Annals Of Boyle* under the preceding year.

1190. [1] *A ship, etc.*—The portion

Conchubar, mac Cathail, mic Urain, mic Toirrdealbaich hUi Chonchubair 7 im Murchadh, mac Conchubair, mic Diarmata, mic Taidhg hUi Mhailruanaigh 7 im Muirgius, mac Uatu, hUa Concheanainn.—Dubeassa, ingean Diarmada, mic Thaidhg, mortua est.—Mor, ingean Toirrdealbaigh Ui Cho[n]chubair, mortua est.'—Diarmaid[d] hUa Rabartaigh, abb Durmaige, quievit.—Alle, ingean Riaca[i]n hUi Mailruanaidh, mortua est.—Mail-Seachlaind hUa Neattain 7 Gilla-Beraigh hUa Sluaigeadaigh do marbad la Toirrdealbach, mac Ruaidri hUi Conchubair, Anno Domini 1190.[d]

B 56d Kal. Ian. 3. f., L 11., Anno Domini M.° c.° xc.° 1° (uel'.—11.[aa])

(Ruaidri[b] hUa Conchubair d' fagbail Chonnacht 7 a dul hi Cenel-Conaill.[b])

[bis] Kal. Ian. [1111.[a] f.,[a]] L x. 111., Anno Domini M.° c.° xc.° 11.° Dorus[b] proinntigi in Duibreiclera is a denum la U[a] Cata[i]n na Croiche 7 la ingin hUi Indeirgi.[b]

(Taichleach[c] hUa Dubda, ri hUa-n-Amalgaid 7 hUa-Fhiacrach-Muaidi, do marbad do da mac a meicc fein. —Aed hUa Flainn, taireach Shil-Mhaili-Ruain, mortuus est.[c])

A.D. 1190. [d-d] t. m., n. t. h., A; om., B, C.
A.D. 1191. [a-a] added, B; om., C. The ferial and epact shew that the reading is erroneous. [b-b] n. t. b., A; om., B, C.
A.D. 1192. [a-a] blank space, A; .ui. f., B. [b-b] Given under A.D. 1191°. vel—2°, B; under A.D. 1191, C. [c-c] n. t. h., A; om., B, C.

within square brackets is supplied from the *Annals of Loch Ce* (ad an.) The other entries are found in the order here observed, but with variations in detail, in the same Annals under this year. The first, second, third and fifth are given in substance in the *Annals of Boyle*.

[2] *Dubeassa*.—Wife of Cosnamach O'Dowda, according to the *Annals of Loch Ce*.

[3] *Alle*.—Wife, according to the same Annals, of the Ua Radhuibh who was drowned, as told in the first item of this year.

[4] *Gilla-Beraigh*.—Devotee of [St.]

Conchubhar, son of Cathal, son of Uran, son of Toirrdeal- [1190] bhadh Ua Conchubair and including Murchadh, son of Conchubhar, son of Diarmait, son of Tadhg Ua Mailruanaigh and including Muirgius Ua Concheanainn, son of Uatu.—Dubeassa,[2] daughter of Diarmait, son of Tadhg [Ua Mailruanaidh], died.—Mor, daughter of Toirrdhealbach Ua Conchubhair, died.—Diarmait Ua Rabartaigh, abbot of Dur-magh, rested.—Alle,[3] daughter of Riacan Ua Mailruanaidh, died.—Mail-Seachlainn Ua Neachtain and Gilla-Beraigh[4] Ua Sluaigheadhaigh were killed by Toirrdhealbach, son of Ruaidhri Ua Conchubair, A.D. 1190.)

Kalends of Jan. on 3rd feria, 2nd of the moon, A.D. [1191] 1191 (or -2).

(Ruaidhri[1] Ua Conchubhair left Connacht and went to the Cenel-Conaill.)

Kalends of Jan. on 4th feria, 13th of the moon, A.D. [1192 Bis.] 1192. The door of the Refectory of the Penitentiary [of Daire] was made by Ua Cathain of the Craib and by the daughter[1] of Ua Inneirghi.

(Taichleach[2] Ua Dubhda, king of Ui-Amhalghaidh and Ui-Fiacrach of the [river] Muaidh, was killed by the two sons of his own son.—Aedh[3] Ua Flainn, chief of Sil-Maili-Ruain, died.)

Berach (of Kilbarry, co. Roscommon, whose feast was Feb. 15).

1191. [1] *Ruaidhri.*—Given under 1190 in the *Annals of Boyle*. According to the *Four Masters*, Roderic went to Tirconnell, Tyrone, the English of Meath and finally to Munster, seeking in vain for aid to recover Connaught. At length, he was recalled and had lands assigned him by his sept.

1192. [1] *Daughter.*—She was most probably the wife of Ua Cathain (O'Kane).

[2] *Taichleach.*—Under the preceding year in the *Annals of Boyle*, with omission of "*of the Muaidh*" and "*by the two,*" etc.

[3] *Aedh.*—" Aed Ua Floind moritur," *Annals of Boyle*, 1191.

P 2

Kal. Ian. 6ª. f., l. xx. 1111.ª, Anno Domini M.º c.º xc.º 111.º
Eocaiḋᵇ O Daiġill do marbaḋ do hUiḃ-Fiacraċ.—Mael-
patraic O Cobťaiġ do éc.ᵇ—Caťalᶜ Maġaiťne do éc.ᶜ

(Diarmait,ᵈ mac Conbroġam hUi Dhiumaraiġ
taireaċ Chlainne-Mailiġra ⁊ fi hUa-Fhailġe fri ré
fada, mortuus est.— Caťal oḃur, mac Meġ Carrťaiġ,
occisus est.—Derforġaill, inġen Murcaiḋ hUi Mhail-
Sheaclaind, mortua est imMainistir Droċait-aťa.—
Muirċeartac, mac Murcaiḋ Mic Murcaḋa, ri hUa-
Ceinnrelaiġ, mortuus est.ᵈ)

Kal. Ian. [uii.ª] f.,ª l.ᵇ u.,ᵇ Anno Domini M.º c.º xc.º 1111.º
Domnallᶜ hUa¹ Briain (macᵈ Toirrḋealḃaiġ,ᵈ doṅ.ᵉ ri
Mumanᵉ) do éc.—Ġaill do ťiaċtain ar Innri hUa¹-
Finntain ⁊ a cur ar eiġin di.—Cú-Miḋe hUa Flainn do
marbaḋ do Ġallaiḃ.ᶠ

(Macᶠ mic Conċuḃair, mic Domnaill ġearrlamaiġ
hUi Briain, do ťallaḋ ⁊ do rboiċteaḋ la Ġallaiḃ.—
Sluaiḋeaḋ la Ġillibert Mac Ġoirdealḃ ġu hEar-ruaiḋ
⁊ ro impo arréin ġan nac tarḃu d'a fluaḋaḋ.ᶠ)

Kal. Ian. [i.ª f.,ª] l. x. ui.,ᵇ Anno Domini M.º c.º xc.º u.º
Eċmarcaċ¹ hUa Caťa[i]n do éc i Reicler Phoilᵃ—
Conċobur Maġ Fhaċtna do éc i [n-ḋub-?] reicler

A.D. 1193. ᵃ⁻ᵃ .uii. f., l. u., B. These belong to A.D. 1194. The two
previous epacts, which he gives accurately, prove that the compiler of B
deviated from his original in antedating by a year. · Similar evidence is
the retention of the A.D. notation from 1192 to 1195, both inclusive,
though inconsistent sometimes with the ferial, sometimes with the epact,
sometimes with both, as given in the (B) MS. ᵇ⁻ᵇ Given under A.D.
1192, B, C. No loċo—or locho—is placed as another reading of Eoċaiḋ,
l. m., t. h., A. ᶜ⁻ᶜ om., B, C. ᵈ⁻ᵈ n, t. h., A; om., B, C.

A.D. 1194. ¹ O, A. ᵃ⁻ᵃ blank space, A; i. f., B. ᵇ⁻ᵇ l. xui., B. The
ferial and epact of B belong to A.D. 1195. ᶜ⁻ᶜ Given under A.D. 1193, B, C.
ᵈ⁻ᵈ c. m., n. t. h., A; om., B, C. ᵉ⁻ᵉ itl., n. t. h., A; om., B, C. ᶠ⁻ᶠ n. t. h.,
A; om., B, C.

A.D. 1195. ¹ Eaċ—, B. ᵃ⁻ᵃ blank space, A; ii. f., B. ᵇ xxuii., B.
The B criteria belong to A.D. 1196. ᶜ⁻ᶜ Given under A.D. 1194, B, C.

Kalends of Jan. on 6th feria, 24th of the moon, A.D. [1193] 1193. Eochaidh O'Baighill was killed by the Ui-Fiachrach [of Ard-sratha].—Mael-Patraic O'Cobhthaigh died. —Cathal Ma[c] Gaithne died.

(Diarmait,[1] son of Cubrogam Ua Diumasaigh, chief of Clann-Mailighra and king of Ui-Failghe for a long time, died.—Cathal the Swarthy, son of Mac Carrthaigh, was slain.—Derfhorgaill,[2] daughter of Murchadh Ua Mail-Seachlainn, died in the Monastery of Drochait-atha.—Muircheartach, son of Murchadh Mac Murchadha, king of Ui-Ceinnselaigh, died.)

Kalends of Jan. on 7th feria, 5th of the moon, A.D. [1194] 1194. Domnall Ua Briain (son of Toirrdhealbach, that is, king of Munster) died.—The Foreigners came upon the Island of the Ui-Finntain and they were put by force therefrom.—Cu-Midhe Ua Flainn was killed by the Foreigners.

(The grandson[1] of Conchubhar, son of Domnall Ua Briain the Short-handed, was blinded and emasculated by the Foreigners.—A hosting by Gillibert Mac Goisdealbh to Eas-ruadh and he returned therefrom without any advantage from his hosting.)

Kalends of Jan. on 1st feria, 16th of the moon, A.D. [1195] 1195. Echmarcach[1] Ua Catha[i]n died in the Regular Canons' house of St. Paul [in Ard-Macha].—Conchobur

---

1193. [1]*Diarmait, etc.*—These four items are given in this order in the *Annals of Loch Cé* (*ad an.*). The second and third are in the *Annals of Boyle* at 1193.

[2] *Derfhorgaill.*—See 1186, note 5, supra.

1194. [1] *The grandson, etc.*—These two entries are in the *Annals of* *Loch Cé*. The second is in the *Annals of Boyle*, 1194.

For grandson the *Annals of Inisfallen and Loch Cé* have son. He is called Muircertach in the *Annals of Boyle*, according to which he was blinded by his grand-uncle, Muircertach.

1195. [1]*Echmarcach.*—Horse-rider.

222 annala ulaoh.

Daire.ᵈ—Sacart° mór ia do éc.°—Macᵈ in Cleirig hUi Catala[i]n do marbad.ᵈ—Sitriuc° hUa gailmredaig do marbad do Mac Duinnsleibe.°

(Florint,ᵃ mac Riaca[i]n hUi Mailruanaid, epistopus Olaxind, in Christo quieuit.—Sluaigead la hEoin Do-Cuirti 7 la mac hUgo De-Laci do gabail neirt ar Ghallaib Laigean 7 Mumhan.—Domnall hUa Finn, comarba Chluana-feartaBrenaind, quieuit.°)

[b₁ϥ] Kal. Ian. 11.ᵃ f., L.xx. uii., Anno Domini M.° c., xc.° ui.ᶜᵇ
A 55b Reicles° Poil 7 Petair co n-a templaib 7 co m-bloid moir do'n rataib do lorcad.—Sluagad la Ruaidri Mac Duinnsleibe, co n-Gallaib 7 co macaib rig Connact docum Cene[oi]l-Eogain 7 Airrter. Tangatur dono Cenel-n-Eogain Telca-óac 7 Errter co Macaire Airo-Maca, co tucrat cat doib 7 cur' mebaid ar Mac Duinnsleibe 7 romarbad derg ar a muinnter iann, idon, da mac rig déc do Connactaib.—Muircertac, mac Muircertaig hUi Loclainn, ri Cene[oi]l-Eogain 7
B 57a ridomna Erenn uile, | idon, tuir gairrcid 7 egnoma¹ Leiti Cuinn, dircailiud Gall 7 cairtel, tercbail cell 7 cadur, do marbad do Donncad, mac Blorcaid hUi Cata[i]n, a comairli Cene[oi]l-Eogain uile: idon, iar tabairt na tri Scrine 7 Canoine Patraic sfir i tempall

A.D. 1195. ᵈ om., B, C. ᶜ⁻ᵇ n. t. h., A ; om., B, C.
A.D. 1196. ¹ egnom (nom. sg.), B. ᵃ⁻ᵃ blank space, A. ᵇ —u,° B. That is, the year is made 1195. But the ferial and epact are those of 1196. In B they are assigned to 1195 and 1196. ᶜ⁻ᶜ All the entries are given under the preceding year (1195), B, C.

---

² *Arch-priest.*—See *Adamnan*, p.' 365. This obit escaped the notice of the learned editor in compiling the *Chronicon Hyense* (*ib.* p. 409).

³ *Florence.*—This and the Domnall obit are given in the *Annals of Boyle*, 1195. The second entry is in the *Annals of Lock Cé* and the *Four Masters*.

The *Annals of Boyle* state that Florence was third abbot of Boyle and equate 1195 of his death with the (Eusebian) Mundane year 6394.

⁴ *Successor.—Comarba.* So called

ANNALS OF ULSTER. 223

Mac Fachtna died in the Penitentiary of Daire.—The arch-priest[2] of I[on]a died.—The son of the Cleric Ua Cathala[i]n was killed.—Sitriuc Ua Gailmredhaigh was killed by [Maghnus] Mac Duinnsleibhe [Ua Eochadha]. [1195]

(Florence,[3] son of Riacan Ua Mailruanaidh, bishop of Oilfinn, rested in Christ.—A hosting by John De-Courcy and by the son of Ugo De-Lacy to obtain sway over the Foreigners of Leinster and Munster.—Domnall Ua Finn, successor[4] of Cluain-ferta of [St.] Brenann, rested.)

Kalends of Jan. on 2nd feria, 27th of the moon, A.D. 1196. The house of the Canons Regular of Paul and Peter [in Ard-Macha] with its churches and a large portion of the Close was burned.—A hosting by Ruaidhri Mac Duinnsleibhe [Ua Eochadha] with the Foreigners and with the sons of the kings of Connacht to Cenel-Eogain and the Airthir. Howbeit, the Cenel-Eogain of Telach-oc and the Airthir came to the Plain of Ard-Macha and gave them battle and defeat was inflicted upon Mac Duinnsleibe and stark slaughter of his people took place there, namely, twelve sons of the kings of Connacht.—Muircertach, son of Muircertach Ua Lochlainn, king of Cenel-Eogain and royal heir of all Ireland, namely, tower of championship and valour of the Half of Conn, dissolver of the Foreigners and of castles, upholder of churches and dignities, was killed by Donnchadh, son of Bloscadh Ua Catha[i]n, by counsel of all Cenel-Eogain: that is, after pledging the three Shrines[1] and the Canon of Patrick[2] to [1196 Bis.]

---

in the *Annals of Boyle* likewise. The *Annals of Innisfallen* have *abbatis*. Whence it may be inferred that he was abbot and bishop.

1196. [1] *Three shrines.*—See at 733(=734) *supra;* where commo-tacio signifies not enshrining of the relics, but their being carried about, to ensure payment of the offerings prescribed by the "Law."

[2] *Canon of Patrick.*—That is, the Book of Armagh.

veirceptač Aird-Maċa reime rin⁴ 7 rucad co Daire Coluim-cille 7 pohadnaiced co honorač.—Mac Olorcaið hUa Cuipin do apcain Tepmainn Dabeó[i]cc 7° pomapbad é péin inn co n-dep gáp a muinntepe pe' pulbud'cenn mír, tpia mipbuil Dabeó[i]c.'—Ipin bliadain rin dono dobrir² Domnall, mac Diapmata Meg³ Cappťaig, cať ap Gallaið Muman 7 Luimnič in pomapð a n-depg ap 7 in podičuíp a Luimníuč⁴ iať iap péin 7 pobrir dá maiðm aile béor.⁰

Kal. Ian. iiii.ª r.,ª L ix, Anno Domini M.º c.º xc.º uii.°, Sluagad la hEoan Do-Chuipt co n-Gallaid Ulad co hErr-craide, co n-depnrat caiptel Cille-Santa[i]n, cor'ralmaiceð¹ truča-ced Ciannačt² doid.º Irin³ caiptel⁴ rin imorro ro ragað Roitrel Phitun co gorpaici 'maille rpir. Táinic dono Roitrel Phitun ap creič co Port-Daire, co⁴ roapc Clua[i]n-í 7 Enač 7 Derc-bruač. Ruc imorro⁰ Flaithertač O Maeldoraið (idon,' ri Conaill 7 Eogain') co n-uatað do Chonall 7 d'Eogan roppo, co tucrat maiðm ap⁵ traig na hUatcongbala

ᵃ pobrir, B.   ³Meg, B.   ⁴—neč, B.   ᵈ om., B, C.   ⁺⁺ om., C.   ʰ pia—before, B.

A.D. 1197. ¹ Co roralmaiged, B.   ²—nača, B.   ³ Ir anran—*it is in that*, B.   ⁴ caipteol, A.   ⁵ ror—*upon*, B.   ᵃ⁻ᵃ blank space, A.   ᵇ⁻.ui.°, B. The ferial and epact shew that the year is 1197.   ⁰ leo aran čaiptel rin—*by them from out that castle*, B ; followed by C.   ᵈ ocur—*and*, B, C.   ⁰ u (contraction for *vero*, the Latin equivalent), A, B.   ᶠ⁻ᶠ r. 'm., t. h., A itl., t. h., B ; "King of Kindred-Owen," C.

---

³ *Southern church.*—The *Annals of Loch Cé* say the *northern*, which proves the scribe had no local knowledge. *Cf.* the Book of Armagh: Et his tribus ordinibus [scil. virginibus, poenitentibus et legitime matrimoniatis] audire verbum predicationis in aeclessia aquilonalis plagae conceditur semper diebus dominicis. In australi vero bassilica aepiscopi et presbiteri et anchoritae aeclessiae et caeteri relegiossi laudes sapidas offerunt (fol. 21a).

Cum sanctorum reliquiis in aeclessia australi, ubi requiescunt corpora sanctorum perigrinorum de longue cum Patricio

him in the southern church³ of Ard-Macha before that. [1196] And he was carried to Daire of Colum-cille and was buried honourably.—Ua Curin, the son of Bloscadh, pillaged the Termon of [St.] Dabeocc and he himself was killed therefor, with stark slaughter of his people, before the end of a month, through miracle of Dabeocc.—In that year also, Domnall, son of Diarmait Mac Carthaigh, gained a battle over the Foreigners of Munster and Limerick, in which a great number of them were killed and whereby they were afterwards expelled from Limerick. And he inflicted two other defeats likewise.

Kalends of Jan. on 4th feria, 9th of the moon, A.D. [1197] 1197. A hosting by John De-Courcy with the Foreigners of Ulidia to Ess-craibhe,¹ so that they built the castle of Cell-Santain²[and] the cantred of Ciannachta was desolated by them. Moreover, in that castle was left Roitsel Fitton [and] a force along with him. Then Roitsel Fitton came on a foray to the Port of Daire, so that he pillaged Cluain-i and Enach and Derc-bruach. But Flaithbertach Ua Maeldoraidh (namely, king of [Cenel-]Cona[i]ll and Cenel-Eoga[i]n) overtook them with a small force of the [Cenel-]Cona[i]ll and the [Cenel-]Eoga[i]n, so that he inflicted defeat upon them on the strand of the [N]uathcongbhail [and] they were

---

transmarinorum caeterorumque iustorum (fol. 21b).

The place is omitted in the *Four Masters*.

The translator of C took *tabairt fris* to be *tabairt leis* and applied it to the murdered man: "after bringing the 3 shrines and Canons of Patrick with him into the south church of Armagh."

1197. ¹ *Ess-craibhe.*—*Cataract of the branch[ing tree]*. On the Bann, south of Coleraine (O'D. *F. M.* iii. 107).

² *Cell-Santain.*—*Church of (bishop) Santan* (whose feast was June 10). From the interchange of *s* and *l* arose *Cell Santa[i]l* of B and "Killsandle" of C (east of the Bann, near Coleraine, O'D., *ib.*).

226 ανναλα υλαΌη.

ροΡΡο, co ρομαρbαό α n-αρ ann (ιΌon,⁶ 'mo mac Αρογαιl hUι Loĕlαιnn⁶), τρε μιρbαιl Coluιm-cιlle 7 Cαίnnιĕ 7 bρεcα[ι]n ροαιρζρετaρ ann.—Mac Ζιlla-|ειΌιĕ Όo Chιannaĕτ[αιb] Όo flατ alταρα τεμpoιll μοιρ Όhαιρε Coluιm-cιlle 7 Όo bρειĕ cειĕρι⁶ coρn ιp ferp Όo boι ι n-Eριnn ειρτι, ιΌon, ιm μαc-ριαbαĕ 7 ιm μαc-ρolu[ι]ρ 7 ιm coρn hUι Maeloopaιb 7 ιm cam-coραιnΌ 7 ιm coρn hUι Όoĕαρταιĕ. Robριρʰ ιμoρρo 7 τall α n-ιnnμυρα 7 α Lαρα[b] Όιb. Eριĕ ιμoρρo ιρn τρερ Loα ιαρ n-α n-ζαιτ nα ρεoιτ 7 ιnτί ρoζατ. Ocup ρocρoĕαb é¹ (ιΌon, ιc croιp nα ριαζ⁷) ι⁸ n-εinεĕ Coluιm-cιlle, 'ρα hαlτoιρ ροραραιξεb ann.—Concobuρ O Caĕα[ι]n Όo éc.— | Flαιĕbεpταĕ hUα Maeloopaιb, ιΌon, pι Conαιll ιρ Eoζαιn ιρ Αιρζιαll ιρ coρnumaιĕ Τειμραĕ 7 ριΌαμnα Eρεnn uιle: ιΌon, Conαll αρ loeĕΌaĕτ, Cu-Culαιno ʰ αρ ξαιρcεb, Ζuαιρε ᵇ αρ εinεĕ, Macʲ Luξαĕ αρ oζlαĕuρ,ʲ α éc ιαρ τρεblαιτ τοζαιbε ι⁹ n-Iniρ-8αιμερ, ιᵏ quαρτ Noιn Febραι,ᵏ ιριn τριĕατμαb¹⁰ blιαbαιn α flαιĕuρα¹¹ 7 ιριn noμαb¹² blιαbαιn αρ coιcαιτ¹³ α αιρι. Ocuρ ροαbnαĕτ α n-Όρuιm-τuαμια co honoρaĕ. Ocuρ ζαbαρ Eĕμαρcαĕ hUa Όoĕαρταιĕ ριξι Ceneoιl-Conαιll ρο cετoιρ 7 nι ραιbε αĕτ caιcĕιζιρ ι ριξι, ιnταn ταιnιζ hEoαn Όo-Cuιρτ co ρoĕραιΌε μoιρ

---

⁶.ιιιι., A, B. ⁷ρεαξ, A. ⁸α, A. ⁹α, B. ¹⁰.xxx. μαb, A. ¹¹lαι—(f om.), A. ¹².ιx.-μαb, A, B. ¹³.lαιτ, A; .lατ, B. ᵉ˙ᶠitl., t.h., A, B.; om., C. ʰocuρ—and—prefixed, B. ʲ om., A. ʲ⁻ʲ om., B, C. ᵏ⁻ᵏ in quαρτα ρεριa (on the fourth feria), A. The copyist doubtless mistook fṝ (thus given in B) = Febραι (February) for *feria* and omitted n̄ = Noιn, as being meaningless. Feb. 2 fell on Sunday, not Wednesday, in 1197.

---

² *Cainnech.*—St Canice of Kilkenny was likewise patron of Ciannachta (barony of Keenaght, co. Londonderry), in which he was born.

⁴ *Brecan.*—Ten of the name are given in the Homonymous Lists (Book of Leinster, p. 366f). The Brecan here intended is perhaps the patron of Cenn Bairche, near the source of the Bann, co. Down.

⁵ *Goblets.*—Chalices, as is evident from the context.

⁶ *Jewels.* — Literally, *valuables.*

slaughtered to a large number (namely, around the son of Ardgal Ua Lochlainn), through miracle of Colum-cille and Cainnech[3] and Brecan[4] [whose churches] they pillaged there.—Mac Gilla-Eidich of the Ciannachta robbed the great altar of the great church of Daire of Columcille and took the four [five] best goblets[5] that were in Ireland therefrom, including "the gray son" and "the son of light" and the goblet of Ua Maeldoraidh and "the twisted goblet" and the goblet of Ua Dochartaich. Moreover, he broke off and took away from them their jewels[6] and their setting. But, on the third day after their being stolen, the treasures and he who stole them were found out. And he was hanged (namely, at the Cross of the Executions) in reparation to Colum-cille, whose altar was profaned there.—Conchobur Ua Catha[i]n died.—Flaithbertach Ua Maeldoraidh, that is, king of [Cenel]-Cona[i]ll and [Cenel]-Eoga[i]n and Airgialla, defender of Temhair and royal heir of all Ireland: namely, Conall[7] for championship, Cu-Culainn[8] for prowess, Guaire[9] for generosity, Mac Lughach[10] for athletics, died after choice tribulation in Inis-Saimer, on the 4th of the Nones [2nd] of February, in the thirtieth year of his lordship and in the ninth and fiftieth year of his age. And he was buried honourably in Druim-tuamha. And Echmarcach Ua Dochartaich takes the kingship of Cenel-Conaill immediately. And he was but a fortnight in the kingship, when John De-Courcy came with a large

[1197]

The translation of *lasa[dh]* (*setting*) is conjectural.

[7] *Conall.*—An Ulster hero who lived in the 1st century of the Christian era.

[8] *Cu-Culainn.*—Cuculandus, decantatissimus pugil (*Ogygia*, p. 279). Flourished in Ulster in the 1st century, A.D.

[9] *Guaire.*—See *supra*, 662(=663). His name still lives, denoting a generous person.

[10] *Mac Lughach.*—[Only] *son of Lugha* (his mother). Grandson of

'maille fris tar Tuaim hi Tir-n-Eogain. Ar[r]eic co hArd-rrata; iar rin, timceall co Daire Coluim-cille co rabadar coic oidce and. Imtigit imorro co Cnoc-Narcain d'a n-imacur tairir. Tegait dono Cenel-Conaill im Ecmarcac hUa n-Docartaic dia n-innraigid 7 doratrat cat doib, du in romarbad da cet[14] did, im a rig, idon, im Ecmarcac[l] 7 im Donncad hUa Taircert,[15] idon,[m] rigtoirec Clainni-Sneidgile, idon, cuing einig 7 egnuma 7 comuirle Ceneoil-Conaill uile 7 im Gilla-m-Brigti hUa n-Docartaic 7 im Mac[16] Duda[i]n 7 im Mag Fergail[17] 7 im macaib hUi m-Daigill et alior nobiler. Ocur roairgret Inir-n-Eogain 7 doratrat boroma mó[i]r eirti.—Concobar,[1] mac mic Taidg, rí Mhuig[i]-Luirg 7 Muigi-Ai, cuir ordain 7 airecair, enic 7 comairci Connact uile, a éc iar n-aitrigi togaidi i Mainirtir Ata-do-laarc.—Ma[c] Craic hUa [Fh]laitbertaic, mac rig Tire-Eogain, do marbad 7 Maelruanaig O Fercomair (no[n] O Carpella[i]n[n]), ardtoirec Clainni-Diarmata, do marbad 7 da marcac maiti d'a muinntir do marbad.[j]

Kal. Ian. u.[a] f.,[a] L xx, Anno Domini M.° c.° xc.° uiii.°[b] Gilla Mac Liac[1] hUa Brena[i]n[2] do attur a comurbuir uada 7 Gilla-Crist hUa Cernaig ar toga[3] loet 7 cleirec Tuaire[i]rt Erenn do[4] oirdned[4] i n-a inad i n-abdaine Coluim-cille.

(Macc[c] Briain Bhreiffnig, mic Thoirrdealbaig hUi Choncubair, do marbad la Catal carrac, mac Concubair Mhaenmaige.

[14].c, A, B. [15] Doir—, A. [16] Mag, A. [17] ergail (g om.), A. [1] hUa n-Docartaig—*Ua Dochartaigh*—added, B. [m] om., B, C. [a-a] itl., t. h., MS. (A).

A.D. 1198. [1] Lia (c om.), A. [2] Br (exemplar probably illegible), A. [3] taga, A. [4-4] ro hoirdned—*was instituted*, A; do attur (the infinitive) shews that the B-reading is correct. [c-c] blank space, A. [b]—.an.°, B.

Finn Mac Cumaill, and a famous | tia), in the third century of our
spearsman in the Irish *Fiann* (Mili- | era.

force under him past Tuaim into Tir-Eogain. From here to [1197] Ard-sratha; after that, around to Daire of Colum-cille, so that they were five nights therein. They go then to Cnoc-Nascain, to be carried across it [Lough Swilly]. But the Cenel-Conaill, under Echmarcach Ua Dochartaigh, come to attack them and gave them battle, where two hundred of them [the Irish] were killed, around their king, that is, Echmarcach and around Donnchadh Ua Taircert, namely, royal chief of Clann-Sneidhghile, to wit, the link of generosity and valour and counsel of all Cenel-Conaill and around Gilla-Brighti Ua Dochartaigh and around Mac Dubha[i]n and Mac Ferghail and the sons of Ua Baighill and other nobles. And they [the English] harried Inis-Eogain and carried great cattle-spoil therefrom.—Concobar, grandson of Tadhg [Ua Maelruanaigh], king of Magh-Luirg and Magh-Ai, tower of splendour and principality, of generosity and protection of all Connacht, died after choice penance in the Monastery of Ath-da-laarc.—Ma[c] Craith Ua [F]laithbertaigh, son of the king of Tir-Eogain, was killed and Maelruanaigh O Fercomais (or O'Cairellain[11]), arch-chief of Clann-Diarmata, was killed and two good horsemen of his people were killed.

Kalends of Jan. on 5th feria, 20th of the moon, A.D. [1198] 1198. Gilla Mac Liac Ua Brena[i]n[1] put the succession away from him and Gilla-Crist Ua Cernaigh[1] by choice of laity and clergy of the North of Ireland was ordained in his stead in the abbacy of Colum-cille.

(The son[2] of Brian of Breifni, son of Toirrdealbach Ua Conchubhair, was killed by Cathal Carrach, son of Conchubar Maenmhaighe.

---

[11] *O'Cairellain.* — This is the correct reading. The O'Cairellans were chiefs of Clann-Diarmada (Clondermot, co. Londonderry).

1198. [1] *Ua Brenain; Ua Cernaigh.* —See *Adamnan,* pp. 408-9.

[2] *The son.*—Given at this year in *Annals of Loch Cé* and *Four Masters.*

No ʒumaḋ aɼ ın Ḳallaınꝺ ɼo buḋ coıɼ Ruaıḋɼı hUa Conċobaıɼ ꝺo ḃeıṫ.

U. cccc. ııı.ᶜ)

Ḳal. Ian. uı.ᵃ ꝑ.,ᵃ L. ı., Ɑnno Ꝺomını M. c.° xc.° ıx.° ᵇ Ruaıḋɼı hUa Concobaıɼ (ıꝺon,ᶜ mac Toıɼɼḋealḃaıǧ hUı Conċubaıɼᶜ), ɼı Eɼenn, ın penıtentıa quıeuıt.—Caṫalan⁴ hUa Maelɼabaıll, ɼı Caıɼɼʒı-Ḋɼaċaıḋe, ꝺo maɼbaḋ ꝺ'O Ꝺeɼa[ı]n 7 O Ꝺeɼa[ı]n ꝺo maɼbaḋ annɼeın.ᵈ—8luaǵaḋ la hEoan Ꝺo-Cuıɼt ı Tıɼ-n-Eoʒaın aɼ ꝼut na ceall: ıꝺon, Ɑɼꝺ-ɼɼata 7 Raṫ-boṫ ꝺo mıllıuḋ ꝺó, noᵉ co ɼoaċt Ꝺaıɼe, co ɼaıḃe annɼım¹ ꝺa oıḋċe ꝼoɼ ɼeċtmaın | ıc mıllıuḋ Innɼı-hEoʒaın 7 ın tıɼe aɼċena 7 nı ɼaʒaḋ aɼ ꝼɼı ɼé ꝼota, no coꝼ toɼaċtꝼ Ɑeḋ hUa Neıll, luċt coıc lonʒ, co Cıll . . .ᵍ ıllaṫaɼnu,² co ɼoloıɼc nı ꝺo'n baıle, co ɼomaɼḃ ꝺıɼ teɼta ꝺo ɼıċıt³ annɼeın⁴. Ɑnnɼeın ɼoḃatan ʒaıll Muıʒe-lıne 7 Ꝺal-Ɑɼaıḋe, tɼı cet,⁵ aɼ a cınn, etıɼ ıaɼn 7 cen⁶ ıaɼn 7 nıɼꝼaıɼıǵeꝺuɼ no co ɼoꝺoıɼptɼıt ꝼn-a cenn ıc loɼcaḋ ın baıle. Ɑnnɼeın tucɼat ꝺebaıḋ aɼ láɼ ın baıle, co ɼomaıḃ aɼ ʒallaıḃ 7 tucɼat coıc maḋmannꝺa⁷ o ꝼeın amaċ ꝼoɼɼa no co n-ꝺeċaꝺuɼ ꝼn-a lonʒaıḃ 7 nıɼꝼɼaʒaḋʰ aċt coıceɼ⁸ ꝺo muınntıɼ hUı Neıll. Iaɼ ɼın ɼoımṫıʒ 8heoan, o'tċuala ɼın ɼoɼtea.—Caċaḋ eteɼ Conall ıɼ Eoʒan, ıꝺon, co tucɼat Cenel-Conaıll ɼıǵı ꝺo U[a] Eıcnıǵ. Ɑnnɼeın táınıcˣ ꝼn-a coınne co Teɼmonn-Ꝺaḃeó[ı]c. Táınıc⁹ hUa

The ferial and epact, however, belong to 1198. ᶜ⁻ᶜ n. t. h., A ; om., B, C.

A.D. 1199. ¹ aınnɼeın, A. ² ala—, A. ³ .xx.ıt, A, B. ⁴ anꝺ—*there*, B. ⁵ .c., A, B. ⁶ ʒan, B. ⁷ -man, A. ⁸ coıcıuɼ, B. ⁹ -ʒ, B. ᵃ⁻ᵃ .ıı. ꝑ., n. t. h., on blank space, A. ᵇ-.ııı.°, B. But the ferial and epact of B itself shew that the year is 1199, not 1198. ᶜ⁻ᶜ ıtl., n. t. h., A ; om., B, C. ᵈ om., B, C. ᵉ om., A. ᶠ⁻ᶠ co n-ꝺeaċaıḋ—*untıl went*, B ; with which C agrees. ᵍ blank left for name of church, A, B. "Killabarna," C, as if nothing was wanting. ʰ nıɼꝼaʒɼat—*they left not*, B.

³ *Or, etc.*—This alternative date is correct. O'Flaherty (*Ogygia*, pp. 441-2) quotes a contemporaneous obit which specifies the year by Thursday, moon 20 and the day as Sunday, Dec. 2, moon 27. These criteria accurately designate 1198.

² 5403.—This belongs to the fol-

Or[3] it may be on this year it were right for [the death of] Ruaidhri Ua Conchobair to be.

[A.M.] 5403.[2])

Kalends of Jan. on 6th feria, 1st of the moon, A.D. 1199. Ruaidhri Ua Concobair (that is, son of Toirrdhealbhach Ua Conchubair), king of Ireland, rested in penance.[1]—Cathalan Ua Maelfhabaill, king of Carraic-Brachaidhe, was killed by O'Derain and O'Derain was killed at the same time.—A hosting by John De-Courcy into Tir-Eogain throughout the churches: namely, Ard-sratha and Rath-both were destroyed by him, until he reached Daire, so that he was there two nights over a week, destroying Inis-Eogain and the country besides. And he would not have gone therefrom for a long time, had not [lit. until] Aedh Ua Neill, [with] a force of five ships, reached Cell [ruadh ?[2]] in Latharna, so that he burned a part of the town and killed twenty, wanting two, therein. Then the Foreigners of Magh-Line and Dal-Araidhe were, three hundred [strong], both in mail[3] and without mail,[3] in front of him and they [the Irish] noticed not, until [the Foreigners] poured against them, burning the town. Thereupon they gave battle in the centre of the town and it went against the Foreigners. And [the Irish] gave five defeats to them thenceforward, until they went into their ships and only five of the people of Ua Neill were lost. Thereafter John went away, when he heard that.—Great war between [Cenel-]Cona[i]ll and [Cenel-]Eoga[i]n, so that Cenel-Conaill gave the kingship to Ua Eicnigh. Then he came to meet them to the Termonn of [St.] Dabeoc. Ua Neill with the Men of

---

lowing year. It is based upon the same Reckoning as that inserted at 432 and elsewhere; namely, the Mundane Period = 4204 years.

1199. [1] *Rested in penance.*—According to the obit in O'Flaherty, he died in the monastery of Cong, where he had spent the last thirteen years of his life and was buried at Clonmacnoise. See O'Donovan, *F. M.* iii. 112-3.

[2] *Cell[-ruadh ?].*—The bracketted part is suggested by O'Donovan.

[3] *Mail.*—Literally, *iron.*

Neill co ʀepaıd Maıxı-1ἐa do ἐaıpmeʀc 'n-a coınne, co ʀaca caċ apaıle dıd 7 co ʀomebaıd aʀ hUa n-θıcnıx 7 co ʀáʀxaıd bʀaıxcı. Cʀʀıde, ıʀın loo cecna, Ced hUa Neıll 7 Cenel-Θoxaın, co ʀoaıpxʀec Cenel-Conaıll ımMaċaıʀe Maıxı-hīἐa 7 co cucʀac boʀoma n-dıaıʀmıde[10] leo. Ocuʀ ıʀ do'n cʀeıċhı ʀın do maʀbad Niall hUa Duıddıpma aʀ ʀcéıṁleaḋ. Iaʀʀın,[d] ʀluaxad la hCed hUa Neıll 7 la Cenel-n-Θoxaın co Maċaıʀe Muıxı-1ἐa do ċabaıʀc caċa do Cenel-Conaıll, no co ʀoʀaxʀac Cenel-Conaıll ın Lonxpoʀc 7 co n-depnʀac blaoxod ʀıἐ[a] annʀeın.[d]

(81d[1] do ċenaṁ do Chaċal Chpoıddeaʀx hUa Choncubaıʀ ʀe Caċal Caʀʀaċ, mac Conċubaıʀ Maenmaıxe 7 a ċabaıʀc hıʀcıʀ 7 ʀeʀann do ċabaıʀc do.[1])

A 66a ⟨Cal. Ian. uıı.[a] ʀ.,[a] L x. 11.,[b] Cnno Domını M.[o c] cc.[o c] Mael-Iʀʀu[d] Mac Xılle-θʀaın, aıʀcınneċ Cılle-moıʀe hUa-Ni[a]lla[ı]n 7 adbuʀ comaʀba ʀacʀaıc, ın pace quıeuıc.[d]—Doʀonʀac Xaıll Ulad[c] cʀı cʀeċa ı Cıp-n-Θoxaın 7 ın cʀeʀ cʀeċ doʀonʀac, doxabʀac Lonxpoʀc ıc Domnaċ-moʀ Muıxı-Imclaıʀ. Docuıʀʀec cʀeċ móʀ ımaċ. Táınıx Ced hUa Neıll ı n-aıʀcıʀ na cʀeıċe, co ʀo compuc do 7 na Xaıll 7 co ʀomuıd aʀ Xallaıd 7 co B 57d ċaʀaıc aʀ n-cıaıʀmıde ʀoʀʀo 7 ʀoéladuʀ 'ʀan | aıdċe[s] co n-deċaduʀ[1] ċaʀ Túaım.—Sanċcuʀ Mauʀıcıuʀ[2] Uo baeca[ı]n ı n-hI Colum-cılle ın pace quıeuıc.—Cʀeċ la Ruaıdʀı Mac Duınnʀleıde, co ní do Xhallaıd Mıde, co ʀoaıpxʀec Maınıʀcıʀ Phoıl 7 Pheċaıʀ,[3] co naʀ'ʀaxʀac ıınċı aċc aen boın.—Raoub[d] Mac Raedıx, coıʀeċ Cene[oı]l-Oenxuʀa, do maʀbad do Xhallaıd aʀ cʀeıċ ı

A.D. 1199. [10]-aıpṁe, B. [1-1] n. t. h., A; om., B, C.

A.D. 1200. [1] n-deaċaduʀ, B. [2] Muʀıcıuʀ, A. [3] Pedıʀ, B. [a-a] n. t. h., on blank space, A. [b] .xı., B. This, unless perhaps a scribal error, is an unaccountable reading; xi. not being an epact. [c-c] m. xc. ıx., B. Erroneously. [d-d] om., B, C. [e] an blıaḋaın ʀın—that year—added, B; followed by C.

Magh-Itha came against him, to prevent him, so that each [1199] of them saw the other. And Ua Eicnigh was defeated and left pledges. From here Aedh Ua Neill and the Cenel-Eogain [went] on the same day, until they harried Cenel-Conaill around the Plain of Magh-Itha and took countless cattle-spoil away with them. And it is on that foray Niall Ua Duibhdirma was killed on a surprise party. After that, a hosting [was made] by Aedh Ua Neill and by the Cenel-Eogain to the Plain of Magh-Itha, to give battle to the Cenel-Conaill, so that the Cenel-Conaill abandoned the camp and they made a kind of peace then.

(Peace[4] was made between Cathal Red-Hand Ua Conchubair with Cathal Carrach, son of Conchubar Maenmaighe and [Cathal] was brought into the country and land given to him.)

Kalends of Jan. on 7th feria, 12th of the moon, A.D. [1200 Bis.] 1200. Mael-Isu, son of Gilla-Erain, herenagh of Cell-mor of Ui-Niallain and successor designate of Patrick, rested in peace.—The Foreigners of Ulidia made three forays into Tir-Eogain and the third foray they made, they made a camp at Domnach-mor of Magh-Imclair. They sent a large foray [party] abroad. Aedh Ua Neill came to rescue the prey, until himself and the Foreigners met and defeat was inflicted upon the Forcigners and countless slaughter was put upon them and they stole away in the night, until they went past Tuaim.—The saintly Maurice Ua Raetain[1] rested in peace in I[ona] of Colum-cille.—A foray by Ruaidhri Mac Duinnsleibhe [Ua Eochadha] with some of the Foreigners of Meath, so that they pillaged the Monastery of Paul and Peter [in Armagh] until they left not therein but one cow.—Radub Mac Raedig, chief of Cenel-Oenghusa, was killed by the

---

[4] *Peace.*—This item is found in the *Annals of Boyle* (ad an.).

1200. [1] *Ua Baetain.*—"Baetan, Baithan, Buadan, Baetog, Baedog,

n-Óenarca-Chéin.ᵈ—Rollant,ᵉ mac Uctraig, rí Gall-Gaidel, in pace quieuit.ᶠ

(Donncadˢ Uaitneac, mac Ruaidri hUi Conchubair, do marbad lair na Saxaib dadur hiLluimniuc.ᵉ)

(U.ᵃ ccccu.ᵃ [=A.D. M. cc. 1.])

Kal. Ian. 11.ᵇ f.,ᵇ L.xx. 111., Anno Domini M.º cc.º 1.º Ruaidri Mac Duinnrleibe, rí Ulad 7 cainnel gairsid na h-Erenn uile, do marbad do Ghallaib, idon, tria mírbuilib Poil 7 Petair¹ 7 Patraic² rorarais—Tomaltac hUa Conchobair, comarba Patraic 7 apo-primaitˢ Erenn uile do ecna[i] 7 do crabad, in pace quieuit.—Innarba[d] Catail croibde[i]rg hUi Concobuir 7 rigad Catail carraig i n-a inad (Noᵈ comad ar in Kalaind ri tuartic innarba[d] Catail croibde[i]rg.ᶜ).—Slogad la hAed hUa Neill i foiritin Catail croib-de[i]rg co ferait Muigi-hIta 7 co n-Airgiallaib co rangatar co Tec-Baitin Airtig, co roroiretur ann, co tangadur co hEr-dara 7 co ruc orra Catal carrac co maitib Connact 7 Uilliam burc co n-Gallaib Luimnig imaille friu 7 co romuid ar Thuairceart n-Erenn 7 co rar'gbad and hUa Heicnig, airorig Airgiall et alii multi.—Slogad la Sheoan do-Chuirt co n-Gallaib Ulad 7 mac Ugo de-Laci co n-Gallaib Mide i foiritin Catail

A.D. 1200. ᵗ⁻ᵗ om., C. ᶠ⁻ᶠ n. t. h., A ; om., B, C.
A.D. 1201. ¹ Pedoair, B. ²-raig, B. ³ airoprimrard, B. ᵃ⁻ᵃ n. t. h., A; om., B, C, D. ᵇ⁻ᵇ n. t. h., on blank space, A; om., B, C, D. ᶜ om., B; that is, the year in B (followed by C, D) is 1200,—erroneously, as the epact shews. ᵈ⁻ᵈ l. m., t. h., A; om., B, C, D.

Buadog are all varieties of the same name, and *Baetog* prefixed by *da* [=*do, thy*], the title of endearment, makes Cluain-da-Bhaotog, now Clondavaddog, the name of a parish in Fanad, in the north of Donegal." *Adamnan*, p. 409.

For the Cross of St. Buadon of Clonca (Cluain-catha, Inishowen, co. Donegal), see Proc. R.I.A. Ser. iii. Vol. II., p. 109.

³ *Roland*.—King of Galloway. For some of his doings, see Benedict

Foreigners on a foray in Aenarca-Cein.—Roland,[2] son [1200] of Uchtrach, king of the Foreign-Irish, rested in peace.

(Donnchadh[3] of Uaithne, son of Ruaidhri Ua Conchubhair, was killed by the Saxons that were in Limerick.)

([A.M.] 5405 [A.D. 1201].)

Kalends of Jan. on 2nd feria, 24th of the moon, A.D. [1201] 1201. Ruaidhri Mac Duinnsleibhe [Ua Eochada], king of Ulidia and candle of championship of all Ireland, was killed by the Foreigners, to wit, through the miracles of Paul and Peter and Patrick whom he dishonoured.[1]— Tomaltach Ua Conchobair, successor of Patrick and archprimate of all Ireland for wisdom and piety, rested in peace.—Expulsion of Cathal Red-hand Ua Conchobuir and coronation of Cathal Carrach in his stead (Or perhaps it is in this [preceding] year above the expulsion of Cathal Red-hand comes.).—A hosting by Aedh Ua Neill in aid of Cathal Red-hand with the Men of Magh-Itha and with the Airghialla, until they came to Tech-Baithin of Airtech. They turned there until they came to Es-dara and Cathal Carrach with the nobles of Connacht and William [de] Burgh with the Foreigners of Limerick along with him overtook them. And the North of Ireland was defeated and Ua Eicnigh, arch-king of Airgialla and many others were lost.—A hosting by John De Courcy with the Foreigners and the son of Ugo De Lacy with the Foreigners of Meath in aid of Cathal Red-hand, until they reached Cell-mic-

---

of Peterborough, i. 339—42, ii. 8 (Rolls' ed.).

[3] *Of Uaithne.*—"So called from having been fostered in the territory of *Uaithne*, now Owneybeg, a barony in the north-east of the co. Limerick." (Note to *Annals of Loch Cé*, i. 208.)

The entry is given at 1200 in the *Annals of Loch Cé*; at 1199 and 1200 in the *Four Masters*.

1201. [1] *Dishonoured.*—See the act of profanation under the last preceding year.

cpoiboe[i]pg, co pangaoup Cill mic n-Ouoc. Annpein
táinig Catal cappac co Connactaib imaille fpip 7 co
pocuippec cat 7 co pomuib ap Ghallaib Ulab 7 Mibe.
1 bail ippabaoup[4] na coic[5] cata, ní táinig ap act oa tat
oib.—Aeb hUa Neill oo atpigab la Cenel-n-Eogain | 7
pigab Concobuip Meg Laclainn ooib 7 co n-oepna creic
hi Cip-n-En[n]ai,[6] co tuc bú | oiaipmibe 7 co pomapb
oaine. Annpein táinig Eicnecan hUa Domnaill co
longaip Cenuil-Conaill 7 co n-a flog ap tír, co
pogabpat longpopt ic Gaet-in-caippgin. Iap pin
tangacup Clann-Oiapmata co Popt-poip oo'n Le[i]t
aile oo gabail fpipin loingip. Iap pin poleictea oppa
na tpi longa oéc lan[a] oo fluag, co pomaib ap Clainn-
Oiapmata. Iap pin táinig Mac Laclainn (oon,[a] Concubap beacc[b]) i n-a puipicin, co pogonab a ec 7 co
topcaip oo'n eppap pin la Cenel-Conaill i n-einec
Coluim-cille 7 a comapba 7 a fepine pobomiabaig.
Ocur[f] tpiapan mipbail cetna[g] pomapb Concobup
Mupcab hUa Crica[i]n, pi hUa-Pacpac.

(Concubap[a] na glaipfeine hU Ruaipc oo babub.[a])

Kal. Ian. iii.[a] p.,[a] L. iiii., Anno Domini M.° cc.° ii.°[b]
Niall hUa Flainn[1] oo mapbab oo Gallaib Ulab[c] i
mebail.—Magnup, mac Oiapmata hUi Laclainn, oo

[a] pia—,A. [b] .u. (the Latin equivalent used as a contraction),. A. [c] -n-Ena, A.
[d] itl., n. t. h., A; om., B, C, D. [f] ip—it is—added, B. The sentence is
omitted in D. g pin—that— added, B

A.D. 1202. [1] Flaino, B.—[a,a] n. t. h., on blank space, A. [b] -.i.°, B:
that is, 1201; which is also the year in C, D. [c] om., B, C, D. 1 mebail is
om. in C, D.

[2] *The place, etc.*—Descendentes ad bellum fuerunt numero 15 millia armatorum, ex quibus 8 millia in eodem bello perierunt, D. This is, no doubt, an exaggeration.

[3] *Dishonoured.* — D adds: Et nihilominus ipse O'Donill cum suis persecutus est fugam inter Dermitios et Eoganenses, quos simul oppressit et tandem rediit cum magna preda et victoria.

[4] *Conchubhar.*—Given in the *Annals of Loch Cé, ad an.*

[5] *Na Glaisfheine.*—Of the green

Duach. Then came Cathal Carrach with the Connachtmen along with him and they engaged in battle and the Foreigners of Ulidia and Meath were defeated. The place[2] wherein were the five battalions, there came not therefrom but two battalions of them.—Aedh Ua Neill was deposed by the Cenel-Eogain and the coronation of Conchobar Mac Lachlainn [was effected] by them. And he made a foray into Tir-Ennai, so that he took away cows innumerable and killed people. Then came Eicnechan Ua Domnaill with the fleet of Cenel-Conaill and with their host on land, so that they formed a camp at Gaethin-cairrgin. Thereafter came the Clann-Diarmata to Port-rois on the other side, to act against the fleet. After that, there were sent against them the thirteen ships full of the host, so that [the battle] went against the Clann-Diarmata. Thereupon Mac Lachlainn (namely, Conchubhur the Little) came to their aid, until his horse was wounded and he fell of that fall by the Cenel-Conaill, in reparation of [St.] Colum-cille and of his successor and of his Shrine that he dishonoured.[3] And through the same miracle Conchobur killed Murchadh Ua Crichain, king of Ui-Fiachrach.

(Conchubhar[4] na Glaisfheine[5] U[a] Ruairc was drowned.[6])

[1201]

Kalends of Jan. on 3rd feria, 4th of the moon, A.D. 1202. Niall Ua Flainn was killed by the Foreigners of Ulidia in treachery.—Maghnus, son of Diarmait Ua

[1202]

---

militia; " so called from the colour of their armour or of their standards" (*Pursuit of Diarmuid and Graine*, ed. S. H. O'Grady, *Trans. Ossian. Soc.* iii. 89).

[6] *Drowned.*—In the Erne, near Belleek, flying from a battle gained over Ualgarg O'Rourke and himself by O'Donnell. (*F. M.* A.D. 1200 and O'D.'s note *k.*)

marbaḋ do Muircertaċ hUa[d] Neill. Muircertaċ hUa Neill dono do marbaḋ ann.

(In° t-earcub hUa Mellaiġ quieuit.—Iohannes, presbiter Cardinalis de Monte Celio et legatus Apostolic[a]e Sedis, in Hiberniam uenit. Senuḋ cleireaċ Erenn, icir Ghallaiḃ 7 Ghoeiḋealaiḃ, i n-Aċ cliaṫ imon Cardinail cetna sin. Senuḋ Chonnaċt, icir Laeċaiḃ 7 cleirċiḃ, hic Aṫ-luain hi cind ċaeiciḋis imon Cardinail cetna.—Toirrḋealbaċ, mac Ruaidri, mic Thoirrḋealbaiḋ hUi Conċuḃair, do gabail la Caṫal croiḃderg, la ri Connaċt. Ocus is iat rosgaḃsat e: idon, Donnċaḋ hUa Dubda, ri hUa-n-Amalgaiḋ 7 Conċuḃar got hUa hEaḋra, ri Luigne Connaċt 7 Diarmaid, mac Ruaidri hUi Conċoḃair, idon, mac a aṫar fein 7 Diarmaid, mac Magnusa, idon, mac derbraṫar a aṫar.—Caṫal carraċ, mac Conċuḃair Mhaenmuiġe, mic Toirrdelḃaiġ moir, ri Condaċt, do marbaḋ in bliaḋain si.)

Kal. Ian. iiii.[a] f.,[a] l. x, u., Anno Domini M.° cc.° iii.°[b] Mael-Coluim° hUa Brona[i]n, airċinneċ Toraiḋe, in pace quieuit.—Domnall Carraċ hUa Doċartaiġ, ri Thire-Conaill, do marbaḋ do Mhuinnter-ḃaiġill[1] ar n-argain cell[2] n-imḋa 7 tuaiti.—Mael-Finnen Mac Colma[i]n, airḋsenoir togaiḋe,[3] in pace quieuit.—Domnall hUa Brolċa[i]n, prioir [Ia,[d]] uasalsenoir

[d] Repeated, doubtless by oversight, B. [e-e] Partly on text space, partly on margin, n. t. h., A; om., B, C, D. [f-f] r. m., n. t. h., A; om., B, C, D.

A.D. 1203. [1] Ḃuiġill, B. [2] ċeall, B. [3] togaidi, A.—[a-a] n. t. h. on blank space, A. [b-c] n.° (1202), B; followed by C, D. [c-c] om., B, C, D. The order of the entries in B, C, D is: Mael-Finnen—Domnall Carraċ —Domnall hUa Brolċan. [d] blank left for name of Community, A, B. Not supplied in C, D. For the reading Ia, see Adamnan, p. 409, n. o.

1202. [1] *At the same time.*—Et propterea eodem instanti ipse Mauricius similiter interemptus fuit, D.

[2] *Ua Mellaigh.*—Conn O'Melaigh, bishop of Annaghdown, co. Galway, according to the *Four Masters.*

All the added entries are given in the *Annals of Loch Cé* at this year.

Lachlainn, was killed by Muircertach Ua Neill. Muir- [1202]
certach Ua Neill, however, was killed at the same time.[1]

(The bishop Ua Mellaigh[2] rested.—John,[3] Cardinal
Priest of Monte Celio and Legate of the Apostolic See,
came into Ireland. A Synod of the clergy of Ireland,
both Foreigners and Gaidhil, [assembled] at Ath-cliath
under that same Cardinal.—A Synod of Connacht, both
laics and clerics, [assembled] at Ath-luain at the end of a
fortnight under the same Cardinal.—Toirrdhealbach, son
of Ruaidhri, son of Toirrdbealbach Ua Conchubhair, was
taken prisoner by Cathal Red-hand, [namely] by the king
of Connacht. And it is these captured him,—namely,
Donnchadh Ua Dubda, king of Ui-Amhalgaidh and Conchubhar Ua Eadhra the Stammerer, king of the Luighni
of Connacht and Diarmaid, son of Ruaidhri Ua Conchobhair, to wit, the son of his own father, and Diarmaid, son
of Maghnus, that is, the son of the brother of his father.—
Cathal Carrach,[4] son of Conchubhar Maenmuighe, son of
Toirrdelbach Mor, king of Connacht, was killed in this
year.)

Kalends of Jan. on 4th feria, 15th of the moon, A.D. [1203]
1203. Mael-Coluim Ua Bronain, herenagh of Toraidhe,
rested in peace.—Domnall Carrach Ua Dochartaigh, king
of Tir-Conaill[1] was killed by Muinnter-Baighill after
pillaging many churches and territories.—Mael-Finne
Mac Colmain, arch-senior select, rested in peace.—Domnall Ua Brolchain prior [of Iona], eminent senior select for-

---

[3] *John.*—On August 15 of this year, King John renewed (by Letters) an appeal before the Legate against the bishops of Clogher, Clonmacnoise, Kells and Ardagh, the archdeacon of Armagh and others, who had shown a manifest desire to work against the king's right respecting the then vacant church of Armagh (*Calendar of Documents relating to Ireland*, vol. I. No. 168).

[4] *Carrach.*—Scabidus, D: correctly. For different accounts of his death, see *Annals of Loch Ce* 1202 *F. M.*; 1201.

1203. [1] *King of Tir-Connaill.*—Regius professor Ardmoighair ! D.

togaide ar ceill, ar cruť, ar deilb, ar dutcur, ar mine, ar mordačt, ar midcaire, ar crabad, ar ecna[i], port magnam tribulationem et optimam penitenciam in quinto Kalendar Maii, ingrer[r]ur ert uiam uniuerrae carnir.

(Cončubar ruad, mac Domnaill hUa Briain, do marbad l'a dearbratair fein, idon, la Muirčeartač, mac n-Dhomnaill, mic Thoirrdealbuid hUi Briain.—Toirrdealbač, mac Ruaidri hUi Cončubair, d'etlud ar a geimiul 7 rid do denum do Chatal croibdearg rir 7 ferann du čabairt do. Toirrdealbač d'innarba[d] do Chatal croibderg 7 rid do denum rir ro četoir tre imrdi na n-Gall, idon, Mailrer 7 Uater.)

[Oir.] Kal. Ian. u. f., L. xx. ui., Anno Domini M.° cc.° iiii.°
A 56c Doire do lorcad | o ta relic Mart[a]in co tibrait
B 58b Adomna[i]n.—Diarmait, mac Muircertaig hUi Loclainn, co ni do Ghallaib do čiačtain ar creič i Tir-n-Eogain, co roairgret in Scrin Coluim-cille, co r'uctat orra drem do Ceniul-Eogain, co remaid for Gallaib, co romarbad Diarmait tria mirbailib na Scrine.—Slogad la mac Uga de-Laci co ni do Ghallaib na Mide i n-Ulltaib, co rodicuireour Sheoan do-Chuirt a hUlltaib.—Mainirtir do denum do Celluč ... ar lar croi

A.D. 1203. ⁴—cionem, B. ⁵ penetenciam, B. .u.tar, A; .u.ta, B. ⁶⁻⁸ ar cruť, ar čeill, B; followed by C, D. ¹·⁴ ar eacna, ar aro-crabad—*for wisdom, for exalted piety,* B (C, D). ⁵·⁶ om., B; uitam riniuit, C, D. ʰ·ʰ n. t. h., A; om., B, C, D.

A.D. 1204. ¹ Doiri, A. ² reilic, A. ³ Mairtin, A. ⁴ Lačlainn, B. ⁵ Chupt, with no Do Cuirt—*or* (the name is not *Do Churt,* but) *Do Cuirt* —itl., t. h., B.—ᵃ⁻ᵃ n. t. h. on blank space, A. ᵇ .xx., t. h.; .ui. added, n. t. h., A. ᶜ—iii.° (1203), B, C, D. ᵈ om., B, C, D. ᵉ blank=space for about 8 letters left in MS. (A). The missing words, there can be little doubt, are abbad Ia—*abbot of Iona.*

In the *Annals of Loch Cé* (1202) he is called king of Ard-Midhair (Ardmire, co. Donegal), which shews that the translator of D consulted other authorities.

² *April* 27.—It fell on Sun-

intelligence, for form, for appearance, for disposition, for gentleness, for magnanimity, for benevolence, for piety, for wisdom, entered the way of all flesh, after great suffering and most excellent penance, on the 5th of the Kalends of May [April 27[2]]. [1203]

(Conchubhar[3] the Red, son of Domnall Ua Briain, was killed by his own brother, namely, by Muircertach, son of Domnall, son of Toirrdhealbudh Ua Briain.—Toirrdhealbach, son of Ruaidhri Ua Conchubhair, escaped from his captivity and peace was made by Cathal Red-hand with him and land was given to him. Toirrdhealbach was expelled by Cathal Red-hand and peace was made with him immediately through intercession of the Foreigners, namely, Meyler[4] and Walter[5] [De Lacy].)

Kalends of Jan. on 5th feria, 26th of the moon, A.D. 1204. Doire was burned from the Cemetery of [St.] Martin to the Well of [St.] Adomhnan.—Diarmait, son of Muircertach Ua Lochlainn, with a force of Foreigners came on a foray into Tir-Eogain, so that they plundered the Shrine of [St.] Colum-cille, until a party of the Cenel-Eogain overtook them [and] defeat was inflicted upon the Foreigners [and] Diarmait was killed through miracles of the Shrine. —A hosting by [Ugo] the son of Ugo De Lacy with a force of Foreigners of Meath into Ulidia, so that they expelled John De Courcy out of Ulidia.—A monastery[1] was built by Cellach, [abbot of Iona] in the centre of the [1204 Bis.]

---

day in the present year. This goes to prove that the *Annals of Loch Ce* (followed by the *F. M.*) err in assigning the obit to 1202; in which the 27th fell on Saturday, a day of no particular note. For Ua Brolchain, see *Adamnan*, p. 409, note *o*.

[3] *Conchubhar, etc.*—The additions are given (the last entry with greater detail) in the *Annals of Loch Ce* (*ad an.*).

[4] *Meyler.*—Meyler Fitz Henry (illegitimate son of King Henry I.), Justiciary of Ireland.

[5] *Walter.*—Son of Hugh De Lacy.

1204. [1] *Monastery.*—See *Adamnan*, p. 412.

Ia ᵹan naċ oliᵹeḋ, ꞇaꞃ ꞃaꞃuxuḋ muinnꞇeꞃi Ia, co ꞃomill in baile co móꞃ. Sloᵹaḋ ꝺono la cleiꞃċiḋ Eꞃenn, iꝺon, la Ꝼloꞃinꞇ hUa Ceꞃballa[i]n, la eꞃpuc Ꞇiꞃe-hEoᵹain ⁊ la Mael-Iꞃu hUa n-Ꝺoꞃiᵹ, iꝺon, eꞃpuc Ꞇiꞃe-Conaill ⁊ la abaꝺ ꞃeicleꞃa Ꝑoil ⁊ Ꝑeꞇaiꞃ i n-Ꞓꞃꝺ-Maċa ⁊ la hꞒmalᵹaiḋ hUa Ꝼeꞃᵹail, abaꝺ ꞃeicleꞃa Ꝺoiꞃe ⁊ la hꞒinmiꞃe hUa Coḃċaiꞡ ⁊ ꞃoċaiḋi móꞃ ꝺo muinnꞇeꞃ Ꝺoiꞃe ⁊ ꞃoċaiḋi moꞃ ꝺo cleiꞃċiḋ in Ꞇuaiꞃce[i]ꞃꞇ, co ꞃoꞃcailꞃeꞇ in Mainiꞃꞇeꞃ ꝺo ꞃeiꞃ oliᵹiḋ na hecailꞃi. In ꞇ-Ꞓṁalᵹaiḋ ꞃeṁꞃaiꞇi ꞃin ꝺo xaḃail aḃꝺaine Ia ꞇꞃe ꞇoᵹa ᵹall ⁊ ᵹaiḋel.ᵈ

(Muiꞃċeaꞃꞇaċ' Ꞇeaꞇḃaċ, mac Conċuḃaiꞃ Maenṁuiᵹe, mic Ruaiḋꞃi hUi Conċuḃaiꞃ, ꝺo maꞃbaḋ ꝺo Ꝺhiaꞃmuiꝺ, mac Ruaiᵹꞃi ⁊ ꝺo Ꞓeḋ, mac Ruaiḋꞃi, iꝺon, ꝺá ḃeaꞃḃꞃaċaiꞃ a aċaꞃ ꝼein.—Maiꝺm ꞃia n-Ꝺhomnall, mac Mhecc Caꞃꞃċaiᵹ ⁊ ꞃia n-Ꝺeaꞃṁuiṁneaċaiḋ ꞃoꞃ ᵹalluiḃ, ubi ceciꝺeꞃunꞇ cenꞇum ꞃexaᵹinꞇa uiꞃi, uel ampliuꞃ.ꞁ)

ₖCal. Ian. uii.ᵃ ꝼ.,ᵃ L. uii., Ꞓnno Ꝺomini M.° cc.° u.° ᵇ Siꞇꞃiuc hUa Sꞃuiċein,¹ aiꞃcinneċ na Conᵹḃala, iꝺon,ᶜ cenn hUa-Muꞃċele ⁊ ꞇoiꞃeċ Clainni-Sneiḋᵹile aꞃ ꞇoċuċꞇ, ꞃoꞃꞇ oꞃꞇimam ꞃeniꞇenꞇiam ꝼeliciꞇeꞃ ꝼiniuiꞇ (uiꞇamᵈ) eꞇ ꞃeꞃulꞇuꞃ eꞃꞇ in ꞇemꞃlo quoꝺ ꝼacꞇum eꞃꞇ aꞃuꝺ iꞃꞃum.ᵉ—Mael-Ḃꞃiᵹꞇe' hUa hEꞃaꞃa[i]n ꝺo ꞇoᵹa[ḋ] i comuꞃbuꞃ Ḃꞃenainn ꝺo laꞃ Ꝺaiꞃe Coluim-cille.— hEoan ꝺo-Chuiꞃꞇ, innꞃeḋaċ ceall Eꞃenn ⁊ ꞇuaċ, ꝺo innaꞃba[ḋ] ꝺo mac Uᵹa ꝺe-Laci i Ꞇiꞃ-n-Eoᵹainꞁ aꞃ comuiꞃce Ceniuil-Eoᵹain.

A.D. 1204. ᶠ⁻ⁱ n. t. h., A; om., B, C, D.
A.D. 1205. ¹ Sꞃuiꞇen, B.—ᵃ⁻ᵃ n. t. h. on blank space, A.   ᵇ⁻.ıııı.° (1204), B (C, D); erroneously. ᶜ⁻ᶜ om., B,D; which have quieuiꞇ after Conᵹbala. "Died," C. ᵈ itl, n. t. h., MS. (A). ᵉ⁻ᵉ om., B, C, D. ꝼ-n-Eoᵹan om., probably from oversight, A.

---

³ *Muircertach.*—This and the following entry are given in *Annals of Loch Cé (ad an.).*

1205. ¹ *By himself.*—*Apud ipsum* in the original,—a literal Latin rendering of the Irish *lais féin.*

ANNALS OF ULSTER. 243

encolsure of Iona, without any right, in dishonour of the [1204] Community of Iona, so that he wrecked the place greatly. A hosting, however, was made by the clergy of Ireland, namely, by Florence Ua Cerballain, bishop of Tir-Eogain and by Mael-Isu Ua Dorig, that is, bishop of Tir-Conaill and by the Abbot of the Monastery of Paul and Peter in Ard-Macha and by Amalgaidh Ua Fergail, abbot of the Monastery of Doire and by Ainmire Ua Cobhthaigh and a large number of the Community of Doire and a large number of the clergy of the North, so that they razed the monastery, according to the law of the Church. That Amalgaidh aforesaid took the abbacy of Iona by selection of Foreigners and Gaidhil.

(Muircertach[2] of Tethbha, son of Conchubhar Maenmhuighe, son of Ruaidhri Ua Conchubhair, was killed by Diarmuid, son of Ruaighri and by Aedh, son of Ruaidhri, that is, two brothers of his own father.—Defeat [was inflicted] by Domnall, son of Mac Carthaigh and by the Desmonians upon the Foreigners, where fell one hundred, and sixty men, or more.)

Kalends of Jan. on 7th feria, 7th of the moon, A.D. [1205] 1205. Sitriuc Ua Sruithein, herenagh of the Congbhail, namely, head of Ui-Murthele and chief of Clann-Sneidhgile for ability, after most excellent penance felicitously finished (his life) and was buried in the church that was built by himself.[1]—Mael-Brighte Ua Erarain was chosen into the succession of [St.] Brenann[2] from[3] the Community of Doire of Colum-cille.—John De Courcy, destroyer of the churches and territories of Ireland, was expelled by [Ugo] the son of Ugo De Lacy into Tir-Eogain, to the protection[4] of Cenel-Eogain.

---

[2] *Succession of* [*St.*] *Brenann.*— That is, very probably, was made bishop of Clonfert.

[3] *From.*—Literally, *from the centre*: meaning that he had no previous connexion with the see over which he was placed.

[4] *To the protection.*—The passage is thus translated in D : In eorum protectione receperunt per nomen

}Cal. 1an. 1.ᵃ ꝼ.,ᵃ L. xuɪɪɪ., Anno Domini M.º cc.º uɪ.º ᵇ
Magnuſ hUa Cata[ɪ]n, mac ꞃɪġ Cɪannacht¹ ⁊ ꝼeꞃ-na-
Cꞃaɪbe, tuɪꞃ ġaɪꞃcɪb ⁊ beoxacta ɪn Tuaɪꞃce[ɪ]ꞃt, do
tuɪtɪm le ġuɪn ꞃoɪxoɪ.—Soeꞃbꞃetac hUa Doɪꞃeɪd,
aɪꞃcɪnnec Domnaɪġ-moɪꞃ, ɪn pace quɪeuɪt.—Patꞃaɪcᶜ
hUa² Moxꞃa[ɪ]n quɪeuɪt ɪn pace.

A 56d }Cal. 1an. ɪɪ.ᵃ ꝼ., L xx. ɪx., Anno Domini M.º cc.º uɪɪ.º ᵇ
Domnallᶜ hUa Muɪꞃedaɪx, apꝺꝼeꞃleıxɪnn Daɪꞃe
Coluɪm-cɪlle, poꞃt magnam¹ tꞃɪbulatɪonem [uɪtam]
ꝼelıcıteꞃ ꝼɪnɪuɪt. Ocuꞃ ꞃotoxad Muɪꞃceꞃtac O
Mɪlluxa[ɪ]n (noᵈ, O Maelaxa[ɪ]nᵈ) 'n-a ɪnad.ᶜ—Mael-
ꞃetaɪꞃ hUa Calma[ɪ]n, comaꞃba² Caɪnnɪx, tuɪꞃ cꞃabad
⁊ eɪnɪx Thuaɪꞃce[ɪ]ꞃt Eꞃenn, ɪn pace quɪeuɪt. Ut
dɪxɪt poetaᵉ :

Eaꞃbaɪd hUa Calma[ɪ]n 'n-a cɪll,
Olc 'n-a axaɪd nı aɪꞃmɪm :
Ita ꞃamud³ d 'an ꞃott ꞃɪn,
'Nott ġan cꞃabad 'n-a catꞃaɪx.

A.D. 1206. ¹Cɪannacta, B. ²O, A. ᵃ⁻ᵃblank space, A. ᵇ⁻ᵇu.º (1205), B (C, D); erroneously. ᶜ⁻ᶜom., C, D.

A.D. 1207. ¹ magnum, MS. (A). ² comuꞃba, A. ³ ꞃamad, B. ᵃ⁻ᵃn. t. h. on blank space, A. ᵇ⁻ᵇuɪ.º (1206), B (C, D); erroneously. ᶜ⁻ᶜom., B, C, D. The Flaɪtbeꞃtac entry is also omitted in D. ᵈ⁻ᵈ itl., t. h., MS. (A). ᵉ om., A.

Cumarky ! Comuirce is rendered *safe-conduct* in C.

1206. ¹ *Fell, etc.*—Percussus sagitta cecidit mortuus, D.

1207. ¹ *Cainnech.*—*Laygnii* in D. On the margin, another hand placed: In alio manuscripto *Cainech*; q. *Achad*. ("The other MS." is probably C, which has *Caynech*.) The query refers to St. Canice's foundation of *Ached-bo* (plain of cows), i.e., Aghaboe, Queen's county. But the context shews that a church in the north of Ireland is intended. This was Drumachose, in the native place of St. Canice, barony of Keenaght, co. Londonderry. See O'Donovan *F. M.*, iii. 149 ; *Adamnan*, p. 121.

² *Loss.*—The C-version of this entry may be quoted in full, as typical of the translator's non-acquaintance with the old language. The omission of the third quatrain, *tarcis* in the second and " giveth " (*dobeir*, a reading which, it has to be noted, is erroneous) in the fourth shew that the B-text was his

Kalends of Jan. on 1st feria, 18th of the moon, A.D. [1206] 1206. Maghnus Ua Cathain, son of the king of Ciannachta and Fir-na-craibhe, tower of championship and courage of the North, fell[1] by the wound of an arrow.—Soerbhrethach Ua Doireidh, herenagh of Domnach-mor, rested in peace.—Patrick Ua Moghrain rested in peace.

Kalends of Jan. on 2nd feria, 29th of the moon, A.D. [1207] 1207. Domhnall Ua Muiredaigh, chief lector of Daire of Colum-cille, after great suffering felicitously finished his life. And Muircertach O'Millugain (or O'Maelagain) was chosen in his stead.—Mael-Petair Ua Calmain, successor of [St.] Cainnech,[1] tower of piety and hospitality of the North of Ireland, rested in peace. As the poet said:

> Loss[2] [is] Ua Calmain in his church,
> Evil in comparison therewith I reckon not;
> There[3] is a community silent [with grief] thereat,
> That to-night there is no piety in his abbey.[3]

---

original. The egregious mistake of *easpadh*, loss, for *espoc*, bishop, is specially significant. (In the MS. the lines and verses are written continuously.)

"Mael-Peter O'Calman, coarb of Caynech, a man full of liberality and goodnes of all the North [of Ireland], in pace quievit. Ut poeta dixit:

Eappaoh, etc.: in English:
Bishop O'Colman in his church,
To which I compare noe other evill;
There is a sanctuary which that hurteth,
That this night there is noe prayer in his citty.

[Caperr, etc.:] signifying:
After Cainegh of chast body
Untill he arise over his alter,
[Third line is not translated.]
None shall tye cap on him so good.

Though noe man under heaven
Saved his church from demons,
Who is hee sanctified
That might but O'Colman!

Co[m]arba, etc.: thus:
The coarb of Cainegh of churches,
A want to all in common,
Giveth lamentacion to all the poore,
His death is a great evill."

The author of D merely gives the substance of the first quatrain (in which he shews he understood the meaning of *easpadh*): De quo dictum fuit, quod eo defficiente, relligio defuit in eius ciuitate.

[2,3] *There—abbey.*—Literally,
There is a community to which silence [is] that,
[Namely] to-night without piety in his abbey.

Apeir⁴ Cainnig in čuipp oig
No co p'eipig uap altóip,
Ni ciall vanuppáca⁵ in plait,
Ní piað cába pa čomaið.

Robo° pai ppibinn pciamglain,
Maið pocongbað coeṁpiagail,
Roppecaið tapða i n-gač tan,
Rob° eacnaið ampa, uapal.°

Gen⁶ co paepað neč po nim
In⁷ oubpeiclep ap veṁnaið,
Gia naemčap | cen⁸ loču ap lap,
Dopaeppað copp hUi Calma[i]n.

Comapba² Cainnig na cell,
Ip vič vo cač i coitčenn,
Ip bpon vo gač boču vobip,⁹
Ip móp in t-olc a eapbaið.
        Eapbaið h. C.—

Dič mop ap čainið 7 ap innilið ipin bliaðain pi.—
[Ph]laičbeptach hUa [Ph]laičbeptaig, ppioip Duine-
Géimin, in pace quieuit.—Gilla-patpaic° hUa palačtaig,
aipcinneč Duin-Cpuične, moptu[u]p ert.—Muipceptač
hUa [Ph]laičbeptaig moptu[i]p ert.°—Cpeč mebla la
Cenel-Conaill i n-Uib-phapanna[i]n¹⁰ 7 i Clainn-
Diapmata, co pogabpat bú 7 co pomapbpat voine.
Rucpat oppa Clann-Diapmata 7 hUi-[Ph]aipenna[i]n¹¹
7 hUi-¹² Gailmpeðaig, co pomapbað áp viaipmiðe 7 co
pobaiðeð pocaiðe vib.—Slogað la hUga ve-Laci co n-
gallaib Miðe 7 Laigen i Čoluč-n-óoc, co poloipctea
cealla 7 apbanna. Ocup ni pucpat geill na eivipe
Aeða hUi Neill vo'n čup pin.—Slogað la hUga ve-Laci

⁴Tapeip, B. ⁵—pacca, B. ⁶gin, A. ⁷an, B. ⁸gen, B. ⁹vobeip, B.
¹⁰ Eap- (p om.), A. ¹¹ Aipinnan, B. ¹² Ua, B.

ᵃ *Within it.*—Literally, *on the centre.*

ᵇ *Drowned.*—D says the leader was Ua Domnaill and adds: *tamen*

After Cainnech of the body pure
Until arose [Ua Calmain] above an altar,
It is not known whether [one as good as Ua
    Calmain] saw the [heavenly] kingdom,
There went not [monk's] mantle upon one as good.

He was a master scribe of beautiful execution,
Well used he keep the fair Rule,
He gave useful responses on every occasion.
He was a sage, distinguished, eminent.

Although no one under heaven could save
His penitentiary from demons,
Though he were sanctified without defect within it,[4]
[Yet] the body of Ua Calmain would save it.

The successor of Cainnech of the churches,
It is injury to every one in general,
It is grief to every wretched person,
It is a great evil,—his loss.
        Loss [is] Ua Calmain, etc.

Great destruction on people and cattle in this year.—[F]laithbertach Ua [F]laithbertaigh, prior of Dun-Geimhin, rested in peace.—Gilla-Patraic Ua Falachtaigh, herenagh of Dun-Cruithne, died.—Muircertach Ua [F]laithbertaigh died.—A treacherous foray by the Cenel-Conaill into Ui-Fhearannain and into Clann-Diarmata, so that they seized cows and killed people. The Clann-Diarmata and the Ui-[Fh]airennain and the Ui-Gailm-redhaigh overtook them, so that a countless number of them were slain and a multitude were drowned.[5]—A hosting by Hugo De Lacy with the Foreigners of Meath and of Leinster into Telach-oc, so that churches and crops were burned. And they took not the pledges or hostages of Aedh Ua Neill on that occasion.—A hosting by Hugo

---

Conallii cum magna difficultate predam in suam patriam adduxe- | runt. Both particulars are found in the account given in the *F. M.*

ι Cιannaċτ[αιb], co ροloιρc cella Cιannaċτ uιle 7 co ροξαὖ bú co τιαιρmιȯe.—Comαρba ρατραιc το ὅul co τeċ ριξ 8αxan το ροċuρ ceall ερenn 7 το ċαραιτ ζall ερenn.

[b.ρ.]]cal. 1an. 111.ª ρ.,ª L x.,b Ơnno Ơomιnι m.º cc.º uιιι.º *
Cρeċ la hειznečan hUα n-Ơomnαιll ι ρεραιb-mαnαč, coρ'ζαὖρατ¹ bú 7 co ρucρατ ριρ-mαnαč ρορρα, co ρomαρbαὖ hUα² Ơomnαιll, ρι Chιρe-Conαιll, ann, co n-αρ τιαιρmιȯe το mαιτιὖ Cenιuιl³-Conαιll mαιlle ρριρ.

A 57a]cal. 1an. u.ª ρ.,ª L. xx. 1.,b Ơnno Ơomιnι m.º cc.º ιx.º *
Cρeċρluαξαὖ la hƠċeὖ hUα Neιll ι n-Inιρ-n-εοζαιn 7 ρuc O Ơomnαιll ραιρ, co τucρατ cατ ιn ραmαρbαὖ αρ τιαιρmιȯe ταιne ροp ζαċ Let,¹ bαιl ρomαρbαὖ Ơomnαll, mαc muρčατα, το Chenel-εοζαιn. ρεpζαl ιmoρρο hUα ὑαιξιll 7d Caτbαρρ hUα Ơomnαιllᵈ 7 Coρmαc hUα Ơomnαιll 7 Ơαbιτ hUα Ơοċuρταιξ co ροċαιȯe το mαιτιὖ Ceneoιl-Conαιll ιmαιlle ριu.²—Cαt τucρατ
B 58d meιc | Raξnαιll, mιc 8omuρlιξ, ροp ρεραιὖ 8cιαὖ, τú ιn ραmαρbαὖ αˢ n-αρ.ᵉ

A.D. 1208. ¹ζuρ'—, A. ²O, A. ³Cenel, A.—ᵃˉᵃ n. t. h. on blank space, A. ᵇ .xx., B. ᶜˉᶜ .uιιι.º (1207), B (C, D); erroneously.

A.D. 1209. ¹leατ, A. ²mαιlle (aphaeresis of ι). B. ᵃˉᵃn. t. h, on blank space, A. ᵇ .x., B. But, to be consistent, it should be i.! ᶜˉᶜ.uιιι.º (1208) B (C, D); erroneously. ᵈ om., B, C, D. ᵉˉᵉ αρ τιαιρmηe—*slaughter innumerable*, B.

ᵃ *Successor of [St.] Patrick.*—The archbishop of Armagh. This was Eohdonn (latinized Eugenius) Mao Gille-uidhir. On May 4, 1203, King John granted the see of Armagh and primacy of Ireland (cf. A.D. 1202, note 3, *supra*) to Humphrey of Tikehull. On the 22nd of the same month, he notified the suffragans and subjects of the archdiocese that Eugene, "called the elect of Armagh," had, against the king's consent and after the king's appeal to the Pope, gone to Rome to secure his promotion and commanded them, if he should return, not to receive him as archbishop. Humphrey having died,

De Lacy into Ciannachta, so that he burned the churches [1207] of all Ciannachta and seized cows to a countless number.—The successor of [St.] Patrick[6] went to the court of the king of the Saxons to succour the churches of Ireland and to accuse the Foreigners of Ireland.

Kalends of Jan. on 3rd feria, 10th of the moon, A.D. 1208. [1208Bis.] A foray by Eignecan Ua Domnaill into Fir-Manach, so that they seized cows and the Fir-Manach overtook them, so that Ua Domnaill, king of Tir-Conaill, was killed there, with slaughter innumerable of the nobles of Cenel-Conaill along with him.[1]

Kalends of Jan. on 5th feria, 21st of the moon, A.D. [1209] 1209. A foray-hosting by Aedh Ua Neill into Inis-Eogain and Ua Domnaill overtook him, so that they gave battle, wherein were killed a countless number of persons on each side. Here was killed Domnall Mac Murchadha of the Cenel-Eogain; also Ferghal Ua Baighill and Cathbarr Ua Domnaill and Cormac Ua Domnaill and David Ua Dochurtaigh, with a multitude of the nobles of Cenel-Conaill along with them.—A battle was fought by the sons of Raghnall, son of Somurlech, against the Men of Sciadh, wherein slaughter was inflicted upon them.[1]

---

the king (Feb. 10, 1204) approved of Ralph, archdeacon of Meath, and commanded the clergy and laity to consider him elected and obey him (*Doc. Ire.*, 177, 178, 200).

These letters were disregarded: perhaps, never reached their destination. Echdonn was confirmed by Innocent III. and obtained peaceable possession of the See. We next find the king availing of his services. On July 19 of the present year, he informs the custodians of the See of Exeter that he sends Eugene, archbishop of Armagh and primate of Ireland, to execute the episcopal office in that diocese and commands them to find him suitable maintenance with six horses (*ubi sup.*, 331).

The visit here mentioned may have been one of the reasons that influenced John to go to Ireland three years later.

1208. [1] *Him.*—D adds: Et eius loco filius succedit in regimine.

1209. [1] *Them.*—D adds: Eodem anno O'Donill fecit exercitum ad-

R

(Finghin,' mac Diarmada, mic Cormuic Mheg Carr-taig, ri Dearmugan, interrectur ert a ruir.—Ualgarc hUa Ruairc d'aitrigad 7 Art, mac Domnaill, mic Fheargail hUi Ruairc, do rigad i n-a inad.'—Anno millerimo ducentermoque nono (nonono, MS.), Alaxander, Doctor reuerendur atque Magirter, Doctrinale ruum dedit tunc legendum.')

Kal. Ian. ui.* f.,* l. 11.,[b] Anno Domini M.° cc.° x.° ͨ Gilla-Crirt hUa Cernaig, comarba Condere, in bona penitentia quieuit.—Ri Saxan do taidect i n-Erinn co Longair diairmide, idon,* rect¹ cet¹ long.*

(Art' mac Domnaill, mic Fergail hUi Ruairc, ri Breifne, do marbad tre meabail la Cormac, mac Airt hUi Mhail-Sheaclainn.—Ceile hUa Dubtaig, errcop Mhaigi-Eo na Saxan], in Chrirto quieuit.—Flaitbertac hUa Flainn, idon, comorba Daconna Earra-mic-n-Eirc, [-Eric, MS.] mortuur ert.')

A.D. 1209. ᶠͨ n. t. h., A; om., B, C, D. ᵍ͛ t. m., n. t. h., A; om. B, C, D.

A.D. 1210. ¹⁻¹ dcc., MS. (A) —ᵃ⁻ᵃ n. t. h., on blank space, A. ᵇ To be in keeping with preceding year, the epact of B should be xxi. ᶜ⁻.ix.° (1209), B (C, D); in error. ᵈ In B, C, D, this item follows the Ri Saxan entry. ᵉ⁻ᵉ om., B, C, D. ᶠᶠ n. t. h., A; om., B, C, D.

versus Hugonem O'Nellium et Eogananses et, capta preda magna et obsidibus, pax perpetua stabilita fuit inter O'Nellum et O'Donill, cum promissis de adiutorio hinc inde prestando aduersus quoscunque eorum aduersarios, siue fuissent Angli, siue Hiberni.

This entry is given in the *F. M.* at 1208.

² *Finghin, etc.*—This and the *Ualgharc* entry are in the *Annals of Loch Cé*, 1209.

³ *Alexander.*—Alexander de Villa Dei, or de Villedieu, a Franciscan of Dole. Professor of Latin in Paris, where his chief work, the *Doctrinale Puerorum*, a versified Latin Grammar, was composed in 1209. It held the foremost place as text-book for more than two centuries. The authors of the *Histoire littéraire de la France* (Tome xvi., p. 188-9. Paris, 1824) allow it no merit.

The Biblical Leonine verses attributed to him and which deserve the censure given by the Benedictines (*loc. cit.*) are spurious, according to some. See Joecher:

(Finghin,[2] son of Diarmaid, son of Cormac Mac Carthaigh, king of Desmond, was slain by his own [people].—Ualgharc Ua Ruairc was dethroned and Art, son of Domnall, son of Fearghal Ua Ruairc, was made king in his stead.—In the year [of our Lord] one thousand two hundred and nine, Alexander,[3] reverend Doctor [of Theology] and Master [of Arts], then [first] delivered his *Doctrinal* to be read.)

Kalends of Jan. on 6th feria, 2nd of the moon, A.D. 1210. Gilla-Crist Ua Cernaigh, bishop[1] of Conderi, rested in good penance.—The king[2] of the Saxons [John] came into Ireland with a fleet hard to count, namely, seven hundred ships.

(Art,[3] son of Domnall, son of Ferghal Ua Ruairc, king of Breifni, was killed through treachery by Cormac, son of Art Ua Mail-Seachlainn.—Ceile Ua Dubhthaigh, bishop of Magh-Eo of the Saxons, rested in Christ.—Flaithbertach Ua Flainn, namely, successor of [St.] Dachonna[4] of Easmic-Eirc, died.)

Allgemeines Gelehrten Lexicon, p. 260 (Leipzig, 1750).

1210. [1] *Bishop.*—Literally, *successor* (of the founder, Mac-Cnisse; [only] *son of* [his mother] *Cness*: L. L. 369 f, 372 b).

[2] *The king, etc.*—For the itinerary of John, from "Crook near Waterford" [June 20] to "The mead near Dublin" [Aug. 24th], see *Doc. Ire.* 401—9.

[3] *Art, etc.*—These three items make up all the entries given in the *Annals of Loch Cé* under this year.

[4] *Dachonna.*—O'Donovan (*F. M.* iii., p. 162) and Reeves (*Adamnan*, p. 281) fell into an unaccountable error in making Dachonna the son of Erc. According to the *Genealogies of Saints* (L. L., p. 348b) and the *Nemsenchas* (versified Genealogies: L. Be. [Book of Ballymote], p. 230a ll. 40, 41), Dachonna and Lugaid and bishop Cormac were sons of Echaid, son of Illand, son of Eogan [a quo Cenel-Eogain] (son, L. L., *loc. cit.*, adds, of Niall of the Nine Hostages).

The *son of Erc*, from whom the Cataract (*Ess*: at present, Assylyn, on the Boyle, about a mile west of the town) took its ancient name, was probably Echaid, the last of the Firbolgic kings, who was slain in the battle of Magh Tuired, near Cong.

Kal. 1an. uııı.ᵖ.ᵃ L.,ᴄ.ᵐⁱ·ᵇ,Anno Domini M.° cc.° x.° ı.°°
Gaill do taıdect co' Caeluırgı, .co poıcınoıl Aed hUa
Neill Conaıll,7 Eogaın·7 Oırgıallu,¹ ·co·romarbad leır.

(Toırrdealbac,ᵈ mac Ruaıdrı hUı Concubaır, do
denum creıce ı Mag-Luırg, gu rug leır ırṁ Segaır hí
docuṁ Dıarmoda, a bratar 7 do lean Aed, mac Catail,
he gu n-deacaıd ır Tuaırgırt ar teıcead reıṁe.—
Braıgde Connact do toıgect ı n-Erınn, ıdon, Dıarmaıd
mac Concubaır, Concubar hU Eagra 7 Fınn hUa
Carmacan 7 Toırberd, mac Gall-Gaoıdıl.—Aıreactac
Mac Donncaıd [occısus est].⁴)

[b.r.] Kal. 1an. ı. r., L. xx. 1111., Anno Domini M.° cc.° x.° ıı.ⁿ
Sıtrıuc hUa Laıgena[ı]n, comarba Comgaıll, do éc 7
Aengur Mac Cormaıc do oırdned ı n-a ınad.—Caırtel
Cluana-Eoır dodenam do Ghallaıb (7ᵇ do'n Gaıllergcopᵇ)
7 srecrluagadˡ do denum doıbᵈ ı Tır-n-Eogaın. (Ocurᶜ
tugrad Fır-Mhanac ár mor orra ann.ᶜ)—Aed hUa
Neıll, rí Conaıll 7 Eogaın 7 Aırgıall, do breıt orraᵃ 7
maıdm for Ghalluıb, dú ın romarbad ár dıaırṁıde
doıb.—Tomar, mac Uctraıg, co macaıb Ragnaıll, mıc
Somarlıg, do taıdect do Dhaıre Coluım-cılle co réˢ
longaıd rectmogadˣ 7 ın baıle do mıllıud doıb co mór
7 Inır-Eogaın co huılıbı do mıllıud doıb 7 do Cheniulˢ-
Conaıll.

A.D. 1211. ¹ Aırgıallu, A.—ᵃ⁻ᵃ n. t. h. on blank space, A. ᵇ .xuı.. B.
The scribe mistook ii. for u. ᶜ⁻ᶜ.x.° (1210), B (C, D); erroneously.
ᵈ⁻ᵈ n. t. h., A; om., B, C, D.

A.D. 1212. ¹—aıgad, B. ² forra, B. ³ uı., A, B. ⁴ .lxx.ad, A, B. ⁵—
neol, A.—ᵃ⁻ᵃ .x.° .ı° (1211), B (C, D). The ferial and epact (which are
given in B also) show that the year is 1212. ᵇ⁻ᵇ itl., n. t. h., A; om., B,
C, D. ᵈ om., B.

1211. ¹ *Toirrdhealbach, etc.*— These entries (with the variant Mac Duinnchathaigh in the third) are given in the *Annals of Loch Cé* (*ad an.*).

² *The pledges.*—They were carried by King John the preceding year to England, according to the *Annals of Loch Cé*.

³ *Foreign-Gaidhel.*—See Vol. I.,

Kalends of Jan. on 7th feria, 13th of the moon, A.D. 1211. The Foreigners came to Narrow-Water, until Aedh Ua Neill assembled.[Cenel-]Conaill and [Cenel-]Eogain and the Airghialla, so that they [the Foreigners] were killed by him.

(Toirrdhealbach,[1] son of Ruaidhri Ua Conchubhair, made a foray into Magh-Luirg, until he brought the spoil with him into the Seghas to Diarmod, his kinsman. And Aodh, son of Cathal, followed him, until [Toirrdhealbach] went into the North, fleeing before him.—The hostages[2] of Connacht came [back] to Ireland: namely, Diarmaid, son of Conchubhar [Mac Diarmata], Conchubhar Ua Eaghra and Finn Ua Carmacan and Toibeard, son of a Foreign-Gaidhel.[3]—Aireachtach Mac Donnchaidh [was slain].)

Kalends of Jan. on 1st feria, 24th of the moon, A.D. 1212. Sitriuc Ua Laighenain, successor of [St.] Comgall [of Bangor], died and Oengus Mac Cormaic was instituted in his stead.—The castle of Cluain-Eois was built by the Foreigners (and by the Foreign bishop[1]) and a foray-hosting was made by them into Tir-Eogain (And the Fir-Manach inflicted great slaughter upon them there.)—Aedh Ua Neill, king of [Cenel-]Conaill and of [Cenel-]Eogain and of the Airghialla overtook them and defeat [was inflicted] upon the Foreigners, wherein were killed a countless number of them.—Thomas, son of Uchtrach with the sons of Raghnall, son of Somarle, came to Daire of [St.] Colum-cille with six and seventy ships and the town was greatly destroyed by them and Inis-Eogain was completely destroyed by them and by the Cenel-Conaill.

---

p. 365, n. 10. The *Annals of Loch Ce* state he was one of the stewards of O'Conor.

1212. [1]*Foreign bishop.*—John de Gray, bishop of Norwich; justiciary of Ireland, 1210-13.

254 annala ulaoh.

(Sloiżeaḋ le Connaċtaiḃ tre ḟoxairm in Ġailleprcoiḃ 7 Ġillibert Mic Ġhoiroealḃ ġu hEar-puaiḃ, ġu n-oearnao cairlen Chailuirġe leo.)

A 57b

Kal. 1an. 111.ᵃ f.,ᵃ l. u., Anno Domini M.° cc.° x.ᵃᵇ 111.ᵃ Donċaḋ Mac¹ Cana,¹ toireċ Ceneoil-Aenġura, do éc.— Creċ do venam do Ġhilla fiaclaċ hUa Ḃaiġill 7 do oireim do Ceniul-Conaill ar Ceniul-n-Eoġain 7 riat ar einec Ceneoil-Conaill uile 7 hUi Tairce[i]rt² co ron-

B 59a

raḋaċ. | Ruc imorro hUa Tairce[i]rt rorra 7 rerait' oeḃaio rriu.ᶜ Marḃtar imorro in Ġillá riaḋaċ hUa Tairce[i]rt, ioon, riġtoireċ Clainni-Sneiḋġile 7 Clainni-Finġin, i cornum a éiniġ.—Oruim-cain co n-a tempall do lorcaḋ do Ceniul-Eoġain ġan ceat do' hUa³ Neill.—Ferġal hUa Caťa[i]n, ri Ciannaċt 7 Fer-na-Craiḃe, do marḃaḋ do Ġhallaiḃ.—Domnall hUa⁴ Daimin do marḃaḋ do macaiḃ Meġ Laċlainn i n-dorur reiclera Daire Coluim-cille.

(Cairlen⁴ Chluana-Eoir do lorġuḃ.—Ġillibert Mac Coiroealḃ do marḃaḋ i Cairlen-an-ċail 7 in cairlen do lorġaḋ for ann.—Donnċaḋ hUa heiḋin do ḃallaḋ le hAeḋ, mac Caťail croiḃoerg.—Maiḋm Chaille-nacrann do ťaḃairt do Cormac, mac Airt hUi Mhail-Sheaċlainn, ar Ġhallaiḃ.ᵈ)

Kal. 1an. 1111ᵃ., f.ᵃ, l. x. ui., Anno Domini M.° cc.° x.ᵃᵇ 1111.ᵃᵇ Donn hUa¹ Ḃreirlen do marḃaḋ o'a airiuċt féin i

A.D. 1212. ᵃ⁻ᵃ n. t. h., A ; om., B, C, D.

A.D. 1213. ¹⁻¹ Macana, A. ² Tirc—, B. ³⁻³ oó[=do Ó], A. ⁴ O, A. ⁵ a, B.—ᵃ⁻ᵃ n. t. h., on blank space, A. ᵇ⁻ᵇ x.° 11.° (1212), B (C, D); erroneously. ᶜ⁻ᶜ reraiḋ oeḃaio rorru—*An attack is delivered upon them*, B. ᵈ⁻ᵈ n. t. h., A ; om., B, C, D.

A.D. 1214. ¹ O, A. B. ᵃ⁻ᵃ n. t. h., on blank space, A. ᵇ⁻ᵇ x.° 111.° (1213), B (C, D); erroneously.

---

² *A hosting.*—Given in the *Annals of Loch Cé* (ad an.)

1213. ¹ *Protection.*—Here and lower down, *comuirce* is rightly

(A hosting[2] by the Connachtmen, through summons of the Foreign bishop and of Gillibert Mac Coisdealbh, to Eas-ruadh, so that the castle of Narrow-Water was made by them.) [1212]

Kalends of Jan. on 3rd feria, 5th of the moon, A.D. 1213. Donnchadh Mac Cana, chief of Cenel-Oenghusa, died.—A foray was made by Gilla Fiachlach Ua Baighill and by a party of the Cenel-Conaill upon the Cenel-Eogain, who were all under the protection[1] of the Cenel-Conaill and of Ua Tairchert in particular. Howbeit, Ua Taircheirt overtook them and [his force] gave battle to them. However, the Gilla Riabhach Ua Taircheirt, namely, royal chief of Clann-Sneidhghille and Clann-Finghin, is killed in defence of [those under] his protection.—Druim-cain with its church was burned by the Cenel-Eogain without permission from [the king] Ua Neill.—Ferghal Ua Cathain, king of Ciannachta and Fir-na-craibhe, was killed by the Foreigners.—Domnall Ua Daimin was killed by the sons of Mac Lachlainn at the door of the Monastery of Daire of [St.] Colum-cille. [1213]

(The castle[2] of Cluain-Eois was burned.—Gillibert Mac Coisdealbh was killed in the castle of the Narrow [-Water] and the castle was also burned at the time.—Donnchadh Ua Eidhin was blinded by Aedh, son of Cathal Red-Hand [Ua Conchubair].—The defeat of the Wood of the [High] Trees was given by Cormac, son of Art Ua Mail-Seachlainn, to the Foreigners.)

Kalends of Jan. on 4th feria, 16th of the moon, A.D. 1214. Donn Ua Breislen was killed by his own council [1214]

---

rendered *patrocinium* by the translator of D.
[2] *The castle.*—These four items are found in the *Annals of Loch Ce* (*ad. un.*). The castle, they state, was destroyed by O'Neill.

meḋail.²—Tomáp, mac Uċtpaiɤ 7 Ruaiḋpi, mac Raᵹnaill, do apᵹain Daipi ᵹo huiliḃi 7 do bpeiṫ ṗet Muinntepe Daipe 7 Tuaipce[i]pt Epenn apċena do láp tempaill in peiclepa imaċ.—hUa¹ Cata[i]n, 7 Ṗip-na-Cpaiḃe do ṫiaċ-tain co Daipe do ɤabail taiᵹi 'mo macaiḃ Meᵹ Laċ-lainn, co³ pomapbpat³ celloip mop peiclepa Daipe ettopa. Doṗona Dia 7 Coluim-cille tpa miṗbail moip annṗein: idon, in ṗep tinoil 7 toċaptail, idon, Matᵹamain Maᵹ Ċitne,⁴ do mapbaḋ i n-eineċ Coluim-cille ṗo cetoip i n-dopuṗ in dubpeiclepa Coluim-cille.—Ainmipe hUa Coḃṫaiᵹ, ab peiclepa Daipe, uapalcleipeċ toᵹaiḋe ap* cpabaḋ, ap duṫċup, ap mine, ap mopḃaċt, ap miḋcaipe, ap mópdépċ, ap ecna[i], ap ᵹaċ maiṫ[i]up apċena,* popt optimam penitentiam inᵹpeṗ[p]up ept uiam uniuepṗ[a]e capnip i n-dubpeiclep Coluim-cille.—Captel Cula-paṫain do ḃenum le ᵈ Tomap, mac Uċtpaiᵹ 7 le ɤallaiḃ Ulaḋ. Ocuṗ popcaileḋ peilce 7 claċana 7 cumdaiċi in baile uile, cenmoṫa in tempall amain, cuiceṗein.*—Ri Alban do éc, idon, Uilliam ᵹapm.—Aeḋ hUa³ Neill do ċabaipt ṁaḋma | ap Ɣhallaiḃ 7 depᵹáp Ɣall do ċup ann 7 in Caiplonᵹpopt do lopcaḋ ipin loa cetna, eitip daine 7 innile.

(Ɣilla⁴-na-naeṁ hUa Ruaḋan, epipcopup Luiᵹne, in Chpipto quieuit.—Epipcopup Cluana-mac-Noip, idon,

A.D. 1214. ²meaḃail, B. ³·³ ᵹup m—, A. ⁴-aiċne, B. ⁵ O.A. ⁶·⁶ om., with exception of ap ecna—*for wisdom*—, which is placed after toᵹaiḋe, B; all om., C; "*Aynmire O Coffay, abbas Derensis, mortuus est*," D (in which it is the last item). ᵈ pe, with dot underneath and l overhead, t. h., A,—a clear proof that the exemplar contained the correct form. ᵉ cum in caipteḷ ṗin—*for that castle*, B. C follows A; D, B. ᶠ·ᶠ n. t. h.,

---

1214. ¹*Manciple.* — Literally, *great Cellarer* (*great* being redundant).

The original *celloir* is the equivalent of the Latin *cellarius*, whose duties are thus defined in the Rule of St. Isidore: Iste prebebit hebdomadariis quidquid necessarium est victui monachorum, hospitum, infirmorum. . Is etiam quidquid residuum fuerit pro pauperum usibus reservabit. . . Ad hunc quoque pertinent horrea, greges ovium et pecorum, lana, linum,

in treachery.—Thomas, son of Uchtrach and Ruaidhri, son [1214] of Raghnall, plundered Daire completely and took the treasures of the Community of Daire and of the North of Ireland besides from out the midst of the church of the Monastery.—Ua Cathain and the Men of Craibh came to Daire to seize a house against the sons of Mac Lachlainn, so that between them they killed the great manciple[1] of the Monastery of Daire. But God and [St.] Colum-cille wrought a great miracle therein: the man that assembled and mustered [the force], namely, Mathgamain Mag Aithne, was killed in reparation to Colum-cille immediately, at the door of the Penitentiary of Colum-cille.—Ainmire Ua Cobhthaigh, abbot of the Monastery of Daire, eminent cleric select for piety, for disposition, for meekness, for magnanimity, for benevolence, for great charity, for every goodness besides, after most excellent penance entered the way of all flesh in the Penitentiary of Colum-cille.— The castle of Cuil-rathain was built by Thomas, son of Uchtrach and by the Foreigners of Ulidia. And all the cemeteries and fences and buildings of the town, save the church alone, were pulled down for that.—The King of Scotland died, namely, William[2] Garm.—Aedh Ua Neill gave a defeat to the Foreigners and stark slaughter of the Foreigners was inflicted therein and Carrlongport was burned, both people and effects, on the same day.

(Gilla-na-naemh[3] Ua Ruadhan, bishop of Luighni [Achonry], rested in Christ.—The Bishop of Cluain-mac-

---

aviaria sollicitudo ; cibaria ad ministrandum pistoribus, jumentis, bobus et avibus; industria quoque calciamentorum, cura pastorum et piscatorum (*Concordia Regularum*, xl. 3).

The same officer is called *equomimus* (*oeconomus*) at 781(=782) *supra* =Irish *Fertighe*. The *Four Masters*, not understanding the term, equate it with Prior! The rendering in D is original: Magnus exorcista ! C gives "the great Caller."

[2] *William.*—Died and was succeeded by his son, Alexander II., in December, 1214.

[3] *Gilla-na-naemh.*—(*Servant* (devotee) *of the saints*). This and the

hUa Muiricean, quieuit.—Muircheartach, Mac Briain, do marbadh do Ghallaib.—Irin bliadain [ri] dobi in t-Aedh breicci, ffir a raitea an Cabartach.ᶠ—Iohannes,ᵍ tunc Angli[a]e rex, tuc re Saxana 7 Ere do'n Papa, idon, Innocentius tertius, 7 tuc an Papa do rein apir iad 7 mile marg doran 7 portesir gacha bliadain: idon, recc ced ex Anglia 7 tri ced ex hibernia.ᶠ)

Kal. Ian. u.ᵃ f.,ᵃ L. xx. uii., Anno Domini M.° cc.° x.ᵛ u.ᵇ Crech do denum d'Aedh, mac Mail-Seclainn¹ Meic Lochlainn, ror comarba Coluim-cille 7° caun greisi do argain do° 7 a marbadh fein do Ghallaib irin bliadain cetna, tria mirbail Coluim-cille.—Bean-Mide, ingen hUi Eignigh, ben² Aeda hUi Neill, rig³ Ailigh, in bona penitentia quieuit.—Sluagadh la hAedh hUa Neill i n-Ultaib 7 tuc maidm mor forᵃ Gallaib Ulad.ᵈ—Uilliam, ri Alban, do ec 7° Alaxander, a mac, do oirdnedh i n-a inadh.—[Gener]aleᵉ Concilium [rub] Innocentio Papa.ᶠ

A; om., B, C, D. ᵃ⁻ᵃ n. t. h., B; om., A; given in C, D.
A.D. 1215. ¹ Maeilec̄—(ⱡ om.), B. ² beam, B. ³ ri, A. ⁴ ar—oa, B.—ᵃ⁻ᵃ n. t. h. on blank space, A. ᵇ⁻ᵇ .x.° iiii.° (1214), B (C, D); erroneously. ᶜ⁻ᶜ om., B, C. ᵈ om., B, C. ᵉ om., A. ᶠ⁻ᶠ L m., t. h., A; om., B,

three next items are given in the *Annals of Loch Cé* (ad an.).

⁴ *Aedh*.—Of this person I have found no account elsewhere.

⁵ *John*.—The author of D mistook the meaning: Papa ipsa redonauit regi una cum mille marchia, etc. It is open to doubt whether it was undetstood by the translator of C: "The Pope surrendred them againe to himselfe and a 1000 marcks to him and after every yeare 700," etc.

The history of the donation and re-donation is sufficiently well known. (For an abstract of the Charter, St. Paul's, London, Oct. 3, 1213—not 1214, as in the text—(see *Doc. Irs.* I 489. Cf. *ib. s. vv.* Pope, I; Tribute, II, III, IV.) Of the money, one-half was to be paid on Sept. 29; the other, on the Easter following. By public script, made at Avignon, April 1, 1317, four delegates (deputed *ad hoc* by Letters of Edward II., given Dec. 16, 1216) agreed, on behalf of the king, to discharge the arrears of Henry and Edward II., amounting to 24,000 marks, by yearly payments of one fourth on the festival of St. Michael, commencing with the feast next ensuing.

Two receipts of John XXII., in the form of Letters to Edward III., have been preserved. The first bears date April 7 [1330] and is

Nois, namely, Ua Muiricean, rested.—Muirceartach, son [1214] of Brian, was killed by the Foreigners.—In this year appeared Aedh[4] "of the deceit," who was called "The Helper."—John,[5] then king of England, gave Saxon-land and Ireland to the Pope, namely, Innocent III. And the Pope gave them back to him again, and 1000 marks [were to be paid] to him [the Pope] and to [his] successors every year: to wit, 700 from England and 300 from Ireland.)

Kalends of Jan. on 5th feria, 27th of the moon, A.D. [1215] 1215. A foray was made by Aedh, son of Mael-Sechlainn Mac Lochlainn upon the successor of [St.] Colum-cille and a herd of cattle was carried off by him. And himself was killed by the Foreigners in the same year through miracle of Colum-cille.—Bean-Midhe, daughter of Ua Eignigh, wife of Aedh Ua Neill, king of Ailech, rested in good penance.—A hosting by Aedh Ua Neill into Ulidia and he inflicted great defeat upon the Foreigners of Ulidia.—William,[1] King of Scotland, died and Alexander, his son, was inaugurated in his stead.—A General Council[2] [was held] under Pope Innocent.

---

for the year ending Sept. 29, 1329: Cum pro regno Anglie et terris Hibernie censum mille marcarum sterlingorum annis singulis Romane ecclesie solvere teneris, etc. (Manner of payment set forth.), Nos solutionem et assignationem approbantes easdem, te ac heredes et successores tuos, necnon regnum et terras predictas de dictis mille marchis sic solutis absolvimus et quitamus.

The second, of July 5, 1333, is for the year ending Sept. 29, 1330, and the half year up to Easter [March 31], 1331. The 1,500 marks were paid in 6,000 gold florins, "singulis marchis pro quatuor florenis auri computatis."

This was apparently the last payment. In a Brief, Avignon, June 6 [1365], Urban V. reminds Edward III. that he made no remittance since July, 1333, and states that bearer was empowered to treat of this and other pressing matters. But, with respect to the arrears, the mission seems to have proved fruitless. See Theiner: *Vet. Mon. Hibern. et Scot.*, Romae, 1864, pp. 193, 253, 259, 329.

1215. [1] *William*.—This entry is misplaced. See 1214, note 2, *supra*.

[2] *Council*.—The 12th Ecumenical

(Cathal, mac Diarmoda, in Christo quieuit.—Ordo Minorum confirmatur hoc anno.—Ardgar hUa Concubair, epscopus Shil-Muiredaig, in Christo quieuit.—Combail erscob na Crisdaideacta co Roim i n-aimsir Innocent[ii] Pap[a]e tersi. Is i nuimir na n-erscob badar ann: quadringenti quindecim, inter quos fuerunt septuaginta unus archiepiscopi et primates et octingenti abbates 7 priores. Ocus i feil Martain do bi in comdail sin.)

[b.r.] Kal. Ian. ui. f., l. ix., ACnno Domini M.° cc.° x.° ui.ᵃ Mael-Poil hUa Muiredaig, prioir Duine-Geirmin, do éc.—Oengus hUa Caipella[i]n, toisec Clainni-Diarmata, do marbad d'a braitrib fein.—Donnsleibi hUa Mail-Mena do marbad do Dhal-Araide.—Tsad hUa Mail-fabaill, toisec Ceneoil-Fersura, co n-a braitrib 7 co¹ n-ár mor, do marbad do Muiredac, mac Mormair Lemnac.—Donncad hUa Duibdirma, toisec na Bredca, do éc i n-dubreicles Daire.—Muircad Mac Cathmail, rigtoisec Cheneoil-Feradaig, do éc tria mirbail Colum-cille.—Ruaidri hUa Flainn, ri Daslair, do éc.—Mag Cana, toisec Ceniu[i]l-Oengusa, do marbad dia braitrib fein.—Dionis[i]us hUa Longarga[i]n, airdespuc Cairil, mortu[u]s est Rom[a]e.—Edonn Mac Gille-uidir, comarba Patraic 7 primait Erenn, post Generale Concilium³ Lateranense Rom[a]e feliciter obdormiuit.—Concobur hUa hEnne, epscop Cille-daluia, post idem Concilium³ reuertens in uia quieuit.

C, D. Underneath is another item, now illegible. ᵉ⁻ᵉ itl., at end of first entry, n. t. h., A; om., B, C, D. ʰ·ʰ n. t. h., A; om., B, C, D.

A.D. 1216. ¹su, A. ²primait, B. ³consilium, A, B.—ᵃ⁻ᵃ n. t. h. on blank space, A. ᵇ⁻·u.° (1215), B (C, D); erroueously. ᶜ⁻ᶜ om., B, C, D. In addition, the Mael-Poil entry is omitted in D.

---

and 4th General of Lateran. Held from Nov. 11 to Nov. 30.

³ Cathal.—This and the other native item are found in the Annals of Loch Ce (ad an.).

⁴ Confirmed.—In the Lateran

(Cathal[3] Mac Diarmoda rested in Christ.—The Order of [Friars] Minors is confirmed[4] this year.—Ardghar Ua Conchubhair, bishop of Sil-Muirethaigh, rested in Christ.—A Synod[5] of the bishops of Christendom [was held] at Rome in the time of Pope Innocent III. This is the number of bishops that were therein, 415 ; amongst whom were 71 archbishops and primates. And 800 abbots and priors. And on the festival of [St.] Martin [Nov. 11] this Synod took place.)

Kalends of Jan. on 6th feria, 9th of the moon, A.D. 1216. Mael-Poil Ua Muiredhaigh, prior of Dun-Geimhin, died.—Oenghus Ua Cairrellain, chief of Clann-Diarmata, was killed by his own kinsmen.—Donnsleiþhi Ua Mail-Mena was killed by the Dal-Araidhe.—Trad Ua Mail-fhabhaill, chief of Cenel-Ferghusa, along with his kinsmen and with great havoc, was killed by Muiredach, son of the Great Steward of Lemhain.—Donnchadh Ua Dubdirma, chief of the Bredach, died in the Penitentiary of Daire.—Murchadh Mac Cathmail, royal chief of Cenel-Feradhaigh, died through miracle of [St.] Colum-cille[1].—Ruaidhri Ua Flainn, king of Dairlas, died.—Mag Cana, chief of Cenel-Oengusa, was killed by his own kinsmen.—Dionysius Ua Longargain, archbishop of Cashel, died in Rome.—Echdonn Mac Gille-uidhir, successor of Patrick and Primate of Ireland, felicitously slept in Rome after the Lateran General Council.—Conchobur Ua Enne, bishop of Cell-da-lua, returning after the same Council, slept on the way.

[1215]

[1216 Bis.]

Council. Wadding: *Ann. Min.*, ad an. 1215. p. 161.

[5] *A Synod.*—Given in substantially the same terms in the *Annals of Loch Cé* (ad an.).

1216. [1] *Colum-cille.*—*Cuius sanctuarium antea inuaserat* is added in D; from what source I know not.

ANNALA ULADH.

(Iohones[d], rex Anglie, mortuus est.—Annud hUa Muiredaid, epircopus Conmaicne, in Christo quieuit.[e]—Obiit[°] Innocentius Papa. Succedit [honor]us.—[Or]do Predicatorum confirmatur.[°] A'.D. 1216. Ag ro an bliadain araide Comairle Generalta 'sa Roim, idon, Laterann, ann aroide mile tri ced erpoc.[f])

Kal. Ian. 1. f., l. xx., Anno Domini m.° cc.° x.° uii.°
A 67ᵃ Matgamlain hUa [Fh]laitbertaig, ri Clainni-Domnaill, mortu[u]s est.

(An[b] t-airdersob hUa Ruanada do gabail do Maitiu hUa Conchubair.—Gilla-Arnain hUa Martain, ollum Erenn i m-breiteamnact, mortuus est.[b])

Kal. Ian. 11.ᵃ f.,ᵃ l. 1., Anno Domini M.° cc.° x.° uiii.ᵃ Gilla-Tigernaig, mac Gilla-Rona[i]n, ersus Airgiall 7 cenn Canonac Erenn, in bona penitentia quieuit.—Ingantac[°] Mac Congalaig do ec.[°]

A.D. 1216. ᵈ⁻ᵈ n. t. h., A; om., B, C, D. ᵉ⁻ᵉ l. m., n. t. h., A; om., B, C, D. ᶠ⁻ᶠ n. t. h., B; om., A; given in C, D.

A.D. 1217. ᵃ⁻...uii.°'(1216), B (C, D); erroneously. ᵇ⁻ᵇ n. t. h., A; om., B, C, D.

A.D. 1218. ᵃ⁻ᵃ n. t. h. on blank space, A. ᵇ⁻ᵇ uii.° (1217), B (C, D); erroneously. ᶜ⁻ᶜ om., B, C, D.

---

[2] *Died.*—On St. Luke's Day, October 18.

[3] *Annudh.*—Given in *Annals of Lock Cé (ad an.).*

[4] *Died.*—July 16. Honorius III. was elected on the 18th.

[5] *Confirmed.*—By Honorius III. in two Briefs, dated Dec. 22. The title *Friars Preachers* was first given in a third Letter, dated from the Lateran, Jan. 26, 1217: Honorius, etc., Dilectis filiis Priori and Fratribus Sancti Romani Praedicatoribus in partibus Tolosanis, etc. (*Script. Rer. Pred.*, p. 13-4.)

[6] 1216.—The date, of course, is erroneous. It should be 1215.

1217. [1] *Died.*—After this entry, D gives (1216): Eodem anno Donaldus Magnus O'Donill cum magno exercitu inuasit Clan-Ricard et continuauit ibidem, deuastando patriam, usquedum Mac William prestitit obedientiam and obsides ipsi O'Donill. Et preterea eiecit ex patria Moriachum Lasyndaylle [O'Daly] propter necem cuiusdam Ffyne O'Brologhan: quem dictus O'Donill prosecutus est in Tuomoniam et ipso Moriacho per

(John, king of England, died.²—Annudh³ Ua Muire- [1216]
thaidh, bishop of Conmaicni [Ardagh], rested in Christ.—
Pope Innocent died.⁴ Honorius succeeds.—The Order of
Preachers is confirmed.⁵—A.D. 1216.⁶ This is the year in
which there was a General Council in Rome, namely, of
Lateran, wherein were 1300 bishops.)

Kalends of Jan. on 1st feria, 20th of the moon, A.D. [1217]
1217. Mathgamain Ua Fhlaithbertaigh, king of Clann-
Domnaill, died.¹

(The archbishop² Ua Ruanadha was taken prisoner by
Mail-Isu Ua Conchubhair.—Gilla-Arnain Ua Martain,
ollam of Ireland in jurisprudence, died.)

Kalends of Jan. on 2nd feria, 1st of the moon, A.D. 1218. [1218]
Gilla-Tighernaigh,¹ son of Gilla-Ronain,¹ bishop of Airghialla [Clogher] and head of the Canons of Ireland,
rested in good penance.²—Ingantach Mac Congalaigh
died.

Donogho[-um] Caribragh O'Brien exinde fugiendo peruenit Limericum. Et cum ipse O'Donill cum exercitu illum persequendo ueniret ad portam Limericensem, homicidam reiecerunt ad mandatum ipsius O'Donill. Et sic ab uno ad alterum delatus fuit Dubliniam, nemine audente eum retinere contra mandatum ipsius O'Donill; qui reuersus [est] cum uictoria, perlustrata hinc inde tota Connacia in illa expeditione.

The foregoing is given with more detail in the *Four Masters* at 1213.

² *The archbishop.* — Given in *Annals of Loch Cé* at 1216. The next entry is in the same Annals under 1218.

1218. ¹ *Tighernaigh*; *Ronain.*—

(*Devotee*) *of* (*St.*) *Tigernach* (of Clones); *of* (*St.*) *Ronan* (of Liathross = Fir-roiss, 826-7, 846-7, *supra*?).

² *Penance.*—D adds the following: Quo anno O'Donill cum omnibus principalibus totius Ultonie et Conacie generalem expeditionem fecit per Midenses et alias Anglicanas partes comburendo et deuastando, quonsque uenerunt ad Dubliniam; cum quibus iuncta pace conditionali quod illum alias nominatum Moriachum homicidam eiicerent ex regno: quem propterea in Scociam in exilium remiserunt et deinde statim O'Donill, obtenta undique uictoria, rediit in patriam.

This is given at 1213 by the *Four Masters*.

264 ανναλα υλαοη.

(Diapmaio,ᵈ mac Concubaip Mic Diapmava, pig Muige-luipg, moptuup ept.—Copmac vo gabail pigi v'a eip.—Domnall hUa gabpa moptuup ept.—Mop, ingen hUi bpiain, bean Chatail cpoibvepg, moptua ept.ᵈ)

B 59a Kal. Ian. iii.ᵃ p.,ᵃ l. x.ii., Anno Domini M.° cc.° x.° ix.°ᵇ Diapmaic° hUa¹ gilla-loinne vo mapbab vo Mac gilla-puaib 7 v'a bpaitpib i mebail'.—Muipceptac hUa¹ flainn, pi hUa-Tuiptpi, vo mapbab vo ghallaib.— Congalac hUa Cainn, cainnel gaipcib 7 einigᵈ Tuaipce[i]pt Epenn, pigtoipec Muigi-lugav 7 Sil-Catupaig uile, vo mapbab vo gallaib ipin loo cetna.—gilla-nanaem hUa gopmgaile, pacapt Rata-lupaig, in penitentia quieuit.—Mael-Ipu hUa Daigpi, aipcinnec Daipe Coluim-cille,—dápicit² bliabain [sic] vo i n-aipcinnect—ap n-venum caca³ maituya etep cill 7 tuait, iᵉ pextᵈ io December, i:ᵉ n-Domnac,ᵉ in bono fine quieuit in pace.

(Clemenp,ᶠ epipcopup luigne, in Chpipto quieuit.— Tempall Mainipopeac na buille vo coipecpab.—hoc anno Sanctup fpancipcup, a ppima conueppione eiupvem anno vecimo teptio, mipit de uoluntate Domini pex fpatpep mip[a]e panctitatip ad pegnum Mappochiopum, uidelicet, fpatpem Uitalem, bepalldum, Ochtonem, Accupipcium, petpum et Adiutum. Quopum quinque ultimi anno pequenti puepunt maptipizati pub pege Mappochiopum, Mipamolino nomine.ᶠ)

A.D. 1218. ᵈ⁻ᵈ n. t. h., A; om., B, C, D.
A.D. 1219. ¹ O, A, ². xl., A, B. ³ gaca, B. ⁴⁻⁴ .i. ui., A, B.— ᵃ⁻ᵃ n. t. h., on blank space, A. ᵇ⁻. uii.° (1218), B (C, D); erroneously. ᶜ⁻ᶜ Placed last in D. ᵈ egnoma—of valour, B; "of courage," C; strenuitatis, D. C and D, accordingly, follow B. ᵉ⁻ᵉ in ppima pepia—on the first feria (the week-day name of Sunday), B; om., C; 6° Idus, etc., D. Here B unconsciously supplies additional internal evidence of the correctness of the chronology of A. For Dec. 6 fell on Sunday in 1219; but on Saturday in 1218. ᶠ⁻ᶠ n. t. h., A; om., B, C, D.

(Diarmaid,[3] son of Conchubhar Mac Diarmada, king of Magh-Luirg, died. Cormac took the kingship after him.—Domnall Ua Gadhra died.—Mor, daughter of Ua Briain, wife of Cathal Red-Hand [Ua Conchobair], died.) [1218]

Kalends of Jan. on 3rd feria, 12th of the moon, A.D. 1219. Diarmait Ua Gille-Loinne was killed by Mac Gilla-ruaidh and by his kinsmen, in treachery.—Muircertagh Ua Flainn, king of Ui-Tuirtre, was killed by the Foreigners.—Congalach Ua Cainn, candle of championship and liberality of the North of Ireland, royal chief of Magh Lughad and Sil-Cathusaigh, was killed by the Foreigners on the same day [as Ua Flainn].—Gilla-na naemh Ua Gormghaile, priest of Ragh-Luraigh, rested in penance.—Mael-Isu Ua Daighri, herenach of Daire of Colum-cille—forty years was he in the herenachy—, after doing every goodness to both clergy and laity, by a good ending rested in peace on Sunday,[1] the 6th of the Ides [8th] of December. [1219]

(Clement,[2] bishop of Luigni [Achonry], rested in Christ.—The church of the [Cistercian] Monastery of the Buill was consecrated.—This year[3] Saint Francis, in the 13th year from his first conversion, sent by will of the Lord six Friars of marvellous sanctity to the kingdom of Morrocco, namely, Brother Vitalis, Beraldus, Octo [Otho], Accuristius, Peter and Adjutus. Of whom the five last were martyred the following year, under the king of Morrocco, Miramolinus by name.)

---

[3] *Diarmaid.*—The three entries are given in the *Annals of Loch Ce* (1218).

1219. [1] *Sunday.*—The *Four Masters* place the obit (which they copy from these Annals) at 1218; omitting the day, which would have shewn that the death must have taken place in 1219.

[2] *Clement, etc.*—This entry is in the *Annals of Loch Ce* (ad an.). The next is given in the same Annals at 1220.

[3] *This year, etc.*—Vitalis was the superior. But he fell sick and died at Saragossa. See Wadding, *Ann. Min. ad an.* 1219, p. 213, 237.

[b'r.] Kal. Ian. 4ᵃ ᵃ p.,ᵃ l. xx.iii.,ᵇ Anno Domini M.° cc.° xx.° ᶜ ꝛonaċtan¹ O brona[i]n, comarba Coluim-cille, in pace quieuit. Ocur ᵈ dopala imperain eter Muinntir n-Daire 7 Cenel-n-Eogain im toga i n-a inað. Ir eð dorigneð annrein: doċogadur Muinnter Daire Mac Caṫmail irin comurbur 7 doċog Aeð O Neill 7 Cenel-n-Eogain Flann hUa brolca[i]n. Iar rin tra dopala imperain eter Muinntir Dhaire 7 O brolca[i]n 7 docuireð O brolċa[i]n ar in comurbur. Iar rin tra roṫogadur Muinnter Daire 7 Cenel-n-Eogain Muircertaċ hUa Milluga[i]n, idon, ferleiginn | Daire, irin comurbur. Ocur dobai in firurleiginn 7 in comurbur ri bliaðain aigi, uel paulo plur. Ocur dopala imperain eter Forfraig hUa n-Daigri,. idon, aircinneċ Daire 7 O Milluga[i]n, idon, in comarba, im an firurleiginn, no co n-deċadur doċum breiti comarba Patraic, co n-derna riṫ etarru 7 gur'togað Eoin, mac in firleiginn, irin firurleiginn, do reir comarba Patraic 7 comarba Colum-cille 7 Muinntere Daire arċena.ᵈ

(Aeð° hUa Mail-Eoin, erscob Cluana-mac-Nois, do baṫuð.—Mail-Seaċnaill, mac Concubair Mhaenṁuiðe, mortuur ert.—Hoc anno quinque ꝼanctirrimi fratrer Minorer, rcilicet, berallour, Octo, Accurrius, Petrur et Adiutur, parri runt rub Miramolino, rege Marrochiorum, Kalendir Februarii, aliar decimo reptimo Kalendarum Februarii, Domini Pap[a]e Honorii tercii

A.D. 1220. ¹ ꝛonaċdan, B.—ᵃ⁻ᵃ n. t. h., on blank space, A; .u., B; ᵇ .xxui., B. The scribe probably mistook ii for u. ᶜ⁻ᶜ x.° ix.° (1219), B (C, D); in error. ᵈ⁻ᵈ om., B (followed by C, D), which has: Flann O brolcain do oirdneð i n-a inað irin comurbur—*Flann O'Brolchan was appointed in his stead in the succession.* ᵉ⁻ᵉ n. t. h., A; om., B, C, D.

1220. ¹ *And there ensued, etc.*—The *Annals of Loch Cé* and the *Four Masters* omit the important dispute respecting the Lectorship.

After the entry describing the succession of O'Brolchain, D adds: Eodem anno O'Donill cum exercitu inuasit asperam illam tertiam partem Conacie, que comuniter dicitur *Garurtrian, siue* Aspera Tertia,

Kalends of Jan. on 4th feria, 23rd of the moon, A.D. 1220. [1220 Bis.] Fonachtan Ua Bronain, successor of [St.] Colum-cille, rested in peace. And there ensued[1] contention between the Community of Daire and the Cenel-Eogain, respecting the selection in his stead. It is this was done then: the Community of Daire chose Mac Cathmail into the succession and Aedh Ua Neill and the Cenel-Eogain chose Flann Ua Brolcain. After that, moreover, there ensued contention between the Community of Daire and O'Brolcain and O'Brolcain was put out of the succession. After that, moreover, the Community of Daire and the Cenel-Eogain chose Muircertach Ua Millugain, namely, lector of Daire, into the succession. And he had the lectorship and the succession for a year, or a little more. And there ensued contention between Geoffrey Ua Daighri, namely, herenagh of Daire and O'Millugain, that is, the abbot, respecting the lectorship, so that they appealed to the judgment of the successor of Patrick and he made peace between them. And John, son of the [late] Lector, was chosen into the lectorship, according to the successor of Patrick and the successor of Colum-cille and the community of Daire besides.

(Aedh[2] Ua Mail-Eoin, bishop of Cluain-mac-Nois, was drowned.—Mail-Seachnaill, son of Concubhar Maenmhuidhe [Ua Concobhair], died.—This year five most saintly Friars Minor, namely, Beraldus, Octo [Otho], Acursius, Peter and Adjutus, suffered [martyrdom] under Miramolinus, king of Morrocco, on the Kalends [1st] of February, or on the 17th of the Kalends of February

---

Conaght, nempe patrias O'Royrck et O'Really; a quibus habita ad vota obedientia et obsidibus, rediit per Fermanagh, quam similiter undique, pro maiori saltem parte, deuastauit.

An entry the same in substance is given in the *Four Masters* at 1219.

[2] *Aedh*.—This and the following item are in the *Annals of Loch Cé* (*ad an.*).

anno quarto, fere septem annis ante mortem Sancti Francisci.ᵃ)

Kal. Ian. f. iii.,ᵃ L. iiii. Anno Domini m.° cc.° xx.°ᵇ i.°ᵇ
(Diarmuid,ᶜ mac Ruaidri, do marbad.—Iacobus, Penitentialis et Capellanus Domini Pap[a]e et Legatus tocius Hiberni[a]e, in Hiberniam uenit.—Maelruanaid hUa Dubda do batud.—Sanctus Dominicus obiit hoc anno.—Primus Conuentus predicatorum uenit in Angliam.ᵉ)

A.D. 1221. ᵃ.u., n. t. h. on blank space, A; .ui., B. ᵇ⁻ᵇ.xx.° (1220), B (C, D); erroneously. ᶜ⁻ᶜn. t. h., A; om., B, C, D. Three lines of text-space are left blank for entries in B.

---

³[Jan. 18].—The 17th of Jan., according to Wadding, (ubi sup., ad an. 1220, p. 237).

1221. ¹Diarmuid; Maelruanaidh.—The two native items are in the Annals of Loch Ce (ud an), with greater detail.

²James.—Said to have been Canon of St. Victor, Paris. Sent as Legate to Ireland (and Scotland) by Honorius III. The Brief of appointment, dated Civita Vecchia, July 31 (1220), was superscribed: Regibus Ultonie, Corcaie, Limrith, Conatie, Insularum [of the Isles], cuilibet per se (Theiner, Vet. Mon., pp. 15, 16).

Respecting the Irish Legation, three Papal commissions are extant. In the first (Civita Vecchia, Aug. 6 [1220]), instructions were given to abrogate the custom [introduced by King John, Jan 14, 17, 1216; Doc. Ireland, I. 736, 739] that no Irishman should receive church preferment (Theiner, Vet. Mon., p. 16). But they do not appear to have been carried into effect. The abuse was abolished by Honorius in a Brief addressed to the Irish clergy (Lateran, Ap. 26 [1224]: Theiner, Vet. Mon., p. 23).

In the second (Civita Vecchia, Aug. 8 [1220]), the Legate was directed to remove the grievance reported by the archbishop of Cashel: namely, when an Englishman lost anything and got six other English to swear they believed his oath that the property was taken by an Irishman, the native, though guiltless and of good name and life and prepared to establish his innocence by thirty or more sworn witnesses, was nevertheless compelled to restitution (Theiner, Vet. Mon., pp. 16, 17). In this matter likewise no action was taken. After an interval of more than thirty years, the "damnable custom" was condemned by Innocent IV. in a Brief (Perugia, July 20 [1252]) to the archbishop of Cashel (Theiner, Vet. Mon., p. 56).

In the third (Lateran, March 19 [1221]), he was enjoined to adjudicate upon four complaints of the same archbishop and the king's reply thereto, touching church lands

[Jan. 18ᵗʰ], in the 4th year of the Lord, Pope Innocent III., nearly seven years before the death of Saint Francis.) [1220]

Kalends of Jan. on 6th feria, 4th of the moon, A.D. 1221. [No original entry]. [1221]
(Diarmuid,[1] son of Ruaidhri [Ua Conchobhair], was killed.—James,[2] Penitentiary and Chaplain of the Lord Pope and Legate of all Ireland, came into Ireland.— Maelruanaidh[1] Ua Dubhda [king of Ui-Amalghaidh] was drowned.—Saint Dominick died this year.[3]—The first Convent of Preachers came into England.)

(Theiner, *Vet. Mon.*, pp. 18, 20). Nothing, however, was done. Fourteen years later, Gregory IX. (Perugia, Jan. 4 [1235]) commanded the archbishop of Dublin to report upon the matters in question, mentioning that James had been empowered by his predecessor to decide them; but, on account of his departure, no process, it was reported, took place (sed, propter eius recessum, nullus, ut dicitur, fuit processus. Theiner, *Vet. Mon.* p. 30).

From Letters of Henry III. to the archbishop of Dublin (Jan. 7, 1222: *Doc. Ireland*, I. 1026) and Geoffrey De Marisco (June 26, 1822: *Doc. Ireland*, I. 1037) we learn that the Legate deposed and sent to the Curia the bishops of Killaloe and Ardfert [Travers and John of Limerick, intruded by De Marisco, whilst he was Justiciary]. In a Brief of Honorius III. (Lateran, May 9 [1226]), we read that James imposed perpetual silence upon Travers and caused another to be consecrated in his place (Theiner, *Vet. Mon.*, p. 26).

In the *Annals of Loch Ce (ad an.)*, James is charged with gross simony and said to have left Ireland in the year of his arrival. The second statement is confirmed from independent sources. On Nov. 20, 1220, Henry III. commanded the Justiciary, magnates (archbishops and bishops) and others in Ireland to receive honourably Master James, the Pope's Chaplain and Penitentiary, sent as Legate and, should anything new arise touching the state of the country, to have recourse to his counsel and aid (*Doc. Ireland*, I. 978). On Nov. 1 of the following year, he was one of the witnesses at Westminster to the surrender of Irish castles by deputies, on behalf of Geoffrey De Marisco, late Justiciary (*Doc. Ire.* I., 1015).

That on his departure he ceased to be Legate, may be inferred from his being merely styled "J[ames], Penitentiary of the Pope" in the document last referred to, and "J[ames], Penitentiary of the Pope and late Papal Legate of Ireland" in Henry's Letters (already mentioned) of Jan. 7 and June 26, 1222.

[3] *This year.*—On Aug. 6. The feast is held on Aug. 4.

270 annala ulaoh.

Kal. Ian. p., uii.ᵃ l. xu., CCnno Domini m.° cc.° xx.° ii.°ᵇ
Mac Uga de° Laci do taibect i n-Epinn da inndeoin
pig Saxan, co táinic¹ co hCCed O Neill, co n-decaoup
'maille i n-agaid Gall Epenn 7 co pomillpec mόp i Mide
7 i Laignib 7 i n-Ulltaib 7 co popcailpec caipcel Cula-
paτain 7 co poτnolpaτ² Gall Epenn ceτpi³ caτa pcecᵈ
co Delgain, co táinic¹ CCed O Neill 7 mac in⁴ Ugaᵈ,
ceτpi⁴ caτa, 'n-a n-agaib, co τucpac Gall bpeτᵉ a beoilᶠ
pein d'O Neill.ᶠ

(Copmac,ᵍ abb Comaip, occipup epτ.—Gilla-Mocoinne
hUa Caτail occipup epτ.—Mop, ingen hUi Dhuigill,
bean CCmlaib hUi Dheollan, mopτua epτ.ʰ)

B 59d   Kal. Ian. 1.ᵃ p.,ᵃ l. xxui.,ᵇ CCnno Domini M.° cc.° xx.° iii.°ᶜ
Niall O Neill do papugud Daipe 'mo ingin hUi Caτa[i]n
7 dopoine Dia 7 Colum-cille mipbuil, co¹ pogaipoigedᵈ
a² jnaiτi.²—Taδg O Daigill, (idonᵈ, mac Ceallaigᵈ) ana
Thuaipce[i]pc Epinn [sic], mopτu[u]p epτ.

(Mael-Ipuᵉ hUa Ploinn, ppioip Eapa-mic-n-Eipc, in
Chpipτo quieuiτ.—Mupcad cappac hUa Peapgail do
mapbad i n-Ghpanapd.—CCilbin hUa Maelmuib, epipcop
Peapna, in Chpipτo quieuiτ.ᶠ)

A.D. 1222. ¹ tanig, B.²—ailpaτ, B. ³⁻³ .iiii. caτa .xx.iτ, A, B.
⁴ .iiii., A, B.—ᵃᵃ n. t. h., A ; .ii., B. ᵇ—.i.° (1221), B (C, D); erroneously.
ᶜ om., A. ᵈ Uga laci, B. ᵉᵉ a bpeτ—*his award*, B. ᶠ annpein—*then*
added, B. ᵍᵍ n.t.h., A; om., B, C, D.

A.D. 1223. ¹⁻¹ gu pugaipoiged, A. ²⁻² a n-[p]naτi, B. ᵃᵃ 7 p., n. t. h.,
on blank space, A ; ᵃ p., B. ᵇ 23, B. Scribe, no doubt, took the u in
the xxui of his original for ii. ᶜ—.ii.° (1222), B (C, D) ; erroneously.
ᵈᵈ itl., t. h., B ; om., A. ᵉᵉ n. t. h., A ; om., B, C, D.

1222. ¹ *Four and twenty battalions.*
—D renders : numerati 24 completa
bella, qui faciunt Hibernica numeratione 72 millia armatorum.

² *Four battalions.* — 12 millibus
armatorum, numeratione supra-
scripta, D.

³ *Cormac.*—Given in the *Four
Masters* at 1221.

⁴ *Gilla-Mochoinne* ; *Mor.*—Given
(the first in more detail) in the
Annals of Loch Ce (ad an.).

1223. ¹ *Respecting.*—That is, as
C and D rightly understand, by

Kalends of Jan. on 7th feria, 15th of the moon, A.D. [1222] 1222. The son of Ugo De Lacy came into Ireland in despite of the king of the Saxons, until he came to Aedh O'Neill; so that they went together against the Foreigners of Ireland and destroyed much in Meath and in Leinster and in Ulidia and razed the castle of Cuilrathain. And the Foreigners of Ireland collected four and twenty battalions[1] at [Dun-]delgain, until Aedh O'Neill and the son of Ugo came with four battalions[2] against them, so that the Foreigners gave the award of his own word to O'Neill.

(Cormac,[3] abbot of Comar, was slain.—Gilla-Mochoinne[4] Ua Cathail [king of Cenel-Aedha] was slain.—Mor,[4] daughter of Ua Buighill, wife of Amlaibh Ua Beollain, died.)

Kalends of Jan. on first feria, 26th of the moon, A.D. [1223] 1223. Niall O'Neill profaned Daire, respecting[1] the daughter of Ua Cathain. And God and Colum-cille wrought a miracle, so that his thread [of life] was shortened.—Tadhg O'Baighill (namely, son of Ceallach), splendour of the North of Ireland, died.

(Mael-Isu Ua Floinn,[2] prior of Eas-mic-nEirc, rested in Christ.—Murchadh[3] Carrach Ua Fearghail was killed in Granard.—Ailbin[3] Ua Maelmuidh, bishop of Fearna, rested in Christ.)

---

abduction. She had probably come for devotional purposes and was forcibly carried off whilst thus engaged.

[2] *Ua Floinn.*—In the *Four Masters* at 1222.

[3] *Murchadh; Ailbin.*—Given (the first at greater length) in the *Annals of Loch Ce* (ad an.). For Ua Maelmuidh (O'Mulloy), see O'Donovan's note, *F. M.* iii., p. 202. From a Patent Roll of King John (*Doc. Ireland*, I. 658), we learn that he attended the Council of Lateran, 1215.

A58b[ir.] Kal. Ian. p. 11., L. 111., Ccnno Domini M.° cc.° xx.° 1111.°ᵃ Catal croibbeps hUa Concobuip, pi Connact 7 pi Ʒaibel¹ Epenn ap totuct, aobat 1 Mainipтip Cnuic-Muaibe, quinto Kalenbapum luini. In t-aen Ʒaibel¹ ip fepp tainiʒ o Dpian Doporma anuap ap uaipli 7 ap onoip; toʒbalat тrepaʒmup, totuctat na tuat; ro-baptanat paibbep, puaitniʒ,ᵇ roinemail na pitcana. Doiʒ ip pe [a] peimep do ʒabab dectmaib co olixtet ap tup i n-iat Epenn. Columain cunnail crabbet,² cept-bpiatpatᵇ crevoini 7 cpiptaibecta; ceptaixteoip na cintat 7 na coibbenat; muʒaixteoip na meiplet 7 na malaptat; coimetaiʒ coitcenn catbuabab in pecta poolertaiʒ. D'a tuc Dia deʒonoip 1 talmain 7 in flaitiup nemba tall. Ap n-eʒ 1 n-aibit manait do, iap m-bpeit buaba o doman 7 o deman.—Matʒamain, mac Ceitepnaiʒ hUi Ceipin, pi Ciapaibe Laca-na-naipne, moptu[u]p ert.—Erpuc Conmaicne, 1don, in Ʒall erpuc, moptuup ert.—Domnall hUa Cellaiʒ, tanupti hUa-Maine, moptu[u]p ert.—Mael-Seclainn, mac Taibʒ hUi Cellaiʒ, moptu[u]pᵉ ert.°

(Finoᵈ hUa Cupmacan quieuit.—Mael-Ipu hUa Con-cubaip quieuit.ᵈ—Prredicator[er]ᵉ intpauepunt hi[bep]-niam.ᵉ)

A.D. 1224. ¹Ʒaei-, B. ²cpaibdec, B. ᵃ-.111.° (1223), B (C. D), with uel .111. (or 1224) overhead, B. Over 1223, 1224 is placed by another hand in D. ᵇom., B. ᶜᶜin Chpipto quieuit, B; "died," C; entry om., D. ᵈ⁻ᵈn. t. h., A; om., B, C, D. ᵉ⁻ᵉr. m., n. t. h., A; om., B, C, D.

1224. ¹ *May* 28.—The *F. M.* say Monday. But May 28 fell on Tuesday in this year. The authority they followed forgot that 1224 was Bissextile.ᵃ

ᵃAt Doiʒ (Seems), *etc.*, c.m., n. t. h., B, is: *receptio decimarum in Hibernia*.

² *Foreign-bishop.*—See O'Donovan *F.M.*, iii. 208.

³ *Died.*—D adds (at 1223, with 1224 placed overhead): Eodem anno O'Donill inuasit Conaciam ex omni parte usque ad Cruaghan et pertransiit flumen Sucka, omnia deuastando. Tamen, habita inhabitantium obedientia et selectis obsidibus, rediit.

Kalends of Jan. on 2nd feria, 7th of the moon, A.D. 1224. [1224] Cathal Red-Hand Ua Conchobair, king of Connacht and king of the Gaidhil of Ireland for ability, died in the [Cistercian] Monastery of Cnoc-Muaidhe, on the 5th of the Kalends of June [May 28[1]]. The best Gaidhel that came from Brian Boruma down, for nobleness and for honour; very fortunate and capable preserver of his territories; wealthy, well-disposed, excellent auxiliary of peace. Seems it is in his time tithe was had legally for the first time in Ireland. Fitting, pious, right-judging prop of faith and christianity; punisher of the guilty and of outlaws; destroyer of robbers and of evil-doers; general battle-victorious maintainer of the righteous law. To whom God gave good honour on earth and the heavenly kingdom beyond. He died in the habit of a [Cistercian] monk, after bringing victory from the world and from the demon.—Mathgamain, son of Ceithernach Ua Ceirin, king of Ciaraidhe of Loch-na-nairne, died.—The bishop of Conmaicni [Ardagh], namely, the Foreign bishop,[2] died.—Domnall Ua Cellaigh, tanist of Ui-Maine, died.—Mael-Sechlainn, son of Tadhg Ua Cellaigh, died.[3]

(Finn Ua Carmacan[4] rested.—Mael-Isu[5] Ua Conchubhair rested.—The [Friars] Preachers entered[6] Ireland.)

Given in substance in the *F. M.* at 1223.

[4] *Finn Ua Carmacan.*—Given in the *Annals of Loch Ce* at 1223, where he is said to have been steward of the king of Connacht and to have possessed much land. The next item is also given in the same Annals at 1223.

[5] *Mael-Isu.*—Prior of Inishmaine, according to the *F. M.* (1223). See O'Donovan's note, iii. 204.

[6] *Entered.*—Quetif and Echard (*Scriptores Ord. Pred.*, Lutetiae Par. 1719, p. 22) merely say under 1221: Ex Anglia nostros in Hyberniam trajecisse non diu postea constat ex Actis.

In the Catalogue of Dominican Houses given in Ware's *Irish Writers*, p. 77 (Ed. Harris; Dublin, 1745), the foundation of the Dublin House is dated 1224. This list is copied into the *Hibernia Dominicana.*

274 αππαλα υλαδη.

[Cal. 1αn. 111[ɪ].ᵃ p., L. [x]uıı[ɪ].ᵃ Anno Domini M., cc.ᶜ xx.ᶜ u.,ᵇ Ouapcan hUa hEaʒpa, pı Luıʒne, mopcuup epc.—ʒılla°-ın-Coımoeʒ Mac ʒılla-Cappaıʒ, uapal-ƒacapc 7 peppun Cıʒı-Óaıcın, quıeuıc ın Chpıpco.— Oıonıpıup¹ hUa Mael-Chıapaın, aıpcınneć Apoa-capna, quıeuıc ın Chpıpco.—Mopƒluaıʒeó oo óenum oo Aeó hUa Neıll ı Connaccu le macaıó | Ruaıópı hUı Concubuıp 7 le² coʒaıpm Shıl-Muıpeóaıc uıle, ać Mac Oıapmaca aıhaın, ıoon, Copmac, mac Comalcaıʒ, co n-oećaıó ap puc Connacc buóep co peóaıó³ Aea-luaın, co poıóe oa aıóćı ıc Muıllıó-Uanać 7 ʒup'aıpʒepcap⁴ Lok-n-én⁵ 7 co cuc ʃeoıc hUı Concobaıp leıp ap. Caınıc 'n-a oıaıʒ co Capn-ƒpaıć | 7 ooaıpʒepcaıp⁶ Caıppóelóać, mac Ruaıópı, ann. Ocup oóćuaıó 'n-a luaććeım o'a ćıʒ ap cloıpcećc oo ʃluaıʒ moıp oo Ghallaıó 7 oo Mhuımnećaıó ʃa Oonnćaó Caıpópeć hUa m-Ópıaın 7 ʃa Sheƒƒpaıʒ Maʃep aʒ Aeó hUa Concoóaıp 7 aʒ Mac Oıapmaca ćıınʒe. Ocup, o naćı puscacup ap hUa⁷ Neıll, poleanʃacup macu⁸ Ruaıópı ʒup'caıpnecup⁹ ıac a n-ućc hUı Neıll apı[ć]ıpı. Romapbʃacup Muımnıʒ oo'n oul' pın° Ećmapcać Mac Ópana[ı]n, caıpeć Copco-Alann¹⁰ a Cıll-Cellaıʒ.¹¹ Ap n-oıcup claınne Ruaıópı a Connacca[ıó]¹² amać, ʒabaıp Aeó, mac Caćaıl cpoıboe[ı]pʒ, pıʒı Connacc o'a n-eıp.—Caóʒ hUa hEaʒpa oo éc.— Ecaın, ınʒen Oıapmaca Mıc Oomnaıll, quıeuıc ın Chpıpco.—ʒoıll 7 Muımnıʒ oo óul ʃa cepmunn Caelƒınn¹³ 7 pocuıpeó áp na n-ʒall cpe ƒıpcaıó Cael[ƒ]ıno.¹⁴ Concobup, mac Caıóʒ 7 Apoʒal, mac Caıóʒ [occıʃı

A.D. 1225. ¹ Oıonıp, A. ² pı, A. ³ ʃeʒaıó, A. ⁴ cop'aıpʒec, B. ⁵ -ne (the horizontal stroke above the e (=n) om., probably by oversight), A. ⁶ -ap, B. ⁷ O, A. ⁸ mıc, A, B. ⁹ -caıʃpnıʒeoup, B. ¹⁰ Copcaćlann (by syncope), A. ¹¹ ʒ-Cıll-, B. ¹² -ccu, B. ¹³ -elaıno, A. ¹⁴ Caelƒıno, B.—ᵃ⁻ᵃ n. t. b., on blank space, A; om., B. ᵇ-.ııı.° (1224), B (C, D); erroneously. ᶜ⁻ᶜ om., B, C, D. The Oıonıpup and Ecan entries are also omitted in D. ᵈ om., B. ᵉ⁻ᵉ cupup pın—that expedition, B. ᶠ hUı add'd, B.

Kalends of Jan. on 4th feria, 18th of the moon, A.D. 1225. Duarcan Ua Eaghra, king of Luighni, died.—Gilla-in-Coimdeg Mac Gilla-carraigh, eminent priest and parson of Tech-Baithin, rested in Christ.—Dionysius Ua Mael-Ciarain, herenagh of Ard-Carna, rested in Christ.—A great hosting was made by Aedh Ua Neill into Connacht, by [invitation of] the sons of Ruaidhri Ua Conchobair and by invitation of all Sil-Muiredhaigh, save Mac Diarmata alone, namely, Cormac, son of Tomaltach, so that he went through the length of Connacht eastwards to the woods of Ath-luain, so that he was a night at the Heights of Uana. And they pillaged Loch-nen and he brought the treasures of Ua Conchobair with him therefrom. He came after that to Carn-fraich and Tairrdhelbach, son of Ruaidhri, was crowned there. And he went on a quick march to his house, on hearing that a large force of Foreigners and of Momonians [was making] towards him, under Donnchadh Cairbrech Ua Briain and under Geoffrey Mares [De Marisco], [led] by Aedh Ua Conchobair and by Mac Diarmata. And when they [the Foreigners, etc.,] did not catch Ua Neill, they followed the sons of Ruaidhri, until they drove them to the protection of Ua Neill again. The Momonians on that occasion killed Echmarcach Mac Branain, chief of Corco-Achlann, at Cell-Cellaigh. On the expulsion of the sons of Ruaidhri from out Connacht, Aedh, son of Cathal Red-Hand[1] takes the kingship after them.—Tadhg Ua Eaghra died.—Etain, daughter of Diarmait Mac Domnaill, rested in Christ.—The Foreigners and the Momonians went to the Termonn of [St.] Caelfhinn and slaughter of the Foreigners was inflicted through miracles of [St.] Caelfhinn.—Conchobur, son of Tadhg [Ua Cellaigh] and Ardghal, son of Tadhg [Ua Cellaigh were

[1225]

1225. [1] *Red-Hand.*—In the margin of D, opposite *pugni rubri* (near the end of folio 23b) is cṅoḃ ḋeaṅg, the Irish equivalent.

runt].—Ar mor do ḋainiḃ [ir]in bliaḋain r.—In t-arḃur 'ga buain a haicle na peile Briġci 7 in treaḃaḋ 'ga ḋenam i[15] n-ainreċt.

Kal. Ian.ᵃ u. f.,ᵃ L. xrix., Anno Domini M.° cc.° xx.° ui.°ᵇ Peiḋlimiḋ[1] hUa Concoḃair do ġaḃail caiġ ar Domnall hUa Fhlaiṫbertaiġ, gur'marḃ 7 gur'loirc é réin 7 a braṫair.—Aeḋ hUa Flaiṫbertaiġ do ġaḃail la hAeḋ, mac Caṫail croiḃde[i]rg 7 a ṫabairt illaim' Ġhall.[3]—Tigernan, mac Caṫail hUi Concoḃair, do marḃaḋ la Donnċaḋ hUa n-Duḃdai.[4]—Muirġius Mac Diarmata do marḃaḋ.—Connmaċᶜ O Tarra, erpuc Luiġne, in Chrirto quieuit.ᶜ—Cairlen Cille-moire do rcailiuḋ la Caṫal O Raiġilliḋ.

(Aeḋ[d] hUa Ruairc do marḃaḋ la Caṫal hUa Raigilliḋ 7 la Conċuḃar Mac Cormuic.ᵈ)

B 60b Kal. Ian. ui.ᵃ f.,ᵃ L. x., Anno Domini M.° cc.° xx.° ui.°ᵇ Uilliam Marer, mac Ġiurtir na hErenn, do ġaḃail do Chormac, mac Tomalcaiġ, do riġ na Cairrgi 7 d'Aeḋ hUa Conċoḃair.—Donnfleiḃe O Ġrada (aliaſ. hUa Ġaḋra; idon, ri Sleiḃe-Luġaᶜ) do marḃaḋ do mac a der[ḃ]braṫar rein i rill 7 domarḃaḋ e rein ind ro cetoir, tre imdell Aeḋa hUi Conċoḃuir.—Brian[d], mac

A.D. 1225. ¹⁵ a, A.
A.D. 1226. ¹ Peiḋlim, A. ² a laim, B. ³ n-Ġall, A. ⁴ -da, A.— ᵃ⁻ᵃ .iiii. f., n. t. h., A; .u. f., B. ᵇ⁻.u.° (1225), B (C, D); erroneously. ᶜ⁻ᶜ om., D. ᵈ⁻ᵈ n. t. h., A; om., B, C, D.
A.D. 1227. ᵃ⁻ᵃ .u. f., n. t. h., on blank space, A; .ui. f., B. ᵇ⁻.ui.° (1226), B (C, D); erroneously. ᶜ⁻ᶜ itl., n. t. h., A; om., B, C, D. ᵈ⁻ᵈ om., B, C, D.

---

² *Were slain.*—The *Four Masters* say they were burned in a house which was set on fire by their brothers.

³ *Great des'ruction.*—D, perhaps correctly, connects this and the following entry (1224): Fuit enim eodem anno maxima mortalitas hominum, ita ut circa festum Sanctae Brigide autumnalia blada colligerentur, cum nec tum seminatura futuri anni facta fuisset, occasione predictarum guerrarum.

1226. ¹ *Feidhlimidh Ua Conchbhair.*—According to the *Four Masters* (ad an.) the deed was done

slain[2]]. Great destruction[3] of people in this year.—The corn [1225] was a-cutting on the morrow of the feast of [St.] Brigit [Feb. 1.] and the ploughing was a-doing at the same time.

Kalends of Jan. on 5th feria, 29th of the moon, A.D. [1226] 1226. Feidhlimidh Ua Concobhair[1] seized a house upon Domnall Ua Flaithbertaigh, so that he killed and burned himself and his kinsman.—Aedh Ua Flaithbertaigh was taken prisoner by Aedh, son of Cathal Red Hand[2] and given into the hand[s] of the Foreigners.—Tighernan, son Cathal Ua Conchobair, was killed by Donnchadh Ua Dubhdai.—Muirghius Mac Diarmata was killed.—Connmac O'Tarpa, bishop of Luighni,[3] rested in Christ.—The castle of Cell-mor was razed by Cathal O'Raighillaidh.

(Aedh[4] Ua Ruairc was killed by Cathal Ua Raighillidh and by Conchubhar, son of Cormac [Ua Maelruanaigh].)

Kalends of Jan. on 6th feria, 10th of the moon, A.D. [1227] 1227. William Mares, son of the Justiciary of Ireland, was taken prisoner by Cormac, son of Tomaltach,[1] king of the Rock and by Aedh Ua Conchobair.—Donnsleibhe O'Grada (otherwise, Ua Gadhra; namely, king of Sliabh-Lugha) was killed by the son of his own brother in treachery and he [the slayer] himself was killed therein immediately, through device[2] of Aedh Ua Conchobair.—

---

by the sons of Murtough O'Flaherty, aided by O'Conor. The entry in the *Annals of Loch Ce* makes no mention of Feidhlimidh.

[2] *Cathal Red-Hand.*—That is, O'Conor, King of Connaught.

[3] *Luighni.*—That is, Achonry.

[4] *Aedh, etc.*—Given in the *Four Masters*. It is there stated that O'Rourke was slain on Lough Allen (co. Leitrim).

1227. [1] *Tomaltach.*—Mac Dermot. His residence was the *Rock* of Lough Ce. A full account of the transaction is given in the *Annals of Loch Ce*, whence it has been copied by the Four Masters.

[2] *Device.*—" Devise," C; industria, D. The account in the *Four Masters* states that the nephew seized a house upon the uncle.

Concobair hUi n-Diarmata, do marbaḋ.ᵈ—Dionirius¹
hUa² Morṗea do crogaḋ d'errus Oil-rinn.—Cumara
hUa Domnalla[i]n do marbaḋ i n-geimil do Ruaiḋri
Mac Duinnrleiḃe, a n-diẋail a aṫar 7 ré crorta.

[bir.] Kal. Ian. uiii.ᵃ r.,ᵃ l.ᵇ xx. i.,ᵇ Anno Domini M.° cc.° xx.°
uiii.ᶜᶜ Aeḋ, mac Caṫail croibde[i]rg hUi Concobair, do
marbaḋ do gallaiḃ i meḋail, iar¹ n-a diċur do Chonnaċtaiḃ uaiṫiḃ.—Giurtireċt na hErenn do ẋaḃail do
mac Uilliam burc (ioon,ᵈ Ricardᵈ)—Aeḋ, mac Ruaiḋri,
do ẋaḃail rige Connaċt 7 rohairgeḋ cealla 7 tuaṫa
Connaċt leó 7 rodiċuireḋ* a cleiriẋ 7 a luċt elaḋna
arċena a tiriḃ comaiḋċiḃ,² ar' n-a cur ri ruaċt 7 ri
gorta.—Muirċertaċ, mac Flaiṫbertaiẋ hUi Fhlanna-
ga[i]n, do marbaḋ la macaiḃ hUi Ghaḋra.¹—Ferẋal,
mac Sitriuca hUi Ruairc, do marbaḋ do macaiḃ Neill,
mic Congalaiċ hUi Ruairc.—Niall, mac Congalaiẋ hUi

A.D. 1227. ¹ Dionir, B.² O, B.—* The Dionirur and Cumara entries
are given under 1225 (=1226) in D.

A.D. 1228. ¹ ar (᷾n), B. ²-dci, A.—ᵃ⁻ᵃ n. t. h., on blank space, A;
om., B. ᵇ⁻ᵇ om., B. ᶜ⁻.uiii.ᵒ (1227), B (C, D). B (followed by C and D)
has no entry under this year. There is a blank space of four lines.
Then:—

Kal. Ian. [blank for ferial and epact] A.D. m.° cc.° xx.° uiii.° The
entries follow as in A. The year in advance, caused by the omission
of 1192, being thus abandoned, B (as well as C and D) comes into
harmony with the chronology of A. ᵈ⁻ᵈ itl., n, t. h., A: om., B, C, D.
* After this word, cell was written, but subsequently deleted by having
a dot placed under each of the letters, A, f-f om., B, C, D.

² *Crossed as a Crusader.*—Literally, *signed;* the native equivalent of *cruce-signatus.* " Crucified," C; over which another hand wrote *abdicavit!* Excommunicatus fuit, D; in which the entry is given under 1225.

As O'More resigned in 1229 and died in 1231, his object apparently was not to go in person to the Holy Land, but to gain the indulgence by contributing to the Crusade. In reference to the request of the king of Scotland regarding: Nonnulli milites et alii de regno suo propter paupertatem, alii ob senectutem, quidam vero propter debilitatem, quamplures etiam ob infirmitatem nequeunt personaliter exequi votum, quod

Dionysius Ua Mordha was crossed as a Crusader[3] from [being] bishop of Oil-finn.—Cumara Ua Domnallain was killed in captivity by Ruaidhri Mac Duinnsleibhe, in revenge of his father, he [Cumara] being crossed [as a Crusader].

Kalends of Jan. on 7th feria, 21st of the moon, A.D. 1228. Aedh, son of Cathal Red-Hand Ua Conchobair, was killed by the Foreigners in treachery, after his being put away by the Connachtmen from themselves.—The Justiciate of Ireland was assumed by the son of William de Burgh (namely, Richard[1]).—Aedh, son of Ruaidhri, [and his brothers] took the kingship of Connacht and the churches and territories of Connacht were pillaged by them and moreover its clergy and folk of learning were expelled into foreign countries, after being exposed to cold and to hunger.—Muircertach, son of Flaithbertach Ua Flannagain, was killed by the sons of Ua Gadhra.—Ferghal, son of Sitriuc Ua Ruairc, was killed by the sons of Niall, son of Congalach Ua Ruairc.—Niall, son of Congalach

---

assumpto crucis signaculo, de transeundo in eiusdem Terre subsidium emiserint, a Brief of Gregory IX., dated the Lateran, March 31 (1238), empowers Cardinal Otho, the Papal Legate, to absolve such from the vow of the Cross: recepta prius ab eis sufficienti et idonea cautione (security), quod omnes expensas, quas facturi essent in eundo, morando et redeundo, in manibus tuis assignent: alias laborem itineris pietatis operibus compensando, illam indulgentiam habituri, qu[a]e transeuntibus in ipsius Terre subsidium in Generali Concilio est concessa (Theiner, *Vet. Mon.*, p. 38).

Amongst the charges brought against the bishop of Ardagh, which Innocent IV. (Lyons, Feb. 13, 1245) appointed judges to investigate, was: pecuniam, quam crucesignati decedentes relinquunt in subsidium Terre Sancte, in usus proprios et illicitos . . . convertit.

1228. *Richard.*—On Feb. 15 of this year, Henry III. notified to the citizens of Dublin, Limerick, Drogheda, Waterford, Cork and to " Duncan Carbry " (Donnchad Cairbrech O'Brien) that Richard de Burgh was appointed justiciary of Ireland. (*D[ocuments*]. [*relating to*] *I[r]-land*]., I. 1573.)

Ruaipc, do mapbaд do Apt, mac Aipt hUi Ruaipc 7 Amlaim gepp, mac Neill, do mapbaд du³ Amlaim, mac Aipt, i patpugaд.—Ma[c] Cpait' hUa Mallacta quieuit in Chpipto.ᵉ

(Dauid ͪ O Flainn, taipeć Sil-Mailpuanaiд, d'héc.—Aeд, mac Donncaд i Fepgail, do mapbaд la hAeд, mac Amlaim i Fepgail.ᵇ—Caiplen¹ Chuil-pataain do denum in bliaдain pi.—San Fpoipiap d'onopugaд map gać naem in bliaдain pi leipin Papa, ɪdon, le Gpegopiup nonup, pcilicet, decimo peptimo Kalendap Augupti¹.)

Kal. 1an. 1[i].ª p., L. ii.,ª Anno Domini M.° cc.° xx.° ix.° Duiberra, ingen Ruaidpi, ben Catail Mic Diapmata, do éc i n-a caillić duiд.—Diapmait Macᶦ Cappтaiz, pí Dep-Muman, quieuit in Chpipto.—Dionipᵇ hUa Mopдa, eppuc Sil-Muipeдaiz, do cup a eppucoide uaдa.ᵇ—Gipapd hUa Cata[i]n, canonać | ip eolća dobi² ipin Opd Canonać [in Chpipto quieuit].—Diapmaitᵇ Mac Fiać, abb Reiglepa Gilla-Molaipi hUa[-i] Gillupa[i]n i Tuaim, in Chpipto quieuit 7 a aдnucal i n-Apd-ćapna.ᵇ—Muipeдać hUa Gopmgaile, ppioip peiglepa Indpi-micnepind (no,ᵉ -n-Epin'), duineᵈ ip egnaiдe 7 ip cpaibtigi[u]³ dobi do Coiceд Con[n]ać, in Chpipto quieuit.—Diapmaid Mac Gilla-Chappaig, aipćinneć Tigi-Daićin 7 uapalpacapt 7 duine pob'pepp deipc 7 eineaćᵉ dobi i cenntupᵈ Connać, in Chpipto quieuit.

A.D. 1228. ²do, B.—¹·¹ om. D. ᵇ·ᵇ n. t. h., A; om., B, C, D. ʰ·ʰ r. m., n. t. h., A; om., B, C, D.

A.D. 1229. ¹Mag, B. ²pobot, B. ³-tige, B. ⁴-taip, B.—ᵃ·ᵃ n. t. h., on blank space, A; om., B. ᵇ om., B, C, D. The Gipapd entry is omitted in D. ᶜ·ᶜ itl, n. t. h., A; om., B, C. ᵈ d is doubled by mistake, B. ᵉ daenać—*humanity*, B.

---

² *Amlaim the Short*.—Auly Carr [Garr]; alias, *curtus filius*, D.
³ *David — Aedh — the castle.* —

These three native items are given in the *Four Masters* under this year.

Ua Ruairc, was killed by Art, son of Art Ua Ruairc and Amlaim the Short,[2] son of Niall, was killed by Amlaim, son of Art, in bathing.—Ma[c] Craith Ua Mallachta rested in Christ.

(David[3] O'Flainn, chief of Sil-Mailruanaidh, died.—Aedh,[3] son of Donnchadh O'Ferghail, was killed by Aedh son of Amhlam O'Ferghail.—The castle[3] of Cuil-rathain was built this year.—Saint Francis was honoured[4] like every saint this year by the Pope, namely, by Gregory IX., that is, on the 17th of the Kalends of August [July 16].)

Kalends of Jan. on 2nd feria, 2nd of the moon, A.D. 1229. Duibessa, daughter of Ruaidhri [Ua Conchobair], wife of Cathal Mac Diarmata, died a nun.—Diarmait Mac Carrthaigh, king of Desmond, rested in Christ.—Dionysius Ua Mordha, bishop of Sil-Muiredhaigh [Elphin], put his bishopric away from him.—Girard Ua Cathain, the most learned Canon that was in the Order of Canons [rested in Christ].—Diarmait Mac Fiaich, abbot of the Monastery of Gilla-Molaisi Ua Gillurain in Tuaim, rested in Christ and was buried in Ard-carna.—Muiredach Ua Gormghaile, prior of the Monastery of the Island of Mac-nErind (or, [Mac]-nErin), the most erudite and pious person of the Fifth of Connacht, rested in Christ.—Diarmait Mac Gilla-Charraigh, herenach of Tech-Baithin and eminent priest and the person of best charity and hospitality that was in this side[1] of Connacht, rested in Christ.

[1228]

[1229]

---

[4] *Was honoured, etc.*—He was canonized in the church of St. George, Assisi.

1229. [1] *This side of Connacht.*— That is, the eastern portion, where the compiler lived. The expression is incorrectly rendered "in those parts" in C. The entry in the

Four Masters states that Mac Gillacarry was interred in the (Premonstratensian) monastery of Trinity Island (Loch Ce), after the body lay unburied for three nights in the (Cistercian) abbey of Boyle, the monks of which attempted to retain it.

Kal. Ian. for· Mairt,ª l. x. III.,ª Anno Domini M.°
cc.° xxx.° Gilla-Iru h-Ua Cleirig, epscop Luigne, quieuit
in[b] [Christo[b]].—Gilla-Carrtaig[c] hUa hElgiura[i]n,
canonac 7 angcaire, quieuit in [Christo].[c]—Donnsleibe
hUa Innuine,[1] manac naem 7 maigirter raer, quieuit
in[b] [Christo[b]].—Mael-Muire hUa Mail-Eoin, abb
Cluana-mac-Nois, in Christo quieuit.—Mael-Seclainn[e]
Mac Phirerding, uarailsacart 7 maigistir leiginn,
quieuit in [Christo], i n-a noibirdi i Mainistir na
Buille.°—Gilla-in-Coimded hUa Duillenna[i]n, comarba
Feicin 7 abb reiglera Canonac Era-dara, in Christo[d]
quieuit.[d]—Sluaiged° la hUilliam Burc i Connacta,[2] gur'-
mill[ed] moran leir[f] do Chonnactaib.[f] Donn óg Mag
Oirectaig do marbad doib 7[e] Ectigern, mac in breit-
eman, hUa Mincacain do marbad doib.—Art, mac[h]
Airt hUi Ruarc, do marbad do Ragnall hUa Finn i
medail.—Ma[c] Craith Mac Sherraig, erruc Con-

A.D. 1230. ¹ Iniṁainen, B. ²-ċtaiḃ, B.—ᵃ·ᵃ n. t. h., on blank space, A;
.III. r. (the Latin equivalent), B. ᵇ·ᵇ om., B. ᶜ·ᶜ om., B, C, D. ᵈ·ᵈ quieuit
in, A. ᵉ This and the Art-Aed-Gilla-Iru- and Macraitt entries are
the only items given (in the foregoing order) in D. ᶠ do Chonnaċtaiḃ
leir, B. ᵍ om., A. ʰ mac mic—*grandson*, A.

1230. ¹ *Mac Craith — Joseph.*—Much light is thrown on these obits by the plaint made in person by bishop Jocelin and embodied in a Brief of Gregory IX. (Perugia, April 8, 1235 ; Theiner, *ubi sup.*, p. 30), appointing judges to examine whether the diocese of Ardagh belonged to Tuam, or to Armagh. The archbishop of Tuam consecrated the prior of Inismor (most probably Inishmore—*great island*—in Lough Gamna, co. Longford) bishop of Ardagh. Afterwards, Joseph (Mag Theichidhain), the archdeacon, who had officiated as such at the function, falsely represented to the primate L[uke Netterville], that himself had been elected. Thereby he obtained confirmation, caused himself (non sine symonie vitio) to be consecrated by the authority of Luke's successor (Donatus) and was intruded by lay influence into partial possession of the diocese.

The canonical bishop having died, "Magairy" (=Mac Sherraigh of the text), the new archdeacon, received consecration from the Tuam metropolitan. His death took place within the same year (1230). Whereupon, the intruded obtained total possession and proceeded to

Kalends of Jan. upon Tuesday, 13th of the moon, A.D. [1230] 1230. Gilla-Isu Ua Cleirigh, bishop of Luigni [Achonry], rested in Christ.—Gilla-Carrthaigh Ua Elgiusa[i]n, canon and anchorite, rested in Christ.—Donnsleibe Ua Inmhainen, a holy monk and master-wright, rested in Christ.—Mael-Muire Ua Mail-Eoin, abbot of Cluain-mac-Nois, rested in Christ.—Mael-Sechlainn Mac Fhireidhinn, eminent priest and master of literature, rested in Christ, a novice in the Monastery of the Buill.—Gilla-in-Coimdedh Ua Duillennain, successor of [St.] Feichin and abbot of the Monastery of Canons of Es-dara, rested in Christ.—A hosting by William de Burgh into Connacht, so that much of Connacht was destroyed by him. Donn Mag Oirechtaigh Junior was killed by them and Echtighern Ua Mincachain, son of the Brehon, was killed by them.—Art, son of Art Ua Ruairc, was killed by Ragnall Ua Finn in treachery.—Ma[c] Craith[1] Mac Sherraigh, bishop of Conmaicni

---

alienate the diocesan property. The prior of "St. John's outside the new gate of Dublin" and his fellow judges (appointed *ad hoc* by the Curia, on the complaint of the prior and canons of Kilbixy (co. Westmeath)) quashed the election of Joseph as uncanonical and unconfirmed by his own (Tuam) metropolitan. The execution of the sentence was intrusted to the primate. He, however (quadam pecunie summa et quibusdam procuratoribus symoniace receptis), for the second time, intruded Joseph.

But the church having been long destitute of a pastor and not free from the danger of an invader, the archbishop of Tuam, to whom the right of election had devolved by lapse of time, consecrated Jocelin, "a monk of St. Mary's near Dublin." (This took place either at the close of 1232, or in the beginning of 1233. For on March 1 of the latter year, Henry III. commanded the justiciary, Maurice FitzGerald, to give such possession of the see to Jocelin, consecrated bishop thereof, as Robert (sic), his predecessor, had at his death (*D. I.*, I. 2018).)

On the other hand, the primate (non sine symonie vitio, ut dicitur) confirmed the election of G[elasius = Gilla-Isu], a priest of the diocese, said to have been excommunicated (for whom, see under 1287, *infra*).

A palpable hiatus in the foregoing, namely, the death of Joseph, is supplied by the additional obit of the text. The omission of his demise by the original compiler shows that, in the chronicle from

2 T

maicne⁸, ouine ir mo crabaó 7 eineċ oobi illeiċ Cuinn, in Chriſto quieuiṫ.ᵈ—Aeó hUa Neill, ri Tuairce[i]rt (Erenn¹) 7 ri Leiṫi Cuinn uile 7 oeẋaóbur airorig Erenn uile¹ 7 ouine ir mo romarb 7 rocreċ ᵹullu ᵏ 7 romill cairlena oobai oo Ɣhaióelaib,ʲ aˢ éc 7 ouine ir Luẋuˢ rorailéó o'ragbail bair innur aile aċṫ le Ɣallaib, quieuiṫ in ᵇ [Chriſto].—Floirinṫᶜ hUa Cerballa[i]n, erruc Tire-hEogain, uaralrenoir toẋaiòe, rontiri-catur rui anno quaorageſimo rexto, [a]etatir ru[a]e octogeſimo rexto, in Chriſto quieuiṫ.ᵉ

(Iorer¹ Maᵹ Theiċióain, errcob Conmaicne, quieuiṫ¹ . . . 7ᵐ corr San Fronrer o'atruẋuo oo comarba na m-braṫar cum eaᵹlaire oorigneċ 'n-a onóir rein, 8 Kt. Iunii.ᵐ)

Kal. Ian. rorᵃ Ceatain,ᵃ L.ᵇ xx.iiii.,ᵇ Anno Domini M.° cc.° xxx.° 1.° Feċroliẋ¹ (ioon,ᶜ ben Muirceraiẋ Muimnib, mic Toirróealbaiẋ moir 1 Concubuirᶜ), ingen Concobuir Mic Oiarmata, quieuiṫ in [Chriſto].ᵈ—Oubċablaiẋ,ᵈ ingen Concoḃair Mic Oiarmata, oo éc i Mainiſtir na Ḃuille.ᵈ—Flann hUa Connaċtaiẋ, erruc na Ḃreirne, inᵉ Chriſto quieuiṫ.ᵉ—Sluaẋaó mor Leir O n-Oomnaill oocum hUi² Raiẋillaiẋ, co ruc ben hUi

---

³ -m, B. ⁴ Ɣhaeróealaib B. ⁵ oo (sign of infinitive), B. ⁶ Luẋa, B. i itl., n. t. h., A; text, B, C, D. ʲ om., B. ᵏ Sic, A, B. The first u arises from assimilation with the final. It proves that the original contained the proper case-ending. ¹⁻¹ n. t. h., A; om., B, C, D. ᵐ⁻ᵐ t. m., n. t. h., A; om., B, C, D. The beginning of the entry stood on a line that was cut away in trimming the edge.

A.D. 1231. ¹ Feṫroliẋe, A. ² hI, B.—ᵃ⁻ᵃ n. t. h., A; .m. r. (the Latin equivalent), B. ᵇ⁻ᵇ om., B. ᶜ⁻ᶜ itl., n. t. h., A; om., B, C, D. ᵈ⁻ᵈ om., B, C, D. ᵉ⁻ᵉ om., A; "dead," C; *quieuit in pace*, D.

---

which Maguire copied, Mag Theichidain was passed over as an intruder.

In the *Annals of Loch Ce* (ad an.), Joseph is given first and *quieuit in Christo* applied to both.

² *Christ.*—D adds: Eodem etiam anno, O'Donill cum vi armata

[Ardagh], the person of most piety and generosity that [1230] was in the Half of Conn, rested in Christ.—Aedh Ua Neill, king of the North (of Ireland) and king of all the Half of Conn and worthy future arch-king of all Ireland and the person of the Gaidhil that most killed and pillaged the Foreigners and destroyed castles, died. And the person that it was least thought would find death otherwise than by the Foreigners rested in Christ.[2]— Florence Ua Cerballa[i]n, bishop of Tir-Eogain [Derry], eminent senior select, rested in Christ, in the 46th year of his pontificate, the 86th of his age.

(Joseph[1] Mag Theichidhan, bishop of Conmaicni [Ardagh], rested.— . . And the body of Saint Francis was removed[3] on the 8th of the Kalends of June [May 25] by the Superior of the Friars to the church that was built in his own honour.)

Kalends of Jan. upon Wednesday, 24th of the moon, [1231] A.D. 1231. Fethfolighi (namely, wife of Muircertach the Momonian,[1] son of Toirrdealbach Mor O'Concubuir), daughter of Conchobur Mac Diarmata, rested in Christ.— Dubchablaigh, daughter of Concobhar Mac Diarmata, died in the Monastery of the Buill.—Flann Ua Connachtaigh, bishop of Breifni [Kilmore], rested in Christ.—A great hosting by O'Domnaill against Ua Raighillaigh, so that he took the wife of Ua Raighillaigh away with him,

---

inuasit Conaciam et, licet multa commisit damna, tamen filii Rorici I Conchuir non adheserunt eius consilio illa uice.

This is given in substantially the same terms by the Four Masters at this year.

[3] *Removed.*—For the unseemly brawl that took place on the occasion of the translation, see Wadding, *Annal. Minor. ad an.* 1230, p. 414, *seq.*

1231. [1] *Momonian.* — So called from having been reared in Munster. At 1233, D gives *Odo renenosus,* mistaking *Muimnech* (Momonian) for *neimnech* (venomous).

Raiġillaiġ leir, iḋon, ingin Meġ³ Ṗhiaċpaċ 7 co pucrac ṗeoic 7 innṁupa 7ᵈ maiċiuṗᵈ in ḃaile uile leó.—Conċobup|goċᵈ hUa hEaxpa, pi Luiġne, quieuic inᵈ [Chpiṗco].ᵈ—Dubċeṁpaċ,ᵈ ingen hUi Chuinn, ben [Ṗh]laiċbeṗcaiġ hUi Ṗhlannaġa[i]n, quieuic in [Chpiṗcoᵈ]. —Ṗlaiċbeṗcaċ hUa Ṗlannaġa[i]n, caiṗeċ Clainni-Caċail 7 ḋuine iṗ uaiṗleᶜ ḋobiᶠ ḋo Shil-Muipeḋaiġ, ḋo⁵ éc i n-a oiliċṗi i Mainiṗcip na ḃuille.—Dioniṗuṗ⁶ᵉ hUa Moṗḋa eṗpuc Sil-Muipeḋaiġ, quieuic in Chpiṗco.ᶠ

Aᵇ⁹ᵇ[ⁱʳ·] Ḳal. Ian. poṗᵃ Dapḋain, L u.,ᵃ Anno Domini M.° cc.° xxx.° ii.° Aeḋᵇ hUa Ṗeṗġail, caiṗeċ Muinnceṗi-hAnġaile, ḋo maṗbaḋ ḋ'a ḃṗaiċṗiḃ ṗein.—Maġnuṗ, mac Aṁlaim, mic Caiḋġ Mic Maelpuanaiġ, cainnel einiġ 7 eġnuma¹ 7 cṗabaiḋ, in Chpiṗco° quieuic.ᶜ—Sluaġaḋ la hUilliam Duṗc co caiṗcel Ḃona-Ġaillbi,² co n-ḋeṗnṗac caiṗcel ann.—Maiḋm ḋo ċabaiṗc ḋo na Tuaċaiḃ aṗ Concobuṗ, mac Aeḋa, mic Ruaiḋṗi, coṗ'maṗbaḋ Concobuṗ ann 7 Ġilla-Cpiṗc, mac Donnċaḋa ec alii multi. —Donnċaḋ, mac Comalcaiġ Mic Diaṗmaca, quieuic inᵈ [Chpiṗcoᵈ].—Mac Neill hUi Ġailmpeḋaiġ³ (iḋon,ᵉ Conċobuṗᵉ), caiṗeċ Ceniuil-Moen, quieuic in [Chpiṗco].—Coiṗecṗaḋ cempaill Cille-moiṗe 7 Canonaiġ ḋo ḋenum iṗin baile cecna la Conn hUa Ṗlannaġa[i]n.⁴—Sluaġaḋᶠ

³ Meiġ, B. ⁴ ġoḋ, A. ᵃ *a—his (death took place)*, B. ᵉ Dioniṗ, B. ᶠ⁻ᶠ*mo maicuṗ ḋoboi—of greatest goodness that was*, B. ᵉ⁻ᵉ om., D. Chpiṗco is omitted in A.

A.D. 1232. ¹ eġnoma, B. ²-Ġaillme, B.³ Ġaiṗmle- (by metathesis of l and ṗ), B. ⁴-can, B.—ᵃ⁻ᵃ n. t. h., on blank space, ; om., B. ᵇ This and the following entry are given under 1231 in D. ᶜ⁻ᶜ quieuic in, A. ᵈ⁻ᵈ om., B. This item is the last which D. has in common with A, B, C under this year. ᵉ⁻ᵉ itl., n. t. h., A; om., B, C. ᶠ⁻ᶠ om., B, C.

---

² *Stammerer.*— Incorrectly rendered *mutus* in D. "The adjective *god (got)* in medical Irish MSS. is used to translate the Latin *balbus*, or *balbutiens*" (O'Donovan, *Four Masters*, iii., p. 260).

³ *Ua Mordha.*—The *Annals of Loch Cé* (*ad an.*) state that he died in the establishment of the Canons in Trinity Island (Loch Ce), on Dec. 15 and was succeeded by Donough O'Conor.

namely, the daughter of Mag Fhiachrach. And they [1231] took away the treasures and valuables and chattels of the whole town with them.—Conchobur Ua hEaghra the Stammerer,[2] king of Luighni, rested in Christ.—Dubthemhrach, daughter of Ua Cuinn, wife of [F]laithbertach Ua Flannaga[i]n, rested in Christ.—[The aforesaid] Flaithbertach Ua Flannaga[i]n, chief of Clann-Cathail and the person that was noblest of the Sil-Muiredhaigh, died on his pilgrimage in the Monastery of the Buill.—Dionysius Ua Mordha,[3] bishop of Sil-Muiredhaigh [Elphin], rested in Christ.

Kalends of Jan. upon Thursday, 5th of the moon, A.D. [1232 Bis.] 1232. Aedh Ua Ferghail, chief of Muinnter-Angaile, was killed[1] by his own kinsmen.—Maghnus, son of Amhlam, son of Tadhg Mac Mailruanaigh, candle of generosity and valour and piety, rested in Christ.—A hosting by William de Burgh to the castle of Bun-Gaillbi, so that they built a castle there.—Defeat was inflicted by "the Territories" on Conchobur, son of Aedh, son of Ruadhri [Ua Conchobair], so that Conchobur [himself] and Gilla-Crist son of Donnchadh [Mac Diarmata] and many others were slain there. —Donnchadh, son of Tomaltach Mac Diarmata, rested in Christ.—The son of Niall Ua Gailmredhaigh (namely, Concobur), chief of Cenel-Moen, rested in Christ.—Consecration of the church of Cell-mor [took place][2] and Canons were established in the same place by Conn Ua Flannaga[i]n.—A hosting by Domnall Ua Lochlainn,

---

1232. [1] *Killed.*—According to the *Annals of Loch Cé* (*ad an.*), he was burned (in an ignited house) in the island of Loch Cuile (in Annaly), co. Longford, the territory of the O'Farrells.

[2] [*Took place*]. — By Donough O'Conor, bishop of Elphin (*Annals of Loch Cé, ad an.*). O'Flannagan (*ib.*) was prior of Kilmore (about six miles east of Elphin O'Donovan, *F.M.* iii. 261).

la Domnall hUa Loclainn, la ríg Ceniuil-Eogain, co n-gallaib 7 co n-gaidelaib i Tir-Conaill d'ar'mill mór i ránait 7 i Tir-Chonaill 7 d'a tuc braigti Domnaill hUi baigill 7 hUi Tairce[i]rt lair.—Sluagad la hUa n-Domnall irin bliadain cetna i Tir-nEogain, co riact Tula[č]-nóc, d'ar'marb bú 7 d'ar'loirc arbanna 7 d'ar'-mill mór arčena irin tir 7 tainic ar cul co corguract. Ocur irin bliadain cetna roairg Loing[a]ir Ceniuil-Eogain Mibbad 7 Eagínír 7 dorala buiden do Chenel-Conaill im mac Neill hUi Domnaill cucu 7 d'ar'lad ar na loingri 7 d'ar'marbad mac Neill.'

(Feidlim⁵ O Concubair, rí Connact, do gabail do Ricard a burc, a Milic, a rill 7 rige Connact do Aed mac Ruaidri arir.⁵)

Kal. Ian. [uii.⁵ f., l xui.,²] Anno Domini M.° cc.° xxx.° iii.⁵ Sluagad la Feidlimid¹ hUa Concobuir i Connactaib, co n-dečaib Cormac, mac Tomaltaig i n-a agaid,² co tuc leir é i Mag-Luirg, co n-derna longport ic³ Druim-gregraide 7 co tainic Cormac 7 Concobur amač 7 na tri Tuata 7 da mac Muircertaig Mic Diarmata, idon, Donnčad 7 Muircertač. Ocur ir i comuirli dorongat: točt i⁴ n-diaig Aeda, mic Ruaidri 7 tucrat maidm for Aed, mac Ruaidri, ann, idon, for

A.D. 1232. ¹-¹ om., B, C. ⁵-⁵ n. t. h., A; om., B, C.
A.D. 1233. ¹ Feidlim, A. ² adaig (metathesis of g and d), A. ³ ag, A. ⁴ a, B.—⁵-⁵ blank space, A, B.

---

³ *Was killed.*—The final entry of this year in D is: Eodem anno, pauperrimi Fratres, quos Minoritas vocant, venerunt (sic) in Hiberniam.

⁴ *Feidhlim, etc.*—About the end of August of this year, Henry III. wrote to de Burgh, the justiciary, that he had been informed that de Burgh seized, imprisoned, and grievously and shamefully treated Frethelin (Feidhlim), son of a former king of Connaught. He was commanded to liberate Feidlim, on his finding sureties to abide anything laid to his charge and to certify why he had been imprisoned (*D. I.*, I. 1975).

In consequence, doubtless, of this mandate, Feidhlim (according to the *Annals of Loch Cé* and the initial entry of the following year) was set at liberty. His seizure was perhaps one of the reasons why de

[namely] by the king of Cenel-Eogain, along with the Foreigners and with the Gaidhil, into Tir-Conaill, whereby he destroyed much in Fanat and in Tir-Conaill and took away the hostages of Domnall Ua Baighill and of Ua Taircheirt with him.—A hosting by Ua Domnaill in the same year into Tir-Eogain, until he reached Tulach-oc, whereby he killed cows and burned crops and destroyed much besides in the country and he came back triumphantly. And in the same year the fleet of Cenel-Conaill harried, Midbadh and Eagh-inis and a party of the Cenel-Conaill, under the son of Niall Ua Domnaill, came upon them and thereby was caused destruction of the fleet and the son of Niall was killed.[3]

(Feidhlim[4] O'Concubhair, king of Connacht, was taken prisoner by Richard de Burgh in Milic, in treachery and the kingship of Connacht [reverted thereby] to Aedh, son of Ruaidhri [Ua Conchobair], again.)

Kalends of Jan. on 17th feria, 16th of the moon, A.D. 1233. A hosting by Feidhlimidh Ua Conchobuir into Connacht, until Cormac, son of Tomaltach [Mac Diarmata], went to meet him, so that he [Cormac] took him with him into Magh-Luirg and formed a camp at Druim-Gregraidhe and there came out[1] Cormac and Conchobur [his son] and the three Territories and the two sons of Mac Diarmata, namely, Donnchadh and Muircertach. And the counsel they adopted was to go in pursuit of Aedh, son of Ruaidhri [Ua Conchobair]. And they inflicted defeat in that place upon Aedh, son of Ruaidhri, that is, upon the

---

Burgh was deprived of the office of justiciary in the beginning of the following month (*ib.*, 1977).

1233. [1] *Out.*—*Amach* in the original; the lection followed by C. D has *filius eiusdem*; that is, the translator's text was *a mhac*, meaning that Conchubar was son of Cormac. The *Annals of Loch Ce* and the *Four Masters* have the same reading.

290

ρι₇ Connacc, ₇υρ'mαρbαð ὁ ρειn 7 Cεð Muιmnεč, mac Ruαιðρι 7 α mac 7 Donncαð moρ, mac Dιαρmαcα, mιc Ruαιðρι | 7 ναιne ιmðα[ι] αιlι,⁵ ιαρ ραρυ₇υð Tι₇ιbαιčιn 7 ιαρ⁶ n-α ρlαc ν'Cεð Muιmnεč 7 ιαρ⁶ ρlαc ceαlυρ 7 εεlυρ n-ιmðα αιle,⁷ ₇υρ'čυιcρες⁶ ρειn ι n-ειnεč čεαll 7 nαεṁ Connacc.ᵇ—Cαιρcεl-nα-Cαιllι₇ε 7 cαιρcεl bonα-nα-₇αιllðι νο ρ₇αιlεð lα ρειðlιmιð hUα Concobυιρ.—Uιllιαm νε Lαcι 7 Sεplυρ, mac Cαčαιl hUι Concobυιρ 7 ₇οιll ιmνα[ι] | νο mαρbαð lα Muιnncιρ-Rαι₇ιllαι₇⁸ ι Monαι₇-cραnncαιn.—Mαel-Iρρυ hUα Mαenαι₇, υαραlρασαρc ρο₇αbαð α ραlcαιρ ₇αč n-αεn lα[u], ας Dια-Domnαι₇, quιεuιc ιn⁶ Chριρτο.ᵇ—₇oρρραι₇ hUα Dαι₇ρι, αιρčιnnεαč Dαιρε Colυιm-cιlle, ιn Chριρτο quιεuιc.

(Tραnρlατιο⁶ bεατι Domιnιcι.⁶)

|Kαl. Iαn. [ι.ᵃ ρ., L xxιιι.,ᵃ] Cnno Domιnι Mº cc.º xxxº ιιιι. Cιlιn, mac Uετραι₇, ρί ₇αll-₇αιðεl, moρτυ[υ]ρ εrς.—Domnαll,ᵇ mac Cεðα hUι Nειll, ρί Cεnεοιl-Εο₇αιn 7 αðbυρ ρι₇ Εριnn, νο mαρbαð νο Mhαc Loclαιnn¹ 7 νο Chεnεl-Εο₇αιn ρειn.²—Cεð hUα hΕα₇ρα, ρίο Lυι₇nε,ᶜ νο ṁαρbαð lε Donncαð hUα n-Εα₇ρα.—Snεčcα moρ εcερ νά Nοclαιc ιριn blιαðαιn ριn.ᵃ Sιcc moρ ν'α ειρ, co n-ιmcι₇cιρ ναιne 7 ειč ρο n-ειριð αρ αιðnιð 7 αρ locαιð³ Eριnn.—Dιαρmαιc bUα Cυιnν, cαιρεč Muιnncεριη-hCn₇αιle, νοᶜ ṁαρbαð.ᵉ—Cαč νο

⁵ αιle, A. ⁶αρ—*upon* (temporal), B. ⁷ele, A. ⁸Rαι₇αll-, B. ᵇ om., B, C, D. ᶜ⁻ᶜ t. m., n. t. h., A; om., B, C, D.

A.D. 1234. ¹lαč-, B. ²ρανειn, B. ³lαčαιð, A.—ᵃ⁻ᵃ on blank space, A, B. ᵇ This entry follows the Cεð item, B, C, D. ᶜ⁻ᶜ om., A. ᵈ ρ—*this*, B. ᵉ⁻ᵉ moρcυυρ εrς, B; "died," C. This and the ₇ιllα-nα-nαεṁ and Mαel-Ρεcαιρ entries are omitted in D.

---

² *Castle of the Hag.* — Castrum vetule, D.

³ *Monach-cranncain.* — Bog of beautiful trees. Grunna crannchayn, D. At 855 [=856] *supra*, *Bellum Grunnae magnae* is the Latin rendering

king of Connacht; so that he himself was killed and Aedh the Momonian, son of Ruaidhri and his son and Donnchadh Mor, son of Diarmait, son of Ruaidhri and many other persons [were killed], after the profaning of Tech-Baithin and after the pillaging thereof by Aedh the Momonian and after the pillaging of many other abbeys and churches; so that they themselves fell in atonement of the churches and saints of Connacht.—The Castle of the Hag[2] and the Castle of Bun-na-Gaillbhi were razed by Feidhlimidh Ua Conchobuir.—William De Lacy and Charles, son of Cathal Ua Conchobuir and many Foreigners were killed by the Muinnter-Raighillaigh in Monach-cranncain[3].—Mael-Isu Ua Maenaigh, an eminent priest that used to recite his Psalter every day, save Sunday, rested in Christ.—Geoffrey Ua Daighri, herenagh of Daire of [St.] Colum-cille, rested in Christ.

(Translation[4] [of the body] of Blessed Dominick.)

Kalends of Jan. [on 1st feria, 27th of the moon,] A.D. 1234. Aillin, son of Uchtrach, king of the Foreign-Gaidhil, died.—Domnall, son of Aedh Ua Neill, king of Cenel-Eogain and future king of Ireland, was killed by Mac Lochlainn and by the Cenel-Eogain themselves.—Aedh Ua Eaghra, king of Luighni, was killed by Donnchadh Ua Eaghra.—Great snow between the two Nativities [Dec. 25—Jan. 6] in that year. Great frost thereafter, so that persons and horses went under burdens upon the rivers and lakes of Ireland.—Diarmait Ua Cuinn, chief of Muinnter-Angaile, was killed.—A battle was

---

of *Cath Mona-moire* — Battle of Moin-mor (big bog).

[4] *Translation, etc.*—On May 24, Tuesday in Whitsun week, of this year, during a general Chapter of the Order, the body of St. Dominick was transferred with imposing ceremonial to a more befitting receptacle in the church of St. Nicholas, Bologna. (See Bzovius in *Ann. Eccl.*, 1233, n. 5; Quetif and Echard : *Script. Ord. Præd., tab. chron. inter pp.* 84-5.)

cur do'n Mhararcal 7 do Sallaib Erenn, gor'marbad in Marargal⁴ ann.—Mael-Iṙṙu hUa Sormgaile, rrioir Innri-mic-n-Erin, quieuit in Chriṫro.—Cenguir Mac Sille Ḟinnein, rí Ḟer-Manac, do marbad la hUa n-Domnaill.—Silla⁴-na-naem, mac Cirt hUi Ḃrain, oircinneċ Rora-Comain, quieuit in [Chriṫro].⁴—Mael-Petair⁶ hUa Carmaca[i]n, maigirtir Rora-Comain, quieuit in [Chriṫro].⁴—Erruc hUa⁵-Ḟiaċraċ, hUa⁵ Mailṟagamair,⁶ quieuit in⁶ Chriṫro.⁶

A 59d |Kal. Ian. [ii.ª r., L ix.,ª] Anno Domini M.° cc. xxx.° u.° Loċlainn, mac Eċtigern hUi Ceallaig, do marbad do macaib in Silla riabaig hUi Baigill.—Sluagad mór lerin Siurtir 7 la Mac Uilliam i Connaċta, gur'-airgetur Mainirtir na Buille 7 co n-dernadur creaċ Creti¹ 7 docuaid iar rin irin Mumain, gur'gab braigti hUi² Ḃriain 7 táinic ari[t]r[i] i Connaċta 7 co Calad na-cairgi, gur'ráġ[b]ad in carriacc³ dó 7 gur'cuir Luċt coimeta innti 7 gibeḋ⁴ doráġbad⁵ ari[t]r[i] í 7 do-leġaḋ.

(Ir⁵ ar in Kalaind ri tic Domnall hUa Neill.ᵇ)

[Ḃir.]
B 61b |Kal. Ian. [iii.ª r., L.xx.,ª] Anno Domini M.° cc.° xxx.° ui.° Creċ Sligiġ do denam lerin Shiurtir 7 le Ḃrian, | mac Toirrḋelbaig, gur'gabadur mná imda broidi.¹—

⁴-cal at first; c was altered to g! A. ⁵O, A. ⁶Maeil-, B.—ᶠ⁻ᶠ om., B, C. ᵍ⁻ᵍ om., B, C, D.

A.D. 1235. ¹Creiti, B. ²I, A. ³-ag, A, ⁴gḃeṫ (that is, the siglum for et with dot overhead, used frequently for eḋ), B ; gḃeaḋ, A. ⁵-gaḋ, A.—ᵃ⁻ᵃ blank space, A, B. ᵇ t. m., t. h., A ; om., B. C. D.

A.D. 1236. ¹broiḋe, B.—ᵃ⁻ᵃ blank space, A, B.

1234. ¹ *Marechal.*—Richard, Earl of Pembroke. See the graphic account in Gilbert's *Viceroys*, p. 93, seq.

² *Ua Domnaill.*—D. adds: videlicet Donaldum magnum O'Donill, qui tunc sibi subiecit omnes inhabitantes illius patriae, ita ut sibi et eius filio post ipsum in omnibus parerent concorditer ut suae patrie

fought between the Marechal[1] and the Foreigners of Ireland, so that the Marechal was killed therein.—Mael-Isu Ua Gormgaile, prior of Inis-mic-nErin, rested in Christ.—Oenghus Mac Gille-Fhinnein, king of Fir-Manach, was killed by Ua Domnaill.[2]—Gilla-na-naem, son of Art Ua Brain, herenagh of Ros-Comain, rested in Christ.—Mael-Petair Ua Carmaca[i]n, Master [of the school] of Ros-Comain, rested in Christ.—The bishop of Ui-Fiachrach [Kilmacduagh], Ua Mailfhaghamhair, rested in Christ.

[1234]

Kalends of Jan. [on 2nd feria, 9th of the moon,] A.D. 1235. Lochlainn, son of Echtigern Ua Ceallaigh, was killed by the sons of the Swarthy Gilla Ua Baighill.—A great hosting by the Justiciary[1] and by Mac William [de Burgh] into Connacht, so that they plundered the Monastery of the Buill and effected the pillaging of Creit. And he went after that into Munster, until he received the pledges of Ua Briain and he came again into Connacht, to the Ferry of the Rock, so that the Rock was abandoned to him and he placed a party of guards therein. Notwithstanding, it was abandoned again and pulled down.

[1235]

(It is in [*lit*, on] this year comes [the death of] Domnall Ua Neill.[2])

Kalends of Jan. [on 3rd feria, 20th of the moon,] A.D. 1236. The pillaging of Sligech was done by the Justiciary and by Brian, son of Toirrdhelbach [Ua Con-

[1236 Bis.]

---

homines; qua conditione O'Donill remisit illis omnes retroactas iniurias et damna quaecunque, pro quorum satisfactione illi suas terras et semetipsos eidem perpetuo tradiderunt.

The original of this I have been unable to find.

1235. [1] *Justiciary*.—Maurice, son of Gerald Fitz Gerald.

[2] *Domnall Ua Neill*.—He is said in the text to have been killed in the preceding year. This note is intended to be a correction of that statement.

ʒilla-patraic[b] mac ʒilla-poiv, toirec Cene[oi]l-Oen-
ʒura, moptuur ert.[b]

Kal. 1an. [u.ˢ p., L. 1.,ᵃ] Anno Domini M.° cc.° xxx.° uii.°
Crec Renna-vuin vo tenum la Peivlimiv hUa Concobair[1] ocur vomarbav Concobur buive, mac Toirr-
velbaiʒ 7 Tavʒ, mac Cormaic. Ocur tainiʒ in ʒiurtir
co Termonn-Cailrinv² 7 voloirces in baile 7 voloirces
tempoll Imliʒ-U-Rocava.—Maivm Cluana-ca[ča] tuc
Peivlimiv³ ar macaiv Ruaivri 7 ar Concobur, mac
Cormaic.—Tomar hUa Ruava[i]n, erpuc Luiʒne,
quieuit in [Chrirto].—Erpuc Conmaicne, ivon, hUa
Tormaiv, quieuit in [Chrirto].—Muirceptač mac
Diarmata (mic[b] Ruaiʒri[b]), quieuit in [Chrirto] (no,ᶜ vo
marbav[ᶜ]).

Kal. 1an. [ui.ᵃ p., L. xii.ᵃ] Anno Domini M.° cc.° xxx.°
uiii.° Donnčav uaitnec, mac Aeva, mic Ruaivri, vo
marbav vo Tavʒ, mac Aeva, mic Catail croivve[i]rʒ.
—Donnčav, mac Duarcain hUi Eiʒra, vo marbav v'a
braitrib.— | Sluaʒav¹ mor vočuavur ʒaill² i Cenél-

A.D. 1236. ᵇ⁻ᵇ om., C, D.
A.D. 1237. ¹-buir, A. ² -lainn, A. ³ Peivlim, A.—ᵃ⁻ᵃ blank space,
A, B. ᵇ⁻ᵇ itl., n. t. h., A; om., B, C, D. ᶜ⁻ᶜ n. t. h., A; om., P, C, D.
A.D. 1238. ¹ Sluaʒ, B. ² ʒoill, B.—ᵃ⁻ᵃ blank space, A, B.

1236. ¹ *Captive.*—After this entry, D has: Eodem anno Sanctus Franciscus mortuus est. I do not know any saint of the name who died in this year.

1237. ¹ *Ua Ruadhain.*—O'Ruan, C; O'Ruanj, D. The inflected *d* was omitted in pronunciation.

² *Ua Tormaidh.*—In the *Annals of Loch Ce* (*ad an.*), his Christian name is given as Gilla-Isu. Having obtained confirmation of his appointment from the primate (1230, note 1, *supra*), he, according to bishop Jocelin, collected an armed force and burned the episcopal houses, together with the fort, or close (castrum), of Ardagh church; thereby destroying the stone (round ?) tower of the cathedral (quandam eius turrim lapideam).

Then proceeding against the bishop, who was being vested for celebration of the divine offices, Gelasius would presumably have slain him and his, had they not provided for themselves by flight. Thus expelled, Jocelin proceeded

chobair], so that they took away many women captive.[1]— [1236]
Gilla-Patraic Mac Gillaroid, chief of Cenel-Oengusa, died.

Kalends of Jan. [on 5th feria, 1st of the moon,] A.D. [1237]
1237. The pillaging of Rinn-duin was done by Feidh-limidh Ua Conchobair and there were killed Conchobur the Tawny, son of Toirrdelbach and Tadhg, son of Cormac. And the Justiciary came to the Termon of [St.] Cailfhinn and the town was burned and the church of Imlech-Ua-Rochadha was burned.—The defeat of Cluain-Ca[tha] was inflicted by Feidhlimidh upon the sons of Ruaidhri and on Conchobur, son of Cormac [Mac Diarmata].—Thomas Ua Ruadhain,[1] bishop of Luighni [Achonry], rested in Christ.—The bishop of Conmaicni [Ardagh], Ua Tormaidh,[2] rested in Christ.—Muircertach (son of Ruaighri) Mac Diarmata, rested in Christ (or, was killed[3]).

Kalends of Jan. [on 6th feria, 12th of the moon,] A.D. [1238]
1238. Donnchadh of Uaithne,[1] son of Aedh, son of Ruaidhri [Ua Conchobair], was killed by Tadhg, son of Aedh, son of Cathal Red-Hand[2].—Donnchadh, son of Duarcan Ua Eaghra, was killed by his kinsmen.—The Foreigners went upon a great hosting into Cenel-Eogain.

---

to the Curia for redress. The judges appointed by Gregory IX. were the archbishop of Dublin, the bishop of Ossory and the prior of All Saints, Dublin. (Theiner, *ubi sup.* p. 30-1.) O'Tormey, it seems probable, died before the proceedings were brought to a close, leaving Jocelin in undisputed possession.

On a review of all the circumstances, it seems impossible to acquit Donatus, archbishop of Armagh, of grave dereliction of duty. A question to be decided amicably by canonical process he thrice deliberately submitted to the arbitrament of force.

The total silence of the native Annals respecting a contest of such duration and violence is remarkable.

[3] *Was killed.*—This, according to the *Annals of Loch Cé*, is the true reading.

1238. [1] *Of Uaithne.* — So called perhaps from having been fostered in Uaithne (Owney and Owneybeg, co. Limerick; O'Donovan, *Book of Rights*, p. 45).

[2] *Red-Hand.*—Scabidi, D. The

n-Eoξain.—Ϝlaitbertać[b] Mac Catṁail, aptoireć Cen-e[oi]l-Ϝeraδaiξ, barr ξairció 7 einiξ ξaeiδiul[sic] 7 aptoireć δano Clainni-Conξaile 7 O-Cennϝoδa hi Tir-Manać, a ṁarbaδ δo Donnćaδ Mac Catṁail, δ'a braταir ϝein, 1 meaδail.[b]

Kal. Ian. [uii.[a] ϝ., L xxiii.[a]] Anno Domini M.° cc.° xxx.° ix.° Cat Cairn-Siaδail[1] tuc Domnall Maξ Laclainn, δu ṁar'ṁarbaδ[2] Domnall Tamnaiξi O Neill 7 Maξ Matξaṁna 7 maiti Cheniuil-Moen[3] uile 7 roćaiδe aile 7 δohatriξaδ in[4] bliaδain ϝeime rin é (iδon, Domnall Maξ Laclainn[b]) 7 δoξaδ ari[t̄i]r[i] an riξi cetna a baitli in[δ] maδmu moir rin tuc.

B 61 c [δir.] Kal. Ian. [i.[a] ϝ., L iiii.[a]] Anno Domini M.° cc.° xl.° Ϝeiδlimiδ Ua[1] Conćobuir δo δul tairir co teć riξ Saxan 7 tuc onoir 7 rimiaδ[2] mor leir.—Cormac, mac Tomaltaiξ, δo atriξaδ irin bliaδain rin.[3]—Ϝerξal, mac Conćonnact (i[b] Raiξilliξ[b]), δo marbaδ la Maelruanaiξ, mac Ϝerξail (7[b] la Concubur, mac Cormaic[b]).—Donnćaδ, mac Muirćertaiξ, δo ξaδail riξi[4] na Cairrξi.—Ξilla-na-naeṁ O Drea[i]n, oirćinneć Aroa-carna, quieuit in[c] [Chriτto[c]].

(Dominur[d] Albericur, archiepircopur Aromachanur, iṁ Anξlia in Aromachanum conrecratur ert archi-

A.D. 1238. [bb] om., A ; perhaps, as it was the last item, by oversight. Given in C, D.

A.D. 1239. [1] -t8i-, A. [2] ar'marbaδ, A. [3] Cenel-, B. [4] an, B.—[aa] blank space, A, B. [bb] itl., t. h., A.; om. B, C, D.

A.D. 1240. [1] O, A. [2] ruξṁiaδ, B. [3] ri—this, B. [4] ri, A. (Scribe perhaps thought the meaning was that Donnchadh *took* (captured) *the king*, instead of *took* (assumed) *the kingship*).—[aa] blank space, A, B. [bb] itl., n. t. h., A; om., B, C, D. [cc] om., B, C, D. [dd] n. t. h., A; om.,

translator, by a lapse of memory, took Cathal *Carrach* for Cathal *Croib-derg* (Red-hand).

1239. [1] *Of Tamnach.* — O'Neill was probably reared in Tawny (Tamhnach), co. Fermanagh.

[3] *More.*—Et aliis qui hic non numerantur, D.

—Flaithbertach Mac Cathmail, arch-chief of Cenel-Feradhaigh, crown of championship and generosity of the Gaidhil and arch-chief, moreover, of Clann-Conghaile and Ui-Cennfhoda in Tir-Manach, was killed by Donnchadh Mac Cathmail, by his own kinsman, in treachery. [1238]

Kalends of Jan. [on 7th feria, 23rd of the moon,] A.D. 1239. The battle of Carn-Siadhail was fought by Domnall Mag Lachlainn, wherein was killed Domnall O'Neill of Tamnach,[1] and Mag Mathgamna and the nobility of all Cenel-Moen and a multitude more[2] [were slain]. And he (namely, Domnall Mag Lachlainn) had been dethroned the year before[3] that and he assumed the same kingship again, on the morrow of that great defeat he inflicted. [1239]

Kalends of Jan. [on 1st feria, 4th of the moon,] A.D. 1240. Feidhlimidh Ua Conchobuir went across to the house of the king of the Saxons and brought [back] great honour and respect with him.—Cormac, son of Tomaltach [Mac Diarmata], was dethroned in that year.—Ferghal, son of Cu-Connacht (O'Raighaillaigh), was killed by Maelruanaigh, son of Ferghal (and by Conchubur, son of Cormac [Mac Diarmata]).—Donnchadh, son of Muircertach [Mac Diarmata] took the kingship of the Rock.—Gilla-na-naemh O Drea[i]n, herenagh of Ard-carna, rested in Christ. [1240 Bis.]

(The Lord Alberic [Albert], archbishop of Ard-Macha, was consecrated in England[1] into the archbishopric of

---

[3] *The year before.*—That is, by the force mentioned in the second entry of the preceding year.

1240. [1] *Consecrated in England.*—This can only signify that Albert (of Cologne) was in England when appointed primate. On Jan. 3. 1241, Henry III. granted him letters of protection in going to Ireland. (*D. I.*, I. 2503.)

He had been bishop of Bremen. Albertus, Livoniensis episcopus, obiit. Et Bremensis ecclesia, iure suo potita, Albertum, Bremensem scholasticum, in episcopum elegit; qui postea factus est Primas in Hibernia (*Annal. Stadenses* A.D. 1228-9. *Mon. Germ. Hist.—Script.* xvi. 360). Subsequently he became a Dominican and was Pro-

epircopatum.—Saḋb, ingen 1 Cheinneoiġ, ben Donn-
chaḋa Cairpṙiḋ Uí Ḃriain, vhec.—Aeḋ, mac Ġilla-cruim
1 Sheċnuraiġ, [vo marḃaḋ la] Conċuḃar, mac Aeḋa,
mic Cathail croiḃḋerġ.⁴)

[Cal. Ian. [111.ª f., L. xu.ª], Anno Domini M.º cc.º xl.º i.ª
Domnall mór hUa¹ Domnaill, rí Thire-Connaill 7
Fer²-Manaċ 7 Cairpri 7 Airġiall o Cḃlar anuar,ᵇ a eġ
re haḋart iar m-breiṫ buaiḋe o ṿoman 7 o' ḋeṁan 7 a
aḋnacal a Mainirter Era-ruaiḋ.—Caṫ Caimeirġi tuc
Ḃrian O Neill 7ᵈ Mael-Seċlainn O Domnaill, rí
Ceniuil-Conaill, vo Domnall Maġ Laċlainn, vo ríġ
Tire-hEoġain, ġur'marḃaḋ Domnall Máġ Loclainn ann
7 veiċnebur² v'a verḃḟine fein ime 7 tairġ Ceniuil-
Eoġain uile 7 vaine maiṫi imḋa[i] aili fór 7ᵉ ríġ vo
ġaḃail vo Ḃrian O Neill v'a eir.ᵉ

(Murċaḋᶠ O Flaiṫberṫaiḋ, erpuc Eanaiḋ-ḋuinn, 7
Diarmait, mac Maġnura mic Toirrḋelḃaiġ 7 Taḋġ,
mac Ruaiḋri I Ġaḋra, in Chrirto quieuerunt hoc anno.ᶠ)

B, C, D. The words in square brackets, being illegible in the MS.,
are supplied from the *Annals of Loch Cé* (*ad an.*).

A.D. 1241. ¹ O, B. ² -neabur, B.—ᵃ⁻ᵃ blank space, A, B. ᵇ⁻ᵇ om., A. In
the MS., a blank space=8 letters is left. Given in B, C, D. ᶜ om., A. ᵈ vo
—to, with no, 7—or, and—overhead, t. h. (signifying that Mael-Sechlainn
was the ally, not opponent, of Brian), B. ᵉ⁻ᵉ om., A. ᶠ⁻ᶠ n. t. h., A; om.,
B, C, D.

vincial in England at the date in
the text. (See the additional
entries respecting him under 1242,
1246, *infra*.)

² *Sadhb; Aedh.*—Given in the
Annals of Loch Cé (*ad an.*).

³ *Gilla-crom.*—The stooped gillie.

1241. ¹ *Domnall mor.*—D adds:
filius violentis O'Donil. The translator perhaps took *Egnachan*, which
was the name of his father, to
signify *violent*.

² *The Plain.*—"The plain here
referred to is Machaire Oirghiall,
or the level part of the county of
Louth, which was then in the possession of the English" (O'Donovan,
F. M. iii. 302).

³ *On the pillow.*—That is, a peace-
ful death from natural causes. D
gives: mortuus est in habitu cani
monachi. Illeque Donaldus magnus
diminuit extorsiones aliaque onera
suis subditis, et omnia tam perfecte
in sua patria in ciuili gubernacionis
forma reducta et certis utilibus

Ard-Macha.—Sadhb,[2] daughter of O'Ceinnedigh, wife of Donnchadh Cairpredh Ua Briain, died.—Aedh,[2] son of Gilla-crom[3] O'Shechnusaigh [was killed by] Conchubhar, son of Aedh, son of Cathal Red-Hand [Ua Conchobair].) [1240]

Kalends of Jan. [on 3rd feria, 15th of the moon,] A.D. 1241. Domnall Mor[1] Ua Domnaill, king of Tir-Conaill and Fir-Manach and Cairpri and Airghialla from the Plain[2] downwards, died on the pillow,[3] after bringing victory from the world and from the demon and he was buried in the Monastery of Es-ruadh.—The battle of Cameirghi was given by Brian O'Neill and Mael-Sechlainn O'Domnaill, king of Cenel-Conaill, to Domnall Mag Lochlainn, [namely] to the king of Tir-Eogain, so that Domnall Mag Lochlainn was killed therein and ten of his own tribe around him and all the chiefs of Cenel-Eogain and many other good persons likewise. And the kingship was taken by Brian O'Neill after him. [1241]

(Murchadh[4] O'Flaithbertaidh, bishop of Eanadh-duin, and Diarmait, son of Magnus, son of Toirrdelbach [Ua Conchobair], and Tadhg, son of Ruaidhri O'Gadhra, rested in Christ.)

---

constitutionibus de consilio procerum eiusdem pro communi usu inter dominos et subditos tenentes factis et confirmatis in sua vita egit, ut communi hominum estimatione nemo ex eius generatione a tempore *Odonis Mac*[-*ic*] *Aynmeragh* tam bene rexit ita ut similis *Cowyn centum bellorum* in bellis extirpandis ac *Cormaco*, filio eiusdem, in equitate iudiciorum ac *Arthuro Hynir* in extirpandis et rejiciendis foraneis et dignus socius *Brian Boravo* in bellicosis actibus et religione retinenda diceretur. Cuius bonorum operum fructu regnum Connallie vicit et reliquit suis posteris. Cui successit filius eius, Moelseaghlin.

The original of the foregoing I have not found. His death as a Grey (Cistercian) monk and the comparisons, with exception of the first, are given in the *Annals of Loch Ce* (ad an.). Aed, son of Ainmire, was slain in 597(-8), *supra*. Conn of the hundred battles, Art Aenfhir (the lonely), his son and Cormac, son of Art [not of Conn, as in D], were kings of Ireland who lived in the second century (A.D.). Brian Boruma was slain in the battle of Clontarf, 1014, *supra*.

[4] *Murchadh, etc.*—These three

Kal. Ian. [iiii.ᵃ f., l. xxui.ᵃ], Anno Domini M.º cc.º xl.º
ii.º Donnċaḋ Cairbreċ hUa Briain 7 a mac, Toirrḋelbaċ,¹ do ég i n-aen bliaḋain.—Brian hUa² Duḃḋa,
rí hUa²-Fiaċraċ 7 hUa²-nAṁalgaiḋ | do ég irin bliaḋain
cetna.—Sluaigeḋ mór lerin giurtir 7 le Feiḋlimiḋ
hUa² Conċobair i Tir-Conaill i⁸ n-deagaiḋ Thaiḋg hUi
Conċobair, gur'gabrat braigdi⁴ hUi⁵ Domnaill do'n
ċur rin.—Taḋg hUa² Conċobair do gaḃail le Coin-Chon-
naċt hUa² Ragallaig tre furail Fheiḋlimiḋ in bliaḋain
cetna fór.

(Alibeara,ᵇ airdefrcop Arta-Maċa, do ḋul a Sax-
anaiḃ.—Ugo de Laci, iarla Ulaḋ, quieuit.ᵇ).

Kal. Ian. (f.ᵃ 5, l. 7ᵃ), Anno Domini M.º cc. xl.º
iii.º Cormac, mac Tomaltaig, do gaḃail le Taḋg (macᵇ

A.D. 1242. ¹ -ḋeal-, A. ²O, A. ³α, A. ⁴ -de, A. ⁵ l, A.—ᵃ⁻ᵃ blank space, A, B. ᵇ⁻ᵇ n. t. h., A; om. B, C, D.

A.D. 1243.—ᵃ⁻ᵃ n. t. h., on blank space left by first scribe, A; om., B. ᵇ⁻ᵇ itl., n. t. h., A; om., B, C, D.

---

obits are given in the *Annals of Loch Cé* (ad an.).

1242. ¹ *Donnchadh.*—Thus in D: Donatus Carribragh O'Brien, rex Momonie ac legitimus heres Brien Borui[mh]e in defendendo et retinendo nomen, dignitatem, fidem et famam Momoniensium et principale sustentaculum gubernacionis Hibernie, una cum filio suo, Terlagh, qui expectatus rex erat Momonie, mortuus est.

The foregoing is apparently expanded from the obit in the *Annals of Loch Cé* (ad an.), in which Donnchadh is called the supporter of the faith and fame of the Half of Mogh and tower of splendour and pre-eminence of the South of Ireland.

Donnchad's zeal once produced an unexpected result. In a Letter addressed to the bishops of Annaghdown and Clonfert (dated Jan. 10, 1244), Innocent IV. appoints them judges in a complaint made by the bishop of Killaloe against the archbishop of Cashel. After his consecration, Richard de Burgh, the Justiciary, retained the regalia, refusing to give them up, except on payment of a sum of money. Whereupon the bishop threatened to excommunicate any one paying the mulct. Verum quia tandem, ipso penitus ignorante, a nobili viro, D. Carbrech, domino Tuadomonie, Laoniensis diocesis, contra inhibitionem huiusmodi dicta fuit persoluta pecunia, et per consequens prefata regalia eidem episcopo restituta, idem archiepiscopus,

Kalends of Jan. [on 4th feria, 26th of the moon,] A.D. [1242] 1242. Donnchadh[1] Cairbrech Ua Briain and his son, Toirrdhelbach, died in the same year.—Brian Ua Dubhda, king of Ui-Fiachrach and Ui-Amhalgaidh, died in the same year.—A great hosting by the Justiciary and by Feidhlimidh Ua Conchobhair into Tir-Connaill, in pursuit of Tadhg Ua Conchobair, so that[2] they received the hostages of Ua Domnaill on that occasion.—Tadhg Ua Conchobhair was taken prisoner by Cu-Connacht Ua Raghallaigh, by direction of Feidhlimidh, this year also.

(Alberic [Albert], archbishop of Armagh, went into Saxon-land.[3]—Hugh De Lacy,[4] Earl of Ulster, rested.)

Kalends of Jan. (on 5th feria, 7th of the moon,) A.D. [1243] 1243. Cormac, son of Tomaltach [Mac Diarmata], was

contra eum [episcopum] ex alia causa rancore concepto, ipsum ex hoc reepersum labe symoniaca reputat et multiplici molestatione perturbat. (Theiner, *ubi sup.*, p. 43.)

[2] *So that, etc.*—In D: Et licet multa damna intulerunt patrie, tamen defecerunt ex desiderio, quia Thadeus eis traditus non fuit. Sed postea Connassius O'Raylii eundem Thadeum ad requisitum Fielmei I Conor in vinculis detinuit.

The last sentence is the rendering of the textual *Tadhg* item.

[3] *Went into Saxon-land.*—The object of this journey appears from a mandate of Henry III. (St. Sever, May 6, 1243) to the justiciary of Ireland. A[lbert], archbishop of Armagh, had lately come to the king in Gascony, demanding, in right of his church, restitution of Drogheda, Louth and other vills, and of the manor of Nobber (co. Meath), this last having belonged to Hugh de Lacy, late Earl of Ulster. Fitz Gerald was commanded to take with him the treasurer of Ireland and the Seneschal of Meath and enquire into the archiepiscopal rights; which the king neither will, nor ought to, subtract from. (*D. I.*, I. 2618).

[4] *Hugh de Lacy.*—Erroneously given under next year in the *Annals of Loch Ce.* Henry III. wrote to the justiciary of Ireland (Bordeaux, Feb. 8, 1243) that, by law and custom of Ireland, the king may distrain widows by their lands to take husbands of the king's choice, provided the widows be not disparaged. Fitz Gerald is commanded that, if A[melina], widow of Hugh de Lacy, will not marry Stephen Longespee, as the king had requested her, he shall distrain her to do so, according to the custom of Ireland. (*D. I.*, I. 2600). De Lacy must accordingly have died in the preceding year.

Aeḋa, mic Caṫail croiḃdeirgᵇ) O Concoḃair¹ ic² Mainirtir na Buille 7 a bean, ingen Meg Carrṫaiġ, do ṫaḃairt
do Choin-Connaċt O Raiġillaiġ, don, maṫair Taiḋg
rein.—Taḋg O Concoḃair do ṫallaḋ 7 do rḃoċaḋ do
Coin-Connaċt O Raġallaiġ (treᵇ furail Ġhall ir
Ġaoiḋealᵇ).—Aeḋᶜ O Dhuiḃdirma, dux na Ḃréḋḟa,
mortuur erṫ.ᶜ

(Ġilla-Patraigᵈ hUa hOnluain, ri Oirġiall, do
marḃaḋ le raiġdeoir Connaċtaċ arrd claideaċ.—
Ruairi, mac Aeḋa, mic Caṫail croiḃdeirg, do ḃaṫaḋ
inrin t-Sinoinn, ag Aṫ-liag.—Concuḃar, mac Aeḋa, mic
Caṫail croiḃdeirg, d'ec.ᵈ—Sluagaḋᵉ [la] ri Saxan cum ri
[Franc] an bliadain ri.ᵉ)

[ḃir] Kal. Ian. (r.ᵃ 6, L. 18ᵃ), Anno Domini M.º cc.º xL.º iiii.ᵃ
Concobur, mac Aeḋa hUi Concobuir, quieuit in
[Christo].—Ruaiḋri, mac Aeḋa, a der[b]braṫair, do
ḃaṫaḋ irin t-Sinaind.—Donnċaḋ hUa Concobair, erscop
Oil-finn,¹ in Christo quieut.—Cormac, mac Tomaltaiġ,
quieuit inᵇ Christo.ᵇ

(Cairlenᶜ Dhomnaiġ-ṁaiġean do ċuṁdaċ do ċloċaiḃ
hoc anno.ᶜ)

Kal. Ian. (r.ᵃ 1, L. 29ᵃ), Anno Domini M.º cc.º xL.º u.º
Cagaḋ mor eter ri Saxan 7 Ḃretain¹ in bliaḋain ri.

A.D. 1243. ¹ -buir, A. ²iġ, A.—ᶜ⁻ᶜ om., A; given in B, C, D.
ᵈ⁻ᵈ n. t. h., A; om., B, C, D. ᵉ⁻ᵉ r. m., n. t. h. (the words in square
brackets are illegible), A; om., B, C, D.

A.D. 1244. ¹ Oilerind, A.—ᵃ⁻ᵃ n. t. h., on blank space, A; om., B.
ᵇ⁻ᵇ om., B, C, D. ᶜ⁻ᶜ n. t. h., A; om., B, C, D.

A.D. 1245. ¹ Ḃrea-, B.—ᵃ⁻ᵃ n. t. h., on blank space, A; om., B.

1243. ¹ *By direction, etc.*—Iussu supradicti Feilmei, D.

² *Died.*—D adds: O'Donill, Moelseaġblin, cum suo exercitu multa damna Tirione intulit et magnam predam exinde abduxit. The original is not known to me.

³ *Ruaidhri.*—This and the following item are found in the *Annals of Loch Ce* under the ensuing year. They seem misplaced here, being found in the text at 1244. Or perhaps the interpolator considered this to be the true year.

taken prisoner by Tadhg (son of Aedh, son of Cathal Red-Hand) O'Conchobair, at the Monastery of the Buill and his wife [Etain], daughter of [Finghin Mor] Mag Carrthaigh, was given to Cu-connacht O'Raighillaigh. [She was,] namely, the mother of Tadhg himself.—Tadhg O'Conchobair was blinded and emasculated by Cu-Connacht O'Raghallaigh by (direction[1] of Foreigners and Gaidhil).—Aedh O'Duibhdirma, chief of the Bredach, died.[2]

(Gilla-Patraig Ua Anluain, king of Oirgialla, was killed by a Connacht archer . . . .—Ruai[dh]ri,[3] son of Aedh, son of Cathal Red-Hand, was drowned in the Shannon at Ath-liag.—Conchubhar, son of Aedh, son of Cathal Red-Hand, died.—A hosting by the king of the Saxons against the king of the Franks this year.[4])

Kalends of Jan. (on 6th feria, 18th of the moon), A.D. 1244. Conchobur, son of Aedh Ua Conchubuir, rested[1] in Christ.—Ruaidhri, son of Aedh, his brother, was drowned in the Shannon.—Donnchadh Ua Conchobair, bishop of Oilfinn, rested in Christ.—Cormac, son of Tomaltach [Mac Diarmata], rested in Christ.

(The castle of Domnach-Mhaighean was covered [roofed] with stone this year.)

Kalends of Jan. (on 1st feria, 29th of the moon,) A.D. 1245. Great war[1] between the king of the Saxons and

---

[4] *This year.*—Given also in the *Annals of Loch Cé* and the *Four Masters* under 1243; but erroneously. Henry III. was in Portsmouth on May 5, 1242 (*D. I.*, I. 2564); in Saintes, June 8 (*ib.*, 2565); in Bordeaux, Sept., 6, 1243 (*ib.*, 2638), and in Westminster, Oct. 12 (*ib.*, 2639).

1244. [1] *Rested.*—A (Cistercian) monk in the abbey of Boyle, according to the *Annals of Loch Cé (ad an.)*

1245. [1] *Great war.* — Maxima gurrarum (sic) comotio inter regem Anglie et Brittones, unde vocati fuerunt a rege Justiciarius et Fielmeus O'Conchuir in Angliam et ivorunt, D.

304 ccuнαlα ulαoh.

In ʒıuρcıρ oo ðul caıρıρ 7 ρeıðlímıð² (ıoon,ᵇ α cαbαıρ ρıʒ Sαxαnᵇ) ıρın blıαðαın ρıᶜ ρóρ.ᶜ—Caıρlen Slıʒıʒ³ oo ðenαm le Mαc Muıρıρ (Mıcᵈ ʒeραılcᵈ) ıρın blıαðαın ρı.

(Muρcαðᵉ hUα hCCnluαın o'eloʒ o Inıρ Locα-αnoρoðαıo cρe mıρbuılıb Ραoραıʒ.ᶠ)

|Cal. 1αn. (ρ.ᵃ 2, L 10ᵃ), CCnno Oomını M.° cc.° xL.° ııı.ᵃ Mαc Comαρbα Moðuα oo ʒαbαıl eρρocoıoe ShılMuıρeðαıʒ 7 nıρ'leıʒeð α bec o'α αımρıρ oo ρe ρollαinnuʒuð.—Cαınıʒ ʒıuρcıρ nuα ĉαıρıρ 7 ρohαĉραıʒeð¹ Mαc Muıρıρ.—Oocoʒαð | Comαlcαĉ hUαᵃ Conĉoðαıρ³ oocum eρρocoıoe Oıl-ρınо.—Ceρbαll buıðe O Oαlαıʒ quıeuıc ın Chρıρco.—Muρcαðᵇ O hCCnluαın, ρí Oıρρceρ, oo mαρbαð cρe eραıl Uρıαın hUı Neıll.ᵇ

A 60c

ᵃ Ρeıðlım, A.   ³ Slıʒıð, B.—ᵇᵇ ıtl., n. t. h., A; om., B, C, D.   ᶜᶜ om., P. ᵈᵈ ıtl., n. t. h., B; om., A; given in D. "The castle of Sligo was made this year," C.   ᵉᵉ n. t. h., A; om., B, C, D.

A.D. 1246. ¹ ρo cαρραıʒeð, B. The contraction 7 = eð is here employed in A and B.   ² O, A.   ³ -buıρ, B.—ᵃ⁻ᵃ n. t. h., on blank space, A; om., B.   ᵇᵇ om., A; given in B, C, D.

² *The Justiciary.*—On Jan. 30, 1245, Henry III. wrote to Maurice Fitz Gerald that David, son of Llewellyn, late prince of North Wales, broke the treaty of peace with the king, invaded the king's land of Wales, slew his subjects, and tried to seduce the Welsh barons from their allegiance. The king prays the justiciary, magnates and subjects of Ireland (which he wishes to share in his conquest) to join him in revenging such treachery. Fitz Gerald is commanded, amongst other matters, to certify what provision and force he can despatch to the king's aid and to confer with the magnates thereupon (*D. I.*, I. 2733).

³ *Feidhlimidh.* — On March 29, 1245, letters of safe conduct for one year were issued for him, in coming to the king. On Oct. 21, 1245, letters of protection, dated from the camp at Gannoc (Carnarvonshire), were granted to him until the king's arrival in Ireland (*D. I.*, I. 2738-78).

⁴ *This year.*—D adds: Eodemque anno, Moelseaghlen O'Donill, facto magno exercitu, invasit Anglos et Hibernios inferioris Conacie, a quibus multas vaccas aliaque innumera bona asportarunt.

This is given in the *Four Masters* under the present year.

⁵ *Murchadh.*—See the last (original) entry of the following year.

the Britons this year. The Justiciary[2] and Feidhlimidh[3] [1245] [Ua Conchobair] went across (that is, in aid of the king of the Saxons) in this year[4] also.—The castle of Sligech was built by Fitz Maurice (Fitz Gerald) in this year.

(Murchadh[5] Ua hAnluain escaped from the Island of Loch-an-Drochaid,[6] through miracles of [St.] Patrick.)

Kalends of Jan. on 2nd feria, 10th of the moon, A.D. [1246] 1246. The son of the successor of [St.] Mochua[1] took [possession of] the bishopric of Sil-Muifedhaigh [Elphin] and not [even] a little of his time was left him to govern [it].—A new Justiciary[2] came across and Fitz Maurice was deposed.[3]—Tomaltach Ua Conchobair was raised[4] to the bishopric of Oil-finn [Elphin].—Cerball O'Dalaigh the Yellow rested in Christ.—Murchadh O'hAnluain, king of the Oirrthir, was killed by direction of Brian Ua Neill.

---

[6] *Loch-an Drochaid.*—Lake of the Bridge. See 1053, note 10, *supra*.

1246. [1] *Successor of [St.] Mochua.*—That is, abbot of Balla, co. Mayo. His name was John O'hUghroin. On the death of Donnchadh in 1244, *supra*, John, the archdeacon and Thomas O'Cuinn, abbot of Roscommon, were elected by the dignitaries and the junior canons respectively. Both appealed by procuration to Innocent IV., who was then in Lyons. In a Letter addressed to the archbishop of Tuam, dated July 3 (1245), the Pope decided in favour of John and gave a dispensation in the defect arising from his having been *de soluto genitus et soluta.* See *Annals of Loch Ce*, 1244-5; to be supplemented and corrected by the Papal text in Theiner (*ubi sup.*, p. 44).

[2] *New Justiciary.*—John Fitz Geoffrey. See Gilbert's *Viceroys*, p. 102.

[3] *Deposed.*—Literally, *unkinged.* "*Drawne,*" C; D renders: *executus fuit per regis ministros*,—which is not alone incorrect in the rendering, but a gross historical error. In this (D) Translation his death is rightly given under 1257.

[4] *Was raised.*—On Aug. 26, 1246, the royal assent to his election was notified to the archbishop of Tuam (although, it was added, the dean and chapter made the selection without first obtaining the king's license). (*D. I.,* I. 2844.)

He was consecrated, according to the *Annals of Loch Ce*, on the Sunday before Septuagesima (Jan. 20) of the following year.

(Alibirt° Almaineać, apdeprcop Apd-Maća, d'ażpużuď ćum na hUngaipe.—Eprcop Rata-Lupaiż do ćoluźaď ćum apdeprcopoide Apda-Maća.ᵃ)

Kal. 1an. (p.ᵃ 3, l. 21ᵇ), Anno Domini M.° cc.° xl° uii.° Mael-Sećlaind hUa Domnaill, pí Tipe-Conaill 7 in żilla muinelać hUa¹ Duiżill 7 Mac Somaipliż do mapbað le Mac Muipir i° m-bel-ata-penaiż 7 pożabrat Cenel-Conaill pe peccmain comlain in t-ać, nap'leiżret żall na żaibel taipir dib, no żup'ímip Copmac hUa¹ Concobair cealż pa deipeð: ion, dočuaið Copmac,ᵇ mapcluaż, ap pat³ in muiżi piap 7 doindto iap pin ap put in muiżi cetna, puar co bord in mointiż 7 dočuaið laim pir pair co painic Ać-cuil-uaine ap in Eipne. Ocup nip'aipiżret Cenel-Conaill, co pacadur in mapcluaż mor čuca do'n taibᵃ d'a pabadur do'n abaind. Ocup mapᵇ doᶜ bí Cenel-Conaill 7 a n-aire ap a mapcluaż leić d'a cul, doleiżret⁷ na żoill 'ran⁸ ać, co tapla Cenel-Conaill 7 in żilla muinelać hUaᵃ Duiżill 7 Mac Somaipliż⁹ pe Mac Muipir i° m-bel-ata-penaiż, cor'toitret° ann.ᶜ—Caiplen Mic żoipde[i]lb do leżað le macaib Aeða hUi Concobair.—Caźað mór do denam do Toippdelbać (macᵈ Aeða hUi Choncubairᵈ) 7 do na macaib piż (peᵈ żallaib in bliaðain piᵈ) 7 bailedha imða[i] do lorcað 7 żoill imða[i] do mapbað leó.—

A.D. 1246.—ᶜ⁻ᶜ n. t. h., A; om., B, C, D.

A.D. 1247. ¹ O, A. ² a, A. ³ put, B. ⁴ taeib, B. ⁵ mup, A. ⁶ Repeated by mistake, A. ⁷ żup' leiżretur (so that, etc.), B. ⁸ ipin, B. ⁹ Somuiplaiż B.—ᵃ⁻ᵃ n. t. h., on blank space, A; om., B. ᵇ om. A. ᶜ⁻ᶜ żup'mapbað leip iat—so that they were killed by him, B; followed by C. ᵈ⁻ᵈ itl., n. t. h., A; om., B, C, D.

ᵃ[*Albert*], *etc.*— Postea, idem Albertus, scilicet anno 1246, Papa Innocentio IV., apud Lugdunum, civitatem Galliae, tunc morante, legatus in Pruciam et Livoniam est transmissus. Et sequenti anno, defuncto Iohanne episcopo, residentiam obtinuit in sede Lubicense et demum factus archiepiscopus Rigensis (*Ann. Stad., ubi sup.,* p. 360-1).

His departure took place early in

(Aiberic [Albert]⁵ the German, archbishop of Ard-Macha, proceeded to Hungary [Prussia].—The bishop of Rath-Luraigh was chosen⁶ to the archbishopric of Ard-Macha). [1246]

Kalends of Jan. (on 3rd feria, 21st of the moon,) A.D. 1247. Mael-Sechlainn Ua Domnaill, king of Tir-Conaill, and the [Wry-]necked¹ Gilla Ua Baighill and Mac Somairligh were killed by Fitz Maurice in Bel-Atha-Senaigh. And the Cenel-Conaill held the Ford for an entire week, so that they allowed neither Foreigner nor Gaidhel across, until Cormac Ua Conchobair played a ruse in the end. That is, Cormac went with the horse-host throughout the length of the plain westwards and he turned after that upwards, throughout the length of the same plain, to the edge of the morass and went close thereby eastwards, until he reached the Ford of Cuil-Uaine on the Erne. And the Cenell-Conaill noticed not until they saw the great horse-host [advancing] to them, on the side of the river on which they were. And whilst the Cenel-Conaill had their attention upon the horse-host on their rear side, the Foreigners plunged into the Ford, so that the Cenel-Conaill and the [Wry-]necked Gilla Ua Baighill and Mac Somairligh met Fitz Maurice in Bel-Atha-Senaigh [and] fell there.—The castle of Mac Goisdelbh was pulled down by the sons of Aedh Ua Conchobair.—Great war was made by Toirrdelbach (son of Aedh Ua Conchubhair) and by the sons of the kings [of Connacht] (against the Foreigners this year) and many towns were burned and many Foreigners slain by them.— [1247]

---

the present year. On March 3, it having been intimated to the king that Armagh was vacant by resignation, the justiciary, Fitz Geoffrey, was commanded to take possession of and keep until further orders all the archiepiscopal land and chattels. (*D. I.*, I. 2812.)

⁶ *Was chosen.* — See note on *Raighned* under next year.

1247. ¹ *Wry-necked.*—*Collo Torturatus*, D.

Eaċmaɾcaċ· hUa Caċa[ı]n, ɾı Cıanaċc 7 Ƒeɾ-na-Cɾaıɓe, ɔo ṁaɾbaɔ la Maxnuɾ hUa Caċa[ı]n, aɾ n-ɔul ɔó aɾ cɾeıċ ċuıʒe, co hŒıɾcéɾ-muıxı ı n-Ɔaıl-ɾıacaı.·—Ruaıxɾı hUa Cananna[ı]n ɔo xaɓaıl ɾıxe Cıɾe-Conaıll.—Œɔ Mac Conċaılleaɔ, abb Cluana-Eoıɾ, quıeuıċ.—Raıxneɔ ɔo oıɾ[ɔ]neaɔ ı n-aɾɔeɾɾcoboıɔ[ı] Œɾɔa-Maċa ıɾın Roım.—Muɾċaɔ hUa hŒnluaın, ɾı Oıɾɾċıɾ, ɔo maɾbaɔ an blıaɓaın [ɾı].¹

[bıɾ.] ɟCal. ıan. ɾ.ª [4], L. 2,· Œnno Ɔomını M.° cc.° xl.° uııı.·
Ruaıɓɾı hUa Cananna[ı]n ɔo maɾbaɔ la ʒoɾɾɾaıx,¹ mac Ɔomnaıll moıɾ hUı² Ɔomnaıll 7 ɔaıne ımɔa[ı] eıle aɾaen ɾıɾ 7 ʒoɾɾɾaıx³ ɔo xaɓaıl ɾıxı⁴ Chıɾe-Conaıll ɔ'a eıɾı.—Raıxneɔ,ᵇ aɾɔeɾɾcoɾ Œɾɔa-Maċa, ɔo ċeaċc o'n Roım cum pallıo 7 aı[ɾ]ɾɾınn ɔo ɾaɔa ɔo Leıɾ ı ɾeıl Peaɔaıɾ 7 Poıll ınnŒɾɔ-Maċa.ᵇ

(A)   (B)
ıuɾoıɾ na hEıɾenn ɔo   8loxeɔ· la ʒallaıɓ Eɾenn
ɔul, ɾluax, xu Cuıl-ɾaċaın   co Cuıl-ɾaċaın co n-ɔeaɾ·

A.D. 1247.—ᵃ⁻ᵃ om., A. ᵇ⁻ᵇ om., B, C, D.
A.D. 1248. ¹ʒoɾɾaıɔ, A. ²hI, A. ³ʒoɾɾaıx, B. ⁴ɾıxe, B. ᵃ⁻ᵃ om., B. ᵇ⁻ᵇ om., B, C, D. ᶜ⁻ᶜ This follows the Lonʒa entry in B. It is the text of C and D.

ᵃ *Raighned.*—The apparent inconsistency of this and the final (additional) entry of the preceding year is explained by the Letter, dated Lyons, Oct. 8 (1246), of Innocent IV. directing the Dominican Prior of Drogheda and the Franciscan Guardian of Dundalk to serve citations in the matter of the Armagh succession. When the See became vacant (by resignation of the German, Albert), the Chancellor, against the consent of the rest of the Chapter, postulated Germanus, bishop of Rathluraigh (Derry). The archdeacon appealed to the Pope, who through the aforesaid Prior and Guardian enjoined all concerned to appear before the Curia on, or before, the next *Leture Jerusalem* Sunday (the fourth Sunday of the following Lent, March 10, 1247). (Theiner, *ubi sup.*, p. 45.) The present entry of the *Annals* shows that the election of Germanus was set aside, and Raighned [Reginald ?] made archbishop.

Eachmarcach Ua Catha[i]n, king of Ciannachta and of [1247] Fir-na-craibhe, was killed by Maghnus Ua Catha[i]n, on his going upon a foray to the latter, to Airther-muighi in Dal-riatai.—Ruaighri Ua Cananna[i]n took the kingship of Tir-Conaill.—Aedh Mac Conchailleadh, abbot of Cluain-Eois, rested.—Raighned[2] was instituted into the archbishopric of Ard-Macha in Rome.—Murchadh Ua hAnluain, king of the Oirrthir, was killed this year.

Kalends of Jan. on [4th] feria, 2nd of the moon, A.D. [1248 Bis.] 1248. Ruaidhri Ua Cananna[i] was killed by Geoffrey, son of Domnall Mor Ua Domnaill and many other persons [were killed] along with him and Geoffrey took the kingship of Tir-Conaill after him.—Raighnedh, archbishop of Ard-Macha, came from Rome with the Pallium and Mass was said by him in it, on the feast of [SS.] Peter and Paul [Monday, June 29], in Ard-Macha.

(A)
The Justiciary of Ireland went [with] a host to Cuil-

(B)
A hosting by the Foreigners of Ireland to Cuil-

With respect to the bishopric of Rathluraigh (Rathlurensis), valuable information is contained in another Letter of the same Pope, dated Lyons, May 31 (1247), transferring the See therefrom to Derry. From the time of the delimitation of the dioceses, the See was in Derry. Sed postmodum bonae memoriae Ocophtyg [Ua Cobthaigh], predecessor eiusdem (i.e., of the bishop who postulated to have the See moved back to Derry) sedem ipsam ad villam Rathlurensem, de qua idem predecessor originem duxerat, illectus natalis soli dulcedine, a Sede Apostolica non petita licentia nec obtenta, transtulit motu proprie voluntatis.

The Ua Cobhthaigh (O'Coffey) here mentioned was, no doubt, the bishop of that name who died in 1173, *supra*. The foregoing is strong confirmatory evidence that the *Bishop's Chair* offered to the Abbot Ua Brolchain in 1158 meant the dignity of mitred abbot. It seems incredible that an abbot-bishop of Derry should remove the See from there to Maghera (Rathluraigh).

1248. [1] *Craft.*—"These were cots, or small boats, which were carried by land on the shoulders of men, to be launched on lakes for plundering islands" (O'Donovan, *F. M.*, iii. 330).

7 cairlen 7 oroicead do ꝺenum doiḃ aꝃ Oꞃuim-ċaiꞃꞃiċ.

naꝺuꞃ oꞃoċat na ḃanna 7 caiꞃtel Oꞃoma-taiꞃꞃiꝃ 7 atꞇꞃeḃaḋ in oꞃoma.

Lonꝁa⁴ do ċaḋaiꞃt la Ḃꞃian hUa Neill, la haꞃoꞃuꝃ Tuaiꞃciꞃt Eꞃenn, de Loċ-Feaḋail 1 Maꝃ-niċa, taꞃ Teꞃmonn-Ꝺaḃeo[i]c, illoꞃcc, co ꞃainic Loċ-n-Eiꞃne, co n-ꝺeꞃna cꞃeiċ n-ꝺiaꞃṁiċi 7 ꝃuꞃ'ḃꞃuꞃ caiꞃtel ann.⁴

B 62b

A 62d

Kal. 1an. (ꝼ.ᵃ 6, L 13ᵉ), Anno Ꝺomini M.° cc.° xl.° ix.° Ꝺa ḃliaḋain ꝺec 7 ꞃecꞇ cet ḃliaḋan o ꝺoċuaiḋ Columcille co hI ꝃuꞃ an ḃliaḋain ꞃi.ᵇ—Mac hAnꞃi | ꝺo maꞃḃaḋ la hAeḋ hUa Concoḃaiꞃ, ꝺon, Aeḋ, mac Feiḋlimiḋ¹ 7 Ꝺaiḃit Oꞃiu 7 Ꝃoilmaiċi eile imaille² ꞃiu. —Maiḋm Aċa-na-ꞃiꝃ aꞃ Toiꞃꞃꝺelḃaċ hUaᵇ Concoḃuiꞃᵇ ꝺ'aꞃ'maꞃḃaḋ Aeḋ, mac Aeḋa, ann 7 Ḃꞃian in Ꝺoiꞃe 7 moꞃan ꝺo maiċiḃ Connaċt.—8luaiꝃeꝺ móꞃ leiꞃin ꝃiuꞃtiꞃ 7 le Mac Muiꞃiꞃ (1ᵉ Connaċtaiḃᶜ), coꞃ'innaꞃḃꞃat³ Feiḋlimiḋ aꞃin tiꞃ 7 ꞃoꝼaꝃꞃat Toiꞃꞃꝺelḃaċ,¹ mac Aeḋa, 1 n-a inaḋ.

(Niall⁴ hUa Canana[i]n ꝺo ꝃaḃail ꞃiꝃe Tiꞃe-Conaill an ḃliaḋan ꞃi.—Toꞃaḋ imḃa aꞃ cꞃannaiḃ an ḃliaḋan ꞃi.⁴)

A.D. 1248. ᵈ⁻ᵈ om., A ; given in B, C, D.
A.D. 1249. ¹-limiꝃ, B. ² maille (aphaeresis of 1), A. ³ -ꞃataꞃ, B. ⁴ Taiꞃꞃ-, A.—ᵃ⁻ᵃ n. t. h. on blank space, A; om., B. (They signify the same down to 1254, inclusive.) ᵇ⁻ᵇ om., A ; given in B, C, D. ᶜ⁻ᶜ itl., n. t. h., A; om., B, C; given in D. ᵈ⁻ᵈ n. t. h., A ; om., B, C, D.

1249. ¹ *Twelve years and seven hundred years.*—This is a material error. In A.D. 537, St. Columba was in his seventeenth year. He passed over to Iona when he was forty two years old. Perhaps, however, as the editor of the *Annals of Loch Ce* suggests (*ad an.*), the meaning is 12 years *less* than 700. (That is, for *ocus*—and, we are to read *o*—from.) This would bring the reckoning within a year of A.D. 562, the true date. (See *Todd Lectures*, Vol. III. pp. 21-2.)

² *Them.*—Namely, with the son of Henry Poer and with Drew.

rathain and a castle and bridge were built by them at Druim-tairsech.

rathain, so that they built the bridge of the Bann and the castle of Druim-tairrsech and the mansion of Druim-[-tairrsech]. [1248]

Craft[1] were carried by Brian Ua Neill, [namely] by the arch-king of the North of Ireland, from Loch-Feabhaill into Magh-Itha, past the Termon of [St.] Dabeoc, into Lorc, until he reached Loch-Eirne, so that he took away countless spoil and broke down a castle there.

Kalends of Jan. (on 6th feria, 13th of the moon), A.D. 1249. Twelve years and seven hundred years[1] [have elapsed] since [St.] Colum-cille went to I[ona] to this year.—[Piers] son of Henry [Poer], was slain by Aedh Ua Conchobair, namely, Aedh, son of Aedh, son of Feidhlimidh and David Drew and other Foreign nobles [were slain] along with them.[2]—The defeat of Ath-na-righ [was inflicted] on Toirrdelbach Ua Conchobuir, whereby Aedh, son of Aedh, was killed therein and Brian of the Doire and a great many of the nobles of Connacht [were killed].—A great hosting by the Justiciary and by Fitz Maurice (into Connacht), until they expelled Feidhlimidh out of the country and left Toirrdelbach, son of Aedh, in his stead.[3] [1249]

(Niall Ua Cananna[i]n took the kingship of Tir-Conaill this year.—Great crop on trees this year.)

---

[3] *In his stead.*—D adds: Deinde O'Donill Goffredus inuasit Conaciam inferiorem cum magno exercitu et deuastauit totam patriam a monte Corsleave usque ad flumen Moye et tandem rediit cum magna patrie preda et captiuis ac obsidibus nulla habita resistentia in illa expeditione.

This is given in the *Four Masters* under the present year.

Kal. Ian. (p.ᵃ 7, l. 24ᵃ.), Anno Domini M.° cc.° l.°
Mael-Muire hUa¹ Lactna[i]n, ardespuc Tuama, in
Christo quieuit.—Tainic Feidlim[id] irin tir 7 doteic
Toirrdelbac reime² a n-uct Gall.—Tomar O Meallaid,³
erpuc Enaig-duin, in⁵ Christo quieuit.ᵇ—Beandᶜ tem-
puill moir Dhaire Colum-cille do tuitim, id ert, rexto
Idur Febhuarii.—Seirilin, ingen Mic Laclainn, rigan
Tuaice[i]rt Erenn, mortua, est.ᶜ

(Muirisᵈ Mac Gearailt 7 Catal hUa Raigillaig 7
Eacaid Mhag Matgamna do dul, rluag, a Tir-Chonaill
7 Niall hUa Canannan do marbad leo, idon, ri Thire-
Conaill.ᵈ)

Kal. Ian. (Dominicaᵃ l. 5ᵃ) Anno Domini M.° cc.° l.° i.ᵃ
Floirint Mac Flaind,¹ do toga[d] cun ardespucoide²
Tuama 7ᵇ roba dingmala cuice he ar med egna 7
oligid.ᵇ—Arogal c hUa [Fh]laitbertaig, ridomna Ailig,
cainnel gairid 7 einig Thuaice[i]rt Erenn, mortuur
est.—Gilla-Crist hUa Breirlen, toirec Fana[i]t 7 a
bratair do marbad la Ceallac m-bald hUa m-Baigill.
—Donchad Mac Catmail, toirec Chene[oi]l-Feradaig,
do marbad d'Airgiallaid.ᶜ

(Raignedᵈ airdepscop Arda-Maca, do dul cum na

A.D. 1250. ¹O, A. ²roime, A. ³Meall (with sign of contraction
attached to the final l). Overhead is placed d, n. t. h., in A, to signify
that the ending is—aid.—ᵇ⁻ᵇ om., B. ᶜ⁻ᶜ om., A; given in B, C, D.
ᵈ n. t. h., A.; om., B, C, D.

A.D. 1251. ¹Flond, A. ²aird—, B. ᵇ⁻ᵇ om., B (followed by C, D).
ᶜ⁻ᶜ om., A; given in B, C, D. ᵈ⁻ᵈ n. t. h., A; om., B, C, D.

1250. ¹ *Mael-Muire.*—His death, according to the *A. L. C.* [*Annals of Loch Cé*], took place "a very short time before Christmas," 1249. This is confirmed by the letter of the Dean and Chapter of Tuam, about the end of Dec., 1249, praying the king's licence to elect in room of Marianus. The licence was granted to their proctor, Jan. 16, 1250 (*D. I.*, I. 3028-34).

³ *O'Meallaidh.*—The election of Concordis (Conchobar ?), his successor, was confirmed by Innocent IV., Jan. 12, 1251 (Theiner, p. 53). The royal assent was given (though the election took place without licence) on May 8 (*D. I.*, I. 3131).

Kalends of Jan. (on 7th feria, 24th of the moon, A.D. [1250] 1250. Mael-Muire[1] Ua Lachtna[i]n, archbishop of Tuaim, rested in Christ.—Feidhlimidh [Ua Conchobhair] came into the country and Toirrdhelbach fled before him, into the midst of the Foreigners.—Thomas O'Meallaidh,[2] bishop of Eanach-duin, rested in Christ.—The pinnacle of the great church of Daire of [St.] Colum-cille fell, namely, on the 6th of the Ides [8th] of February.—Cecily, daughter of Mac Lochlainn, that is, queen of the North of Ireland, died.

(Maurice[3] Fitz Gerald and Cathal Ua Raighillaigh and Eachaidh Mag Mathghamna went [with] a host into Tir-Conaill and Niall Ua Canannan, namely, king of Tir-Conaill, was killed by them.)

Kalends of Jan. (on Sunday, 5th of the moon,) A.D. [1251] 1251. Florence Mac Flainn was elected[1] to the archbishopric of Tuaim, and he was fit therefor by the extent of [his] wisdom and legal lore.—Ardghal Ua [F]laithbertaigh royal heir of Ailech, candle of the championship and hospitality of the North of Ireland, died.—Gilla-Crist Ua Breslen, chief of Fanat and his kinsman were killed by Ceallach Ua Baighill the Dumb.—Donnchadh Mac Cathmhail, chief[2] of Cenel-Feradhaigh, was killed by the Airghialla.

(Raighnedh,[3] archbishop of Ard-Macha, went to Rome.

---

[3] *Maurice.*—Given at greater length in the *A. L. C.* (*ad an.*)

1251. [1] *Elected.*—This is a year too late. Shortly before May 27, 1250, the Dean and Chapter of Tuam wrote to the king that, having obtained licence, they unanimously elected Florence, chancellor of their church and sub-deacon of the Pope. The royal assent was given on May 27 (*D. I.*, I. 3044–5). The consecration took place in Tuam on the Christmas day of the same year (*A. L. C.*, A.D. 1250).

[2] *Chief.*—Subregulus, D.

[3] *Raighned, etc.*—These items, with exception of the last, are also given in the *Four Masters* under this year.

Roma.—Imap Maʒmaḋaxan, caireċ Cloinne-Ruaḋraċ, do marbaḋ.—Da mac Ruaiʒri hUi Neill do marbaḋ aʒ Cill-móir hUa-Niallain.—Donnċaḋ Mac Caṫmail do marbaḋ.—Cairlen Duin-ċuile do ḋenum.[d]

[b'r.] Kal. Ian. (r.* 2, L. 16'.) Anno Domini M.° cc.° L.° ii.° Sampaḋ[b] ce irin bliaḋain ri.—Cairlen Cail-uirci do denam le Mac Muirir. Cairlen Muiʒi-coḃa do ḋenam leir (don,[c] le ʒearrolt[c]) ror.—Mael-Ni[o]aeḋoic hUa Beolla[i]n, comarba Coluim-cille i[1] n-Druim-cliaḃ, in[s] c-aen comarba robo mó conaċ ⁊ robo[3] oirrdercu | eineċ ⁊ robo mó caḋur ⁊[d] onoir[d] roboi re [a] linn rein i n-Erinn o ʒallaiḃ ⁊ o ʒhaiḋelaiḃ,[4] in Chrirco quieuic.—Aeḋ[c] Mac Caṫmail morcuur erc.—Conċobur Mac Caṫmaeil riʒcoireċ Cenuil-Feraḋaiʒ ⁊ cuaṫ n-imḋa arċena, cuir einiʒ ⁊ eʒnoma Tuairce[i]rc Erenn, rer rréa Conaill ir Eoʒain ir Airʒiall, a marbaḋ do ruċaiḃ Briain hUi Neill ⁊ ré i cornum a comairce rriu ⁊ re rein ar rlanaċur hUi ʒailmreḋaiʒ ⁊ hUi Caṫa[i]n.—Conċobur hUa Doċarcaiʒ, cairec Airdi-miḋair re heaḋ, morcuur erc.[c]

(Iurcir[c] na hEirenn do ċeaċc, rluaḋ mor, ʒo hArd-Maċa ⁊ arrin i n-Ou-Eaṫaċ ⁊ areiʒ ar a n-air ʒu Cluain-Fiacna ⁊ Brian hUa Neill d'a n-oiʒreir annrin ⁊ do ċabairc a ḋearḃraṫar rein, idon, Ruaiʒri hUa Neill, do ḃraiʒid doiḃ.[f])

A.D. 1252. [1] *a*, B. [2] *an*, B. [3] *rob* (*o* om.), A. [4] ʒhaei—, B.— [b] This item is second in A, B, C. But *also* (*ror*) shews that the *cairlen* entries followed each other immediately. [c-c] r. m., n. t. b., A; om., B, C; given in D. [d-d] om., B. [e-e] om., A; given in B, C, D. [f-f] n. t. b. A; om., B, C, D.

[4] *Mac Cathmhail.*—The person mentioned in the last original entry of the present year.

1252. [1] *Peace-maker, etc.*—The meaning is accurately expressed in D: pacis et concordiae perficiendus auctor singularis inter reges Eoganensium et Connalliae [et Orientalium].

—Imhar Mag Mhadaghan, chief of Clann-Ruadhrach, [1251] was killed.—The two sons of Ruaighri Ua Neill were killed at Cell-mor of Ui-Niallain.—Donnchadh Mac Cathmhail[4] was killed.—The castle of Dun-chuile was built.)

Kalends of Jan. (on 2nd feria, 16th of the moon,) A.D. [1252 Bis.] 1252. A hot summer in this year.—The castle of Narrow-Water was built by Fitz Maurice. The castle of Magh-Cobha was built by him (namely, [Fitz] Gerald) also.—Mael-M[o]edoic Ua Beolla[i]n, successor of [St.] Columcille in Druim-cliabh, the superior of greatest substance and of most distinguished hospitality and of greatest esteem and honour by Foreigners and by Gaidhil [of any] that was during his own time in Ireland, rested in Christ.—Aedh Mac Cathmhail died.—Conchobur Mac Cathmhail, royal chief of Cenel-Feradhaigh and of many territories besides, tower of hospitality and valour of the North of Ireland, peace-maker[1] of [Cenel-]Conaill and [Cenel-]Eogain and the Airghialla, was killed by the routs of Brian Ua Neill, whilst he was defending his protection[2] against them and he himself [was] under the safeguard of Ua Gailmredhaigh and of Ua Catha[i]n.—Conchobur Ua Dochartaigh, chief of Ard-midhair for a time, died.

(The Justiciary[3] of Ireland came [with] a great host to Ard-Macha and therefrom into Ui-Eathach and from here backwards to Cluain-Fiacna. And Brian Ua Neill gave full submission to him then and delivered his own brother, that is, Ruaighri Ua Neill, as a hostage to them.)

---

[2] *Protection.* — Signifying, by metonymy, those whom he had undertaken to protect. In defensione sui patrocinii, ipso etiam existente sub patrocinio et salvo conductu I Gorumlea et I Cahan, D.

[3] *The justiciary.* — John Fitz Geoffrey. The entry is given in the *Four Masters* at this year.

ccmocícc ulccoh.

Kal. Ian. (f.ᵃ 4, L 27ᵃ), Anno Domini M.° cc.° L° iii.°
Sluaġ mor do tinol le Mac Muirir, co n-deacaid i Tir-n-Eoġain 7 nír'ġad nert na tenn¹ innti 7 tucad ar mor ar na ġallaib do'n toirc² rin.—Mael-Pedair' hUa Muiredaiġ, prioir Duine-ġeimin, mortuur ert.—Donatur, archiepircopur Mumoni[a]e, quieuit in [Chrirto].
—Sluaiġeab la Brian hUa Neill, la hairoriġ Thuair-ce[i]rt Erenn, co Maġ-coba d'ar'milled leir in cairtel co n-a daimib 7 cairtela imda eile i n-Ultaib 7 daine imda do'n turur rin.ᵇ·

(Cairlen° Muiġe-caba do rġrir la Brian hUa Neill, riġ Thire-hEoġain.—Mael-Padraiġ hUa Sġannuil do'n Ord Phreirriur do toġa le hardeprcop Arda-Maca, a comairle Innocent Papa, cum errocoide Rata-bot. Et idem archiepircopur conrtituit eum uicarium ruum in prouincia Armachana, portquam conrecratur fuit in monarterio fratrum | Minorum de Dun-dealġan in Dominica prima Aduentur Domini.—Fructur copiorrur in arborribur hoc anno.—Dauid Mhaġ Ceallaiġ, airdeprcop Cairril, quieuit in pace.ᶜ)

Kal. Ian. (f.ᵃ 5, L 9ᵃ), Anno Domini M.° cc.° L° iiii.°
A.D. 1253. ¹ teann, B. ² toirg, A. ᵇ⁻ᵇ om., A; given in B, C, D. ᶜ⁻ᶜ Fol. 60d, f. m.; fol. 61a, t. m., n. t. h., A; om., B, C, D.

1253. ¹ *Donatus.*—This should be David (see the final additional entry of this year). The choice of his successor, David (Mac Carroll), was ratified by Innocent IV., Aug. 17, 1254. The delay arose from the objection of the suffragan bishops that, having been made by the Chapter and not by themselves, the election was invalid. For the conclusive reply, see the Bull of confirmation (Theiner, p. 61 sq). Mac Carroll occupied the See until 1289 (D. I., III. 468). He was succeeded by Stephen O'Bragan, whose election was confirmed by Nicholas IV., Sept. 21, 1290 (Theiner, p. 151 sq).

² *Expedition.*—D adds : Goffredus O Donill cum magno exercitu intravit terras Eoganenses et illic accepit predas et captivos conduxit multos et Brien O Neill in persecutione depredantium, cum illos

Kalends of Jan. (on 4th feria, 27th of the moon,) A.D. [1253] 1253. A large host was collected by Fitz Maurice [Fitz Gerald], so that he went into Tir-Eogain. And he obtained neither sway nor hold therein and great slaughter was inflicted on the Foreigners on that expedition.—Mael-Pedair Ua Muiredhaigh, prior of Dun-geimhin, died.—Donatus,[1] archbishop of Munster, rested in Christ.—A hosting by Brian Ua Neill [that is] by the arch-king of the North of Ireland, into Magh-Cobha, whereby the castle with its people and many other castles in Ulidia were destroyed and many persons were killed by him on that expedition.[2]

(The castle of Magh-Cobha was levelled by Brian Ua Neill, king of Tir-Eoghain.—Mael-Padraig[3] Ua Sgannuil of the Preaching Order was chosen by the archbishop of Ard-Macha, by advice of Pope Innocent, to the bishopric of Rath-both. And the same archbishop constituted him his Vicar[4] in the Province of Ard-Macha, after he was consecrated in the Monastery of the Friars Minor of Dundealgan [Dundalk] on the First Sunday of the Advent of the Lord [Nov. 30].—Copious fruit[5] on trees this year.—David[6] Mag Ceallaigh, archbishop of Cashel, rested in peace.)

Kalends of Jan. (on 5th feria, 9th of the moon,) A.D. [1254]

---

aggredi tentaret, restiterunt fortiter Conallienses et occiderunt multos ex potioribus Eoganensium.

The original is given in the *Four Masters* under 1252.

[3] *Mael-Padraig.*—The archbishop of Armagh was empowered by Innocent IV. (May 23, 1253) to receive personally or by deputy the resignation of his predecessor (Theiner, p. 57). Having gone to Rome to consult with the Pope on the state of his diocese, the bishop of Raphoe obtained (March 21, 1255) power from Alexander IV. to excommunicate contumacious persons and permission to avail of two Dominicans of the Irish Province to aid him by counsel and preaching (Theiner, p. 71).

[4] *Vicar.*—The archbishop was absent in Rome at the time.

[5] *Copious fruit.*—Given in the A. L. C. under the following year.

Muṙċaḋ hUa Mail-[Sh]eċlainn¹ quieuit in [Chriſto ᵇ].
Donnċaḋ, mac Donnċaḋa 7 Aṁlaim hUa Biḃraiġ do
marbaḋ la Connaċtaiḃ.—Ainḋileſ ᶜ hUa hInḋeirġi, tuiṙ
eġnoma Thuaiſceirt Erenn, mortuur eſt.ᶜ—Dedicatio
eccleſi[a]e Sancti Patricii Dublini[a]e.ᵈ

(Teine ᵉ ḋiaitt aiḋċe Doṁnaiġ i ḟeil na Croiċe in
t-saṁraiḋ i m-Baile hUa-Ruaḋagan, i ḟiġ Chonaill 7
noṁur do lorcaḋ a tiġ ann.ᵉ)

Kal. Ian. (f.ᵃ 6,ᵃ l. 20,ᵃ) Anno Domini M.º cc.º L.ᵒ u.ᵒ
Innocenciuſ Papa quieuit in [Chriſto ᵇ].—Tómaſ Mac
Diarmata, arċideoċan Oil-ḟinn,¹ mortuur eſt.—Donn-
ſleiḃe ᶜ hUa Flainn, abb reiġleſa Poil 7 Peadair i n-
Ard-Maċa, mortu[u]ſ eſt.ᶜ

(Donatur,ᵈ idon, an t-oċtṁaḋ abb doḃi imMainiſtir
Poil 7 Pheadair i n-Ard-Maċa, quieuit et Patriciuſ
hUa Muireaḋaiġ, idon, prioir an tiġe cetna, do toġa
cum na habḋaine et benedictur eſt reſ manuſ Mael-
patricii, epiſcopi Rapotenſiſ.ᵈ)

B62d[biſ.] Kal. Ian. (f.ᵃ 7, l. 1ᵃ) Anno Domini M.º cc.º L.ᵒ ui.ᵒ
Ruaiḋri hUa¹ Ġaḋra, ri Sleiḃe-Luġa, do marbaḋ la
Daiḃiċ, mac Ricaird Cuiſin.—Floirint Maġ Fhloinḋ,
airderic Tuama-da-ġualann, quieuit in [Chriſto].—

A.D. 1254. ¹Mael—, B. ᵇom., A, B, D; "died," C. ᶜ⁻ᶜom.,
A; given in B, C, D. ᵈ⁻ᵈom., B, C, D. ᵉ⁻ᵉn. t. h., A; om., B, C, D.

A.D. 1255. ¹Oilḟinn, A.—ᵃ⁻ᵃn. t. h. on blank space, A; blank left in
B (with the same signification to 1260, inclusive). ᵇom., B, C, D.
ᶜ⁻ᶜom., A; given in B, C, D. ᵈ⁻ᵈn. t. h., A; om., B, C, D.

A.D. 1256. ¹O, A.

1254 ¹[*Son, etc.*] — The bracketted words are taken from the *A. L. C.* (*ad an.*); according to which Donchadh and Amlaim were defeated and slain by Cathal O'Conor, at Cloone, co. Leitrim.

² *Tower of valour.* — "The threshold of manhood"! C. Vir magnae estimacionis! D.

³ *Sunday.*—May 3 fell on that day in 1254; which shows that the additional item (not given in the *A. L. C.*, or the *Four Masters*) is correctly dated.

1254. Murchadh Ua Mail-[S]echlainn rested in Christ. —Donnchadh, son of Donnchadh, [son[1] of Gilla-Isa, son of Donchadh O'Raighillaigh] and Amlaim Ua Bibsaigh were killed by the Connachtmen.—Aindiles Ua Inneirghi, tower of valour[2] of the North of Ireland, died.—Dedication of the Church of St. Patrick in Dublin.

(Lightning fire [came] on the night of Sunday,[3] on the feast of the Cross in Summer [May 3], in the town of the Ui-Ruadhagan, at the Wood of Conall and nine persons were burned in a house there.)

Kalends of Jan. (on 6th feria, 20th of the moon,) A.D. 1255. Pope Innocent [IV.] rested in Christ.[1]—Thomas Mac Diarmata, archdeacon[2] of Oil-finn, died.—Donnsleibe Ua Flainn, abbot of the Monastery of [SS.] Paul and Peter in Ard-Macha, died.

(Donatus,[3] namely, the eighth abbot that was in the Monastery of Paul and Peter in Ard-Macha, rested and Patrick Ua Muireadhaigh, namely, prior of the same House, was chosen to the abbacy and he was blessed by the hands of Mael-Patraic [Ua Sgannuil], bishop of Rathboth.)

Kalends of Jan. (on 7th feria, 1st of the moon), A.D. 1256. Ruaidhri Ua Gadhra, king of Sliabh-Lugha, was killed by David, son of Richard Cussen.—Florence Mag Floinn, archbishop of Tuaim-da-ghualann, rested in Christ.[1]—The Muinnter-Raghallaigh were killed by Aedh,

---

1255. [1] *Rested in Christ.*—This is erroneous; Innocent IV. died in Naples, Dec. 7, 1254. The *A. L. C.* also give his obit under 1255.

[2] *Archdeacon.*—The *Four Masters*, against A, B, C, D and the *A. L. C.*, call him herensgh.

[3] *Donatus.*—The *Donnsleibhe* of the preceding entry; *Donatus* being the meaningless Latin alias.

1256. [1] *Rested in Christ.*—At Bristol, according to the *A. L. C.* (*ad an.*). On June 29, 1256, the Dean and Chapter of Tuam re-

Muinnter-Raȝallaiȝ do marbad le hAed, mac Feidlimthe² hUi Conchobuir (7° le Conchubur, mac Tiȝernain hUi Ruairc°), idon, Cathal 7 Domnaill 7 Cu-Connacht 7 in ȝilla caech 7 Ȝarffraiȝ 7 maithi Muin[n]teri-Raȝallaiȝ³ 7 hUa¹-m-briuin uile ar aen lathair aȝ Allt-na-heillti, or bealuch-na-beithiȝe, i cinn Sleibe-in-iarainn. Domarbadur Muinnter-Raȝallaiȝ³ Diarmait hUa¹ Flannaȝ[i]n 7 Flann Maȝ Oirechtaiȝ 7 Murchad finn hUa Ferȝail. Doȝonadur 7 domarbadar daine imda[i] eili nach airmiter⁴ funn.

(Raiȝned,ᵈ airderp[s]or Airḋ-Macha, ḋh'ec i¹in Roim.ᵈ)

Kal. Ian. (f.ᵃ 2, l. 12ᵃ), Anno Domini M.° cc.° L° uii.°

(A.)
Muirir Mac Ȝeraild quieuit in [Christo].— Cairlen Cail-uirci do leaȝad le ȝoffraiȝ O n-Domnaill 7 techt ar a aithle dó 7 do Ceniul-Conaill d'innroiȝid Shliȝiȝ 7 do comfaic re ȝallaib in baile

(B.)
Ieoan° birret, malartach ceall 7 ȝaeidel, rubita morte reruit.— Muirir Mac Ȝeraild, iurtir Erenn ri head, dirfailted ȝaeidel 7 ceall n-Erenn, mortuur ert.— Scainner croda do tabairt do Shof-

A.D. 1256. ²—miȝ, B. ³ Raȝillaiȝ, A. ⁴ airmiter, B.—ᵇ opposite this entry, l. m., n. t. h., is Cat Muiȝe—Slecht—*Battle of Magh-Slecht*. A In B, r. m., t. h., Marbad Mhuinnteri—Raȝallaiȝ—*Slaying of Muinnter. Rugallaigh*. ᶜ⁻ᶜ itl, n. t. h., A; om., B, C, D. ᵈ⁻ᵈ n. t. h., A; om., B, C, D.

A.D. 1257. ᵃ C and D follow B.

ceived through Reginald, chaplain and Maurice Lumbard, clerk, royal licence to elect an archbishop. The choice fell upon a Franciscan, James O Lachtnain. The king assented on Oct. 16, and wrote to the Pope to confirm the postulation (*D. I.*, III. 507-21).

² *Allt-na-heillti*.—*Height of the Doe*.

³ *Belach-na-beithighe*.—*Pass of the birch (tree)*. Apud vallem [!] na Hally, prope viam na betbij. D.

⁴ *Sliabh-in-iaraian*.—*Mountain of Iron*.

⁵ *Persons*.—The remaining words

son of Feidhlimidh Ua Conchobuir (and by Conchubur, son of Tigernan Ua Ruairc). Namely, [those killed were] Cathal and Domnall and Cu-Connacht and the Blind Gillie and Geoffrey [Ua Raghallaigh] and all the nobles of Muinnter-Raghallaigh and the Ui-Briuin on one spot, at Allt-na-beillti,[2] over Belach-na-Bcithighe,[3] in front of Sliabh-in-iarainn.[4] The Muinnter-Raghallaigh killed Diarmait Ua Flannaga[i]n and Flann Mag Oirechtaigh and Murchadh Ua Ferghail the Fair. They [likewise] wounded and killed many other persons[5] that are not reckoned here.

(Raighned,[6] archbishop of Ard-Macha, died in Rome.)

Kalends of Jan. (on 2nd feria, 12th of the moon,) A.D. 1257.

(A)
Maurice Fitz Gerald rested in Christ.[1] — The Castle of Narrow-Water was levelled by Geoffrey O'Domnaill and he and the Cenel-Conaill came therefrom on the morrow, to attack Sligech. And he met with the Foreigners of the town and

(B)
John Bisset, destroyer of churches and of Gaidhil, perished by a sudden death. Maurice Fitz Gerald, Justiciary of Ireland for a time, dissolver of the Gaidhil and of the churches of Ireland, died.—A courageous encounter was fought by

---

are omitted in D, which adds: O Donil Goffredus cum magno exercitu perlustrauit patrias de Fearmanagh et Brieni O Roirke, ex quibus predas, redemptiones et obsides accepit et rediit.

This is given in substance by the F. M. under the present year.

[6] *Raighned.*—From a charter of assent (Oct. 2, 1254) to the election of the bishop of Meath (inserted in the Papal confirmation), which

begins with *Frater R.*, we learn that he was a friar, probably a Dominican. From the date of the royal licence to elect his successor, Feb. 20, 1257, it may be inferred that he died towards the close of 1256 (*D. I.*, III. 531).

1257. [1] *Rested in Christ.*—In the Franciscan (or south; to distinguish it from the north, or Dominican) Monastery of Youghal. C and D translate the B-text.

7 cuc maiom foppo ag Cpe-
opan-Cille, ipRop-ceipe,
1 Cpic-Caippi. Ocur vo-
gonaṫ hUa Domnaill ann
7 mina gabaic a gona
grema ve, pobiaṫ maiom
foppa co Muaiṫ. Ocur
voloiſeṫ 8ligeċ leo 7
vohairgeṫ (7ᵇ vogabaṫ mac
Grifin ann, ivon, pivipe
maiṫᵇ).— Cancobur, mac
Cigernain (hUiᵇ Ruaipcᵇ),
vo marbaṫ le Muinncip-
Raigillaig (ivon,ᵇ le Maṫa
hUa Raigillaigᵇ). — Cuc
O briain maiom mop ar
Ghallaiṫ irin bliaṫain pi.

fpaig hUa Domnaill, ri
Thipe-Conaill 7 vo Ghal-
laiṫ Connacṫ (ivon,¹ 1 Cpe-
opan-cilli, 1 Rop-ceivi, 1
Cpic-Caipppi¹) 7 maiṫm ar
na Gallaiṫ 7 tri pcic,¹ no
ni ar mo, vo marbaṫ vo na
Gallaiṫ. Ocur vogonaṫ O
Domnaill ann 7 Donncaṫ,
mac Cormaic hUi Dom-
naill, tuir einig 7 egnoma
Thipe-Conaill, vo guin annrein 7 a eg vi.—Caircel
Cail-uirci vo leagaṫ le
Gorfraig hUa n-Domnaill.
—Concobar, mac Cigernain, vo marbaṫ le Muinn-
cir-Ragallaig.—Cuc hUa
briain maiom mor arGhallaiṫ irin bliaṫain pi.

(Caṫal,ᵉ mac Aeṫa, mic Caṫail croibvergg, vo ṫallaṫ la hAeṫ O Concuḃair 7 Caṫal cuircec O Concuḃair vo ṫallaṫ mar aen pir.ᵉ—Abrahamᵈ hUa Conallan vo vul cum na Roma taperr a toig[ṫ]a cum airverpucoive Arva-Maca.—Macroḃiur, aḃ Cluana-Eoir, vh'ec.—Mael-Muire Mag Murchaiṫ, taireċ Muintire-birn, vo marbaṫ, ivon, o n-a braiṫriḃ fein, ig Cill-irrill.ᵈ)

A.D. 1257. ᵇ⁻ᵇitl., n. t. h., A. ᶜ⁻ᶜl. m., n. t. h., A; om., B, C, D.
ᵈ⁻ᵈn. t. h., A; om., B, C, D   ᶠ⁻ᶠr. m., t. h., B; om., C; aputd Creopan, D.

---

² *Cathal.* — Given at greater length in the *A. L. C.* (*ad an.*).

³ *Ua Conallan.*—According to a royal mandate (about Feb. 6, 1257: *D. I.,* III. 569) regulating the issues and rents of the See during his detention in Rome, O'Conallan had been arch-presbyter of Armagh.

On Dec. 21, 1258, he obtained permission from Alexander IV. to borrow 500 marks sterling for the use of his diocese (Theiner, p. 30-1).

⁴ *Macrobius.*—Made into *Mac*

inflicted defeat upon them at Credran-cille, in Ros-cheidi, in the country of Cairpre. And O'Domnaill was wounded there and had his wounds not taken hold of him, there would have been defeat [inflicted] upon them to the [river] Muaidh. And Sligech was burned by them and pillaged. (And Mac Grifin, namely, a good knight, was taken prisoner there.)—Conchobur, son of Tigernan (Ua Ruairc), was killed by the Muinnter-Raighillaigh (namely, by Matthew Ua Raighillaigh). —O'Briain gave a great defeat to the Foreigners in this year.

Geoffrey Ua Domnaill, king of Tir-Conaill and the Foreigners of Connacht (namely, in Credran-cilli, in Ros-cheidi, in the territory of Cairpre). And defeat was inflicted upon the Foreigners and three score, or something more, were killed of the Foreigners. And O'Domnaill was wounded there and Donnchadh, son of Cormac Ua Domnaill, tower of hospitality and valour of Tir-Conaill, was wounded there and he died thereof.—The castle of Narrow-Water was levelled by Geoffrey Ua Domnaill.—Conchobar, son of Tigernan, was killed by the Muinnter-Raghallaigh. —Ua Briain gave a great defeat to the Foreigners in this year.

[1257]

(Cathal,[2] son of Aedh, son of Cathal Red-hand, was blinded by Aedh O'Conchubair and Cathal O'Concubair the Long-haired, was blinded along with him.—Abraham Ua Conallan[3] went to Rome after his election to the archbishopric of Ard-Macha. — Macrobius,[4] abbot of Cluain-Eois, died.—Mael-Muire Mac Murchaidh, chief of Muinnter-Birn, was killed, namely, by his own kinsman, at Cell-issel.)

Robias by the *Four Masters* (ad an.). But such a native name does not exist. The abbot's designation in was religion *Macrobius*, perhaps

the martyr of Nicomedia, who is commemorated in the *Martyrology of Tallaght* at May 7 (*L.L.*, p. 360b).

A 61b Kal. 1an. (f.ᵃ 3, l. 23ᵃ) Anno Domini M.° cc.° L.° uiii.°
Goffraix hUa Domnaill, ri Thire-Conaill, quieuit in [Christo].—Siurtan Gaileang do marbad la Mac Somairlid ar oilén mara i n-1artar Connact 7 daine maiti imda eile araen¹ ris.—Sluax² mór la hAed, mac Feidlimte 7 la Tadg hUa³ m-Briain i coinne Briain hUi Néill co Cael-uirce (idon,ᵇ ag Leicc hUi Maeildoraixᵇ). Ocus tucadur na maiti sin uile ardcennur do Brian hUa³

B 63a Neill: idon, braixdi mic Feidlimte dóron 7 braixdi | Mhuinntiri-Ruixillaix d'Aed hUa Concobuir 7 braixdi hUa-m-Briuin uile o Chenannusᶜ co Druim-cliab.— Domnall hUa Domnaill do rixad an tan sin 7 tucsat Cenel-Conaill uile braixdi 7 tixernus dó.—Mac Craitᵈ Mag Thigernain, tairec Thellaix-Duncada, do marbad la Domnall Mac Tigernain.ᵈ—Amlaim, mac Airt, ri Breifne, quieuit in [Christo].—In manac hUa³ Cuirnin quieuit in Christo.

A.D. 1258. ¹araen, B. ²Sluagad, B. ³O, A. ⁴Cheanannsur! B. ᵇ⁻ᵇitl., n. t. h., A; om., B, C, D. ᶜom., B. ᵈ⁻ᵈom., D.

1258. ¹ *Ua Domnaill.*—Thus in D: O'Donnill Goffredus[-o] sub cura medicorum toto anno existente in Insula Lochbeatha post bellum Credrayn, Brien O'Neill, collecto magno exercitu ad invadendum Connalliam, missis nunciis ad O'Donill petiit ab eo submissionem et obedientiam, una cum obsidibus ab inhabitantibus Tire Connill pro continuanda obedientia, ipsis tunc non habentibus competentem dominum ex illa generatione post Goffredum. Et aliquali responso dato nunciis, ipse Goffredus in articulo mortis existens iussit tot quot vixerunt in Connallia viros habiles ad arma gerenda ad eum venire. Quibus ita collectis, ipse Goffredus, cum aliter eos precedere non posset, iussit corpus suum in feretro cum quo ad sepulturam mortuos ferre solent, poni et sic asportari ad resistendum Brien O'Neill.

Quo facto, exhortavit suos viriliter resistere eorum inimicis, quamdiu spiritus in eius corpore remaneret. Et sic in magna fiducia per gentes obviam dederunt inimicis apud flumen Soilli [Swilly]. Et fortiter hinc inde decertantibus, tandem O'Neillius coactus [est] redire, relictis multis occisis cum ingenti numero equorum. Et redeuntibus O'Donill cum suis, adeptâ illâ fortunatâ victoriâ, prostrato feretro, in quo Goffredus ad tunc vivens existit, apud Congawill[Conghbhail; Con-

Kalends of Jan. (on 3rd feria, 23rd of the moon), A.D. [1258] 1258. Geoffrey Ua Domnaill,[1] king of Tir-Conaill, rested in Christ.—Jordan Gaileang [de Exeter] was killed by Mac Somhairlidh on an island of the sea in the West of Connacht and many other good people [were killed] along with him.— A great host [was led] by Aedh, son of Feidhlimidh [Ua Conchobhair] and by Tadhg Ua Briain, to meet Brian Ua Neill, to Narrow-Water (namely, at the Flagstone of Ua Maeldoraigh). And all those nobles gave the arch-headship to Brian Ua Neill: that is, the hostages of the son of Feidhlimidh [were given] to him [Brian] and the hostages of Muinnter-Raighillaigh [were given] to Aedh Ua Conchobuir and the hostages of all Ui-Briuin from Cenannus to Druim-cliabh.[2]—Domnall Ua Domnaill was made king that time and all Cenel-Conaill gave pledges and lordship to him.—Mac Craith Mag Tigernain, chief of Tellach-Dunchadha, was killed by Domnall Mac Tigernain.— Amlaim, son of Art, king of Breifni, rested in Christ.— The monk, Ua Cuirnin, rested in Christ.

---

wal, near Letterkenny], in ipso instanti ex convulsione vulneris recepti in bello Credrayn emisit spiritum. Qui in morte, sicuti in vita, fortem et strenuum se mundo ostendit, habita victoria contra suos aduersarios cunctos usque ad horam illam et in ipsa hora.

The original, which is somewhat more diffuse, is given by the *Four Masters* at this year.

[2] *Drum-cliabh.* — D goes on, omitting the next entry : Tandem O'Neillius petiit subiectionem et obsides ab inhabitantibus Connalliae, qui, obtento certo tempore, consultantes [-tabant] quem eligerent in gubernatorem, quia nullum habuerunt ante dominum a morte Goffredi. Interim Donaldus Iuuenis O'Donill venit ex Scotia anno aetatis decimo octavo. Cui statim omnes Connalliae inhabitantes voluntariam et promptam supremitatem et obedientiam prestarunt, nemini id admirante, cum ipse Donaldus heres legittimus illius patrie existeret. Et ad inde nullos obsides dederunt O'Nellio, aut alicui, Donaldo veniente. Cuius adventus ita opportunus et necessarius pro tunc assimulatum fuit aduentui *Twoweill Teachtmair* ex transmarinis regionibus post dispersionem et anihillationem eius [Tuathalii] gentis. Qui statim accepit totius regni supremam regalitatem; deinceps uniendo et

(Tomaltac͡° hUa Conc͡ubaip do t͡oxa cum aipdeppcopoide Tuama. — Abpaham, aipdeppcop Apd-Maca,
pallium impetpatup a Cupia Romana et Mippam cum
eo celebpauit, quapto Nonap Iunii, apud Apdmacham.ᵃ)

}Cal. Ian. (p.ᵃ 4, l. 4,ᵃ) Anno Domini M.° cc.° ix.°
Cat͡al Mac Con[-Sh]nama do dallad.—Milid Mac
Soipte[i]lbᶦ quieuit in [Chpipto].—Sigpaid O baigill do
mapbad d'a bpait͡pib pein.—Dpaigoi hUa²-m-Dpiuin do
dallad la hAced, mac peidlimid.³—Copmac hUa Luimluin
eppuc Cluana-pepta, quieuit in [Chpipto] (iᵇ n-a peanoip
naeimeagnaigᵇ).

(Tomaltac͡,ᵇ mac Toippdealbaig, mic Mhailt͡peac-
lainn hUi Chonc͡ubaip, do gabail aipdeppcopoide Tuama.
—Tadg O Dpiain, adbup pi Muman, dh'ecᵇ).

A.D. 1258. ᵃ⁻ᵃ n. t. h., A; om., B, C, D.
A.D. 1259. ¹ Soipteald, B. ² O, A. ³ Peidlim, A. ᵇ⁻ᵇ n. t. h., A; om., B, C, D.

defendendo suam patriam contra exteros usque ad finem suae vitae·

The original, which is more prolix, forms in the *Four Masters* a continuation of the account given in the preceding Note. Donal, according to Charles O'Conor, was son of Donal Mor by a daughter of Cathal Red-hand, king of Connacht.

In the second century, the Attacots cut off the Milesian nobility, with the exception of the queen, who was pregnant. She escaped to Scotland, where she gave birth to a son, Tuathal *Techtmar*, (*wealthy*). In time he returned: was received favourably and re-established the Milesian dynasty.

³ *Ua Conchubhair*.—On May 29, 1257, Alexander IV. set aside the election of James Ua Lachtnain (1156, note 1, *supra*) and appointed Walter, Dean of St. Paul's, London and Papal Chaplain, to the archbishopric of Tuam. Walter was consecrated by the Pope, most probably in Viterbo, where the Bull is dated. He died at latest early in the following year. On April 22, 1258, the archbishop being deceased, a royal mandate was issued to the escheator of Ireland to take the lands and tenements of the See into possession. (*D. I.*, III. 576.) O'Conor had been bishop of Elphin (*ib.* 621-2-4). He is called *Thomas* (the Latin name which most resembled *Tomaltach*) in the royal documents just referred to, and in

(Tomaltach Ua Conchubhair[3] was elected to the arch- [1258] bishopric of Tuaim.—Abraham, archbishop of Ard-Macha, obtains the Pallium from the Roman Curia and celebrated Mass therewith on the 4th of the Nones [2nd] of June,[a] at Ard-Macha.)

Kalends of Jan. (on 4th feria, 4th of the moon,) A.D. [1259] 1259. Cathal Mac Con[-Sh]nama was blinded.—Milidh Mac Goisdeilbh rested in Christ.—Sigraidh[1] O'Baighill was killed by his own kinsmen.—The hostages of the Ui-Briuin were blinded by Aedh, son of Feidhlimidh[2] [Ua Conchobair].—Cormac[3] Ua Luimluin, bishop of Cluain-ferta, rested in Christ (a holy-minded spiritual director).

(Tomaltach,[4] son of Toirrdhealbach, son of Mael-Seachlainn Ua Conchubhair, assumed the archbishopric of Tuaim.—Tadhg O'Briain, future king of Munster, died.)

a Brief of Alexander IV. (April 29, 1259), empowering him to contract a loan of 2,400 marks for diocesan purposes (Theiner, p. 81). Himself and two of the canons of Elphin were in the Curia at the time. They attended perhaps to procure confirmation of his election to Tuam.

[a] *2nd of June.*—It fell on Sunday in this year.

1259. [1] *Sigraidh.*—Thus in D: Sygray O'Broychill, subregulus trium Tuoha [of the three Territories], qui fuit vir bone fame et liberalitatis et summe estimationis in re militari, occisus fuit a propriis germanis fraudelenter.

A similar entry is given in the *Annals of Loch Ce* (ad an.).

[2] *Feidhlimidh.*—D adds: O'Donill, Donaldus Iuuenis, collecto magno exercitu, hostiliter invasit Tironiam et ex altera parte Hugo Flavus O'Neill venit in eius occursum cum consimili exercitu. Et insimul devastatâ undique patriâ illâ, progressi [sunt] ulterius devastando usque ad orientales limites Ultonie, habitâ undique victoriâ et obedientiâ, nemo [nemine] eis obsistente, usque dum redierunt.

The original is probably an entry in the *Four Masters* at this year.

[3] *Cormac.*—He died before July 20 of this year. On th..t day, royal licence was given to th Dean and Chapter to elect in place of Charles, late bishop of Clonfert (*D. I.*, III. 620).

[4] *Tomaltach.*—This (in greater detail) and the following item are in the *A. L. C.* (ad an.). *Assumed* means entered into possession of the See.

[b·ſ.] Kal. Ian. (ꝑ.ᵃ 5, l. 15,ᵃ) Anno Domini M.ᵒ cc.ᵒ lx.ᵒ Caṫ Droma-de[i]ꞃg (inᵇ loco qui dicitur Dromma-dergᵇ), ag Dun-da-leaṫglar tuc¹ brian hUa Neill 7 Aeḋ, mac Feiḋlimiḋ, do Ghallaiḃ Tuaiꞃce[i]ꞃt Erenn, ait i n-aꞃ-marbaḋ moran do ṁaitiḃ Gaiḋeal, idon, brian hUa² Neill 7 Domnall hUa² Caiꞃꞃe 7 Diarmait Mag Laċ-lainn 7 Magnur hUa³ Caṫa[i]n 7 Cian hUa² hInneiꞃġi 7 Donnrleiḃe Mag Cana 7 Concobur O Duiḋoirma 7 Aeḋ, a mac 7 Aṁlaim hUa² Gairmleaġaiḋ 7 Cú-Ulaḋ hUa² hAnluain. Aċt aen ní, romarbaḋ coic³ rir dég do ṁaitiḃ Cloinne-Caṫain ar an⁴ lataiꞃ rin. Romarbaḋ do Connactaiḃ annᵉ : Gilla Criꞃt, mac Concobaiꞃ, mic Cormaic hUi Mailruanaig,⁵ rí Muigi-Luirg 7 Caṫal, mac Tigernain hUi Concobaiꞃ 7 Maelruanaiḋ, mac Donncaḋa 7 Caṫal, mac Donncaḋa, mic Muiꞃceꞃtaig 7

A 61c Aeḋ, mac | Muiꞃceꞃtaig finn 7 Taḋg, mac Caṫail, mic briain hUi Mailruanaiḋ 7 Diarmait, mac Taiḋg, mic Muiꞃeḋaig, mic Tomaltaig hUi Mailruanaig 7 Conco-bur Mac Gille-Arraiṫ 7 Taḋg, mac Cein hUi Gaḋra 7 Gilla-beraig hUa Cuind 7 daine imda aili.⁶—Domnall,

B 63b mac Concobuiꞃ, | mic Tigernain, do marbaḋ la Teallaċ-n-Dunċaḋa.—Abratam hUa² Conalla[i]n, comarba Patraig,⁷ in Christo quieuit.

(Aoḋᵈ buiḋe hUa Neill du rigaḋ ꝼor Thir-n-Eugain.ᵉ)

Kal. Ian. (ꝑ.ᵒ 7, l. 26ⁱ), Anno Domini M.ᵒ cc.ᵒ lx.ᵒ i.ᵒ Maiṫi cleireċ Cene[oi]l-Conaill do marbaḋ la Conco-

A.D. 1260. ¹tug, B. ²O, A. ³.u. (the Latin equivalent), A, B. ⁴in, A. ⁵Maeil—, B. ⁶eile, A. ⁷ꝑao—, A.—ᵇ⁻ᵇ itl, n. t. h., A ; om., B, C, D. ᵉ roon--*namely*—added, B. ᵈ n. t. h., A ; om., B, C, D.

1260. ¹*Nobles.* — "15 of the best," C ; quindecim selecti viri, D.

²*Rested in Christ.*—Apparently towards the close of the year. On Feb. 27, 1261, royal licence was given to elect his successor (D. I., III. 702).

D adds : Eodem anno, post Dunense bellum O'Donill cum suo exercitu invasit Eoganenses eosque cum igne et gladio devastauit et per continuas incursiones ferme depopulauit.

Kalends of Jan. (on 5th feria, 15th of the moon), A.D. [1260] 1260. The battle of Druim-derg [was fought] (in a place which is called Dromma-derg) at Dun-da-leathglas by Brian Ua Neill and Aedh, son of Feidhlimidh [Ua Conchobair], against the Foreigners of the North of Ireland, wherein were killed many of the nobles[1] of the Gaidhil, namely, Brian Ua Neill and Domnall Ua Cairre and Diarmait Mag Lachlainn and Maghnus Ua Catha[i]n and Cian Ua Inneirghi and Donnsleibhe Mag Cana and Concobur O'Duibhdirma and Aedh, his son, and Amlaim Ua Gairmleaghaidh and Cu-Uladh Ua hAnluain. But one [notable] thing [happened]: fifteen men of the nobles of Clann-Cathain were killed on that spot. There were killed of the Connachtmen there: Gilla-Crist, son of Conchobar, son of Cormac Ua Mailruanaigh and king of Magh-Luirg and Cathal, son of Tighernan Ua Conchobair and Maelruanaidh, son of Donnchadh [Ua Mailruanaigh] and Cathal, son of Donnchadh, son of Muircertach and Aedh, son of Muircertach the Fair and Tadhg, son of Cathal, son of Brian Ua Mailruanaigh and Diarmait, son of Tadhg, son of Muiredhach, son of Tomaltach Ua Mailruanaigh and Conchobur Mac Gille-Arraigh and Tadhg, son of Cian Ua Gadhra and Gilla-Beraigh Ua Cuinn and many other persons.—Domnall, son of Concobur, son of Tigernan [Ua Conchobair], was killed by the Tellach-Dunchadha.—Abraham Ua Conalla[i]n, successor of Patrick, rested in Christ.[2]

(Aedh Ua Neill the Tawny was made king over Tir-Eoghain.)

Kalends of Jan. (on 7th feria, 26th of the moon), A.D. 1261. [1261] The [most] worthy[1] of the clergy of Cenel-Conaill were

---

1261. [1] *The [most] worthy.*—Literally, *the good (clergy)*, κατ' 'εξοχήν. | They had probably assembled for some ecclesiastical function.

bur hUa Neill 7 pe Cenel-Eogain i n-Óoipe Coluim-cille, im Choncobuṙ hUa pṙɼiL. Concobur hUa Neill ꝺo marbaṙ ꝺono[b] a cetoip ꞇpe mipbuil Coluim-cille la Ꝺonn hUa[1] m-Ḃpeirlen, ꞇaipeċ Ḟána[i]ꞇ.—Caṫal hUa heɼpa ꝺo marbaṙ ꝺo Ɣhallaiḃ.—Sluaɼ[c] la hCCeṙ, mac Ḟeiꝺlimċe, 'rin m-Ḃpeiṙne, ɼup'loiṙc bailꞇi imḋa 7 apbanna. Córꞇur maṫma ꝺo ṫabaipꞇ ap ꝺpéim ꝺ'a púꞇaiḃ, ɼup'marbaṙ moran ꝺiḃ°.—Seón Ḟi[ꞇz] Ꞇomar[1] 7 in ḃarpaċ mór ꝺo marbaṙ la Ḟinɼin Maɼ Carrċaiɼ 7 la Ꝺearmuimneċaiḃ[e] arċena 7 moran ꝺo Ɣhallaiḃ ailiḃ.[2]—Ḟinɼin, Ma[c][3] Carrċaiɼ[3] ꝺo marbaṙ la Ɣallaiḃ.—CCeṙ buiṙe hUa[1] Neill expulrur[e] erꞇ[e] 7 Niall Culanaċ O Neill (ḟraꞇer[e] Oꝺonir[e]) ꝺo pɼaṙ.—Niall hUa[1] Ɣaipmleɼaiṙ, ꞇaipeċ Ceniuil-Moain, morꞇuur eṙꞇ.—Ṗilib Mac Cinaeṫa,[4] ꞇaipeċ an ꞇpiċa-ceꞇ, occirur erꞇ per Ɣilla-Mupa hUa[1] Caipre.

(Paꞇpiciur[b] (iꝺon,[1] Mael-Paꝺpaiɼ') hUa Sɼanuil, epircopur Raꞇhpoꞇeirir, elecꞇur erꞇ concorꝺiꞇer in arċiepircopum Apꝺmachanum eꞇ pporeɋuuꞇur ḟuiꞇ elecꞇionem ꝺe re ḟacꞇam aꝺ Seꝺem Aporꞇolicam.—Amalɼaiṙ hUa Ruaꝺaɼan, riɼ hO-ḃeaꞇaċ, ꝺo ṁarbaṙ per Ꝺonaꞇum hUa Caipre eꞇ Ꝺonaꞇur hUa Caipre ꝺo ṁarbaṙ ar in laṫaip ceꝺna[h].)

A.D. 1261. [1] O, A. [2] ḟi., B; eile, A. [3-3] Maɼ C—, B. [4] Cinaeꞇ, A. [a-a] n. t. h. on blank space (for 26 the MS. has 23, the scribe having misread the *xxvi.* of his text as *xxiii.*), A; blank in B. In B, C, D, the CCeṙ buiṙe and Niall entries are placed after the Marꞇi item. [b] om., A. [c-c] om., B, C, D. [d] In A a blank=two letters is left between Ḟi and Ꞇomar. Seon Ḟi ocur Ꞇomar—*John Fi and Thomas* (Fi)! B. [e] Ꝺer-Mhumain—*Desmond*, B. [f] n. t. h. on blank left by t. h., A. [g-g] itl., n. t. h., A; om., B, C, D. [h-h] n. t. h., A; om., B, C, D. [i] itl. by the hand that wrote the additional entry.

---

[2] *Donn.*—Called *Domnall* by mistake in the *A. L. C.* (*ad an.*).

[3] *John Fitz-Thomas.*—C, following B, has: "John Fy and Thomas!" D, however, is far worse; Carolus O'Gara occisus fuit per Soen Fith Seon et Thomas Fith Thomas; in quo anno Bar-

killed by Conchobur Ua Neill and by the Cenel-Eogain in Doire of [St.] Colum-cille, around Conchobur Ua Firghil. Conchobur Ua Neill was, however, killed immediately, through miracle of Colum-cille by Donn[2] Ua Breslen, chief of Fanat.—Cathal Ua Egbra was killed by Foreigners.— A hosting [was made] by Aedh, son of Feidlimidh [Ua Conchobhair], into Breifni, so that he burned many towns and the crops. Complete defeat was given to a force of his routs, so that a great number of them were killed.— John Fitz Thomas[3] and the Barrymore were killed by Finghin Mag Carrthaigh and by the Desmonians likewise and a large number of other Foreigners [were killed].— Finghin Mac Carrthaigh was killed by the Foreigners.— Aed Ua Neill the Tawny was expelled and Niall Culanach O'Neill (brother of Aedh) made king.—Niall Ua Gairmlegaidh, chief of Cenel-Moain, died.—Philip Mac Cinaetha, chief of the Cantred, was slain by Gilla-Muire Ua Cairre.[4]

(Patrick (that is, Mael-Padraig) Ua Sganuil, bishop of Rath-both, was elected unanimously as archbishop of Ard-Macha and he defended[5] at the Apostolic See the election made of himself.—Amalgaidh Ua Ruadhagan, king of Ui-bhEathach, was killed by Donatus Ua Cairre and Donatus Ua Cairre was killed on the same spot.)

[1261]

---

ragh more occisus fuit per Fynioum Makartii et Desmonienses et alios Anglicanos.

The A-text shows that O'Hara (Ua Eagbra) was not killed by John or Thomas; that the slayers in D had no existence; that John Fitz Thomas, as well as Barrymore, was slain by Mac Carthy; finally, that "the other English," instead of assisting to kill Barrymore, were killed themselves.

[4] *Ua Cairre.*—D adds: Eodem anno, O'Donill, videlicet Donaldus Oge, obtinuit magnam victoriam adversus Niellanum Culanagh O'Neill, in qua non solum multi erant occisi, verum etiam magnus erat numerus captivorum Eoganensium quos O'Donill secum adduxit ex illa victoria, una cum Makawal [Mac Cathmhail], subregulo Generationis Fearaii [Cenel-Feradhaigh].

The original is the final entry of this year in the *Four Masters.*

[5] *Defended.*—That is, attended at the Curia to secure confirmation of his election. He was at the Papal Court at the time.

332   αnnαlα ulαδh.

Kal. 1an. (p.⸱ 1, l; 7, aliap 4ᵃ) Anno Domini m.° cc.ʳ lx.°
11.° Sluaᵇ mop le Mac Uilliam i Connaċtaiḃ, gup-
milleḋ mopan leip. Peiḋlimiḋ hUa Conċobuip 7 Aeḋ,
a mac 7 maiċi Sil-Muipeḋaiᵹ do dul co hEp-puaiḋ
pompo co hupmóp bó Connaċt leo ap a ṡaṡaḋ, co n-
depnpat piḋᵇ.—Cpeaċ móp do ḋenum la hAeḋ, mac
Peiḋlimċe,¹ ap Gallaiḃ Sléiḃe-Luṡa 7 a Ciapaiḋe, co
tucpat buap imḋa leo 7 po mapbpat Goill imḋa.—
Mael-Seaċlainn, mac Taiḋᵹ hUi Conċobaip, | eppuc Oil-
find, in Chpipto quieuit.—Copmac, mac Domnaill
ᵹuid Meᵹ Cappċaiᵹ, do mapbuḋ le Gallaiḃ.

[A.D. M.° cc.ʳ lx.° 111.] Domnall hUa² Domnaill do mapbaḋ (Dhuinn⸱) Ο⸱ [Ui] Ḃpeiplen i³ cuipt in eppuic ipRaiċ-
boċ.—Daḃiḋ hUa Find, ab na Ḃuille, in Chpipto quieuit.
—Diapmait, mac Copmaic, quieuit in [Chpipto].—
Aenᵹur hUa² Clumain, eppuc Luiᵹne, quieuit in
[Chpipto].—Tomap hUa² Ceallaiᵹ, eppuc Cluana-pepta
quieuit in [Chpipto].—Eḃdonn, pi Loċlann, do éᵹ i n-
inpib Opc ic⁴ teċt a n-Epinn.—Sampaḋ te ipin bliaḋain
pi.—Donnpleibe Mac Caṫmail, taipeċ Ceniuil-

A.D. 1262. ¹—Limiḋ, B. ²O, A. ³a, B. ⁴iᵹ, A. ᵃᵃ n. t. h. on blank
space (The alternative reading refers to the epact 23[+11—30=4], erroneously given as that of the preceding year.), A; blank space left in B.
ᵇ⁻ᵇom., B, C, D (in which the Donnpleibe and Aeḋ buiḋe follow the Cpeaċ
item). In A, the original reading was do mapbaḋ do Donn O Ḃpeiplen

---

1262. ¹ *Mael-Sechlainn.*— Before this entry another hand placed (q.⸱ [aere] 1263) on the margin of C; meaning that the remaining items belonged perhaps to that year.

[1263] ¹ *Domnall.* — Here the A. L. C. begin 1263 with the annual luni-solar criteria. The re-adjustment of the chronology, chiefly in accordance with the A. L. C., is given within square brackets. Confirmatory data are set forth under the several years. The textual arrangement has thus been preserved intact. The original dates (placed within round brackets on the margin) are, as a rule, correct in reference to the later items. The additions, namely, were made under the respective years to which they were considered to belong.

Kalends of Jan. (on 1st feria; 7th, otherwise 4th, of the moon), A.D. 1262. A great host [was led] by Mac William [de Burgh] into Connacht, so that much was destroyed by him. Feidhlimidh Ua Conchobuir and Aedh, his son and the nobles of Connacht went to Es-ruadh before them with very great part of the cows of Connacht with them for the war, so that they made peace.—A great foray was made by Aedh, son of Feidhlimidh, on the Foreigners of Sliabh-Lugha and into Ciaraidhe, so that they took many cows away with them and killed many Foreigners.—Mael-Sechlainn,[1] son of Tadhg Ua Conchobair, bishop of Oilfinn, rested in Christ.—Cormac, son of Domnall Mag Carrthaigh the Stammerer, was killed by Foreigners.

[A.D. 1263] Domnall[1] Ua Domnaill killed Donn O'Breislen in the court of the bishop in Rath-both.— David Ua Finn, abbot of the Buill, rested in Christ.— Diarmait, son of Cormac [Mac Diarmata], rested in Christ. —Aengus Ua Clumain, bishop of Luighni [Achonry], rested in Christ.—Thomas Ua Ceallaigh, bishop of Cluainferta, rested in Christ.[2]—Ebdonn,[3] king of Lochlann, died in the Isles of Orc in coming to Ireland.—A hot Summer in this year.[4]—Donnsleibe Mac Cathmail, chief of Cenel-

[1262]

[1263]

C and D represent O'Donnell as slain by O'Breslen. This error has been dealt with in the textual note c-c.

[2] *Rested in Christ.*—The Dean and Chapter of Clonfert wrote for royal licence to elect, Thomas, the bishop, having died on the Epiphany [Jan. 6], 1263 (*D. I.*, III. 742). This goes to prove that the *Loch Ce* chronology is correct at this year.

[3] *Ebdonn.*—"According to the *Saga Hakonar Hakonarsonar*, the Irish had sent ambassadors to king Hakon, offering to submit themselves to him, if he would come and expel the English. See *Saga Hakonar Hakonarsonar*, c. 322 (Fornmanna Sögur. Kaupmannahöfn, 1835, vol. 10, p. 131) and Munch's *Norske Folks Historie*, Christiania, 1858, vol. i., part iv., p. 407. The Chron. Mannie at 1263 says: Venit Haco, rex Norwegiae, ad partes Scotiae (i.e. Hiberniae?) et nihil expediens reversus est ad Orcades et ibidem apud Kirkwall mortuus." Note by Editor of *A. L. C.* (*in loco*).

[4] *This year.*—D adds: In quo

ꞅepaḃaiᵹ, occiꞅuꞃ eꞃc ꞃeꞃ Aeḋ buiḋe.—Aeḋ buiḋe
icepum ꞇo ꞃiᵹaḋ 7 Niall Culanaċ ꞇo ınnapḃaḋ.

(ꞅaꞇꞃıcıuꞅ,ᵃ iꞇon, Mael-ꞃaꞇꞃaiᵹ, hUa 8ᵹannuil,
apchıeꞅıꞅcoꞅuꞅ Apꞇ[a]-Maċa, aꞃ ꞃaḋa Aiꞅꞅꞃınn cum
pallio, in cꞃaꞅꞇino Iohannıꞅ ḃaꞅꞇıꞅꞇ[a]e ı n-Apꞇ-Maċa.
—Aꞃ moꞃ aꞃ ḋaınıḃ an bliaḋain ꞅı ꞇo ꞅlaıᵹ 7 ꞇo
ᵹoꞃꞇaᵈ.)

Kal. Ian. (ꞅ.ᵃ 2, l. 18,ᵃ) Anno Domini M.º cc.º lx.º ııı.ᵇ
[-u.ᶜ]. Feiḋlim[ıḋ] hUa Choncoḃuıꞃ, aıꞃꞇꞃı Connaċc, in¹
ꞇ-aen ᵹaıḋel ꞃoḃ' ꞅeꞃꞃ² maıꞇ[ı]uꞅ ꞇoḃı⁴ i³ n-Eꞃınn ı n-a
ꞃéımeꞃ ꞅein, moꞃꞇuuꞅ eꞅc.—Caċal, mac Caıꞇᵹ hUı
Concoḃaıꞃ, ꞇo maꞃḃaḋ le hAeḋ hUa Concoḃaıꞃ.—
Tómaꞅ hUa⁴ Maıcın, eꞅꞃuc Luıᵹne, quıeuıꞇ ınᵉ [Chꞃıꞅꞇo].
—Tomáꞅ, mac Pheꞃᵹaıl Mıc Diaꞃmaꞇa, eꞅꞃuc Oıl-
ꞅınꞇ, quıeuıꞇ ınᵉ [Chꞃıꞅꞇo].—Caıꞅlen 8lıᵹıᵹ ꞇo leaᵹaḋ
la hAeḋ, mac Feıḋlımċe⁵ 7 le Doṁnall hUa n-Doṁ-
naıll.—Muıꞃeḋac hUa⁴ Ceꞃbaıll, ꞇaıꞅeċ Calꞃaıᵹı⁶;
Caċal Maᵹ Raᵹnaıll, ꞇaıꞅeċ Muınnꞇeꞃı-hEolaıꞅ,
quıeueꞃunꞇ in [Chꞃıꞅꞇo].—ᵹılla-na-Naem hUa⁴ Cuinn,
ꞇaıꞅeċ Muınnꞇeꞃı-ᵹıllᵹa[ı]n, moꞃꞇuuꞅ eꞅc.—Fꞃaꞇeꞃ

—*Domnall was killed* (lit. *to be killed*) *by Donn O'Breislen*. Do was marked
underneath by the text hand, to shew that it was to be omitted (the meaning
thus being that Donn was killed by Domnall). But the scribe forgot to
change Donn O into the genitive, Duınn Uı. Then the later hand under-
marked Donn and placed Dhuınn hUı Leıꞅ overhead, making the sense:
(*Domnall Ua Domnaill* [nom. abs.], *the killing of Donn Ua Breislen* [*was
done*] *by him*. In B (followed by C, D) ꞇo Donn hUa Bꞃeıꞅlen—*by Donn
Ua Breislen*—is given. But the slayer, as appears from an entry under
the next year, was O'Donnell. ᵈ⁻ᵈ n. t. h., A; om., B, C, D.

A.D. 1263. ¹ an, A. ² ꞅeaꞃꞅ, A. ³ a, A. ⁴ O, A. ⁵ Feiḋlım, B. ⁶ -ꞇḋe, B.
ᵃ⁻ᵃ n. t. h., on blank space, A; blank in B. ᵇ Above the date a modern
hand placed 1265, B. In C, another hand added (*rectius* 1265). The
Tomaꞅ (*bis*), ᵹılla-na-naeṁ and Caċal Maᵹ Raᵹnaıll entries are
omitted in D. ᶜ om., B.

| O'Donill, collecto magno exercitu, | I Roirk et Asperam Tertiam |
| invasit Fearmanagh [et] Breniffiam | [Garb-Trian] Connacie usque ad |

Feradhaigh, was slain by Aedh [Ua Neill] the Tawny.— Aedh the Tawny again became king and Niall Culanach was expelled.

(Patrick, that is, Mael-Padraig, Ua Sganuil, archbishop of Ard-Macha, said Mass with the Pallium on the morrow [of the feast] of John the Baptist[1] [Sunday, June 25] in Ard-Macha.—Great destruction [was inflicted] on people this year by plague and by famine.)

[The original entries under 1263 belong to 1265.]

Kalends of Jan. (on 2nd feria, 18th of the moon), A.D. 1263[1][-5]. Feidhlimidh Ua Conchobuir, arch-king of Connacht, the Gaidhel of most goodness that was in Ireland in his own period, died.—Cathal, son of Tadhg Ua Conchobuir was killed by Aedh Ua Conchobair.—Thomas Ua Maicin, bishop of Luighni [Achonry], rested in Christ.[2] —Thomas, son of Ferghal Mac Diarmata, bishop of Oilfinn,[3] rested in Christ.—The castle of Sligech was levelled by Aedh, son of Feidhlimidh and by Domnall Ua Domnaill.—Muiredhach Ua Cerbaill, chief of Calraighe; Cathal Mag Raghnaill, chief of Muinnter-Eolais, rested in Christ.—Gilla-na-naem Ua Cuinn, chief of Muinnter-

---

Granardiam. Et obtenta victoria et obsidibus undique, rediit absque ulla resistentia.

The original is given at 1262 in the *Four Masters*.

(1262) [1] *Morrow of John the Baptist*.—The *Four Masters* read *in the Octave*; which is meaningless here. The Chronicler noted the day, which, being Sunday, was naturally selected for the first appearance of the archbishop in the Pallium.

[1265] [1] *1263*.—The entries of this (textual) year are dated 1265 in the *A. L. C.* For the correctness thereof, see Notes 2, 3, 5, *infra*.

[2] *Rested in Christ*.—In a letter, given in the church of Achonry on the morrow of Trinity Sunday [Monday, June 1], 1265, the Dean and Chapter pray for royal licence to elect, by reason of the death of Bishop Thomas (*D. I.*, II. 774).

[3] *Bishop of Oilfinn*.—Towards the end of 1265, the Dean and Chapter of Elphin pray for royal licence to elect in place of Thomas, the late bishop (*D. I.*, II. 781). It was

ρατρισιυρ Ο Sgannail, airoerpuc Cīroa-Maċa, ap⁴ n-oenam⁴ Caiboleaċ coitcinne a n-Oroiċeat-áta in bliaδain ρι (ρeρia* ρecunoa, τερτia et quarta ρort ρertum Omnium Sanctorum*).

(Oono' hUa Upeiρlen oo ṁaρbaδ la Oomnall hUa n-Oomnaill i Raiċ-boċ i cúiρt an eaρρuiξ.—Ceδ buiδe hUa Neill oo ċabaiρt inξine Mic Soiroealbaiξ in uxorem'.)

[b₁ρ.] Kal. Ian. [ρ.ᵃ 111., L. xxix.*], Cnno Oomini m.° cc.° lx.° 1111.°ᵇ Oomnall hUa heξρa,¹ ρι Luiξne, oo maρbaδ oo Shallaiδ.—Maċgamain, mac Ceiċeρnaiξ hUi Cheiρin, ρι Ciaρaiδe, oo maρbaδ oo Shallaiδ.—Cúṁuiδe hUa² Caċa[i]n, ρι Cian[n]aċt, captur ert ρeρ Ooneṁ' ρlauum.°

(A)   (B)

(A)	(B)
Ciroerpuc Croa-Maċa, ioon, M a e l - ρ a τ ρ a i c O Sgannail, oo δenum oiξe τimcell Croa-Maċa 7 bρaiċρi Minuρa oo ċabaiρt co hCρo-Maċa leρin ρear cetna iρin bliaδain ρi.	Uρaiċρi Minúρa oo ċabaiρt co hCρo-Maċa leρin airoerρcop, ioon, le Mael-ρaoρaiξ hUa Sgannail 7 an ρeρ cetna, ioon, Mael-ρaoρaiξ, oo δenum oiξe τimceall Croa-Maċa in bliaδain ρi.

A D. 1263. ᵈ⁻ᵈ oo δenaṁ, B. ᶜ⁻ᶜ itl., n. t. h., A; om., B, C, D. ᶠᶠ n. t. h., A; om., B, C, D.

A.D. 1264. ¹ hEaξρa, B. ² O, A. ᵃ⁻ᵃ Blank space, A, B (with the same meaning down to the textual year 1314, inclusive). ᵇ 1266 overhead, n. t. h., B; *alias* 1266, C. ᶜ⁻ᶜ Ceδ buiδe (the Irish equivalent), B.

---

granted through Maurice, their clerk (*ib.*, 786-7).

ᵃ *This year.*—D adds: In quo O'Donill cum magno exercitu ivit in occursum Odonis I Conchuir ad Coresleave, exinde ad Cruaghan et ultra flumen Suka ad Clan-Ricard, usque ad montes Eaghtai. Et in reditu ad Galliviam et Odone O'Connor redeunte ad propria. O'Donill cum suis pertransivit flumina Sruthair et Roba et undique devastatione facta, in Tirtawaillii [Tir-Amhalghadha] rediit,

Gillga[i]n, died.—Friar Patrick O'Sgannail, archbishop of Ard-Macha, held a General Chapter in Drochet-atha this year[4] (the 2nd,[5] 3rd and 4th week-days after the Feast of All Saints).

(Donn[1] Ua Breslen was killed by Domnall Ua Domnaill in Rath-both in the court of the bishop.—Aedh Ua Neill the Tawny took the daughter of Mac Goisdealbaigh to wife.)

Kalends of Jan. [on 3rd feria, 29th of the moon], A.D. 1264.[1] Domnall Ua Eghra, king of Luighni, was killed by the Foreigners.—Mathgamain, son of Ceithernach Ua Ceirin, king of Ciaraidhe, was killed by Foreigners.— Cumhuidhe Ua Catha[i]n, king of Ciannachta, was taken prisoner by Aedh the Tawny.

(A)
The archbishop of Ard-Macha, namely, Mael-Patraic O'Sgannail, made a ditch around Ard-Macha and Friars Minor were brought to Ard-Macha by the same person in this year.

(B)
Friars Minor were brought to Ard-Macha by the archbishop, namely, by Mael-Padraig Ua Sgannail and the same person, that is, Mael-Padraig, made a ditch around Ard-Macha this year.

---

citra flumen Moye, cum multis armentis et obsidibus, habitâ victoriâ in toto suo progressu illa vice.

The original is given in the *Four Masters* at 1263.

[5] *The 2nd, etc.*—The interlineation shows that the date was 1265. In that year All Saints' Day (Nov. 1) fell on Sunday. In 1263, it fell on Wednesday.

(1263) [1] *Donn.* — This agrees with the chronology of the *Annals of Loch Cé*, which place the death of O'Breslen in 1263. See above, the first entry under [1263].

[1264] [1] Of the entries under this year, the 1st, 3rd and 4th are given in the *A. L. C.* at 1264; the 2nd is at 1266; the 1st is repeated at the latter year.

A 62a
(Aedh buidhe hUa Neill, ri Thire-hEogain, do gabail
tigerndair Oirghiall.— | Benedictio fratrir Catholici,
precentoris domur Aportolorum Petri et Pauli de
Aromacha, ad abbaciam domur ranctae Mariae de
Clochar.—Frater Patriciur hUa Mureadaigh, abbar
monarterii Apostolorum Petri et Pauli, deponitur
ert et rubrtituitur ert abbar de Daeri, rcilicet,
Cirtianur Mhagramragan.ᵈ)

Kal. Ian. [f.ᵃ uii., L. ii.ᵃ], Anno Domini M.° cc.° lx.° .uᵇ
[-uiii.ᶜ]. Cagadh mor eter ri Saxan 7 Simunn Muford.
—Murchadh Mac Suibne do gabail la Domnall Mac
Magnura 7 a tinnlacudh illaim inˡ Iarla 7 a eg irinˀ
priron.—Feidhlimidhᶜ hUa Conchobair,³ ri Connacht mortuur ert.

(Fraterᵈ Patriciur hUa Mureadaigh ar n-a gabail
arir chum a abdaine rein.—Aedh buidhe hUa Neill 7
Uater a buirc, doon, Iarla Uladh, do dul a Tir-Conaill,
rluadh, 7 nir' gabadar teann, na treirˑ.ᵈ)

[b ir.]
Kal. Ian. [f.ᵃ i., L. xiii.ᵃ] Anno Domini M.° cc.° lx.°
ui.ᵇ ᵇ[-uiii.ᶜ] Concobur hUa Briain, ri Tuadh-Muman, do
marbadh la Diarmait, mac Muircertaigh hUi Briain 7
B 63d
ri [a] mac, Seoinin 7 daine | imdha ailiˡ (7ᵉ Brian ruadh,
a mac, do gabail a inaidhᵉ).—Toirrdelbach, mac Aeda

A.D. 1264. ᵈ⁻ᵈ n. t. h., A ; om., B, C, D.

A.D. 1265. ¹an, A. ²iran, A. ³—buir, A. ᵇ 1267, overhead, n. t. h.,
B; *alias* 1267, C. ᶜ Opposite this word, l. m., n. t. h., B, is : *supra in initio
paginae*, referring to the top of the column, where the obit is also recorded,
under 1263[-5]. This duplicate entry is given in A, B, C, D. ᵈ⁻ᵈ n. t. h.,
A; om., B, C, D.

A.D. 1266. ¹eile, A; ii., B. ᵇ 1268, overhead, n. t. h., B ; *rectius*
1268, C. ᶜ⁻ᵉ r. m., t. h., B ; om., A, C ; given in D.

[1267] ¹ *1265.*—Henceforward, to 1378 (=1373 of text), after which year the chronology is correct, in Text and Translation, the square-bracketted Ferial and Epact correspond with the similarly placed A.D. All the items are given under

(Aedh Ua Neill the Tawny, king of Tir-Eogain, took the lordship of Oirghialla.—Benediction of Friar Catholicus, Precentor of the House of the Apostles Peter and Paul of Ard-Macha, to the abbacy of the House of St. Mary of Clochar.—Friar Patrick Ua Muireadhaigh, abbot of the Monastery of the Apostles Peter and Paul, was deposed and the abbot of Daire, namely, Christian Mag Shamhragan, was substituted.)

[The entries of 1266 are omitted.]

Kalends of Jan. [on 7th feria, 2nd of the moon], A.D. 1265[1][-7]. Great war[2] between the king of the Saxons and Simon Montfort.—Murchadh Mac Suibhne was taken prisoner by Domnall Mac Maghnusa and he was handed into the custody of the Earl [de Burgh] and he died in the prison.—Feidhlimidh Ua Conchobair, king of Connacht, died.[3]

(Friar Patrick Ua Muiredhaigh was taken back to his own abbacy.—Aedh Ua Neill the Tawny and Walter de Burgh, namely, Earl of Ulster, went into Tir-Conaill with a host and they gained neither hold nor sway.)

Kalends of Jan. [on 1st feria, 13th of the moon], A.D. 1266[-8]. Concobur[1] Ua Briain, king of Thomond, was killed along with [his] son, Johnikin, by Diarmait, son of Muircertach Ua Briain. And many other persons [were slain with him]. (And Brian the Red, his son, took his

---

1265 in the *A. L. C.* The two first are, however, repeated at 1267. The true year is determined if the opening entry refers to the battle of Evesham, which was fought Aug. 6, 1265.

[2] *Great war.*—Expanded thus in D: Maxima belli expectatio ac violentarum guerrarum commotio.

[3] *Died.*—Repetition of an obit at 1265 (=1263 of text), *supra*.

[1268] [1] *Conchobur.*—The four original items of the textual year, 1266, are given under 1268 in the *A. L. C.*

hUi Concobuip, valta hUa²-mbpiuin, quieuit in[d] [Chpirto].—Concobup hUa Ceallaiᵹ quieuit in[d] [Chpirto].—Diapmait hUa Opiain, in pep lep'mapbab Concobup, do mapbab ind.

(Ecclepia* maiop ranctı Patpicii in Apomachenre [ciuitate] inrra murum incepta ert pep Apchiepircopum Apomachanum, id ert, Mael-Padpaiᵹ hUa Sᵹannaill.—Laclainn Macana extra portam curi[a]e Domini Apchiepircopi in ulcionem Mupcaib hUi Anluain pep Eacmarcac hUa hAnluain ert ocripur.—Cimiterium fratrum Minorum de Apomacha conrecratum ert pep eundem Patricium, Apchiepircopum et Dominor Rapotenrem, Dunnorenrem et Conderenrem.—Frater Capbricur hUa Scuaba conrecratur ert in Rapotenrem [epircopum*].

Kal. Ian. [p.ᵃ iii., l. xxiii.,ᵃ] Anno Domini M.° cc.° lx.° uii.° ᵇ[-ix.°] Cairlén Rora-Comain do benam la Roibert D'Urroit, iurtir na hErenn¹ 7 le ᵹallaib Erenn re riᵹi,² Aeba, mic Feiblimte hUi* Concobuir* 7 Aeb rein i n-ᵹalur an tan rin 7 rorrecab 7 rohairᵹeb móran do Connactaib cum in cairlein rin.—Cairlen Sliᵹiᵹ do benum le Mac Muirir.—Taᵭᵹ,* mac Neill Mic Muire-

A.D. 1266. ᵃO, A. ᵈom., B. ᵉ*n. t. h., A; om., B, C. The last item is given in D.
A.D. 1267. ¹ind, B. ²riᵹe, B. ᵇ 1269, overhead, n. t. h., B; *alias* 1269, C. ᶜ*om., B, C; given in D.

---

² *Was killed therefor.*—D adds: in ecclesia magna Ardmaghnensi, de consensu et industria archiepiscopi Patricii I Skanill. The translator apparently confounded this with the following (additional) entry.
(1266) ¹ *Church.*—Placed, no doubt correctly, by the *Four Masters* under 1268.
² *Ua Scuaba.*—The *A. L. C.* call him a Dominican, adding that he was consecrated in Armagh in 1266. On the translation of O'Sgannel to Armagh (1261, *supra*), the minority of the Chapter elected the arch-

place.)—Toirrdhelbach, son of Aedh Ua Conchobuir, the [1268] foster-son of the Ui-Briuin, rested in Christ.—Conchobur Ua Ceallaigh, rested in Christ.—Diarmait Ua Briain, the person by whom was killed Conchobur, was killed therefor.²

(The larger church¹ of St. Patrick in the city of Ard- (1266) Macha within the wall was commenced by the archbishop of Ard-Macha, namely, Mael-Padraig Ua Sgannail.— Lachlainn Ma[c] Cana was slain outside the door of the court of the Lord Archbishop by Eachmarcach Ua Anluain, in revenge of [the slaying of] Murchadh Ua Anluain.— The Cemetery of the Friars Minor of Ard-Macha was consecrated by the same Patrick, archbishop and the Lords [bishops] of Rath-both, Dun and Conneri.— Friar Cairbre Ua Scuaba² was consecrated bishop of Rath-both.)

Kalends of Jan. [on 3rd feria, 24th of the moon], A.D. [1269] 1267¹[-9]. The castle of Ros-Comain was built by Robert D'Ufford, Justiciary of Ireland and by the Foreigners of Ireland during the reign of Aedh, son of Feidhlimidh Ua Conchobuir. And Aedh himself was in sickness at that time and much of Connacht was despoiled and harried for [the building of] that castle.—The castle of Sligeach was built by Fitz Maurice,²—Tadhg, son of Niall Mac Muired-

---

deacon, Henry; the majority, the abbot of "the Monastery of Nigracella" [Dub-Recles] of Derry. The archbishop of Armagh annulled the election of the archdeacon, who proceeded to Rome to prosecute an appeal and died there. On Dec. 3, 1263, Urban IV. passed over the abbot and appointed John de Alneto, a Franciscan resident in Ireland (Theiner, pp. 92-3). On the 28th April, 1265, John was excused on the plea of incurable infirmity by Clement IV., who reserved the appointment to himself (ib., p. 96). The result appears in the present entry.

[1269] ¹ *1267.*—The original entries of the (textual) year 1267 are given in the *A. L. C.* under 1269.

² *Fitz-Maurice.*—D adds: Quod antea O'Donill et Odo O'Connor funditus prostrarunt.

ḃaıġ, do marbaḋ ı n-Oıl-ḟınn do ḟerrenaċ doċnaıċ do muınnċır a braṫar ṡeın.ᶜ—Aeḋ, mac Domnaıll hUı Ferġaıll, do marbaḋ do Ġallaıḃ 7 d'a braıṫrıḃ ṡeın. —Aeḋ hUa Ḟınn, raı oırṡoıġ, quıeuıt ın³ [Chrısto].— Brıan,ᵈ mac Domnaıll duıb hUı Eaġra, do marbaḋ la Ġallaıḃ.ᵈ

(Dauıḋᵉ hUa Braġan, erḃaġ Cloċaır, quı uırtuosse et ṡıdelıter pro deṡencıone ıurtıcı[a]e et ıuŗıṡ eccleṡı[a]e Clochorenṡıŗ per tempuṣ uıt[a]e eıuṣ laborauıt, obııt hoc anno. Ocuŗ a aḋlacaḋ ımMaınıṡtır Mhellı-ṣoınt, oır dobo manaċ d'a manċaıḃ ṡeın he roımerın.ᵉ)

Kal. Ian. [ṣ.ᵃ ıııı., l. u.,ᵃ] Anno Domını M.º cc.º lx.º uııı.º ᵇ[-lxx º] Maıḋm Aṫa-ın-ċıŗ le hAeḋ, mac Feıḋ-lımṫe 7 le Connaċtaıḃ aŗ ın Iarla, don aŗ Uáteŗ¹ a ḃurc 7 aŗ Ġallaıḃ Erenn arċena, dú ı tucaḋ áŗ dıaırmıḋe² | aŗ Ġallaıḃ 7 doġabaḋ ann Uıllıam óġ a ḃurc 7 ŗomarbaḋ é ıardaın ıṡın laım cetna. Ocuŗ nı mó corġaıŗ ná ṡaċırġal d'a tuċṡat Ġaıdhıl do Ġallaıḃ ı n-Erınn rıam ınaŗ. Uaıŗ ŗomarbaḋ Rıcard na coılle, braṫaır an Iarla, 7 Seon Buıtıléŗ 7 rıderedaḋ³ ımda aılı⁴ 7 Ġoıll 7 Ġaıdıl dıaırmıḋe 7 ŗoṡaġaḋ ċeṫ⁵ d'euċaıḃ co n-a luırecaıḃ 7 co n-a n-dıllaıtıḃ.—Comarbaᶜ Radŗaıġ, don, Mael-Radŗaıġ hUa Sġandaıl, quıeuıt ın [Chrıstoᶜ].—Ġorta móŗ do[ṡ]olaċtaᵈ ıᵇ n-Erınn ırın

A.D. 1267. ³ om., B. ᵈ⁻ᵈ om., B, C, D. ᶜ⁻ᶜ n. t. h., A; om., B, C, D.
A.D. 1268. ¹ Bhaı-, B. ²—ṁe, A. ³ rıderġa (=eḋa), A; —eḋa, B. ⁴ eıle, A; ıı., B. ⁵ .c. (the Latin equivalent), A, B. ⁶ a, A. ᵇ 1271 (*alias* 1270), overhead, n. t. h., B; *rectius* 1270, n. t. h., C. ᶜ⁻ᶜ om., A; given in B, C, D. ᵈ om., B, C, D.

(1267) ¹ *Ua Bragan.*—His death is given by the *F. M.* at 1269. But the present obit appears to have been composed by one well acquainted with the date.

² *Before that.*—That is, the context shows, before he was made bishop. The *F. M.* omit the words; whence O'Donovan (iii. 406) erroneously concluded that O'Bragan "had retired into the monastery some time before his death."

haigh, was killed in Oil-finn by an ill-mannered servitor [1269] of the retinue of his own kinsman.—Aedh, son of Domnall Ua Ferghaill, was killed by the Foreigners and by his own kinsmen.—Aedh Ua Finn, master of harmony, rested in Christ.—Brian, son of Domnall Ua Eaghra the Black, was killed by the Foreigners.

(David Ua Bragan,[1] bishop of Clochar, who laboured (1267) courageously and faithfully in defence of justice and the right of the church of Clochar during the time of his life, died this year. And he was buried in the Monastery of Mellifont, for he was a monk of its monks before that.[2])

Kalends of Jan. [on 4th feria, 5th of the moon], A.D. [1270] 1268[1][-70]. The defeat of Ath-in-chip[2] [was inflicted] by Aedh, son of Feidhlimidh [Ua Conchobair] and by the Connachtmen on the Earl, namely, on Walter de Burgh and on the Foreigners of Ireland besides, wherein was committed slaughter innumerable on the Foreigners. And William de Burgh junior was taken prisoner there and he was killed afterwards in the same captivity. And not greater than it was any defeat, or battle-rout that the Gaidhil ever gave to the Foreigners in Ireland previously. For there was killed Richard of the Wood, kinsman of the Earl, as well as John Butler and many other knights and Foreigners and Gaidhil innumerable. And there were abandoned one hundred horses[3] with their breastplates and with their saddles.—The successor of [St.] Patrick,[4] namely, Mael-Padraig Ua Sgannail, rested in Christ.—

[1270]. [1] *1268.*—The original items of the (textual) year 1268 are given in the *A. L. C.* at 1270; except the last, which is placed under 1269. The second is also given at the latter year.

[2] *Ath-in-chip.*—*Ford of the beam.* Apud Vadum trabis, vulgo dictum Agh kipp, D.

[3] *Horses, etc.*—Centum equi Anglico aparatu circumdati, una cum militum armatura relicti fuerunt, D.

[4] *Successor of Patrick.*—That is, archbishop of Armagh. The textual date, we have abundant proof, is two years in advance. Brictius (presumably, the Latin alias of

bliaḋain ṛi.—Cṛiṛcina, ingen hUi Neċcain, bean Ḋiaṛmaca Miḋiẋ Mic Ḋiaṛmaca, in bean ṗob' ṛeṛṛ ḋelb[d] 7 eineaċ[d] 7 cṛaḃaḋ ṛoḃai i* n-aen aimṛiṛ ṛia* 7 iṛ mó cuc ḋo'n Oṛḋ Liaṫ, quieuic in Chṛiṛco.[d]

(Mael-Ṗaḋṛaiẋ[e] hUa Ṡgannail, aiṛḋeaṛḃaẋ Aṛḋ-Maċa, ḋo ḋul gu ceaċ ṛiẋ Saxan an bliaḋain ṛi 7 a ṫeaċc anoiṛ aṛiṛ an bliaḋain ċecna mailli ṛe cumaċcain inoiṛ.—Eaċṁaṛcaċ hUa Anluain, ṛi Oiṛṛṫiṛ, ḋo ẋaḃail ṛeṛ Ualceṛum Maiṛeṛ, iḋon, Conṛcabla Ṛiuṛ-na-caiṛge 7 ḋoċeṛno uaḋa aṛiṛ an bliaḋain cecna.—Michael Mac an-c-Shaiṛ, Oiṛṛicel Aṛḋ-Maċa, ḋo ċonṛecṛaicc le haiṛḋeaṛḃoẋ Aṛḋ-Maċa, i n-a eaṛḃoẋ i Cloċuṛ, in cṛaṛcino Naciuicaciṛ Ḃeacae Maṛi[a]e.')

|Cal. Ian. [ṛ.[a] u., L. x.iii.,[a]] Anno Ḋomini M.° cc.° Lx.° ix.°[b] [-lxx.° i.°] | Mac Seoa[i]n Iḃeṛḋuin ḋo maṛbaḋ le Uáceṛ[1] a ḃúṛc.—Simon Maẋ [C]ṛaiṫ. ḋeẋanaċ Aṛḋa-caṛna, quieuic in [Chṛiṛco].—Maṫgamain Maẋ[c] Caṛṛṫaiẋ ḋo maṛbaḋ.—Ḃháceṛ a ḃúṛc, Iaṛla Ulaḋ 7 ciẋeṛna Connaċc, moṛcuuṛ eṛc.—Caiṛlen Ṫaiẋi-cempla ḋo bṛiṛiuḋ la hAeḋ hUa Conċoḃuiṛ.—Ḋonnċaḋ Mhaẋ Shamṛuḋain quieuic in [Chṛiṛco].—Caiṛlen Ṛoṛa-

A.D. 1268.—[d-d] om., B, C, D. [e-e] i n-a haimṛiṛ—*in her (own) time*, B (followed by C, D). [f-f] n. t. h., A ; om., B, C, D.

A.D. 1269. [1] Ḃhái—, A. [c] mac Mheẋ (Caṛṛṫaiẋ)—*son of Ma: (Carr-thaigh)*, B.

Mael-, or Gilla-, Brigte), canon of Armagh, having gone to Henry III., with letters of the Dean and Chapter announcing the death of Patrick, the archbishop, licence to elect was granted (*D. I.*, II. 869) in the beginning of May, 1270.

The election of Nicholas, canon of Armagh, was confirmed (Theiner, p. 101) by Gregory X., July 13, 1272. (The delay was apparently owing to the interregnum between the demise of Clement IV., Nov. 29, 1268, and the coronation of Gregory X., Jan. 27, 1272.) The confirmation having been notified to the king by the Curia, the temporalities were restored to the archbishop on the ensuing Sept. 25 (*D. I.*, II. 927).

Great, unbearable famine in Ireland this year.—Christina, [1270] daughter of Ua Nechtain, wife of Diarmait Mac Diarmata the Midian, the woman that was of best shape and generosity and piety that was in one time with herself and that gave most to the Grey Order,[5] rested in Christ.

(Mael-Padraig Ua Sgannail, archbishop of Ard-Macha, (1268) went to the house of the king of the Saxons this year and came from the east again the same year with great power. —Eachmarcach Ua Anluain, king of the Oirthir, was taken prisoner by Walter de Marisco, namely, the Constable of Ros-na-cairge and he escaped from him the same year.— Michael Mac-an-tshair,[1] Official of Ard-Macha, was consecrated bishop in Clochar by the archbishop of Ard-Macha, on the morrow of the Nativity of Blessed Mary [Sept 8[2]].

Kalends of Jan. [on 5th feria, 16th of the moon], A.D. [1271] 1269[1][-71]. The son[2] of John de Verdon was killed by Walter de Burgh.—Simon Mag Craith, dean of Ard-carna, rested in peace.—Mathgamain Mag Carrthaigh was killed.—Walter de Burgh, Earl of Ulster and lord of Connacht, died.[3]—The castle of Tech-templa was broken down by Aedh Ua Conchobuir.—Donnchadh Mag Shamhrudhain rested in Christ.[4]—The castle of Ros-comain and

---

[5] *Grey Order.*—Namely, the Cistercian.

(1268) [1] *Mac-an-tshair.—Son of the wright.* Generally anglicized Carpenter.

[2] *Sept.* 8.—In 1268 it fell on Sunday, one of the days prescribed for conferring episcopal consecration.

[1271] [1] *1269.*—Of the entries of the (textual) year, 1269, the first, fourth, fifth, and seventh (except the *Ros-Comain* item) are given in the *A. L. C.* at 1271. The sixth,

Ros-Comain of the seventh, the eighth, ninth and eleventh are placed under 1272 in the same Annals.

[2] *The son.*—Called Nicholas in the *A. L. C.*; which state that he was slain by Geoffrey O'Ferrall and the people of Annaly (co. Longford).

[3] *Died.*—In Galway castle, according to the *A. L. C.*

[4] *Rested in Christ.*—In the *A. L. C.* he is said to have been slain by his brother, Thomas.

Comain 7 caiplen Sliziz 7 caiplen Aēa-liaz do lezað la hAeð, mac Peiðlimēe.

[bp.] [A.D. M.° cc.° Lxx.° 11.°] Muipzip, mac Donncaða, tizepna Chipe-hOilella, neč dob' pepp eineč 7 tinnlacað do Connačtaið, do éz a Mupbač illonzpopt hUi Domnaill 7 a bpeiē co Mainiptep na Ouille 7 a aðnucal indti co honopač.—Clann-Muipceptaiz do ðul i n-Iaptap Chonnačt, zup'mapbað leo hOiopi Mac Mheupic 7 hAnpi Ouitillép.—Caiplen Renna-duin do leazað la hAeð hUa Concobuip.—Taðz dall, mac Aeða, quieuit in Chpipto.

kal. Ian.[p. 1., L.1x.], Anno Domini M.° cc.° Lxx.°[-iii.]° Concobup buiðe, Mac Aipt hUi Ruaipe, pí Opeipne, do mapbað la mac Concobuip, mic Chizepna[i]n hUi Concobuip 7 pomapbað in t-é pomapū.—Eačaið Máz A 62c Matzamna quieuit in [Chpipto].— | Cpeč do ðenum do Shiuptan d'Eipetpa ipin Copunn 7 becan do macaið piz Connačt do bpeit poppa 7 aimzlicup do denum tpe pupail dpočðaine, zup'mapbað Domnall, mac Donnčaða, mic Mazhupa 7 Maznup, mac Aipt 7 Oipečtač Mac Aeðuzain 7 Aeð hUa Oipn 7 daine imða aili.

(Lodouicup, idon, Loðaip naem, piz Fpanc, do dul cum nime, decimo quapto Kalendap Septembpip, in bliaðain pi, 1270; idon, Loðaip, mac Loðaip.)

A.D. 1269. ² a long—, A. ³ Mhepic, A. The t. h. wrote mec; pí was inserted, n. t. h. ᵇ 1272, overhead, n. t. h., B; alias 1271, n. t. h., C. ᶜ mac Mhez (Cappταιz)—son of Mac (Carrthaigh), B. ᵈ om., A.

A.D. 1270. ¹ cpeač, B. ²—zan, A. ²·eile, A; ii, B. ᵇ 1273, overhead, n. t. h., B; alias 1272; rel 1273, n. t. h., C. ᶜ·ᵈ t. m., t.h., A; om., B, C, D.

[1272] ¹ *Maurice, etc.*—From this entry to the textual year 1281 (= 1284) inclusive, these Annals are three years antedated.

² *Clann-Muircertaigh.*—Descendents of *Muircertach* (the Momonian, son of Turlough Mor O'Conor, king of Connacht).

³ *Tadhg the Blind.*—Grandson of Cathal Red-hand O'Conor, king of

the castle of Sligeach and the castle of Ath-liag were [1271] levelled by Aedh, son of Feidhlimidh [Ua Conchobair].

[A.D. 1272]. Maurice,[1] son of Donnchadh [Ua Mael- [1272 Bis.] ruanaigh] lord of Tir-Oilella, one that was the best of the Connachtmen for hospitality and gratuity, died in Murbach, in the camp of Ua Domnaill and he was carried to the Monastery of the Buill and honourably buried therein.—The Clann-Muircertaigh[2] went into the West of Connacht, so that Hoidsi Mac Mebric and Henry Butler were killed by them.—The castle of Rinn-duin was levelled by Aedh Ua Conchobuir.—Tadhg the Blind,[3] son of Aedh, rested in Christ.

Kalends of Jan. [on 1st feria, 9th of the moon,] A.D. [1273] 1270[1][-3]. Conchobur the Tawny, son of Art Ua Ruairc, king of Breifni, was killed by the son of Conchobur, son of Tigernan Ua Concobuir and he who killed [him] was killed therein.—Eochaidh Mac Mathgamna [king of Oirghialla] rested in Christ.[2]—A foray was made by Jordan de Exeter into the Corann. And a few of the sons of the kings of Connacht overtook them and an imprudence was committed [by the Connacht leaders] through advice of evil persons, so that Domnall, son of Donnchadh, son of Maghnus [Ua Conchobair] and Maghnus, son of Art [Ua Conchobair] and Oirechtach Mac Aedhugain and Aedh Ua Birn and many other persons were killed.

(Louis,[1] namely, Saint Louis, king of the French, went (1270) to heaven on the 14th of the Kalends of September [Aug. 19] this year, 1270. That is Louis [IX.], son of Louis [VIII.].)

Connacht, according to the *A. L. C.*; which add that he was blinded by the O'Reillys (co. Cavan).

[1273] [1] *1270.*—All the entries of the (textual) year 1270 are given in the *A. L. C.* under 1273.

[3] *Rested in Christ.*—But the *A. L. C.* state that he and many others along with him were slain by O'Hanlon and the Cenel-Owen.

(1270) [1] *Louis.*—Died Aug. 25 (*L'Art de vérif. les dates*), 1270;

z 2

348 ANNALA ULAOH.

B 64b |Cal. 1an. [p.ᵃ 11., l. xx.ᵃ], Anno Domini M.° cc.° lxx.° 1.°ᵇ [-iu.°] Domnall, mac Magnupa, mic Muipcepcaig Muimnig hUi Concobuip, pai bpuinnci 7 peicem coicceann, comlanᶜ do'n ciniud daenna, quieuic in [Chpipco].—Gilla-na-naem O Fepgail, aen pagu¹ caipec Epenn i² n-a² aimpip pein, quieuicᵈ in [Chpipco].ᵈ—Aed, mac Feid-limce³ hUi Concobuip, pi Connact 7 adbup aippig Epenn, pep ba mó gpain 7 copgap dobí i n-Epinn, quieuic in [Chpipco].—Tigepnan, mac Aeda hUi Ruaipc, pi Dpeipne, quieuic in [Chpipco].—Eogan, mac Ruaidpi hUiᵉ Concobaip, pi Connact pe paici, a mapbad i Mainipcip na m-bpacap i Rop-Comain (laᵉ a bpacpuib pein°).—Aed, mac Cacail doill hUi Concobuip, pi Con-nact pe caeicidip, quieuic in [Chpipco] ('Domapbadᶠ la Tommalcac Mhag Oipeactaig 7 do comaiple Gilla-Cpipt hUi Bhipn.ᵉ).—Cacal Mag Fhlannchada, caipec Dapcpaigi, quieuic in [Chpipco].—Tadg hUaᵍ Dalmg (idon,ᶠ mac Cepbail buide, d'ap n-doigᶠ), pai maic pe dan, quieuic in [Chpipco].—Caipbpi hUa Sguaba, eppuc Tipe-Conaill, (inᵉ Chpipco quieuic etᵉ) in Cupia obiit.

(Mail-Seaclainn,ʰ mac Amlaim, mic Aipt hUi Ruaipc, pig Dapcpaige, do mapbad la Conchbap, mac Domnaill, mic Neill hUi Ruaipc.ʰ)

A.D. 1271. ¹-a, B. ²⁻²na (aphaeresis of i), A. ³-mid, B. ⁴1, A.
ᵃ O, A. ᵇ 1274 overhead, n. t. h., B; *rectius* 1274, n. t. h., C. ᶜ om., B. ᵈ⁻ᵈ om., A. ᵉ⁻ᵉ itl., n. t. h., A; om., B, C, D. ᶠ⁻ᶠ itl., t. h., B; om., A; given in C, D. ᵍ⁻ᵍ *in Christo quieuit* is the textual reading in B. *Et in curia obiit* is interlined, t. h. C has *in Christo quieuit*, with *in curia* interlined. D gives *quievit*. ʰ⁻ʰ n. t. h., A; om., B, C, D.

---

canonized by Boniface VIII., Aug. 11, 1297.

[1274]¹ *1271*.—The first of entry the (textual) year 1271 is dated 1273 in the *A. L. C.* The others (except the last, which is under 1275) are given at 1274 in the same Annals.

² *Aedh*.—Thus freely rendered in

D: Odo Mac Feilem I Conor, rex Conaciae, qni fuit expectatus futurus rex Hibernie propter sua magnalia acta contra Anglicanos, cum quibus cunctis diebus sue vite incessanter luctabat, quieuit.

In the *A. L. C.*, Aedh is said to have died on Thursday, May 3, the

Kalends of Jan. [on 2nd feria, 20th of the moon], A.D. 1271 [-4]. Domnall, son of Maghnus, son of Muircertach Ua Conchobuir the Momonian, eminent donor and a general, perfect benefactor to the human race, rested in Christ.—Gilla-na-naem O'Ferghail, the most choice of the chiefs of Ireland in his own time, rested in Christ.—Aedh,[2] son of Feidhlimidh Ua Conchobuir, king of Connacht and future arch-king of Ireland, the man most feared and victorious that was in Ireland, rested in Christ.—Tigernan, son of Aedh Ua Ruairc, king of Breifni, rested in Christ.—Eogan, son of Ruaidhri Ua Concobair, king of Connacht for a quarter [of a year], was killed in the Monastery of the Friars in Ros-Comain (by his own kinsmen).—Aedh, son of Cathal Ua Concobuir the Blind, king of Connacht for a fortnight, rested[3] in Christ. (He was killed by Tomaltach Mag Oirechtaigh and by counsel of Gilla-Crist Ua Birn.)—Cathal Mag Flannchadha, chief of Dartraighe, rested in Christ.—Tadhg Ua Dalaigh (namely, son of Cerball the Tawny, in our opinion), a good master in poetry, rested in Christ.—Cairbre Ua Sguaba, bishop of Tir-Conaill, (rested in Christ and) died in the Curia.[4]

(Mail-Sechlainn,[1] son of Amlaimh, son of Art Ua Ruairc, king of Dartraighi, was killed by Conchubhar, son of Domnall, son of Niall Ua Ruairc.)

[1274]

(1271)

---

feast of the Finding of the Holy Cross. Accordingly, at this year the *Annals of Ulster* are three years in advance. In 1274, May 3 fell on Thursday; in 1271, on Sunday.

[3] *Rested.*—Namely, died a natural death. So the two MSS. and the two translations. But there can be no doubt, from the proofs given in the A. L. C., that he was slain. The correction interlined in A is consequently well founded.

[4] *Died in the Curia.*—That is, in the Papal Court. 'Ware (*Bishops*, ed. Harris, p. 271) states on the authority of the "*Annals of Loch-Kee*" that Bishop O'Scoba died at Rome; but it is clear that Ware did not quote from the original of the present volumes, as there is no mention of Rome either in this MS., or in the so-called *Annals of Connacht*.' (Note to A. L. C., i. p. 478.) Ware most probably quoted from C, in which *in Curia* is interlined over *in Christo*.

(1271) [1] *Mail-Sechlainn.*—Given

Kal. Ian. [r.ᵃ iii., L. i.ᵃ], Anno Domini M.° cc.° lxx.° ii.°ᵇ [-u.°] Art, mac Catail riabaig, rí Breifne, mortuus ert.—Ruaidri, mac Toirrdelbaig hUi Concobuir, do gabail d'a bratair féin, do Thadg, mac Thoirrdelbaig hUi Concobair (7 Tadg, mac Catail, mic Diarmoda, do argain uile leirᶜ) 7 Concobur, mac Fergail, mic Donncada, mic Muircertaig, do marbad d'a bratair féin.—In t-erpuc hUaˡ Laidig,¹ erpuc Cille-alad, quieuit in [Christo].

(Ruaigriᵈ hUa Concudair d'elog 7 Concudar hUa hAinli do breit leir 7 a leanmuin gu mait 7 breit ar Concudar 7 a marbad.—Cairbre hUa rguaba, erscop Rata-bot, quieuit.—Art, mac Catail riabaig, ri Breifne, do marbad do Mhuintir-Ghearudan.—Tomar Mhacc Shamrugain do marbad la Cinel-Luacan.ᵈ)

[bis.] Kal. Ian. [r.ᵃ iiii. L. xii.ᵃ], Anno Domini M.° cc.° lxx.° iii.°ᵇ[-ui.°] Aed Muimnec, mac Feidlimte,¹ do tiactain arin Mumain imerc Connact 7 tiact² do Clainn Tairr-

A.D. 1272. ¹⁻¹ Uallaidig, A.—ᵇ 1275 overhead, n. t. h., B ; *alias*, 1275, n. t. h., C. ᶜ⁻ᶜ om., B, C, D. The portion within brackets is itl., n. t. h. ᵈ⁻ᵈ n. t. h., A ; om., B, C, D.

A.D. 1273. ¹-mid, B. ²tact, B. ᵇ 1276, overhead, n. t. h., B ; *alias*, 1276, n. t. h., C.

under 1274 in the *A. L. C.* It is accordingly misplaced here.

[1275] ¹ *1272*.—The entries, both original and added, of the (textual) year 1272 are dated 1275 in the *A. L. C.*

² *Died*.—The second additional entry (which was inserted perhaps to correct this and with which the *A. L. C.* agree) states that he was killed.

³ *By his own kinsman*.—Omitted in D, which adds : O'Donill asportatis nauiculis ad Luagh Earne et exinde ad Luagh Uoghtiar et ibi circumiacientium omnium diuitias reperit et tandem, subiugatis circumquaque incolis illarum terrarum, cum summa victoria rediit.

The original is given in the *Four Masters* at 1272.

⁴ *Laidhig*.—Laydin, C ; Lagaire, with *Laidin* overhead, D.

(1272) ¹ *Ua Scuaba*.—See [1274], note 4, *supra*.

² *Thomas*.—See [1271], note 4, *supra*.

Kalends of Jan. [on 3rd feria, 1st of the moon,] A.D. [1275] 1272¹[-5]. Art, son of Cathal the Swarthy [Ua Ruairc], king of Breifni, died.²—Ruaidhri, son of Toirrdhelbach Ua Concobuir, was taken prisoner by his own kinsman,³ [namely] by Tadhg, son of Toirrdhelbach Ua Conchobair (and Tadhg, son of Cathal Mac Diarmoda was despoiled completely by him) and Conchobur, son of Ferghal, son of Donnchadh, son of Muircertach, was killed by his own kinsman.—The bishop Ua Laidhig,⁴ bishop of Cell-aladh, rested in Christ.

(Ruaighri Ua Conchubhair escaped and took Conchu- (1272) bhar Ua Ainli with him. But they were well followed and Conchubar was caught and killed.—Cairbre Ua Sguaba,¹ bishop of Rath-both, rested.—Art, son of Cathal the Swarthy [Ua Ruairc], king of Breifni, was killed by the Muinnter-Ghearudhan.—Thomas² Mag Shamhrughain was killed by the Cenel-Luachan.)

Kalends of Jan. [on 4th feria, 12th of the moon], A.D. [1276 Bis.] 1273¹[-6]. Aedh² the Momonian, son of Feidhlimidh [Ua Conchobair], came out of Munster into the midst of Connacht and the children of Toirrdhelbach [Ua Conchobair]

[1276] ¹ *1273.*—The entries of the (textual) year 1273 are given in the *A. L. C.* under 1276.

² *Aedh.*—This item is rather a mnemonic note than a historical record. Its brevity is misleading, as well as obscure. According to Mageoghegan's Version of the *Annals of Clonmacnoise*: "A base son was presented to Felym Mac Cahall Crovederg O'Connor, after the death of said Ffelym a long space, who was called Hugh Moyneagh, because he was nurished and brought up in Munster and came to Connoght from thence.

And as soon as he came and was known to be the son of Felym, Silmoreye [Sil-Muiredhaigh, the O'Conors] and Clann Moyleronie [Sil-Mailruanaigh, the O'Flynns] accepted of him and had him in great accoumpt and reverence."

On being accepted as king, the sons of Toirdelbach (Torlough), Ruaidhri and Tadhg, fled into Tirconnell to O'Donnell. Their *coming into the country* is the foray mentioned in the first additional entry. They were slain in 1278(= 1275 of the text).

352 ccnnala ulaoh.

A 62d δelbaiξ aρτιρ.ᶜ—Διaρmaιτ, mac Ξιlle-Mυιρe! hUi Mhoρna, ρι Ulaδ, quιeuιτ ιn [Chριρτo].—Cρeč¹ δο δenum δo mac Fheιδlιmče aρ Claιnn-Mυιρceρταξ 7 ι τορaιδečτ na cρeιče ρomaρbaδ Ξιlla-na-n-aιngel O Conρaι.ᵈ—Δomnall, mac Neιll, mιc Conξalaιξ hUi Ruaιρc (ριρᵉ a ρaιτea Ξιlla ιn ιnmeᵉ), δo maρbaδ la hUa Nečταιn.

(Cρeačᶠ δo δenum le Cloιnn Τοιρρδealbaιξ aρ mac Fheιδlιm[č]e 7 aρ macaιδ Mιc Δhιaρmmoδa 7 Ξιlla-Cριτδ hUa Maιl-Δρenaιnn δο maρbaδ leο an la ριn.—Ξιlla-Cριτδ hUa Neačταιn 7 Uιllιam hUa Neačταιn δο maρbaδ la Ruaιξρι, mac Τοιρρδealbaιξ hUi Conču-δaιρ.ᵍ)

B 64c Kal. Ian. [ρ.ᵃ ιιι., l. xx.ιιι.ᵃ] Anno Domιnι M.º cc.ºlxxᵉ ιιιι.º ᵇ[-uιι.] Ξιlla-na-naem hUa¹ Διρn quιeuιτ ιn [Chριρτo].—Δριan ρuaδ hUa Δριaιn quιeuιτ ιn [Chριρτo].—Δρaen hUa Maιl-močeιρξι,² ab Cenannρa,³ ιnᶜ Chριρτο quιeuιτ.ᶜ

A.D. 1273. ᵉιρn τιρ—*into the country*. B, C; om., D. ᵈ⁻ᵈ om. B, C, D. ᵉ⁻ᵉ itl., n. t. h., A; om., B, C, D. ᶠ⁻ᶠ n. t. h., A; om., B, C, D.

A.D. 1274. ¹ O, A. ² Maeιl—, B. ³ Cenanδρa, B.—ᵇ 1277, over-head, n. t. h., B; *alias*, 1276, n. t. b., C. ᶜ⁻ᶜ quιeuιτ ιn, B.

³ *Son.*—The *Four Masters* give Mag Giolla Muire, omitting Ua Morna. (The editor of the *A. L. C.,* i. p. 479, says by oversight that they call him *O'Gillamuire.*) They add that he was lord of Leth-Cathail (Lecale, co. Down).

⁴ *Clann-Muircertaigh.*—See [1272] note 2, *supra.*

⁵ *Domnall.*—Donaldus O'Roirk occisus per O'Neachten, D. It adds: O'Donill, Donaldus Iuuenis, collecto magno exercitu ex Conacia et Connallia, invasit Tironiam et depredata undique patria rediit victoriosus cum obsidibus multis et ingenti preda omnis generis.

The original is given in the *Four Masters* at 1273.

(1273) ¹ *A foray.*—This and the following entry are given in the *A. L. C.* at 1276. They were placed here perhaps as having reference to the main subject matter of the textual year.

[1277] ¹ *1274.*—The two events of the (textual) year, 1275, are given in the *A. L. C.* at 1277.

² *Rested in Christ.*—That is, died a natural death. But this is a very

came into the country [to oppose him].—Diarmait, son[3] of Gilla-Muire Ua Morna, king of Ulidia, rested in Christ.—A foray was made by the son of Feidhlimidh on the Clann-Muircertaigh[4] and in driving the prey Gilla-na-naingel Ua Conrai was killed.—Domnall,[5] son of Niall, son of Conghalach Ua Ruairc (who was called "Gillie of the butter"), was killed by Ua Nechtain.

(A foray[1] was made by the children of Toirrdhealbach on the son of Feidhlimidh and on the sons of Mac Diarmoda and Gilla-Crisd Ua Mail-Brenainn was killed by them that day.—Gilla-Crisd Ua Neachtain and William Ua Neachtain were killed by Ruaighri, son of Toirrdhelbach Ua Conchubhair.)

Kalends of Jan. [on 6th feria, 23rd of the moon], A.D. 1274[1][-7]. Gilla-na-naem Ua Birn rested in Christ.—Brian Ua Briain the Red, rested in Christ.[2]—Braen[3] Ua Mail-mocheirghi[4] abbot of Cenannus, rested in Christ.—

[1276 Bis.]

(1273)

[1277]

---

considerable error. The event is thus described in the Remonstrance addressed (Theiner, p. 201) by the Irish Magnates, through the Nuncios, Cardinals Jocelin and Luke, to Pope John XXII., about 1318 : Item, Dominus Thomas de Clare, Comitis Gloverniae [Gloucester] frater, vocans ad domum suam praeclarissimum virum, Brianum Rufum, principem Totmoniae, suum compatrinum, cum, in maioris confoederationis et amiciciae signum, de eadem Hostia consecrata in duas divisa partes nequiter communicavit, ipsum denique de consilio nephandae gentis praedictae subito de mensa et convivio arreptum in caudem trahi fecit equorum ; amputato quoque capite, truncum corporis per pedes suspendi fecit in ligno

(Fordun : *Scotichronicon*, O x o n., 1722, iii. 917-8).

The *Annals of Clonmacnoise* (Mageoghegan's version, O'D. F. M. iii. 426-7) agree with the account given in the second additional entry of the following year.

[3] *Braen*.—Brien O'Molmocherri quieuit, D ; which adds : Hoc anno Eoganenses venerunt in Connalliam, sperantes sumere vindictam pro precedenti anno. Et collectâ magnâ predâ, O'Donill cum suis eos insequentes ad confines montes Tireone [*recte*, ad confinem Montis Truim] irruit in eos et habitâ victoriâ restituit sua cum multis equis et armatura.

The original is in the *Four Masters* at 1275.

[4] *Mail-mocheirghi*. — *Devotee of early rising*.

(Σilla-Cpıρυᵈ hUa bıρn, ρeaρ σραδα Œeδa hUı Chon-
ĉuδaıρ, υο ṁaρδaδ υο'n Σılla ρυaδ, mac Loĉlaınn hUı
Chonĉuδaıρ.ᵈ)

Kal. Ian. [ρ.ˢ uıı., L. ıııı.ᵃ], Œnno Domını M.° cc.ˢ lxx.ˢ
u.ᵃᵇ[-uııı.ᵃ] Taδσ, mac Toıρρδelbaıξ, υο maρδaδ la
claınn Caĉaıl Mıc Dıaρmaτa.—Ruaıδρı, mac Toıρρδelbaıξ, υο maρδaδ la Σılla-Cρıρτ Maσ Fhlannĉaδa 7 le
Daρτaaıξı aρĉena, aρ boρυ Dρoma-clıaδ 7 ın ρeρρun
ρıaδaĉ, mac Tıσeρnaın hUı Conĉobuıρ 7 υaıne aılı¹ naĉ
aıρıṁτeρ ρunn.—Donnĉaδ 7 Feρξal, δa mac Muıρσıρa,
mıc Donnĉaδa, mıc Tomalτaıξ, υο maρδaδ, la Taδσ,
mac Domnaıll Iρρaıρ.—Flaıĉbeρτaĉ hUa Daımín, ρı
Feρ-Manaĉ, quıeuıτ ın Chρıρτo (ıυon,ᶜ ı τeρτ Noın mıρ
Fheδρa:).—Maıυm Cuınĉı υο ĉabaıρτ υο Donnĉaδ, mac
bρıaın ρuaδ 7 υο macaıδ aılıδ² hUı bρıaın aρ ın ıaρla
O³ Claıρe (σuρ'loıρσρeaυᵈ τeampull Cuınĉe ı ceann a
ṁuınnτeρı, σu τuσταυ aρ υıaıρm[ıδ]e ρoρρa, eτıρ loρσaυ
7 maρδaδᵈ).—Tomaρ hUa Cuınn, eρρuc Cluana-mac-
Noıρ,⁴ quıeuıτ ın [Chρıρτo].—Tomalτaĉ Mac Oıρeĉτaıξ,
ρıξταıρeĉ Shıl-Muıρeδaıξ, υο maρδaδ υο na Tuaĉaıδ.

(Σılla-na-n-aınσel,ᵃ ab Leρa-σabaıl, moρτuuρ eρτ
Nonıρ Maρcıı.—bρıan ρuaδ, mac Conĉuδaıρ hUı

A.D. 1274. ᵈᵈ n. t. h., A ; om., B, C, D.
A.D. 1275. ¹ eıle, A ; ıı., B. ² ıı., A, B. ³ om., B. ⁴ mıc—, B. ᵇ 1278,
overhead, n. t. h., B ; *alias*, 1278, n. t. h., C. ᶜ⁻ᶜ ıtl., υ. t. h., A ; ıtl., t. h.,
B ; om., C, D. ᵈ⁻ᵈ ıtl., n. t. h., A ; om., B, C, D. ᵉ⁻ᵉ n. t. h., A ; om.,
B, C, D.

(1274) ¹ *Gilla-Crisd (Devotee of Christ)*.—Given in the *A. L. C.* under 1277.

[1278] ¹ *1275*.—The events of the (textual) year, 1275, are in the *A. L. C.* at 1278.

² *The Swarthy Parson*.—Rector fuscus, D.

³ *And other, etc.*—" And other men not here nombred," C.

⁴ *The defeat, etc.*—" Donnough Mac Bryen Roe O'Bryen gave the overthrow of Coynche to Thomas de Clare (the Earle before mentioned) and burnt the church of Coynche over the heads of the said Earle and his people; where infinite numbers of people were both slain and killed therein and escaped narrowly himself: for

(Gilla-Crisd[1] Ua Birn, confidant of Aedh Ua Conchubhair, was killed by the "Red Gillie," son of Lochlann Ua Conchubhair.) (1274)

Kalends of Jan. [on 7th feria, 4th of the moon], A.D. 1275[1][-8]. Tadhg, son of Toirrdhelbach [Ua Conchobair], was killed by the children of Cathal Mac Diarmata.—Ruaidhri, son of [the aforesaid] Toirrdhelbach, was killed by Gilla-Crist Mac Flannchadha and by the Dartraighi besides, on the border of Druim-cliabh and "the Swarthy Parson,"[2] son of Tigernan Ua Conchobuir, and other[3] persons that are not reckoned here [were killed].—Donnchadh and Ferghal, two sons of Muirghius, son of Donnchadh, son of Tomaltach [Ua Conchobair], were killed by Tadhg, son of Domnall [Ua Conchobair] of Irras.—Flaithbertach Ua Daimin, king of Fir-Manach, rested in Christ (namely, on the 3rd of the Nones [3rd] of the month of February).—The defeat[4] of Cuinche was given by Donnchadh, son of Brian [Ua Briain] the Red, to the Earl of Clare (so that they burned the church of Cuinche over the heads of his people [and] inflicted slaughter innumerable upon them, both by burning and killing).—Thomas Ua Cuinn,[5] bishop of Cluain-mac-Nois, rested in Christ.—Tomaltach Mac Oirechtaigh, royal chief of Sil-Muiredhaigh, was killed by "the Territories." [1278]

(Gilla-na-naingel,[1] abbot of Lis-gabail, died on the Nones [7th] of March.—Brian the Red,[2] son of Conchu- (1275)

---

which escape myne author [i.e., the chronicle which he translated] sayeth that himself was sorry for." Mageoghegan, 1278.

The original of "myne author" is given in the *A. L. C.*: "But, alas! the son of the Earl went thereout from them secretly" (1278).

[3] *Ua Cuinn.* — A Franciscan.

Elected in 1253 (*D. I.*, II. 151). Died probably towards the close of 1278 (cf. *ib.* 1713).

(1275) [1] *Gilla-na-naingel.—Devotee of the angels.* The original of this entry is not known to me.

[2] *Brian the Red.*—This is the true version of the second item in the (textual) year 1274 (=1277).

ḃhṗiain, ṗiġ Ṫuaḋṁumun, do ġaḃail le mac Iaṗla hO Claiṗe. Ocuṗ ṗiaḋ aṗ cuṗ a ḟola i n-aen ṗoiġteaċ 7 aṗ n-ḋenum caiṗoiuṗa-Cṗiṗo 7 aṗ ṫoḃeṗt ṁinn 7 ċloġ d'a ċele. Ocuṗ a ċaṗṗaing etiṗ ṗoeḋaiḃ ḋeiṗ a ġaḃala.')

[Cal. 1an. [ṗ. 1., l. xu.ª], Anno Domini M.º cc.º lxx.º ui.º ʰ[-ix.º] Ṫomaltaċ hUa Conċoḃuiṗ, aiṗdeṗpuc Ṫuama, ṗai Eṗenn aṗ eineċ 7 aṗ uaiṗli, aṗ ṗoċṗaideċt 7 aṗ eiḋlucaḋ,¹ quieuit in [Chṗiṗto].—Mael-Sheċlainn,ᶜ mac Ṫoiṗṗḋelḃaiġ, occiṡuṗ eṡt.ᶜ—Conċoḃuṗ, mac Diaṗmata, mic Maġnuṗa hUi Conċoḃuiṗ, occiṡuṗ eṡt.—Ġilla-in-Choimḋeḋ hUa Ceṗḃalla[i]n, eṗpuc Ṫiṗe-hEoġain, quieuit inᵈ [Chṗiṗto].—Muṗċaḋ | hUa² Neaċtain do maṗḃaḋ do Domnalleᵉ hUa² Neaċtain. Ocuṗ compac' d'ṗuaġṗa[ḋ] do Roiḃeṗt hUa² Neċtain, do deṗḃṗaṫaiṗ

A.D. 1276. ¹ eiḋlacuḋ, B. ² O, A. ᵇ 1279, overhead, n. t. h., B; *aliter*, 1279, n. t. h., C. ᶜ⁻ᶜ om., B, C, D. ᵈ om., B. ᵉ Choṗmac—*Cormac*,

---

³ *Blood in one vessel.*—For the antiquity of this method of covenanting, see L.L., p. 302b (*History of the Boruma*). The king of Ulster saw in a dream a vat one-third full of human blood, one-third of new milk and one-third of wine, in the centre of his house. The narrative then goes on: Atċondaiṗc iaṗum Conċoḃuṗ inn aiṗlingte ṗin. Ocuṗ iṡ amlaid atċonnaic Laigin 7 Ulaid 'má'n daḃaiġ ic a hól. Ocuṗ "ṗoṗetaṗṗa," aṗ ṡe, "iṡ é in cottaċ ṗotaiṗṡġeṗed andṡin. Uaiṗ iṡ í ind ṗuil atċeṡṡ iṡṡin daḃaċ ṗuil na da Coiċed i compaċ. Iṡ é in lemnaċt in ċanóin ċomḋeta ċanait cleṗiġ na da ċoiċed. Iṡ é in ṗin Coṗp Cṗiṡt 7 a Ṗhuil eḋṗṗait na cleṗiġ.
Conchobur saw that vision afterwards. And he saw thus,— the Lagenians and the Ultonians around the vat a-drinking therefrom. And "I know," quoth he, "that is the covenant that was prophesied then. For the blood that was seen [by us] in the vat is the blood of the two Fifths [Ulster and Leinster] a-contending. The new milk is the Canon of the Lord which the clergy of the two Fifths chant. The wine is the Body of Christ and His Blood which the clergy offer."
See also the *Yellow Book of Lecan*, T.C.D., H. 2. 16, col. 313 (the reference to which I owe to a Note in the *A. L. C.*, i. 460-1): "Do ḋenam ṗita iteṗ ṗil Taiḋg, mic Cein 7 ṗil Eoġain, mic Neill, tanac," ol ṡe. Do ġniteṗ iaṗum coḋaċ annṡin etaṗṗu 7 cumaiṡċo Caiṗneċ a ṗuil i n-oen leaṗtaṗ

bhar Ua Briain, king of Thomond, was taken prisoner by the son of the Earl of Clare. And they were after putting their blood in one vessel³ and after making gossipred and after pledging relics and bells to each other. And he was drawn between steeds after his capture.) (1275)

Kalends of Jan. [on 1st feria, 15th of the moon], A.D. 1276¹[-9]. Tomaltach Ua Conchobuir,² archbishop of Tuaim, formost in Ireland³ for generosity and for nobility, for succouring and for bestowal, rested in Christ.—Mael-Sechlainn, son of Toirrdhelbach [Ua Conchobuir], was slain.—Conchobur, son of Diarmait, son of Maghnus Ua Conchobuir, was slain.—Gilla-in-Coimded⁴ Ua Cerballain, bishop of Tir-Eogain, rested in Christ.—Murchadh⁵ Ua Neachtain was killed by Domnall Ua Neachtain. And [1279]

oiblinib 7 rrubair amal doronrat in caoac aimrin 7 arbert Muircertach . . .
Cumarcter a ruil co bect.
A mic Erca co mornert,
Co rcribtar i lebar lem
Coaac Eogain ir Gaileng.
"For the making of peace between the seed of Tadg, son of Cian and the seed of Eogan, son of Niall, came I," quoth he. Thereupon the covenant was made there and Cairnech mingles the blood of both in one vessel and writes how they made the covenant there and Muircertach said . . .
[A quatrain, bidding St. Cairnech depart. The latter replies in *Debide* metre, saying *inter alia* :]
  Let the blood be mingled duly,
  Thou son of Erc of great power,
  That there be written in a book by me
  The covenant of Eogan and of the Gailenga.
[1279] ¹*1276*.—The entries of the (textual) year 1276 are given in the *A. L. C.* under 1279.

² *Ua Conchobuir.*—See 1258, note 3, *supra*. The text is here three years antedated. About June, 1279, the primate wrote to the king in favour of the Franciscan, Malachy, who, when Tuam lately became vacant by the death of T[omaltach], was postulated by the dean, archdeacon and some of the canons (*D. I.*, II. 1576).
At the election, five canons voted for canon Nicholas; the dean and the remaining two, for Malachy. The matter was referred to the Curia. The protracted proceedings that ensued are detailed in the Bull of Honorius IV. (July 12, 1286) transferring Stephen de Foleburne from Waterford to Tuam (Theiner, pp. 135–6).
³ *In Ireland.*—Genitive in the original.
⁴ *Gilla-in-Coimded.* — *Servant of the Lord.*
⁵ *Murchadh, etc.* — "Morrogh O'Neaghten was killed by Donnole

Murċaḋa hUi Neaċtain, aṗ Ḋomnall, 7 Roibert do
marbaḋ ann (do'n ḟir ċetna irin compuc rin).

(Ḋomnall, mac Ġilla-Criṡd hUi Neaċtain, do
marbaḋ la hAeḋ hUa Conċeanainn.)

[bir.]
[B 64d]

Kal. Ian. [f. 11., l. xxvi.,] Anno Domini M.° cc.° lxx.°
uii.° [-lxxx.°] | Aeḋ Muimneċ hUa Concobuir (idon, riġ
Connaċt in tan ro) do marbaḋ la clainn Muircertaiġ
(aġ Caill-in-daingean). Caṫal, mac Concobuir ruaiḋ,
do riġaḋ do Connaċtaiḃ.—Seoan hUa Laiḋiġ, erpuc
Cille-alaḋ, quieuit in [Chrirto].—Mail-Seċlainn hUa
Ġairmleġaiḋ, tairec Cenuil-Moein 7 Concobur hUa
Ġairmleġaiḋ occiri runt per Tellaċ-Modoran.

(Aemann O Congaile, oircinneaċ Ros-orcer, raoiḋ-
cleireċ, mortu[u]r ert.)

Kal. Ian. [f. iiii., l. uii.], Anno Domini M.° cc.° lxx.°
uiii.° [-lxxx.° i.°] Taḋġ, mac Caṫail Mic Diarmata, ri
Muiġi-Luirġ, rai n-einiġ 7 n-eġnoma, quieuit in
[Chrirto].—Caṫ Dirirt-da-criċ eter Conall 7 Eoġan,
dú i troċair Ḋomnall hUa Ḋomnaill (le hAeḋ m-

B, C, D. ¹Copmac—*Cormac*, B, C, D. ⁵⁻⁵ om., B, C, D. This is a most
extraordinary misconception. The compiler of the B text mistook *compac*,
(*single*) *combat*, for the personal name *Cormac*. Then, by substitution and
omission, he makes *Cormac* (not Domnall) the slayer; and says *Cormac
was challenged* (*d'ḟuaġra[ḋ]*) by Robert (instead of Robert challenging
Domnall) to combat. C and D follow B, but render *d'ḟuaġra[ḋ]* by
banishment! The final clause C translates: "and Robert killed in that";
D: *in quo Robertus occisus fuit.* ᵇ⁻ᵇ n. t. h., A; om., B, C, D.

A.D. 1277. ¹-eaġ—, A. ²Moan, A. ³O, A. ⁴-eaġ—, B. ᵇ 1280
overhead, n. t. h., B; *alias* 1280, n. t. h., C. ᶜ⁻ᶜ itl, n. t. h., A; om., B,
C, D. The first is the only entry given in D. ᵈ⁻ᵈ n. t. h. (nor the hand
that made the previous additions), A; om., B, C, D.

A.D. 1278. ¹topċ—, B. (Both readings are equally good.) ᵇ 1281,
overhead, n. t. h., B; *alias* 1281, n. t. h., C. ᶜ⁻ᶜ itl, n. t. h., A; om., B, C, D.

O'Neaghten; whereupon Robert | Morrough, challenged him single
O'Neaghten, brother of the said | combatt of hand to hand, which

combat was challenged by Robert Ua Nechtian, [namely] [1279] by the brother of Murchadh Ua Nechtain, on Domnall and Robert was killed therein (by the same man in that combat).

(Domnall,[1] son of Gilla-Crisd Ua Neachtain was killed (1276) by Aedh Ua Concheanainn.)

Kalends of Jan. [on 2nd feria, 26th of the moon], A.D. [1280 Bis.] 1277[1][-80]. Aedh Ua Concobuir the Momonian (namely, king of Connacht at this time) was killed by the Clann-Muircertaigh (at the Wood of the Stronghold).—Cathal, son of Concobur [Ua Conchobair] the Red, was made king by the Connachtmen).—John Ua Laidhig,[2] bishop of Cell-aladh, rested in Christ.—Mail-Sechlainn Ua Gairmleghaidh, chief of Cenel-Moein and Concobur Ua Gairmleghaidh were slain by the Tellach-Modoran.

(Edmond O Congaile, herenagh of Ros-orcer, a learned (1277) cleric, died.)

Kalends of Jan. [on 4th feria, 7th of the moon], A.D. [1281] 1278[1][-81]. Tadhg, son of Cathal Mac Diarmata, king of Magh-Luirg, eminent for hospitality and prowess, rested in Christ. The battle of Disert-da-crich [was fought] between [Cenel-]Cona[i]ll and [Cenel-]Eoga[i]n, where fell Domnall Ua Domnaill[2] (by Aedh Ua Neill the Tawny

---

the said Daniel answered and killed Robert also." Mageoghegan, 1279.

The *F. M.* also understood it rightly (*ad an.*).

(1276) [1] *Domnall, etc.*—Given in the *A. L. C.* and *F. M.* at 1279.

[1280] [1] *1277.*—The entries of the (textual) year 1277, with the exception of the last, are given in the *A. L. C.* under 1280.

[2] *Ua Laidhig.*—On Dec. 9, 1280, letters of licence to elect were issued to the Dean and Chapter of Killala, who had notified the death of J[ohn], their late bishop (*D. I.*, II. 1770). They elected Donatus [=Donnchadh], the dean, who received the royal assent, April 16, 1281. (*Ib.* 1816.)

The events of this year are accordingly three years predated.

[1281] [1] *1278.* = 1281 of the *A. L. C.*

[2] *Ua Domnaill.*—This, very probably, is the *Oudonnildus*, whose proclaimed head Thomas de Maundeville caused to be carried to the Exchequer, Dublin; for which the

buiðe hUa Neill 7 le Mac Maipcin ͨ), ɪᴅon,ᵈ ꝼep ꝺap'-
ȝiallaꝺup ꝼip-Manač 7 Oipȝialla 7 upmóp ȝaiðel
Connačc 7 Ulaꝺ, accmaꝺ bec 7 ꝼip-Opeipnȝ uile. In
c-en Ȝhaiðel pob' ꝼepp einec͘ 7 oipečup; peicem coiccenn
ɪapčaip na hEoppa. Ocup a aðnacul i Mainipcep na
m-ꝺpačap i n-Ooipe Coluim-cille, ap m-bpeič buaða
ȝač uile ṁaič[i]upa. Ocup ap ɪaꝺ ꝼo ba ꝼepp ꝺomap-
baꝺ ann: ɪᴅon, Maelꞅuanaiȝ O ꝺaiȝill, caipec͘ na cpi
cuač 7 Eoȝan, mac Mail-cShečlainn hUi Oomnaill 7
Cellač Uaˢ ꝺuiȝill, in c-én caipec͘ pob' ꝼepp einec͘ 7
ciðnacul (ꝺobiͨ) i n-aen aimpip ꝼpip 7 Ȝilla Mac
ꝼlanncaða, caipec͘ Oapcpaiȝi 7 Oomnall Mac Ȝille-
ꝼhinnén, caipec͘ Mhuinncepi-Peoꝺača[i]n 7ᵈ Ainꝺilep
O ꝺaiȝill 7 Ouꝺȝall, a mac 7 Enna hUaˢ Ȝaipmleaȝaið,
pȝcairecͨ͘ Censuil-Moein⁴ 7 Copmac, mac ɪnꝺ ꝼipleiȝinn
hUi Oomnaill, caipec͘ ꝼana[i]c 7 Ȝilla-in-Choimꝺeȝˢ
O Maelaꝺuin, pi Luipȝ 7 Capmac, mac Capmaic hUi
A 63b Oomnaill 7 Ȝilla-na-n-óc Mac Calpeꝺocaip | 7 Mael-
Sečlainn, mac Neill hUi ꝺuiȝill 7 Ainꝺilep, mac
Muipcepcaiȝ hUi Oomnaill 7 Maȝnup Mac Cuinn 7
Ȝilla-na-naem O hEoċaȝa[i]n 7 Muipcepcač hUa ꝼlaič-
bepcaič 7 Muipcepcač Mac-ɪn-Ullcaiȝ 7 ꝼlaičbepcač
Maȝ ꝺuiðeča[i]n 7 ꝺaine ɪmꝺa aili⁶ ꝺo macaiꝺ piȝ 7
caipec͘ 7 ꝺ'oȝlačaiꝺ nač aipimčep punn.—Cač ecep na
ꝺaipeꝺačaiꝺ 7 in⁷ Cimpóȝač, ꝺú in pomebaiꝺ ap na
B 65a ꝺaipeꝺačaiꝺ 7 ꝺ'ap'mapbaꝺͨ ann Uilliam ꝺaipeꝺ | 7
Aꝺam ꝼleimenn 7 ꝺaine ɪmꝺa aili⁸ 7 ꝺobaꝺup ꝺiap
Ȝaiðelač ap leč in Cimpoȝaiȝ ꝺočinnꝼec ap ꝺeoȝačc 7

ᵃ ꝼep-m—(g. pl.), B; erroneously. ᵇ O, A. ⁴-Moan, A. ˢ Ȝillan—(=ȝilla-
in—), A. ⁶ eile, A; ſi., B. ⁷ an, A. ⁸ ſi., A, B. ᵈ om., A. ͨ itl., n. t. h., A; om.,
B. ᶠ piȝ, itl., n. t. h., A. ᵍ ꝺo mapbaꝺ (ꝺo for po and the relative om.), B.

---

justiciary, De Foleburne, bishop of Waterford, was twice commanded (Feb. 14, 16, 1283) to pay what was due to him (D. I., II. 2049-51). If so, the textual date is three years in advance.

and by Mac Martain); namely, the man to whom were [1281] subject Fir-Manach and Oirghialla and very great part of the Gaidhil of Connacht and Ulidia, save a little and all Fir-Breifne. The one Gaidhel that was best of hospitality and principality; the general guarantor of the West of Europe. And he was buried in the Monastery of the Friars in Doire of [St.] Colum-cille after gaining victory of every goodness. And these were the best that were killed there: namely, Maelruanaigh O'Baighill, chief of "the Three Territories" and Eogan, son of Mail-Sechlainn Ua Domnaill and Cellach Ua Baighill, the one chief of his own time that was best of hospitality and bestowal and Gilla Mac Flannchadha, chief of Dartraighi and Domnall Mac Gille-Fhinnen, chief of Muinnter-Peodacha[i]n and Aindiles O'Baighill and Dubhghall, his son and Enna Ua Gairmleaghaidh, royal chief of the Cenel-Moein and Cormac, son of the Lector Ua Domnaill, chief of Fanat and Gilla-in-Choimdegh O'Maeladuin, king of Lurg and Carmac,[3] son of Carmac[3] Ua Domnaill and Gilla-na-noc[4] Mac Calredocair and Mael-Sechlainn, son of Niall Ua Baighill and Aindiles, son of Muircertach Ua Domnaill and Maghnus Mac Cuinn and Gilla-na-naem O'Eochaga[i]n and Muircertach Ua Flaithbertaich and Muircertach Mac-in-Ulltaigh[5] and Flaithbertach Mag Buidhecha[i]n and many other persons of the sons of kings and chiefs and of men-at-arms that are not reckoned here.—A battle [was fought] between the Barrets and the Cusack, where defeat was inflicted on the Barrets and whereby were killed William Barret and Adam Fleming and many other persons. And there were two Gaidhil on the side of Cusack who surpassed many of the other

---

[3] *Carmac.*—Rightly, *Cormac*. The *o* was assimilated to the *a*.

[4] *Gilla-na-noc.*—*Servant (devotee) of the virgins.*

[5] *Mac-in-Ulltaigh.* — *Son of the Ultonian;* anglicized Mac Nulty.

2 A

ap Lamað ap mopan do daimb ailib,ᵍ idon, Taiclec O Dubda ⁊ Taiclec O baiξill.

Kal. 1an. [p.ª u., L. xuiii.ª], Anno Domini M.° cc.° Lxx.° ix.° ᵇ[-Lxxx.°ii.°] Taiclec, mac Maelpuanaiȝh hUi Dhubda, pi hUa¹-piacpac, in duine pob' pepp einec ⁊ eȝnum ⁊ innpoiȝid do° Ȝaidelaib dobí i n-a aimpip,ᶜ a mapbad le hAdam Cimpóȝ ap tpaiȝ Eotaille.—Lapaip-pina, inȝen Catail cpoibde[i]pȝ, [in] ten pob' uaipte i' n-Epinn i ⁿ-a haimpip,ᵈ quieuit in [Chpipto].—Mata (puad°) O Raiȝillaiȝ do eȝ.—Ȝilla-Ippu³ mop Maȝ Thiȝepna[i]n, taipec Thellaiȝ-Duncada ⁊ Lettpomán na bpeipne, quieuit in [Chpipto].—Cacal, mac Ȝilla-na-naem, hUa pepȝail quieuit in Chpipto.ᶠ—Nluipcep-tac Mac Mupcada, pi Laiȝen, do mapbad do Ȝhallaib ⁊ a depbpatáip (eile,ᵍ idonʰ), Apt Mac Mupcada.—Snecta mop ⁊ picc o Hollaic co peil bpiȝdi ipin blia-dain pi.ʰ

Kal. 1an. [p.ª iii., L. xxix.ª], Anno Domini M.° cc.° Lxxx.° [-iii.°] Tadȝ, mac Domnaill Ippaip hUi Concobuip, do mapbad la Luiȝnib.—Aed buide¹ hUa Neill do mapbad le Maȝ Matȝamna (idon,ᶜ La bpian° ⁊ᵈ Leip hUa [Raȝallaiȝ]ᵈ.)

A.D. 1278. ᵃ ii., A, B.
A.D. 1279. ¹ O, A. ² a, A. ³ Ipa, A. ⁴ -uiȝ, B. ᵇ 1282, overhead, n. t. h., B; *alias* 1282, n. t. h., C. ᶜ⁻ᶜ om., B, C, D. ᵈ⁻ᵈ i n-a dutaid— *in her country*, B; om., C, D. ᵉ itl., n. t. h., A; om., B, C, D. ᶠ om., A. ᵍ itl., n. t. h., A; om., B, C, D. ʰ om., B, C; given in D.
A.D. 1280. ¹ buidi, B.— ᵇ 1283, overhead, n. t. h., B; *alias* 1283, n. t. h., C. ᶜ⁻ᶜ itl., n. t. h., A; om., B, C. Given in D. ᵈ⁻ᵈ n. t. h., A; om., C, D. The word in square brackets is supplied from the *Annals of Loch Cé* (1283).

[1282] ¹ *1279 = 1282 of the A. L. C.*
² *Prop.—Supressor*, D.
³ *Mac Murchadha.—*One of the charges brought against De Fol-burne, as justiciary, related to the head-money of these two Mac Mur-roughs. (D. I., II. 1999, 2333-4;

persons for courage and for dexterity, namely, Taichlech O'Dubhda and Taichlech O'Baighill. [1281]

Kalends of Jan. [on 5th feria, 18th of the moon], A.D. 1279¹[-82]. Taichlech, son of Maelruanaigh Ua Dubhda, king of Ui-Fiachrach, the person of the Gaidhil that was best in hospitality and valour and attack in his time, was killed by Adam Cusack on the strand of Eothaill.—Lasairfhina, daughter of Cathal Red-hand [Ua Conchobair], the woman that was noblest in Ireland in her time, rested in Christ.—Matthew (the Red) O'Raighillaigh died.—Gilla-Issu mor Mag Tigerna[i]n, chief of Tellach-Dunchadha and prop² of Breifni, rested in Christ.—Cathal, son of Gilla-na-naem Ua Ferghail, rested in Christ.—Muircertach Mac Murchadha,³ king of Leinster, was killed by the Foreigners and his (other) brother, (namely) Art Mac Murchadha [was killed by them].—Great snow and frost from the Nativity [1281] to the feast of [St.] Brigit [Feb. 1] in this year. [1282]

Kalends of Jan. [on 6th feria, 29th of the moon], A.D. 1280¹[-3]. Tadhg, son of Domnall Ua Conchobuir of Irras, was killed by the Luighni.—Aedh Ua Neill the Tawny² was killed by Mag Mathgamna (that is, by Brian and by Ua Raghallaigh). [1283]

III. 2.) From the date of No. 1999, (Ap. 29, 1282) the year in which they were slain can be inferred.

(1283) ¹ *1280* = 1283 of the A. L. C.

² *Aedh the Tawny.*—Thus amplified in D: Hugo Flauu*, alias Eadh Boy O'Neill, a quo dicitur Clanhuboy, omni estimatione, potentia et principalitate dignus inter Hibernos sui temporis, occisus fuit per Mac Mahowny, nominatum Brien, hoc anno.

It adds : Guerra crudelis inter Odonem O'Donill et suum fratrem, Terleum, qui coegit Odonem permanere in Tireonia, unde ipse O'Donill ueuastauit magnam part-m Tireoniae.

I have not found the original of the foregoing entry.

364   ccнraia ulacoh.

A63c [Bis.] Kal. Ian. [p.* uii., l. x.*], Œnno Domini M.° cc° lxxx.°
1.° b[-iiii.°] Muirir hUa¹ Concobuir, errur Oil-rinn,² in'
Chrirro quieuit.*—Donncaḋ hUa¹ briain, ri Tuaḋ-
Muman, do marbaḋ la Toirrḋelbac hUa m-briain.—
Œmlaim ͩ O Tomoltaiġ, toġa conrirmaiti erircori Oil-
rinn,² quieuit in [Chrirto].ᵈ—Oubġall, mac Maġnura
hUi baiġill, toireć Cloići-Cinnraelaiḋ, do marbaḋ la
muinnter hUi Mailġaići.—Mac na haiḋće³ Mac
Dorćaiḋ, toireć Cenuil-Luaćain (no°-Duaćain'), quieuit
in [Chrirto].

(Ġilla-Iru' Mac Tiġernain, arḋ toireać Chinel-
brenainn, mortuur ert.'—No,' ġumaḋ uire ro, rcilicet
[Œ.D.] 1281, Mata hUa Raiġillaiġ, ri breirne.')

B 65b Kal. Ian. [p.* ii, l. xxi.*], Œnno Domini M.° cc° lxxx.°
ii.° b[-u.°] Simon hUa¹ Ruairc, errur na breirne,
quieuit in [Chrirto.—Maiḋm do ćabairt do Maġnur
hUa¹ Concobuir ar Œoaiḋ Cimroġ 7 ar Ġallaiḃ Iartair
Connact aġ Ear-dara, du inar'marbaḋ daine imḋa 7
inar'ġabaḋ Colin Cimróġ, a derbratair, a m-braiġdenur
do cinn na riġeḋ do leġaḋ ḋó rein, tareir a muinntera
do marbaḋ co mór.—Maiḋm° tuc Pilib Mac Ġor-
de[i]lb, ar muinnter Maġnura hUi Concobuir ar
Sliab-ġam, ġur'marbaḋ moran do ġlarlać ann.'—Eru

A.D. 1281. ¹ O, A. ² Oilerinn, A. ³-ci, A. ⁴ Mhag—, B. ᵃ⁻ᵃ Blank
space, A, B. ᵇ 1284, overhead, n. t. h., B; rectius 1285, n. t. h., C.
ᶜ⁻ᶜ quieuit in [Chrirto], B. ᵈ⁻ᵈ om., B, C, D. ᵉ⁻ᵉ itl., t. h., B; above the
l of Luaċain, in A, the t. h. placed no, D—or D—, meaning that the word
may have commenced with D' not L. Hence the note in B. Ch—l;
D, D' ᶠ⁻ᶠ n. t. h., A; om., B, C, D. ᵍ⁻ᵍ t. m., t. h., A; om., B, C, D.

A.D. 1282. ¹ O, A.— ᵇ 1285, overhead, n. t. h., B; rectius 1286, n. t.
h., C. ᶜ⁻ᶜ om., B, C, D.

[1284] ¹ 1281 = 1284 of the   ² Ua Conchobuir.—See 1263 (=
A. L. C.   1265), note 3, supra.

Kalends of Jan. [on 7th feria, 10th of the moon], A.D. [1281 Bis.] 1281¹[-4]. Maurice Ua Conchobuir,² bishop of Oil-finn, rested in Christ.—Donnchadh Ua Briain, king of Thomond, was killed by Toirdhelbach Ua Briain.—Amlaim O'Tomoltaigh, bishop-elect [and] confirmed³ of Oil-finn, rested in Christ.—Dubghall, son of Maghnus Ua Baighill chief of Cloch-Cinnfhaelaidh, was killed by the people of Ua Mailgaithi.—"Son of the night" Mac Dorchaidh, chief of Cenel-Luachain (or,-Duachain), rested in Christ.⁴

(Gilla-Isu¹ Mac Tigernain, arch-chief of Cinel-Brenainn, (1281) died.—Or, it may be on this year, namely, 1281,² [the death of] Matthew Ua Raighilluigh, king of Breifni [ought to be].)

Kalends of Jan. [on 2nd feria, 21st of the moon], A.D. [1285] 1282¹[-5]. Simon Ua Ruairc, bishop of Breifni [Kilmore], rested in Christ.—Defeat was given by Maghnus Ua Conchobuir to Adam Cusack and to the Foreigners of the West of Connacht at Eas-dara; where were killed many persons and Colin Cusack, his brother, was taken in security, to allow [Adam] himself to go away, after great havoc had been made of his people.—Defeat was inflicted by Philip Mac Goisdeilb on the people of Maghnus Ua Conchobuir on Sliabh-gamh, so that many recruits

---

³ *Bishop-elect [and] confirmed.*—Literally, *choice of a confirmed bishop.* (For the idiom, see 1126, note 2, *supra.*) His death took place after confirmation of the election (by the archbishop of Tuam) and before consecration.

⁴ *In Christ.*—D adds, from what source I know not: O'Donill ad predandum inferiorem Conaciam inuasit eam et finito proposito rediit victoriosus.

(1281) ¹ *Gilla-Isu, etc.*—This is a repetition of the fourth entry of the textual year 1279(=1282), *supra.*

² *1281.*—The obit of *Ua Raighillaigh* is given as the third item at 1279(=1282), *supra.* The *A. L. C.* call him chief of Muinter-Maelmordha (the O'Reilly's of Breifny).

[1285] ¹ *1282*=1285 and 1286 of the *A. L. C.*

Mac Gille-Phinnein do marbaḋ.—Ruaiḋri hUa¹ Gaḋra, ri Sleiḃe-Luġa, do marbaḋ la Mac Pheorair ar a loč rein.

[CC.D. M.° cc.° lxxx.° ui.°] Sluaġ mór la hIarla Ulaḋ i Connaċtu,² gur'mill moran do ċellaiḃ 7 do ṁainirtreċaiḃ. Ocur ger'b'eḋ, doġaḃ nert ġač conair rainic 7 doġaḃ braiġdi³ Connaċt⁰ 7⁰ Conaill 7 Eogain 7 doairṁiġ Domnall hUa Neill (idon,ᵈ Domnall, mac Brain⁴) 7 tuc riġi do Niall Culanač hUa¹ Neill.—Muirir mael Mac Geralt quieuit in [Chrirto].

Kal. Ian. [f.ᵃ iiii., l. x.iii.ᵃ] Anno Domini M.° cc.° lxxx.° iii.°ᵇ[-uii.°] Mata, mac Muirġira, mic Caṫail, quieuit in [Chrirto].—Diarmait⁰ Miḋeč (macᵈ Diarmada, mic Caṫail Mic Diarmoda, idon, ri Muinntire-Mailruanaidᵈ) quieuit in Chrirto.ᵉ—Ploirint O Ġibella[i]n, arciḋeočun Oil-finn. fellrum eolair 7 inntliuċta,¹ quieuit in [Chrirto].—Ġilla-na-nóġ O Mannaċa[i]n, ri na Tuaṫ, quieuit in Chrirto.—Mael-Seċlainn,ᶜ mac Tomaltaiġ, Mac Oireċtaiġ do marbaḋ la Toirrḋelbač, mac Eogain hUi Concobuir, a n-ḋiġailt a aṫar do tregaḋ do Tomaltač cetna do macaiḃ Toirrḋelbaiġ.ᵉ— Adam Cimróġ quieuit in [Chrirto].—| Bean-Muman, ingen hUi Caṫa[i]n, mortua ert.

A.D. 1282. ²-ta, A. ³-ḋe, B. ᵈ⁻ᵈitl., n. t. h., A; om., B, C, D.

A.D. 1283. ¹ inṫ—, B. ᵇ 1286, overhead, n. t. h., B; *alias* 1287, n. t. h., C. ᶜ⁻ᵉ om., B, C, D. ᵈ⁻ᵈ itl., n. t. h., MS. (A).

---

² *Killed.*—Cruciatus occisus est (*cruciatus* without warrant in the original), D. The entry in the A. L. C. states that he died a natural death.

³ *Mac Fheorais.*—Son of Pierce; the Irish patronymic assumed by the Berminghams. The eponymous head was probably the Pierce mentioned [1305] *infra*.

[1286] ¹ *A great host, etc.*—This and the following entry are given in the A. L. C. under 1286.

Henceforward, down to 1309 of the text (= 1313), the dating is four years in advance.

[1287] ¹ *1283* = 1287 of the A. L. C.

² *Gilla-na-nog* (*devotee of the Virgins*).—*Gilla-na-neave* (*devotee of the saints*), D.

³ *Rested in Christ.*—On Sept. 7, according to the A. L. C. This tends to prove that the text is four years in advance. In 1287, Sept. 7 fell on Sunday. In 1283 it was

were killed therein.—Henry Mac Gille-Fhinnein was killed.[2]—Ruaidhri Ua Gadhra, king of Sliabh-Lugha, was killed by Mac Fheorais[3] on his own lake. [1285]

[A.D. 1286]. A great host[1] [was led] by the Earl of Ulster into Connacht, so that he destroyed many of the churches and monasteries. And moreover, he obtained sway in every direction he went and received the pledges of Connacht [and Cenel-]Conaill and [Cenel-]Eogain. And he deposed Domnall Ua Neill (namely, Domnall, son of Brian) and gave the kingship to Niall Culanach Ua Neill.—Maurice Fitz Gerald the Bald rested in Christ. [1286]

Kalends of Jan. [on 4th feria, 13th of the moon], A.D. 1283[1][-7]. Matthew, son of Maurice, son of Cathal [Mac Diarmata], rested in Christ.—Diarmait the Midian (son of Diarmad, son of Cathal Mac Diarmoda, namely, king of Muinnter-Mailruanaidh) rested in Christ.—Florence O'Gibellain, archdeacon of Oil-finn, distinguished in knowledge and intelligence, rested in Christ.—Gilla-na-nog[2] O'Mannacha[i]n, king of "The Territories," rested in Christ.[3]—Mael-Sechlainn, son of Tomaltach Mac Oirechthaigh, was killed by Toirdhelbach, son of Eogan Ua Concobuir, in revenge of his father having been abandoned by the same Tomaltach to the sons of Toirdhelbach.[4]—Adam Cusack[5] rested in Christ.—Beau-Muman, daughter of Ua Catha[i]n, died. [1287]

Tuesday,—an incidence devoid of note.

[4] *Sons of Toirdhelbach.* — The editor of the *A. L. C.* suggests *sons of Tomaltach*; because, as the sentence stands, Toirdelbach takes vengeance on Tomaltach for having abandoned the father of Toirdelbach to the sons of Toirdelbach. Perhaps, however, there existed a family feud between Toirdelbach and his father on the one side and the sons of Toirdelbach on the other.

The *F. M.*, as was their wont, omitted the passage containing the difficulty.

[5] *Cusack.*—He died at the close of the year, as his name appears in a Roll of receipt, Nov. 15, 1287. (*D. I.*, III. 341.)

368 ccmccla ulaoh.

[b̔ır.] Kal. Ian. [ɼ.ˢ u., L xx.ııı.,ᵃ] Anno Domini M.ᵒ cc.ᵒ lxxx.ᵒ ıııı.ᵒ[-uıııı.ᵒ] Michael Mac-ın¹-t-ṡaıɼ, eɼpuc Clocaıɼ, moɼtuuɼ eɼt.—Maġnuɼ hUa Concobuıɼ (ıɒon,ᶜ mac Concubaıɼ ɼuaıɒᵉ), maɼaen le ɼuaıɼ ɒo Connactaıb 7 hUı-mbɼıuın [hUa-] 7 Conmaıcne, ɒocect laıɼ ɒo ġabaıl ɼıġe Connact ɒó ɼeın. Ocuɼ ɒo haɼɼıgaɒ Catal ɼuaɒ, a ɒeɼbɼataıɼ 7 toct ɒoıbˊ² co hCE-Slıɼen, muɼ aɼoıbe Catal co n-a ɼocɼaıɒe 7 cumuɼc ɒoıb let aɼ let 7 Catal ɒo ġabaıl aıġıᵈ 7 maıɒm ɒo cabaıɼtaɼa muın[ɴ]ceɼ. Ocuɼ ɒohaıɼgeɒ uɼṁoɼ Connact ɒoˊnˊ³ ɒul ɼın 7 ɼıġı Connact ɒo ġabaıl aɼ eıgın ɒo Mhaġnuɼ.—Donncaɒᵉ ɼıabac, mac Maġnuɼa, mıc Muıɼceɼtaıġ hUı Concobuıɼ, quıeuıt ın [Chɼıɼto].ᶠ—Tec ɒo ġabaıl aɼ Mhaġnuɼ hUa Concobuıɼ ɒo Thoıɼɼɒelbac, mac Eoġaın hUı Concobuıɼ, ıɼın Ɽoɼ-
B 65c móɼ 7 Maġnuɼ ɒo lot ann 7 Ɽaġ|nall Mac Ɽaġnaıll, taıɼec Muıntcıɼı-hEolaıɼ, ɒo maɼbaɒ ɒˊen uɼcuɼ ɼoıġɒı 7 ɒoloıteɒ Nıall ġelbuıɒe hUaᵍ Concobuıɼ 7 ɒomaɼbaɒ ɒaıne aılıᵍ 7 ɒo beanaıɒ eıc maıtı ɒıb.—Sloıġʰ le Maġnuɼ O Concobuıɼ aɼ éıɼ a leıɼıɼ a Sıl-Muıɼeɒaıġ, ġuɼˊġaɒ a neɼt 7 a m-bɼaıġɒe.—Sluaġ leıɼan ıaɼla (ıɒon,ⁱ an t-ıaɼla ɼuaɒˁ) ɒocum Connact, co taınıc co Ɽoɼ-comaın 7 cum Maġnuɼa hUı Concobuıɼ, ɼı Chon-nact 7 ı n-aɒaıġ muınteɼı ın ɼıġ 7 Mıcᵏ Ġeɼaılt 7 ɒo-ġɼeannaıġeɒuɼ ın t-ıaɼla ım toct ɼeca ɼın 7 ní toɼɼact ıteɼ. Sġaılıɼ a ɼluaġ 7 a ɼocɼaıɒe ġan tenn ɒo ġabaıl.—Steaɼan, aɼɒeɼpuc Tuama 7 Ġıuɼtıɼ na hEɼenn, ın

A.D. 1284. ¹ an, B. ² ɒaıb, A. ³ ɒo (stroke over o=n omitted by oversight), A. ⁴ O, A. ⁵ ii., A, B. ⁶ mac, MS. (A). ᵇ alias 1287, over-head, n. t. h., B ; alias 1288, n. t. h., C ; 1288, on margin, D. ᶜ itl, n. t. h., A; om., B, C, D. ᵈ ann—in that (place), B. ᵉ om., B, C, D. ᶠ ᵍitl., n. t. h., MS.

[1288]. ¹ *1284* = 1288 of the A. L. C.

² *Michael, etc.*—See (1268) notes 1, 2, supra.

³ *Stephen.*—De Foleburne. He was transferred from Waterford (which he had held since 1274) by Honorius IV., July 12, 1286 (Theiner, p. 135-6) and died before July, 1288. A notable memoran-

Kalends of Jan. [on 5th feria, 24th of the moon,] A.D. [1288 Bis.] 1284¹[-8]. Michael² Mac-in-tshair, bishop of Clochar, died.—Maghnus Ua Concobuir (namely, son of Concubhar the Red), along with what he got to join him of the Connachtmen and of the Ui-Briuin and of Conmaicni, came to take the kingship of Connacht to himself. And Cathal the Red, his brother, was deposed. And they came to Ath-Slisen, where Cathal was with his force and they fought side for side and Cathal was taken by him and defeat inflicted on his people. And very large part of Connacht was harried on that occasion. And the kingship of Connacht was taken by force by Maghnus.— Donnchadh the Swarthy, son of Maghnus, son of Muircertach Ua Concobuir, rested in Christ.—A house was seized on Maghnus Ua Conchobuir by Toirdhelbach, son of Eogan Ua Conchobuir, in Ros-mor and Maghnus was injured therein and Raghnall Mac Raghnaill, chief of Muinnter-Eolais, was killed by one shot of an arrow and Niall Ua Conchobuir the Tawny was injured and other persons were killed. And good horses were taken from them.—A host [was led] by Maghnus O'Conchobuir after his healing into Sil-Muiredhaigh, so that he obtained sway over them and [obtained] their hostages.—A host [was led] by the Earl (namely, the Red Earl) to Connacht, until he came to Ros-Comain and to Maghnus Ua Conchobuir, king of Connacht and against the people of the king and Fitz Gerald. And they challenged the Earl to go beyond that and he went not accordingly. He disperses his host and his force without obtaining sway.— Stephen,³ archbishop of Tuaim and Justiciary of Ireland,

---

dum of the chattels belonging to him found in Tuam and Athlone was made in the beginning of that month. (*D. I.*, III. 406.) For his doings from his arrival in Ireland as "brother of the Hospital of St· John of Jerusalem in England" (*ib.*, II. 886) in 1270 to his death as justiciary, see the references under *Foleburne; Waterford, Brother Stephen* (*ib.* II.); *Waterford, Stephen; Tuam, Stephen* (*ib.* III.).

Chpıpτo quıeuıτ.—Caċal mac τaıdg, mıc Caċaıl Mıc Ɖıapmaτa, ꝺo ჳadaıl pıჳı Muıჳı-Luıpჳ.—Uıllıam Mac Ƒheopaıp, ꝺo ṫoჳa[d] cum aıpꝺeppocoıꝺe τuama.

|Cal. 1an. [p.ᵃ uıı., l. u.,ᵃ] Ccnno Ɖomını M.° cc.° lxxx.° ıı.°ᵇ[-ıx.°] τaꝺჳ hUa Ƒlannaჳa[ı]n, τaıpeċ Claınnı-Caċaıl, quıeuıτ ın [Chpıpτo].—Maṫa O 8ჳınჳın, aıpꝺṗenċaıd Epenn uıle, mopτuup epτ.—Mıleṗ, eppuc Conmaıcne, ıꝺon, ın Ɉaılleppuc. quıeuıτ ın [Chpıpτo].— Simon hUa¹ Ƒınaċτa, aıpcınneċ Oıl-ṗınn, quıeuıτ ın [Chpıpτo].— | Sluaჳad la Rıcapꝺ Ɖıuıꝺ 7 le Ɉallaıd na Mıde—7 Maჳnup hUa Conċobuıp, pı Connaċτ, leıpcum [U]ı Maıl-[Sh]eċlaınn, co τucad maıꝺm mop oppa° (ıꝺon,° maıꝺm ın Cpoıṗ-pleıde°) 7 pomapbad Rıċapꝺ Ɖıuıꝺ ann, ın Ɓapun mopuapalᵈ 7 a bpaıṫpeċa 7 8ecup hUa Cellaıჳ, ıꝺon, mac ın eppuıc.—Ƒıaċpa hUa Ƒlaınn, τaıpeċ 8ıl-Maılpuanaıჳ, ın τ-aen ꝺuıneˢ pob' ṗepp eıneċ 7 eჳnom 7 comaıpce ꝺobı ı Connaċτaıd, ꝺo° ꝺul ꝺo denum cleamnupa pe Ɉallaıd, ჳup'mapb mac Rıcaıpꝺ ṗınn aᶠ Ɓupc 7 Mac Uıllıam 7 Mac Ƒheopaıp ı meɓaıl e.—

A 64a

A.D. 1285. ¹O, A. ²opτa, A. ³-nı, B. ᵇ1289, overhead, n. t. h., B; *alias* 1289, n. t. h., B; 1289, on margin, D. The Mıleṗ item is omitted in D. ᶜˑᵈ l. m., t. h., A, B; om., C, D. ᵈmoṗ, B; followed by C. ᵉ a—*his*, B. ᶠom., A

ᵍ *Elected.*—Having gone to Rome for the purpose, he got his election confirmed by Nicholas IV., May 2, 1289. (Theiner, p. 142-3.) Thereupon, he was promoted from subdeaconship to deaconship and empowered (May 26) to receive priest's Orders from any bishop he should chose (*ib.* 144). On the same day the bishops of Killala and Clonfert were directed, either of them, with two other suffragans, to give him episcopal consecration (*ib.*). In addition to being rector of Athenry in Tuam, he held a benefice in Cashel, Killaloe and Killala respectively! To discharge the church debts of Tuam and support the archiepiscopal dignity, he was allowed (Aug. 5, 1289) to retain these four preferments for three years and to receive one year's revenue of every benefice vacated during the three years next ensuing, due provision being made for the cure of souls. The bishops of Lis-

rested in Christ.—Cathal, son of Tadhg, son of Cathal [1288]
Mac Diarmata, took the kingship of Magh-Luirg.—
William Mac Fheorais [Bermingham] was elected[4] to the
archbishopric of Tuaim.

Kalends of Jan. [on 7th feria, 5th of the moon,] A.D. [1289]
1285[1][-9]. Tadhg Ua Flannaga[i]n, chief of Clann-
Cathail, rested in Christ.—Matthew O'Sgingin, arch-
antiquary of all Ireland, died.—Miles,[2] bishop of Conmaicni [Ardagh], namely, the Foreign bishop, rested in
Christ.—Simon Ua Finachta, herenagh of Oil-finn, rested
in Christ.—A hosting by Richard Tuit [of Athlone] and
by the Foreigners of Meath—and Maghnus Ua Conchobuir,
king of Connacht, [was] with him—to [attack] Ua Mail-
[S]echlainn, so that a great defeat (namely, the defeat of
Crois-sliabh) was inflicted upon them. And Richard Tuit,
the great, noble Baron was killed[3] therein, as well as his
kinsmen and Jacques Ua Cellaigh, namely, the son of the
bishop.[4]—Fiachra Ua Flainn, chief of Muinnter-Mail-
ruanaigh, the best person for hospitality and prowess and
protection that was in Connacht, went to make marriage
alliance with the Foreigners, so that the son of Richard
de Burgh the Fair and Mac William [de Burgh] and
Mac Fheorais killed him in treachery.—A great host [was

---

more and Killaloe were to execute the terms of the concession (*ib.* p. 145).

[1289] [1]*1285* = 1289 of the *A. L. C.*

[2] *Miles.*—Of Dunstable. Appointed at the close of 1255, or early in 1256. (*D. I.*, II. 486.) As the temporalities were restored to his successor, Matthew, canon of Ardagh, Jan. 28, 1290 (*ib.* III.

574), Miles, it can scarcely be doubted, died in 1289. The text is consequently four years predated.

[3] *Killed.*—From a grant of custody of his lands and tenements issued Sept. 2, 1290 (*D. I.*, III. 764), it may be inferred that Tuite was slain in that year.

[4] *Bishop.*—Thomas O'Kelly, of Clonfert, who died in [1263], *supra.*

372 αηηαλα υλαοh.

Sluaξ mor le Mac Fheoραιr cum in⁴ Chalbaiξ hUi Concobuir 7 na mac⁵ riξ Laiξnec,⁶ co tucαð maiom mor rorro 7 gur'marbαð Mailir d'Eiretra 7 Goill imða aili⁷ 7 eic imða do buain de.

Kal. 1an. [f.ᵃ 1, L x.ui.ᵃ], Anno Domini M.° cc.° lxxx.' ui.°ᵇ[-xc.°] William Mac Fheoραιr do ξaðail αrdespo-coide [Tuamaᶜ].—In t-erροc hUa¹ Sedeca[i]n, idon, erρuc Cille-mic-n'Ouac, quieuit in [Chριrto].—Cairρri hUa Mail[-Sh]eclainn, ρi Miðe, in mac|αm ir moirg-nimαici² dobi i n-Eρinn i n-α aimrir, do marbað (le⁴ Ma[c] Coclanᵈ).—Sluαιξeð la Domnall, mac Oριαin hUi Neill i Cenel-nEoγαin, gur'cuir Niall hUa¹ Neill (idon,ᵈ Niall Culanacᵈ) αρ eiγin eirci 7 gur'γab rein riξi αρ lor α lαmα.—Aeð hUa³ Domnaill do αtriξαð d'α derbrαταιr rein, idon, do Toirrðelbac hUa³ Dom-naill, tre cumactain cinið α matar, idon, Clainni-Domnaill 7 Galloγlac n-imða aile⁴ (7' riξi do γaðail do rein αρ eiγinᵈ).

(hocᵉ anno Iohannes de Ianua, frater Ordinis Prae-dicatorum, auctorem qui dicitur Catholicon perfecit, reu αd finem perduxit, Nonis Marcii.ᶠ)

A.D. 1285. ⁴an, B. ⁵mic (which is meaningless), B. ⁶-eaca, A; -eca, B. The sense requires the gen. pl. ⁷eile, A; ii., B.

A.D. 1286. ¹O, A. ²-αιξι, B. ³O. B. ⁴eile, A; ii., B. ᵇ 1290, over-head, n. t. h., B; alias 1290, n. t. h., C; 1290, on margin, D. ᶜ Given in D. Cf. the last item of 1284. Here in A, l. m., t. h., is: αnnρo de rυo tuar—Here [under this year] comes that [entry regarding Mac Feorsii given] above [under 1284]. ᵈ⁻ᵈ itl., n. t. h., A; om., B, C, D. ᵉ˒ᶠ On text space, n. t. h., A; om., B, C, D.

---

³ *De Exeter.*—His name appears in a Roll of receipt, May 10, 1289 (*D. I.*, III. 475); which confirms the accuracy of the *Loch Cé* date.

[1290] ¹ *1286* = 1290 of the *A. L. C.*

²[*David*!].—Elected apparently in 1284 (*D. I.*, II. 2182). "David, bishop of Kilmacduagh," appears in a Roll of receipt, May 20, 1286 (*ib.*, III. 215). Nicholas, canon of the church, having announced the death of David, licence to elect was granted, June 13, 1290 (*ib.*,

led] by Mac Fheorais against the Calbach Ua Concobuir [1289] and the sons of the kings of Leinster, so that great defeat was put upon them. And Meyler de Exeter[5] and many other Foreigners were killed and many horses were taken from him.

Kalends of Jan. [on 1st feria, 16th of the moon,] A.D. [1290] 1286[1][-90]. William Mac Fheorais took [possession of] the archbishopric of Tuaim.—The bishop [David][2] Ua Sedechain, namely, bishop of Cell-mic-Duach, rested in Christ.—Cairpri Ua Mail-[S]echlainn, king of Meath, the most noble-deeded youth that was in Ireland in his time, was killed[3] (by Ma[c] Cochlan).—A hosting by Domnall, son of Briain Ua Neill, into Cenel-Eogain, so that he put Niall Ua Neill (namely, Niall Culanach) by force therefrom and took the kingship himself by power of his force.—Aedh Ua Domnaill was deposed by his own brother, namely, by Toirdhelbach Ua Domnaill, through the power of the tribe of his mother, namely, the Clann-Domnaill and many other Gallowglasses[4] (and he took the kingship to himself by force).

(This year John of Genoa,[1] Friar of the Order of (1286) Preachers, perfected, or brought to end, the Author that is called *Catholicon*, on the Nones [7th] of March.)

---

680). The textual date is thus four years in advance.

[3] *Killed.*—Treacherously, according to the *A. L. C.*

[4] *Gallowglasses.*—Literally, *Foreign youth* (a collective substantive). See Grace's Annals (*Ir. Arch. Soc.*), p. 71.

(1286) [1] *John of Genoa.*—John De Balbis, a Dominican, born in Genoa. Of the *Catholicon*, Quetif and Echard (*Script. Ord. Praed.*, p. 462) write: Opus continct Orthographiam, Prosodiam, Grammaticam, Rhetoricam, Etymologiam: proptereaque dicitur *Catholicon*, id est, opus universale. Cuius potissima pars est Vocabularium voces omnes primae, mediae et infimae Latinitatis complectens. Titulus in codicibus, qua manuscriptis, qua impressis: Incipit Summa, quae vocatur *Catholicon*, edita a F. Joanne de Janua, Ord. F. P. Ad calcem: Immensas omnipotenti Deo Patri et Filio et Spiritui Sancto gratiarum referimus actiones, qui nostrum *Catholicon* ex

Kal. Ian. (p.ˣ 11., l. xx.uii.ˣ), Anno Domini M.° cc.°
lxxx.° uiii. 1.° ᵇ[-xc.1.°] Toirrdelbač, mac Eogain hUi Concobuir, in duine ir° mo 7 ir° aille 7 rob' ferr eineč 7
egnom 7 corcur¹ dobí i n-Erinn, do⁴ marbad la Niall n-
gelbuide hUa Concobuir.—Sluag le Ricard a Burc, le
hIarla Ulad (idon,ᵉ in t-Iarla ruad'), i Tir-nEogain,
d'ar'atrig ré Domnall, mac Briain hUi Neill 7 dorigad
leir Niall Culanač O' Neill' 7 mur dorag² in t-Iarla in
tir, domarbad Niall Culanač le Domnall hUa Neill.
Ocur dorigad a huč an Iarla cetna le Mac Mairtin
7 le Mac Eoin mac Aeda buide hUi Neill (idon,ᵉ Brian,
mac Aeda buideᵉ) 7 rogagaid Domnall in tir.—Sluag
leirin | Iarla i Tir-Conaill cum Toirrdelbaig, gur'airg
in tir, eter cill 7 tuait 7 co tainic i Connactaibˢ co
hOil-finn 7 co tucadur Connacta felbraigde do.—

A.D. 1287. ¹-gur, A. ²-gaib, B. ³-čta, B. ᵇ 1291, overhead, n. t. h.,
B; *alias* 1291 n. t. h., C; 1291 on margin, D. ᶜ⁻ᵉ rob'—*that was*, B. ᵈ a
—*his*, B. ᵉ⁻ᶠ itl., n. t. h., A; om., B, C, D. ᶠᶠ om., B, C; given in D.

---

multis et diversis doctorum textu-
ris elaboratum atque contextum,
licet per multa annorum curricula,
in M.CC.LXXX.VI. Anno Domini,
Nonis Martii, ad finem usque perduxit.

The concluding words shew that
the person who made the additional
entry at this year had the *Catholicon*
before him.

Erasmus pokes fun at the *Catho-
licon* in the *Synodus Grammaticorum*:
Albinus: Quinam erant [libri]?
Bertulphus: Oh, praeclari omnes :
Catholicon, etc. (Erasmi *Colloquia*,
Amstelodami, Typ. Lud. Elzevirii,
1650, p. 417.)

Its chief interest lies in the fact
that it was, according to Trithe-
mius, the first example of block
printing. Treating of John of
Guttenberg and John Fust, he
says (*Chron. Hirsaug. a.l an.* 1450):
Imprimis igitur characteribus lit-
terarum in tabulis ligneis per
ordinem scriptis formisque compo-
sitis vocabularium *Catholicon* nun-
cupatum impresserunt : sed cum
iisdem formis nihil aliud potuerunt
inscribere, etc. Six other additions
of the work appeared up to 1506.

The Authors of the *Histoire
Litteraire de la France* do not fail
to turn his confession to account:
Balbi de Gênes, l'un de plus célèbres
grammariens dont l'Italie pût alors
s'enorgueillir, avoue qu'il ne sait
pas bien la langue d'Homère : mihi
non bene scienti linguam Graecum
[sic] (p. 142).

Kalends of Jan. (on 2nd feria, 27th of the moon,) A.D. [1291]
1287[1][-91]. Toirdhelbach, son of Eogan Ua Concobuir, the person who was greatest and handsomest and who was best of hospitality and prowess and triumph that was in Ireland, was killed by Niall Ua Concobuir the Tawny.—A host [was led] by Richard de Burgh [namely] by the Earl of Ulster (that is, the Red Earl) into Tir-Eogain, whereby he deposed Domnall, son of Brian Ua Neill and Niall Culanach O'Neill was made king by him. And when the Earl left the country, Niall Culanach was killed by Domnall Ua Neill. And the son of Aedh[2] Ua Neill the Tawny (namely, Brian, son of Aedh the Tawny) was made king, with assent of the same Earl, by Mac Martin and by Mac Eoin. And Domnall left the country.—A host [was led] by the Earl into Tir-Conaill against Toirdhelbach [Ua Domnaill], so that he harried the country, both church and territory. And he came into Connacht to Oil-finn and the Connachtmen gave deceptive pledges[3] to him.—

[1291] [1] *1287* = 1291 of the *A. L. C.*

[2] *Son of Aedh*—(*namely, Brian*).—The collocation of the subject (after the agent) has led the authors of C and D astray. C gives: "And was made king after by the consent of the Earle aforesaid by Mac Martin and Mac Eoin Mac Hugh Boy O'Neale." Read "The son [*mac*] of Hugh Boy [*the Tawny*] was made king," etc. D has: Bernardus [*recte*, Brianus], filius Odonis Flauui, regnauit authoritate Comitis et per institutionem Mag Martin et Macke Euoyne, filium Odonis Flaui. *Mac Eoin* and *mac Aedha* are here erroneously taken to be in apposition.

A scribal error, which passed unnoticed by the editor, occurs in the *A. L. C.* (1291). The person who was made king is called Niall, son of Aedh. In the entry of his death at 1295 in the same Annals, he is rightly named Brian, son of Aedh.

[3] *Deceptive pledges.*—That is, they intended nevertheless to cast off his authority as soon as they could. C makes an extraordinary blunder in this place: "Connaght made him the Feast of St. Briget!" That is, *fel*, deceit is taken for *feil*, feast and *braighde*, pledges, for *Brighde*, gen. of *Brigit*, a personal name. D also errs: Inhabitantes tradiderunt eidem *viles* tantum obsides. The *F. M.* omit *fel*, which is the chief word.

Concobuɩn hUa Ouɓɒa, ɲɩ hUa-Ρɩaɕɲaɕ,⁴ ɒo baɕaɓ aɲ ɩn
ɕ-Sɩnaɩnn.—Comɕoʒbaɩl ɒo ɓenum ɒo Chaɕal hUa
Concobuɩn 7 ɒo Nɩall ʒelbuɩɓe 7 ɒo luɕɕ ʒaɕa coɩmeɩɲʒɩ
ɒ'a ɲaɩbe acu, eɕeɲ ʒallaɩɓ 7 ʒaɩɓelaɩɓ, ɒ'aɩɕɲɩʒaɓ
Maʒnuɲa 7 ɩmɲeɲaɩn ɒo ɕabaɩɲɕ ɒoɩɓ ɩ Caɲaɩɓ-Culaɩnɒ
(alɩaɲ*-Chulṁaɩle*). Ocuɲ Caɕal ɒo loɕ ann 7 Muɲɕaɓ,
mac Caɩɒʒ hUɩ Concobuɩɲ, ɒo maɲbaɓ ann 7 ɒaɩne eɩle
7 eɩɕ ɩmɓa ɒo ɓuaɩn ɒo ṁuɩnnɕeɲ Maʒnuɲa 7 maɩɒm
ɒo ɕabaɩɲɕ aɲ ɲeɩn 7 a ɒul aɲ ɲo laɩm 7 cɲeɕa moɲa ɒo
ɓenum ɒo muɩnnɕeɲ Caɕaɩl [U]ɩ Concobuɩɲ 7 ɒo Nɩall
ʒelbuɩɓe aɲ n-ʒuɩn Caɕaɩl ɩ Caɩɲɲɩ. Ocuɲ Maʒnuɲ
O Concobaɩɲ, aɲ ɕeɕɕ ɒo Shɩl-Muɩɲeɓaɩʒ ɕuɩʒɩ 7 a aeɲ⁵
ʒɲaɒa ɲeɩn 7 ʒall[aɩɓ] Rora-|Comaɩn ɒ'a ɲoɩɲɩɕɩn aɲ
naṁaɲaɕ aɲ eɩɲ ɩn maɒma, ɕoɕɕ ɒó ɩ n-aɩɲɲɕɩɲ⁶ na cɲeɕ
(Cɲᵍ bɲeɩɕ⁶ ɒo ɲoɲɲo aɲ Sɲaɕ-ɩn-ɲeɲaɩn[n] ɲo'nʰ Œnaɕ,
ɩn cɲeɕ uɩle ɒo buaɩn ɒɩɓ 7 Nɩall ɲeɩn ɒo ɓul aɲ eɩʒɩn
aɲ 7 Comaɲ Mac ʒoɩɲɒelɓ ɒo maɲbaɓ ann 7 a bɲaɕaɩɲ,
Ɒaɩɓɩɕ Mac ʒoɩɲɕelɓ, ɒo ʒabaɩl ann 7 a maɲbaɓ ɩɲɩn
laɩṁ ɲɩnᶦ 7 moɲan aɩle⁷ ɒo'n ɕ-ɲloʒ ɲɩn ɒo maɲbaɓ ann,
eɕeɲ ʒallaɩɓ 7 ʒaɩɓelaɩɓ. Ocuɲ ɕeɕɕ ɒo Nɩall aɲ ɲɩɕ
aɲɕɩɲ 7 a ɲeɲann ɲeɩn ɒo ɕabaɩɲɕ ɒó. Ɒoɲɩʒneɓʲ eɕeɲ-
caɲaɩɕ moɲ 7 ɩnnlaɕ aɒɓul eɕuɲɲu : ɲuabaɩɲɕ ɩn ɕɩɲe ɒo
ʒabaɩl ɒo Nɩall ; cɲeɕ moɲ ɒo ɓenum ɒo Mhaʒnuɲ aɲ
Nɩall 7 a aɲʒaɩn uɩle.ᶦ—Œɓ hUa Ρallaṁaɩn quɩeuɩɕ ɩn
[Chɲɩɲɕo].—Conʒalaɕ Mác Eoɕaʒa[ɩ]n, ɕaɩɲeɕ Cene[oɩ]l-
Ρhɩaɕaɩɓ, moɲɕuuɲ eɲɕ.

(Bɲɩanᵏ O Ρlaɩnn, ɲɩ O-Cuɩɲɕɲɩ, occɩɲɲuɲ eɲɕ.—
Coɩɲɲɓealbaɕ hUa Ɒomnaɩll ɒo aɕɲɩʒaɓ ɒ'a bɲaɕaɩɲ

A.D. 1287. ⁴O—, A. ⁵aeɲa (gen.) A. ⁶-ɲɕ, A. ⁷eɩle, A; ñ, B.
ᶠᶠocuɲ bɲeɕ—*and (he) overtook*, B; followed by C, D. ʰ ɲoɲ an—*upon
the*, B. ᶦ ceɕna—*the same*, B, C. ᴶᴶom., B, C, D. ᵏᵏ n. t. h., A; om.,
B, C, D.

⁴*Secretly.*—Literally (as rendered in C), *under hand*. It means that he was not recognised. Fauore, potius quam propriâ industriâ, euasit, D.

⁵*Maghnus.*—Here, by the native idiom, nom. absolute.

⁶*With difficulty.*—"Escaped hardly," C ; valide, licet fugiendo, euasit, D.

(1287). ¹*Brian.*—This item is in the *F. M.* (who have *died*, instead of *was slain*) at 1291. The other

Concobur Ua Dubhda, king of Ui-Fiachrach, was drowned [1291] in the Shannon.—A general muster was made by Cathal Ua Concobuir and by Niall the Tawny and by all the folk that they had capable of rising out, both Foreigners and Gaidhil, to depose Maghnus. And they gave battle in Caradh-Culainn (otherwise, [Caradh]-Chulmaile) and Cathal was injured therein and Murchadh, son of Tadhg Ua Conchobuir and other persons [were killed there]. And many horses were taken from the people of Maghnus and defeat was inflicted upon himself and he went therefrom secretly.[4] —And many preys were made by the people of Cathal Ua Conchobuir and by Niall the Tawny [in revenge] for the wounding of Cathal in Cairpre. And Maghnus[5] O'Concobhair, when the Sil-Muiredaigh came to him and [when] his own retinue and the Foreigners of Ros-Comain [came] to his aid on the morrow after the defeat, he went to the rescue of the preys. On his overtaking them at Srath-infherainn and close by the Aenach, all the prey was taken from them and Niall himself escaped with difficulty[6] therefrom. And Thomas Mac Goistelb was killed there and his kinsman, David Mac Goistelb, was captured there and much more of that host, both Foreigners and Gaidhil, was killed there. And Niall came, on peace [being made], into the country and his own land was given to him. Great recrimination and contention [however] happened between them: the direction of the country was assumed by Niall; a great foray was made by Maghnus on Niall and he was completely despoiled by him.—Aedh Ua Fallamhain rested in Christ.—Conghalach Mag Eochaga[i]n, chief of Cenel-Fiachaidh, died.

(Brian[1] O'Flainn, king of Ui-Tuirtri, was slain.— (1287) Toirdhealbach Ua Domnaill was deposed by his own kins-

two entries are in the *A. L. C.* under 1291. Perhaps the Continuator placed them here, though at the wrong year, because they were given at the same date as the foregoing textual events in the source whence he drew.

378 ανναλα υλαδη.

ϝein, iꝺon, ꝺ'Ϲeꝺ hUa Ꝺomnaill 7 ꝛiġi ꝺo ġaꝺail ꝺo
ϝein aꝛiꝛ.—Ϲeꝺꝛu Mhaġꝛaṫ, abb na Tꝛinoiꝺe aꝛ Loċ-
Che, in Chꝛiꝛco quieuiꞇ.*)

[b.ꝛ.] Kal. ian. [ꝛ.* iii., l. ix.,*] Ϲnno Ꝺomini M.° cc.° lxxx.°
uiii.°ᵇ[-xc.ii.°] Sluaġ leꝛin iaꝛla ceꞇna cum Maġnuꝛa,
no co ꝛainic co Ros-Comain 7 ꝺoim[ṫ]ic ġan bꝛaiġꝺe,
ġan neꝛꞇ ꝺo'n ꞇuꝛuꝛ ꝛin. Roleꞇ imoꝛꝛo Maġnuꝛ in ꞇ-
iaꝛla co Miliuġ 7 ꝺoꝛiġne a oiġꝛeiꝛ ann.*—Ꝺonnċaꝺ,
mac Eoġain hUi Conċobuiꝛ, quieuiꞇ in [Chꝛiꝛco].—
Somaiꝛliꝺ O Ġaiꝛmleġaiꝺ ꝺo maꝛbaꝺ la hUa¹ Neill—
Niall ġealbuiꝺe hUa Conċobuiꝛ ꝺo maꝛbaꝺ ꝺo Thaꝺġ,
mac Ϲinnꝛiaꝛ hUi Conċobuiꝛ 7 ꝺo Thuaṫal, mac Muiꝛ-
ceꝛꞇaiġ.—Maġ Coċla[i]n, ꝛi Ꝺelḃna, ꝺo maꝛbaꝺ | ꝺo
Shiꝛin Mac Pheoꝛaiꝛ ꞇꝛe ꝝoꝛġoll in² iaꝛla.—Ϲinꝺileꝛ
O Ꝺoċaꝛꞇaiġ, ꞇaiꝛec Ϲꝛꝺa-Miṫaiꝛ, quieuiꞇ in Chꝛiꝛco.

Kal. ian. [ꝛ.* u., l. xx.,*] Ϲnno Ꝺomini M.° cc.° lxxx.°
ix.°ᵇ[-xc.° iii.°] Maġnuꝛ hUa Concobuiꝛ, ꝛi Connaċꞇ ꝛe
coic¹ bliaꝺna co leiṫ, in ϝeꝛ ꝺenṁa ꝛiꝺa 7 caġaiꝺ ꝛobo
mó ġꝛain 7 cuꝛġuꝛ 7 ꝛob' ϝeꝛꝛ einec 7 eġnom i n-a
aimꝛiꝛ ϝein ꝺo Ġhaiꝺelaiꝺ, iaꝛ m-beiṫ ꝺó ꝛaiṫi i n-
ġalaꝛ, moꝛꞇuuꝛ eꝛꞇ.—Caṫal hUa Conċobuiꝛ ꝺo maꝛbaꝺ
ꝺo Ruaiꝺꝛi, mac Ꝺonnċaꝺa ꝛiaḃaiġ.—Caṫal ꝛuaꝺ hUa
Conċobuiꝛ (iꝺon,ᵈ mac Concubaiꝛ ꝛuaiꝺᵈ) ꝺo ġaꝺail ꝛiġi
Connaċꞇ iaꝛ n-ġabail Ϲeꝺa, mic Eoġain. Ocuꝛ Caṫal
ceꞇna ꝺo maꝛbaꝺ i cinn ꝛaiṫi ꝺo Ruaiꝺꝛi, mac Ꝺonnċaꝺa ꝛiaḃaiġ hUi Conċobuiꝛ 7 Ϲeꝺ, mac Eoġain, ꝺo

A.D. 1288. ¹O, A. ²an, A. ᵇ1292, overhead, n. t. h., A; *alias*
1292, n. t. h., C; 1292, on margin, D. ᶜ⁻ᶜom., B, C, D.

A.D. 1289. ¹.u. (the Latin equivalent used here and elsewhere as
contraction), A, B. ᵇ1293, overhead, n. t. h., B; *alias* 1293, n. t. h., C;
1293, on margin, D. ᶜ om. (probably by mistake), A. ᵈ⁻ᵈitl., n. t. h.,
A; om., B, C, D.

² *Trinity*.—The Premonstratensian abbey, Trinity Island, Loch
Ce.

[1292] ¹*1288* = 1292 of the
A. L. C.
² *Son of Andrew*.—D adds: mic

man, namely, by Aedh Ua Domnaill and the kingship was [1291] taken by himself again.—Aedru Magrath, abbot of the Trinity[2] in [*lit.* on] Loch-Che, rested in Christ.)

Kalends of Jan. [on 3rd feria, 9th of the moon,] A.D. [1292 Bis.] 1288[1][-92]. A host [was led] by the same Earl against Maghnus [Ua Conchobair], until he reached Ros-Comain, and he went without hostage, without sway, on that expedition. Maghnus, however, followed the Earl to Miliug and complied with his full demand there.—Donnchadh, son of Eogan Ua Conchobuir, rested in Christ.—Somhairlidh O'Gairmleghaidh was killed by Ua Neill.—Niall Ua Conchobuir the Tawny was killed by Tadhg, son of Andrew[2] Ua Conchobuir and by Tuathal, son of Muircertach.—Mag Cochla[i]n, king of Delbna, was killed by Sifin Mac Feorais [Birmingham], through direction of the Earl.—Aindiles O'Dochartaigh, chief of Ard-Midhair,[3] rested in Christ.

Kalends of Jan. [on 5th feria, 20th of the moon,] A.D. [1293] 1289[1][-93]. Maghnus Ua Concobuir, king of Connacht for five years and a half, the man of the Gaidhil for making peace and war that caused most terror and triumph and was best in hospitality and benevolence in his own time, after being a quarter [of a year] in illness, died.—Cathal Ua Conchobuir was killed by Ruaidhri, son of Donnchadh the Swarthy.[2]—Cathal Ua Conchobuir the Red (namely, son of Concubar the Red) took the kingship of Connacht after the capture of Aedh, son of Eogan [Ua Conchobair]. And the same Cathal was killed at the end of a quarter [of a year] by Ruaidhri, son of Donnchadh Ua Conchobuir

---

Bria[i]n Luaigne—son of Brian of Luighni. This is given in the *A. L. C.* (1292).

For Tuathal, see the final entry of following year.

[3] *Ard-Midhair.*—D adds: communis omnibus hospitalitate. The original of the expression is in the *F. M.* at this year.

[1293] [1] *1289* = 1293 of the *A. L. C.*

Donnchadh the Swarthy.—Donati fusci, D.

ανναλα υλαδη.

Leȝan ap 7 puȝi Connact do ȝabail do͡c ꞇpe nepꞇ in Ȝhiupꞇip.—Caiplen 8liȝiȝ do ꞇenum do 8heon p[ꞇ] Tomup 7 a ꞇul ꞇaipip co ꞇec piȝ 8axan.—Aed, mac Eoȝain hUi Concobuip, do ȝabail piȝi Connact | 7 a piȝad do'n Ȝiupꞇip 7 do muinnꞇep* in² piȝ 7 an³ decmad⁴ la iap' n-a piȝad, a ȝabail do Mac Ȝepailꞇ i⁵ medail 7 coica⁶ da muinnꞇep do mapbad 7 cpeca mopa do ꞇenum aip.—Mupcad hUa Mail-[8h]eclainn, pi Mide, quieuꞇ in [Chpiꞇo].—Peȝal hUa Raȝaillaiȝ, pi Muinnꞇep-Mhailmópda, mopꞇuup epꞇ.—Taippi padpaic⁷ 7 Columcille 7 bpiȝde do poillpuȝud do Nicol Mac Mail-Ippu, do Chomapba padpaic,⁷ do beꞇ 8abull padpaic⁷ 7 a ꞇoȝbail do 7 iap n-a⁸ ꞇoȝbail, pepꞇa mopa 7 mipbuileda do ꞇenum 7 a cup dopun a pcpin cumdaiȝ co honopac.—Mop, inȝen Peidlimꞇe hUi Concobuip, quieuꞇ in [Chpiꞇo].—Ploipinꞇ hUa Cepballa[i]n, eppuc Tipe-hEoȝain⁵ (aliap,ᵈ eppuc Doipeᵈ), quieuꞇ in [Chpiꞇo]—Muipcepꞇac hUa Plannaȝa[i]n, ꞇaipec Clainni-Caꞇail, quieuꞇ in [Chpiꞇo].—Tuaꞇal,ᵇ mac Muipcepꞇaiȝ (hUi⁴ Choncubaipᵈ), do mapbad la Muinnꞇep-Eaȝpa.

(Caꞇal' Mac Diapmada, piȝ Mhuiȝe-Luipȝ, do ȝabail le hAed, mac Eoȝain hUi Choncubaip, im meadail 7 he pein do ꞇul ap eiȝin ap ꞇopad a lama ap a cuidpiȝid 7 cpeac do ꞇenum do ap cloinn Chaꞇail hUi Phlannaȝan. Ocup milled⁹ Connacꞇ do ꞇeacꞇ do na holcaid dopinded annpin eꞇip ȝabail 7 mapbad.'—Aed,ʲ mac [Eo]ȝain

A.D. 1289. ² an, A. ³ in, B. ⁴ .x. mad, A, B. ⁵ a, A. ⁶ .L (the Latin numeral used as contraction), A, B. ꞇ.-15, B. ⁸ n-o, A. ⁹ mill 7, (A) MS. ᶜ a huccꞇ an Ȝiupꞇip 7 muinnꞇepi—*by the power of the Justiciary and the people (of the king),* B; "by the power of the deputy," C. ᶠ ap--on (=after), A. ᵉ Doipe—*of Doire*, with: no, Chipi-hEoȝain—*or, of Tir-Eogain*, itl, t. h., B; followed by C and D. ᵇ om., D. ¹⁻¹ n. t. h., A; om., B, C, D. ʲ-ʲ l. m., n. t. h., but different from that of ¹⁻¹, A; om., B, C, D.

³ *Justiciary.*—William de Vesey, 1290–1294.

⁴ *Fitz Thomas.*—Fitz Gerald of Offaly. For the wager of battle between him and de Vescy (in connection with which he went to England), see *D. I.,* IV. 147.

Opposite this entry, L m., Latin hand, is: *Reedificatio Sligiae per Anglos.*

the Swarthy. And Aedh, son of Eogan, was liberated and [1293] the kingship of Connacht taken by him through the power of the Justiciary.[3]—The castle of Sligech was built by John Fitz Thomas[4] and he went across to the house of the king of the Saxons.—Aedh, son of Eogan Ua Conchobuir, took the kingship of Connacht and he was made king by the Justiciary and by the people of the king and the tenth day after his being made king, he was captured in treachery by Fitz Gerald. And fifty of his people were killed and great preys were made upon him.—Murchalh Ua Mail-[S]echlainn, king of Meath, rested in Christ.— Ferghal Ua Raigbaillaigh, king of Muinnter-Mailmordha, died.—The relics[5] of [SS.] Patrick and Colum-cille and Brigit were revealed to Nicholas Mac Mail-Issu, [namely] to the successor of Patrick, to be in Sabhall of Patrick. And they were taken up by him and, after their being taken up, great deeds and marvels were done and they were placed honourably by him in an ornamental shrine.—Mor, daughter of Feidhlimidh Ua Conchobuir, rested in Christ. —Florence[6] Ua Cerballa[i]n, bishop of Tir-Eogain (otherwise, bishop of Daire), rested in Christ.—Muircertach Ua Flannaga[i]n, chief of Clann-Catbail, rested in Christ.— Tuathal, son of Muircertach (Ua Conchubair), was killed by the Muinnter-Eaghra.

(Cathal[1] Mac Diarmada, king of Magh-Lurg, was taken (1289) prisoner by Aedh, son of Eoghan Ua Conchubhair, in treachery. And he himself went by force, by dint of his own power, out of his fetters and a foray was made by him on the children of Cathal Ua Flannagan. And destruction of Connacht came of the evils that were done then, both

---

[5] *The relics, etc.*—O'Donovan (*F. M.* iii. 456 sq.) adduces reasons to shew that this discovery did not take place.

[6] *Florence.*—On April 22, 1293, four years later than the textual date of his death, he paid a fine of 20s. for not coming to parliament (*D. I.*, IV. 21). He died the same year, before October 10 (*ib.* 91).

(1289) [1] *Cathal, etc.*—The additions belong to 1293. The first

h[Ui Concu]buir, inci[ri]t re[gn]are. — Reliqui[a]e [sanct]orum patricii, Columbae [et] brigiDae [hoc] anno in[uen]tae runt.¹)

Kal. Ian. [f.ª ui., l. 1.,ª] Anno Domini M.º cc.º xc.'' [·1111.º] Aeo,ª mac Eogain, do benum cred mor ar Clainn-Muircertaig.—Muircertac, mac Magnura hUi Concobuir, abbur coicebaig¹ ir ferr do bi d'a ciniud² fein, do marbad le Domnall, mac Taidg 7 le Tadg.—I Domnall hua hEgra, ri Luigne, quieuit in [Chrirto].— Mael-Seclainn hUa³ Flannaga[i]n, tairec Clainni-Catail, do marbad la Catal, mac Taidg Mic Diarmata, ar rraid Sligig.⁴—Donncad Mac Con[Sh]nama, tairec Muinntere-Cinaeta,⁵ quieuit in [Chrirto].— Duarcan Mac⁶ Tigernain, tairec Teallaig-Duncada, quieuit in [Chrirto].—Catal mac Taidg Mic Diarmata, ri Muige-Luirg, quieuit in [Chrirto].—Carrac-in-cairn Mag Tigernain, tairec Thellaig-Duncada, quieuit in [Chrirto].—Cairlen Sligig do leagad le hAed, mac Eogain hUiᵈ Concobuir.ᵈ—Derbail,ᵉ ingen Taidg Mic (Catailᶠ Mic') Diarmata, quieuit in [Chrirto].— Maelruanaig, mac Gilla-Crird Mic Diarmata, do gabail rig Maigi-Luirg.ᵍ—In t-Iarla (idon,ʰ Ricard a burc, idon, an t-Iarla ruadᵍ) do gabail do Mac Geroilt 7 buaidred Erenn uile do tect trid an* gabail' rin.— Creacᵃ mora mebla do benum do Mac Geroilt 7 do

A.D. 1290. ¹-Taig, B. ²cineD, A; ³O, A. ⁴-gd, A. ⁵-ant, B. ⁶Mag, B. 1294, overhead, n. t. h., B; *alias* 1294, n. t. h., B, C; 1294 on margin, D. ᶜ This item is omitted in D. ᵈ⁻ᵈ om., B, C; given in D. ᵉ⁻ᵉ om., B, C, D. ᶠ⁻ᶠ itl., n. t. h., (A) MS. ᵍ⁻ᵍ itl., n. t. h., A; om., B, C. D. Opposite the entry, r. m., t. h., A, B, is Gabail Maic Geroilt ar in Iarla—*Fitz Gerald's capture of the Earl*; literally: *capture of Fitz Gerald on the Earl.*

---

is given in the *A. L. C.* at that year; the second and third are respectively found (with more de- tail) in the third and eighth of the original entries of this year.

[1294] ¹*1290*=1294 of the *A. L. C.*

by capturing and killing.—Aedh, son of Eogan Ua Conchobuir, begins to reign.—The relics of Saints Patrick, Columba and Brigid were found this year.) (1289)

Kalends of Jan. [on 6th feria, 1st of the moon,] A.D. 1290¹[-4]. Aedh, son of Eogan [Ua Conchobair], made a great foray on the Clann-Muircertaigh.—Muircertach, son of Maghnus Ua Concobuir, the one of his own sept best fit to be king of a Province, was killed by Domnall, son of Tadhg and by Tadhg [Ua Conchobair].—Domnall Ua Eghra, king of Luighni, rested in Christ.—Mael-Sechlainn Ua Flannaga[i]n, chief of Clann-Cathail, was killed by Cathal, son of Tadhg Mac Diarmata, on the street of Sligech.—Donnchadh Mac Con[Sh]nama, chief of Muinnter-Cinaetha, rested in Christ.—Duarcan Mac Tigernain, chief of Tellach-Dunchadha, rested in Christ. —Cathal, son of Tadhg Mac Diarmata, king of Magh-Luirg, rested in Christ.—Carrach-in-cairn² Mag Tigernain, chief of Tellach-Dunchadha, rested in Christ.—The castle of Sligech was levelled³ by Aedh, son of Eogan Ua Conchobuir.—Derbail, daughter of Tadhg (son of Cathal) Mac Diarmata, rested in Christ.—Maelruanaigh, son of Gilla-Crisd Mac Diarmata, took the kingship of Magh-Luirg.— The Earl (namely, Richard de Burgh, that is, the Red Earl) was taken prisoner⁴ by Fitz Gerald and disturbance of all Ireland came through that capture. — Great treacherous forays were made by Fitz Gerald and by Mac [1294]

---

² *Carrach - in - Cairn.* — *Scabidus acervi lapidum*, D. The origin of the soubriquet is unknown to me. The editor of the *A. L. C.* (i. 510) says the *F. M.* call him Duarcan. The explanation is, they give Duarcan's obit (the next preceding entry but one) and omit this.

Levelled.—See the third original entry of [1293], *supra*.

⁴ *Taken prisoner.*—At the close of 1294, or early in 1295 (*D. I.*, IV. 191: the Roll referred to by O'Donovan, *F. M.* iii. 462, note n). According to Clyn's Annals the earl was taken on Saturday [Dec. 12] before the feast of St. Lucy [Dec. 13] 1294. Hence the text is four years antedated.

Mac Fheoŗaiŗ aŗ Connaċtaiḃ 7 Ceḋ, mac Eogain, do ṛamailt d'aẓṛiẓaḋ. In tiŗ do ṁilliuḋ doiḃ 7 níŗ'ẓabŗat neŗt eili buḋ mo na ṛin.—Daibiṫ Mac Ʒille-Aŗŗaiṫ do maŗbaḋ la macaiḃ Domnaill duiḃ hUi Eẓŗa.[a]

(Ʒilla-Adoṁnain[b] Maʒŗaiṫ, comaŗba Teŗmuinn-Dabeó[i]ʒ, quieuit decimo teŗtio Kalendaŗ Nouembŗiŗ hoc anno.[b])

Kal. Ian. [ŗ.[a] uii., L. x.ii.,[a]] Anno Domini M° cc.° xc.° i.[ob] [-u.] In t-Iaŗla cetna do légun aŗ do Mac Ʒeŗailt tŗe neŗt ŗiʒ Saxan aŗ bŗaiẓdiḃ maiṫi[ḃ] d'a ċineḋ ŗein.— | Bŗian, mac Aeḋa buiḋe hUi Neill, ŗi Cenuil-Eogain,[1] do maŗbaḋ la Domnall (mac[c] Bŗiain[c]) hUi[-a] Neill 7 aŗ moŗ do Ʒhallaiḃ 7 do Ʒhaiḋelaiḃ 'maille ŗŗiŗ (Maiḋm[d] na Cŗaiḃe[d]).—Domnall hUa[2] Cellaiʒ, ŗi hUa[2]-Maine, in t-aen Ʒhaiḋel iŗ glicu 7[e] iŗ linaiẓi[u][f] 7 iŗ[f] ŗeŗŗ comuiŗle dobi i n-a ḋutaiḋ[g] ŗein a[b] n-Eŗinn,[h] a éʒ i n-aibit manaiẓ 7 a aḋnucal i Cnoc-Muaiḋe.— Conn[i] Mac Bŗana[i]n, taiŗeċ Coŗc[a]-Aċland, occiŗuŗ eŗt.[i] Tomaltaċ[k] Mac Bŗana[i]n, in taiŗeċ doŗẓneḋ 'n-a inaḋ, do maŗbaḋ do ṁuinnteŗ Chonalla[i]n a n-dizailt a n-aṫuŗ do maŗbaḋ dóŗum.[b]—Coʒaḋ[3] móŗ i Tiŗ-Conaill iŗin[4] bliaḋain ŗin.[j]—Caʒaḋ móŗ eteŗ ŗi Saxan 7 ŗi Fŗanʒc.—Caiŗlen[k] [Muiʒe-Duma[k]] 7 caiŗlen in Ḃaile-nua 7 caiŗlen Muiʒi-Ḃŗecŗaiḋe do leaʒaḋ la Seaŗŗŗaiẓ hUa Feŗʒail.

A.D. 1290. [h-h] t. m., n. t. h., A; om., B, C, D.

A.D. 1291. [1] Cenel—, A. [2] O, A. [3] caʒaḋ, A. [4] iŗ (short form of the textual word), B. [b] 1295, overhead, n. t. h., B; *alias* 1295, n. t. L., C; 1295, on margin, D. [c-c] itl., t. h., A; om., B, C, D. [d-d] r. m., t. h., A; l. m., t. h., B; om., C, D. [e-e] om., A, D; given in B, C. [f] dob'—*that was*, B. [g] aimŗiŗ—*time*, B, C; om., D. [h-h] om., B, C, D. [i] om., D; eŗt is omitted in A. [j] ŗi—*this*, B. [k-k] om., B, C, D: a blank is left in the MS. for the name, which is here supplied from the *Annals of Loch Cé* (1295).

Feorais on Connacht and Aedh, son of Eogan, seemed to be deposed. The country was destroyed by them; but they got no power that was greater than that.—David Mac Gille-arraith was killed by the sons of Domnall Ua Eghra the Black. [1294]

(Gilla-Adomhnain Magraith, superior of Termonn-Dabeo[i]g, rested on the 13th of the Kalends of November [Oct. 20] this year.) (1290)

Kalends of Jan. [on 7th feria, 12th of the moon], A.D. 1291[1][-5]. The same Earl was liberated by Fitz Gerald,[2] through power of the king of the Saxons, for good hostages of his own sept.—Brian, son of Aedh Ua Neill the Tawny, was killed by Domnall (son of Brian) Ua Neill and great havoc [was wrought] of Foreigners and Gaidhil along with him (The Defeat of the Craibh).—Domnall Ua Cellaigh, king of Ui-Maine, the one Gaidhel the most prudent, the most perfect and of best counsel that was in his own district in Ireland, died in the habit of a monk and was buried in Cnoc-Muaidhe.—Conn Mac Brana[i]n, chief of Corca-Achlann, was slain. Tomaltach Mac Brana[i]n, the chief that was made in his stead, was killed by the family of Cu-alla[i]n, in revenge of their father having been killed by him.—Great war in Tir-Conaill in this year.—Great war[3] between the king of the Saxons and the king of the French.—The castle of [Magh-Duma] and the castle of Newtown and the castle of Magh-Brecraidhe were levelled by Geoffrey Ua Ferghail. [1295]

[1295] [1] *1291* = 1295 of the A. L. C.

[2] *Fitz Gerald.*—He was in Westminster at the time, having submitted to the king's will respecting the caption of de Burgh and other treasonable offences laid to his charge (*D. I.*, IV. 246).

[3] *War.*—Edward I.'s abortive expedition for the recovery of Gascony in 1295. For the connexion of Ireland therewith, see *D. I.*, IV. Index *Gascony*.

A65a[b1г.] [Cal. Ian. [р.ᵃ 1., L. xx.111.ᵃ]. Anno Domini M.° cc.° x.'
11.° ᵇ[-111.°] Aeḋ, mac Eoġain hUi Conċobuir, ḋ'aṫrigaḋ
ḋ'a oireċt fein 7 Clann-Muircertaiġ ḋo ṫabairt arip
i n-a inaḋ 7 cennur 7 braiġdi do ṫabairt do Choncobur
ruaḋ, mac Caṫail 7 in tir uile, eter cill 7 tuaiṫ, do
milliuḋ trefan aṫriġaḋ rin. Cric-Cairpri uile do
lorcaḋ 7 do milliuḋ la Clainn-Muircertaiġ 7 dul fa
ṫemplaiḋ in tire doiḃ. Ocur dodiġail Dia 7 Colum-
cille 7 Muire baintiġerna, ira tempuill dofairġeḋur.—
Sluaġ mór do tinol do'n Aeḋ cetna rin do Ġallaiḃ 7
do Ġaiḋelaiḃ fa Uilliam Búrc 7 fa Teḋoir a Búrc, co
raḃaḋur ceiṫri⁴ hoiḋce irtir 7 roṁilleaḋur arbanna 7
imenna in tire uile 7 tanġaḋur tairis in tire 'n-a teċ
annrin. Ruġaḋur leó iad co teċ in Iarla, do ḋenum
fita Aeḋa. Ocur ġe roġellfat, nir' ċomaillret in fit
7 do aentaiġeḋur arir ar teċt ḋ'a tiġ Lerin Clainn
cetna rin. In t-Aeḋ cetna fin do toiḋeċt irna Tuataiḃ.
O Ferġail 7 Maġ Raġnaill co n-a n-imirciḃ do ṫabairt
ḋó leir. Ocur teċta do ċur cum Mac Diarmata 7
O Flannaġa[i]n 7 innroḋ ḋoiḃ irtir trefan teċtairect
rin 7 Concobur ruaḋ do ᵈ lenṁain 7 creċ do ḋenum dó
forro. Impoḋ doiḃ forro, idon, ar in creiċ 7 ᵉ Concobur'
ruaḋ, mac' Caṫail,ᶠ do marḃaḋ le Mac Diarmata' ar
toraiḋeċt na' creiċe. Ocur Loċlainn, mac Concobuir, do
ġaḃail 7 Maġnur, mac Tomaltaiġ, do ġaḃail 7 becan ⁿ do
ḋainiḃ eile do marḃaḋ ann.ᵇ Ocur ir ann dorinneḋ rin,
i Cinn-Ceidi Ṫire-Tuatail.—Aeḋ hUa² Concobuir 7
Mac Diarmata 7 O Ferġail 7 na hoirecta arċeana do

A.D. 1292. ¹n-Diar—, B. ²O, A. ᵇ 1296, overhead, n. t. h., B;
alias 1296, n t. h., C; 1296, on margin, D. ᶜᵈom., B, C, D. ᵈ Over o is
placed a, n. t. h., to make the reading da [=do a]—(*followed*) *them*, MS.
(A). ᵉ B has idon—*namely* (*quia*, D), introducing the punishment that
was inflicted on the profaners of the churches.

[1296] ¹*1292* = 1296 of the
A. L. C.
² *Church and territory.*—"Both
spirituall and temporall," C; in
utroque foro, D.

Kalends of Jan. [on 1st feria, 23rd of the moon], A.D. [1296 Bis.] 1292¹[-6]. Aedh, son of Eogan Ua Conchobuir, were deposed by his own tribe and the Clann-Muircertaigh were brought into the country in his stead and headship and hostages were given to Concobur the Red, son of Cathal [Ua Conchobair]. And the whole country, both church and territory,² was destroyed through that deposition. All the district of Cairpre was burned and destroyed by the Clann-Muircertaigh and the churches of the territory were attacked by them. And God and Colum-cille and Mary, the Queen, whose churches they profaned, avenged [this].—A great host was mustered by the same Aedh of Foreigners and Gaidhil under William de Burgh and under Theobald de Burgh, so that they were four nights in the country and they destroyed the crops and chattels of all the country. And the chiefs of the country came into their house [i.e., submitted] then. They took them with them to the house of the Earl [Richard de Burgh], to make peace with Aedh. And though they promised, they kept not the peace and they united again with that same Clann on returning to their homes. That same Aedh came into "The Territories." O'Ferghail and Mag Raghnaill with their forces he brought with him. And messengers were sent to the Mac Diarmatas and O'Flannaga[i]ns and they returned into the country in consequence of that message. And Conchobur the Red followed and made a foray upon them. They turned upon these, namely, upon the foray force and Concobur the Red was killed by Mac Diarmata, in driving the prey. And Lochlainn, son of Concobur, was taken and Maghnus, son of Tomaltach, was taken and a small number of other persons were killed there. And where that was done is in Cenn-Ceidi of Tir-Tuathail. Aedh Ua Concobuir and Mac Diarmata and O'Ferghail and the allies also made large retaliatory forays on the people of Clann-Muircertaigh the

ɖenum cpeć móp n-ꝺɩx̄la ap muınnꞇɩp' Claınnı-Ϻuıp-ceptaıx̄ ın la ceꞇna.—ɪn' laclann ceꞇna pın, mac Con-cobuıp, ꝺo ɖallaɖ 7 a éx̄ a n-ućup a ɖallꞇa.'—X̄ılla-ɪap' Ϻac-ın-lɩaċanaıx̄, eppuc Oɩl-pınn, quıeuıꞇ ın [Chpıpꞇo]. — Ϻael-peꝺuıp O 'Ꝺuıɓx̄enna[ɪ]n, apċıꝺeoċan na ɓpeıpne, o Ꝺpuım-clıaɓ co Cenannup, quıeuıꞇ ın Chpıpꞇo.'—Ϻoppluax̄[3] le pıx̄ Saxan ı n-Alban, x̄up'x̄aɓ nepꞇ Alban uıle 7 x̄up'ṁıll | ꞇuaċa 7 x̄up'px̄up oıpeċꞇa[4] 7 ex̄lupa 7 x̄u ponnpaɓaċ maínıpꞇep ɓpaċap, co nap'pax̄[5] cloċ ap aıꞇ ꝺı 7 x̄up'mapɓ pıp[u] x̄paıɓ 7 mná ımɓa. Ocup ꝺobaꝺup maıċı pep n-Epenn ap ın pluax̄ pın, ıꝺon, Rıcapꝺ a ɓupc, ɪapla Ulaɓ 7 Ϻac X̄epaılꞇ, ıꝺon, Seón pı[ꞇz] Tomup.

Kal. ɪan. [p.* ııı., l. ıııı.*,] Anno Ꝺomını Ϻ.° cc.* xc.* ııı.°[b][-uıı.°] Concobup, mac Taıċlıx̄, mıc Ꝺıapmaꞇa, mıc° Concobuıp (mıc[d] Taıɓx̄[d]) Ϻıc Ꝺıapmaꞇa,[c] pı Ϻuıx̄ı-luıpx̄ 7 Aıpꞇıx̄, pınpepbpaċaıp 7 ꞇıx̄epna Ϻuınnꞇepı-Ϻaelpuanaıx̄ uıle, pep pob' pep[1] ꞇpoıꝺ[c] 7 ꞇaċup,[c] x̄al 7 x̄aıpceɖ, ınnpaıx̄ıꝺ[a] 7 anaɖ,[a] ꝺın[a] 7[c] ꞇepmonn, pıpınne[f] 7 plaıċemnup ı n-a comaımpıp, quıeuıꞇ ın [Chpıpꞇo] (7[d] a aɖlucuɖ ımϺaınıpꝺıp na ɓuılle[d]). — Ϻax̄nup O hAınlı,[2] ꞇaıpeċ Cenıuıl-Ꝺobċa,[3] quıeuıꞇ ın [Chpıpꞇo].—

A.D. 1292. ᵃ-pluaıx̄eɖ, B. ⁴-peċꞇ, B. ⁵-x̄aıɓ, B. ᶠ ᶠ om., A, D; given in B, C. ᵍ om., B (C). The word having reference to what is not given in that text. ʰ ʰ ꝺaıne aılı [lı MS.] ꝺo mapbaɖ—*other persons were killed*, B (C). Note the omission of ann—*in that place*, which refers to what is not given in B. ¹ om., B, C, D. ʲ This item is omitted in D.

A.D. 1293. ¹pepp, B. ²-lıꝺe, B. ³-ꝺopa (the phonetic form), A. ᵇ 1297, overhead, n. t. h., B; *alias* 1297, n. t h., C; 1297 on margin, D. ᶜ ᶜ om., B, C, D. ᵈ ᵈ ıꞇl., n. t. h., MS. (A). ᵉ ᵉ placed after plaıċemnup,

---

[3] *Mac-in-Liathannigh.—Son of the Grey* (O'Conor). According to the *A. L. C.*, he had been abbot of the Trinity, Loch Ce, and was chosen bishop on the death of O'Tomaltey, 1284, *supra*. On Sept. 10, 1296, the king informed Wogan, the Justiciary, that Trinotus [*Gilla-na-Trinoite*, Devotee of the Trinity] O'Thomelty [probably brother of the bishop-elect just mentioned] and Denis of Roscommon, canons

same day.—That same Lochlainn, son of Conchobur, was [1296] blinded and he died in the illness of his blinding.—Gilla-Isa Mac-in-Liathanaigh,[3] bishop of Oil-finn, rested in Christ.—Mael-Pedair O'Duibhgenna[i]n, archdeacon of Breifni from Druim-Cliabh to Cenannus, rested in Christ. —A great host [was led] by the king of the Saxons into Scotland, so that he got command of all Scotland and destroyed territories and despoiled shire-lands and churches and particularly a Monastery of Friars,[4] so that he left not a stone of it in place. And he killed many ecclesiastics and women. And there were nobles of the Men of Ireland on that expedition, namely, Richard de Burgh,[5] Earl of Ulster and Fitz Gerald, that is, John Fitz Thomas.

Kalends of Jan. [on 3rd feria, 4th of the moon], A.D. [1297] 1293[1][-7]. Concobur, son of Taichlech, son of Diarmait, son of Conchobur (son of Tadhg) Mac Diarmata, king of Magh-Luirg and Airtech, elder brother and lord of all Muinnter-Maelruanaigh, the man of best courage and prowess, valour and championship, attack and resistance, protection and asylum, truth and governance in his own time, rested in Christ (and he was buried in the Monastery of the Buill). —Maghnus O'hAinli, chief of Cenel-Dobtha, rested in

of Elphin, prayed for licence to elect in place of Brother Gelasius [*Gilla-Isu*], their late bishop (*D. I.*, IV. 322). For the sequel, see [1297], note 5, *infra*. The text is accordingly four years in advance.

[4] *Monastery of Friars.*—According to the *A. L. C.* they were Dominicans. The house, as the editor suggests, was probably St. Andrew's. The expedition took place in 1296.

The entry is thus unsatisfactorily summarized in D : Hoc anno Rex Angliae cum potenti armatura invasit Scotiam eamque funditus devastando ecclesiasque et monasteria comburendo et subuertendo.

[5] *De Burgh, etc.*—Amongst the expenses in the account of the Irish treasurer for 1295-6 is an item of £5,011 13s. 4d., to pay wages to Richard, Earl of Ulster, John Fitz Thomas, Theobald de Boteler and others, leaving for the king's service in Scotland, at Pentecost, a. r. 24 [1296] (*D. I.*, IV. 346).

[1297] [1] *1293* = 1297 of the *A. L. C.*

henpi Mag Oipeċtaiξ, eppuc Connipe, manaċ liaṫ quieuiꞇ in [Chpipꞇo] (7ᵈ a aḋlucuḃ ꞁ Mainipꞇip Opoċaiḃaꞇaᵈ).—Uilliam O Ḋubċaiξ, eppuc Cluana[-mac-Noip],ᵉ ꝺo mapbaḋ ꝺ'epcupᶠ ap ꞇoiꞇim ꝺó ꝺ'a eoċ pein.—Moppluaiξeḋᵍ le hEꝺubapꝺ, le puξ Saxan, ipin Ppaingc go moippmenmnaċ 7 ꞇainic gan ꞇpen, gan ꞇpeipi eipꞇi.— Mael-[Ṡh]eċlainn Mac Ḃpiain, ab na Ḃuille, ꝺo ꞇoξa[ḋ] cum eppocoiꝺe Oil-pinn 7 Mapian O Ꝺonꝺobuip, bpaꞇaip Ppeciup, ꝺo ꞇoξa[ḋ] peiṁe 7 a ꝺul ꝺo'n Roim ꞁ n-imcopnum na heppocoiꝺe ceꞇna 7 a éξ ꝺo'n ꞇupup pin.ᶜ —Cu-Ulaḋ O hAnluain, pí Oippċep 7 a ꝺepbpaꞇaip 7 Aenξup Mhag Maꞇξamna 7 mopan ꝺo maiċiḃ a ṁuinnꞇepi ꝺo mapbaḋ la ξallaiḃ Ꝺuin-Ꝺelξan, aξ impoḋ ꝺ'a ꞇiξiḃ o'n lapla.—Ꝺepḃ[p]opξaill,ᵇ inξen h[U]i Floinꝺ Epa[-Uꞁ Floinꝺ], quieuiꞇ in [Chpipꞇo].ᶜ

B; om., C, D. ᵇ cap, B. ᶜ om., B, C, D. ᵍ pepꞇa (Clonfert) is given in B, but it was deleted; *Clonmacnois*, C; *Cluain mac noys*, on margin, D.

---

² *Connor.*—In Antrim. Achonry, B, C, D. The true reading is Derry. Henry, a Cistercian, was chosen bishop of the latter see by the primate in 1294 (*D. I.*, IV. 156; *cf. ib.* 195-7). He died early in 1297 (*ib.* 371) and was succeeded by Geoffrey Mac Loughlin (*ib.* 405). The contemporary bishop of Connor was John, elected at the close of 1292, or the beginning of 1293 (*ib.* 12).

³ *Cluain-mac-Nois.* — Forgetting that Clonmacnoise was *par excellence* the *Cluain*, the *F. M.* read Clonfert, an error adopted by O'Donovan (iii. 469) and the editor of the *A. L. C.* (i. 519). The Franciscan, William O'Duffy, was elected bishop of Clonmacnoise in 1290 (*D. I.*, III. 726-35) and died before Aug. 5, 1297 (*ib.* IV. 429).

The bishop of Clonfert at the time was Robert, a Benedictine of Christ Church, Canterbury, appointed by Boniface VIII. (Jan. 2, 1279: Theiner, p. 158), in succession to John of Alatri (collector of the papal tenth in Ireland) promoted to the archbishopric of Benevento.

⁴ *Hosting.*—The war in Flanders is intended. Edward crossed over in Aug. 1296 and returned in March 1297. (*D. I.*, IV. p. xvi.)

⁵ *Went.*—According to the *F. M.* both went (α n-ꝺol apaon) and Melaghlin died on the journey. In support hereof, the editor (iii. 468) quotes the A-text, with α n-ꝺul (they went) for α ꝺul (he went)! But the *A. L. C.*, a reliable authority in the present instance, agree with the *Annals of Ulster*. Furthermore, amongst the charges

Christ.—Henry Mag Oirechtaigh, bishop of Conniri [Connor],[2] a Grey [Cistercian] monk, rested in Christ (and he was buried in the Monastery of [Mellifont at] Drochaidatha).—William O'Dubthaigh, bishop of Cluain[-macNois],[3] was killed by concussion, on falling from his own horse.—A great hosting[4] [was made] very courageously by Edward, [namely] by the king of the Saxons, into France and he came without conquest, without sway, therefrom.—Mael-Sechlainn Mac Briain, abbot of the Buill, was elected to the bishopric of Oil-finn and Marian O'Dondobuir, a Friar Preacher, was elected before him and went[5] to Rome to maintain[6] [his election to] the same bishopric and died on that journey.—Cu-Ulad O'Anluain, king of the Oirrthir and his brother and Aenghus Mag Mathgamna and many of the chiefs of his people were killed by the Foreigners of Dun-delgan, in returning to their houses from the Earl.[7]—Derbhfhorgaill, daughter of Ua Floinn of Es[-Ui Floinn], rested in Christ.

[1297]

---

made against William Birmingham, archbishop of Tuam, by the dean of Annaghdown in person at the Curia, which Boniface VIII. (July 20, 1303) appointed judges to investigate, the following appears: Cumquequondam Frater Marianus, tunc Electus Elfinensis, ab eodem archiepiscopo, pro eo quod electionem de ipso ad episcopatum Elfinensem de eadem provincia canonice celebratam renuerat confirmare, ad Sedem [Apostolicam] appellasset predictam ac eiusdem electionis confirmationem a Sede obtinuisset eadem: prefatus archiepiscopus, horum nequaquam ignarus, in eiusdem Sedis contemptum, Malachiam, tunc abbatem Monasterii de Buellio Elfinensis diocesis, qui nunc pro episcopo Elfinensi se gerit, receptâ propter hoc ab eo quadam pecunie summâ, in episcopum Elfinensem non absque simoniaca labe preficere, quin potius intrudere, non expavit. Sicque, eodem electo, antequam ad ecclesiam ipsam Elfinensem accederet, nature debitum persolvente, predictus Malachias occupavit eandem et adhuc detinet occupatam. (Theiner, pp. 171-2.)

It is somewhat noteworthy to find the (apparently studied) meagreness of the local chronicles thus supplemented from a foreign source.

[6] *Maintain*.—That is, to defend the validity of his election before the Curia: a course usual, either personally or by procuration, with bishops-elect at that time.

[7] *Returning from the Earl.*—They had probably accompanied him on

Kal. Ian. [p.ª iiii., L x.u.ª], Anno Domini M.° cc.° xc.°
iiii.° ᵇ[-uiii.°] Tomar p̣[tz] Muirir, barun mór do
Clainn-Ẓerailt, [f]hiri n-abairtea in t-eiẓri cam,
quieuit in [Christo].—Tomar O hOirectaiẓ, ab Eara-
ruaiḋ, quieuit in [Christo].—Saḋḃ, ingen Aeḋa buiḋe
hUi Neill, ben Taiḋg, mic° Anriar ͨ hUi Concobuir,
quieuitᵈ in [Christoᵈ].—Brian Breẓac̈² Maẓ Shampra-
ḋain, taireč Thellaiẓ-Eatač, do marbaḋ la hAeḋ m-
Breirneč hUa² Concobuir 7 la Clainn-Muircertaiẓ
aircena.—Donnčaḋ,ͨ mac Domnaill hUi Eaẓra, in t-
aen mač riẓ ir rerr eineač 7 rob' rerr dobi a cornum
a čire, do marbaḋ la Brian Carrač O n-Eẓra, d'a
bratair rein, i meḋail.ͨ

(Ercoboiḋͨ Chluana[-mac-Noir] do ẓabail d'Uilliam
hUa N-[f]innan, d'abbaiḋ Chille-beaẓain.ͨ)

Kal. Ian.[p. u.,L.xx.ui.ª], Anno Domini M.ͨ cc.ͨ xc.° u.ͨᵇ
[-ix.]ͨ Alaxandair Mac Domnaill, in duine¹ rob' rerr
eineč 7 maič[i]ur dobi i² n-Erinn 7 i n-|Albain, a
marbaḋ le hAlaxandair Mac Dubẓaill maille re hár
diairṁiḋe³ d'a muinnter | rein ͨ uime.ͨ—Ferẓal hUa⁴
Firẓil, erpuc Rata-boč, in t-aen erpuc ẓaiḋelač rob'
rerr eineč 7 dérc 7° daenačtͨ 7 crabaḋ dobi i n-Erinn,
quieuit in [Christo].—Cač do tabairt do riẓ Tairtri
7 do riẓ Fermenia (im feil Muire moir in foẓṁuirᵈ),

A.D. 1294. ¹Breaḋač, A. ²O, B. ᵇ 1298, overhead, n. t. h., B; *alias*
1298, n. t. h., C; 1298, on margin, D. ͨ⁻ͨ om., B, C, D. ᵈ⁻ᵈ mortua ert,
B, C, D. ͤ⁻ͤ n. t. h., A; om., B, C, D.

A.D. 1295. ¹⁻ni, A. ²a, A. ³-riṁe, A. ⁴O, A. ᵇ 1299, overhead,
n. t. h., B; *alias* 1299, n. t. h., C; 1299, on margin, D. ͨ⁻ͨ om., B, C,
D. ᵈ⁻ᵈ itl., n. t. h., A; om., B, C, D.

---

the expedition into Scotland the previous year.

[1298] ¹*1294* = 1298 of the A. L. C.

²*Fitz Maurice*.—Justiciary of Ireland, March — October, 1295 (*D. I.*, IV. 202-67). Died on the Wednesday after Trinity Sunday [June 4], a. r. [Edward I] 26 [1298] (*ib.* 561).

Kalends of Jan. [on 4th feria, 15th of the moon], A.D. 1294¹[-8]. Thomas Fitz Maurice,² a great baron of the Clann-Gerald, who was called The crooked Heir,³ rested in Christ.—Thomas O'hOirechtaigh, abbot of Eas-ruadh, rested in Christ.—Sadhbh, daughter of Aedh Ua Neill the Tawny, wife of Tadhg, son of Andrew Ua Concobuir, rested in Christ.—Brian Mag Shamradhain the Bregian, chief of Tellach-Eathach, was killed by Aed Ua Concobuir the Brefnian and by the Clann-Muircertaigh besides.—Donnchadh, son of Domnall Ua Eaghra, the one son of a king that was best in generosity and that was best in defence of his country, was killed by Brian Carrach O'Eghra, [that is] by his own kinsman, in treachery.

[1298]

(The bishopric of Cluain[-mac-Nois] was taken by William Ua Ninnan,¹ namely, by the abbot of Cell-began.)

(1294)

Kalends of Jan. [on 5th feria, 26th of the moon], A.D. 1295¹[-9]. Alexander Mac Domnaill, the person who was the best for hospitality and excellence that was in Ireland and in Scotland, was killed, together with a countless number of his own people that were slaughtered around him, by Alexander Mac Dubghaill.—Ferghal Ua Firghil, bishop of Rath-both, the one Gaidhelic bishop who was the best for hospitality and charity and humanity and piety that was in Ireland, rested in Christ.—Battle² was given by the king of Tartary and by the king of Armenia (about the great

[1299]

---

³ *The Crooked Heir.*—"That was called the crooked heire," C; quique dicebatur haeres obliquus, D.

(1294) ¹ *Ua-Ninnan.* — Rightly, Ua n-Finnain. The *f,* when *eclipsed* by *n,* was silent and consequently omitted by the copyist. The entry is correctly given under 1298 in the *A. L. C.* O'Finnen succeeded O'Duffy, [1297], note 3, *supra.* He died (probably in Aug.) 1302 (*D. I.,* V. 121).

[1299] ¹ *1295* = 1299 of the *A. L. C.*
² *Battle.*—Of Damascus, Aug. 15, 1300.

2 C

maille ré ruarapur do comtorbail,* do Shó[l]oan na
baibiloine 7 do na Sarrairdin:b arcena ([Ccr]ᵈ dıarṁe
do tabairt ar an So[l]oan").

(Muirir' hUa hógan, erscop Cille-da-lua, quievit.')

[bɪr.] Kal. Ian. [r.* iii., L. iii.*], Anno Domini M.° cc.° xc.°
iii.°ᵇ[-ccc.°] Teboit¹ buitiller, barun mór, uaral,
mortuur ert.—hEoanᵉ Prinnoregar do marbad le mac
Fiacra hUi Phloinn.ᶜ—Adam Sdondin, barun mor
aile,² quievitᵈ in [Chrirtoᵈ].—Cairlen Ata-cliat-in-
Conainn do tinnrgedal Lerin Iarla.—Seoinínᵉ óg Mac
Muirir do marbad (laᵉ Concubur, mac Fiacra hUi
Phloinn').ᶜ—Feidlimid Mag Carrtair, adbur rig Der-
Muman, quievit in [Chrirto].—Congalac hUa Loclainn,
erruc Corcumruad, rai n-einig 7 craba[i]d, quievit in
[Chrirto].—Gairm coittenn do tett o Roim i³ n-aimrer
bonarair Papa ra'n Crirtaidectᵗ uile' 7 gaca cetmad
bliadain ticᵟ in gairm rin 7 bliadain Rata a hainm rin.
Ocur rluaig diarṁide a huilid tirid na Crirdaidacta⁶
do dul ra'n gairm rin d'a n-oilidri co Roim 7 logad a
recad uile' d'ragbail doib.

A.D. 1295. ᵃ aile (ii., MS.)—other, added, B. ᶠ⁻ᶠ n. t. h., A; om., B, C, D.

A.D. 1296. ¹Teabord, B. ²ii., A, B. ³a, A. ⁴-daigact, A. ⁵og,
⁵⁻igacta, A. ᵇ1300, overhead, n. t. h., B; rectius 1300, n. t. h., C;
rectius anno 1300, on margin, D. ᶜ⁻ᶜ om., B, C, D. ᵈ⁻ᵈ mortuur ert, B,
D; moricur, C. ᵉ⁻ᵉ a. m., n. t. h., A; om., B, C, D. ᶠ om., B, C; given
in D.

[D ends with this year.]

(1295) ¹ O'Hogan. — Formerly precentor of Killaloe. Elected bishop Nov. 12, 1281 (D. I., II. 1286); died Oct. 1298 (ib. IV. 556). The obit is incorrectly given in the A. L. C. under 1299.

[1300] ¹ *1296 = 1300* of the A. L. C.

² *Butler; Stanton.*—They were amongst those whom Edward addressed, May 4, 1297, for aid towards the Gascon war (D. I., IV. 396).

³ *Ua Locklainn.*—Formerly dean of Kilfenora. Elected bishop about Aug. 1281 (D. I., II. 1843-56); died Dec. 1298 (ib. IV. 577). (Charles is the alias of Congalach, *locc. citt.*)

⁴ *Incitation.*—The Bull of Boniface VIII., Feb. 2, 1300, instituting the Jubilee every hundredth year

feast of Mary of the Harvest [Aug. 15]), along with what [1299] assistance they could find, to the Sultan of Babylon and to the Saracens besides (Slaughter innumerable was inflicted on the Sultan).

(Maurice O'Hogan,[1] bishop of Cell-da-lua, rested.)

Kalends of Jan. [on 6th feria, 7th of the moon], A.D. [1300Bis.] 1296[1][1300]. Theobald Butler,[2] a great, noble baron, died.—John Prendergast was killed by the son of Fiachra Ua Floinn.—Adam Stanton,[2] another great baron, rested in Christ.—The castle of the Hurdle-ford of the Weir was begun by the Earl.—Johnikin Fitz Maurice junior was killed (by Conchubur, son of Fiachra Ua Floinn).— Feidhlimidh Mag Carrthaigh, future king of Desmond, rested in Christ.—Congalach Ua Lochlainn,[3] bishop of Corcumruadh [Kilfenora], eminent in hospitality and piety, rested in Christ.—A general invitation[4] came from Rome in the time of Pope Boniface [VIII.] throughout all Christendom and every hundredth year[5] comes that invitation and the *Year of Grace*[6] is its name. And a countless host[7] from all countries of Christendom went on that invitation on their pilgrimage to Rome and remission of all their sins was obtained by them.

This Jubilee has been immortalized in the Divina Commedia (Inf., c. 18, v. 28 ; Par., c. 2, v. 28 sq.).

[5] *Hundredth year.*—This goes to prove that the present entry is contemporaneous. Urban VI.(Ap. 11, 1389) fixed the Jubilee term at 33 years ; Paul II. (Ap. 19, 1470), at 25.

[6] *Year of Grace.*—"And that year is called the year of Happiness" (with *Jubile* placed above the last word), C; annumque ipsum annum prosperitatis nuncupabant, D.

[7] *Countless host.*—"Innumerable troopes and sortes went and got an absolution of their sinns," C 200,000 is the estimated number.

At the end of this year D concludes with the following Note: Ab hoc anno usque ad annum Domini 1420 nihil reperitur in hoc libro, quia pars libri aliquo fortuito casu ex ipso libro ablata fuit. Ergo nunc historia cessare oportet, quousque illa pars ablata vel ex aliquo alio consimili libro contenta reperiri poterit.

396 ccnnala ulaoh.

(Muiṗċeaṙtaċ,ᵉ mac Íṁuiṙ húí Ḃhiṙnn, ᴅ'hec aṙ ṙliġiġ na hoiliéṙi cetna ṙin.ᶠ)

Ḱal 1an. [ṙ.ᵃ 1., L x.uiii.ᵃ], Anno Domini M.º cc.º xc.º uii.º ᵇ[-ccc.º 1.º] Finnġuala, inġen Ṗheiḋlimée húí Conċobuiṙ, banaḃ Cille-Craeḃnaḋa,¹ quieuit in [Chṙiṙto].— Uilliam Maġ [Ṗh]lannċaḋa,² taiṙeċ Ḋaṙtraiġe, ᴅo maṙḃaḋ la húal[ġ]aṙġ, mac Ḋoṁnaill, mic Aiṙt húí Ruaiṙc.—Caiṙpṙi, mac Coṙmaic húí Mail-[Sh]eċlainn, ᴅo maṙḃaḋ tṙe ḟoṙġall³ a ḃṙaċaṙ⁴ ḟein, iᴅon,⁵ mac Aiṙt húí Mail-[Sh]eċlainn.—Creaċᶜ móṙ ᴅo ḋenum ᴅ'Aeḋ, mac Caṫail húí Conċobuiṙ 7 ᴅo Clainn-Muiṙceṙtaiġ aṙ Taḋġ, mac Annṙian, a Muiġ-cetne.ᵈ— Sluaiġeḋ⁶ la ṙiġ Saxan i⁷ n-Alban 7 Mac Ġeṙailt 7 Mac Ṗheoṙair 7 maiṫí Ḃharun⁸ Eṙenn uile, a n-inġnaiṙ Íaṙla Ulaḋ, leiṙ aṙ in ṙluaiġeḋ ṙin 7 beiṫ ᴅoiḃ a n-Alban o caeiciḋiṙ ṙe Luġnuṙaḋ co⁹ Samuin 7 ġan | a loṙneṙt ᴅo ġaḃail ᴅoiḃ ċ-[ṙ]oiṙ.

A 65d

Ḱal 1an. [ṙ.ᵃ ii., L xxix.ᵃ], Anno Domini M.º cc. xc.º uiii.º ᵇ[-ccc.º ii.º] Domnall ruaḋ Maġ Caṙṙṫaiġ, ṙí

A.D. 1296. ᵉ⁻ᶠ n. t. h., A; om., B, C, D.

A.D. 1297. ¹-naᴅ, B. ²ḟ om., A. ³ ḟeṙġal (apparently a personal name), with aliaṙ, ḟoṙġal—*or, order,* itl., n. t. h., A. ⁴ ḃṙaċaṙ (ac., to agree with ḟeṙġal), A. ⁵ om., A. These three variants seem to prove that the scribe of A took the meaning to be that Cairpri was slain by Fergal, his kinsman, son of Art. The translator of C committed a similar error in rendering the B text : "killed by Forgall, his owne brother." But ḃṙaċaṙ, the word which he had before him, is gen., not ac. Moreover, the name of the slayer (which is passed over in C) shews that he was not "owne brother" of his victim. The compiler of B understood the sense. ⁶⁻⁷, A. ⁷ a, A. ⁸⁻naḋ, A. ⁹ ġu, B. ᵇ 1301, overhead, n. t. h., B; *alias* 1301, n. t. h., C. ᶜ⁻ᵈ om., B, C.

A.D. 1298. ᵇ 1302, overhead, n.t.h., B; *alias* 1302, n. t. h., C.

[1301] ¹ *1297* = 1301 of the A. L. C.

² *Finnghuala.* — Literally, *fair-shoulder;* anglicized Finola.

³ *Cairpri.*—Called Cormac in the A. L. C.

⁴ *Chiefs of the barons.*—See the list of those (amongst whom are

ANNALS OF ULSTER.   397

(Muircertach, son of Imbur Ua Birn, died on the way of that same pilgrimage.) (1296)

Kalends of Jan. [on 1st feria, 18th of the moon], A.D. 1297¹[1301]. Finnghuala,² daughter of Feidhlimidh Ua Conchobuir, abbess of Cell-Craebhnada, rested in Christ.—William Mag [F]lannchadha, chief of Dartraighi, was killed by Ual[gh]arg, son of Domnall, son of Art Ua Ruairc.—Cairpri,³ son of Cormac Ua Mail-[S]echlainn, was killed by direction of his own kinsman, namely, the son of Art Ua Mail-[S]echlainn.—A great foray was made by Aedh, son of Cathal Ua Conchobuir and by the Clann-Muircertaigh on Tadhg, son of Andrew [Ua Conchobair], in Magh-Cetne.—A hosting [was made] by [Edward] the king of the Saxons into Scotland and [John Fitz Thomas] Fitz Gerald and Mac Feorais [Birmingham] and the chiefs of the barons⁴ of all Ireland, except⁵ the Earl of Ulster, [were] with him on that hosting. And they were in Scotland from a fortnight before Lammas⁶ [Aug. 1] to November Day.⁷ But full sway was not obtained by them in the East.⁸ [1301]

Kalends of Jan. [on 2nd feria, 29th of the moon], A.D. 1298¹[1302]. Domnall Mag Carrthaigh the Red, king of Des- [1302]

---

the two here mentioned) addressed for aid by the king, D. I., IV. 785.

⁵ *Except, etc.*—See *ib.* 849.

⁶ *Lammas.*—Literally, *Lugh-commemoration*: i.e. funeral games (cf. O'Curry: *Manners, etc.*, Introd. cccxxv., sq.) annually held by the Tuatha-de-Danann king, Lugh, in memory of his wives Nas (*unde* Naas, co. Kildare) and Bai (*unde* Cnoc-Bai, Cnogba, Knowth, Meath).

The celebration took place at Telltown, Meath, on the first of August. (L. Be. p. 362 a, l. 35 sq.; L.L. p. 200 b, ll. 33-4.)

⁷ *November Day.* — Literally, *Summer-ending* (*Book of Rights*, p. liii.).

⁸ *East.*—Namely, Scotland; so called from the situation in reference to Ireland.

[1302] ¹ *1298* = 1302 of the A. L. C.

Der-Muman, quieuit in [Chpipto].—|Milep, eppuc Luimniʒ, mac mic eipein do'n iapla Laiʒneċ, quieuit in [Chpipto].—Eppuc Copcaiʒe, manaċ liaṫ, quieuit in [Chpipto].—Ruaiḋpi, mac Domnaill hUi hEaʒpa, aḋḃup piʒ Luiʒne, quieuit in [Chpipto].—Ḃóoiṫ móp in bliaḋain pin¹ ap ceṫpa.—Cpeċ mop do ḋenum d'Aeḋ, mac Caṫail, ap Taḋʒ, mac Annpiap 7 ap Shitpiuʒ, mac in Caipniʒ Meʒ Laclainn, [i Maʒ-]Cetne.—Donn Maʒ Uiḋep, pi Fep-Manaċ, idon, cetna pi Fep-Manaċ do macaiḃ Meʒ Uiḋip, quieuit in [Chpipto].—Maiʒiptep Soiamna O Ḃpaʒain, aipdeppuc Caipil, quieuit in [Chpipto].

Kal. Ian. [p. iii., L. x.], Anno Domini M.° cc.° xc.° ix.° [M.° ccc.° iii.°] Nicol Mac-Mail-Ipu, aipdeppuc Apda-Maċa, in t-aen cleipeċ ip diaʒa 7 ip cpaḃdiʒi[u]² dobi i n-Epinn i n-a aimpep pein, quieuit in [Chpipto]. —Mael-Sheclainn Mac Ḃpiain, eppuc Oil-pinn, quieuit in [Chpipto]. Donnċaḋ hUa³ Flannaʒa[i]n, abb na Ḃuille, do ʒaḃail na heppocoide cetna d'a eipi.—Diapmait hUa⁴ Flannaʒa[i]n, taipeċ Tuaiṫi-Raṫa 7 a ḃa mac 7 mopan aile⁵ do mapḃaḋ do dpoinʒ do Luċt tiʒe Domnaill, mic Taiḋʒ hUi Concobuip, i⁶ m-Ḃun-duiḃe, a topaiḃeċt cpeiċe puc pe Leip a Muiʒ-Cetne.—Toippḋel-

A.D. 1298. *Marescal* [=Marshall], r. m., n. t. h., B. ᵈ⁻ᵈ om., B; "dead," C. ᵉ⁻ᵉ om., B, C. ᶠ⁻ᶠ om., A; placed after *Christo* in B; given in C.

A.D. 1299. ¹·piuċ, A. ²·ʒe, A. ³O, B. ⁴O, A. ⁵ii, B; eile, A. ⁶a, B. ᵇ 1303, overhead, n. t. h., B; *alias* 1303, n. t. h., C.

---

² *Miles.*—The Christian name was Gerald. Formerly archdeacon of Limerick; elected bishop in 1272 or —3 (*D. I.*, II. 943); died apparently in 1302 (*ib.*, V. 59). (No. 779, *ib.* IV., giving the death in 1301, appears out of place.)

³ *Grandson, etc.*—This is confirmed by the surname, le Marshall (*D. I.*, II. 945). The grandfather was probably William Marshall the younger, Earl of Pembroke, who died, without legitimate issue, in 1231 (*D. I.*, I. 1872).

⁴ *Bishop of Cork.*—Robert (called Mac Donnchadha in the *A. L. C.*), a Cistercian, was elected in 1277 (*D.I.*, II. 1346) and died in 1302 (*ib.* V.

mond, rested in Christ.—Miles,[2] bishop of Limerick—that [1302] person was grandson[3] to the Leinster Earl—rested in Christ. —The bishop of Cork,[4] a Grey [Cistercian] monk, rested in Christ.—Ruaidhri, son of Domnall Ua Eaghra, future king of Luighni, rested in Christ.—Great murrain that year on cattle.—A great foray was made by Aedh, son of Cathal [Ua Conchobair], on Tadhg, son of Cathal [Ua Conchobair] and on Sitrec, son of the Cairnech Mag Lachlainn, [in Magh-]Cetne.—Donn Mag Uidhir, king of Fir-Manach, namely, the first king of Fir-manach of the sons of Mag Uidhir, rested in Christ.—Master Stephen[5] O'Bragain, archbishop of Cashel, rested in Christ.

Kalends of Jan. [on 3rd feria, 10th of the moon,] A.D. [1303] 1299[1] [1303]. Nicholas[2] Mac-Mail-Isu, archbishop of Ard-Macha, the one cleric the most godly and pious that was in Ireland in his own time, rested in Christ.—Mael-Sechlainn[3] Mac Briain, bishop of Oil-finn, rested in Christ. Donnchadh[4] Ua Flannaga[i]n, abbot of the Buill, assumed the same bishopric after him.—Diarmait Ua Flannaga[i]n, chief of Tuath-Ratha, and his two sons and many others were killed by a party of the house-folk of Domnall, son of Tadhg Ua Concobuir, in Bun-duibhe, in driving away a prey he took with him from Magh-Cetne.—Toirdhelbach

---

64). (No. 782, ib. IV., assigning the obit to 1301 seems misplaced).

[5] *Stephen.*—See 1253, note 1, supra. Died July 25, 1302, (*D. I.,* V. 93) and was succeeded by Maurice, the archdeacon, whose election was confirmed by Benedict XI., Nov. 17, 1303 (Theiner, p. 173).

[1303] [1] *1299* = 1303 of the *A. L. C.*

[2] *Nicholas.*—See [1270], note 4, supra. Died in the first half of 1303 (*D. I.,* V. 235). His successor, John, was appointed by Clement V., Aug. 27, 1305 (Theiner, p. 174). The causes of the delay are set forth in the Bull.

[3] *Mael-Sechlainn.*—See [1297], note 5, supra. Died before March 8, 1303 (*D. I.,* V. 179).

[4] *Donnchadh.*—Donatus is the Latin alias in the royal assent to his election, June 28, 1303, (*ib.* 233-4).

400

bać hUa Domnaill, rí Tire-Conaill 7 Muircertać Mag fhlannćada⁷ 7 Donn O Catha[i]n 7 Donnćad Mac Menman 7 Aed Mac Menman, [da] mac [mic] ind fhirleiginn hUi Domnaill 7 Niall, mac Neill hUi Buigill 7 Mac hUgorai 7 a mac 7 a derbratair 7 Adam Sandal, Goill 7 Gaeidil imda aili⁵ orin amać do marbad⁴ la hAed hUa n-Domnaill, le [a] derbratair (rein,ᵉ idon, tairec Muinteri-Feo[da]cain]ᶠ).—Niall Mac Gilla-Fhinnen quieuit in [Christo].—Creć' mór do denum la Clainn-Muirćertaig a Muinnter-Cinaeta 7 Muircertać Mac Con[Sh]nama, adbur tairig Muinnteri-Cinaeta, do marbad doib ar in creić rin.ᶠ—Sluag mór le rig Saxan i⁸ n-Albain 7 sathraća imda do gabail

A 66a

doib 7 in t-Iarla 7 Goill 7 Gaeidil do dul a hErinn, cablać mor 7 nert do gabail ar Albanćaib doib. Tedoid a burc, derbratair inᵍ Iarla, d'eg ar toideći dó do'n t-sluaged rin i Carraig-Ferguса, adaig Notla[i]c.¹⁰—Domnall óg (alias,ʰ ruadʰ) Mag Carrtaig, rí Dermuman, quieuit in [Christo].—Magnur Mag Shamrada[i]n, tairec Tellaig-Eatać, mortuur ert.

(Shearoid¹ Fitomar, oigri Cloinne-Gerailt, mortuur ert.¹)

B67c[bir.] Kal. Ian. [f.ᵃ iiii., L xx.i.,ᵃ] Anno Domini M.º ccc.ᵒᵇ [-iiii.ᵒ] In Cunntair, ben¹ Ricaird a burc, Iarla Ulad, mortua ert.—Uaiter² a burc, oigri in Iarla cetna,³ mortuur ert.—Concobur, mac Aeda hUi Concobair, do marbad la hoibert hUa Flaitbertaig iarᶜ n-denum mebla dóron ar Dhonnćad hUa Flaitbertaig 7 in t-Oibert hirin do tuitim ar in Lataír cetna.ᶜ

⁷ fh om., A. (Da and ṁic in l. 3 are from the A. L. C.) ⁸ a, A. ⁹ an, B. ¹⁰ Nod lag, B. ¹ ri—this, B. ᵉ om., B, C. ᵈ orin, added by a scribal error, A. ᵉ⁻ᵉ itl., n. t. h. (The letters within square brackets are worn away.), A ; om., B, C. ᶠ⁻ᶠ om., B, C. ᵍ Opposite this entry, r. m., n. t. h., B, is : Surub' uime rin ar cormail gur' b'e doroinde [Te]bood—so that for that reason it is likely that this was (the castle) Tibbot built. ᵇ⁻ʰ c. m., n. t. h., A ; om., B, C. ⁱ⁻ⁱ n. t. h., A ; om., B, C.

A.D. 1300. ¹ bean, A. ² baiter, A. ³ cedna, B. ᵇ 1304, overhead n. t. h., B; alias 1304, n. t. h., C. ᶜ⁻ᶜ om., B, C.

Ua Domnaill, king of Tir-Conaill and Muircertach Mag Flannchadha and Donn O'Catha[i]n and Donnchadh Mac Menman and Aedh Mac Menman, [i.e. two grand-]son[s] of the Lector Ua Domnaill and Niall, son of Niall Ua Buighill and Mac Ughosai and his son and his brother and Adam Sandal[and] many other Foreigners and Gaidhil in addition were killed by Aedh Ua Domnaill, [namely] by his (own) brother (that is, the chief of Muinnter-Feodachain).—Niall Mac Gilla-Fhinnen rested in Christ.—A great foray was made by the Clann-Muircertaigh into Muinnter-Cinaetha and Muircertach Mac Con[Sh]nama, future chief of Muinnter-Cinaetha, was killed by them on that foray.—A great hosting[5] [was made] by the king of the Saxons into Scotland and many cities were taken by them. And the Earl [Richard de Burgh] and Foreigners and Gaidhil went with a large fleet and they got sway over the Men of Scotland. Theobald de Burgh, brother of the Earl, died on his return from that hosting, in Carraic-Ferghusa, on the night of the Nativity.—Domnall Mag Carrthaigh, Junior (otherwise the Red), king of Desmond, rested in Christ.—Maghnus Mag Shamhradha[i]n, chief of Tellach-Eathach, died.

(Gerald [son of John][1] Fitz Thomas, heir of the Clann-Geralt [of Offaly], died.)

Kalends of Jan. [on 4th feria, 21st of the moon], A.D. 1300[1][-4]. The Countess,[2] wife of Richard de Burgh, Earl of Ulster, died.—Walter de Burgh, heir of the same Earl, died.—Concobur, son of Aedh Ua Concobair, was killed by Hubert Ua Flaithbertaigh, after [Aedh] had practised deceit on Donnchadh Ua Flaithbertaigh and the same Hubert fell on the same spot.

---

[5] *A great hosting,' etc.*—The invasion of Scotland by Edward I. in 1303.

(1299) [1] [*Son of John*].—These words are supplied from Clyn's *Annals*, A.D. 1303.

[1304] [1] *1300* = 1304 of the A. L. C.

[2] *The Countess.*—Margaret, cousin of Eleanor, queen-consort of Edward I. (*D. I.*, II. 2102).

Kal. Ian. [f.ᵃ ui., l. 11.ᵃ] Anno Domini M.° ccc.° 1.°ᵇ [-u.°] Muircertach hUa Concobuir Fhailgi 7 Mael-morda, a bratair 7 in Calbach hUa Concobair, maille fri nónbur ar ficit¹ do maithib a muinntheri, do marbad do Shar² Piarur³ Mac Feorair tre feall 7 tre mebail i cairlen Fheorair.—Cairlen Inri-hEogain do denam lerin Iarla.—Mata óg O Raigillaig do marbad do Chellach-nDunchada.—Aed óg hUa Ferghail [mortuus est].—Maidm la hAed, mac Catail hUi Concobuir 7 le Clainn-Muircertaig archena ar Muinnter-Ragaillaig, co n-dorchair⁴ and Pilip hUa⁵ Ragaillaig 7 oigri Clainni-Suibne 7 Mag Uirrce, cenn na n-Galloglach, maille fri cet⁶ ar cethorchat⁶ do dainib ailib.⁷—Toirrdelbach, mac Neill ruaid hUi Briain, quieuit in [Christo].

(No,ᵈ gumad ar an Kalainn fo bud choir Donn Mhag Uidir do beith.ᵈ)

A.D. 1301. ¹.xx., A; .xx.it, B. ² fapa, A. ³ pépur, A. ⁴ n-dorcair, B. ⁵ O, A. ᵈ˙ˢ .c ar xlat, A, B. ⁷.fi., B; aile, A. ᵇ 1305, overhead, n. t. h., B; *alias* 1305, n. t. h., C. ᶜ om., A. Opposite this entry, l. m., n. t. h., B, is: cairlen nuad Inri-hEogain per Anglos—*the new castle of Inis-Eogain (was built) by the English.* ᵈ c. m., opposite the date, n. t. h., A; om., B, C.

[1305] ¹ *1301* = 1305 of the *A. L. C.*

² *Castle.* — Castle-Carbury, co. Kildare (O'D., *F. M.* iii. 480). The assassination is thus described in the Irish Remonstrance (1277, note 2, *supra*) :

Anglici enim, nostram inhabitantes terram, qui se vocant mediae nacionis, sic sunt ab Anglicorum de Anglia ceterarumque nacionum moribus alieni, quod non mediae, sed extremae perfidiae nacio propiissime possunt appellari. Ab antiquo enim fuit illis haec reproba et abusiva consuetudo, quae apud illos nondum desinit, sed quotidie magis invalescit et roboratur: viz. quando invitant ad convivium aliquos nobiles nacionis nostrae, inter ipsas epulas, vel dormitionis tempore, invitatorum hospitum, nil mali suspicancium, sine misericordia effuderunt sanguinem suum: detestabile convivium hoc modo terminantes. Quo taliter facto, interfectorum amputata capita eorum inimicie pro pecuniis vendiderunt.

Sicat fecit Petrus Brunychehame, baro, proditor nominatus et nimis solemnis, Mauricio de S[*lege:* [Of]faly?], compatrino suo et Calvacho, fratri suo, viris valde

Kalends of Jan. [on 6th feria, 2nd of the moon], A.D. [1305] 1301¹[-5]. Muircertach Ua Concobuir Failghi and Mael-mordha, his kinsman and the Calbach Ua Concobhair, along with nine and twenty of the nobles of their people, were killed by Sir Pierce Mac Feorais [Birmingham], through treachery and through deceit, in the castle² of Mac Feorais.—The castle³ of Inis-Eogain was built by [Richard de Burgh] the Earl.—Matthew Ua Raighillaigh Junior was killed by the Tellach-Dunchadha.—Aedh Ua Ferghail Junior [died].—A defeat [was inflicted] by Aedh, son of Cathal Ua Concobuir and by the Clann-Muircertaigh also on the Muinnter-Raghaillaigh, so that Philip Ua Raighillaigh and the heir of Clann-Suibhne and Mag Buirrce, head of the Gallowglasses, together with one hundred and forty other persons, fell there.—Toirdhelbach, son of Niall Ua Briain the red, rested in Christ.

(Or it may be on this year¹ [the death of] Donn Mag (1301) Uidhir should be.)

ingenuis et valde apud nos nominatis, invitans ipsos ad convivium in festo Sanctissimae Trinitatis [Jun. 13], ipso die, refectione completa, statim cum surrexerunt de mensa, cum viginti quatuor hominibus de sequela sua, crudeliter jugulavit, ipsorum capita care vendens eorum inimicis. Et cum pro isto scelere regi Angliae [Eduardo I.], patri scilicet istius regis [Ed. II.], accusatus fuisset, nullam de tam nephando proditore fecit correcionem (pp. 916-7).

The truth of the foregoing is amply confirmed. On July 2, 1305—within a month after the massacre—a writ was directed to the Treasurer and Chamberlains of Dublin for payment to Peter de Bermengeham of £100 granted to him by the justiciary and council of Ireland, with consent of Richard de Burgh, Earl of Ulster, and Geoffrey de Genville [for whom see Grace's Annals, pp. 37, 54], to subdue Irish felons of Offaly, of the race of O'Conoghers and to decapitate the chiefs of the same race. Peter had already sent to Dublin the heads of Moriordagh [Muircertach] and Malmorthe [Maelmordha] O'Conoghers, chiefs of the race aforesaid and also 16 heads of others of the same race and their accomplices. Witness, J[ohn] Wogan, justiciary of Ireland. Dublin. (*D. I.*, V. 434.)

²*The castle.*—Perhaps Green Castle, co. Donegal. (See O'D. iii. 481.)

(1301) ¹ *This year.*—See the last entry but one, [1302], *supra*.

{Cal. Ian. [p.,ᵃ uii., L. xiii.ᵃ], Anno Domini M.° ccc.° ii.°ᵇ[-ui.°] Toirrdelbach hUa Briain, ri Tuad-Muman, in t-aen duine rob' oirexda¹ 7 rob' ferr ax² 7 exnum, rerᶜ lan do dérc 7 do crabad 7 robo mó rat͡ꞇ dobi i n-Erinn i n-a aimrir fein, quieuit in Chrirto.ᵈ Donnchad hUa Briain, a mac, do rixad i n-a inad.—Fergal Mag Raxnaill, tairec Muintire-hEolair, do marbad le [a] derbrat͡ꞃir³ fein* 7 la bloix d'a oirect i⁴ medail.— Cagad͡ʾ mor eter Aed, mac Eogain hUi Concobuir, ri Connact 7 maiti Sil-Muiredaix ar aen rir 7 Aed, mac Cat͡ꞇail hUi Concobuir 7 moran do macaib tairec Connact mar aen re toirecaib 7 oirectaib na Breifne arcena 'mun Sinainn re ré tri mír no cetair, co n-dernadur drem do macaib rix Aeda, mic Cathail, forbair irna Tuatraib mar aen re rocraide, xur'xabrat creacha 7 airgn[i] flann, mac Fiacra [U]i Fhloinn, adbur tairix Sil-Mailruanaix 7 Brian, mac Donnchada riabaix hUi Concobair, mar aen re dainib imda[ib]⁵ ailib⁵ do marbad ar lurg na creice do'n toir. Moran d'fardox do na creachaib 7 blox aile⁶ do breit ar. Ir iat tra ba ferr dobi annrin: Ruaidri, mac Cat͡ꞇail hUi Concobuir 7 Donnchad, mac Concobuir in copain, mic Fergail, mic Donnchada, mic Muircertaix Mic Diarmata, adbur rix Sil-Mailruanaix ar ax, ar einech, ar exnum, connice in la rin. Ir éd rainic reime co Longport [U]i Choncobuir 7 loirgir rairir rix Connact, mar aen re tigb in Longport. Beirir fair Aed hUa Concobuir 7 benair an crec de 7 marbtar é iartain.ᶜ—Donnchad hUaᵇ Flaithbertaix, errur Cille-alad, rai n-einix 7 crabaid

A.D. 1302. ¹x om., A. ²ad, B. ³-recaib, A. ⁴a, A. ⁵it, MS. (A). ⁶O, A. ᵇ1306, overhead, n. t. h., B; *alias* 1306, D. ᶜ⁻ᶜ om., B, C. ᵈ om., A; *quieuit*, C.

[1306] ¹ *1302* = 1306 of the A. L. C.
² *Cell-aladh.*—Killala. See [1280],

note 2, *supra*. O'Flaherty died before the end of May, 1306 (*D. l.*, V. 527).

Kalends of Jan. [on 7th feria, 13th of the moon], A.D. [1306] 1302¹[-6]. Toirdhelbach Ua Briain, king of Thomond, the one person the most distinguished and best in victory and prowess, a man full of charity and piety and of most prosperity that was in Ireland in his own time, rested in Christ. Donnchadh Ua Briain, his son, became king in his stead.—Ferghal Mag Raghnaill, chief of Muinnter-Eolais, was killed by his own brothers and by a part of his sept, in treachery.—Great war [took place] between Aedh, son of Eogan Ua Concobuir, king of Connacht and the nobles of Sil-Muiredhaigh with him and Aedh, son of Cathal Ua Concobuir and many of the sons of the chiefs of Connacht together with the chiefs and septs of Breifni also, along the Shannon for the space of three months or more, until a party of the sons of kings [on the side] of Aedh, son of Cathal, made an encampment in "The Territories" with a strong force, so that they took many preys and spoils. Flann, son of Fiachra Ua Floinn, future chief of Sil-Mailruanaigh and Brian, son of Donnchadh Ua Conchobair the Swarthy, along with many other persons, were killed in the rere of that prey by the pursuing party. Much of the preys was held fast and another part was wrested. These indeed are the best that were there: Ruaidhri, son of Cathal Ua Concobuir and Donnchadh, son of Concobur "of the Goblet," son of Fergal, son of Donnchadh, son of Muircertach Mac Diarmata, one fit to be king of Sil-Mailruanaigh for felicity, for generosity, for prowess up to that day. This is [what Donnchadh did]: he went forward to the stronghold of Ua Conchobuir and burned the palace of the kings of Connacht, along with the houses of the stronghold. Aedh Ua Concobuir overtakes him and wrests the prey from him and he is killed after.—Donnchadh Ua Flaithbertaigh, bishop of Cell-aladh,² most eminent of the Gaidhil for liberality and piety, died in Dun-buinne, in the end of Spring before

na n-ʒaıδel, do eʒ ı⁷ n-Ꝺun-buınne ı⁷ n-ꝺereδ⁸ eppaıc
peımepın, aʒ ꝺul ꝺo Aċ-clıaċ 7 [a] aꝺnuc|al 'pn⁹
Muılınn-cıpp,¹⁰ ı taıʒ Muıpe co honópaċ.—Maıʒıpтep
Tómaр О Náán, apcıꝺeoċan Raċa-boċ 7° тoʒa eppuıc na
heclu[ı]pe ceтna,ᶜ ın Chpıpтo quıeuıт.—Roıbepт a
bpıuıp, mopmaep, ꝺo ʒabaıl pıʒı n-Alban* ap eıʒın ı n-
aʒaıδ¹¹ pıʒ Saxan.—Ꝺomnall Tuıpтpeċ О Neıll ꝺo
mapbaδ ı⁴ тuıpıl¹² le luċт тıʒı hUı Neıll.—Sap Uıllıam
Pпınnꝺpaʒap, pıꝺıpe óʒ ba mó¹³ nóı· 7 eıneċ 7° laʒ pobı
ı n-Epınn ı n-a aımpep peın, mopтuup epт.—Cпeċ mór
ꝺo ꝺenum ꝺo Claınn-Muıpcepтaıʒ ı Cpıċ-Caıppпı, ꝺu
ap'mapbaδ Ꝺaıbıт hUa Caema[ı]n, bpuʒaıδ mór conaıċ
7 Ꝺonnċaδ Maʒ buıδeċa[ı]n 7 ꝺaıne ımꝺa eıle.—
bpıan cappaċ О h-Eaʒra ꝺo mapbaδ hUı Flannaʒa[ı]n.
—Peтpup О Tuaċala[ı]n, bıcaıp Cılle-eppuıc-[b]poın,
quıeuıт ın Chpıpтo.ᶜ—Nıcol hUaᶜ Ꝺonnċaδa, pacapт óʒ
ꝺobí ı n-Ꝺpuım-clıaδ, ꝺo mapbaδ ꝺo'n Ꝋeppan ꝺuδ ꝺo
na baıpeꝺaċaıδ ʒan cın, ʒan aꝺbup, aċт mapтpa ꝺ'ımípт
paıp. Ocup ʒaċ aen ʒeδup Paıтep ꝺo paıċ a anma,
aтaıт pe¹⁴ pċıт¹⁴ la loʒaıδ aıʒı ʒaċ meıncı[u] ʒebтap¹⁵
ꝺo.

(No,' ʒumaδ ap ın Kalaınn pı buꝺ cóıp Ꝺonn
Maʒ Uıꝺep.')

A.D. 13C2. ⁷a, B. ⁸⁻·⁷, A. ⁹pa, B. ¹⁰-leann-ċeapp, B. ¹¹-aꝺ, A.
¹²-el, B. ¹³mór (the positive), B. ¹⁴,¹⁴ .uı, xx.ıc, A, B. ¹⁵ʒeδup,—*he
recites* (*it*), B; followed by C. *ı n-Albaın—*in Scotland*, B. ᵗ·ᵈ 66a.
f. m., n. t. b., A; om., B, C.

---

³ *Bishop-elect.*—See [1284], note 3, *supra.*

⁴ *Robert Bruce.*—He married Elizabeth, daughter of Richard de Burgh, Earl of Ulster, in 1303 (Grace). As his assumption of the Scottish crown took place in 1306, there is a prolepsis of four years in the textual date.

⁵ *Took, etc.*—The translator of C misunderstood the construction: "taken by king of Scotland per force, against the king of England's will."

⁶ *Cell-espuip* [B]*roin.*—*Church of Bishop Bron* (Brunus, episcopus, L. A., 12d): now Killaspugbrone,

that, in going to Ath-cliath. And he was buried honour- [1306] ably in the Muillen-cerr [Mullingar], in the house of Mary. —Master Thomas O'Naan, archdeacon of Rath-both and bishop-elect[3] of the same church, rested in Christ.—Robert Bruce,[4] Great Steward, took[5] the kingship of Scotland by force against the king of the Saxons.—Domnall O'Neill of Tuirtre was killed by accident by the household of Ua Neill.—Sir William Prendergast, a young knight of the best repute and liberality and disposition that was in Ireland in his own time, died.—A great foray was made by the Clann-Muircertaigh into the country of Cairpre, wherein were killed David Ua Caema[i]n, a large, substantial yeoman and Donnchadh Mag Buidhecha[i]n and many other persons.—Brian Carrach O'Eaghra killed Ua Flannaga[i]n.—Peter O'Tuathala[i]n, vicar of Cell-espuic-[B]roin,[6] rested in Christ.—Nicholas Ua Donnchadha, a young priest that was in Druim-cliabh, was killed by the "Black Horse" of the Barrets, without guilt, without reason, except to inflict a violent death upon him. And every one that shall say a *Pater* for the good of his soul, there are six score days[7] of indulgence for him, as often as it is said by him.

(Or it may be on this year[1] [the death of] Donn Mag (1302) Uider should be.)

---

bar. of Carbury, co. Sligo (O'D., F. M. iii. 482).

[7] *Six score days.*—On Oct. 8, 1309, Clement V., in view of his devotion to God and the church, granted to the soul of the knight, John Havering, at the request of his son, the archbishop-elect of Dublin : omnibus vere penitentibus et confessis, qui devotis orationibus divinam pro eius anima misericordiam imploraverint, singulis diebus, quibus apud Deum huiusmodi orationes effundent, viginti dies de iniunctis sibi penitentiis misericorditer relaxamus. Presentibus post triennium non valituris (Theiner, p. 180).

(1302) [1] *This year.*—See (1301) note 1, *supra.*

408

A 660

[Cal. Ian. [p.ˢ ı., l. xx.ıııı.ᵃ], Anno Domini M.° ccc.° ııı.ᵃ [-uıı.°] Luipint hUa¹ Lachtna[i]n, erpuc Cılle-mıc-nDuach, manach Liath, quıeuıt ın [Chpirto].—Echuim O-Maine do Lorcad Le dpeim do macaıb pıg O-Maıne. —Goill Rora-comain uile d'[f]orba do mapbad la Donnchad O Cellaig, pı hUa¹-Maine, ag At-erpach-Cuan, dú ıtrochaıp Pilip Muınntep⁷° 7 Sean Muındtep° 7 Maıu Dpuv map aen pe daınıb aılıb,² etep mapbad 7 fagbaıl³ 7 gabaıl. Do gabad ann Diapmaıt gall Mac Diap-mata 7 Cormac Mac Cethernaıg 7° poleıged⁴ ap a pochaıdeda po cumur. Ocup pogabad ann forᵉ Seıppıamᵈ Rora-Comaın 7 do leıged⁴ ap ıat ap tpıll 7 doponpat pat ap pon ın⁵ baıle do° Lorcad pe hemunn Buıtıllep.ᶜ— Eoubapd, pí Saxan, tıgepna na hepenn 7 Bpetan 7 Alban, moptuur ert.—Donnchad O flannaga[ı]n, erpuc Oıl-fınd,⁵ quıeuıt ın [Chpirto].—Domnall, mac Taıdg, mıc Bpıaın, mıc Annpıar, mıc Bpıaın Luıgnıg, mıc Toırpdelbaıg moıp, tanurtı Connacht, fep lan d'egnum 7 d'eınech, paıᵉ coıtcenn,ᵉ a mapbad la hAed m-Bpeıpnech, mac Catail puaıd hUı Concobuıp.—Tadg,ᵉ mac Maıl-[Sh]echlaınn, mıc Donnchada, mıc Domnaıll, mıc Magnupa, mıc Toırpdelbaıg, feıchem coıtcenn ím bıad 7 ím ellach, a mapbad do Catal, mac Domnaıll, mıc Taıdg.ᶜ—Donnchad Muımnech O Ceallaıg, pı O-Maıne, paı coımdep° ím° gach nı, quıeuıt ın [Chpirto].—Uılliam

A.D. 1303. ¹ O, A. ² ií., B; eıle, A. ³ fogbaıl, A. ⁴ -7, MS. (A). ⁵ an, A. ⁶ Oılepınn, A. ᵇ 1307, overhead, n. t. h., B; *alias* 1307, n.t.h., C. ᶜ᪲ om., B, C. ᵈ 7—and (given in C) is required before this word in B. The omission was, no doubt, accidental. ᵉ᪲ coıtcen[n] ı n—(*general in*), B, C.

[1307] ¹ *1303.* = 1307 of the A.L.C.

² *Ua Lachtnain.*—Elected in 1290 (D. I., III. 759); died before March, 1307 (*ib.* V. 622).

³ *Ath-escrach-Cuan.*—Ford of the ridge of [St.] Cuan; Ahascragh, co. Galway, "where the memory of St. Cuan is still held in great veneration" (O'D., *F. M.* iii. 187).

⁴ *And, etc.*—Literally, *together with other persons, between killing, and abandoning, and capturing.*

⁵ *Sheriff.*—Perhaps Richard de

Kalends of Jan. [on 1st feria, 24th of the moon,] A.D. [1307] 1303¹[-7]. Laurence Ua Lachtna[i]n,² bishop of Cell-mic-Duach, a Grey [Cistercian] monk, rested in Christ.—Echdruim of Ui-Maine was burned by a party of the sons of kings of Ui-Maine.—The Foreigners of all Ros-comain were in great part killed by Donnchadh O'Cellaigh, king of Ui-Maine, at Ath-escrach-Cuan,³ where fell Philip Munnter and John Munnter and Matthew Drew and⁴ other persons were either killed, or left [wounded], or captured. Diarmait Mac Diarmata the Foreigner and Cormac Mac Ceithernaigh were taken there and their forces were allowed to depart under condition. And the Sheriff⁵ of Ros-comain was also taken there [along with his force] and they were all allowed to depart upon sufferance. And they made peace. [This happened] because the town [of Ahascragh] was burned by Edmund Butler.—Edward, king of the Saxons, lord of Ireland and the Britons and Scotland, died.⁶ —Donnchadh⁷ O'Flannacha[i]n, bishop of Oil-finn, rested in Christ.—Domnall, son of Brian, son of Tadhg, son of Andrew, son of Brian of Luighni, son of Toirdhelbach Mor [Ua Conchobair], tanist⁸ of Connacht, a man full of prowess and of generosity, a general scholar, was killed by Aedh the Brefnian, son of Cathal Ua Conchobuir the Red. —Tadhg, son of Mail-[S]echlainn, son of Donnchadh, son of Domnall, son of Magnus, son of Toirdhelbach, general benefactor respecting food and cattle, was killed by Cathal, son of Domnall, son of Tadhg [Ua Conchobhair].—Donnchadh O'Cellaigh the Momonian, king of Ui-Maine, expert

---

Exon, keeper of the castle of Ros-common (D. I., V. Index, Roscommon : Richard de Exon).

⁶ Died.—July 7, 1307. Hence, there is a prolepsis of four years in the text at this year.

⁷ Donnchadh.—See [1303], note 4,

supra. According to the eulogistic obit in the A. L. C., he died June 22, 1307.

⁸ Tanist.—From the Irish tanaise, second. It signifies the next to the kingship, the heir-presumptive.

Mac Fheopaip, apoerpuc Tuama, | oo oul [co' Roim'].—
Coporn oo tabaipt oo pig Saxan 7 Opetan 7 Epenn,
roon, o'Eoubapo og.—Ailbi, ingen Taog [U]i Concobuip,
moptua ept.—Clann-Muipceptaig oo tect 1 Mag-Cetne
7 apbanna Cpici-Caippp 7 mopan o'apbup Tipe-hOilella
7 in Copainn oo lopcad leo. Ocup oo'n toipc pin oo
mapbad Taog, mac Magnupa. Do mapbad lapin Catal
cetna.—Mail-[Sh]etlainn O Gaipmlegaid, taipet Cene[oi]l-Moá[i]n, quieuit in .[Chpipto].—Magnup Mag
Oipettaig quieuit in Chpipto.

[Oip.] Kal. Ian. [ii.ª p., l. u.ª], Anno Domini M.º ccc.º iiii.º
[-uiii.º] Moipcpeat oo oenum oo Maelpuanaig Mac
Diapmata ap macaid Domnaill hUi Concobuip 1 Cpic
Caippp. Cpeata mopa oo oenum oo Clann-Muipceptaig ap na macaid cetna 7 piat ap n-oenum pita peime
piu 7 ap tabaipt bpaiget ooid 7 oo peallaoup oppa
iaptain. | Ocup oo gluaipeoup na meic pompo co Sliad-én
7 ní pucaoup leo att a n-eit 7 a n-eioed 7 a n-gpoige. Ap
n-a cloiptin pin oo Ghallaid O-piactat 7 Luigne, oo tinoileaoup cucu 7 oo leanuoup iat co mullat Sleide-én 7
oo inntóoup meic Donntada 7 meic Domnaill piu,
gup'teiteoup na goill pompo 7 co tucad maiom poppo
co leic Epa-oapa. Ocup oo mapbad leo Tomag Mac

A.D. 1303. ¹⁻¹ om. in MS. (A); owing, most probably, to the similarity between copoim and copoin (the opening word of the next entry).

---

⁹ *To Rome.*—Doubtless, in reference to the charges brought against him [1297], note 5, *supra*.

C ends this year with: "William Brimingham, archbishop of Tuam;" leaving the entry incomplete, as it stands in B.

¹⁰ *Young Edward.*—Edward II. was crowned Feb. 24, 1308. "But the years were computed from July 7, as appears from the *Red Book of the Exchequer*: Data regis E., filii regis E., mutatur singulis annis in festo Translationis S. Thomae, Martyris, viz. VII. Idus Julii." Hampson: *Medii Aevi Calendarium*, London (no date), vol. 2, p. 413.

The meaning of the native annalist is that he succeeded to the crown on the death of Edward I.

¹¹ *Same Cathal.*—Son of Domnall, mentioned in the seventh entry of this year.

proficient in every thing, rested in Christ.—William Mac Feorais [Birmingham], archbishop of Tuaim, went to Rome.[9]—The crown was given to the king of the Saxons and Britons and Ireland, namely, to young Edward.[10]— Ailbi, daught of Tadhg Ua Concobuir, died.—The Clann-Muircertaigh came into Magh-Cetne and the crops of the country of Cairpre and much of the corn of Tir-Oilella and the Corann were burned by them. And on that expedition was killed Tadhg, son of Maghnus [Ua Conchobair]. He was slain by the same Cathal [Ua Conchobair].[11]—Mail-[S]echlainn O'Gairmlegaidh, chief of Cenel-Moa[i]n, rested in Christ.—Maghnus Mag Oirechtaigh rested in Christ.

Kalends of Jan. [on 2nd feria, 5th of the moon], A.D. 1304[1][-8]. A great foray was made by Mailruanaigh Mac Diarmata on the sons of Domnall Ua Conchobuir in the country of Cairpre. Great forays were made by the Clann-Muircertaigh on the same sons, although these[2] had made peace previously with them and had given pledges to them; but they acted treacherously towards them afterwards. And the sons went forward to Slaibh-en and took nothing with them except their steeds and their accoutrements and their [pack-]horses. When that was heard by the Foreigners of Ui-Fiachrach and of Luighni, they assembled their forces and followed them to the summit of Sliabh-en. And the sons of Donnchadh and the sons of Domnall turned upon them, so that the Foreigners fled before them and defeat was put upon them as far as the Flagstone of Es-dara. And Thomas, son of Walter [de

[1307]

[1308 Bis.]

[1308] [1] *1304* = 1308 of the *A. L. C.;* which, however, fall into a serious error (repeated by Magsoghegan in his Annals) by stating that Easter fell in March in this year. It was (XVII. F) April 14.

[2] *These.*— Namely, the Clann-Muircertaigh (for whom see O'Donovan, *F. M.* iii. 492–3).

balltaiρ, Conρtabla bona-ρinne · 7 a ԁeρbρaťaiρ 7
ԁaine aili.—Cρeč ԁiξalta ԁo ťenum ԁ'Ceԁ, mac Caťail,
aρ Ruaiԁρi, mac Caťail, aρ a ԁeρbρaťaiρ ρein. Ocuρ
Maξnuρ, mac Maξnuρa, ԁo maρbaԁ leiρ 7 ԁaine aili.—
Iṁaρ Mac ξeibennaiξ quieuit in [Chρiρto].—8oiξnen
ťeineԁ ԁo ťoitim i Mainiρtiρ na m-bρaťaρ i Roρ-Comain,
ξuρ'bρuρ in Mainiρtiρ.—Ԁomnall, mac Comaρba Comain,
aiρciԁeoťan Oil-ρinn, quieuit in Chρiρto.— . . , bicaiρ[b]
Clain-innρi, moρtuuρ eρt quinto Iԁuρ ρebρuaρii.

kal. Ian. [ρ.* iiii., l x.ui.,*] Cnno Ԁomini M.° ccc.* u.*
[-ix.°] Ceԁ, mac Eoξain, mic Ruaiԁρi, mic Ceԁa, mic
Caťail Cρoiԁԁeiρξ, mic Toiρρԁelbaiξ moiρ hUi Concobuiρ, ρi Connačt 7 ԁeξaԁbuρ aiρԁρiξ Eρenn 7 in t-aen
ξaiԁel ρob' ρeρρ eξnum 7 eineč; ρo bo mó 7 ρob' ρeρρ
ԁelԁ tainic O bρian boρuma anuaρ, ԁo maρbaԁ le hCeԁ
m-bρeiρneč,. mac Caťail hUi Cončobuiρ, (7[b] in ԁael
hUa 8očlača[i]n ԁo ρin lam ԁo ԁ'a ṁaρbaԁ le tuaiξ,
iԁon, boԁač ρuԁaiρe[b]) i Coill-in-clačain 7 moρan ԁo
maiťiԁ a muinnteρi. Ocuρ iρ iat ρo na maiťi ρin:
iԁon, Concobuρ Mac Ԁiaρmata 7 Ԁiaρmait ρuaԁ, mac
Taiԁξ hUi Concobuiρ 7 Ԁiaρmait, mac Caťail caρρaξ,
Mac Ԁiaρmata 7 Ceԁ, mac Muiρceρtaiξ, mic Taiԁξ, mic
Mailρuanaiξ. Ԁiaρmait O hEiliԁe, ρlaitbρuξaiԁ ρob'
ρeρρ i n-a aimρiρ ρein 7 ξilla-na-naem Mac Ceԁuξa[i]n,
ollaṁ Connačt 7 Eρenn 7 ρai coimԁeρ i n-ξač ceiρԁ, ԁo
ťoitim ԁo'n lučt ρoiρ 'ρin lo cetna 7 ρaξaρtač O

A.D. 1304.   [b-b] 66o, f. m., t. h.; the first part of the entry is illegible.
A.D. 1305.   [b-b] r. m., n. t. h. (A) MS.

[3] *Fell.*—On the night (eve) of St.
Stephen's Day, according to the
A. L. C. and Mageoghegan.

[4] *Successor of* [*St.*] *Coman.*—That
is, abbot of Roscommon. The
A. L. C. state his name was
O'Conor.

[1309] [1] *1305* = 1309 of the
A. L. C.

[2] *Coill-in-clachain.*—*Wood of the
(stepping) stones.* "In Kilcloaghan,
in the territory of the Bre[f]ne,"
Mageoghegan. Probably (O'D.,
F. M. iii. 490), Kilclogha, parish of

Burgh], constable of Bun-finne and his brother and other [1308] persons were killed by them.—A retaliatory foray was made by Aedh, son of Cathal [Ua Conchobhair], on Ruaidhri, son of Cathal, that is, on his own brother. And Maghnus, son of Maghnus [Ua Conchobhair] and other persons were killed by him.—Imhar Mac Geibennaigh rested in Christ.—A bolt of fire fell[3] on the Monastery of the Friars in Ros-comain, so that it broke down the Monastery.—Domnall, son of the Successor of [St.] Coman,[4] archdeacon of Oil-finn, rested in Christ.— . . . , Vicar of Clain-inis, died on the 5th of the Ides [9th] of February.

Kalends of Jan. [on 4th feria, 16th of the moon], A.D. [1309] 1305[1][-9]. Aedh, son of Eogan, son of Ruaidhri, son of Aedh, son of Cathal Red-hand, son of Toirdelbach Ua Concobuir the Great, king of Connacht and one worthy to be arch-king of Ireland and the one Gaidhel that was best of prowess and hospitality; that was greatest and best of figure that came from Brian Boruma downwards, was killed by Aedh the Brefnian, son of Cathal Ua Conchobuir, (and "the Chafer" Ua Sochlacain, namely, a boorish tanner, it was that stretched out a hand towards him to kill him with a hatchet) in Coill-in-clachain.[2] And many of the nobles of his people [were slain likewise]. And these are the nobles: to wit, Concobur Mac Diarmata and Diarmait the Red, son of Tadhg Ua Concobuir and Diarmait, son of Cathal Carrach Mac Diarmata and Aedh, son of Muircertach, son of Tadhg, son of Mailruanaigh [Ua Conchobair]. Diarmait O'hEilidhe, a chieftain-yeoman that was the best in his own time and Gilla-na-naem Mac Aedhuga[i]n, ollam of Connacht and of Ireland and accomplished sage in every science, fell by the eastern[3]

Drumgoon, barony of Clankee, co. Cavan.

[3] *Eastern*.—Namely, the Brefnian portion of the forces.

Doibilen do lucht tigi Tomaltaig Mic Donnchaid.—Creċ do ḋenum la hAeḋ, mac Cataıl hUı Concobuır, ar Muirgir Mac Donnċaid 7 a ġabaıl fein.—Cataḷ, mac ın Liaṫanaıġ, abb na Trınoıdı, do toġa[ḋ] cum erpucoıde Oıl-finn.—Uıllıam Burc do tect co hOıl-finn ar eır [U]ı Concobuır to marbad ı Connaċtaıḋ 7 Sıl-Muıre-ḋaıġ do ṫabaırt tıġernu[ı]r do mac Cataıl° hUı Concobuır.—Ruaıdrı, mac Cataıl° 7 O Flaınn | do dul, marcluaıġ, ar a Maċaıre 7 mac Mıc Fheorar do marbaḋ leo.—Coınne do ḋenum d'Uıllıam Burc 7 do Chonnaċtaıḋ re mac Cataıl 'ma Aṫ-rlıren. Brıreḋ coınne etorra 7 maıdm do ṫabaırt ar mac Cataıl ann. Dream d'a muınntır do marbaḋ. Uıllıam Burc do dul co Maınıſtır na Buılle 7 Clann-Muırcertaıġ do teċt ı Tır-n-Oılella. Arbur ımḋa do lorcaḋ 7 do ṁıllıuḋ doıḃ. Mac Uıllıam do teċt ar Corr-ſlıaḃ anúar. Mac Cataıl do cur ar a Longport dó 7 Donnċaḋ O Fınaċta do marbaḋ do ṫoraċ rluaıġ Mıc Uıllıam 7 daıne aılı.—Creċ do ḋenum le Mac Uıllıam ı Clıond-Fherṁuıġe. Creċ aıle leır co Beınn-Gulban 7 ní ır rada rír.—Concobur, mac Brıaın ruaıḋ hUı Brıaın, do marbaḋ.

A.D. 1305. ° Baıl (=Cataıl), (A) MS.

ᶜ *Cathal.*—Born in 1270, according to the *A. L. C.* On the death of Donough O'Flannagan ([1307], note 7, *supra*), the canons elected Malachy (Mac Aedha, Mac Hugh), canon of Elphin, who was in Minor Orders. The dean, however, refused to take part in the election, betook himself elsewhere and, having nominated Charles (Cathal), "abbot of the monastery of the Holy Trinity of Loch Ke of the Premonstratensian Order," got his selection confirmed (archiepiscopo in remotis agente) by Master Reginald, Official of the Armagh curia, and had his nominee consecrated bishop (in Armagh, *A. L. C. ad an.* 1307). Whereupon, Malachy appealed to the Curia (in Avignon). After due canonical proofs, which are detailed in the Bull of appointment, O'Conor, who appeared neither in person, nor by proxy,

people on the same day and Faghartach O'Doibhilen by [1309] the household people of Tomaltach Mac Donnchaidh.—A foray was made by Aedh, son of Cathal Ua Concobuir, on Maurice Mac Donnchaidh and [Maurice] himself was taken prisoner.—Cathal,[4] son of the Liathanach [Grey-Ua Conchobair], abbot of the Trinity [Island, Loch Ce], was chosen to the bishopric of Oil-finn.—William de Burgh came to Oil-finn after [Aedh] Ua Concobuir was killed in Connacht and the Sil-Muiredhaigh gave lordship to [Ruaidhri] the son of Cathal Ua Concobuir.—Ruaidhri, son of Cathal and O'Flainn went on the Plain [of Connacht] and the son of Mac Feorais [Birmingham] was killed by them.—A meeting was held between William de Burgh and by the Connachtmen [on the one side] with [Ruaidhri] son of Cathal, [on the other] near Ath-slissen. The meeting was broken up between them[5] and defeat inflicted on the son of Cathal there. Some of his people were killed. William de Burgh [then] went to the Monastery of the Buill and the Clann-Muircertaigh came into Tir-Oilella. Much corn was burned and [much] destroyed by them. Mac William came down past Corr-sliabh. The son of Cathal was put out of his stronghold by him and Domnall O'Finachta and other persons were killed by the van of the host of Mac William.—A foray by Mac William in Clann-Fermuighe. Another foray by him to Benn-Gulbain and farther downwards.[6]—Concobur,[7] son of Brian Ua Briain the Red, was killed.

---

was deprived of the See and Malachy appointed thereto by Clement V., June 22, 1310 (Theiner, p. 180-1).

The *A. L. C.* state he enjoyed the revenue for three years and a half. The text is consequently four years predated in this place.

His death took place in [1343], *infra.*

[5] *Meeting-them.*—Literally, *breaking of meeting* [*took place*] *between them.*

[6] *Downwards.* — Towards the north, which is the reading of the *A. L. C.*

[7] *Concobur.*—See the first entry of the following year.

416 annala ulaoh.

Kal. 1an. [u.ᵃ p., l. xx.uii.ᵃ], Anno Domini M.º ccc.ᵃ ui.º [-x.º] Concobur hUa Briain, mac riz rob' repr do leit Moza, do marbad do na Zallaib duba i medail.— Creca mora dizla do denum le hAed m-Breirnec 7 le Clainn-Muircertaiz arcena ar Maelruanaiz Mac n-Diarmada 7 Donncad, mac Donncada, d'arzain 7 do zabail 7 a muinnter do marbad 7 do zabail 7 do lorcad. Ocur a ben do marbad, idon, ingen hUi Flannaga[i]n 7 mna 7 rirᵇ imda aili ror.—Ferzal Maz Dorcaid quieuit in [Chrirto].—Una, ingen Aeda, mic Feidlimte, d'ez.— Sluaized le Serrraiz O Ferzail co Dun-Uadair, ait ar'marbad Domnall, mac Aeda oiz [U]i Fherzail 7 Aed, mac Mail-Iru 7 Zarrraiz, mac Muircertaiz.— Cairlen Bona-Finne do lorcad 7 d'arzain, eter cruacaib 7 tizib, le Ruaidri, mac Catail 7 le hAed, mac Maznura 7 le muindtir Aeda Breirniz arcena.—Finnzuala, ingen Maznura [U]i Choncobuir, d'ez.—Aed Breirnec O Concobuir, dezaddur airdriz Connact 7 in mac riz ir rerr tainic o Murcad, mac Briain [Boruma], anuar, a marbad le Mac Uidilin (idon,ᶜ Seonaz Mac Uidilinᶜ), idon, buana do bi ar conzmail aizi rein, i feall 7 a medail ar cennaidect do ronad.—Fici tunna rina do cur ro tir i Maz-Cetne in tan rin.—Cairlen Slizib do denum leirin Iarla.—Feidlimib, mac Aeda, mic Eozain,

A.D. 1306. ᵇ rer (i.e. r with siglum for er overhead), MS.   ᶜ il., n. t. h., MS.

[1310] ¹ *1306* = 1310 of the *A. L. C.*

² *Black Foreigners.*—"Probably used to denote the English lately come over, who were black strangers in comparison with the English-Irish" (O'D. *F. M.* iii. 494).

³ *Burned.*— From the burnings that took place on the occasion the incursion was called *Crech-in-toiten* (foray of the conflagration), according to the *A. L. C.*

⁴ *The castle, etc.*—This is copied by the *Four Masters.* A longer account is given in the *A. L. C.*

⁵ *Killed.*—See the fuller description in the *A. L. C.* (*ad an.*) and in Mageoghegan (O'D. iii. 496).

⁶ *Mercenary.*—The *buana* was a soldier paid partly in money, partly in victuals. This system of payment was called *buanacht* (Anglo-Irish, bonaght). A proportion of "wages in money," "dietts in

Kalends of Jan. [on 5th feria, 27th of the moon], A.D. [1310] 1306¹[-10]. Conchobur Ua Briain, the son of a king that was the best of the Half of Mogh was killed by the Black Foreigners² in treachery.—Large retaliatory forays were made by Aedh the Brefnian, and by the Clann-Muircertaigh also on Maelruanaigh Mac Diarmata and Donnchadh, son of Donnchadh [Mac Diarmata] was despoiled and taken prisoner and his people were [either] killed or taken prisoners, or burned.³ And his wife was killed, namely, the daughter of Ua Flannaga[i]n and many other women and men also [were killed].—Ferghal Mac Dorchaidh rested in Christ.—Una, daughter of Aedh, son of Feidhlimidh [Ua Conchobair], died.—A hosting by Geoffrey O'Ferghail to Dun-Uabhair, a place where was killed Domnall, son of Aedh Ua Ferghail junior and Aedh, son of Mail-Isu and Godfrey, son of Muircertach [Ua Ferghail].—The castle⁴ of Bun-finne was burned and despoiled, both [corn-]reeks and houses, by Ruaidhri, son of Cathal [Ua Conchobair] and by Aedh, son of Maghnus [Ua Conchobair] and by the people of Aedh [Ua Conchobair] the Brefnian besides. —Finnghuala, daughter of Maghnus Ua Concobuir, died. —Aedh Ua Conchobuir the Brefnian, worthy heir of the arch-king of Connacht and the son of a king the best that came from Murchadh, son of Brian [Boruma], downwards, was killed⁵ by Mac Uidilin (namely, Johnock Mac Uibhilin): that is, a mercenary⁶ that was kept by himself [as a body-guard] did it in treachery and deceit for a price.—Twenty tons of wine were put [i.e., washed] ashore in Magh-Cedne that time.—The Castle of Sligech was built by the Earl.—Feidhlimidh, son of Aedh, son of

---

money," and "dietts in victuells" "in the Bonaghte" is set forth in "The rate of the wages of the Galloglas," etc. (*Tracts relating to Ireland*, Ir. Arch. Soc., II. p. 87 sq.). For the two kinds of Bonaght, see

Dymmok's *Treatise of Ireland* (*ib.* p. 8).

In a secondary sense, Bonaght signified the soldiery thus maintained.

a n-inað a atar rein.—Cormac O Flannaga[i]n, tairec Tuaet-rata, do marbað le Henri Mac Gille-Fhinnein, tairec Muinnteri-Peodaca[i]n, a reall.—Ma[c] Craet Mag Uidir, ridamna Fer-Manac 7 Domnall Mac Gille-Micil, tairec Clainni-Congaile, do milliud 7 do lorcad le Roolb Mag Mhatgamna.—Amlaim{d} Mag Uidir, idon, mac Duinn carraig, tairec Muinnteri-Peodaca[i]n, mortuus ert 14 Kal. Iulii, 1306.{d}

Kal. Ian. [ui.{a} f., l. ix.,{a}] Anno Domini M.° ccc.° uii.° [-xi.°] Creč mor do denum le Clainn-Muircertaig i Connacta 7 Gilla-Crist, mac Muirgira, mic Donncada Mic Diarmata, do marbað ann 7 Aed, mac Cormaic 7 Uilliam Mac Gille-arraič 7 Donncað mac Tomaltaig 7 daine imda aili.—Da Mac Uilliam leič a burc do marbað do na macaib rig Laixneca[ib].—Sluaiged mor le hUilliam burc irin Mumain i n-agaid in Clarait 7 cat do tabairt doib 7 maidm do tabair tar in Claraic ann 7 Uilliam burc ar derbð a muinnteri ag lenman in mađma. Ocus gibe ro gabað, is aigi do bi corcur in mađma.—Tadg O hAinlide do marbað la Siurtan d'Eiretra.—Sagað mor i Tuað-Mumain irin bliadain si 7 cat do tabairt do Dhonncað Mac Conmara 7 d'a oirect, idon, do Trica-cet O-Cairin, i n-agaid h[U]i briain 7 Fer Muman uile. Ocus Donncað Mac Conmara do marbað ann 7 maiti a oirecta uile 7 Domnall O Grada, tairec Cene[oi]l-Dungaile. Ocus ar diairmide etorra, let ar let.—Donncað O Briain, ri Muman 7

A.D. 1306. {d-d} 67a, f. m., t. h., MS.

[1311]. {1} *1307* = 1311 of the A. L. C.

{2} *Battle was given.*—At Bunratty, co. Clare, on Ascension Day, 1310 (Clyn); May 20, 1311 (Grace). These data supplement and correct each other, enabling the true year to be determined. In 1311 (I. C.), Easter fell on April 14; Ascension Day, on May 20. The text consequently anticipates by four years.

{3} *Killed.*—The *A. L. C.* state that

Eogan [Ua Conchobair, became king] instead of his own father.—Cormac O'Flannaga[i]n, chief of Tuath-Ratha, was killed by Henry Mac Gille-Finnein, chief of Muinter-Peodacha[i]n, in treachery.—Ma[c] Craith Mag Uidhir, royal heir of Fir-Manach and Domnall Mac Gille-Michil, chief of Clann-Conghaile, were pillaged and burned by Ralph Mac Mathgamna.—Amhlaim Mag Uidhir, namely, son of Donn Carrach, chief of Muinter-Peodacha[i]n, died on the 14th of the Kalends of July [June 18], 1306.

Kalends of Jan. [on 6th feria, 9th of the moon], A.D. 1307[1][-11]. A great foray was made by the Clann-Muircertaigh into Connacht and Gilla-Crist, son of Maurice, son of Donnchadh Mac Diarmata, was killed therein and Aedh, son of Cormac [Mac Diarmata] and William Mac Gille-Arraith and Donnchadh, son of Tomaltach [Mac Diarmata] and many other persons [were killed].—Two sons of William de Burgh the Grey were slain by the Leinster sons of kings.—A great hosting [was made] by William de Burgh into Munster against De Clare and battle was given[2] by them and defeat was inflicted on De Clare there. And William de Burgh was at the rere of his force in following up the defeat. And, though he was captured, it is with him the triumph of the defeat remained.—Tadhg O'hAinlidhe was killed[3] by Jordan de Exeter.—Great war in Thomond in this year and battle was given by Donnchadh Mac Conmara and by his sept, namely, by the Cantred of Ui-Caisin, against Ua Briain and all the Men of Munster. And Donnchadh Mac Conmara was killed therein and all the chiefs of his sept and Domnall O'Grada, chief of Cenel-Dunghaile [were killed]. And countless slaughter [took place] between them, side for side.—

[1311]

O'Hanly was slain in pursuit of the party led by de Exeter into Magh Luirg (barony of Boyle, co. Roscommon).

aobuρ ρiξ Eρenn, do maρbað a meðail do Muρčað, mac Matξamna [U]ı Bρiain.—Loclainn ριabač O Deaξað do maρbað le Matξamain, mac Domnaill Connačtaiξ [U]ı Bρiain.—Seonaξ Mac Uıξılın do maρbað ın Zρuelaıξ ı m-baıle-tobaıρ-Bρıξde 7 a maρbað ρeın ınd. Ocuρ ıρ do'n ξeρρρa[m]ètaıξ d'aρ'maρð ρe Cað Bρeıρneč O Concobuıρ, ρı Connačt, do maρbað e ρeın.—Cρeč do ðenum le Feıðlımıð O Concobuıρ, ρı Connačt, aρ Claınn-Muıρceρtaıξ, aρ boρd Muıξı-Cetnı. Ocuρ Mael-Seclaınn, mac Concobuıρρuaıð, ρıρı ρaıtea Ceann ın meıξıl, do maρbað ann 7 daını eıle.—Domnall hUa Ruaıρc, ρı Bρeıρne, moρtuuρ eρt.—Dıaρmaıt Cleıρeč hUa Bρıaın moρtuuρ eρt.—Muıρceρtač O Bρıaın do ρıξað.—Domnall O Bıρn, taıρeč Tıρe-Bρıuın, quıeuıt ın [Chρıρto].—Zılla-Iρu O'Dalaıξ, ollam dana, quıeuıt ın [Chρıρto].

A67q[bıρ.] Kal. 1an. [uıı.ª ρ., L xx.ª], Cnno Domını M.º ccc.º uıı.º [-x.º 11.º] Uıllıam Mac Fheoρaıρ, aıρdeρρuc Tuama, ın Chρıρto quıeuıt.—Beınıðečt O Bρaξa[ı]n, eρρuc Luıξne, quıeuıt ın [Chρıρto].—Malacı Maξ Cæða, eρρuc Oıl-ρınd, do èoξa[ð] cum aıρdeρρucoıde Tuama.

Kal. 1an. [ıı.ª ρ., L 1.ª], Cnno Domını M.º ccc.º ıx.º [-x.111.º] Clemenρ ρapa moρtuuρ eρt.—Rex Fρancı[a]e moρtuuρ eρt.—Zılla-Iρu Maξ Doρcaıð do maρbað do

---

⁴ *Gruelach.*—The name here intended has not been identified.

⁵ *Baile-tobair-Brigde.*—Town of the *well of* [St.] *Brigit* (Balintober, co. Roscommon). The well "from which the place took its name is yet in existence here, but not regarded as a holy well" (O'D. iii. 500).

⁶ *Killed.*—In [1311], *supra*.

⁷ *Head of the Harvest-band.*—So called, in all probability, from having devoted himself to agriculture rather than to warfare.

[1312] ¹ *1308* = 1312 of the *A. L. C.*

² *Malachy.*—On the death of Birmingham, the Chapter elected (per viam compromissi) Philip, dean of Tuam. He having refused to consent, the Chapter in the same manner chose Malachy of Elphin ([1309], note 4, *supra*). The bishop

Donnchadh Ua Briain, king of Munster and one fit to be [1311] king of Ireland, was killed in treachery by Murchadh, son of Mathgamain Ua Briain.—Lochlainn O'Deaghadh the Swarthy was killed by Mathgamain, son of Domnall Ua Briain the Connacian.—Johnock Mac Uighilin killed the Gruelach[4] in Baile-tobair-Brighde[5] and himself was killed [immediately] therefor. And it is with the short [handled-] axe wherewith he killed[6] Aedh O'Concobuir the Brefnian, he was killed himself.—A foray was made by Feidhlimidh O'Conchobuir, king of Connacht, on the Clann-Muircertaigh, on the verge of Magh-Cetne. And Mael-Sechlainn, son of Concobur the Red, who was usually called Head of the harvest-band[7] and other persons were killed therein.—Domnall Ua Ruairc, king of Breifni, died.—Diarmait Ua Briain the Cleric died.—Muircertach Ua Briain was made king.—Domnall O'Birn, chief of Tir-Briuin, rested in Christ.—Gilla-Isu O'Dalaigh, professor of poetry, rested in Christ.

Kalends of Jan. [on 7th feria, 20th of the moon], A.D. [1312Bis.] 1308[1][-12]. William Mac Feorais [Birmingham], archbishop of Tuaim, rested in Christ.—Benedict O'Braga[i]n, bishop of Luighni [Achonry], rested in Christ.—Malachy[2] Mac Aedha, bishop of Oil-finn, was chosen to the archbishopric of Tuaim.

Kalends of Jan. [on 2nd feria, 1st of the moon], A.D. [1313] 1309[1][-13]. Pope Clement [V.] died.[2]—The king of France died.[3]—Gilla-Isu Mag Dorchaidh was killed by

---

submitted himself in the matter to the decision of the Curia and proceeded to Avignon, in company with the capitular proctors. Having been questioned and approved by three examiners deputed ad hoc, he was transferred to Tuam by Clement V., December 19, 1312 (Theiner, p. 185-6). The text accordingly is antedated by four years.

[1313] [1] *1309* = 1313 of the *A. L. C.*

[2] *Died.*—This obit is five years antedated. Clement V. died April 20, 1314.

[3] *Died.*—A similar prolepsis of five years. Philip le Bel of France lived until 1314.

422 ANNALA ULAOh.

Conċobuṗ Cappaċ Mac Ḋiaṗmata. — Taḋg, Mac Annṗiaṗ, d'ég.—Caṫal, mac Muṗċaḋa Cappaiġ h[u]i Ḟeṗgail, quieuit in [Chṗiṗto].

Kal. Ian. [iii.ᵃ f., l. xii.ᵃ] Anno Domini M.° ccc.° x.° [-x.° iiii.°] Niall O Domnaill occiṗuṗ eṗt.—Maiḋm Muinnteṗi-Raiġillaiġ ic Ḋṗuim-leṫan le Ruaiḋṗi, mac Caṫail [U]i Concobuiṗ.—Maġnuṗ, mac Domnaill h[u]i Eaġṗa, do maṗbaḋ le Maġnuṗ, mac Uilliam [U]i Eaġṗa, i ṗeall.—Niall, mac Ḃṗiain hUi Neill, in t-aen mac ṗiġ ṗo bo linmuiṗe 7 ṗob' ṗeṗṗ maiṫ[i]uṗ bo bí a n-Eṗinn i n-aen aimṗiṗ ṗiṗ ṗein, quieuit in [Chṗiṗto].

Kal. Ian. [iii.ᵃ f., l. x.ii.] Anno Domini M.° ccc.° x.° i.° [-x.° iiii.°] Maṫa Mag Tiġeṗna[i]n do maṗbaḋ do Chaṫal O Ruaiṗc.—Niall O Domnaill do maṗbaḋ le hAeḋ O n-Domnaill.—Maṫa Mag [Oh]uiḋne, eṗpuc na Ḃṗeiṗne, d'ég.—Roolḃ Mag Maṫgamna do maṗbaḋ d'a ḃṗaiṫṗiḃ ṗein.

Kal. Ian. [iiii.ᵃ f., l. xx.iii.] Anno Domini M.° ccc.° x.° ii.° [-x.° u.°] Sluaġ-loinġeṗ moṗ do ṫeċt a hAlbain le deṗḃṗaṫaiṗ ṗiġ Alban, le hEoudaṗd, i cṗiċaiḃ Ulaḋ. Cṗeċa moṗa do ḋenum dó aṗ muinntiṗ in Iaṗla 7 aṗ Ġallaiḃ na Miḋe. Sluaġ moṗ do ṫinol do'n Iaṗla i n-aġaiḋ na n-Albanaċ. Ḟeiḋlimiḋ, mac Aeḋa hUi Choncobuiṗ, ṗi Connaċt, do ḋul leiṗiu. Sluaġ moṗ aile
A 67d do tinol | le Ruaiḋṗi, mac Caṫail [U]i Choncobuiṗ, i

---

⁴ *Tadhg.*—According to the eulogistic account in the *A. L. C.*, he was grandson of Turlough Mor O'Conor, and died a monk in the abbey of Boyle.

[1314] ¹ *1310* = 1314 of the *A. L. C.*

² *Niall.*—The entry in the *Four Masters* states that he was grandson of Turlough O'Donnell, who was slain [1303], *supra*.

³ *1311* = 1314 of the *A. L. C.* From this to the textual year 1366 (=1369) inclusive, the dating is three years in advance.

⁴ *Niall.*—A repetition (with the name of the slayer added) of the first entry of the textual year 1310 (=1314).

Conchobur Carrach Mac Diarmata.—Tadhg,[4] son of Andrew [Ua Conchobair], died.—Cathal, son of Murchadh Carrach Ua Ferghail, rested in Christ. [1313]

Kalends of Jan. [on 3rd feria, 12th of the moon], A.D. 1310[1][-14]. Niall[2] O'Domnaill was slain.—Defeat of the Muinter-Raighillaigh [was inflicted] at Druim-lethan by Ruaidhri, son of Cathal Ua Concobuir.—Maghnus, son of Domnall Ua Eaghra, was killed by Maghnus, son of William Ua Eaghra, in treachery.—Niall, son of Brian Ua Neill, the one son of a king who was most bountiful and best in goodness that was in Ireland at the same time as himself, rested in Christ. [1314]

Kalends of Jan. [on 3rd feria, 12th of the moon], A.D. 1311[3][-14]. Matthew Mag Tigerna[i]n was killed by Cathal O'Ruairc.—Niall[4] O'Domnaill was killed by Aedh O'Domnaill.—Matthew Mag [Dh]uibhne, bishop of the Breifni [Kilmore], died.—Ralph Mag Mathgamna was killed by his own kinsmen.

Kalends of Jan. [on 4th feria, 23rd of the moon], A.D. 1312[1][-15]. A great fleet-host came from Scotland with the brother of the king of Scotland, that is, with Edward [Bruce],[2] into the territories of Ulidia. Great forays were made by it on the people of the Earl [de Burgh] and on the Foreigners of Meath. A great host was collected by the Earl against the Scotch. Feidhlimidh, son of Aedh Ua Concobuir, king of Connacht, went with that. Another great host was collected by Ruaidhri,[3] son of Cathal Ua [1315]

[1315] [1] *1312* = 1315 of the *A. L. C.*

[2] *Edward [Bruce].*—For the proceedings of the Bruces in Ireland, see Gilbert's *Viceroys*, p. 134 sq.

[3] *Ruaidhri.*—According to the *A. L. C.*, instead of employing the force to aid Bruce (the ostensible purpose for which it was raised), Ruaidhri marched unopposed through the province, in the absence of Feilim, and had himself inaugurated king of Connaught.

Connaċta. Cairſena do loſgaḋ 7 do briſiuḋ.—Aeḋ, mac Maġnuſa [U]ı Conċobuıſ, do maſbaḋ le Caṫal, mac Domnaıll [U]ı Concobuıſ. Maġnuſ, mac Maġnuſa, ın mac ríġ ſob' ſeſſ eıneċ 7 eġnom do bí do Connaċtaıḃ 7 Domnall, a deſbſaṫaıſ, do maſbaḋ ın la aſ namaſaċ leſın ſeſ cetna. Dıaſmaıṫ, mac Sımoın n a t ſ a ξ a, do maſbaḋ ın la do maſbaḋ Aeḋ, mac Maġnuſa [U]ı Concobuıſ, leſın Claınn cetna a n-dıġaıl a n-aṫaſ.—Cat do'n ıaſla d'on d-aſa leṫ 7 d'Eoubaſd co n-a ſedaın do'n leṫ aıle, ξuſ'maıdm[eḋ] aſ ın ıaſla 7 aſ ξallaıḃ aſċena. Ocuſ do ξabaḋ ann Uıllıam Búſc 7 da mac Mıc-ın-Mhılıḋ.—Matġamaın Maξ Raξnaıll, taıſeċ Muınnteſı-hEolu[ı]ſ, do maſbaḋ le Maelſuanaıξ Mac n-Dıaſmata, ſí Muıξe-Luıſξ 7 O Maılṁıadaıξ, taıſeċ Muınnteſı-Ceaſballa[ı]n 7 moſan do Muınntıſ-Eolu[ı]ſ aſaen ſıu. Conċobuſ ſuaḋ, mac Aeḋa Bſeıfnıġ, do maſbaḋ ann.—Maelſuanaıξ Mac Dıaſmata 7 ξılleberd Mac ξoıſdelḃ do ṫeċt ı Maξ-Luıſξ 7 cſeaċa do denum doıḃ. Ocuſ ſucaduſ ben Dıaſmata ξa[ı]ll leo 7 do aıſξeoaſ uıle muın[n]tıſ Dıaſmata ξa[ı]ll.—Taınıc Aeḋ O Domnaıll ſa ċaıſlen Slıξıḋ 7 do cuaſ ſaıſ leıſ. Ruaıdſı, mac Domnaıll [U]ı Concobuıſ, do maſbaḋ le Deſboſξaıll, ınξen Maġnuſa [U]ı Choncobuıſ, aſ cennaıḋeċt do ceıṫſı ξallóξlaċ.

Father. — Domnall O'Conor, father of Cathal, was slain in an encounter with Hugh O'Conor the Brefnian [1307], *supra.* According to the *A. L. C.*, he was wounded in the contest by Dermod, son of Simon. Hence the vendetta here mentioned.

Was fought.—At Connor, co. Antrim (*A. L. C.* and Grace).

William de Burgh.—Probably, the son of the Earl.

Mathgamain, etc.— See the *A. L. C.*, ad an. (Rolls' ed., i. 175).

Maelruanaigh, etc.—See the *A. L. C.* (*ib.* 577).

Derborgaill. — According to Mageoghegan (O'D. iii. 509-10) and the *A. L. C.*, the reduction of Sligo and the assassination of Rory were to avenge the slaying of her father (second entry of this year) by Domnall, brother of Rory.

Was done.—Given at 1216 in

Conchobuir, in Connacht. Castles were burned and [1315] broken down.—Aedh, son of Maghnus Ua Conchobuir, was killed by Cathal, son of Domnall Ua Concobuir. Maghnus, son of Maghnus, the son of a king who was best of hospitality and prowess that was of the Connachtmen and Domnall, his brother, were killed on the morrow by the same man. Diarmait, son of Simon of the Strand, was killed on the day on which was killed Aedh, son of Maghnus Ua Concobuir, by the same Clan, in revenge of their father.[4]—A battle [was fought][5] by the Earl on the one side and by Edward [Bruce] with his force on the other side, so that defeat was given to the Earl and to the Foreigners besides. And William de Burgh[6] and the two sons of Mac-in-Mhilidh were taken prisoners there.—Mathgamain[7] Mag Raghnaill, chief of Muinter-Eolu[i]s and O'Mailmhiadhaigh, chief of Muinter-Cerballa[i]n and many of Muinter-Eolu[i]s along with them were killed by Maelruanaigh[8] Mac Diarmata. Concobur the Red, son of Aedh [Ua Conchobair] the Brefnian, was killed there.—Maelruanaigh[8] Mac Diarmata and Gilbert Mac Goisdelbh came into Magh-Luirg and forays were made by them. And they took away with them the wife of Diarmait [Mac Diarmata] the Foreigner and plundered all the people of Diarmait the Foreigner.—Aedh O'Domnaill came against the Castle of Sligech and it was reduced by him. Ruaidhri, son of Domnall Ua Concobuir, was killed by Derborgaill,[9] daughter of Maghnus Ua Concobuir. [The deed was done[10]] for stipend by a band of gallowglasses.

---

the *A. L. C.*, according to which O'Donnell entered the country of Cairpre a second time, with a large force. On that occasion, Rory separated himself from his brothers, made peace with O'Donnell and received the lordship of Cairpre Nevertheless, "in violation of the relics of Tir-Conaill," he was slain as stated in the text.

426

Bó8a[bɪr.] [Cal. Ian. [u.ᵃ f.°, L. 1111.ᵃ] Anno Domini M.° ccc.
x.° 111.°ᵇ [-x.° uɪ.°] Sluaġ mor do tinol le Feiḋlimiḋ
O Concobuir 7 le Mac Fheorair 7 le Gallaiḃ Iartair
Connact. Tect doib co Tocur Mona-Coinneda. Ruaiḋri
hUa¹ Concobuir do ḋul 'n-a n-aġaiḋ 7° cumur[c] doiḃ
ar a ceile. Ruaiḋri hUa¹ Concobuir, ri Connact, do
marbaḋ ann 7 Diarmait Gall Mac Diarmata, ri
Muiġi-Luirg 7 Cormac Mac Ceiṫernaiġ, ri Ciaraiḋe 7
galloglaca uairli 7 daine imda aili.² Riġe in Coiciḋ do
gabail d'Fheiḋlimiḋ³ arir. Ocur fluaġ mor leir
d'innraiġiḋ Aṫa-Leṫain 7 in baile do lorgaḋ leir. Ocur
Sleimne d'Eiretra, tiġerna in baile, do marbaḋ leo 7
in Goganac, in t-aen barun ba raire⁴ do bi a n-Erinn, do
marbaḋ leo 7 Goill imda aili.² Ocur edala mora
d'faġbail doiḃ. A' nór 7 a n-allaḋ do ḋul fa Erinn,
gur'ġiallfat moran doiḃ.ᶠ—Sluaiġeḋ mor do ͫ comoraḋ ͫ
le ᵇ Feiḋlimiḋ ᵇ | mar aen re maiṫiḃ an coiciḋ 7 Donn-
caḋ O Briain, ri Muman 7 O Mael-[Sh]eclainn, ri
Miḋe 7 Ual[ġ]arc O Ruairc, ri Breifne (Ual[ġ]arcⁱ
O Ruairc do ġabail riġi in irto anno.ⁱ) 7 O Ferġail, ri
Muinnteri-hAngaile 7 Taḋg O Cellaiġ, ri O-Maine 7
Maġnur, mac Domnaill hUi Concobuir, tanurti Connact
7 Art O hEaġra, ri Luiġne 7 Brian O Dubḋa, ri O-Fiacrac.
A n-dul rin uile co hAṫ-na-riġ. Goill Iartair Connact
uile do tinol 'n-a n-aiġiḋ : idon, Uilliam Burc 7 in
barun Mac Feorair, tiġerna Aṫa-na-riġ 7 Goill Leiṫ

A.D. 1313. ¹O, A. ²ii, B; eile, A. ³⁻lim, B. ⁴ raire, A. ᵇ 1316 overhead, n. t. h., B. ᶜ om, A. ᵈ Opposite this place, Ruaiḋri, ri Connact—*Ruaidhri, King of Connacht*—is placed, l. m., t. h., B. ᵉ .u. (the Latin equivalent for the Irish coic—*five*) with ro overhead, A, B. ᶠ⁻ᶠ om., B. ᵍ⁻ᵍ docum omoraḋ, which is meaningless, B. It can signify *against* (literally *unto*) [the] *Ui-Mordha*. But this sense is inapplicable here. The reading is a misconception of the A-text. ʰ⁻ʰ do—*by him* (Fedhlimid), A. ⁱ⁻ⁱ t. m., t. h., A ; om., B.

[1316] ¹ *1313* = 1316 of the A. L. C.
² *Killed.*—Fidelmeus O Conghur interfecit Rororicum, filium Catholi O Conghur (Grace, *ad an.* 1315[= 1316]. His A.D. notation com-

Kalends of Jan. [on 5th feria, 4th of the moon], A.D. [1316 Bis.] 1313¹[-16]. A large host was mustered by Feidhlimidh Ua Concobair and by Mac Feorais [Birmingham] and by the Foreigners of the West of Connacht. They came to the Causeway of Moin-Coinnedha. Ruaidhri Ua Concobuir went against them and they engaged with each other. Ruaidhri Ua Concobuir, king of Connacht, was killed[2] there along with Diarmait Mac Diarmata the Foreigner, king of Magh-Luirg and Cormac Mac Ceithernaigh, king of Ciaraidhe and noble gallowglasses and many other persons. The kingship of the Fifth was assumed by Feidhlimidh again. And a large host was led by him to the assault of Ath-lethan and the place was burned by him. And Slevin de Exeter, lord of the town and de Cogan, the noblest baron that was in Ireland and many other Foreigners were killed by them. And many chattels were got by them. Their fame[3] and their renown went throughout Ireland, so that many submitted to them.—A great hosting was undertaken by Feidhlimidh, together with the nobles of the Fifth [of Connacht] and with Donnchadh O'Briain, king of Munster and O'Mael[-Sh]eclainn, king of Meath and Ual[gh]arc O'Ruairc, king of Breifni (Ual[gh]arc O'Ruairc took the kingship that year) and O'Ferghail, king of Muinter-hAnghaile and Tadhg O'Cellaigh, king of Ui-Maine and Maghnus, son of Domnall Ua Concobuir, tanist of Connacht and Art O'hEaghra, king of Luighni and Brian O'Dubhda, king of Ui-Fiachrach. They went, all those, to Ath-na-righ. The Foreigners of the West of Connacht all assembled against them: to wit, William de Burgh and the Baron Mac Feorais [Birmingham],[4] lord of Ath-na-righ and all the

---

mences on March 25; the change of the Dominical Letter, on the preceding Jan. 1).

[3] *Their fame, etc.*—A partisan exaggeration. How transient was

O'Conor's pre-eminence, is shown in the following entry.

[4] *Birmingham.*—It is worthy of note that he was on the side of O'Concr in the previous expedition.

Cuinn⁵ uile d'urṁor. Caṫ do comoraḋ leo 7 maiḋm do ṫabairt ar Ḡaiḋelaiḃ ann. Feiḋlimiḋ O Concobuir (mac¹ Aeḋa, mic Eoġain¹), rí Connaċt, do marbaḋ ann: in t-aen duine* iṡ mo re' raiḃe aire Fer n-Erenn uile 7 roḃ' fer eineċ 7 eġnum. Taḋg hUa¹ Ceallaiġ, rí O-Maine, do marbaḋ ann 7 oċtar ar fiċit d'ar'ḋual riġ do Clainn-Cellaiġ do marbaḋ ann. Art O hEaġra, ri Luiġne, do marbaḋ ann. Aċt aen ní, nír'marbaḋ 'rin aimsir ri i n-Erinn in coimlin do marbaḋ ann do macaiḃ riġ 7 tairec 7 do daíniḃ imḋa aili² orin amaċ. Ruaiḋri, mac 'Donnċaḋa, mic Eoġain hUi Concobuir, do riġaḋ do Connaċtaiḃ.—Sluaġ' le hUilliam Burc i Sil-Muireḋaiġ.' O Concobuir 7 Connaċta do ḋenum ria, aċt Mac Diarmata. Teċt' do Mac Uilliam i Maġ-Luirg. Creċa mora do ṫabairt leo o Aṫ-in-ċip 7 o Uaċtar-tire 7 in tir uile do lorcaḋ 7 do ṁilliuḋ doiḃ. Imteċt doiḃ arir amaċ iar rin.' In Ruaiḋri cetna do aṫriġaḋ le Mac Diarmata iar rin.—Derborgaill,'ingen Maġnura hUi Concobuir, d'eg.'

B 68b

Kal. Ian. [uii.ᵃ f., l. x.u.,*] Anno Domini M.° ccc.° x.° iiii.°ᵇ [-x.° uii.°] Toirrdelbaċ, mac Aeḋa,¹ mic Eoġain, do riġaḋ le Connaċta.—Roibeat a Briuir, ri Alban, do teċt a n-Erinn maille° re galloglaċaiḃ imḋaiḃ i furtaċt Eḋubairḋ, a braṫar rein, do ḋiċur Ḡall a hErinn.—Mailir d'Eiretra, tiġerna Aṫa-leṫain, do marbaḋ le

⁵ The MSS. have q for cu.—⁶ 1316, overhead, n. t. h., B. From Sluaġ to ann, inclusive, is translated in C at 1312, [alias] 1316. The next year is 1486. ʲʲitl, t. h., A; om., B. ᵏ Ḡaiḋel—Gaidhel, B. ¹ riri (same in meaning as the word in A), B.

A.D. 1314. ¹ Oaeḋa! B. ³ O, B. ᵇ 1317, overhead, n. t. h., B. * Faraaen (same signification as the A word), B. ᵈ⁻ᵈom., B.

---

⁵ *Battle, etc.*—On the feast of St. Lawrence (August 10), according to the *A. L. C.*, Clyn and Grace.

⁶ *Made peace.*—Namely, with de Burgh.

⁷ *Mac Diarmata.*—Who had not made peace with de Burgh.

⁸ *Derborgaill.*—See [1315], note 9, supra.

Foreigners of the greater part of the Half of Conn. Battle[5] [1316 Bis] was engaged in by them and defeat inflicted on the Gaidhil there. Feidhlimidh O'Concobuir (son of Aedh, son of Eogan), king of Connacht, was slain there: the one person on whom the attention of the Men of all Ireland was most directed and who was best in generosity and prowess. Tadhg Ua Cellaigh, king of Ui-Maine, was slain there and eight and twenty of the Clann-Cellaigh that had right to kingship [of Ui-Maine] were slain there. Art O'hEghra, king of Luighni was slain there. But [for] one thing, there was not slain in this time in Ireland the amount that was slain there of sons of kings and of chiefs and of many other persons in addition.—Ruaidhri, son of Donnchadh, son of Eogan Ua Concobuir, was [then] made king by the Connachtmen.—A hosting [was made after that] by William de Burgh into Sil-Muiredhaigh. O'Concobuir and the Connachtmen, with the exception of Mac Diarmata, made peace.[6] Mac William [de Burgh] came into Magh-Luirg. Great preys were brought by them from Ath-in-chip and from Uachtair-tire and the whole country was burned and pillaged by them. They went from out the country afterwards. The same Ruaidhri was deposed by Mac Diarmata[7] after that.—Derborgaill,[8] daughter of Maghnus Ua Concobuir, died.

Kalends of Jan. [on 7th feria, 15th of the moon], A.D. [1317] 1314[1][-17]. Toirdelbach, son of Aedh, son of Eogan [Ua Conchobair] was made king by the Connachtmen.—Robert Bruce, king of Scotland, came to Ireland[2] along with many gallowglasses in aid of Edward, his brother, to expel the Foreigners from Ireland.—Meyler de Exeter, lord of Ath-

---

[1317] [1] *1314* = 1317 of the *A. L. C.*

[2] *Came to Ireland.*—Bruce, according to Clyn, came about Christmas,

1316. But, having regard to Clyn's A.D. notation ([1327], note 4, *infra*), this does not exclude the beginning of 1317.

Catal, mac Domnaill hUí Concobuir, ap bopn Dpoma-
cliað 7 Domnall, mac Caiðg, mic Domnaill Ippaip, do
mapbað ann 7 ceitpi fip déc aili.—Caiplen Ata-cliat-
in-copainn do buipiuð.[d]—Donncað hUa[2] | Opiain, pi
Muman, occippup ept.—Concobup[d] buiðe Mag Tiżep-
na[i]n, taipeć Tellaiż-Dunćaða, occippup ept immaiom
Cille-móipe [7] Matzamain Mag Tiżepna[i]n 7 in
Zilla puað, mac in Aipcinniż 7 mopan aile d'a
cinniuð 7 Nicol Mac-in-Mhaiżiptip 7 mopan d'a aicme.
—Maiom Cille-moipe ap mac Ruaiðpi n-Zallozlać
7 ap fepaið Opeifne 7 ap Mhuinntip-Peoðaca[i]n, du'
inap'ćuit mopan do ðainið.—Mael-Ipu puað Mac
Aeðuza[i]n d'eź.—Ragnall[d] Mag Ragnaill do żaðail 7
Sefrpaiż Mhag Ragnaill, taipeć do denum ðe.[d]—
Zopta mop ipin bliaðain pi.[f]

[Kal. Ian. 1.[a] f.[*], [L[b] xx.ui.[b]] Anno Domini M.° ccc.° x.° u.°[c]
[-u.° iii.°] Maiom[d] i n-Eliṫ ap Zallaið leip O Cepðaill,
dú ap'mapbað Adam Maipeip 7 Zoill imda eile.[d]—
Sluaż mop do tinol le Maelpuanaiż Mac n-Diapmata
7 ip iat po: idon, Coippðelbać O Concobuip, pi Connaćt
7 Concobup O Ceallaiż, pi O-Maine 7 Ual[ż]apc[i] O
Ruaipc, pi Opeifne 7 Comaltać Mac Donnćaið, tiżepna
Thipe-hOilella, d'innpaiżið Cataill, mic Domhnaill, co
fápað-coille. Ocup tapzad[2] Catal comaða mopa do
Mac Diapmata do cinn gan teaćt ćuizi do'n toipc pin.[e]

A.D. 1314   e-e om., A.   f pin—that, B.
A.D. 1315.   L-g, A.   ²-ɡaið, B.   a-a om., A.   b-b Blank space, A, B.
c 1318, overhead, n. t. h., B.   d om., B.   e-e om., A.

---

[3] *Conchobur, etc.*—This item should follow the next.

[4] *The Herenagh.*—Namely, Mag Tighernain.

[5] *Mac-in-maighistir.*—*Son of the master.* "This name is still extant in the co. Cavan, but generally anglicised Masterson" (O D. iii. 516).

[6] *Mac Aedhaga[i]n.*—"The best learned in Ireland in the Brehon Lawe, in Irish called Fenechus" (Mageoghegan). See the Introduction (p. x.) to the lithographed edition of the Lebar Breac (*Speckled Book* [of the Mac Egans]).

[7] *Great dearth.*—Frumenti magna caritas: cranocus valebat 24s,

lethan, was killed by Cathal, son of Domnall Ua Concobur, [1317] on the border of Druim-cliabh and Domnall, son of Tadhg, son of Domnall [Ua Conchobair] of Irras and fourteen other persons were killed there.—The Castle of the Hurdle-ford of the Weir was broken down.—Donnchadh Ua Briain, king of Munster, was slain.—Conchobur[3] Mag Tigherna[i]n the Tawny, chief of Tellach-Dunchadha, was slain in the defeat of Cell-mor and Mathgamain Mag Tigherna[i]n and the Red Gillie, son of the Herenagh[4] and many more of his tribe and Nicholas Mac-in-maighistir[5] and many of his sept [were slain].—The defeat of Cell-mor [was inflicted] on the Gallowglass, son of Ruaidhri [Ua Ruairc] and on the Men of Breifni and on the Muinter-Peodachs[i]n, wherein fell a great number of persons.—Mael-Isu Mac Aedhaga[i]n[6] the Red died.—Raghnall Mag Raghnaill was taken prisoner and Geoffrey Mag Raghnaill was made chieftain.—Great dearth[7] in this year.

Kalends of Jan. on 1st feria, [26th of the moon], A.D. [1318] 1315[1][-18]. Defeat[2] [was inflicted] in Eili on the Foreigners by O'Cerbhaill, where Adam de Marisco and many other Foreigners were killed.—A great host was mustered by Maelruanaigh Mac Diarmata and these are [they who came]: to wit, Toirdelbach O'Concobuir, king of Connacht and Concobur O'Ceallaigh, king of Ui-Maine and Ual[gh]arc O'Ruairc, king of Breifni and Tomaltach Mac Donnchaidh, lord of Tir-Oilella, to attack Cathal, son of Domnall [Ua Conchobair], to Fasadh-coille. And Cathal proffered large donatives to Mac Diarmata for the sake of

---

avenae 16s, vinum 8d. Universa enim regio devastata a Scotis et Ultoniis (Grace, A.D. 1317). Fames irrationabilis prevaluit, adeo quod mensura tritici de la Cronnock continens 4 galones solvebatur pro xxiii. s (Dowling's Annals, 1317).

[1318] [1] *1315.*—The ferial number (1) proves that the true year is 1318.
[2] *Defeat, etc.*—According to Clyn (1318), about two hundred of the force of Edmund Butler were slain by Donatus (Donough) O'Carroll.

Ocuf nif'gabaḋ uaḋa, gur'innraiẋeḋur na roḃraiḋeaḋa rin co³ lar a Longruirt 7 nír'time 7 nir'teiceḋ do Caṫalim in toirc rin. Innraigir⁴ Caṫal arna tiẋiḃ amaċ 7 cumurcit ar a ċeile. Aċt en ní, marḃtar⁵ Conċoḃur O Ceallaiẋ, ri O-Maine 7 Ḃrian, mac Toirr-ḋelḃaiẋ [U]i Conċoḃuir, aḋḃur riẋ Connaċt 7 daine imḋa aili, eter marḃaḋ 7 leaṫaḋ. Caṫal cetna d'innraiẋiḋ Connaċt 7 do haṫriẋaḋ Toirrdelḃaċ O Conċoḃuir. Ocur do ẋaḃ Caṫal riẋe Connaċt 7 do roine creċa mora ar Mac n-Diarmata.—Seán, mac Dom-naill hUi Neill, do marḃaḋ le hAeḋ O n-Domnaill.—Ricard a Clara do marḃaḋ.—Eoudard a Ḃruir, rear millti Erenn co⁶ coitcenn, eter Ghallaiḃ 7 Ghaiḋelaiḃ, do marḃaḋ le Gallaiḃ Erenn tre nert caṫaiẋ[ṫ]i aẋ Dun-Dealgan. Ocur do marḃaḋ 'n-a focair Mac Ruaiḋri, ri Innri-Gall 7 Mac Domnaill, ri Aer[ṫ]er-Ghaiḋel,⁷ mar aen re hár na n-Albanaċ uime. Ocur

B 68c

A 68c

ni derrnaḋ | o ṫur domain ẋnim buḋ feirr d'Eirinncaiḃ ina'n ᵈ ẋním rin.ᵈ Uair tainic gorta 7 diṫ daine re [a] linn a n-Erinn uile | co coitcenn re ᵈ heaḋ tri m-bliaḋan co leṫ ᵈ 7 do itoir na daine a ċeile gan amurur ar fut Erenn.—Seffraiẋ hUa⁸ Fergail, tairec na hAnẋaile, quieuit in [Chrirto].—Snechta mor irin bliaḋain rin.ᶠ—Seann O Fergail do marḃaḋ d'aen urċur roiẋne.

A.D. 1315. ³ẋu, A. ⁴-ẋur, A. ⁵-tur, A. ⁶ẋa, B. ⁷Oirir-gaiḋil, B. ⁸O, A. ᶠno—or, B. ᵉ om., B.

---

³ *There was not fear, etc.*—Meaning that it was not through dread of his foes, but to avoid bloodshed, the offer of Cathal had been made. Hence there is no warrant for Mageoghegan's: "which he seeing, having none other remedy, *he tooke heart anew*."

⁴ *Killed.*—In Derry, according to the *A. L. C.*

ᵇ *De Clare.*—The battle (for an account of which, see *Historical Memoir of the O'Briens* by J. O'Donoghue, p. 126-7), we learn from Clyn, was fought on the morning of Thursday, May 11. This concurrence denotes 1318. The text is thus three years pre-dated.

⁶ *Dun-Delgan.*—Dundalk. "The

not coming against him on that expedition. And they [1318] were not accepted from him and those forces penetrated to the centre of his camp. And there was not fear[3] and there was not flight for Cathal respecting that expedition Cathal sallied from the houses forth and they engage with each other. But [for] one thing, Conchobhar O'Ceallaigh, king of Ui-Maine and Brian, son of Toirdelbach Ua Conchobhuir, one fit to be king of Connacht, were killed and many other persons [were lost] both by killing and by wounding. The same Cathal invaded Connacht and Toirdelbach O'Concobhuir was deposed. And Cathal took the kingship of Connacht and made great forays on Mac Diarmata.—John, son of Domnall Ua Neill, was killed[4] by Aedh O'Domnaill.—Richard de Clare[5] was killed.—Edward Bruce, the destroyer of Ireland in general, both Foreigners and Gaidhil, was killed by the Foreigners of Ireland by dint of fighting at Dun-Delgan.[6] And there were killed in his company Mac Ruaidhri, king of Insi-Gall [Hebrides] and Mac Domnaill, king of Airthir-Gaidhil [Argyle], together with slaughter of the Men of Scotland around him. And there was not done[7] from the beginning of the world a deed that was better for the Men of Ireland than that deed. For there came dearth and loss of people duing his time in all Ireland in general for the space of three years and a half and people undoubtedly used to eat each other throughout Ireland.—Geoffrey O'Ferghail, chief[8] of the Anghaile, rested in Christ.— Great snow in that year.—John O'Ferghail was killed by one shot of an arrow [by his own son[9]].

---

battle was fought near the hill of Faughard, within two miles of Dundalk, and the natives still point out the spot where he [Edward Bruce] fell" (O'D. iii. 520).

The date is accurately determined by the criteria in Clyn: "1318 on the feast of blessed. Calixtus, Pope and Martyr [Oct. 14], on the morning of Saturday."

[7] *There was not done*, etc.—For the opposite view, see Gilbert, *Viceroys*, p. 140 sq.

[8] *Chief.*—For six and thirty years, according to the *A. L. C.*

[9] *By—son.*—From the *A. L. C.*

434 annala ulaoh.

Kal. 1an. [11.ᵃ p., L. uııı.ᵃ], Anno Domini M.° ccc.° x.°ᵇ uıı.°ᶜ [-ıx.°] Enpi Mac-ın-Cporaın, erpuc Rata-bot, ın Chpırto quıeuıt.ᵈ Tomar, mac Capmaıc hUı Domnaıll, abb Erra-ruaıb, do toxa[b] cum erpucoıde Rata-bot.— Erpuc Doıre ın Chpırto quıeuıt.—Erpuc Clocaır ınᵈ Chpırto quıeuıt.ᵈ—Erpuc Cluana - ferta - Brenaınn quıeuıtᵈ ın [Chpırtoᵈ].—Aıne,ᵉ ıngen Mıc Dıarmata, ben Mıc Con[8h]nama, quıeuıt ın [Chpırto°].—Tomaltac° O Mael-Brenaınn 7 Etmarcac Mac Branaın, taıret Corco-Aclann, do marbab a ceıle.°—O Bana[ı]n, erpuc Oırgıall, d'eg.ᶠ—Brıan, Mac Domnaıll h[U]ı Neıll, do marbab le Cla[ı]nn-Aeba-buıbe.

[bır.] Kal. 1an. [111.ᵃ p., L. x.uıııı.ᵃ], Anno Domini M.° ccc.° x.° uıı.°ᵇ [-xx.°] Coınne° mór eter Catal O Concobuır 7 Maelruanaıg Mac Dıarmata: rıt do benum doıb 7 taıııc Mac Dıarmata artır ıar rın.° Feall do benum do['n] Catal cetnaᵈ ar Mac n-Dıarmata ı¹ Mullac- Dorabruc 7 a gabaıl ann 7 Graıne, ıngen Mıc Magnura a ben, do gabaıl 'rın lo cetna ı² Port Calad-na-caırgı. Ocur do lomaırged ın tıre uıle. Ocurᵉ porᶠ do gabab Mael-Iru donn Mac Aebaga[ı]n 7 a macᶠ 7ᵍ Tomaltac

A.D. 1316. ᵇ .x. was omitted at first and put overhead afterwards in paler ink, B. ᶜ 1319, overhead, n. t. h., B. ᵈ⁻ᵈ quıeuıt ın [Chpırto], B. ᵉ⁻ᵉ om., B. ᶠ lection of d-d, B.

A.D. 1317. ¹ a, B. ² a, A. ᵃ⁻ᵃ Blank space, A; none left in B. ᵇ 1320, overhead, n. t. b. (The correction is made in this place, except at 1335, by the same hand at each year down to 1373(=1378), where the misdating ends.), B. ᶜ⁻ᶜ om., B. ᵈ O Concobuır—O Conchobuir, B. The words were necessary (in consequence of the omission of the previous entry) to identify Cathal. ᵉ⁻ᵉ ror 7, B. ᶠ⁻ᶠ Placed (with ocur—and —prefixed) after Tıre-hOılella, B. ᵍ om., B.

[1319] ¹ *1316* = 1319 of the A. L. C.

² *Bishop of Doire.*—Hugh O'Neill, 1316-1319 (Ware, *Bishops*, p. 289).

³ *Clochar.*—This obit is omitted in the *A. L. C* and *Four Masters.*

It may have reference to the subject of the seventh entry of this year.

⁴ *Cluain-ferta.*—Gregory O'Brogy, 1308-1319 (Ware, *ib.*, p. 639).

⁵ *Echmarcach.*—He died of his

Kalends of Jan. [on 2nd feria, 7th of the moon], A.D. [1319] 1316¹[-19]. Henry Mac-in-Crosain, bishop of Rath-both, rested in Christ. Thomas, son of Cormac Ua Domnaill, abbot of Ess-ruadh, was chosen to the bishopric of Rath-both.—The bishop of Doire² rested in Christ.—The bishop of Clochar³ rested in Christ —The bishop of Cluain-ferta⁴ of [St.] Brenann rested in Christ.—Aine, daughter of Mac Diarmata, wife of Mac Con[Sh]nama, rested in Christ.—Tomaltach O'Mael-Brenainn and Echmarcach⁵ Mac Branain, chief of Corco-Achlann, killed each other.—O'Bana[i]n,⁶ bishop of Oirghialla [Clogher], died.—Brian, son of Domnall Ua Neill, was killed by the Clann-Aedba-buidhe.⁷

Kalends of Jan. [on 3rd feria, 18th of the moon,] A.D. [1320 Bis.] 1317¹[-20]. A great meeting between Cathal O'Conchobuir and Maelruanaigh Mac Diarmata: peace was made between them and Mac Diarmata came into the country after that. Deception was [nevertheless] practised by the same Cathal on Mac Diarmata in Mullach-Dorabruch and he was taken prisoner there and Graine,² daughter of Mac Maghnusa, his wife, was taken prisoner on the same day at the landing-place of the Ferry of the Rock. And the country was laid bare completely. And moreover Mael-Isu Mac Aedhaga[i]n the Brown and his son and Tomal-

---

wounds within three days (*A. L. C.*).

⁶ *O'Bana[i]n.* — His Christian name, according to Ware, was Gelasius. If so, he may have been the Gelasius, elect of Clogher, whom the primate, Roland de Jorse, was charged with having confirmed and consecrated, whilst Roland lay under sentence of excommunication (Theiner, p. 223).

⁷ *Clann-Aedha-buidhe.* — *Clan of Hugh [O'Neill] the Tawny*, anglicised Clannaboy.

[1320] ¹ *1317* = 1320 of the *A. L. C.*

² *Graine.* — "And also took Graine . . . whom he found staying for a boat, to pass over into the Island of Carrick Logha Ke [Rock of Lough Ce]," Mageoghegan.

436   annala ulaḋh.

Mac Donnċaıḋ, tıǵerna Tıre-hOılella 7 ruaraḋur moranh d'ulc.—Mor, ınġen Uı Daıġıll,³ ben h[U]ı Ferġaıl, d'ec.⁴—Matġaṁaın, tanuṙtı O Brıaın, quıeuıt ın [Chrırto].ᵉ

Kal. Ian. [u.ᵃ f., l. xx.ıx.ᵃ,] Anno Domını M.º ccc.º x.º uııı.ºᵇ [-xx.º ı.º] Graıne, ınġen Mıc¹ Maġnura, banrıġan ᵉ Muıġı-Luırġ,ᶜ ben Maelruanaıġ Mıc Dıarmata, d'eġ.—Ruaıḋrı, mac Donnċaḋa, rı Connaċt, do marbaḋ le Caṫal, mac Aeḋa² hUı Concobuır.—Carracc ᶜ Loċa-Cé do leaġaḋ le Caṫal O Conċobuır.ᵉ—Maġnur O hAnluaın do ḋallaḋ la Nıall O n-Anluaın.—Nıall O hAnluaın, rı Oırrıṫer, do marbaḋ do Ġhallaıḃ Duın-Dealġan ı meḃaıl.—Maıdm ᵉ mor do ṫaḃuırt do Anrıu Mac Fheoraır 7 do Ġallaıḃ na Mıḋe ar macaıḃ rıġ O-Faılġı.ᵉ—Boıṫ mor ar ᶜ fur ᶜ Erenn ᵈ uıle co coıtċenn.ᵈ

Kal. Ian. [uı.ᵃ f., l. x.ᵃ,] Anno Domını M° ccc.º x.º ıx.ºᵇ [-xx.º ıı.º] Coġaḋ mór eter rí Saxan 7 a ıarlaḋa.—Mata O hEoṫaıġ, errup Ardd-aċaḋ, quıeuıt ın [Chrırto].—Murċaḋ O Ferġaıl, ṫaıreċ na hAnġaıle, do marbaḋ le Seoan O Ferġaıl, le mac a derbraṫar. Muırcertaċ ᵉ hUa Ferġaıl do marbaḋ le [a] braṫaır feın for 'rın lo cetna.—Donnċaḋ, mac Donnċaḋa Mıc Dıarmata, quıeuıt ın [Chrırto].ᵉ—Ġıllıbert O Ceallaıġ, rı O-Maıne, d'eġ (ıᵈ No[ı]n Auġuırt ᵈ).—Enrı Mac Ġıllı-

A.D. 1317. ³ Duı—, B. ⁴-ġ. A. ʰ mor, *much (adjective used as substantive)*, B.
A.D. 1318. ¹ Meġ, A. ² Aoḋa, B. ᵃ⁻ᵃ bl. [blank space], A, B. ᵇ 1321, B. ᶜ⁻ᶜ om., B. ᵈ⁻ᵈ ı n-Erınn ın blıaḋaın rı—*in Ireland this year*, B.
A.D. 1319. ᵃ⁻ᵃ bl., A, B. ᵇ 1322, B. ᶜ⁻ᶜ om., B. ᵈ⁻ᵈ r. m., t. h., B ; om., A.

---

³ *Mathgamain.*—Son of Domnall and grandson of the Domnall O'Brien who died 1194, *supra.*

⁴ *Rested in Christ.*—The A. L. C. state he was slain by the Clan-Cuilen (Mac Namaras).

[1321] ¹ *1318 = 1321* of the A. L. C.

² *Graine.*—Mentioned in the last entry but two of the preceding year.

³ *The Rock.*—See 1187, note 1 *supra.*

⁴ *Cathal.*—Son of Domnall. He was slain in [1324], *infra.*

tach Mac Donnchaidh, lord of Tir-Oilella, were captured [1320] and received much injury.—Mor, daughter of Ua Baighill, wife of Ua Fergail, died.—Mathgamain[3] O'Briain, tanist of the O'Briains, rested in Christ.[4]

Kalends of Jan. [on 5th feria, 29th of the moon], A.D. [1321] 1318¹[-21]. Graine,[2] daughter of Mac Maghnusa, queen of Magh-Luirg, wife of Maelruanaigh Mac Diarmata, died· —Ruaidhri, son of Donnchadh [Ua Conchobair], king of Connacht, was killed by Cathal, son of Aedh Ua Concobuir. —The Rock[3] of Loch-Ce was razed by Cathal[4] O'Conchobuir.—Maghnus O'hAnluain was blinded[5] by Niall O'hAnluain.—Niall O'hAnluain, king of the Oirrthir, was killed by the Foreigners of Dun-Delgan in treachery. —A great defeat[6] was given by Andrew Mac Feorais [Birmingham] and by the Foreigners of Meath to the sons of the kings of Ui-Failghi.—Great cow destruction throughout all Ireland in general.

Kalends of Jan. [on 6th feria, 10th of the moon], A.D. [1322] 1319¹[-22]. Great war[2] between the king of the Saxons and his Earls.—Matthew O'hEothaigh, bishop of Ardachadh, rested in Christ.—Murchadh O'Ferghail, chief of the Anghaile, was killed by John O'Ferghail, [namely] by the son of his brother. Muircertach O'Ferghail was killed by his own brother likewise on the same day.— Donnchadh, son of Donnchadh Mac Diarmata, rested in Christ.—Gilbert O'Ceallaigh, king of Ui-Maine, died on the None [5th] of August.—Henry Mac Gille-Finnein,

---

[5] *Blinded.*—On the Wednesday in Holy Week (*A. L. C.*).

[6] *Great Defeat.*—Circa festum Philippi et Jacobi [Ma. 1] occiduntur de O'Konchours circa 300 in confinio Midie et Lagenie per Andream de Brimegham (Clyn, A.D. 1321).

[1322] ¹ *1319* = 1322 of the *A. L. C.*

² *Great war.*—This belongs to 1322, when Edward II. crushed the barons by the capture and decapitation of Lancaster. Clyn says the Earl was beheaded on Monday [March 22], the morrow [of the

438

Ḟhinnein, ṫaiṙeċ Muinnṫeṙi-Ṙeoḋaċa[i]n, do maṙḃaḋ do clainn Amlaim Meg Uiḋiṙ.—Ḃaṙun̄ Mac Ḟeoṙaiṙ d'eġ.—Uilliam liaṫ, mac Uilliam móiṙ, do ecc.¹

Kal. Ian. uii. f., [L.ᵃ xx.i.ᵃ], Anno Domini M.° ccc.° xx.°ᵇ [-iii.°] Caiṙṗṙi O Mael[-Sh]eċlainn¹ occiṡuṙ eṙt.—Seoinin̄ O Ḟeṙġail do maṙḃaḋ do clainn Sheoain [U]i Ḟeṙġail—O hEaẋṙa do maṙḃaḋ do hUa Connmaca[i]n in bliaḋain ṡin.°

[b.ṙ.] Kal. Ian. i. f., [L.ᵃ ii.ᵃ], Anno Domini M.° ccc.° xx.° i.°ᵇ [-iiii.°] Uilliam Ḃuṙc, mac Uilliam móiṙ, moṙtuuṡ eṙt.—In boḋiṫ ceṫna aṙ fuṫ Eṙenn, idon,ᶜ Maeldomnaiġ.¹ᵃ—Caṫal, mac Domnaill, mic Taiḋg, mic Ḃṙiain, mic Annṙiaṡ, mic Ḃṙiain Luiġniċ, mic Toiṙṙḋelḃaiġ ṁoiṙ, idon, ṙi Connaċt, aen duine iṡ beoḋa 7 buḋ mó aiṫuṡ 7 tuṙċuṙ do bi i² n-aen aimṡiṙ ṙiṡ, do¹ maṙḃaḋ le Toiṙṙḋelḃaċ O Conċoḃuiṙ 7 le Connaċtaiḋ aṙcena 7 Mael-Seċlainn, mac Toiṙṙḋelḃaiġ hUi Domnaill 7 Ġilla-Cṙiṡt og Mac Donnċaiḋ do° maṙḃaḋ ann̄ 7 daine imda aili.³ Toiṙṙḋelḃaċ (macʰ Aeḋa, mic Eoġainᵏ) hUa⁴ Concoḃuiṙ, do ġaḃail ṙiġi Connaċt.—Raġnall¹ óg Mag Raġnaill, ṫaiṙeċ Muinnṫeṙi-hEolaiṙ, do maṙḃaḋ.¹

A.D. 1319. ¹⁻¹ d'eġ, A. ᶜ⁻ᶜ om., B.
A.D. 1320. ¹ Maeil—, B. ᵃ⁻ᵃ bl., A, B. ᵇ 1323, B. ᶜ⁻ᶜ om., B.
A.D. 1321. ¹ Mol—, A. ² a, B. ³ ii., B; eile, A. ⁴ hUi (gen.), A; O, B. ᵃ⁻ᵃ bl., B; none left in A. ᵇ 1324, B. ᶜ⁻ᶜ r. m., t. h., A; itl., t. h., B. ᵈ om., A. ᵉ ṙa—(that) was, B. ᶠ a—his, B. ᵍ om., A. ʰ⁻ʰ itl., t. h., A; om., B. ⁱ⁻ⁱ om., B.

---

feast] of St. Benedict, 1321-2. For the others hanged and drawn, see ib.

³ Sons.—By his brothers, Lochlainn and Robert, according to the A. L. C.

⁴ Died.—In the beginning of Autumn (Clyn).

[1323] ¹ 1320 = 1323 of the A. L. C.

² Cairpri.—King of Meath; slain treacherously by O'Mulloy (chief of Fir-cell, King's co.), FourMast.

³ Ua Conmaca[i]n.—"The name is still extant in the district of Ballycroy, co. Mayo, and is now generally anglicised Conway" (O'D. iii. 528-9).

[1324] ¹ 1321 = 1324 of the A. L. C.

² William, etc.—A repetition of the final obit of [1322], supra.

chief of Muinter-Peodacha[i]n, was killed by the sons[3] of Amlam Mag Uidhir.—The Baron [Richard] Mac Feorais [Birmingham] died.[4]—William [de Burgh] the Grey, son of William Mor, died. [1322]

Kalends of Jan. [on 7th feria, 21st of the moon], A.D. 1320[1][-3]. Cairpri[2] O'Mael[-Sh]eclainn was slain.—Jenkin O'Fergail was killed by the sons of John O'Fergail.—O'hEaghra was killed by Ua Connmaca[i]n[3] in that year. [1323]

Kalends of Jan. on 1st feria [2nd of the moon], A.D. 1321[1][-4]. William[2] de Burgh, son of William Mor, died.—The same[3] cow-destruction (namely, the Mael-domnaigh[4]) [prevailed] throughout Ireland.—Cathal, son of Domnall, son of Tadhg, son of Brian, son of Andrew, son of Brian of Luighni, son of Toirdhelbach Mor [Ua Conchobair], king of Connacht,[5] the person the most active and of most goodness and success that was in the same time with him, was killed by Toirdhelbach O'Conchobuir and by the Connachtmen likewise. And Mael-Sechlainn, son of Toirdhelbach Ua Domnaill and Gilla-Crist Mac Donnchaidh junior and many other persons were killed there. Toirdhelbach (son of Aedh, son of Eogan) Ua Concobuir took the kingship of Connacht.—Raghnall[6] Mag Raghnaill junior, chief of Muinter-Eolais, was killed. [1324Bis.]

Clyn states he died on Septuagesima [Sunday, Feb. 11], 1323-4: he true date, judging from the precision of the diurnal notation.

[3] *Same.*—Mentioned in the last entry of [1321], *supra.*

[4] *Mael-domnaigh.*—The meaning of this word in connection with a murrain is unknown to me. (The literal sense is *devotee of Sunday.*)

Item, hoc anno, scilicet 1324, fuit pestis gravis boum et vaccarum in multis locis Hibernie (Clyn).

Fuit pestis communis vaccarum et etiam aliorum animalium, quae dicebatur in Hibernia *Mal-dow-*[*naigh?*] (*Annal. Rossen.*, A.D. 1324).

It may accordingly be concluded that there is a prolepsis of three years in the textual date.

[5] *King of Connacht.*—Since [1318], *supra.*

[6] *Raghnall, etc.*—Omitted in the A. L. C.; given in the *Four Masters.*

440   annala ulaoh.

A 69a   Kal Ian. (111.ª f, l. x.111.ª), Anno Domini M.º ccc.º xx.º
ii.ºᵇ [-u.º] Domnall, mac Briain hUi Neill, ri Tire-
hEogain, quieuit in [Chriſto].—Gilla-Criſtº cleireć
Mac Diarmata d'eg.—Diarmait O Mail-Brenainn,
tairec Clainne-Concobuir, quieuit in [Chriſto].ᶜ—Cu-
Ulað, mac Domnaill, mic Briain h[U]i Neill, deſaobur
airdrig Erenn, do marbað le macaið Neill, mic Briain.
Derbrataiṙ rein a atar run.—In bodit ceonaſ¹ n-Erinn
arir.ᵈ—Brianº O Gaðra quieuit inˢ [Chriſto].ᶜ

B 69a   Kal. Ian. [1111. f.ª, l. xx.1111.,ᵉ] Anno Domini M.º ccc.º
xx.º 111.ºᵇ [-ui.º] Riſdard a burc, iarla Ulað (anᶜ t-
iarla ruaðᶜ), aen raguˡ Gall 7 Gaiðel Erenn. d'eg—
Cogað² mor eter riᵈ Saxan 7 ri Franc.ᵈ—Luirint O
Lactna[i]n, eſruc Oil-rinn, quieuit in [Chriſto].
Maigiſterᵉ Seoan O Finacta do toga[ð] cum na herru-
coide cetna.ᵉ

    Kal. Ian. [u.ª f., l. u.,ᵃ] Anno Domini M.º ccc.º xx.º
1111.ºᵇ[-uii.º] Cogað¹ mor eter ri Saxan 7 a-ben rein, ingen
riġ² Fraingc 7 ri Saxan d'atrigað le 7 a mac rein do
gabail a n-agaið a atar tre forgall a matar, idon, na
riġna 7 coroin riġ do tabairt do'n mac cetna tre

A.D. 1322. ¹α, A. ᵃ⁻ᵃbl., A, B. ᵇ 1325, B. ᶜ⁻ᶜom., B. ᵈ beoſ—still, B.
A.D. 1323. ¹roga, B. ²Ca—, A. ᵃ⁻ᵃbl., A, B. ᵇ 1326, B. ᶜ⁻ᶜl. m.,
t h., B; om., A. ᵈ⁻ᵈri Frang 7 ri Saxan, B. ᵉ⁻ᵉom., B.
A.D. 1324. ¹Ca—, A. ²ri, B. ³O, A. ᵃ⁻ᵃbl., A, B. ᵇ 1327, B.

[1325] ¹ *1322* = 1325 of the A. L. C.

² *Rested in Christ.*—At Lough Laeghaire (bar. of Clogher, co. Tyrone), according to the *Four Masters.*

³ *One—arch-king.*—Literally, excellent material of an arch-king.

⁴ *The same.*—Mentioned in the second entry of the previous year.

[1326] ¹ *1323* = 1326 of the A. L. C.

² *De Burgh.*—According to the eulogistic obit in Clyn, he died on the Tuesday [July 29] before St. Peter ad Vincula [Aug. 1], 1326. This is confirmed by the date, Aug. 5, a. r. Ed. II. 20, of the writs issued respecting the goods and chattels of the deceased Earl. (*Ib.* note, p. 102-3.) The textual date is thus three years too early.

³ *War.*—Declared by Edward II. against Charles le Bel on account

Kalends of Jan. [on 3rd feria, 13th of the moon], A.D. 1322¹[-5]. Domnall, son of Brian Ua Neill, king of Tir-Eogain, rested in Christ.²—Gilla-Crist Mac Diarmata, the Cleric, died.—Diarmait O'Mael-Brenainn, chief of Clann-Concobuir, rested in Christ.—Cu-Uladh, son of Domnall, son of Brian Ua Neill, one full worthy to be arch-king³ of Ireland, was killed by the sons of Niall, son of Brian. That [man, Cu-Uladh, was] the brother of their father.—The same⁴ cow-destruction [prevailed] in Ireland again.—Brian O'Gadhra rested in Christ.

Kalends of Jan. [on 4th feria, 24th of the moon], A.D. 1323¹[-6]. Richard de Burgh,² Earl of Ulster (the Red Earl), unique choice of the Foreigners and Gaidhil of of Ireland, died.—Great war³ between the king of the Saxons and the king of the French.—Lawrence O'Lachtna[i]n,⁴ bishop of Oil-finn, rested in Christ. Master John O'Finachta was chosen to the same bishopric.

Kalends of Jan. [on 5th feria, 5th of the moon], A.D. 1324¹[-7]. Great war² between the king of the Saxons and his own wife,³ the daughter of the king of the French and the king of the Saxons was deposed by her and her own son was accepted against his father through suggestion of his mother, namely, of the queen and the royal crown was given⁴ to the same son through advice⁵ of the

---

of the invasion of Guienne and detention of his queen and of the heir presumptive.

⁴ *O'Lachtna[i]n.*—On the translation of Malachy to Tuam ([1312], note 2, *supra*), the Dean and Chapter of Elphin postulated Lawrence, priest and canon. He was appointed bishop by Clement V., (Avignon) Jan. 21, 1313. On Feb. 18, he was empowered to contract a loan of 1,000 gold florins and receive consecration from any archbishop or bishop he should choose, assisted by two or more bishops. (Theiner, p. 187.)

[1327] ¹*1324* = 1327 of the A. L. C.

² *Great war.*—The "war" (the invasion of the queen and the flight and capture of Edward) took place in 1326. It is mentioned to render what follows intelligible.

³ *Wife.*—Isabella, daughter of Philip le Bel.

⁴ *Was given.*—To Edward III.

comairpli Shaxan.—Gormlaiṫ,ᶜ ingean Mic Diarmaca, morcua erc.—Plaiṫberzaċ Maz Uiḋir, ri Ṡer-Manaċ, morcuur erc.—Mail[-Sh]eċlainn hUa³ Flannaga[i]n, cairec Tuaiṫ-raṫa, do marbaḋ le n-a braiṫriḃ rein.— Eouḃarv, rí Saxan, ar m-buain a riże ḋe, morcuur erc. —Ceiom galair bric ar ruc Erenn uile.—Fergal, mac Ual[ż]airg hUi Ruairc, v'eg.ᵈ—Cuilen hUa Dimaraig v'eg.ᵈ—Saḋḃ,ᶜ ingen Mic Ceḋaga[i]n, v'eg.ᶜ

[b₁r.] Kal. Ian. [ui.ᵃ r., l. x.ui.ᵃ], Anno Domini M.° ccc.° xx.° u.°ᵇ[-uiii.°] Mael-Seċlainn O Raiżillaiż, ri Muinncer-Mailmorḋa, vo gabail 7 vo loc vo Ghallaiḃ na Miḋe. Ocur a fuarlucuḋ¹ ar braiżoiḃ 7 a eg 'n-a ciż rein v'a

A 69b żonaiḃ.—Brian, | mac Tomalcaiż Illic Donnċaiḋ, vo marbaḋ vo Brian, mac Taiḋg.—Toirneċ 7 ceinnceċ anḋail irin bliaḋain rin. gur'milleour coraḋᶜ 7 arbanna Erenn,co rabaour rinna rar.—Ceiomᵈgalair coicċinn ar ruc Erenn uile,riri n-abairċea S l a e v a n, re heḋ cri lá no ċeċair ar gaċ neċ, gur'ba canairci bair é.—Gilla-nanaingel O Taicliż, airċinneċ Dam-innri, morcuur erc.ᵈ —Imar Maz Ragnaill, cairec Muinncire-hEolu[i]r, occirur erc.—Sar hEoan Mac Pheorair, Iarla Lugbaiḋ, in c-aen Gall ro bo beoḋa 7 rob' rerr eineċ² 7ᵈ egnomᵈ vo bi i n-Erinn, vo marbaḋ ar' n-venum feille v'a

A.D. 1324. ᶜ The order in B is: Eouḃarv—Plaiṫberzaċ—Maeileċlainn —Gormlaiṫ. ᵈ morcuur erc, B. ᵉ⁻ᵉ om., B.

A.D. 1325. ¹-gaḋ, A. ²-eaċ, A. ᵃ⁻ᵃbl., A, B. ᵇ 1328, B. ᶜ carréi (pl. of the word in A), B. ᵈ⁻ᵈ om.,B. ᵉ⁻ᵉ via muinncir rein a rell—*by his own people in treachery*, B.

He was crowned, according to Clyn, on Sunday [Feb. 1], the vigil of the Purification [Feb. 2], 1326(= 1327. The Dominical Letter was changed in Clyn's Annals on Jan. 1 ; the A.D. notation on the ensuing March 25).

⁵ *Advice.*—This and the colourless obit of Edward II. (*infra*) would seem to show that the compiler was in favour of Isabella.

⁶ *Gormlaith.*—Married (*A. L. C.* and Mageoghegan) first to Manus O'Conor, tanist of Connaught ; next, to O'Kelly of Hy-Many ; thirdly, to O'Hara (of Leyny, co. Sligo).

⁷ *Died.*—According to Clyn (who employs the misleading *obiit*), on the feast of SS. Eustachius and Companions [Sept. 20] next following his deposition. That the death

Saxons.—Gormlaith,[6] daughter of Mac Diarmata, died.— [1327]
Flaithbertach Mag Uidhir, king of Fir-Manach, died.—
Mael[-Sh]echlainn Ua Flannaga[i]n, chief of Tuath-ratha,
was killed by his own kinsmen.—Edward [II.], king of
the Saxons, after his kingship was taken from him, died.[7]
—A plague of small-pox[8] [prevailed] throughout all
Ireland.—Fergal, son of Ual[gh]arg Ua Ruairc, died.—
Cuilen Ua Dimasaigh died.—Sadhbh, daughter of Mac
Aedhaga[i]n, died.

Kalends of Jan. [on 6th feria, 16th of the moon], A.D. [1328 Bis.]
1325[1][-8]. Mael-Sechlainn O'Raighillaigh, king of
Muinter-Mailmordha, was taken prisoner and injured
by the Foreigners of Meath. And he was liberated for
hostages and died in his own house of his wounds.—Brian,
son of Tomaltach Mac Donnchaidh, was killed by Brian,
son of Tadhg [Mac Donnchaidh].—Excessive thunder and
lightning in that year, so that they injured the fruit and
crops of Ireland, until[2] they were quite withered.—A
plague of general disease throughout all Ireland, which
was called a C o l d :[3] for the space of three days or four
[it continued] on each person, so that he was nigh unto
death.—Gilla-na-naingel O'Taichligh, herenagh of Daim-
inis, died.—Imar Mag Raghnaill, chief of Muinter-
Eolu[i]s, was slain.—Sir John Mac Feorais [Birmingham[4]],
Earl of Lughbaidh, the one Gaidhel the [most] spirited
and best of generosity and prowess that was in Ireland,

---

was violent became known in Ireland at the time. The Annals of
Clonmacnoise (Mageoghegan) state
"he was pressed to death by pressing a great table on his belly ..
with many other tortures."

[8] *Small-pox.*—Literally, *speckled
disease* ("pied pox, or little pox,"
Mageoghegan). "Throughout the
province of Connaught, galap

bpeac means the small-pox; but
in the south of Ireland, where
bolgac is used to denote the small-
pox, galap bpeac is used to denote
the spotted fever" (O'D. iii. 537).

[1328][1] *1325*=1328 of the *A.L.C.*

[2] *Until, etc.*—Literally, *until they
were white [and] empty.*

[3] *Cold.*—Namely, the Influenza.

[4] *Birmingham.*—Slain, according

muinnτip ꝼein aip.ᵃ Mopanᶠ do ʒallaiḃ 7 do ʒaiḃelaiḃ maiτi[ḃ]ᵍ do mapḃaḋ ꝼopʰ ap in laτaip ceτna. In' Caeċ Mac Cepḃaill, idon,ⁱ Maelpuanaiʒ,ⁱ aen paʒa τimpanaċ Epenn 7 Alban 7 in domain uile 7ᵈ ni depḃτap a leiċeid do ċeċτ piaṁ o ċup domain pipin elaḋain pin,ᵈ aⁱ mapḃaḋ ꝼein ᵈ 7 depḃpaτaip maiτ eile doᵈ ap in laτaip ceτna.ᵏ — Muipip O ʒibeala[i]n, apdmaiʒipτip Epenn a n-oliʒiḃ nua 7 a ꝼein oliʒiḃ, a Canoin 7 a Lex, ꝼellpam ꝼepaᵈ 7ᵈ eolaip,ⁱ paiᵈ n-dana 7 n-oʒmopaċτa 7 elaḋan imda aile,ᵈ Cananaċ copaḋ i Τuaim-da-ʒualann 7 i n-Oil-ꝼinn 7 i n-Aċaḋ-Conaipe 7 i Cill-alaḋ 7 i n-Eanaċ-duin 7 i Cluain-ꝼepτa; Oiꝼꝼidel 7 | bpeiτiṁ coiτċenn na haipdeppucoide, quieuiτ in [Chpiꝛτo]. — Τomap O Mellaiʒ, eꝛpuc Eanaiċ-duin, moꝛτuuꝛ eꝛτ i Cuiꝛτ inˢ Phapa. — Τaḋʒ, mac Τoippdelḃaiʒ hUi Concoḃuip, occiꝼuꝛ eꝛτ la Diapmaiτ O n-ʒaḃpa i meḃail. — Coindeᵈ moꝛ eτep ḃaiτeꝛ a ḃupc 7 ʒilliḃepτ Mac ʒoiꝛdelḃ do'n d-apa leτ 7 Maelpuanaiʒ Mac Diapmaτa 7 Τomalτaċ, a mac 7 Τomalτaċ Mac Donnċaiḃ 7 Muinnτep-Mailpuanaiʒ apċena do'n leτ eile, ꝼa Aċ-cinn-Loċa-Τeiċed. — Ḃꝛeiꝛim maḋma ap Mac Uilliam d'ap'mapḃaḋ Ḃpian, mac Τaiḋʒ, le [a] ḃpaτaip ꝼein a n-diʒail Ḃpiain, mic Τomalτaiʒ Mic Donnċaiḃ, do mapḃ in ꝼep ceτna. — Moꝛꝼluaiʒeḋ le hIapla Ulaḋ 7 le Τoippdelḃaċ O Concoḃuip, pi Connaċτ 7 le Muipceꝛτaċ O m-Ḃpiain, pi Muman, i n-aʒaiḋ Ḃpiain [U]i Ḃpiain. Maidm le Ḃpian O m-Ḃpiain, du

ᵃ an, A. ᶠ Oċuꝛ—and—prefixed, B. ᵍ ailiḃ—other—added, B. ʰ om. B. ⁱ·¹ l. m., t. h., B. ʲ do (the verbal particle), B. ᵏ Oċuꝛ depḃpaτaip maiτ aile do mapḃaḋ i n-a ꝼoċaip— and another good brother was killed along with him—added, B. (The reading is a scribal alteration of the A text.) ˡ oċuꝛ mnτleċτa—and of intelligence—added, B.

---

to Clyn, on the vigil of Pentecost and of St. Barnabas the Apostle, 1329. These criteria are accurate: Easter (XIX. A), April 23; Pentecost, June 11 (feast of St. Barnabas).

Two of his brothers, nine of his name and over 160 retainers fell on the occasion (id.).

ˢ Blind.—Of an eye. Vocatus Cam O'Kyrwyll, quia luscus erat,

was killed by his own people practising treachery upon [1328] him. Many of the foreigners and of the Gaidhil were killed in the same place likewise. The Blind[5] Mac Cerbail, namely, Maelruanaigh, the most choice timpanist[6] of Ireland and of Scotland and of the whole world—and it is not verified that an equal to him in that art ever came from the beginning of the world—was killed, and another good brother of his [was killed] on the same spot.—Maurice O'Gibillain, arch-master of Ireland in new jurisprudence and in old jurisprudence, [i.e.] in the Canon and in the Civil Law, one eminent in wisdom and knowledge, professor of poetry and Ogmic and many other arts, canon chorister in Tuaim-da-ghualann and in Oil-finn and in Achad-Conaire and in Cell-aladh and in Enach-duin and in Cluian-ferta; Official and general judge of the archbishopric, rested in Christ.—Thomas O'Mellaigh, bishop of Enach-duin, died in the court of the Pope.—Tadhg, son of Toirdelbach Ua Concobuir, was slain by Diarmait O'Gadhra in treachery.—A great meeting between Walter de Burgh and Gilbert Mac Goisdelbh of the one side and Maelruanaigh Mac Diarmata and Tomaltach, his son and Tomaltach Mac Donnchaidh and the Muinter-Mailruanaigh besides of the other side, near the Ford of the Head of Loch-Teiched.—Defeat was inflicted on Mac William, wherein was killed Brian, son of Tadhg [Mac Donnchaidh] by his own kinsman, in revenge of Brian, son of Tomaltach Mac Donnchaidh; whom the same man[7] killed.—A great hosting by the Earl of Ulster and by Toirdhelbach O'Concobuir, king of Connacht and by Muircertach O'Briain, king of Munster, against Brian Ua

---

nec habebat oculos rectos, sed oblique respiciens (Clyn, 1329).

[6] *Most choice timpanist.*—Literally, *unique choice of the timpanist.* Thus amplified by Clyn (*ib.*): Et si non fuerat artis musice cordalis primus inventor, omnium tamen predecessorum et precedentium ipsum et contemporaneorum corrector, doctor et director extitit.

[7] *Same man.*—That is, Brian, son of Tadhg.

αnnαlα ulαδh.

ιnαη'mαηβαδ Concobuη O βηιαιn, δeξαδbuη ηιξ Εηenn
αη δeιlδ 7 αη ειδnucαl, mαιlle ηe ceιεηι ηιεειδ, ετεη
mαιε 7 ηαιε.ᵈ—Άιne, ιngenᵉ Τηeηξαιl | ηUι Ραιξιllιξ,
ben Ομαλταιξ Mιc Διαημαεα, μοηευα εηε.—Donnεαδᵈ
Ξαll, mαc Δomnαιllᵐ ηUι Concobuιη, δo μαηβαδ lα
ηΆεδ, mαc Ταδξ, mιc Mαξnuηα.ᵈ

Κal. 1αn. [1.ᵃ ξ., L. xx.uιι.ᵃ], Anno Domιnι M.° ccc.° xx.°
uι.°ᵇ [-ιx.°]   Cαεαl, mαc Δomnαιll ηUι Ρυαιηc, εennαδ-
buη ηιξ Βηeιηne, mαcᶜ ηιξ ιη noημυιηe 7 ιη ξnιmαιεί δo
bι δo βηeιηneεαιδ,ᶜ δo μαηβαδ δo Ξαllαιδ ι ηell 7
δαιne αιlι.¹—Μυιηceηεαε, mαc Δomnαιll, mιc Ταδξ
ηUι Concobuιη, εαξεηnα Cαιηηηι 7 Cαlηαιξι, mαcαm nα
mαc ηιξ, μοηευυη εηε.—Δαbυξᶜ δοnn Mαc Uιllιαm,
ηιδιηe μοηconαιξ, quιeuιε ιn .[Chηιεεο].—Cαξαδ ετεη
Τοιηηδelbαε ηUα Concobuιη 7 Μυιnnειη-Mαιlηυαnαιξ.
—Cαεαl, mαc Άεδα, mιc Εοξαιn, δo δίευη αη ειξιn αηnα
ηeδαιδ 7 α Τιη-Mαιne εηe ηοηξοll δαιεeη α δυηc αη
Clαιnn-Ceαllαιξ.—Ταδξ, mαc Τοιηηδelbαιξ Μιc Μαε-
ξαmnα [μοηευυη εηε].—Άυξυηειn, αβ Leηα-ξαδαιl ηοη
Loε-Eιηnι, μοηευυη εηε ηηιδιε Κalenδαη Nουembηιη.ᶜ

Κal. 1αn. [ιι.ᵃ ξ.,ᵃ L. ιx.ᵃ], Anno Domιnι M.° ccc.° xx.°
uιι.°ᵇ [-xxx.°]   Μαξnuη, mαc Άeδα Βηeιηnιξ ηUι Concο-
buιη, δo μαηβαδ leιηιn° Cαεαl ceεnα ηιn° 7ᵈ 8ιmon Μαc-
αn-ηαιlξιδ δo μαηβαδ αnn ηοη, αη ιn lαεαιη ceεnα.—

<small>A.D. 1325. ᵈ-eαn, B.   ᵐΔιαημαεα was written after Μαc, but deleted by dots placed underneath, A.

A.D. 1326. ¹ ff., B; eιle, A.   ᵃ⁻ᵃ bl., A, B.   ᵇ 1329, B.   ᶜ⁻ᶜ om., B.

A.D. 1327. ᵃ⁻ᵃ bl., A, B.   ᵇ 1330, B.   ᶜ⁻ᶜ lα Cαεαl, mαc Άεδα, mιc Εοξαιn—*by Cathal, son of Aedh, son of Eogan*, B. This was necessary in consequence of the omission of the *Cathal* entry (the last but two) of the previous year.   ᵈ⁻ᵈ om., B.</small>

<small>ᵃ *Defeat, etc.*—Eodem anno (1329), 14 Kal. Aug., Breyn O'Breyn apud Urlef [Thurles], interfecit de exercitu Willelmi de Burgo, Comitis Ultonie, Walterum, filium Hillarii de Burgo, Konkur O'Breyn [fratrem Muircertachi], Nicholaum Mac Nemare, cum aliis nobilibus de Totmonia (Clyn).

[1329] ¹ *1326* = 1329 of the A. L. C.

² *Foreigners.*—According to the</small>

Briain [the Fair]. Defeat[3] [was inflicted upon them] by Brian O'Briain, wherein was killed Concobur O'Briain, well worthy to be king of Ireland for figure and bestowal, together with four score, both noble and base.—Aine, daughter of Ferghal Ua Raighillaigh, wife of Tomaltach Mac Diarmata, died.—Donnchadh the Foreigner, son of Domnall Ua Concobuir, was killed by Aedh, son of Tadhg, son of Maghnus [Ua Conchobair]. [1328]

Kalends of Jan. [on 1st feria, 27th of the moon], A.D. 1326[1][-9]. Cathal, son of Domnall Ua Ruairc, excellent material of a king of Breifni, the son of a king the best disposed and most accomplished that was of the Brefnians, was killed along with other persons by the Foreigners[2] in treachery.—Muircertach, son of Domnall, son of Tadhg Ua Concobuir, lord of Cairpre and Calraighi, select son of the sons of kings, died.—Dabug Mac William [de Burgh] the Brown, a knight of great substance, rested in Christ. —War [arose] between Toirdelbach Ua Concobuir and the Muinter-Mailruanaigh.—Cathal, son of Aedh, son of Eogan [Ua Conchobair], was put by force from out the Fedha and from Tir-Maine, through injunction of Walter de Burgh [imposed] on the Clann-Ceallaigh.—Tadhg, son of Toirdelbach Mac Mathgamna [died].—Augustine, abbot of Lis-gabhail upon Loch-Erne, died on the 2nd of the Kalends of November [October 31]. [1329]

Kalends of Jan. [on 2nd feria, 9th of the moon], A.D. 1327[1][-30]. Maghnus, son of Aedh Ua Conchobuir the Brefnian, was killed by that same Cathal[2] and Simon Mac-an-fhailgidh[3] was killed there likewise, on the same spot. [1330]

---

entry in the *F. M.* (A.D. 1329), he was treacherously slain [probably at a banquet] by the sons of John O'Farrell [of Annaly, co. Longford] and the English of Meath, in the house of Richard Tuite at the monastery of Fore [Westmeath].

[1330] [1] *1327* = 1330 of the *A. L. C.*
[2] *Same Cathal.* — Mentioned in the third entry of the preceding year.
[3] *Mac-an-fhailgidh.* — Anglicised Mac Anally, or Mac Nally. The

Amuṙ longpuiṙt le Toiṙṙḋelḃaċ O Concobuiṙ aṙ ḃaiṫeṙ Mac Uilliam a ḃuṙc 7 a ṙuáżaḋ aṙ ḟaḋ Muiżi. Żilliḃeṙt Mac Żoiṙḋelḃ ḋo teċt, ḟeḋan moṙ, ḋ'ṙuṙtaċt Mic Uilliam. Inntoḋ ḋu na ṙluażaiḋ ṙin, leaṫ aṙ leṫ, aṙ O Conċobuiṙ, no co ṙanżaḋuṙ aṫ Ḋiṙiṙt-Nuaḋat. ḃecan ḋo muinntiṙ [U]ḣ Conċobuiṙ ḋo maṙḃaḋ annṙin 7 O Conċobuiṙ ḋ'imteċt o'n Aṫ co ḃeoḋa, noṙmuṙ iṙna Tuaṫaiḋ 7 longṙoṙt ḋo żaḃail le Mac Uilliam i Cill-Lomat. Siṫ cunnail, caiṙḋemail ḋe ḋenum ḋ'O Chonċobuiṙ 7 ḋo Mac Ḋiaṙmata.—Mael-Seċlainn Mac Caṙmaic, ḃṙużaiḋ coitċenn, ḋ'eż.ᵈ—Mael-Iṙu ḋonn Mac Aeḋażain¹ ḋ'eż.—Sluaiżeḋ le hUal[ż]aṙc² O Ruaiṙc, ṙi Ḃreiḟne, co ṙiḋ-in-aṫa. Żoill in ḃaile ḋ'eṙ|żi ḋaiḃ, żuṙ'-maṙḃaḋ Aṙt O Ruaiṙc ann, aḋḃuṙ ṙiż Ḃreiḟne 7ᶜ moṙan aile.'—Ḃeiniḋeċtᵈ O Ḟlannaża[i]n, ṙṙioiṙ Cille-moiṙe Tiṙe-Ḃriuin, in Chṙiṙto quieuit.ᵈ— Żilla-Iṙu hUaˢ Raiżillaiż, ṙi Muinnteṙi-Mailmoṙḋa 7 na Ḃreiḟne uile ṙe moṙan ḋ'aimṙiṙ, a eż i n-a ḟenoiṙ⁴ ṙaṫmuṙ, iaṙ m-ḃṙeiṫ ḃuaḋa o ḋoman 7 o ḋeṁon.—Maiḋmᵈ moṙ le Concoḃuṙ, mac Taiḋż, mic Ḃṙiain, mic Anṙṙiaṙ, mic Ḃṙiain Luiżniż, aṙ Ḋaiṙtṙaiżiḃ, żuṙ'maṙḃaḋ moṙan ḋiḃ leiṙ.ᵈ

(Noᶠ żumaḋ aiṙ an Kallainn ṙo ḃuḋ ċoiṙ Maeileaċ-lainn hUa Raiżilliż, in ḟeṙto Natalis Ḋomini, ṙcilicet [A.Ḋ.] 1327.ᶠ)

A.D. 1327. ¹-użan, A. ²-ż, A. ³O, A. ⁴ḟean—, B. ᶜ⁻ᵃ et alii multi (the Latin equivalent of the A reading), B. ᶠ⁻ᶠt. m., t. h., A; om., B.

---

meaning of *failgidh* has not been determined.

ᶜ *Desert-Nuadhat.—Desert* [hermitage] *of* [*St.*] *Nuadu*. He is the Nuadu, anchorite, commemorated in the Martyrology of Tallaght at Oct. 3 (L.L. 563d). One of the interpolations in the *Tripartite Life* (Part II.) is a prophecy attributed to St. Patrick respecting this saint. By the usual phonetic changes, *Ath-desirt-Nuadhat* became Easternsnow (bar. of Boyle, co. Roscommon). See O'Donovan, *F. M.*, iii. 546-7.

ᵈ *Cell-Lomat.* — *Church of* [*St.*] *Lomu* (Killumod, bar. of Boyle, co. Roscommon : O'D., *ubi sup.*).

ᵉ *Mac Diarmata.*—He had joined

—A camp assault [was delivered] by Toirdhelbach [1330] O'Concobuir on Walter Mac William de Burgh and [Toirdhelbach] routed him throughout Magh[-Luirg]· Gilbert Mac Goisdelb came with a large force to aid Mac William. Those hosts turned, side by side, on O'Conchobuir, until they reached the Ford of Desert-Nuadhat.[4] A few of the force of Ua Conchobuir were killed there and O'Conchobbuir went from the Ford spiritedly, orderly into The Territories and camp was taken by Mac William in Cell-Lomat.[5] Peace, honorable [and] cordial, was made by O'Conchobuir and by Mac Diarmata.[6]— Mael-Sechlainn Mac Carmaic, a general entertainer, died. —Mael-Isu Mac Aedhagain the Brown, died.—A hosting by Ual[gh]arc O'Ruairc, king of Breifni, to Fidh-in-atha.[7] The Foreigners of the town arose against them, so that Art O'Ruairc, material of a king of Breifni and many others were killed there.—Benedict O'Flannaga[i]n, prior of Cell-mor of Tir-Briuin,[8] rested in Christ.—Gilla-Isu Ua Raighillaigh, king of Muinter-Mailmordha and of all the Breifni for a long time, died a prosperous senior, after gaining victory from world and from demon.—Great defeat [was inflicted] by Concobur, son of Tadhg, son of Brian, son of Andrew, son of Brian [Ua Conchobair] of Luighni, on the Dartraighi, so that many of them were killed by him.

(Or[1] perhaps it is on this Kalend [year] it were right (1327) for [the death of] Maeileachlainn Ua Raighillaigh [to be], on the festival of the Nativity of the Lord, namely, [A.D.] 1327.)

Walter de Burgh against O'Conor on this occasion.

[7] *Fidh-in-atha.*—*Wood of the ford* (on the stream which connects Lough Sheelin and Lough Inny: anglicised Finae. O'D. iii. 544-5.)

[8] *Tir-Briuin.* — One of the Three Territories forming a deanery of ten parishes in Elphin diocese.

(1327) [1] *Or, etc.*—The suggested correction has reference to the first entry of the textual year 1325(= 1328), *supra.*

Kal. Ian. (iii.ᵃ f., l. xx.ᵃ), Anno Domini M.° ccc.° xx.°
uiii.°ᵇ [-xxx.° 1.°] Maelruanaiġ Mac Diarmata, rí
Muiġi-Luirg, d'faġbail a riġi 7 do ġabail aibide manaċ¹
liaċ¹ i Mainirtir na buille. Tomaltaċ Mac Diarmata,
a mac, do ġabail na riġi cetna, in' reirreḋᵈ la iar m-
bealltaine.—Ferġal, mac Mail[-Sh]eċlainn Charraiġ
Mic Diarmata, do marbaḋ le Taḋg, mac Caṫail, mic
Domnaill hUi Concobuir.—Sluaġ le baiter Mac
Uilliam i Maġ-Luirg 7 in tir uile do lorcaḋ, aċt na
cealla 7 tuc comuirce doibrein.ᶜ

Kal. Ian. [iiii.ᵃ f., l. 1.ᵃ], Anno Domini M.° ccc.° xx.°
ix.°ᵇ [-xxx.° 11.°] baiter Mac Uilliam do ġabail lerin
iarla 7 a breiṫ do leir co Cairlen Innri-hEoġain 7 a eg
iran rrirun do ġorta.—Maiṫi' Alban do marbaḋ
lerin Aiḋelbaċ.°—| Maidm berna-in-mil ar Tomaltaċ
Mac n-Diarmata 7 ar Mac Uilliam, ait aᵈ r'marbaḋ
moran do muinntir Mic Uilliam annᵃ [la] mac in iarla
7 Tomaltaċ Mac Donnċaiḋ.ᶜ

Kal. Ian. [ui.ᵃ f., l. x.ii.ᵃ], Anno Domini M.° ccc.° xxx.°¹
[-iii.°] Tomaltaċ, mac Donnċaḋa Mic Diarmata,
mortuus ert.—Uilliam a burc, iarla Ulaḋ, | do

A.D. 1328. ¹·¹ manaiġ leit (sg. of the A reading), B. ᵃ⁻ᵃ bl., A, B.
ᵇ 1331, B. ᶜ⁻ᶜ om., B. ᵈ .ui. (the Latin equivalent), with eó placed above.
(A) MS.
A.D. 1329. ᵃ⁻ᵃ bl., A, B. ᵇ 1332, B. ᶜ⁻ᶜ om., B. ᵈ ı n-a—*in which*, B.
A.D. 1330. ᵃ⁻ᵃ bl., A, B. ᵇ 1333, B.

[1331] ¹ *1328* = 1331 of the A. L. C.
² *Took, etc.*—According to the Clonmacnoise Annals (Mageoghegan): "within a short while after died, after whose death his sonne," etc.
³ *A host, etc.*—In retaliation for the defection of Mac Dermot ([1330], note 6, *supra*). The *A. L. C.* add that Mac Dermot attacked de Burgh, but was defeated with heavy loss; which, however, he did not suffer to remain unavenged (apparently, by making sudden attacks on the retiring force of de Burgh).
[1332] ¹ *1329* = 1332 of the A. L. C.
² *Castle.*—Green Castle, at the western entrance to Lough Foyle, according to O'Donovan (*F. M.* iii.

Kalends of Jan. [on 3rd feria, 20th of the moon], A.D. [1331] 1328¹[-31]. Maelruanaigh Mac Diarmata, king of Magh-Luirg, abandoned his kingship and took the habit of the Grey [Cistercian] monks in the Monastery of the Buill. Tomaltach Mac Diarmata, his son, took² the same kingship the sixth day after May-Day.—Fergal, son of Mael[-Sh]echlainn Carrach Mac Dairmata, was killed by Tadhg, son of Cathal, son of Domnall Ua Conchobuir.—A host³ [was led] by Walter Mac William [de Burgh], into Magh-Luirg and the whole country was burned, except the churches and he gave protection to those.

Kalends of Jan. [on 4th feria, 1st of the moon], A.D. [1332 Bis.] 1329¹[-32]. Walter Mac William [de Burgh] was taken prisoner by the Earl [de Burgh] and carried by him to the castle² of Inis-Eogain and he died in that prison of want.—The nobles of Scotland were slain³ by the Baliol.—The defeat of Berna-in-mil [was inflicted] on Tomaltach Mac Diarmata and on Mac William, where were killed many of the people of Mac William [by]⁴ the son of the Earl and Tomaltach Mac Donnchaidh.

Kalends of Jan. [on 6th feria, 12th of the moon], A.D. [1333] 1330¹[-33]. Tomaltach, son of Donnchadh Mac Diarmata, died.—William de Burgh, Earl of Ulster, was killed² by

---

550). But the New Castle of the *A. L. C.* rather identifies it with the castle mentioned in the "Names of all the chiefe places in O'Dowghertie's Cuntry, that is called Eunsheun (Inishowen)" contained in the Munich MS. 68ᵃ, fol. 60b : " First, on the south syde of the cuntry, at the coming in [to Lough Swilly], is an old castle called Newcastle." ([Unpublished] Report on Rymer's *Foedera*, p. 171. Cf. Suppl. to Ap., *ib.* p. 51.)

³ *Slain.*—At Dupplin Moor, Pertshire, in 1332. Hence there is a prolepsis of three years in the textual date.

⁴ *By.*—Taken from the *A. L. C.*
[1333] ¹ *1330* = 1333 of the *A. L. C.*

² *Killed.*—Clyn says on July [June] 6, the Octave of Trinity Sunday (Easter—IV. C—was Ap. 4 ; Trin. Sun., May 30. Hence July is a scribal error for June. The latest Octave in question is June 27.). There is accordingly a prolepsis of three years in the textual date.

marbaḋ le Ġallaıḃ Ulaḋ ⁊ na Ġoıll ꞅeın ꞃo ṫoıcım ann, eꞇeꞃ cꞃoċaḋ ⁊ marbaḋ ⁊ ꞇaꞃꞃaınġ, ꞃo' muınnꞇıꞃ ꞃıġ Saxan.—Ġıllıbeꞃꞇ Mac Ġoıꞃꞃelḃ ꞃo marbaḋ le Caṫal Mac Ꞃıaꞃmaꞇa Ġall, aꞃ laꞃ a caıꞃleın ꞅeın.—Aeḋ, mac Ꞃomnaıll hUı Ꞃomnaıll, ꞃı Ṫıꞃe-Conaıll, aen ꞃuıne ꞃa[d] mo ġꞃaın ⁊ coꞃcuꞃ, ꞅeıċıum coıꞇċenn,[1] neoċ ꞃob' ꞅeꞃꞃ ꞅmaċꞇ ⁊ ꞃıaxaıl ꞃobı ı[2] n-aen aımꞅıꞃ ꞃıꞅ, aꞃ m-bꞃeıṫ buaḋa o ꞃoman ⁊ o ḋemʰan, aꞃ n-ġabaıl aıbıꞇı manaıċ leıṫ uıme, a eġ ı[3] n-a[3] lonġꞃoꞃꞇ ꞅeın ⁊ a aḋnucal ı ꞇempall[c] Maınıꞅꞇꞃeċ[f] Eꞃa-ꞃuaıḋ. Conċobuꞃ, mac Aeḋa ceꞇna, ꞃo ġabaıl ꞃıġı Ṫıꞃe-Conaıll aꞃ[g] eıꞅ a aṫaꞃ. Imcoꞃnam eꞇeꞃ Aꞃꞇ hUa[5] n-Ꞃomnaıll ⁊[h] Con-cobuꞃ,[h] mac a aṫuꞃ ꞅeın, ım[ı] an[ı] ꞃıġe ⁊ Aꞃꞇ ꞃo ġabaıl le Concobuꞃ ⁊ a maꞃbaḋ a ceꞇoıꞃ leıꞅ.—Ꞃonnċaḋ,[k] mac Aeḋa hUı Cellaıġ, ꞃo ġabaıl le Toıꞃꞃḋelbaċ O Conċobuıꞃ, ꞃı Connaċꞇ.—Aeḋ Mac Con[Sh]naına moꞃꞇuuꞃ eꞅꞇ.—Ꞃomnall Mac Con[Sh]nama, ꞇaıꞃeċ Muınnꞇeꞃı-Cınaıṫ, moꞃꞇuuꞃ eꞅꞇ.—M a c n a h a ı ṫ c e Maġ[ꞃh]lannċaḋa, aꞃbuꞃ ꞇaıꞃıġ Ꞃaꞃꞇꞃaıġı, ꞃo maꞃbaḋ le Connaċꞇaıḃ.

Kal. Ian. [uıı.[a] ꞅ., l. xx.ııı.[a]], Anno Ꞃomını M.° ccc.° xxx.° ı.°[b] [-ıııı.°] Sluaġaḋ le Connaċꞇaıḃ, eꞇeꞃ Ġall ⁊ Ġaıḋel, ꞅa Mumaın cum Ma[ı]c Conmaꞃa. Bꞃaıġꞃe[1] ⁊ neꞃꞇ ꞃo ġabaıl ꞃoıḃ aꞃ Mac Conmaꞃa. Ꞇempoll ꞃo loꞅcaḋ le

A.D. 1380. [1]-ċınn, B. [2] a, A. [3-3] n-a (aphaeresis of ı), A. [4] ꞇaꞃ, B. [5] O, A. [c] le—by, B. [d] ıꞅ—(who) is, A. [e] om., B. [f] Maınıꞅꞇꞃı—(in) the Monastery, B. [g] (eꞇeꞃ) Concobuꞃ ⁊—(between) Concobur and, R. [h-h] om., B. By this and the preceding variant the order of the proper names in the Imcoꞃnam item, as given in A, is inverted. [ı-ı] 'mm (aphaeresis of ı), B.

A.D. 1331. [1] bꞃaıġꞃı, (pl. of A word), B. [a-a] bl., A, B. [b] 1334, B.

[a] *Fell, etc.*—According to Clyn, the slayers and more than 300 of their associates were slain by John de Mandeville on one day within two months after the slaying of de Burgh. On the other hand, Grace asserts (1333) that John Darcy, the justiciary, proceeded to Ulster, defeated the homicides, captured some and slew others. Mageoghegan states the "king of England [by the justiciary?] caused the said Englishmen to be hanged, drawn and quartered."

[b] *Killed.*—Treacherously (*A. L. C.* and Mageoghegan).

the Foreigners of Ulidia and those Foreigners fell[3] there-   [1333]
for, either hanged, or slain, or drawn, by the people of the
king of the Saxons.—Gilbert Mac Goisdelbh was killed[4] by
Cathal Mac Diarmata the Foreigner, in the centre of his
own castle.—Aedh, son of Domnall Ua Domnaill,[5] king of
Tir-Conaill, the one person that caused most fear and
triumph, general guarantor, the one of best sway and rule
that was in the same time as he, after gaining victory
from world and from demon, after taking the habit of a
Grey [Cistercian] monk upon him, died in his own stronghold[6] and was buried in the church of the Monastery of
Ess-ruadh. Conchobur, son of the same Aedh, took the
kingship of Tir-Conaill after his father. Contention
[arose] between Art Ua Domnaill and Concobur, the son
of his [Art's] own father, respecting the kingship, and
Art was taken prisoner by Concobur and killed immediately by him.—Donnchadh, son of Aedh Ua Cellaigh,
was taken prisoner by Toirdhelbach O'Conchobuir, king
of Connacht.—Aedh Mac Con[Sh]nama died.—Domnall
Mac Con[Sh]nama, chief of Muinter-Cinaith, died.—
Son of the night Mag [Fh]lannchadha, material of
a chief of Dartraighi, was killed by the Connachtmen.

Kalends of Jan. [on 7th feria, 23rd of the moon,] A.D.   [1334]
1331[1][-4]. A hosting by the Connachtmen, both
Foreigner and Gaidhel, into Munster, against Mac Conmara. Pledge and sway were gained by them on Mac
Conmara. A church was burned by a party of the host,
wherein were two score and one hundred[2] persons, both

---

[5] *Ua Domnaill.*— Died [1281], *supra.*

[6] *His own stronghold.*—Inis-saimer (*Four Masters*). "A small island in the river Erne, close to the cata- ract of Assaroe at Ballyshannon. It is to be distinguished from the monastery of Assaroe [in which O'Donnell was buried], which is situated on the north side of the river, about one mile to the west of the town of Ballyshannon" (O'D. iii. 552).

[1334] [1] *1331* = 1334 of the A. L. C.

[2] *Two score and one hundred.*— "Some of the said armie burnt a church, wherein 180 persons [the number given in the *A. L. C.*] with two priests were alltogether burnt and turnt to asshes" (Mageogho- gan).

opeim do'n t-ṡluaẋ ippabatoup da picit 7 cet do ḋainiḃ, etep uaṛal 7 iṛel 7 diaṛ do ṛacaptaiḃ oib ṛin 7 aꞌ loṛcaḋᶜ ṛin uile.—Deicnebuṛᵈ do ṁuinntip Dhonnċaḋa piabaiẋ, mic Mail[-sh]eċlainn Caṛṛaiẋ Mic Diaṛmata, do baċuḃ ap Loċ-Teiċed.—Taḋg, mac Caṫail, mic Dom-naill, quieuit in [Chṛisto].ᵈ

|Cal. 1an. [i.ᵃ ṛ., L. 1111.,ᵃ] Anno Domini M.° ccc.° xxx. 11.°ᵇ [-u.°] Seaanᶜ O'hEaẋṛa do ẋabail le mac in Iaṛla 7 ṛoṛgla a ṁuinntipe d'aṛgain.—Cṛeċ le clainn Dom-naill ap Ẑallaiḃ, idon, ap Clainn Muiṛiṛ Shuẑaiẋ Mic Ẑeaṛailt. Cṛeċ mop le Clainn-Muiṛiṛ ap a[n] clainn cetna. Iaṛṫap Chonnaċt do ṁilliuḃ uile le Uilliam buṛc. Daine imda do maṛbaḋ 7 cṛeaċa 7 loiṛcti 7 uile diaiṛmiḃe ap mac in Iaṛla 7 ap Chlainn-Ricaiṛd a buṛc do ḋenum ḋo. Siḋ etep na buṛcaċaiḃ cetna.ᶜ

A70b[biṛ.] |Cal. 1an. [11.ᵃ ṛ., L.x.u.ᵃ], Anno Domini M.° ccc.° xxx. 111.°ᵇ [-ui.°] Tomaltaċ Mac Diaṛmada, ṛi Muiẑi-Luiṛg,
B 69d ṛeṛ ṛo bo mo | ẑṛain 7 coṛcup 7 ṛob'ᶜ ṛeṛṛ ṛiṫ 7 cocaḋ,¹ oeṛcᵈ 7 daenaċtᵈ ṛo° ḃi aᵈ n-Eṛinnᵈ i n-a aimṛip ṛein, a eẑ aᵈ n-Domnaċ na Tṛinoide,ᵈ i n-a Longṛoṛt ṛein, i Calaḋ na Caiṛṛẑeᵉ 7 a aḋnucal iꜰ Mainiṛtip na Buille,ꜰ

A.D. 1331. ᶜ⁻ᶜ alloṛcaḋ, B. ᵈ⁻ᵈ om., B.
A.D. 1332. ᵃ⁻ᵃ bl., A, B. ᵇ 1335, B. ᶜ⁻ᶜ om. (i.e. the year is blank), B.
A.D. 1333. ¹ caẑaḋ, A. ² caiṛṛiẑi (doubtless a scribal mistake for caiṛṛiẑ), A. ᵃ·ᵇ 1336, B. ᶜ vob', B. ᵈ⁻ᵈ om., B. ᵉ vo, B. ꜰ im, B. ꜰ 7 aṛaile—and the rest (of the A text, which the compiler deemed it unne-cessary to transcribe)—added, B.

[1335] ¹ *1332* = 1335 of the *A. L. C.*

² *Earl.*—Richard de Burgh, the Red Earl, who died [1326], *supra*.

³ *Domnall.*—O'Conor, mentioned in the final entry of the preceding year.

⁴ *Gerald.*—Taken from Mageo-ghegan: "The sonns of Donnell O'Connor took a prey from the sonns [descendants] of Gerald Succkagh [Merry] and killed Mac Morishe himself. This is Mac Morish of the Bryes, he is of the Geraldines" (1335).

From this it may be concluded that the founder of the family of Mac Maurice of the Bryes (or Brees: a castle in the par. of Mayo, bar. of Clanmorris, co. Mayo, O'D.

noble and base and two priests were of them and those all were burned.—Ten of the people of Donnchadh the Swarthy, son of Mael[Sh]echlainn Carrach Mac Diarmata, were drowned on Loch-Teiched.—Tadhg, son of Cathal, son of Domnall [Ua Conchobair] rested in Christ. [1334]

Kalends of Jan. [on 1st feria, 4th of the moon,] A.D. 1332[1][-5]. John O'hEaghra was taken prisoner by the son of the Earl[2] and considerable part of his people were plundered.—A foray was made by the sons of Domnall[3] on the Foreigners, namely, on the Clan of [Gerald[4]] the Merry [Mac] Maurice Fitz Gerald. A great [retaliatory] foray [was made] by the Clann-Maurice on the same sons of Domnall.—The West of Connacht was all destroyed by William de Burgh.[5] Persons numerous were killed and preys and burnings and ills innumerable were done by him on the son[6] of the Earl and on the Clann-Ricaird[7] de Burgh. Peace [was made] between the same de Burghs. [1335]

Kalends of Jan. [on 2nd feria, 15th of the moon], A.D. 1333[1][-6]. Tomaltach Mac Diarmata, king of Magh-Luirg, the man who wrought most fear and triumph and was the best for peace and war, charity and humanity that was in Ireland in his own time, died on the Sunday of the Trinity,[2] in his own stronghold, at the Strath of the Rock[3] and was buried in the Monastery of the Buill with an [1336 Bis]

---

iii. 638) was the Gerald the Merry who died in 1251 (A. L. C.).

[5] *William de Burgh.*—This should be Edmond Mac William de Burgh (A. L. C.). He was the eponymous head of Mac William Ichtar, or Lower.

[6] *Son.*—William, mentioned in the first entry of this year. He took the name of Mac William Uachtar, or Upper.

[7] *Clann-Ricaird.*—Descendants of Richard (de Burgh, the Red Earl); anglicised Clanrickard. The tribe was Mac William Upper.

[1336] [1]$1333 = 1336$ of the A. L. C.

[2] *Sunday of the Trinity.*—May 26. May 24, A. L. C. and Mageoghegan, but erroneously; Easter (VII. F) fell on March 31 in 1336.

co[d] roċraıḋ onoraċ. Quicunque legerit, oret.[d] Concobur, mac Tomaltaıġ Mıc Dıarmata, do ġabaıl ríġı ar[b] eır[b] a aṫar.—Teboıt a ḃurc mortuur ert.—Maılır[d] Mac Sıurtan d'Eretra, quieuıt ın [Chrırto].—Maıdm le hEogan hUa Maduġa[ı]n ar Claınn-Rıcaırd a ḃurc, du ıtroċaır reırrer 7 trı rıċıt, eter maıṫ 7 raıt.[d]— Domnall, mac Seaa[ı]n, mıc Domnaıll [U]ı Concobuır, mortuur ert.—Nıall,[d] mac Concobuır Mıc Taıḋġ, occirur eıt d'aen urċur roıġdı.—Trınoıt O Naa[ı]n, maıġırter coıtcenn ı n-ealaḋnaıḃ eraṁlaıḃ, ı n-Dlıġeḋ ċanonda 7 ıller, mortuur ert.—Creċ mor le macaıḃ Dıarmad[a] ġall ar Claınn-nġoırdelḃ 7 do marbaḋ Maıuġ, mac ḃaıltrın Mıc [ġh]oırdealḃ.—Creċ mor le hEmonn Mac Uıllıam ar Claınn-Caṫaıl, du ar'haırġed Conċobur O Flannaġa[ı]n 7 moran aıle do luċt ın tıre. Ocur do marbaḋ Mael-Seċlaınn, mac Aeḋa hUı Fhlannaġa[ı]n, ar toraıdeċt na creıċe 7 do ġabaḋ leoran mac Mıc-ın-Mılıḋ.—Cancobur Mac Dıarmata, rí Muıġı-Luırġ 7 Aeḋ, mac Aeḋa 7 luċt tıġe h[U]í Conċobuır 7 Clann-Donnċaıḋ 7 ġlarlaċ Crıċe-Caırrrı ım Cormac, mac Ruaıḋrı, do ḋul ar creıċ hı Tır-Fhıaċraċ, co ranġadur Mullaċ-raṫa. Ocur ba ın tıre do ċeıċeḋ rompa. Maırbedala mora 7 capaıll ımḋa do ṫabaırt doıḃ leo 7 le Connaċtaıḃ arċena.[d] Caırlen mor Mıc ġoırdelḃ do leġaḋ[3] le Toırrdelḃaċ 7 le Connaċtaıḃ arċena.

Ḳal 1an. [1111.ª r., l. xx.uı.ª], Anno Domını M.º ccc.º xxx.º 1111.º[-uıı.º]. Sıṫ[c] do ḋenum do mac ın 1arla re Ḃrıan m-ban O m-Ḃrıaın.—Sıṫ do ḋenam d'Aeḋ remur hUa Neıll (ıdon,[d] Aeḋ meıṫ[d]) re hOırġıallaıḃ 7 re

---

A.D. 1333. [3] leaġan, A. [h-h] d'eır (same in meaning as the A reading, B).

A.D. 1334 [a-a] bl., A, B. [b] 1337, A. [c-c] om., B. [d-d] itl., t.h., (A) MS.

---

[3] *The Rock.*—Of Lough Ce. See O'Donovan, *F. M.*, iii. 556.

[4] *Son of Domnall.*—Son of Eogan, B; against the *A. L. C.*

[5] *Clann-Cathail—Descendants of*

Cathal: the tribe name of the O'Flannagans (co. Roscommon).

[6] *Son of Aedh.*—Son of Feidhlimidh, son of Aedh, son of Eogan O'Conor, *A. L. C.*; son of Feidh-

honourable funeral. Whoso reads, let him pray. Concobur, son of Tomaltach Mac Diarmata, took the kingship after his father.—Theobald de Burgh died.—Meyler Mac Jordan de Exeter, rested in Christ.—Defeat [was inflicted] by Eogan Ua Madugha[i]n on the Clann-Ricaird de Burgh, wherein fell three score and six, both good and bad.—Domnall, son of John, son of Domnall[4] Ua Concobuir, died.—Niall, son of Concobur Mac Taidhg, was slain by one shot of an arrow.—Trinity O'Naa[i]n, general master in divers arts, in the Canon Law and [Civil] Law, died.—A great foray by the sons of Diarmait [Mac Diarmata] the Foreigner on the Clann-Goisdelbh and Maiug, son of Waltrim Mac [G]oisdelb, was killed.—A foray [was made] by Edmond Mac William [de Burgh] on the Clann-Cathail,[5] wherein Conchobur O'Flannaga[i]n and many more of the people of the country were plundered. And Mael-Sechlainn, son of Aedh Ua Flannaga[i]n, was killed in the pursuit of the foray and the son of Mac-in-Milidh was taken prisoner by them.—Concobur Mac Diarmada, king of Magh-Luirg and Aedh, son of Aedh[6] and the household force of Ua Conchobuir and the Clann-Donnchaidh and the recruits of Crich-Cairpri under Cormac, son of Ruaidhri [Ua Conchobair] went on a foray into Tir-Fiachrach, until they reached Mullach-ratha. And the beeves of the country fled[7] before them. Large inanimate chattels and many horses were brought by them and by the Connachtmen also with them. The great castle of Mac Goistelb[8] was levelled [on that occasion] by Toirdhelbach and by the Connachtmen likewise.

[1336]

Kalends of Jan. [on 4th feria, 26th of the moon], A.D. 1334[1][-7]. Peace was made by [William] the son of the Earl [de Burgh] with Brian O'Briain the Fair.—Peace was made by Aedh Ua Neill the Stout (that is, Aedh the

[1337]

limidh, son of Aedh O'Conor, Mageoghegan.

[7] *Fled.*—That is, were driven off hastily.

[8] *Great castle of Mac Goistelb.*—

Anglicised Castlemore - Costello (bar. of Costello, co. Mayo. O'D. iii. 558-9).

[1337] [1] *1334* = 1337 of the A.L.C.

Ḟeraiḃ-Manaċ.—Ḟarlonġporc do ḃenum le Toirrḋelḃaċ hUa Concobuir 15 Æc-liacc i n-aḋaiġ Emoind a ḃurc.—Seoan O Ḟallamann, cairec Clainni-hUadaċ, morcuur erc.ᶜ—Caḋġ Maġ Ḟlannċaiḃ, cairec Darcraiġi, do marbaḋ le Cormac, mac Ruaiḋri, mic Domnaill, maraen re roċraide aile,¹ | aᵃ n-diġail Seaain Mic Domnaill. Ocur creaċa mora do ḃenum ar Darcraiġiḃ 7 mac Muirir Meġ Ḟlannċaiḃ do marbaḋ an la cecna.ᵃ—Caḋġᵃ 7 Mail[-Sh]eċlainn, da mac Iṁair Meġ Raġnaill, do ġabail do Caċal Máġ Raġnaill Uilliam, mac Macġamna 7 in blaḋ aile do clainn Imair, idon, Concobur 7 Comalcaċ, riġaḋburr Muinncer-hEolu[i]r, do cinol d'a ċóraideċc 7 Caċal Mac Raġnaill 7 Maġnur, mac Ḟerġail, do marbaḋ doiḃ. Cairec do ḃenum do Caḋġ Maġ Raġnaill.ᶜ—Domnall ruaḋ² O Maille 7 Cormac O Maille, a mac, do marbaḋ do Clainn-Meiḃric 7 do Ġallaiḃ ailiḃ maille friú, aḋaiġ feil Scefain in bliaḋain ri.ᵃ—Comár, mac Carmaic hUi Domnaill, erpuc Ciri-Conaill, faí n-eġna 7 craḃaḋ coiccennᵃ fa biaḋ 7 fa ellaċ d'eiġriḃ 7 d'ollamnaiḃ in Beċa,ᵃ in Chrirco quieuic.

Kal. Ian. u. f., [L.ᵃ uiii.ᵃ], Anno Domini M.ᵒ ccc.ᵃ xxx. u.ᵇ[-uiii.ᵒ]. Ruaiḋri (inᵃ einiġ, mac Ḟlaiċberċaiġ, mic Ḋhuinn oiġ, aliar Carraiċᵃ) Maġ Uiḋir, ri Ḟer-Manaċ 7 Laċa-Eirne (perᵃ quacuordecim annor; aliar, per duor annorᶜ), in fer ir mo ro ċiḋlaic d'airġed 7 d'innmur, d'eċaiḃ 7 d'alṁaiḃ 7 d'inniliḃ, do ḋul d'eġ re haḋarc,

A.D. 1334. ¹oile, A. ²-ġ, A.
A.D. 1335. —ᵃ bl., A, B. ᵇ 1338, c. m., B. ᶜitl., t. h., A; om. (except in einiġ) B.

---

² *Edmond de Burgh.*—The Lower (or northern) Mac William.

³ *In revenge, etc.*—From this it can be inferred that John O'Conor had been slain by the Mac Clancys (Maic Flannchadha).

⁴ *Mathgamain, Fergal.*—Brothers The former treacherously slew the latter in 1306 (*A. L. C.*). Hence the feud between their sons.

⁵ *Bishop.*—Since [1319], *supra*. [1338] ¹*1335.*—The ferial (5) proves that the true year is 1338.

Fat) with the Oirghialla and with the Fir-Manach.—A [1337] fortress was made by Toirdhelbach Ua Concobuir at Athliacc against Edmond de Burgh.² —John O'Fallamain, chief of Clann-hUadach, died.—Tadhg Mag Flannchaidh, chief of Dartraighi, was killed, together with a multitude besides, by Cormac, son of Ruaidhri, son of Domnall [Ua Conchobair] in revenge³ of John, son of Domnall [Ua Conchobair]. And great forays were made on Dartraighi and the son of Maurice Mag Flannchaidh was killed the same day.—Tadhg and Mael[-Sh]echlainn, two sons of Imhar Mag Raghnaill were taken prisoners by Cathal Mag Raghnaill. William, son of Mathgamain⁴ [Mag Raghnaill] and the other part of the children of Imar, namely, Concobur and Tomaltach, royal heirs of Muinter-Eolu[i]s, assembled to pursue them and Cathal Mag Raghnaill and Maghnus, son of Fergall⁴ [Mag Raghnaill], were killed by them. Tadhg Mag Raghnaill was [in consequence] made a chieftain of.—Domnall O'Maille the Red and Cormac O'Maille, his son, were killed by the Clann-Mebric and by other Foreigners along with them, the night of the feast of Stephen [Dec. 26] this year.—Thomas, son of Carmac Ua Domnaill, bishop⁵ of Tir-Conaill [Raphoe], eminent in wisdom and in general benevolence in food and in cattle to the learned and the poets of the world, rested in Christ.

Kalends of Jan. on 5th feria, [7th of the moon], A.D. [1338] 1335¹[-8]. Ruaidhri (of the hospitality, son of Flaithbertach, son of Donn junior, otherwise Carrach) Mag Uidhir, king of Fir-Manach and of Loch-Eirne (for fourteen² years; otherwise, for two years), the man that most bestowed of money and of goods, of horses and of

---

² *Fourteen.*—*Recte*, eleven. Ruaidhri succeeded Flaithbertach in [1327], *supra*.

ιαρ m-buaiὅ⁴ o· éιϛριὅ 7 o ollamnaiὅ.·—Μac ιαρlα Ulaὅ do ξabail d'Emonn a burc 7 a cur illoc-Oirbren. Uilc° mora 7 cagaὅ coitcenn i Connactaiὅ trid rin.— Taὅϛ mac Ruaiὅri, mic Catail hUi Concobuir, do ξabail do Tomar Μaϛ 8ampaὅain 7 moran d'a muinntir do marbaὅ. Μaϛ 8hampaὅa[i]n do dul do ciϛ [U]i Concobuir in bliaὅain cetna 7 a tect arir i n-a [f]ritteing 7 aircir do tabort do Clainn-Muircertaiϛ air 7 do Muinntir-Eolu[i]r 7 do coimtinol na breifne, eter ϛaiὅel 7 ϛalloϛlac. Ocur Μaϛ 8ampaὅa[i]n do ξabail 7 moran d'a muinntir do marbaὅ.·—Ceὅ in cleitiϛ, mac Ruaiὅri [U]i Concobuir, do lot ar deriὅ creice 'ra bolegan 7 a eϛ ὅe.—Derbail,· ingen Catail Μic Murchaiὅ, ben Donncaὅa, mic Ceὅa oiϛ, d'eϛ.·

Kal. Ian. ui. f., [l.° x.uiii.°] Anno Domini Μ.° ccc.° xxx.° ui.°ᵇ[-ix.°] 8luaϛ¹ mor la hCeὅ remar² hUa Neill cum Tire-Conaill, dar'marbaὅ mac | Seaain hUi Neill 7 ϛarfraiϛ hUa Domnaill la muinntir hUi Docartaiϛ.— Ruaiὅri O Ceallaiϛ, ri hUa³-Maine, do marbaὅ la Catal, mac Ceὅa, mic Eoϛain, ar° n-dul a tiϛ Toirrdelbaiϛ hUi Concobuir d'a tiϛ fein. Sai Erenn ϛan imperain fein.·—Emonn Μac Uilliam a burc d'innarba[ὅ] in bliaὅain ri.ᵈ—beanᵉ mic Iarla Ulaὅ, idon, ingen Toirrdelbaiϛ hUi briain, do tabairt do Toirrdelbac hUa Concobuir, do riϛ Connact, in bliaὅain ri 7 Derbail, ingen Ceὅa [U]i Domnaill, do leϛan do.— Tomar Μaϛ 8ampaὅa[i]n, do bi illaim i[c] Clainn-

A.D. 1335. ᵈ 7 apaile—and so on—added, B. ᵉom, B.
A.D. 1336. ¹.₅₇, B. ²rea—, A. ³O, A. ᵃbl., A, B. ᵇ 1339, B.
ᶜom., B. ᵈ om., B.

---

³ *Put into.*—With a stone tied to his neck, according to the *A. L. C.* and Mageoghegan.

⁴ *Went to the house.*—See [1339], note 4, *infra*.

⁵ *Of the Quill.*—Mageoghegan, according to O'Donovan (iii. 564), says the soubriquet was applied to Aedh, because his mother could weave.

[1339] ¹ *1336.*—The ferial (6) proves that the true year is 1339.

herds and of cattle, died on the pillow after victory [of [1338] praise] from learned and from poets.—[Edmond] son of the [red] Earl of Ulster was taken prisoner by Edmond de Burgh and put into[3] Loch-Oirbsen. Great evils and general war [arose] in Connacht through that.—Tadhg, son of Ruaidhri, son of Cathal Ua Conchobuir, was taken prisoner by Thomas Mag Samhradha[i]n and many of his people were killed. Mag Shamhradha[i]n went to the house[4] of Ua Concobuir the same year and he came back again and on his return an attack was made by the Clann-Muircertaigh and by Muinter-Eolu[i]s and by the muster of the Breifni, both Foreigner and Gallowglass, on him. And Mag Shamhradha[i]n was taken prisoner and many of his people were killed.—Aedh of the Quill,[5] son of Ruaidhri Ua Conchobuir, was [mortally] injured in the rere of a foray in the Bolcgan and he died thereof.—Derbhail, daughter of Cathal Mac Murchadha, wife of Donnchadh, son of Aedh [Mag Uidhir] junior, died.

Kalends of Jan. on 6th feria, [18th of the moon], A.D. [1339] 1336[1][-9]. A great host [was led] by Aedh Ua Neill the Stout to Tir-Conaill, whereby were killed the son of John Ua Neill and Geoffrey Ua Domnaill by the people of Ua Dochartaigh.—Ruaidhri O'Ceallaigh, king of Ui-Maine, was killed by Cathal, son of Aedh, son of Eogan [Ua Conchobair], after going from the house of Toirdelbach Ua Concobuir to his own. The most eminent in Ireland without dispute [was] that man.—Edmond Mac William de Burgh was expelled[2] this year.—The wife of the son of the Earl of Ulster, namely, the daughter of Toirdelbach Ua Briain, was taken [to wife] by Toirdelbach Ua Concobuir, [that is,] by the king of Connacht, this year and Derbail, daughter of Aedh Ua Domnaill, was abandoned by him.—Thomas Mag Samradha[i]n, who

---

[2] *Expelled.*—This was the second expulsion. See the account of the first in the *A. L. C.* under 1338.

Muircertaig, do ḃul ar in bliaḋain rin, ar n-ḋiulταḋ
ḋ'ingin Donnċaḋa riabaig rir 7 a ḋa mac d'eloġ irin
bliaḋain rin ror.ᶜ—Plaiġᵈ mor do rnecτa 7 do ric in
bliaḋain rin, o cenn caiciḋiri do ġeimreḋ co tainic bloḋ
d'errac, co n-deacaiḋ moran d'ellaċ Erenn d'eg ann 7
guirτ gemair Erenn do ḃul a muguḋa in bliaḋain ceτna.ᵉ

B 70a[ḃir.] Kal. Ian. uii.ᵃ r.,ᵃ [L.ᵇ xx.ix.ᵇ], Anno Domini M.º ccc.º
xxx.º uii.º[-xl.ᶜ] Comτóġbailᵈ mor caġaiḋ eτer Maine-
ċaiḋ, iḋon, eτer Taḋg, mac Taiḋg [U]i Cheallaiġ 7
Uilliam, mac Donnċaḋa Muimniġ [U]i Cheallaiġ 7
Donnċaḋ, mac Aeḋa [U]i Chellaiġ, d'a τuc Toirrḋelbaċ
O Concobuir urlamur O-Maine, do Taḋg 7 moran d'a
cineḋ rein ror, gur'τeilgreτ Uilliam arτir imaċ. Ocur
rolenraτ uile e, gur'impo Uilliam orra 7 gur'marbaḋ
Donnċaḋ, mac Aeḋa [U]i Cellaiġ 7 gur'gabaḋ Taḋg
O Cellaiġ 7 gur'loiτeḋ 7 co n-deacaiḋ d'eg d'a loiτiḃ.ᵈ—
Mael-Seċlainn hUa¹ Gairmleaġaiḋ, τairec Cene[oi]l-
Moa[i]n, d'eg.—Toircᵈ docóḋar meic Ual[ġ]airc hUi
Ruairc, iḋon, Domnall 7 Aeḋ 7 Gilla-Criḋd 7 Ruaiḋri,
ar sreiċ cum Caṫail, mic Aeḋa Ḃreirniġ 7 do rinneaḋur

A.D. 1336. ᶠ-ḃ, B. ᵉ om., A.
A.D. 1337. ¹O, B. ᵃ⁻ᵃom., B. ᵇ⁻ᵇbl., A, B. ᶜ1340, B. ᵈ⁻ᵈom., B.

ᵃ *Was set free.*—Literally, *went out of it* (the captivity, by consent of his custodians).

ᵈ *Donnchadh.*—Namely, O'Conor.

ᵇ *Was renounced.*—From this it appears that the "going to the house of O'Conor," mentioned in the previous year, was to contract a marriage alliance, the rescission of which was the condition of Magauran's release.

The *A. L. C.* and Mageoghegan merely state that he was set at liberty.

ᵉ *Snow, etc.*—"This year was very stormy and hurtful to men and animals; for from the feast of All Saints [Nov. 1, 1338] to Easter [March 28, 1339] for the most part there was rain, snow, or frost. From the feast of St. Andrew [Nov. 30, 1338] tillage operations ceased on account of the snow and frost, which at that time abounded almost continuously.... This year [1339] oxen and cows were dying, and sheep especially were almost destroyed: so that, according to common report, scarce a seventh part of the sheep escaped the

was in custody with the Clann-Muircertaigh, was set free[3] [1339] in that year, after the daughter of Donnchadh[4] the Swarthy was renounced[5] him and his two sons escaped that year likewise.—A great plague of snow[6] and of frost [prevailed] that year from the beginning of a fortnight of winter until a part of spring came, so that much of the cattle of Ireland suffered death and the green crops of Ireland went to nought the same year.

Kalends of Jan. on 7th feria, [29th of the moon,] A.D. [1340 Bis.] 1337[1][-40]. Great levy of war [took place] between the Ui-Maine, namely, between Tadhg, son of Tadhg[2] Ua Cellaigh and William, son of Donnchadh Ua Ceallaigh the Momonian[3] and Donnchadh son of Aedh Ua Cellaigh, to whom[4] Toirdelbach O'Concobuir gave the governance of Ui-Maine, [namely] to Tadhg[5], and [between] great part of their own tribe likewise, so that they cast William from the country forth. And they all followed him, until William turned upon them and Donnchadh, son of Aedh Ua Cellaigh, was killed and Tadhg O'Cellaigh was taken[6] prisoner and wounded and underwent death of his injuries. —Mael-Sechlainn Ua Gairmleghaidh, chief of Cenel-Moen, died.—An expedition was gone upon by the sons of Ual[gh]arc Ua Ruairc, namely, Domnall and Aedh and Gilla-Crisd and Ruaidhri, on a foray against Cathal, son of Aedh [Ua Conchobair] the Brefnian and they made an

---

plague; but there was greater loss of lambs. Also in this year, in Lent, sallows produced roses in England, which were carried to different countries as a sight " (Clyn).

[1340] [1] *1337.*—The ferial (7) proves that the true year is 1340.

[2] *Tadhg.*—Slain in the battle of Athenry, co. Galway [1316], *supra.*

[3] *Donnchadh the Momonian* (reared in Munster).—King of Ui-Maine; died [1307], *supra.*

[4] *To whom—Tadhg.*—This clause should have been inserted after *son of Tadhg Ua Cellaigh.*

[5] *Gave to Tadhg.*—After the slaying of Ruaidhri in the preceding year.

[6] *Was taken, etc.*—"And at his taking was hurt grievously, of which hurt Teig died afterwards" (Mageoghegan).

cpeč aobal ʒan ımpeɼaın 7 ꝺo ṁaɼḃaꝺup Concobuɼ, mac
Ꝺonnčaḃa ɼıabaıʒ 7 moɼan aıle. Ꝺo ɼınne Catal
ꝺoɼaıḃ maıč, ꝺaɼ'ꝼaɼꞇo moɼan ꝺo'n cɼeıč 7 ꝺaɼ'maɼbaḃ
Ꝺomnall O Ruaıɼc, aen ɼaʒa mac ɼıʒ na ḃɼeıꝼne 7
moɼan ꝺ'a muınnꞇıɼ maɼaen ɼıɼ 7 ꝺaɼ'ʒabaḃ ann
Ʒılla-Cɼıꞇꝺ O Ruaıɼc 7 Mac Con[ɾh]nama. Ꞇaḋʒ, mac
Ruaıḋɼı Uı Concobuıɼ, ꝺo bı ıllaım aʒ O Ruaıɼc, ꝺo
leʒan amač ꞇɼe comꝼuaɼluʒaḃ Ʒılla-Cɼıꞇꝺ [U]ı Ruaıɼc.
—Ꞃeḃ, mac Ꝼeıḋlımıḃ Uı Concobuıɼ, ꝺo ʒabaıl ꝺo
Ꞇhoıɼɼḃelḃač O Cončobuıɼ, ꝺo ɼıʒ Connačꞇ 7 caʒaḃ
ꝺ'eıɼʒı ꞇɼıꝺ ɼın eꞇeɼ O Cončobuıɼ 7 Concobuɼ Mac n-
Ꝺıaɼmaꞇa, | ɼí Muıʒı-Luıɼʒ 7 ʒuɼ'mılleḃ moɼan eꞇoɼɼa.
—Sıuɼꞇan ɼuaḃ Mac Ʒoıɼꝺelb ꝺo maɼbaḃ ꝺo Caꞇal
Mac Ꝺıaɼmaꞇa Ʒall.—Ꞇaḃʒ Mac Ꝺonnčaıḃ ꝺo ʒabaıl
ꝺo Concobuɼ Mac Ꝺıaɼmaꞇa ın blıaḋaın ɼın.[d]—Caꞇal
Mac Ꝺıaɼmaꞇa Ʒall, aen ɼaʒu[2] mac ɼıʒ Connačꞇ aɼ[d]
ʒoıl 7 aɼ ʒaıɼceḃ, aɼ ꞇɼeıɼı 7 aɼ aʒmuıɼe 7 aɼ ınnɼaıʒıḃ,
aɼ coɼnum Ꞃıɼꞇıʒ 7 Sleıbe-Luʒa ꝺo aɼ ꞇaɼaḃ a laṁa
laıꝺıɼe,[d] ꝺo maɼbaḃ ꝺo Ꝺhonnčaḃ ɼıabač, mac Maıl
[-ɾh]ečlaınn Chaɼɼaıʒ, ꞇɼe ꝼell ıʒ Lıɼ-ꝼelbaıʒ ı Cloınꝺ-
Cončobuıɼ.—Maʒnuɼ,[d] mac Caꞇaıl, mıc Ꞃnnɼıaɼ, ꝺo
maɼbaḃ ꝺo Caꞇal, mac Ꞃeḋa ḃɼeıꝼnıʒ.[d]—Ḃɼıan oʒ Maʒ
Samɼaḃa[ı]n ꝺo maɼbaḃ ꝺo Ꞇhellač-Ꝺunčaḃa.—Eoʒan[d]
hUa heıʒın, ɼı O-Ꝼıačɼač-Ꞃıḋne, ꝺo maɼbaḃ ꝺ'a
bɼaıꞇɼıḃ ꝼeın.—Eoʒan, mac Seɼɼaıʒ Meʒ Raʒnaıll 7
Ꞃeḃ O Maılmıaḋaıʒ ꝺo maɼbaḃ a čeıle.—Ꞃḃaṁ Maʒ
Ꞇheıčeḃa[ı]n ꝺ'eʒ.—Ꝑılıb O Ꝺuıḃʒenna[ı]n, ɼaı ʒan
ımɼeɼaın, ꝺ'eʒ.—Inıuʒ, ınʒen Mıc Ʒoıɼꝺelb, ben Eoʒaın

A.D. 1337. [2]-a, B.

---

[7] *Donnchadh.*—Grandson of Murtough O'Conor the Momonian, *A. L. C.* They add that this was the first rupture between the O'Rourkes and the descendants of Murtough the Momonian.

[8] *In custody.*—See the third entry of [1338], *supra.*

[9] *Aedh, etc.*—This entry is given with more detail in the *A. L. C.* and *F. M.* (Mageoghegan's version is quoted in the latter, iii. 569).

[10] *Son of Andrew.*—Son of Domnall, *A. L. C.* (apparently with more accuracy).

indisputably enormous foray and killed Concobur, son of [1340]
Donnchadh[7] the Swarthy and many others. Cathal made
good pursuit, whereby much of the prey was wrested and
Domnall O'Ruairc, the choicest of the sons of the kings of
the Breifni and many of his people along with him were
killed and Gilla-Crisd O'Ruairc and Mac Con[Sh]nama
were captured. Tadhg, son of Ruaidhri Ua Concobuir,
who was in custody[8] with O'Ruairc, was left out for the
co-liberation of Gilla-Crisd Ua Ruairc.—Aedh,[9] son of
Feidhlimidh Ua Concobuir, was taken prisoner by Toirdhelbach O'Conchobuir, [namely] by the king of Connacht.
And war arose through that between O'Conchobuir and
Concobur Mac Diarmata, king of Magh-Luirg and much
was destroyed between them.—Jordan Mac Goisdelb the
Red was killed by Cathal Mac Diarmata the Foreigner.—
Tadhg Mac Donnchaidh was taken prisoner by Concobur
Mac Diarmata that year.—Cathal Mac Diarmata the
Foreigner, the choicest of the sons of the kings of Con-
nacht for spirit and for prowess, for excellence and for
felicity and for attack, for defending Airtech and Sliabh-
Lugha by virtue of his strong hand, was killed by Donn-
chadh the Swarthy, son of Mail[-Sh]echlainn Carrach
[Mac Diarmata], through treachery, at Lis-selbaig in
Clann-Conchobuir.—Maghnus, son of Cathal, son of
Andrew[10] [Ua Conchobair], was killed by Cathal, son of
Aedh Ua Conchobair the Brefnian.—Brian Mag Samrad-
ha[i]n junior was killed by the Tellach-Dunchadha.—Eogan
Ua hEighin, king of Ui-Fiachrach-Aidhne, was killed by
his own kinsmen.—Eogan, son of Geoffrey Mag Raghnaill
and Aedh O'Mailmiadhaigh killed each other.—Adam
Mag Teichedha[i]n died.—Philip O'Duibhgenna[i]n, a
sage[11] without question, died.—Iniug, daughter of Mac

---

[11] *Sage.*—O'Duigenan, according to the *A. L. C.*, was ollam (his- torian) of Conmaicni (i. e. the O'Rourkes, co. Leitrim).

Mic Fingin, d'eg.—Uilliam, mac Gillibert Mic goirdelb, do marbad ar gneir 'ra breirne do Cellac-Eacac. —Ruaidri, mac Magnura [U]i hEagra, d'eg.—Mata, mac Annaig hUi Raigillaig, do marbad d'Annriar, mac briain hUi Raigillaig 7 creca mora do denum 'rin bolgan do'n toirc rin.[d]

Kal. Ian. ii. f., l. [x.ª], Anno Domini M.° ccc.° xxx. uiii.°[-xl.° i.°] Maidm mor do tabairt do Mac Uilliam burc ar Clainn-Muirir, du inar'marbad Comar Mac Muirir, Muirir, mac Seonag ruaid 7 deicnebur 7 tri ficit ar aen riu.—Domnall' Mag Dhorcaid, tairec Cene-[oi]l-Luaca[i]n, d'eg.—Donncad, mac M i c n a h a i d c e Meg [Fh]lanncada, do marbad d'Aed, mac Caidg Meg [Fh]lanncada.—O Gairmleagaid d'eg.—brian O Flaind, tairec Sil-Mailruanaig, d'eg.—Catal Mac Ceitearnaig do marbad d'ergur.[c]—Cairlen Rora-Comain do gabail do Thoirrdelbac hUa[1] Concobuir. Ocur Aed, mac Feidlimid, do bi illiam 'ra cairlen, do treig d'O Choncobuirie.—Seaan Mag Matgamna do cur a hA[i]rgiallaib. —Cu-Chonnact[c] O Cuind, tairec Muinntir-Gillga[i]n, mortuur ert.[c]

(Muirceartac[d] Mac-in-gabann, abb Clocair, mortuur ert Kalendir Februarii.[d])

A 71b Kal. Ian. iii. f., l. [xx.i.ª], Anno Domini M.° ccc.° xxx.° ix.°[-xl.° ii.°] In Gilla dub Mag Uidir do batud ar Loc-Eirne ar dered creice.—Sagad[b] mor d'eirgi eter Thoirrdelbac O Concobuir, ri Connact 7 Concobur Mac

A.D. 1338. [J] O, B. ª.xx.° ii°, A, B. This epact does not occur in the Decemnovennal Cycle. [b] 1341, B. [c-c] om., B. [d-d] n. t. h., A, om., B.
A.D. 1339. ª.xx.° iiii.°! A, B. [b] 1342, B. [c-c] om., B.

---

[12] *Were made.* — By Andrew O'Reilly (*A. L. C.*)

[1341] [1] *1338.*—The ferial (2) proves that the true year is 1341.

[2] *J. knock.*—Mac Maurice.

[3] *Three score and ten.* — Seven score, *A. L. C.* The *Four Masters* adopt the textual number.

[4] *O'Gairmleghaidh.* — Chief of Cenel-Moen (the tribal name of the O'Gormleys), *A. L. C.*

Goisdelb, wife of Eogan Mac Fingin, died.—William, son [1340] of Gilbert Mac Goisdelb, was killed on a night-foray in the Breifni by the Tellach-Eachach.—Ruaidhri, son of Maghnus Ua hEaghra, died.—Matthew, son of Annagh Ua Raighillaigh, was killed by Andrew, son of Brian Ua Raighillaigh and great forays were made[12] in the Bolegan during that expedition.

Kalends of Jan. on 2nd feria, [10th of the moon,] A.D. [1341] 1338¹[-41]. Great defeat was inflicted by Mac William de Burgh on the Clann-Maurice, wherein were killed Thomas Mac Maurice, son of Johnock² the Red and three score and ten³ along with them.—Domnall Mag Dorchaidh, chief of Cenel-Luacain, died.—Donnchadh, son of Son of the Night Mag [F]lannchadha, was killed by Aedh, son of Tadhg Mag [F]lannchadha.—O'Gairmleghaidh⁴ died.—Brian O'Flainn, chief of Sil-Mailruanaigh, died.—Cathal Mac Ceithernaigh was killed by a fall.—The castle of Ros-Comain was taken by Toirdhelbach Ua Conchobuir. And Aedh, son of Feidhlimidh [Ua Conchobair], that was in custody⁵ in the castle, betrayed it to O'Concobuir.—John Mag Mathgamna was put out of Airghialla.—Cu-Connacht O'Cuinn, chief of Muinter-Gillga[i]n, died.

(Muircertach¹ Mac-in-ghabann,² abbot of Clochar, died (1338) on the Kalends [1st] of February.)

Kalends of Jan. on 3rd feria, [21st] of the moon, A.D. [1342] 1339¹[-42]. The black Gillie Mag Uidhir was drowned on Loch-Eirne in the rere of a foray party.— Great war arose between Toirdelbach O'Conchobuir, king

---

⁵ *In custody.* — See the fourth entry of the preceding year.

(1338) ¹*Muircertach, etc.*—Given in the *Four Masters* under 1341.

² *Mac-in-ghabann.*—Son of the Smith; "generally anglicised Mac Gowan in the north of Ireland, but in Meath and Leinster it is often translated Smith" (O'D. iii, 571).

[1342] ¹ *1339.*—The ferial (3)

468 αннαlα ulαɒh.

Ɒιαρmαtα, ρι Mυιξε-Lυιρξ. emonɒ α bυρc ɒ'eιρξι le Mαc Ɒιαρmαtα 7 Œeb, mαc ϝειblιmče 7 Ɒonnčαb O bιρn. Ocυϝ ιn τ-O bιρn hιϝeιn ɒo čυρ [U]ι Concobυιρ ι τempoll Oιl-ϝιnɒ αρ n-ɒυl ɒó ɒo ξαbαιl ξιll cρειče ɒo ρυιnneɒυρ Mυιnnτερ-bιρn αρ hoιbeρτ α bυρc 7 ní ɒ'α ξαlloξlαčαιb ɒo mαρbαb ϝα'n Conϝταblα, ιɒon, ϝα Mαc Rυαιbρι. Ρυbυρ móρ 7 olc αɒbαl 7 cαξαb coιτčenn ɒ'eιρξι τριɒ ϝιn ι Connαčταιb υιle 7 Clαnn-Mυιρcερταιξ ɒ'eιρξι le O Concobυιρ αρ τυρ α n-αξαιb Mιc Ɒιαρmαtα 7 ιmρob ɒoιb αριϝ le Mαc Uιllιαm 7 le Mαc Ɒιαρmαtα. Ϝeαll ɒo benυm αρ Clαιnn-Uιllιαm bυρc τρe υραιl [U]ι Concobυιρ, ɒαρ'mαρbαb Τomαϝ α bυρc ι ϝell ξραnnα 'n-α n-oιρečτυρ ϝeιn, le Clαιnn-Mυιριϝ 7 8εoιnιn α bυρc ɒo mαρbαb αρ ιn lατάιρ (noᵈ, αρ ιn αιϝτιᵈ) ceτnα ɒo Clαιnn-Rιcαιρɒ. Cαčαl, mαc ξιllα-Cριϝτ, Mαc Ɒιαρmαtα ɒo mαρbαb ɒ'ϝερξαl hUα Ταιbξ αρ ιn cαξαb ceτnα. Ϝερξαl, mαc ξιllα-Cριϝτ ϝιnɒ Mιc Coρmαιc, ɒo mαρbαb αρ ιn cαξαb ceτnα.—bρειριm bρoξ[b]α ɒo čαbαιρτ ɒo Concobυρ Mαc Ɒιαρmαtα 7 ɒ'α mαcαιb ριξ αρ O Concobυιρ ϝα bhel-αčα-ϝlιϝen, ɒαρ'lιnξeb ιn τ-αč co τoξbα ταιριb 7 ɒ'αρ'mαρbαb αnn Ɒιαρmαιτ, mαc bριαιn [U]í Ϝhερξαιl, ιn τ-αen mαc ταιριč nα αeρα ɒob'-ϝερρ ɒo bι 'n-α αιmριρ ɒo Conmαιcnιb 7 mαc hoιbeρτ α bυρc, mιbαč ξαn eρbαb 7 Concobυρ, mαc Ɒonnčαbα ɒυιb [U]ι eιlιbe.ᶜ—8eααn Mαξ Mατξαmnα, ϝαί n-eινιξ 7

A.D. 1339. ᵈ⁻ᵈ itl., t. h., (A) MS.

---

proves that the true year is 1342.

² *O'Birn.*—Lord of Tir-Briuin, the O'Beirnes' country, in co. Roscommon.

³ *To take.*—By force: "to distrain for a prey that O'Byrne tooke before from Hobert Burke," Mageoghegan, 1342.

⁴ *Mac Ruaidhri.* — Mac Rory "was leader of a Scottish band of gallowglasses from the western islands of Scotland, who were at this period in the pay of the king of Connaught" (O'D. iii. 573).

⁵ *Assembly.*—*Oirechtus* in the original: anglicised *Iraghte*. "Item, he shall not assemble the queen's

of Connacht and Concobur Mac Diarmata, king of Magh- [1342] Luirg. Edmond de Burgh and Aedh, son of Feidhlimidh [Ua Conchobair] and Donnchadh O'Birn[2] rose out with Mac Diarmata. And that O'Birn forced Ua Conchobuir into the church of Oil-finn, on his having gone to take[3] a pledge for a foray committed by the Muinter-Birn on Hubert de Burgh and portion of his gallowglasses were killed under the Constable, namely, under Mac Ruaidhri.[4] Great loss and evil excessive and general war arose through that in all Connacht. And the Clann-Muircertaigh rose out with O'Concobuir in the beginning against Mac Diarmata and they turned again with Mac William and with Mac Diarmata. Treachery was practised on the Clann-William de Burgh, through instigation of O'Conchobuir, whereby Thomas de Burgh was killed in ugly treachery in their own assembly[5] by the Clann-Maurice and Jenkin de Burgh was killed in the same place (or, in the [same] transaction) by the Clann-Ricaird. Cathal, son of Gilla-Crist, Mac Diarmata, was killed by Fergal Ua Taidhg in the same war. Ferghal, son of Gilla-Crist Mac Cormaic the Fair, was killed in the same war.—A crushing defeat was inflicted by Conchobur Mac Diarmata and by his sons of kings on O'Concobuir near Bel-atha-slissen, whereby the Ford was crossed in a masterly manner[6] past them and Diarmait, son of Brian Ua Ferghail, the best son of a chief of the [same] age that was in his time of the Conmaicni and the son of Hubert de Burgh, [an] honourable [man] without defect and Concobur, son of Donnchadh Ua hEilidhe the Black, were killed there.—John Mag Mathgamna,[7] eminent for generosity and prowess

---

people upon hills, or use any Iraghtes, or parlees, upon hills," Privy Council Book, 25 Eliz., quoted in Hardiman: *Irish Minstrelsy*, ii. 159 (O'D. iii. 574).

[6] *In a masterly manner.*—Literally, *choicely.*

[7] *Mag Mathgamna.* — Namely, Mac Mahon, king of Oriel.

n-exnuma, a* marbaδ ap verεδ cρειčε¹ co n-a ʒalloʒla-
čaιδ vo lučt τιξε¹ Ccεδa, mιc Rooιlδ 7 vo Claιnn-
Ceallaιξ ι° τoραιδεčτ.° Ocup ιr common vo maρbaδ 7
vo baτaδ ιατ.—Diaρmaιτ' puaδ, mac Coρmaιc όιʒ Mιc
Diaρmaτa, v'εξ ι n-aιbιτ manaιč leιč ι Maιnιrτιρ na
buιlle, ʒan aen ʒuτ a n-vιaιδ a anma ra eιneč, no ra
cρabaδ.°—Concobuρ puaδ Maʒ Eočaʒa[ι]n vo maρbaδ
vo ʒallaιδ.—Coρmac,° mac Ruaιδρι, mιc Domnaιll [U]ι
Končobuιρ, vo ʒabaιl le Končobuρ, mac Taιδʒ 7 le
Ruaιδρι, mac Caτaιl [U]ι Končobuιρ 7 Concobuρ vo
ʒabaιl le Bριan, mac Ruaιδρι 7 a τabaιρτ ιllaιm Concobuιρ Mιc Diaρmaτa 7 a cup vo ρen v'a coιmev ι
Caρρaιʒ Lača-Cé.—Domnall hUa Dočaρτaιξ, aρvτaιρεč
Aρva-Mιδaιρ 7 noč° n-εδ amaιn, uaιρ ιr bec nač | ρaιδι
τιξερnuρ Innρι-hEoʒaιn 7 τιξερnuρ' Tριča-cετ Thιρι-
hEnna 7° ρo bo τερc a n-Eριnn τaιρεč 'ʒ aρ' lιa vaιne 7
ba mό maρcrluaʒ 7 ba rερρ ʒoιl 7 ʒaιρceδ, eιneč 7
τιδnucal ιnnáρ.° Ocup' a vul v'εξ aρ laρ a τιξε ρeιn' 7
Seaan hUa² Dočaρτaιξ vo ʒabaιl a ιnaιδ.—Sιl-Muιρε-
δaιξ,° ετερ veoιn 7 aιnveoιn, vo διlrιuξuδ ριξ Connacτ,
ιvon, Toιρρvelbač, mac Ccεδa, ma[ι]c Eoʒaιn [U]ι Concobuιρ. Ocup ιr ιατ ιr oιρεʒδa vo eιριʒ vo: Emonv
Mac Uιllιam a buρc 7 Concobuρ Mac Diaρmaτa, ρι
Muιʒι-Luιρʒ, co n-a bραιτριδ 7 co n-a oιρεčτ. Ocur
Ccεv, mac Ccεδa Bρειrnιʒ, mιc Caτaιl puaιδ 7 rorραιve
na Bρειrnε 7 Conmaιcnι aρ aen rú 7 Ccεδ, mac reιδ-
lιmτε, ρι Connačτ. Ocur a ιnnaρba[δ] aρτιρ amač
leρna cuιbρεnnaιδ rιn. Ocur aρ ι comuιρle τucρατ a
caιρve vό: vul vo τιξ Mιc Diaρmaτa 'ran aιδcι. Ocur

A.D. 1339. ¹·¹, B. ²O, A. *vo (verbal particle), B. ¹·¹ a eξ ι n-a
τιξ rειn—*he died in his own house*, B. ⁵·⁵ a n' ιnaιδ—*in his stead*, B.

---

⁸ *Equal number, etc.*—Literally,
it is equally great they were slain
and they were drowned.

⁹ *Without — name.* — Literally,
without any voice [of reproach]
after his name.

¹⁰ *Some—constraint.* — Literally,
between willingness and unwilling-
ness.

was killed with his gallowglasses in the rere of a foray-party by the household force of Aedh, son of Ralph [Mag Mathgamna] and by the Clann-Ceallaigh, in the pursuit. And an equal[8] number were slain as were drowned.—Diarmait the Red, son of Cormac Mac Diarmata junior, died in the habit of a Grey [Cistercian] monk in the Monastery of the Buill, without[9] leaving reproach to his name respecting hospitality or respecting piety.—Conchobur Mag Eocha-ga[i]n the Red was killed by Foreigners.—Cormac, son of Ruaidhri, son of Domnall Ua Conchobuir, was taken prisoner by Conchobur, son of Tadhg and by Ruaidhri, son of Cathal Ua Conchobuir and Concobur was taken prisoner by Brian, son of Ruaidhri and given into the hand of Concobur Mac Diarmata and placed by him in keeping in the Rock of Loch-Ce.—Domnall Ua Dochartaigh, arch-chief of Ard-Midhair—and it is not this alone, for there was little wanting from his having the lordship of Inis-Eogain and the lordship of the Cantred of Tir-hEnna and there was scarcely in Ireland a chief that had more people and a larger horse-host and better spirit and valour, hospitality and bestowal than he—and he died in the centre of his own house and John Ua Dochartaigh took his place.—The Sil-Muiredhaigh, some[10] willingly and some by constraint, disowned the king of Connacht, namely, Toirdelbach, son of Aedh, son of Eogan Ua Concobuir. And these are the chiefest that rose against him: Edmond Mac William de Burgh and Concobur Mac Diarmata, king of Magh-Luirg, with their kinsmen and with their sept. And Aedh, son of Aedh the Brefnian, son of Cathal [Ua Conchobair] the Red and the muster of the Breifni and the Conmaicni along with them and Aedh, son of Feidhlimidh [Ua Conchobair], king of Connacht. And he was expelled from the country by those allies. And this is the advice his friends [then] gave him: to go to the house of Mac Diarmata by night. And the Clann-Muir-

[1342]

ruapaoup Clann-Muipcepταιξ α fip pin 7 σο innleoup
pen ap pliξτιϐ·7 ap capanaiϐ 7 ap bepnaϐaiϐ-beaϐail in
Longpuipt. Ocur τainic τpempa pin 'pan aiϐci pé σοpċa,
σiap no τpiup mapcaċ. Ocur σο eipξeϐ σο ap τoċup in
Longpuipt 7 τainic uaiτiϐ ap τapaϐ a lama laiσipe 7
σο loit pé Caτal, mac Ceϐa Ɓpeipniξ. Ocur ní paiϐe a
fip pin aξ Mac Σiapmaτa no co cuala pe na comaipc 7
in mallaċaϐ 'ξa σenum ap puτ in Longpuipt. O pin σοiϐ
co lá ap namapaċ 7 ap paξail a fepa σο Mac Σiapmaτa,
σο ċuip σaine τaipipi cuiξi σ'a ċup 'pa Chappaiξ 7 σο bí
popξla peċτmuine innτi. Ocur σο τeiξσip σaine maiτ in
τipe pa peċ ξaċ lae cuiξi. Ocur σa n-σepnτai ap Mac
n-Σiapmaτa,σο ξenτai pτ pip. Ocur o naċ σepnaσ, σο
[τ]innlaic é co Caiplen Ροpa-Comain 7 popaξaiϐ annpin
é.—Simon, mac Concobuip, mic Simoin Mic Ξille-
Cppaiτ, τaipeċ σο τaipeċaiϐ Luiξne, mopτuup eπc·—
Ceϐ, mac Ceϐa Ɓpeipniξ, σο ξabail piξi Connaċτ Σia-
Luain,° iσοn, in ceτ Luan σο ξeimpeξ.°—Concobup hUa³
Σomnaill, pí Τipe-Conaill 7 poiτeċ σinξbala² σ'aipσpiξ
n-Epenn ξan amupup é ap cpuτ 7 ap ceill 7° ap ceτpaϐ,
ap uaill 7° ap eineċ 7 ap oippσepcup, ap⁵ menmnaiξi 7
ap mop τoipbepτaiξi, ap cpoϐaċτ 7 ap caτipξail, ap
uaipli 7 ap ailξine, ap σaenaċτ 7 ap σeξ cpabaϐ,⁶ a
mapbaϐ la Niall hUa² n-Σomnaill, la mac a aċap pein,
ap τabaipτ amaip⁴ Longpuipτ paip. Ocur° τeinnτi 7
τennala σο ċup ipin τeċ mόp 7 O Σomnaill | σ'eipξi
amaċ 7 a τoiτim a n-σopup a τiξi pein, ap m-bpeiτ
buaϐa o σoman 7 o σeṁan. Ocur ip σilliuċτa an eiξi,
7 an elaϐa ξan pep a himoċaip, na a halτpuim τapeir

A.D. 1339. ³⁻ξihala, B. ⁴amup (pl.), B.

A 71d

---

¹¹ *And—fortress.*—This is a prolepsis; it should follow **morrow**
of the next sentence.

¹² *Fortress.*—This, according to
the entry in the *Four Masters*, was
Murbhach (Murvagh), a place
about three miles south-west of the
town of Donegal (O'D.iii. 417, 578).

certaigh got tidings thereof and they lay in wait on the roads and on the paths and on the gaps of danger of the fortress. And he came through those in the night, owing to the darkness, [with] two or three horsemen. And an attack was made on him on the causeway of the fortress and he came [safe] from them by virtue of his strong hand and he injured Cathal, son of Aedh the Brefnian. And[11] news thereof reached not Mac Diarmata, until he heard the frays and the execration a-doing throughout the fortress. Thus was it with them till the morrow. And on Mac Diarmata receiving tale thereof, he sent trusty persons to him to put him into the Rock. And he was the greater part of a week therein. And the noble persons of the country used to go secretly every day to him. And if it had been done for Mac Diarmata, peace would have been made with him. And, as it was not made, he [Mac Diarmata] escorted him to the castle of Ros-Comain and left him there.—Simon, son of Concobur, son of Simon Mac Gille-Arraith, a chief of the chiefs of Luighni, died. —Aedh, son of Aedh [Ua Conchobair] the Brefnian, took the kingship of Connacht on Monday, namely, the first Monday of Winter.—Conchobur Ua Domnaill, king of Tir-Conaill—and fitting vessel for the arch-kingship of Ireland [was] he without dispute, for shape and for sense and for intellect, for highmindedness and for generosity and for pre-eminence, for magnanimity and for great bestowal, for courage and for battle-vigour, for nobility and for gentleness, for humanity and good piety—was killed by Niall Ua Domnaill, [namely] by the son of his own father, after assaulting his fortress.[12] And [his death happened thus:] fires and brands were put into the palace. And O'Domnaill came out and fell in the door of his own house, after gaining victory from world and from demon. And orphaned are wisdom and science without a man to

[1342]

The *A. L. C.* state it was in Finnros (*fair-wood*), which has not been

474 . . ᴀɴɴᴀʟᴀ ᴜʟᴀᴆh.

in ecca rin.ᶜ—flann óg O Domnall[i]n, ollaṁ Connacc, inʰ Chpirco quieuic.ᵇ—Domnall O Coinoliр, pencaiò рuaбamail 7ᶜ caibleoiр glan[p]oclaċ na gaiδilgi, бо маpбaб la h[U]iб-Diapmaca, gaipiᶜ pe Caipc.ᶜ—бpugaiδ coiccenn, ciallᵃ conaix,ᶜ бo bi ap loc-Eiрne, gan биulcaδ бо ċpuag, no бо cpen, iбon Маċa Мас Магнура, б'eg in bliaδain rin¹ (14ᶜᵈ Kalenбар Sepcimbрирᶜᵈ).—Tomap° Mac gilli-Coiрgli, рai n-egna, in Chpirco quieuic.—Caδg Mac Donncaiб, рi Cipe-hOilella, б'innарba[δ] le Concobup Мас n-Diapмaca· б'a cigерna 7 б'a bpacaip pein 7 feрgal, mac Tomalcaig Мic Diapмaca, бо gabail Cipe-hOilella ар a eiр.ᶜ

B 70b Kal. Ian. 1111.f., L. 11ᵃ., Anno Domini M.° ccc.° xL.ᵇ[-xL.° 111.ᶜ] Slaine, ingen [U]i Бриаin, ben Coippбelbaig [U]i Concobup 7 бepbрup a маċар pein рор, моpcua eрc.—Dерbail, ingen [U]i Domnaill, in aen bean poб' реpр cainic б'a cineб pein piam, бо ċeċc¹ ap cuaipc cum Concobup Mic Diapмaca co hInip-Doigpi 7 galap a heжa б'a gabail 7 a haδnucal² i³ Mainircip na buille.—Dubċablaċ,ᶜ ingen Concobup Mic Diapмaca, ben [U]i биpn, рai mna gan impepain, моpcua eрc.ᶜ—Tómap Маg Sampaбa[i]n, aen раxu caipeċ Epenn, моpcuup eрc.—Muipcepcaċ O Bpiain, рi Tuaб-Muman,⁴ б'eg 7 Diapмaic hUa⁵ Bpiain бо рixaб i⁶ n-a inaб 7ᶜ a inбарba[δ] рen Le Bрian O m-Bpiain 7 maiċi Tuaб-Muman бо cpeiбium бо.ᶜ—Uilliug, mac Ricaipб, mic Uilliam Leiċ, macam gall Epenn apᶜ eineċ 7 ap egnum, моpcuup eрc.—Caċalᶜ O Мабuxa[i]n бо маpбaб le

A.D. 1339. ʰ⁻ʰ quieuic in [Chpir co], B. ¹ рi—*this*, B.
A.D. 1340. ¹ ċoċc, A. ² haбlucaб, B. ³ a, B. ⁴ Tuag—, A. ⁵ O, A.
⁶ om., A. ᵃ .u., A, B. Scribe mistook ⁊ for u. ᵇ 1343, B. ᶜ⁻ᶜom., B.

---

identified. It may be concluded that, like Murvagh, it was in Tir-Aedha (Tirhugh).

[1343]¹*1340*.—The ferial (4) and amended epact (2) prove that the true year is 1343.

²*Slaine*. — Mentioned in the fourth entry of [1339] *supra*.

support or to foster them, after that deed.—Flann O'Domnalla[i]n junior, ollam of Connacht, rested in Christ.—Domnall O'Cuindlis, excellent historian and pure-worded exponent [?] of the Gaidhilic, was killed by the Ui-Diarmata, shortly before Easter.—A general entertainer, of considerable substance, that was on Loch-Erne, without refusal to powerful or to weak, namely, Matthew Mac Maghnusa, died this year (on the 14th of the Kalends of September [Aug. 19]).—Thomas Mac Gille-Coisgli, an eminent sage, rested in Christ.—Tadhg Mac Donnchaidh, king of Tir-Oilella, was expelled by Concobur Mac Diarmata, [namely] by his own lord and by his own kinsman and Fergal, son of Tomaltach Mac Diarmata, took Tir-Oilella after him. [1342]

Kalends of Jan. on 4th feria, 2nd of the moon, A.D. 1340[1][-3]. Slaine,[2] daughter of Ua Briain, wife of Toirdelbach Ua Concobuir and sister of his own mother likewise, died.—Derbail,[3] daughter of Ua Domnaill, the best woman that ever came of her own tribe, came on a visit to Conchobur Mac Diarmata to Inis-Doighri and the illness of her death seized her and she was buried in the Monastery of the Buill.—Dubchablach, daughter of Concobur Mac Diarmata, wife of Ua Birn, a choice woman without dispute, died.—Thomas Mag Samradha[i]n,[4] unique choice of the chiefs of Ireland, died.—Muircertach O'Briain, king of Thomond, died and Diarmait Ua Briain was made king in his stead. And he was expelled by Brian O'Briain, who was acknowledged by the nobles of Thomond.—Ulick, son of Richard, son of William [de Burgh] the Grey, the best Foreign youth of Ireland for generosity and for valour, died.—Cathal[5] O'Madugha[i]n was killed by the Clann- [1343]

---

[3] *Derbail.*—Repudiated wife of O'Conor. See the reference in note 2.

[4] *Mag Samradha[i]n.*—Lord of Tellach-Echach (bar. of Tullyhaw, co. Cavan).

[5] *Cathal.* — Chief of Sil-Anmchadha (O'Madden's country, com-

Clann-Ricaiṗd 7 ro bo do maiṫiḃ Ērenn dó.—Donnċaḋ cleireċ O Mail-Ḃrenaind, canonaċ coraḃ i n-Oil-finn, a marbaḋ d'aen urċur roiġdi le muinntir hoiḃert, mic Daiḃiṫ duinn Mic Uilliam.—Caṫal Mac-in-Liaṫanaiġ, ab na Trinoide, mortuur ert.ᵃ—Maidm mor le Clainn-Fheoṗair 7 le Clainn-Ricaiṗd ar [U]ib-Maine, du inar'-marbaḋ⁷ en mac riġ deġ do Clainn-Cellaiġ, ra Concoḃur cerrḃaċ hUa⁵ Ceallaiġ.—Aenġur hUa⁵ Domnaill do riġaḋ leir hUa⁵ n-Doċartaiġ 7 le Domnall duḃ⁸ hUa⁵ m-Ḃaiġill 7 le nert Aeḋa reaṁair [U]i Neill 7 Niall hUa⁵ Domnaill d'aṫriġaḋ leó. Ġairid ar a aiṫle rin co tucrat | imerain d'a ceile 7 do marbaḋ le hAenġur 7 le Clainn-Muirċertaiġ Ainḋiler O Ḃaiġill, taireċ Tiri-hAinmireċ 7 a mac 7 Eoġan, mac Airt [U]i Domnaill 7 daine imda aili eturru, leṫ ar leṫ.—Iohanneṛᶜ Ol-laitim, erpuc Cille-alaḋ, in Ċhrirto quieuit.—Seoan Mac Eoaiġ, macam ruiḃerpuc Ērenn, idon, erpuc Con-maicne, quieuit in [Ċhrirto]ᶜ.—Concoḃur Mac Diar-mata, ri Muiġi-Luirġ, 7 Airtiġ 7 Tiri-hOilella 7 Tiri-Tuaṫail 7 na Renn 7 reċt m-baile do Clainn-Caṫail 7 in fer fir nar'ġaḃaḋ ġan urraim do buain do ġaċ aen d'a teġmaḋ fir—oirᶜ do derḃadur uġdair no haimriri ri ġur'ḃ'e rin aen raġa urriġ na hĒrenn, ar crut 7 ar ċeill, ar blaḋ 7 ar ḃuantiḋlucaḋ, ar einiċ 7 ar eġnum, ar aġ 7 ar firuairliᶜ, co⁹ nar' ḃ'inimarḃaġa neċ fir do'nᵒ fine Ġaiḋelaiġ iᵇ n-a aimrir fein⁴. Coᵃ 'n-a der-baḋ rinᵃ aduḃert in¹⁰ file an duain d'a dan fein:

A 72a

A.D. 1340. ⁷ a ṗ'm—, A. ⁸ n-d—, A. ⁹ ġu, A. ¹⁰ an, A. ᵈ om., A. ᵃ⁻ᵉ Amail—As, B.

prising part of Galway co. and part of King's).

⁶ *Cathal.*—See the fourth entry of [1309], *supra.* The omission of his election to the bishopric of El-phin is noteworthy.

⁷ *Gave battle.*—At Achadh-mona [*bog-field*], according to the *Four Masters* (Aghawoney, a townland in par. and bar. of Kilmacrenan, co. Donegal, O'D. iii. 582.)

⁸ *Clann - Muircertaigh.* — They had been expelled shortly before from Breifny and had Tirhugh granted to them by Aenghus O'Donnell (*A. L. C.*)

Ricaird and he was one of the noble[st] persons in Ireland. [1343] —Donnchadh O'Mail-Brenainn, the Cleric, canon chorister in Oil-finn, was killed by one shot of an arrow, by the people of Hubert, son of David Mac William [de Burgh] the Brown.—Cathal[d] Mac-in-Liathanaigh, abbot of the Trinity, died.—Great defeat [was inflicted] by the Clann-Feorais [Birmingham] and the Clann-Ricaird on the Ui-Maine, where were killed eleven sons of kings of the Clann-Cellaigh, under Concobur Ua Ceallaigh the Longhaired. — Aengus Ua Domnaill was made king by Ua Dochartaigh and by Domnall Ua Baighill the Black and by the power of Aedh Ua Neill the Stout and Niall Ua Domnaill was deposed by them. A short time after that, they gave battle[7] to one another and there were killed by Aengus and by the Clann-Muircertaigh[8] Aindiles O'Baighill, chief of Tir-hAinmirech and his son and Eogan, son of Art Ua Domnaill and many other persons between them, side for side.—John O'[Fh]Laitim, bishop of Cell-aladh, rested in Christ.—John Mac Eoaigh, most distinguished of the learned bishops of Ireland, that is, the bishop of Conmaicni [Ardagh], rested in Christ.—Concobur Mac Diarmata, king of Magh-Luirg and Airtech and Tir-Oilella and Tir-Tuathail and the Renna and the seven towns of Clann-Cathail and a man with whom a contest was not entered upon without his wresting superiority from every one that engaged with him—for the authors of this time certified that he was the choicest of the sub-kings of Ireland for shape and for sense, for renown and for substantial bestowal, for generosity and for prowess, for disposition and for true nobleness, so that no one was to be vaunted of beside him of the Gaidhilic stock in his own time. Hence, to certify that, the poet said this poem in his own art:

---

[9] *Stanza.*—the metre is *Debide*, for which see *Todd Lectures*, Vol. iii. p. 102 sq.

[10] *Conn.*—Of the Hundred Battles; slain A.D. 187 (*Todd Lect.*, iii. 308.)

Rann⁴—Ða n-ꝺeꞃnainn ımuꞃbaıᵹ aꞃ,
Mac Ðıaꞃmaꞇa, 'ꞃ nı ꝺeꞃnuꞃ,
Cennuꞃ Ꞇeṁꞃa ⁊ Claınnı Cuínn,
Ðo baꞃꞃ beꞃba ꝺo beꞃaınꝺ.

Ní° ꝼaıcım a n-Inıꞃ-Ꝼaıl
Ꝼeꞃ coımeꞃa a ᵹ-cleıṫ ımḃaın;
Ní ꝼuıl co ꞇeċ Cınn-ċoꞃaḃ
Neċ aꞃ naꞃ'cınn Concobuꞃ.

Imuꞃbaıᵹ nı ꝺenꞇa ꝺam
Re ꝼeꞃaıḃ Eꞃenn aꞃꞃan,—
Ᵹan ımaꞃbaıꝺ ꝼuaıꞃ an ᵹeall
Sluaıᵹ ꝼınnuꞃlaıꞃ na hEꞃenn°.—

a éᵹ ın uꞃꞃıᵹ ꞃın ı ꞇaıᵹ ṁóꞃ na Caıꞃꞃᵹı, aꞃ' m-bꞃeıṫ buaḋa o ꝺoman ⁊ o ḋeṁon, ꞃeċꞇmaın° ꞃe Samaın, Ðıa-Saṫaıꞃn ꝺo ꞅonnꞃuḋ ⁊ a aḋnacal ı Maınıꞃꞇıꞃ na buılle°. Ocuꞃ ᵈ Ꝼeꞃᵹal Mac Ðıaꞃmaꞇa, a ꝺeꞃbꞃaṫaıꞃ ꝼéın°, ꝺo ꞃıᵹaḋ 'n-a ınaḋ.

(No ʰ, ᵹumaḋ aꞃ ın Ꞣallaınn ꞃı buḋ coıꞃ Nıcol Maᵹ-ꞃaıṫʰ.)

[bıꞃ.] Ꞣal. Ian. u. ꝼ., L.ᵃ [x.ııı.ᵃ], Anno Ðomını M.° ccc.° xL.° 1.°ᵇ [-ııı.°] Eꞃpuc Luıᵹne¹ ꝺ'eᵹ. Muꞃċaḋ°, mac Maılmuaḋ [u]ı Eaxꞃa, ab na buılle ⁊ aꝺbuꞃ eꞃpuıc Luıᵹne, quıeuıꞇ ın [Chꞃıꞃꞇo].—Maṫa, mac Ᵹılla-Cꞃıꞃꞇ cleıꞃıᵹ Mıc Ðıaꞃmaꞇa, ꝺo maꞃbaḋ le Muınꞇıꞃ-nEılıḋe aꞃ ın Coıꞃꞃ-ꞅlıaḃ.—Uıllıam, mac Maꞇᵹamna Meᵹ Raᵹnaıll, ꝺo maꞃbaḋ le macaıḃ Caṫaıl Meᵹ Raᵹnaıll°.

A.D. 1340. ᶠıaꞃ—*after*, B. ᵉ om., B. ʰ⁻ʰ 71d, f. m., n. t. h., A; om., B.
A.D. 1341. ¹-ní, A. ᵃᵃ bl., A; L., with blank for epact, B. ᵇ 1344, B. ᶜᶜ om., B.

---

¹¹ *A week—Saturday.*—This concurrence is another proof that the text is three years antedated in this place. In 1343, Oct. 25 and Nov. 1 fell on Saturday (E); in 1340, on Wednesday (A).

Stanza:[9]   If I had made a vaunt of him, [1343]
Mac Diarmata and I made [it] not,
Headship of Tara and of the Clan of Conn[10]
To the chief of Berbha I should give.

I see not in Inis-Fail
A man to be compared to him;
There is not as far as the house of Cenn-choradh
One whom Concobur surpassed not.

Vaunting shall not be done by me
Before the Men of Ireland out of that,—
Without vaunting he obtained the pledge
Of the host of the fair surface of Ireland.—

the death of that sub-king [took place] in the great house of the Rock, after gaining victory from world and from demon, a week[11] before November-Day, Saturday precisely, and he was buried in the Monastery of the Buill. And Fergal Mac Diarmata, his own brother, was made king in his stead.

(Or[1] it may be on this Kalend [year] it were right [for (1340) the death of] Nicholas Magraith [to be].

Kalends of Jan. on 5th feria, [13th] of the moon, A.D. [1344Bis.] 1341[1][-4]. The bishop of Luighni[2] died.—Murchadh, son of Maelmuadh Ua Eaghra, abbot of the Buill and likely to be bishop[3] of Luighni, rested in Christ.—Matthew, son of Gilla-Crist Mac Diarmata the Cleric, was killed by the Muinter-Eilidhe on the Corr-sliabh.—William, son of Mathgamain Mag Raghnaill, was killed by the sons of Cathal Mag Raghnaill.—Aedh, son of Ralph Mag Math-

---

(1340) [1] *Or, etc.*—See the second additional entry under next year.

[1344] [1] *1341.*—The ferial (5) proves that the true year is 1344.

[2] *Luighni.*—That is, Achonry.

[3] *Likely to be bishop.*—The original expression (*material of a bishop*), in all probability, signifies that the character of the abbot would have ensured his election to the bishopric.

From this obit, Ware (*Bishops*, p. 659) erroneously infers that he was bishop.

Aeb, mac Roailb Meg Matgamna, ri Oirgiall, o'eg 7 Murċaḋ óg Mhag Matgamna do ċoxa[ḋ] ı² n-a inaḋ 7 a eg ı° cinn ṙeċtmaine. Magnup, mac Eaċaḋa, Mac Rooilḃ do xaḃail rig¹ n-Oirgiall—Apt hUa⁴ Mail-[Sh]eċlainn, ri Miḋe, do marbaḋ le Cormac m-ballaċ O Mail[-Sh]eċlainn 7 e ṙein do rixaḋ ı² n-a inaḋ.

(Urian, mac Ruaigri Mheg Uiḋir, 15 Kalendar Febpuarii quieuit.—Nicol Magrait, comarba Termuinn Daḃeog, mortuur ert Nonir Septimbrir⁴.)

A 72b
B 70c

Kal Ian. uii. ṗ., [L⁴ xx.iiii²], Anno Domini M.° ccc.° xl.° ii.°ᵇ[-u.°] Tomar°, mac Caṫail riabaig [U]i Ruairc, do marbaḋ le Clainn-Muircertaig ir t-[ṙ]ampaḋ°.— Ṫoirroelbaċ hUa¹ Concobuir, ri Connaċt, 7 aoḃur rig⁴ Erenn, neċᵈ ṙo bo mó 7 ṙoḃ' uairli 7 ṙoḃ' [ṙ]erṙ einec 7 egnum do bí i n-Erinn i n-aen aimrir rir, do ḋul do cungnum le Taḋg Mag Raxnaill, la tairec Muinnteri-hEolu[i]r, co Loċ-Oirind a n-aigaiḋ Clainni-Muircertaig. Ocut Clann-Muircertaig d'a innraigiḋ 7 bloḋ do Muinntir-Eolu[i]r leó 7 a lenmain doiḃ co Fiḋ-Doruḃa 7 aen urċup roigdi d'a marbaḋ ann 7 ní ṙer cia tuc. Ocur airmiṫ ugḋair na haimrir ri gurab' é rin gnim ir mó do rinneḋ le roigid a n-Erinn riam. Ocur bennaċt na heigri 7 na helaḋna ar a anmain in airorig rin; oir ní himda aici ṙer a himcair na a haltruma ar a eir. Et in Artumno ert oc[ċ]irur⁴.—

A.D. 1341. ²om. (by aphaeresis), A. ³a, B. ⁴O, A. ᵈ⁻ᵈ n. t. h., A; om., B.

A.D. 1342. ¹ O, A. ᵃ⁻ᵃ bl., A, B. ᵇ 1345, B. ᶜ om., B. ᵈ airorig— arch-king, B. ᵈ⁻ᵈ do marbaḋ le Clann-Muircertaig 7 le curo do Muinntir-Eolu[i]r d'en urċup roigde—was killed by the Clann-Murcertaigh and by a portion of Muinter-Eoluis with one shot of an arrow, B.

(1341) ¹ *Brian-Nicholas.*—Given in the *Four Masters* under 1344.

² *Mag Uidhir.*—King of Fermanagh; died [1338], *supra.*

[1345] ¹ *1342.*—The ferial (7) proves that the true year is 1345.

² *Killed.*—Interlined in a Latin hand in B is: *13 [15] Octobris. Vide Clinn.* The account in Clyn (1345) varies from that of the text: Item, die Sabbati, in crastino Calixti Pape, occiditur in parlia-

gamna, king of Oirghialla, died and Murchadh Mag [1344] Mathgamna junior was chosen in his stead and died at the end of a week. Maghnus, son of Echaidh, son of Ralph, took the kingship of Oirghialla.—Art Ua Mail[-Sh]echlainn, king of Meath, was killed by Cormac O'Mail[-Sh]echlainn the Freckled and himself was made king in his stead.

(Brian,[1] son of Ruaighri Mag Uidhir,[2] rested on the 15th (1341) of the Kalends of February [Jan. 18].—Nicholas[1] Magraith, incumbent of the Termon of [St.] Dabeog, died on the Nones [5th] of September.)

Kalends of Jan. on 7th feria, [24th of the moon], A.D. [1345] 1342[1][-5]. Thomas, son of Cathal Ua Ruairc the Grey, was killed by the Clann-Muircertaigh in the Summer.— Toirdhelbach Ua Concobuir, king of Connacht and one fit to be king of Ireland and one who was of the greatest and noblest and best generosity and prowess that was in Ireland at the same time as he, went to assist Tadhg Mag Raghnaill, chief of Muinter-Eolu[i]s, to Loch-Oirinn, against the Clann-Muircertaigh. And the Clann-Muircertaigh and part of Muinter-Eolu[i]s with them attacked him and he was pursued by them to Fidh-Dorudha and one shot of an arrow killed[2] him there and it is not known who discharged it. And the authors of this time narrate that this is the greatest deed that ever was done with an arrow in Ireland. And the blessing of wisdom and of science on the soul of that arch-king; for not many a man have they to support, or to foster them after him. And in Autumn was he slain.—Brian Ua Ferghail, material

---

mento [Parle ; for which see [1342], note 5, supra] a suis consanguineis Tir Halwaht [Toirdelbach] O'Konkur, rex Conactie, ex discordia orta inter eos, una cum [lege cum una] sagitta, projecta ad interitum ad comunem populum, eum in genu percussit, statim interiit, aliis illesis omnibus permanentibus.

In 1345, the morrow (Oct. 15) of the feast of St. Calixtus (Oct. 14) fell on Saturday ; in 1342, on Tues-

bnian hUa¹ ferjail, cnbuŗᵉ aŗncaıŗıξᶜ Conmaıcne 7ʹ aen ŗaξu mac caıŗeċ Eŗenn ɪ n-a aımŗıŗ ŗeın, aŗ m-bŗeıċ buaoa o oomon 7 o oeṁon [o'eξ]ᶠ. Ocuŗᶜ ŗaınıc ʒan aen ʒuċ aċmoŗaın o eıʒŗıḃ 7 o ollamnaıḃ Eŗennᶜ.

(Nualaıċˢ, ınʒen Meʒ Maċʒamna, moŗcua eŗc 6 Kalenoaŗ ɪuɪnɪˢ.—Maıξıŗceŗʰ Comaŗ Mac ʒılla-Coıŗʒle oo ċuŗ [CC.'D.] 1342ʰ.)

Kal. Ian. ɪ. ŗ., [L˙ u.˙], Cnnoᵇ 'Domını M.˙ ccc.˙ xl˙ ɪɪɪ.ᵒᵇ[-uɪ.ᵒ]

(A)
Caʒaḃ moŗ eceŗ Mac n-'Dıaŗmaca 7 Maξnuŗ Mac 'Dıaŗmaca ʒall ın blıaóaın ŗın 7 ŗell oo ḃenaṁ oo claınn baıllcŗın Mıc ʒoıŗ-oelb 'n-a cıξ ŗeın aŗ Maξ-nuŗ Mac 'Dıaŗmaca ʒall 7 a maŗbaḃ ann 7 Coŗmac caec Mac ŗınʒın oo maŗbaḃ ann.

(B)
Maξnuŗ Mac 'Dıaŗmaca ʒall oo maŗbaḃ a ŗell oo claınn baıllcŗın Mıc ʒoıŗ-celb 'n-a cıξ ŗeın 7 Coŗbmac caec Mac ŗınʒın oo ṁaŗ-baḃ ann beoŗ.

Caʒaḃᶜ moŗ o'eıŗξı eceŗ Ual[ξ]aŗc O Ruaıŗc 7 Ruaıóŗı, mac Caċaıl [U]ı Conċobuıŗ 7 cŗoıo oo ċabaıŗc oıb o'a ċeıle 7° maıom oo ċabaıŗc aŗ hUa¹ Ruaıŗcᵈ oo Ruaıóŗı, mac Caċaılᵉ 7 ʒallóʒlaċa hUɪ² Ruaıŗc uıle oo maŗbaḃᶠ, ɪoon Maʒ buıŗŗce 7 mac Neıll caım 7 a muınnceŗ uıle o' ŗoŗʒla. Ocuŗ O Ruaıŗc ŗeın oo len-muın 7 a maŗbaḃᶠ oo Maelŗuanaıʒ Mac 'Donnċaıḃ.

A.D. 1342. ᵉ⁻ᵉ ɪoon, caıŗeċ—*namely, chief*, B. ᶠᶠ *moŗcuuŗ eŗc*, B. ᵍ⁻ᵍ n. t. h., A; om., B. ʰ⁻ʰ t. m., n. t. h., A; om., B.

A.D. 1343. ¹ O, A. ² hɪ, B. ᵃ⁻ᵃ bl., A, B. ᵇ⁻ᵇ *Cnno 'Domını 1343*, in paler ink, on space originally left blank, t. h., A; t. h., B; 1346, B., ᶜ⁻ᶜ om., B. ᵈ ɪoon, aŗ Ualaŗʒ hUa Ruaıŗc—*namely, on Ualarg Ua Ruairc*, ıtl., t. h., B. ᵉ hUı Concobuıŗ—*Ua Concobuir*, ıtl., t. h., B. Both these interlineations became necessary, in consequence of the omission of the opening portion of the entry as found in A. ᶠ ann—*therein*, added, B.

day. The textual date is accordingly three years in advance.'

(1342) ¹ *Nualaith*.—This entry I have not found elsewhere.

² *Thomas*.—See the last item but one [1342], *supra*.

[1346] ¹*1343*.—The ferial (1) proves that the true year is 1346.

of an arch-chief of Conmaicni and the choicest of the sons of chiefs of Ireland in his own time, after gaining victory from world and from demon, died. And he passed without [incurring] any voice of reproach from the learned and from the poets of Ireland.

(Nualaith,[1] daughter of Mag Mathgamna, died on the 6th of the Kalends of June [May 27].—Master Thomas[2] Mac Gilla-Coisgle was buried [A.D.] 1342.)

Kalends of Jan. on 1st feria, [5th of the moon], A.D. 1343[1][-6].

(A)[2]

Great war between [the] Mac Diarmata and Maghnus Mac Diarmata the Foreigner this year and treachery was committed by the sons of Waltrin Mac Goisdelb in his own house on Maghnus Mac Diarmata the Foreigner and he [Maghnus] was killed there and Cormac Blind[-eye] Mac Fingin was killed there.

(B)[2]

Maghnus Mac Diarmata the Foreigner was killed in treachery by the sons of Waltrin Mac Goistelb in his own house and Cormac Blind [-eye] Mac Finghin was killed there likewise.

Great war arose between Ual[gh]arc O'Ruairc and Ruaidhri, son of Cathal Ua Conchobhair. And battle was given[3] by them to each other and defeat was inflicted on Ua Ruairc by Ruaidhri, son of Cathal and the gallow-glasses of Ua Ruairc were all slain, namely, Mag Buirrce and the son of Niall the Lame and all their people, [or] for the chief part. And O'Ruairc himself was pursued and slain by Maelruanaigh Mac Donnchaidh. And this

---

[2] *A, B.*—The A recension is given in the *A. L. C.* (1346); B is followed in substance by the *Four Masters.*

[3] *Was given.*—In Calry-Lough-Gill (bar. of Carbury, co. Sligo), *A, L. C.*

[4] *Cormac.*—King of Cashel; slain in the battle of Ballaghmoone, co. Kildare, 907 (-8), *supra.*

Ocur° ir é rin ꙅnim ar mo do rinneḋ o bar Cormaic, mic Cuilennain, anuar i n-Erinnᶜ.—Ceiṫri meic Caṫail, mic in³ ċaiċ⁴ Meꙅ Raꙅnaill, do ꙅabail ar Loċ-in-rꙅuir do Concobur Maꙅ Raꙅnaill 7 Tomaltaċ Maꙅ Raꙅnaill d'a m-breiṫ leir co Cairel-Corcraiꙅ 7 a marbaḋ annˢ, —rꙅelᶜ ir truaiꙅi do rinneḋ 'ran aimrir rinᶜ.— | Comarba Padraiꙅ, idon, Daibid Maꙅ Oireċtaiꙅ, mortuur erṫ.—Cu-Ulaḋ Mac Caṫṁail, ardtaireċ Cene[oi]l-Feradaiꙅ, do marbaḋ do Domnall Mac Caṫmail.—Maidm la Brian Maꙅ Mhaṫꙅamna ar Ꙅhallaiḃ, d'a rainic tri ceṫ cenn co Laṫair.—Niallᶜ O Domnaill 7 Clann Muirceartaiꙅ 7 mac Feidlimṫe 7 Maꙅnur Mac Diarmata do lenṁuin Ruaiḋri, mic Caṫail, i Culṁail 7 maidm imirceṫ do ṫabairt rair 7 ar Clainn-Donnċaiḋ 7 ár adbal do ṫabairt rorro, eter baṫaḋ 7 leṫ[r]aḋ 7 foilleċ 7 do creċaiḋ mora[iḋ] leirᶜ.

Kal. Ian. 11. f., [L.ᵃ x.ui.ˢ,] Anno Domini M.° ccc.° xl.° 1111.°ᵇ [-uii.°] Ꙅilla-na-naem hUa¹ Ferꙅail, taireċ Muinntiri-hAnꙅaili,ᶜ an ᵈ duine ir mó do rinne do

A.D. 1343. ³an, B. ⁴ċaeiċ, A. ˢ 7 araile—*and so on* (referring to the concluding statement in A), B.

A.D. 1344. ¹ O, A, ᵃᵃ bl., A, B. ᵇ 1347, B. ᶜ mortuur erṫ, added, B. ᵈᵈ om., B.

ᵃ *David.*—From the Bull of appointment (by John XXII., Avignon, July 4, 1334) we learn that, on the death (1333) of Stephen (Segrave), the Chapter unanimously chose David, canon and priest of Armagh. The elect and capitular proctors proceeded to the Curia to obtain confirmation of the postulation. After examination and approval by three deputed ad hoc, David was appointed to the See. On July 26, having received consecration in the meantime, he was empowered to proceed to his church. (Theiner, p. 263.)

The Nuncio in England, Pelegrini, having fulminated censures against the archbishop to recover 700 marks, fourteen arrears of fifty marks payable by the primate at his triennial visitation to the Apostolic See, Clement VI., on the petition of David, who pleaded inability to pay, directed (Avignon, August 3, 1344) security to be taken for the amount, the process to be discontinued and absolution imparted. (Theiner, p. 281-2.)

The words, nuper diem clausit extremum, of the Bull (July 31, 1346) appointing his successor (for

is the greatest deed that was done in Ireland from the death of Cormac,[4] son of Cuilennan, downwards.—Four sons of Cathal, son of Mag Raghnaill the Blind[-eye], were taken prisoners on Loch-in-sguir by Concobur Mag Raghnaill. And Tomaltach Mag Raghnaill took them with him to Caisel-Coscraigh and they were killed there,— the saddest tale that was done in that time.—The successor of [St.] Patrick, namely, David[5] Mag Oirechtaigh, died.—Cu-Uladh Mac Cathmail, arch-chief of Cenel-Feradhaigh, was killed by Domnall Mac Cathmail. —Defeat[6] [was inflicted] by Brian Mag Mathgamna on the Foreigners, whence came[7] three hundred heads [of slain to be counted] at[8] the place.—Niall O'Domnaill and the Clann Muircertaigh and the son of Feidhlimidh[9] and Maghnus Mac Diarmata pursued Ruaidhri, son of Cathal,[9] into Culmhail and dispersing defeat was inflicted upon him and on the Clann-Donchaidh and slaughter enormous was inflicted upon them, both by drowning and lacerating and wounding. And large preys were carried off by him.

[1346]

Kalends of Jan. on 2nd feria, [16th of the moon] A.D. 1344[1][-7]. Gilla-na naem[2] Ua Ferghail, chief of Muinter-hAnghaile, the person that did most of good deeds for

[1347]

---

whom see the seventh entry of [1360], *infra*) show that he died in the first half of 1346. The textual date is consequently three years in advance.

[6] *Defeat.*—This is probably the event mentioned by Clyn: Item, circa festum Baptiste [Jun. 24] occiduntur de hominibus [Anglis] Erglaie [Oriel] et Dundalk cccc. per Hibernicos (1346).

[7] *Came, etc.*—The idiomatic turn of phrase is intended to emphasize the obstinacy of the contest. The vanquished fell on the field, not in the flight.

[8] *At.*—Literally, *to*.

[9] *Feidhlimidh, Cathal.*—O'Conor.

[1347] [1] *1344.*—The ferial (2) proves that the true year is 1347.

[2] *Gilla-na-naem.*—Son of Jeffrey, who died [1318], *supra*. He and Cathal were grandsons of Gilla-na-naem, who died [1274], *supra*.

gnimarcaib maiti[b] do Dia 7 do duine, d'eg, ar m-breit buada o doman 7 o deman do.ᵈ Catal° mac Murcada [U]i Fergail, do ̄ᵈ gabail ᵈ a' inaiḋ'.—Muirġir MacDiarmata, aenᵈ ragaᵈ mic uprig Erenn ͫ 'n-a aimpir pein ͫ, do marbad la Seoan ruaḋ² Mac Daibit a burc.—Taḋg ʰ Mag Ragnaill tairec Muinntire-hEolu[i]p, do gabail do Clainn-Muircertaig in bliadain rin.—Uilliamᵈ Mac Daibit bimilip, do marbad do Thadg ruad, mac Diarmata gall, a m-baile-in-tobair in bliadain rin.—Fergal Mac Cormaic do marbad 7 ni fer cia do marbᵈ.—Tempall Cille-Ronain do denum la Fergal hUa ͥ n-Duibgenna[i]n in bliadain rin.ͥ—Finnguala, ingen Mic Fhingin, ben Fhergail [U]i Duibgennain,ᶜ inᵈ ben pob' ferr re [a] cerd rein do mnai duine elaḋna do bi i n-Erinn, d'eg in bliadain rinᵈ.—Tomar Mac Arta[i]n, (noʲ Mag Cartainʲ) ri O-nEatac Ulad, do crocad doᵏ Ghallaiḋ ͥ. Ocurᵈ nir' crocad o Dhia anuar gnim bud móᵈ (do ͥ rgel ͥ).—Finnguala ᵈ, ingen Mail[-Sh]eclainn [U]i Raigillaig, d'eg—In Gilla du ḃ Mac Gilla-Cua d'eg.ᵈ

[b ͥ r] Kal. Ian. iii. f., [Lª xx.uiii.,ᵃ] Anno Domini M° ccc.° xl.° u.° [-uiii..°] Catal hUa ͥ Fergail, tairec Muinntir hAnġaile, d'eg ͨ.—Cagadᵈ d'eirġi eter Fergal Mac n-Diarmata 7 Ruaidri, mac Catail, | mic Annriar 7 Longport Mic Diarmata do lorcad do mac Catail

A 72d

A.D. 1344. ²-ġ, A. ᵃ Ocur — *And* — prefixed, B. ᵇᵇ i n-a inaḋ—[*was received*] *in his stead*, B. ᵍᵍ pob fepp i n-a aimpip—*who was best in his time*, B. ʰ This entry follows the Tomar item, and is, consequently, the last of the year, in B. ͥ om., B. ʲ itl., n. t. h., A ; om., B. ᵏ le (same meaning as the A—reading), B. ͥ in bliadain ri—*this year*—added, B.

A.D. 1345. ͥ O, A. ᵃᵃ bl., A, B. ᵇ 1348, B. ᶜ mortuur ertc, B. ᵈᵈ om., B.

---

³ *Murchadh.*—Slain [1322], *supra.*
⁴ *Bimilis.*—The meaning of this word is obscure.
⁵ *MacCormaic.*—The editor of the

A. L. C. says that the meaning may be *son of Cormac* (*Mac Dermot*).
⁶ *The church, etc.*—This entry is omitted in the *A. L. C.*, which

God and for man, died, after gaining victory from world and from demon. Cathal, son of Murchadh,[3] Ua Ferghail took his place.—Maurice Mac Diarmata, unique choice of the son of a sub-king of Ireland in his own time, was killed by John Mac David de Burgh the Red.—Tadhg Mag Raghnaill, chief of Muinter-Eolu[i]s, was taken prisoner by the Clann-Muircertaigh that year.—William Mac David Bimilis[4] [de Burgh] was killed by Tadhg the Red, son of Mac Diarmata the Foreigner, in Baile-in-tobair that year. —Fergal Mac Cormaic[5] was killed and it is not known who killed him.—The church[6] of Cell-Ronain[7] was erected by Fergal Ua Duibgenna[i]n that year.—Finnguala, daughter of Mac Finghin, wife of Fergal Ua Duibgennain, the woman who was the best that was in Ireland in her own sphere as the the wife of a learned man, died that year.—Thomas Mac Arta[i]n (or, Mag Cartain), king of the Ui-nEathach of Ulidia, was hanged by the Foreigners. And there was not a hanging from [that of] God downwards that was a deed of more [pitiable] (tale).—Finnghuala, daughter of Mail[-Sh]echlaim Ua Raighillaigh, died.—The Black Gillie Mac Gilla-Cua[8] died.

[1347]

Kalends of Jan. on 3rd feria, [27th of the moon], A.D. 1345[1][-8]. Cathal Ua Fergail, chief of Muinnter-hAnghaile, died.—War arose between Fergal Mac Diarmata and Ruaidhri, son of Cathal, son of Andrew,[2] and the fortress[3] of Mac Diarmata was burned by the son of

[1348 Bis.]

---

state that the church was built by O'Duigenan (who was the hereditary herenagh) in 1339, and burned in 1340. The re-building is consequently here intended.

[7] *Cell-Ronain.*—*Church of* (St.) *Ronan.* See 1218, note 1, *supra*.

[8] *Cua.*—*Mo-Chua* (the devotional form of the name; *cf.* 1246, note 1, *supra*) in the *A. L. C.* The person in question thus apparently belonged to Mayo.

[1348] [1] *1345.*—The ferial (3) proves that the true year is 1348.

[2] *Son of Andrew.*—This should be *son of Domnall* (O'Conor), *A. L. C.* (1348). Mageoghegan (1347).

[3] *Fortress.*—Not the rock of Lough Ce, but a fortification situated on Longford Hill. (O'D. iii. 593.)

Mac Diarmata do tinol Connact 7 gluarrad doib a n-diaiġ mic Cataıl 7 nır' lamad cenn do togbaıl doib co pangadur longport mic Cataıl, ıdon, Baıle-ın-muta. Ocur do luaċloırced eter cloıċ 7 teċ 7 tucadur ı paıbe do braıġdıb ann leó, ra mac [U]ı Ruaırc 7 do cudoun reın rlan d'a tıġıbᵈ.— | Nıall hUa¹ Domnaıll do marbad la Maġnur hUa¹ n-Domnaıll—Maıl[-Sh]eċlaınn Maġ Oıreċtaıġ, taıreċ Muınntıre-Raduıb, ımper ın eınıġᵒ 7ᵈ reıċmeoır na reıle 7 dıdneoır na daennaċta, quıeuıt ın [Chrırto]. Ocur dabrır craıbı na heıġrı 7 na heladna do cumaıd ın caemtaırıġ rın, co naċ ınrı- baıl, ıdon, d'a eırᵈ.—Donnċad Maġ Bradaıġ, taıreċ Cuıle-Brıġdın, d'eġᵒ.—Ġılla-na-naemᶠ hUa Cıana[ı]n, ab Leara-ġabaıl, mortuur ert ı Prıd ıd Auġurtᵍ.

Kal. ıan. u. r., [Lˡ ıx.,ª] Anno Domını M.ᵒ ccc.ᵒ xlᵒ. uı.ᵒᵇ[-ıx.ᶜ] Eoın dub Mac Domnaıll do marbad la Maġnur, mac Eċada Meġ Mhaġamna.—Ġılla-na- naem hUa¹ hUıġınd,² ınᵒ rıle ġrıbda, ġlanroclaċ ır coıt- ċınne do bı ı cerdıb na rılıdeċta ı n-Erınn, a eġ caıcıdır re Caırc, ar m-breıċ buada o doman 7 o demonᶜ.— Maıdm do tabaırt la Aed hUa Ruaırc ar Flaıt- bertaċ hUa¹ Ruaırc 7 ar Donnċad hUa¹ n-Domnaıll 7 ar Darrraıġıb 7 Aed Maġ [Fh]lannċada, taıreċ Darrraıġe, do marbad ar aen rur 7 Ġılla-Crırt Maġ [Fh]lannċada 7 Laċlaınn, mac Aındılır [U]ı Baıġıll,

A.D. 1346. ᵉ mortuur ert, added, B. ᶠ 172 c., f. m., t. h., A ; 70 c., f. m., t. h., B.

A.D. 1346. ¹ O, A. ² =1345ᶜ. ᵃ⁻ᵇ bl, A, B. ᵇ 1342, B. ᶜ⁻ᶜ om., B.

---

⁴ *No attempt—them.*—Literally, It was not attempted to raise a head to [=against] them.

⁵ *Son of Ua Ruairc.*—Hence it may be inferred that he was made prisoner in the defeat mentioned in the second entry of [1346], *supra*.

⁶ *Niall, Maghnus.*—Respectively called *Garbh* (Rough) and *Meblach* (Guileful).

⁷ *Slain.*—A detailed account is given in the *Four Masters* (1348).

⁸ *Died.*—The obit occurs in the *F. M.* at 1345 and 1348.

Cathal. Mac Diarmata mustered Connacht and they proceeded after the son of Cathal, and no attempt[4] was made to oppose them until they reached the fortress of the son of Cathal, namely, Baile-in-muta. And it was quickly burned, both stone [structure] and [wooden] house, and they took what was there of hostages with them, including the son of Ua Ruairc,[5] and they went themselves safe to their houses.—Niall[6] Ua Domnaill was slain[7] by Maghnus[6] Ua Domnaill.—Mail[-Sh]echlainn Mag Oirechtaigh, chief of Muinter-Radhuibh, emperor of generosity and guarantor of hospitality and protector of benevolence, rested in Christ. And the heart of wisdom and learning broke of grief for the fair chieftain, so that it cannot progress after [the loss of] him.—Donnchadh Mag Bradaigh, chief of Cuil-Brighdin, died.—Gilla-na-naem Ua Ciana[i]n, abbot of Lis-gabhail, died[8] on the 2nd of the Ides [12th] of August.

Kalends of Jan. on 5th feria, [9th of the moon], A.D. 1346[1][-9]. John Mac Domnaill the Black was killed by Maghnus, son of Echaidh Mag Mathgamna.—Gilla-na-naem Ua hUiginn, a poet the readiest, most pure-worded and most general in the arts of poetry that was in Ireland, died a fortnight before Easter[2], after gaining victory from world and from demon.—Defeat was inflicted by Aedh Ua Ruairc on Flaithbertach Ua Ruairc and on Donnchadh Ua Domnaill and on the Dartraighi and Aedh Mag [Fh]lannchadha, chief of Dartraighi, was slain along with him,[3] and Gilla-Crist Mag [Fh]lannchadha and Lachlainn, son of Aindiles Ua Baighill, were slain

---

[1349] [1] *1346.*—The ferial (5) proves that the true year is 1349.
[2] *A fortnight before Easter.*—Namely, on Sunday, March 29;
Easter (I. D) falling on April 12.
[3] *Him.*—That is, Flaithbertach (anglicised Flaherty).

490

do marbaḋ ann ror 7 daine imda aili² nac͂° airmiṫer.—
Mac mic in Iarla do ṫec͂t i Connaċtaiḃ 7 creċ do ġabail
do 7 Mac Uilliam 7 Mac Feorair do breiṫ air 7
maidm arḋal do ṫabairt air 7 mac mic an Iarla do
ġabail ann 7 moran do Clainn-Ricairḋ do ġabail 7
do marbaḋ ann ror.—Caġaḋ mor d'eirġi eter Ruaiḋri,
mac Caṫail 7 Feṙġal Mac Diarmata, ġur'ṫinoil Mac
Diarmata Ġoill 7 Ġaiḋil Connaċt uile 7 Cenel-Conaill
7 Clann-Muirceartaiġ, ġur'cureḋ mac Caṫail i Clainn-
Fermuiġe. Ocus nir'ḟetsat Ġoill na Ġaiḋil ni do, ġur'-
inntoḋur uile uaḋa ġan ġiall, ġan eidere, ġur'loisc-
riun 7 ġur'mill 7 ġur'airg urmor Maiġi-Luirg d'a eiri.
—In plaiġ mor in ġalair coitcenn do bi ar fud Erenn
a Muiġ-Luirg in bliaḋain rin, co tucaḋ ar mor daine
innti. Maṫa, mac Caṫail [U]i Ruairc, d'eġ de.—Donnċaḋ riabaċ Mac Diarmata do ġabail do Cormac boḋor
Mac Diarmata 7 a breiṫ do leir a n-Airteċ 7 a
marbaḋ i dunataiṫ do Luċt Airtiġ°.—Risdeard hUa¹
Raiġilliġ, ri Breifne, d'eġ in^d bliaḋain r^d.—Ġilleberd
hUa¹ Flannaġa[i]n, tairec͂ Tuaiṫi-Raṫa, do° marbaḋ°
A 73a. do macaiḃ Briain [U]i Flannaġa[i]n.— | Muirceartaċ
Riaġanaċ Maġ Aenġusa do marbaḋ d'a braitriḃ rein
in^d bliaḋain r^d.—Donn° hUa Daimin, tairec͂ Tire-
Cennroda, mortuus est.°

Kal. Ian. ui. f., [L.ª xx.ª], Anno Domini M.° ccc.° xl.°
-uii.°ᵇ[-L.°] Feṙġal, mac Ual[ġ]airc [U]i Ruairc, do
marbaḋ do mac Caṫail cleiriġ Mic Donnċaiḋ.—Brian
Mac Diarmata, adbur riġ Muiġi-Luirg, do marbaḋ a

A.D. 1346. ² eile, A.   ᵈ⁻ᵈ om., A.   ⁻⁻72 d, f. m., t. b, A; om., B.
A.D. 1347. ⁻⁻bl., A, B.   ᵇ 1350, B.

---

⁴ *Earl.*—Richard de Burgh, who died [1326], *supra*.

⁵ *Or.*—Literally, *and*. Some were made prisoners and others slain.

⁶ *Cathal.*— Son of Domnall O'Conor.

⁷ *Plague.*—See the vivid account of Clyn (who himself fell a victim to the pestilence), A.D. 1348-9, and

there also, and many other persons that are not numbered. [1349]
—The grandson of the Earl[4] came into Connacht and a prey was seized by him, and Mac William and Mac Feorais overtook him and inflicted enormous defeat on him, and the grandson of the Earl was taken prisoner there, and many of the Clann-Ricaird were taken prisoners or[5] slain there likewise.—Great war arose between Ruaidhri, son of Cathal[6] and Fergal Mac Diarmata, whereupon Mac Diarmata assembled the Foreigners and Gaidhil of all Connacht and the Cenel-Conaill and Clann-Muircertaigh, so that the son of Cathal was forced into Clann-Fermhuighe. And the Foreigners or the Gaidhil could do nothing to him, whence they all turned away from him without pledge or hostage. And he burned and pillaged and harried the greater part of Magh-Luirg after them.—The great plague[7] of the general disease that was throughout Ireland [prevailed] in Magh-Luirg this year, so that geat destruction of people was inflicted therein. Matthew, son of Cathal Ua Ruairc, died thereof.—Donnchadh Mac Diarmata the Swarthy was taken prisoner by Cormac Diarmata the Deaf and brought with him to Airtech and killed secretly by the people of Airtech.—Richard Ua Raighillaigh, king of [East] Breifni, died this year.—Gilbert Ua Flannaga[i]n, chief of Tuath-Ratha, was killed by the sons of Brian Ua Flannaga[i]n. Muircertach Riaganach Mag Aenghusa was killed by his own kinsmen this year.—Donn Ua Daimin, chief of Tir-Cennfota, died.

Kalends of Jan. on 6th feria, [20th of the moon], A.D. [1350] 1347[1][-50]. Ferghal son of Ual[gh]arc Ua Ruairc, was killed by the son of Cathal Mac Donnchaidh the Cleric.—Brian Mac Diarmata, one fit to be king of Magh-Luirg,

---

the notes in the Ir. Arch. Soc. edition (pp. 33, 65).

[1350] [1] *1347.*—The ferial (6) proves that the true year is 1350.

m-baile Rora-Comain leirin errus hUa¹ Finacta
d'aen² urcur roigde. Ocur in³ t-é⁴ ar ar'cuired in t-ur-
cur do cirrbad 7 do marbad ann, doon, Ruaidri in
t-reompa h[U]a¹ Donncada.—Brian hUa¹ brian do
marbad a reall do macaid Me[c] Ceo[t]ac.—Aed, mac
Aeda breirnig hUi° Concobuir,° ri Connact, do marbad
la hAed hUa¹ Ruairc ar Muig-Engaide. Aengur hUa¹
hEoguya, rai coitcenn, coimder a cerdaid na rilidacta,
d'eg.—Aengur ruad⁵ hUa¹ Dalaig (doon,ᵈ mac Donncada, mic Aenguya, mic Donncada moirᵈ), rai gan uirer-
baid, moptuur ept.—Ruaidri, mac Catail, mic Domnaill [U]i Concobuir, do marbad do macaib Ferġail
Mic Donncaid.—Aed, mac Amlaim Meg Uidir, mortu[u]r ert.

Kal. ian. uii. r., [Lᵃ 1.,ᵃ] Anno Domini M.° ccc.° xl°
uiii.°ᵇ [-Lᵃ 1.°] Pilib Mag Uidir (doonᶜ, taireč Muinn-
tiri-reodača[i]nᵉ) moptuur ept.—Enna hUa¹ Flan-
B 71a naga[i]n, taireč eile, moptuur ept.— | Eogan Mac
Suibne do marbad la Magnur hUa¹ n-Domnaill.—Aedᵈ
O Ruairc do gabail ic tett o Cruaic-Patraic do mac
Pilbin Mic Uilliam 7 Fergal Mac Diarmata d'eirġi
trid 7 cagad coitcenn i Connactaib 7 Mag-Luirg uile
do lomargain tridᵈ.—Matgamain Mac Con[-Sh]nama
do marbad do clainn Donncada Mic Con[-Sh]nama—
Fuagraᵉ coitcenn O Uilliam hUa¹ Cellaig ar damaib

A.D. 1347. ¹ O, A. ² d'aon, B. ³ an, B. ⁴ t-1, B. ⁵ -g, B. ᵃ⁻ᵃ om., A.
ᵈ⁻ᵈ itl., t. h., A ; om., B.

A.D. 1348. ¹ O, A. ᵃ⁻ᵃ bl., A, B. ᵇ 1351, B. ᶜ⁻ᶜ itl., t. h., A, B.
ᵈ⁻ᵈ om., B. In B, Aed is written with dots underneath, showing the compiler omitted the entry designedly. ᵉ garrm—*invitation*, B.

³ *With the bishop.*—The *A. L. C.* (1350) state that he was slain by mischance by the bishop's people.

³ *Ua Finachta.*—Bishop of Elphin [1326], *supra* ; 1354, *infra*.

⁴ *To whom—home.*—Literally, on whom was placed the shot.

⁵ *Brian.*—Grandson (son of Dom-nall) of Brian the Red, who was murdered by Thomas de Clare, [1277], *supra*.

was killed in the town of Ros-Comain, [whilst he was] with [1350] the bishop² Ua Finachta,³ with one shot of an arrow. And the person to whom⁴ [the discharge of] the shot was brought home⁴ was mangled and killed therefor, namely, Ruaidhri Ua Donnchadha of the Chamber.—Brian⁵ Ua Briain was killed in treachery by the sons of Mac Ceo[th]ach.—Aedh, son of Aedh Ua Concobuir the Brefnian, king of Connacht, was killed by Aedh Ua Ruairc on Magh-Enghaide.—Aenghus Ua hEoghusa, a general, expert proficient in the arts of poetry, died.—Aengus Ua Dalaigh the Red (namely, son of Donnchadh, son of Aengus, son of Donnchadh Mor), a sage⁶ without defect, died.—Ruaidhri, son of Cathal, son of Domnall Ua Concobuir, was killed by the sons of Ferghal Mac Donnchaidh. —Aedh, son of Amblam Mag Uidhir, died.

Kalends of Jan. on 7th feria, [1st of the moon], A.D. [1351] 1348¹[-51]. Philip Mag Uidhir (namely, chief of Muinter-Peodacha[i]n) died.—Enna Ua Flannagain, another chief,² died.—Eoghan Mac Suibhne was killed by Maghnus Ua Domnaill.—Aedh O'Ruairc was taken prisoner by the son of Philpin Mac William [de Burgh], in coming from Cruach-Patraic³ and Fergal Mac Diarmata rose out on account of that, and there was general war in Connacht and Magh-Luirg was all laid bare through it.—Mathgamain Mac Con[Sh]nama was killed by the sons of Donnchadh Mac Con[Sh]nama.—A general invitation⁴ [was issued] from William Ua Cellaigh to the learned of

---

⁶ *Sage.*—The most eminent poet of Ireland, according to the *A. L. C.*

[1351] ¹ *1348.*—The ferial (7) proves that the true year is 1351.

² *Another chief.*—Of Fermanagh. O'Flanagan was lord of Tuathratha (Tooraah: bar. of Magheraboy), which adjoined Muinter-Peodachain (bar. of Clanawley).

³ *From Cruach-Patraic.*— See 1115, note 1, *supra.*

⁴ *Invitation.*—See Mageoghegan's account, quoted in the *F. M.* iii. 600-1.

ę̄renn, 7 tangaḋup co m-buıḋeċ uaḋa.—Cpıpcınup' hUa
Leanna[ı]n, ab Lepa-gabaıl, mopcuup ept . . 1ḋup'
Cppılıp.ᵈᶠ

(1ohannep⁵ Cnḋree, excellentıppımup ḋoctop, quiᵇ
ppoppıa Sextı, Clementıp, atque Nouellap, hıepoɲymı
Lauḋep, Speculıque ıupa pepegıt,ʰ obııt hoc anno, ḋıe
7mo menpıp 1ulıı, pepḋıpae pepcıp pato, et pepulcup
ept ın ecclepıa Sancti Ḋomınıcı ın cıuıtate Ḃononıenpı.ᶠ)

[bıp.] Ical. 1an. 1. p., L [x. 11.ᵃ], Cnno Ḋomını M.° ccc.° xl.°
ıx.° ᵇ[-L.° 11.°] Ceḋ, mac Toıppḋealbaıg, ḋo ḡabaıl pıḡe
Connacc° ap eıgın cap ḡallaıḃ 7 cap Ḡhaıḋelaıḃ.—Nu-
alaıg, ıngen Mıc Ḋıapmata, ḋ'eg.—Ceḋᵈ O Mael-
ḃpenaınn 7 a ḋa mac ḋo mapbaḋ ḋ'Ceḋ, mac Fheıḋ-
lımıḋ hUı Conċobuıp.—Taḋg, mac Secupa hUı Cellaıg,
ḋ'egᵈ.—Ceḋ hUaᶦ Ruaıpc ḋo mapbaḋ la Claınn-Muıp-

ᶠ⁻ᶠ f. m., t. h., A; text, B. The numeral before Idus is illegible. ᵉ⁻ᵉ n. t.
h., A; om., B. ʰ⁻ʰ Slightly altered from the second and third of the four
hexameters forming the epitaph:
    Primus qui Sextum Clementis, quique Nouellas,
    Hieronymi laudes, Speculi quoque iura peregit.
A.D. 1349. ᵃ .x.° 111.° , A, B.   ᵇ 1352, B.   ᶜ om., B.   ᵈ⁻ᵈ om., B.

(1348) ¹ *John Andreae.*—A Florentine, doctor of Civil and Canon Law, and professor at Bologna. In a *Notice and Commendation* of him appended to the *Sixth*, it is said (inter alia): qui, contra consuetudinem hominum nostri temporis, quamvis uxoris esset vinculis alligatus, incredibile tamen studium literis impendit.

² *Sixth.*—A collection of Decretals issued by Boniface VIII., A.D. 1296, to supplement the Five Books (whence the title) promulgated by Gregory IX. in 1234. The work of Andreae here referred to is the *Mercuriales,* or Commentary on the (eighty-eight) legal Rules (*Regulae Juris*), which form the final Title (V. 13) of the *Sixth.*

³ *Clement[ine].* — Constitutions made public by John XXII. about 1416, and so called as consisting mainly of the Decrees of Clement V. (1305-14). One of the items in the printed title is: *vna cum profundo apparatu domini Ioannis Andreae.* The quotation given Vol. I., p. 13, supra, belongs to a gloss of Andreae on the title, *De Magistris* (Clem. V. 1), the Decretal of Clement V. in the Council of Vienne, A.D. 1312, respecting the teaching of Hebrew, Arabic and

Ireland, and they came gratefully from him.—Christian [1351]
Ua Leanna[i]n, abbot of Lis-gabhail, died on the .. Ides
[13th] of April.

(John Andreae,[1] most excellent doctor, who explained (1348)
the peculiar Rules of the *Sixth*,[2] the Laws of the *Clemen-
t[ine]*,[3] and composed the *Novellae*,[4] the *Praises of* [*St.*]
Jerome,[5] and explained the enactments of the *Speculum*,[6]
died this year,[7] on the seventh day of the month of July,
of the very dire pestilence, and was buried in the church
of St. Dominic in the city of Bologna).

Kalends of Jan. on 1st feria, [12th] of the moon, A.D. [1352 Bis.]
1349[1][-52]. Aedh, son of Toirdelbach,[2] took the kingship of Connacht by force against the Foreigners and
against the Gaidhil.—Nualaith, daughter of Mac Diarmata,
died.—Aedh O'Mael-Brenainn and his two sons were slain
by Aedh, son of Feidhlimidh Ua Conchobuirr.—Tadhg
son Jacques Ua Cellaigh, died.—Aedh Ua Ruairc was

Chaldaic in the Curia, and in the Universities of Paris, Oxford, Bologna and Salamanca.

[4] *Novellae.*—Most of the summaries and glosses of the *Sixth* were written by Andreae. (His well known Tree of Consanguinity is inserted at the end of the Fourth Book. Two of the laudatory lines at foot run:

Ioanni celebres Andreae dentur
  honores;
Arboreos fructus quo mediante
  legis.)

These he styled *Novellae*, in honour of his daughter, Novella, who sometimes, it is said, supplied her father's place in the lecture chair.

[5] *Praises of St. Jerome.*—One of the works of Andreae. In the prologue of the *Novellae* he calls St. Jerome *patrinus meus*.

[6] *Speculum.*—The *Speculum Juris* was edited with additions by Andreae. It was the work of Durandus (thence called *Speculator*), a canonist of Provence, who died at Rome in 1296. The *Rationale divinorum officiorum* of the same author is better known.

[7] *This year.*—The *Notice* agrees with the present obit as to the year, but omits the day of the month.

[1352] [1] *1349.*—The ferial (1) proves that the true year is 1352.

[2] *Toirdelbach.* — Turlough O'Conor.

certaix.—Aengur hUa¹ Domnaill do marbad la
Magnur hUa¹ n-Domnaill.—Tomar Mag Ragnaill
mortuur ert.—Commac baile-in-duin la hAed, mac
| Toirrdelbaig hUi Concobuir 7 dit bó 7 caepac ann.—
Concobur, mac Muirgira Mic Donncaid, rai᷎ coitcenn
im ellac 7 im biad᷎, d'eg¹.—Dabug Dilmain, mac
Uilliug Umaill, cenn ceitern² 7᷎ Dilmainec Connact᷎,
mortuur᷎ ert᷎.—Daibit᷎ hUa hEogain, aircinnec Innri-
cain ror Loc-herne, mortuur ert 12 Kalendar Iuini.

Kal. Ian. iii. f., L. xx[iii.], Anno Domini M.° ccc.° L.°
[-L° iii.°] Gormlait, ingen [U]i Domnaill, ben¹ [U]i
Neill, quieuit᷎ in [Christo]᷎.—Aed, mac Ruaidri h[U]i
Neill, d'eg.—Tadg Mag Ragnaill, ardtairec Muinn-
teri-hEolu[i]r, macan᷎ tairec Erenn,᷎ do marbad do
clainn t-Sheffraig Meg Ragnaill.

(Eoin᷎ hUa Cairbri, comorba Tigernaig i Cluain-Eoir,
d'heg in bliadain [ri] Kalendir Februarii.᷎)

Kal. Ian. iiii. f., L. [iiii.᷎], Anno Domini M.° ccc.° L°
i.°᷎ [-iiii.°] brian hUa¹ Dubda, ri Tire-Fiacrac, mortuur ert.—Sitriug Mag Samrada[i]n d'eg.—Derborgaill, ingen¹ [U]i Concobuir, mortua ert.—Tadg Mac
Senlaic² d'eg.᷎—Catal, mac Neill [U]i Ruairc, d'eg᷎.—
Ruaidri hUa¹ Morda, ri Laigeir, do marbad d'a brai-

A.D. 1349. ¹ O, A. ² ceitirne (sg. of the A reading), B. ᶜ⁻ᶜ om., A.
¹⁻¹ 73 a, f. m., t. h., A; om., B.

A.D. 1350. ¹ bean, A. ᵃ 1353. B. ᵇ⁻ᵇ d'heg, with 14 Aprilis overhead, n. t. (Latin) h., B. ᶜ⁻ᶜ om., B. ᵈ⁻ᵈ n. t. h., A; om., B.

A.D. 1351. ¹ O, A. ² Seann—, A. ᵃ .uii., A, B. The first two n
were mistaken for u. ᵇ 1354, B. ᶜ mortuur ert, B.

---

³ *Slain.*—The A. L. C. add that great slaughter was inflicted on the gallowglasses of the Mac Sweeneys on the occasion.

⁴ *Slain.* — A fuller account is given in the F. M. (1352).

⁵ *Breaking down.* — *Commach* = *combach*, for which see the Stowe Missal, 64a (Tr. R. I. A., xxvii. 250).

⁶ *Baile-in-duin.* — *Town of the moated fort* (Cf. O'Curry: *Man. and*

slain[3] by the Clann-Muircertaigh.—Aenghus Ua Domnaill [1352] was slain[4] by Maghnus Ua Domnaill.—Thomas Mag Ragnaill died.—The breaking down[5] of Baile-in-duin[6] [was effected] by Aedh, son of Toirdhelbach Ua Conchobuir and destruction of cows and sheep [was wrought] there.—Concobur, son of Maurice Mac Donnchaidh, general benefactor respecting cattle and food, died.—Dabug Dillon, son of Ulick of Umall, head of the kerns and of the Dillons of Connacht, died.—David Ua hEogain, herenagh of Inis-cain upon Loch-Erne, died on the 12th of the Kalends of June [May 21].

Kalends of Jan. on 3rd feria, [23rd] of the moon, A.D. [1353] 1350[1][-3]. Gormlaith, daughter of Ua Domnaill, wife of Ua Neill,[2] rested in Christ.—Aedh, son of Ruaidhri Ua Neill, died.—Tadhg Mag Raghnall, arch-chief of Muinter-Eolu[i]s, the choicest of the chiefs of Ireland, was slain by the sons of Geoffrey Mag Raghnaill.

(John[1] Ua Cairbri,[2] successor of [St.] Tigernach in Cluain-Eois, died this year on the Kalends [1st] of February).

Kalends of Jan. on 4th feria, [4th] of the moon, A.D. [1354] 1351[1][-4]. Brian Ua Dubhda, king of Tir-Fiachrach, died.—Sitric Mag Samradha[i]n died.—Cathal, son of Niall Ua Ruairc, died.—Ruaidhri Ua Mordha, king of Laighis, was killed by his own kinsmen and by the folk

---

Cust. s. v. Dun): Ballindoon, near Lough Arrow, bar. of Tirerrill, co. Sligo (O'D. iii. 602).

[1353] [1]*1350.*—The ferial (3) proves that the true year is 1353.

[2] *Ua Neill.*—Aedh, or Hugh, king of Ulster.

(1350) [1] *John, etc.*—The obit is given in the *Four Masters* at 1353, which most probably is the true date.

[2] *Ua Cairbri.*—The Domhnach Airgid (for an account of which reliquary see Petrie, Tr. R. I. A., xviii. 16 sq., O'Curry, *MS. Mat.*, p. 322 sq.) perpetuates his name in one of its two inscriptions: JOHANNES O KARBRI, COMORBANUS SANCTI TIGERNACII, PERMISIT [OPERIMENTUM FIERI].

[1354] [1]*1351.* — The ferial (4) proves that the true year is 1354.

éμιδ ϝein 7 o'a luċṫ ṫιξι.—Eμpuc 8ιl-Muιροδαιξ, ιοοn, Maιξιμτeμ Seoan hUa¹ ϝιneċτa, ν'ecᵈ.—ϝeμξal Μάξ Θοċαξα[ι]n ν'eξ, ιοοn,' ταιμeċ Ceniuιl-ϝιαċαιξ'.—Eμpuc Connaċṫ, hUa¹ Laċṫna[ι]n, quιeuιτ ιn' [Chμιμτο]ᶠ.—8eμ-ϝμαιξ Μαξ Ραξnaιll ν'eξ.—8eμ[ϝ]μαιξ hUa¹ Ραιξιl-laιξ ν'eξ (nonoᵉ νιe menμιμ Μαμcιι).—Μαc Μuμċαδα νο ṫaμμaιnξ νο ξhallaιδ 7 caξαδ mon eτeμ ξhallaιb 7 ξαιδelaιδ τμιν μιn.—Œeδ Μαξ 8αμμαδα[ι]n ν'eξ ν'α lοιτιδ, αμ n-α ξuιn ν'hUa³ ϝhala[ι]n.—ϝeμξal' Μαξ Θοċαξα[ι]n, ταιμeċ Cene[οι]l-ϝιαċαιξ, ν'ec'.—Ðμιαn, mac Œeδα moιμ hUι Neιll, ν'éc, ϝαι coιτċenn.—Ruαιδμι, mac Seoaιn Μeξ Μhaṫξamna, νο maμbaδ ιllοnξμομṫ Μeξ Μαṫξamna.—Œb[b] 8μuṫμα, mac' Caṫaιl, ν'eξ': ιοοn, Μuμċαδ, mac Caṫaιl [U]ι ϝeμξaιl, ν'eξ.

(ριlιbʰ Μαξ Uιδιμ, ταιμeaċ Μuιnτιμe-ϝeονaċan, ν'hec ιnΝοιn ϝheaδμa.ʰ)

B 71b ̷Cal. 1an. [u.ᵃ ϝ., l. xu.ᵃ] Œnno Ðomιnι Μ.° ccc.° L°
 11.°ᵇ [-u.°] Μuιμιμ, mac Τομαιμ (1αμlαᵃ Ðe[μ]-Μumanᵉ),
A 73c | ξιuμτιμ na hEμenn, ν'eξ.—Νιαll Μαξ Μαṫξαμna νο maμbaδ νο claιnn Seoaιn Μeξ Μhaṫξαμna.—Ðomnall, mac Seaaιn hUι ϝeμξaιl, ταιμeċ Μuιnnτιμe-hŒnξaιle,

A.D. 1351. ³ν'O, A. ᵈν'heξ, μομτuuμ eμṫ! B. ᵉ⁻ᵉ om., A. ᶠ⁻ᶠ om., B. ᵍ⁻ᵍ itl., n. t. h., A; om., B. ʰ⁻ʰ n. t. h., A; om., B.

A.D. 1352. ᵃ⁻ᵃ bl., A, B. ᵇ 1355, B. ᶜ⁻ᶜ r. m. (which is partly cut off), t. h., B; om., A.

---

² *Ua Finachta.* — Shortly before the demise of Clement VI. (Dec. 1352), a report reached Avignon that Rodulph, bishop of Down, was dead. That pope not having acted upon it, his successor, Innocent VI., nominated (Jan. 29, 1353) Gregory, priest and provost of Killala, and had him consecrated at the Curia. (Theiner, p. 302-3.) Though the rumour proved un- founded, Rodulph died soon after. The Chapter elected Richard, prior of the Benedictine House of Down, and he was confirmed by Innocent, Dec. 4, 1353 (*ib.* p. 305). Having received consecration, he was directed (Dec. 23) to proceed to the church (*ib.* p. 305-6). Though the collation had been reserved to the Pontiff, to impose a selection made before the vacancy arose would have

of his house.—The bishop of Sil-Muiredhaigh [Elphin], namely, Master John Ua Finachta,[2] died.—Fergal Mag Eochaga[i]n, namely, chief of Cenel-Fiachaigh, died.—The bishop of Connacht,[3] Ua Lachtna[i]n, rested in Christ.—Geoffrey Mag Raghnaill died.—Geoffrey Ua Raighillaigh died (on the 9th day of the month of March).—Mac Murchadha was drawn [asunder] by the Foreigners and a great war [arose] between the Foreigners and Gaidhil through that.—Aedh Mag Samradha[i]n died of his injuries on being wounded by Ua Fala[i]n.—Fergal[4] Mag Eochaga[i]n, chief of Cenel-Fiachaigh, died.—Brian, son of Aedh Mor Ua Neill, a general sage, died.—Ruaidhri, son of John Mag Mathgamna, was killed in the fortress of Mag Mathgamna.—The abbot of Sruthair, the son of Cathal, died: that is, Murchadh, son of Cathal Ua Ferghail, died.

(Philip Mag Uidhir, chief of Muinter-Feodachan, died on the None [5th] of February).

Kalends of Jan. [on 5th feria, 15th of the moon,] A.D. 1352[1][-5]. Maurice[2] Fitz Thomas (Earl of Desmond), Justiciary of Ireland, died.—Niall Mag Mathgamna was slain by the sons of John Mag Mathgama.—Domnall, son of John Ua Fergail, chief of Muinter-Anghaile, died.—

[1354]

[1355]

---

appeared too arbitrary. Hence, doubtless, the silence of the second Bull respecting the existence of the first.

Gregory thus remained (evidently at the Papal Court) bishop of no church, until he was appointed to succeed John in the diocese of Elphin, Feb. 27, 1357 (*ib.* p. 310-1). Whence it may be inferred that the death of O'Finaghty took place towards the close of 1354.

[3] *Connacht.*—Perhaps the same as Richard O'Loughlain, bishop of Kilfenora (Ware, p. 624).

[4] *Fergal, etc.*—A repetition of the sixth entry.

(1351) [1]*Philip, etc.*—The first obit of [1351] *supra*+the day of the month.

[1355] [1]*1352*=1355 of the *A.L.C.*

[2] *Maurice.*—Grace states that he became Justiciary in 1355 (July 8, note, p. 145) and died soon after. One item in his encomium of Desmond is that he well chastised the Irish.

d'eg.—Concobur Mac Con[8]nama, erpuc na Breifne o' Druimcliab co'Cenannur¹, d'ég'.—Diarmait⁴ O Mailmiadaig, taireċ Muinntire-Cerballa[i]n, do marbaḋ do Muinntir-Birn 7 moran do Muinntir-Eolair ar aen rir⁴.—Prioir na Trinoide, Mac Gall-Gaidil, mortuur[h] erṫ[h].—Caṫal⁴ O Cuind, taireċ Muinntire-Gillga[i]n, do marbaḋ 7 coicer d'a braiṫriḃ do clainn Aeḋa 7 do clainn t-Seoain⁴.—Aḋug Mac Uidilin² do marbaḋ d'Oirrṫeraiḃ.—Cormac Mag Raġnaill, taireċ Muinntire-Eolu[i]r, do marbaḋ do clainn Imair Meg Raġnaill 7 Conn, mac Tomaltaiġ, do marbaḋ ann.—Borgaill,⁴ ingen [U]i Fherġail, d'eg⁴.

(A) (B)

Donnċaḋ O Domnaill do marbaḋ (idon¹, le Donn Mac Murċaḋa i Longport Aeḋa ruaiḋ¹) ic tabairt ingine Meg Uidir ar eigin Leir, idon, (Gormlaiṫ) ingen Aeḋa ruaiḋ.

Donnċaḋ hUa Domnaill do marbaḋ ic tabairt ingine Meg Uidir Leir ar eigin, idon, ingen Aeḋa ruaiḋ Meg Uidir (idon Gormlaiṫ). Ocur le Donn Mac Murċaḋa do marbaḋ e illongport Meg Uidir, 7 araile.

Taḋg Mac Aeḋaga[i]n d'eg.

[bir]. Kal. Ian. [u]i. r., L x[x.ui.,] Anno Domini M.° ccc.l° iii.°⁴ [-ui.°] Mor, ingen [U]i Concobuir, ben [U]i Ferġail, d'eg.—Ruaidri, mac Aeḋa [U]i Concobuir, d'éc—

A.D. 1352. ¹-ntur, B. ³ Uib—, B. ᵈ a (the Latin equivalent), overhead, n. t. (Latin) h., B. ᵉ usque ad (the Latin rendering) overhead, n. t. (Latin) h., B. ᶠ quieuit in Chrirto, B. ᵍ⁻ᵈ om., B. ʰ⁻ʰ om., A. ⁱ itl., t. h., (A) MS.

A.D. 1353. ᵃ 1356, B.

---

³ *Breifni.*—That is, the diocese of Kilmore.

⁴ *Mac Gall-Gaidhil.* — There is little likelihood that a native of Galloway (Vol. I., p. 365-6, *supra*) was a member of the Trinity Community, Lough Ce, at this time. Mac Gall-Gaidbil (*son of a Foreign Gaidhel*), we may thus conclude, was a patronymic. The prior, in

Concobur Mac Con[Sh]nama, bishop of the Breifni[3] from [1355] Druim-cliabh to Cenannus, died.—Diarmait O'Mailmiadhaigh, chief of Muinter-Cerballa[i]n, was slain by the Muinter-Birn, and many of the Muinter-Eolais [were slain] along with him.—The Prior of the Trinity, Mac Gall-Gaidhil,[4] died.—Cathal O'Cuinn, chief of Muinter-Gilgain, and five of his kinsmen were slain by the sons of Aedh[5] and the sons of John[5].—Adug Mac Uidhilin was slain by the Oirthir.—Cormac Mag Raghnaill, chief of Muinter-Eoluis, was slain by the sons of Imar Mag Raghnaill and Conn, son of Tomaltach [Mag Ragnaill], was slain there.—Borgaill, daughter of Ua Ferghail, died.

(A)
Donnchadh O'Domnaill was slain (namely, by Donn, Mac Murchadha, in the fortress of Aedh [Mag Uidhir] the Red) in carrying the daughter of Mag Uidher by force with him; that is, (Gormlaith) the daughter of Aedh the Red.

(B)
Donnchadh Ua Domnaill was slain in carrying the daughter of Mag Uidhir with him by force; that is, the daughter (namely, Gormlaith) of Aedh Mag Uidhir the Red. And by Donn Mac Murchadha was he killed in the fortress of Mag Uidhir, and so on.

Tadhg Mac Aedhaga[i]n[6] died.

Kalends of Jan. on [6th] feria, [26th] of the moon, A.D. [1356 Bis.] 1353[1][-6]. Mor, daughter of Ua Concobuir, wife of Ua Ferghail, died.—Ruaidhri, son of Aedh Ua Concobuir,

---

all probability, descended from the Toibeard mentioned 1211, *supra*.

[5] *Aedh, John.*—From these the two branches of the O'Farrells derive their respective tribe-names, *Clann-Aedha* (Clann-Hugh) and *Clann-Seain* (Clann-Shane).

[6] *Mac Aedhagain.*—According to the obit in the *F. M.*, Mac Egan was a proficient in the Feinechas (inter-tribal law).

[1356] [1]*1353*=1356 of the *A. L. C.*

Muircertaigh, mac Seaain, mic Domnaill, mic Briain hUi Neill, do marbad (quinto Nonis Marcii) do Philib Mag Uidir.—Diarmait, mac Diarmata Meg Carrtaig 7 a mac, Donncad, do marbad do mac hUi Shuilleba[i]n¹. — Giurtir° Aed-cliat d'eg. — Mac Feórair do marbad do Ghallaib.—Toirrdelbac, mac Aeda hUi Concobuir, do marbad la Clainn-Donncaid.—Aed, mac Toirrdelbaig hUi Concobuir, ri Connact, do marbad do macaib hUi Cheallaig tre ed.—Dubgall' Mac Suibne do marbad la Domnall O Concobuir⁵.—Donncad Mac Conmara do marbad la Sil-mBriain.—Domnall, mac Aed Breifnig, mortuus ert.—Nicol Mac Catúraig, erpuc Oirgiall, mortuus ert (irin Fogmar') 7 Brian Mac Catmail do togal[d] i n-a inad.—Solam hUa² Mella[i]n, maer Cluig in Udact[a], feicem coit-cenn, quieuit in [Christo].—Donncad° Proirtec do marbad do bir d'a muinntir fein.—Gearoidin Tribel do tarraing do Saxanaib ar faitci Aed-cliat'.—Feid-lim', mac Aeda, mic Domnaill hUi Domnaill, ri Tir-Conaill, do marbad le mac a derbrátar fein, idon, Seaan, mac Concobuir, mic Aeda, mic Domnaill [hUi Domnaill], i cornum rigi frir'.—Murcad, mac Briain hUi | Neill, d'eg.—Brian', mac Magnura, mortuus ert rexto Idur Aprilir'.

A.D. 1353. ¹Shuilduban, A. ²O, A. ᵇᵇitl., t. h., A. B; quarto, B. ᶜᵈom., B. ᵈᵈitl., t. h., A, B. Erpuc Clocair—*bishop of Clochar*—is placed on r. m., t. h., B. *In Autumno* (the Latin equivalent), over-head, n. t. (Latin) h.; B. ᵉ om. (by aphaeresis), A. ᶠᶠ om., A

---

² *Justiciary*.—Thomas de Rokeby. He became justiciary for the second time in 1356 and died the same year in Kilkea castle (co. Kildare), Grace.

³ *Ua Cellaigh*.—Donough, in revenge for the abduction of whose wife Aedh (Hugh) O'Conor was slain, *A. L. C.*

⁴ *Sil-Briain*.—*Seed of Brian* (Boruma): the O'Briens of Thomond.

⁵ *Aedh*.—O'Conor.

⁶ *Oirgialla* (Oriel). — Clogher diocese. Mac Casey succeeded on

died.—Muircertach, son of John, son of Domnall, son of [1356] Brian Ua Neill, was slain (on the 5th of the Nones [3rd] of March) by Philip Mag Uidhir.—Diarmait, son of Diarmait Mag Carthaigh and his son, Donnchadh, were slain by the son of Ua Suillebha[i]n.—The Justiciary[2] of Ath-cliath died.—Mac Feorais was slain by the Foreigners.—Toirdhelbach, son of Aedh Ua Conchbuir, was slain by the Clann-Donnchaidh.—Aedh, son of Toirdelbach Ua Concobuir, king of Connacht, was slain by the sons of Ua Cellaigh[3] through jealousy.—Dubghall Mac Suibne was slain by Domnall O'Concobuir.—Donnchadh Mac Conmara was slain by the Sil-Briain.[4]—Domnall, son of Aedh[5] the Brefnian, died.—Nicholas Mac Cathusaigh, bishop of Oirgialla,[6] died (in the Harvest), and Brian Mac Cathmail was chosen in his stead.—Solomon Ua Mella[i]n, keeper of the Bell of the Testament,[7] general protector,[8] rested in Christ.—Donnchadh Proistech was slain by two of his own people.—Gerodin Tyrrell was drawn [asunder] by the Saxons on the green of Ath-cliath.—Feidhlimidh, son of Aedh, son of Domnall Ua Domnaill, king of Tir-Conaill, was slain by the son of his own brother, namely, John, son of Concobur, son of Aedh, son of Domnall,[9] in contesting the kingship with him.—Murchadh, son of Brian Ua Neill, died.—Brian, son of Maghnus,[10] died on the 6th of the Ides [8th] of April.

---

the death of O'Banan, [1319], supra. Nicholaus Clokerensis was one of the bishops present in the church of Armagh, when the Bull of John XXII. against Louis of Bavaria was published by the primate, Stephen (Segrave), June 25, 1325. (Theiner, p. 230).

[7] *Bell of the Testament.*—See 552 (-3), supra; O'Donovan, *F. M.* iii.

609; Reeves, *Columba*, 323-6. A bequest of a bell by St. Patrick is not mentioned in the Tripartite Life, or the Book of Armagh.

[8] *Protector.*—Of poets and learned men.

[9] *Domnall.*—O'Donnell]

[10] *Maghnus.*—Maguire. Perhaps the reading is Mac Maghnusa (Maguire).

Ical 1an. [1.ᵃ] p., L [uɪɪ.ᵇ]. Anno Domini M.° ccc.° L.°
iiii.°[-uɪɪ.ᵉ]. Maᵹnup (macᵈ Eaċaḋaᵉ) Maᵹ Mhaṫ-
ᵹamna, pi Oipᵹiall, o'eᵹ (ipinᵈ Eppaċᵈ).—Loċlainnᵉ, mac
Muipceptaiᵹ hUi Concobuip, o'eᵹᵉ.—Seaan, mac Opiain
hUi Raiᵹillaiᵹ, oo mapbaḋ oo Ḟhallaiḃ.—Maṫaᵉ, mac
Tomaip hUi Ruaipc, cenn ᵹaipciḋ na Opeipne o'eᵹᵉ.—
Niall hUa¹ Fapceallaiᵹ oo mapbaḋ o'en upċup poiᵹoe
le Cenel-Luaċain. Ocup oa maipeḋ, po bo comapba ap
naṁapaċ.—Fepᵹal hUa¹ Ouiḃᵹenna[i]n, ollam na
Opeipneᶠ [pe oan], o'eᵹ.

O° Ouiḃᵹenna[i]n, tpen a tpep,
A bponnaḋ noċo bpeiᵹmep ;
Calma pe conaḋ a cnep,
Aḋḃa ollaṁ ip éiᵹep.

Fepᵹal, pep oana nap'ḋaep,
Senċaiḋ muipneċ ip mac caem ;
Caċ poluḃ peċup 'n-a ṫeċ,
Ollaṁ up ip oipcinneċᵉ.

Siṫ coitcenn etep oa Caṫal, ioon, Caṫal, mac Caṫail
7 Caṫal, mac Aeḋa Opeipniᵹ.—Donnpleiḃe Mac Cep-
baill, paep maiᵹipter na penma, o'éc, in t-aen ouine
pob' pepp pe [a] ealaḋain pein i n-Epinnᵉ.—Opian, mac
Ᵹilla-Cpipt [U]i Ruaipc, o'eᵹᵉ.—Maᵹnup buioe Maᵹ
Sampaoa[i]n oo mapbaḋ a Rút Mic Uioilin le hAeḋ
hUa¹ Néill.—| Cleminc hUa¹ Ouiḃᵹenna[i]n (ioon,ᵇ
paᵹapt na Sinnaċᵇ), bicaip Cille-Ronain, quieuit in
[Chpipto].—Mail-Seċlainn Mac Domnaill, taipeċ
Clainni-Ceallaiᵹ, o'éᵹ.

A.D. 1354. ¹O, A. ᵃ.ɪɪ, A, B. ᵇ xx.ɪ, A, B. ᶜ 1357, B. ᵈ⁻ᵈ itl.,
t. h., A ; om., B. ᵉ⁻ᵉ om., B. ᶠ After this word a space = 6 letters is
left blank, A. The context suggests the bracketted words. ᵍ om., A.
ʰ⁻ʰ itl., t. h., A, B.

[1357] ¹₁₃₅₄=1357 of the A. L.
C.

²Eachaidh.—Mac Mahon, king
of Oriel, who died [1273], supra.

Kalends of Jan. on [1st] feria, [7th] of the moon, A.D. [1357] 1354¹[-7]. Maghnus (son of Eachaidh²) Mag Mathgamna, king of Oirghialla, died (in the Spring).—Lochlainn, son of Muircertach Ua Concobuir, died.—John, son of Brian Ua Raighbillaigh, was slain by the Foreigners.—Matthew, son of Thomas Ua Ruairc, head³ of the prowess of the Breifni, died.—Niall Ua Fairceallaigh was killed by one shot of an arrow by the Cenel-Luachain. And had he lived, he would have been Superior⁴ on the morrow.—Fergal Ua Duibhgenna[i]n, ollam of the Breifni, died:

> O'Duibhgennain,⁵ strong his prowess,
> To grant [this] is not a false decision;
> Excellent
> Abode of ollams and of learned.

> Fergal [was] a poet that was not bitter,
> A historian impartial and a bounteous person,
> Every comfort is supplied in his house,
> A perfect ollam and herenagh.

General peace [was made] between the two Cathals: namely, Cathal, son of Cathal⁶ and Cathal, son of Aedh⁶ the Brefnian.—Donnsleibhe Mac Cerbaill, noble master of melody, the person that was best in his own art in Ireland, died.—Brian, son of Cilla-Crist Ua Ruairc, died.—Maghnus Mag Samradha[i]n the Tawny was killed in the Route of Mac Uidhilin by Aedh Ua Neill.—Clement Ua Duibgenna[i]n (namely, the priest of the Foxes⁷), vicar of Cell-Ronain, rested in Christ.—Mail-Sechlainn Mac Domnaill, chief of Clann-Cellaigh, died.

---

³ *Head, etc.*—"Chief man for hardiness and vallour of his hands of the Bre[f]nie," Mageoghegan (1357).

⁴ *Superior.*—Namely, abbot of Drumlane, co. Cavan.

⁵ *Ua Duibhgennain, etc.*—The metre is Debide.

⁶ *Cathal, Aedh.*—O'Conor.

⁷ *Priest of the Foxes.*—"It is not easy to determine why he was so called, as he does not appear to

Kal. Ian. 11. f., l. [xui]11., Anno Domini M.˚ ccc.˚ l.˚ u.˚ᵃ[-uiii.˚] Domnall hUa¹ hEgra, ri Luigne, d'eg im⁰ Chairc⁰. — Magnur Mag Uidir (don, mac Aeda ruaid⁽), do marbad (12ᵈ Kalendar Mai⁽ᵈ⁾), do Clainn-Catmail—Concobur hUa¹ hAinlide, tairec Ceniuil-Dobta, d'ec.—Maidm mor do tabairt d'Aed hUa¹ Neill ar Oirgallaib [7] ar Feraib-Manac.—Aed Mac Caba do marbad ann 7 mac in erruic [U]i Dubda 7 daine imda aili².—Maidm mor do tabairt do³ hUa³ Morda ar Ghallaib Aea-cliat 7 da ficit dec do marbad dib.—Cit mor do tect irin Samrad rin a Cairbri 7 nir' lug-u na⁴ fiadugall anabaid gac aen⁵ mell dib.—Brian Mac Catmail, erpuc Oirgiall, quieuit in Christo⁰.—Seinicin Mac Uidilin, aobur Conrtabla Coicid Ulad, d'ec.—Mac⁰ Ainoriu Mic Fheorair d'ec⁰.—Toirrdel-bac⁽, mac Aeda na Fiodaidi hUi Neill, occirur ert quinto Kalendar Iuini⁽.

(Crecrluaiged⁽ mor do denum do hUa Neill (don⁵, d'Aod mor, mac Toirdelbaig. .⁰) i Tir-Conaill, d'ar'-comairmed rect cata deg do bocrud, a n-fegmur saerac 7 gabar 7 muc 7 tri ficit groid do groidib. Ocur a m-braigdi a n-diaig na creac, [A.O.] 1355.⁽)

A.D. 1355. ¹O, A. ²eile, A. ³·³d'O, A. ⁴ina, B. ⁵ein, B. ᵃ¯ᵃ 1358, B. ᵇ¯ᵇom., B. ᶜ¯ᶜitl., n. t. h., A; itl., t. h., B. ᵈ¯ᵈitl., n. t. h., A; om., B. ᵉom., B. ᶠ¯ᶠn. t. h., A. For Iuini, B reads Ianuarii. ᵍ¯ᵍ 74 a, t. m., n. t. h., A; om., B. ʰ¯ʰ Placed overhead; portion being cut away in trimming the edge, (A) MS.

---

have had any connexion with the Sinnachs, or Foxes, chiefs of Teffia, in Westmeath " (O'D. iii. 611).

[1358] ¹ *1355*=1358 of the *A.L.C.*

² *Bishop Ua Dubda.*—William of Killala. By a rare exception, the patronymic is given in the Bull of his appointment. After the death of O'Lahiff ([1343], *supra*), one portion of the Chapter chose James Birmingham, canon and priest; the other, William O'Dowda, canon and acolyte. The former assented to his election; the latter, holding himself indifferent and reasonably anticipating, what the event veri-fied, that James would get himself consecrated by Malachy (Mac

ANNALS OF ULSTER. 507

Kalends of Jan. on [2nd] feria, [18th] of the moon, A.D. 1355[1][-8]. Domnall Ua hEghra, king of Luighni, died about Easter.—Maghnus Mag Uidhir (namely, son of Aedh the Red) was killed (on the 12th of the Kalends of May [April 20]) by the Clann-Cathmhail.—Concobur Ua hAinlidhe, chief of Cenel-Dobtha died.—Great defeat was inflicted by Aedh Ua Neill on the Oirgialla and on the Fir-Manach. Aedh Mac Caba was killed therein, and the son of the bishop Ua Dubda[2] and many other persons [were slain therein].—Great defeat was inflicted by Ua Mordha on the Foreigners of Ath-cliath, and twelve score were slain of them.—A great shower came in that Summer in Cairbre and not less[3] than a very ripe [full-grown] apple was every stone of them.—Brian Mac Cathmail,[4] bishop of Oirgialla, rested in Christ.—Jenkin Mac Uidhilin, one fit to be Constable of the Fifth of Ulster, died.—The son of Andrew Mac Feorais [Birmingham] died. — Toirdelbach, son of Aedh Ua Neill of the Wood, was slain on the 5th of the Kalends of June [May 28]. [1358]

(A great[1] foray-hosting was made by Ua Neill (namely, by Aodh Mor, son of Toirdelbach) into Tir-Conaill, whereby were reckoned [to be driven off] seventeen herds of cattle chattel, besides sheep and goats and swine and three score choice steeds of their steeds. And their hostages [came] in the rear of the preys, A.D. 1355). (1355)

Hugh), the metropolitan of Tuam, referred the matter to the Curia.

During the proceedings that ensued, bishop Birmingham died in attendance, and O'Dowda, himself likewise present and promoted to the diaconate in the interim, was appointed to the see by Clement VI., June 26, 1346. (Theiner, p. 285.) He died in 1350 (*A. L. C.*)

[3] *Not less, etc.*—"Every stone thereof was not less than a crabb," Mageoghegan (1358).

[4] *Mac Cathmail.*—He succeeded Mac Casey as bishop of Clogher, [1356] note 6, *supra*.

(1355) [1] *A great, etc.*—Not given in the *A. L. C.*, Mageoghegan, or the *Four Masters*.

2 K 2

508 ανηαία υlαοη.

A 74a |Cal. 1an. [iii.ª] p., l. [xx.ix.ᵇ], Anno Domini M.° ccc.° L°
iii.°[ix°]. Cormac Mag Carrcaig, ri Oer-Muman,
d'ecᵈ.—Domnall, mac Taiδg [U]i Maξamna, mortuur
ert.—Aeδ, mac Concobuir Mic Aeδaga[i]n, adbur ruaδ¹
re breitemnur, d'éc.—Maiom mor (Maiom⁺ Actareanaiξᵉ) do tabairt do. Chatal óg, mac Catail [U]i
Concoδair, ra Act-renaiξ ar Conallcaiδ (idonⁱ, ar Seaan,
mac Concobuir hUi Domnaill 7ᶠ) Seaan hUa² Doċartaiξ, tairec Arda-Miδair 7 Eoξan Connactac 7 Toirrdelbac Mac Suiδne do ξabail le mac [U]i Con[c]obuir.
Mata Mag Samraδa[i]n, adbur tairiξ Tellca-Eacac,
do lot in la rin 7 a éξ 'g a tiξ rein. Riξi Tire-Conaill
do ξabail do mac [U]i Concobuir.—Donncaδ Mag Uiδir
do marbaδ le mac Duinoᵍ (idonʳ, Arogal oξˢ), mic Flaitbertaiξ Meg Uiδir (7ʰ la hArt, mac Flaitbertaiξᵏ).—
Magnurˡ Meblac hUa Domnaill do ξabail Tire-Conaill
inᵗ bliaδain ri 7 ξan ξairm riξ rairʲ.—Catalᵏ boδur,
mac Catail [U]i Ruairc, do marbaδ ar a caξaδ cetna.
Ocur [e rein 7] Mael-Seclainn hUa² ξairmleξaiδˢ [do]
comtuitim re ceile.—Muircertac, mac Tomair [U]i
Fhloind, adbur riξ hUa²-Tuirtri, do marbaδ a rell
d'Aeδ, mac Uriain, mic Aeδa buiδe [U]i Neill.—Murċaδ óg Mac Matξamna, adbur riξ Corco-δairrinn, do
marbaδ le Sil-mU[r]iain.—Urian Mac Donncaiδ,
B 71d adbur riξ hUa²-nOilella, | do marbaδ do Mac Senca
d'oirect [U]i ξaδraⁱ.— Haenri,ᵐ mac Uilliug, mic
Ricairδ, d'eξ.ᵐ

A.D. 1356. ¹-ξ, A. ²O, A. ³n-Ouinn, A. ⁴an, B. ⁵-leoaiξ (metathesis of ξ and o), B. ª .iiii., A, R. ᵇ xiii., A, B. ᶜ 1359, B. ᵈ After
this word, Aeδ (the first word of the third entry) was placed, but deleted
afterwards, B. ᵉ⁻ᶠ l. m. t. h., A, B. Some of the letters are cut away in
B. ᶠ⁻ᶠ itl, t. h., A. In B, the text is: ra Act-reanaiξ, idon, ar Sheaan,
mac Concobuir hUi Domnaill 7 ar Conallaiδ. Seaan, .. Close to
Ath-seanaigh, that is, on John, son of Concobur Ua Domnaill and on the
Conailli. John,|etc. ᵍ⁻ᵍ itl., t. h., A; in text, after Meg Uiδir, B. ʰ⁻ʰ itl.,
t. h., A; text, B. ⁱ⁻ⁱ l. m., t. h., A; text, B. ʲ om., B. ᵏ The order in
B is: Catal-Donncaδ-Magnur. ˡ idon, in bliaδain ri—namely, this
year—added, B. ᵐ⁻ᵐ om., B.

Kalends of Jan. on [3rd] feria, [29th] of the moon, A.D. 1356¹[-9]. Cormac Mag Carthaigh, king of Desmond, died.—Domnall, son of Tadhg Ua Mathgamna, died.—Aedh son of Concobur Mac Aedhaga[i]n, who was² to be chief professor of jurisprudence, died. A great defeat (the defeat of Ath-seanaigh) was inflicted by Cathal junior, son of Cathal Ua Concobhuir, near Ath-senaigh on the Conailli: (namely, on John, son of Concobar Ua Domnaill and) John Ua Dochartaigh, chief of Ard-Midhair and Eogan³ the Connacian and Toirdelbach Mac Suibhne were taken prisoners by the son of Ua Concobuir. Matthew Mag Samradha[i]n, who was to be chief of Tellach-Eachach, was [mortally] injured that day and died at his own house. The kingship⁴ of Tir-Connaill was taken by the son of Ua Concobuir.—Donnchadh Mag Uidhir was killed by the son of Donn (namely, Ardgal junior), son of Flaithbertach Mag Uidhir (and by Art, son of Flaithbertach).—Maghnus Ua Domnaill the Guileful took the kingship of Tir-Conaill this year, but without the title of king [being bestowed] upon him.—Cathal the Deaf, son of Cathal Ua Ruairc, was slain in the same war. And⁵ he and Mail-Shechlainn Ua Gairmleghaidh fell by one another.—Muircertach, son of Thomas Ua Floinn, who was to be king of Ui-Tuirtri, was slain in treachery by Aedh, son of Brian, son of Aedh Ua Neill the Tawny.—Murchadh Mac Mathgamna junior, who was to be king of Corco-Baiscinn, was killed by the Sil-Briain.—Brian Mac Donnchaidh, who was to be king of Ui-Oillella, was killed by Mac Sencha of the sept⁶ of O'Gadhra.—Henry, son of Ulick, son of Richard [de Burgh], died.

[1359]

[1359] ¹ *1356* = 1359 of the *A.L.C.*
² *Who was, etc.*—Literally, *material of a chief professor.* For the *suadh*, see O'Curry, *Man. and Cust.* iii. 510.
³ *Eogan.*—Mac Sweeney. He was called the Connacian from having been fostered in Connaught.
⁴ *The kingship—Ua Concobuir.—*

"The Four Masters, who had the Annals of Ulster before them, have suppressed this passage, thinking that it would derogate from the glory of the O'Donnells!" (O'D. iii. 616).
⁵ *And.*—Supply: his death took place thus:
⁶ *Sept. — Oirecht*: whence the

510

[b͟r.] Kal. Ian. [1111.ᵃ] f., l. [x.ᵇ], Anno Domini M.º ccc.º L.º uııı.ºᶜ[-lx.º] Maelruanaiġ,¹ mac Ġille muinelaiġh [U]h baiġill, d'éc.—Sar Roibert Sabair d'eg.—Amlaim,ᵈ mac Serraiġ Meg Raġnaill, do marbaḋᵈ.—Loirceí² mora irın³ aimrir cetna, ıdon, baile Rora-Comain 7 Daim-ínır 7 Sliġeċ 7 Mainırtır Lera-ġabail 7 Fiġnaċ 7 Druim-liar.—Seaan, mac Ġılla-Crırt [U]h Ruairc, do marbaḋ la hAeḋ Mac Dorċaıḋ.—Diarmait O hAinliḋe, d'éc.—Primaitᵈ Arda-Maċa, fer-ınaitᵈ Patraiġᵈ, quieuit ın [Chrırto].—Ferġal,ᵈ mac Serraiġ Meg Raġnaill; Caċal, mac ın caiċ, do marbaḋ.—Seaan, mac Simuġ Mic Uıḋılın, do marbaḋᵈ.—Naemuġ hUaᵉ Duibġenna[ı]n d'eg.—Diarmait,ᵈ mac Donnċaḋa rıabaıġ Mıc Diarmata, do marbaḋ le Caċal og, mac Caċail [U]h Concobuirᵈ.—Inġen Toirrdelbaıġ [U]h Concobuir, ben Ferġail [U]h Raiġıllaıġ, do marbaḋ d'ergur.—Mac ruġ Saxan do ċeċt ıᶠ n-Erinn.—Ġılla-na-naem O Connmaiḋ, ollam Tuad-Muman, ıdonᶜ, re tımpanaċt,ᶜ d'éġ.—Maċġamaın Ġallta Mag Uıḋir, ıdon,ᵈ mac ... ᵈᵈmortuur ert reftimoᵈ Kalendar Aprilirᵈ.

A 74b Kal. Ian. [uı.ᵃ] f., l. [xx.ᵇ] Anno Domini M.º ccc.º L.º uıııı.ºᶜ[-lx.º 1.º] Beiniḋeċtᵈ O Moċa[ı]n, oirċınneċ Cille-

A.D. 1357. ¹ Maol-ḋ, B. ²-rce, A. ³ ran, B. ⁴—mraıt, B. ⁵ O, A. ⁶ a, A.— ᵃ.uı., A, B. ᵇ .xuıı., A, B. ᶜ 1360, B. ᵈ⁻ᵈ om., B. ᵉ⁺l m. t. h., A; text, with ıdon—*namely*—om., B. ᶠ A blank= space for 14 letters left by scribe, A; no lacuna in B.

A.D. 1358. ᵃ.uıı., A, B. ᵇ.u., A, B. ᶜ 1361. B. ᵈ The order of this and the following entry is reversed in B.

Hiberno-Latin, *de Iraghto suo* (of their sept), in the Patent Roll of 32 Ed. III. (Grace, p. 148, note n.)

[1360] ¹ *1357* = 1360 of the *A. L. C.*

² *Savage*.—Grace gives his obit and eulogium at 1360. He was buried in the Dominican House of Coleraine. The textual A.D. is thus three years in advance.

³ *Slain*.—O'Donovan, by an oversight, has "died" (iii. 617).

⁴ *Happened*.—Accidentally.

⁵ *Primate*.—Richard Fitz Ralph. On the death of David Mageraghty in [1346], *supra*, being then dean of Lichfield, he was unanimously nominated by the Chapter of Armagh and appointed by Clement VI., July 31, 1346. (Theiner, p. 286). He died in the Curia (at Avignon), Dec. 16, 1360. For a summary of his energetic life and

Kalends of Jan. on [4th] feria [10th] of the moon, A.D. [1360 Bis.] 1357¹[-60]. Maelruanaigh, son of the [Wry-]necked Gillie Ua Baighill, died.—Sir Robert Savage² died.—Amlaim, son of Geoffrey Mag Raghnaill, was slain.³—Great burnings [happened⁴] at the same time, namely, [those of] the town of Ros-Comain and Daim-inis and Sligech and the Monastery of Lis-gabail and Fighnach and Druim-lias.—John, son of Gilla-Crist Ua Ruairc, was slain by Aedh Mac Dorchaidh.—Diarmait O'hAinlidhe died.—The Primate⁵ of Ard-Macha, vicar of [St.] Patrick, rested in Christ.—Ferghal⁶ son of Geoffrey Mag Raghnaill; Cathal, son of the Blind [Mag Raghnaill], were slain.—John, son of Simug Mac Uidhilin, was killed.—Naemug Ua Duibgenne[i]n died. — Diarmait, son of Donnchadh Mac Diarmata the Grey, was killed by Cathal junior, son of Cathal Ua Concobuir.—The daughter of Toirdelbach Ua Concobuir, wife of Ferghal Ua Raighillaigh, was killed by a fall.—The son⁷ of the king of the Saxons came into Ireland.—Gilla-na-naem O'Conmaidh, cllam of Thomond, namely, iu timpan⁸-playing, died.—Mathgamain Mag Uidhir the Foreigner, namely, son . . , died on the 7th of the Kalends of April [March 26].

Kalends of Jan. on [6th] feria, [21st] of the moon, A.D. [1361] 1358¹[-61]. Benedict O'Mocha[i]n, herenagh of Cell-

---

memorable controversy with the Mendicant Orders, see Bellesheim: *Geschichte der Kathol. Kirche in Irland*, I. 520 sq.

⁶ *Ferghal.*—The *A. L. C.* state he died a natural death. This, in all probability, is correct. Had he been slain, his name would have been included with that of his brother in the third obit of this year.

⁷ *Son.*—Lionel, duke of Clarence, third son of Edward III. According to Grace, he landed, Sept. 15, 1361, with his wife, Elizabeth (only child of William de Burgh, who was slain [1333], *supra*).

⁸ *Timpan.*—See 1177, note 7, *supra*.

[1361] ¹ *1358*=1361 of the *A. L. C.*

Aṫracṫ, in Chpipṫo quieuiṫ.—Apt Mac Muṗcaḋa, ṗi
Laiġen | 7 Domnall ṗiabaċ, aḋḃup ṗiġ Laiġen, a n-
ġaḃail a ḟell do mac ṗiġ Saxan 'n-a ṫiġ ḟein 7 a' ṫeṗoail
aiġe'.—Copmac ballaċ hUa¹ Mail[-Sh]eċlainn, ṗi Miḋe,
d'éġ.—Donnċaḋ hUa¹ Loċlainn, ṗi Copcumṗuaḋ², d'éġ.—
Nicol' O Ḟinaċṫa d'éc.—Tomalṫaċ Mac Neill do
maṗḃaḋ'.—Saṗ Remunn a ḃuṗc d'eġ.—Duḃóġ, inġen
Aeḋa Meġ Uiḋiṗ, ben Con-Chonnaċṫ, mic Pilib Meġ
Mhaṫġamna, d'eġ in' bliaḋain ṗi'.—Cluiċe in ṗiġ do
ḃeiṫ co ṫiuġ iṗin bliaḋain ṗin¹ i³ n-Eṗinn. Ṗiṗḋeṗḋ
Saḋaiṗ d'ec ḋé.—Caṫal 7 Muiṗceṗṫaċ, da mac Aeḋa,
mic Eoġain, d'éc.—Remunn, mac Ḃuṗcaiḋ in Muine,
d'éc.—Uaiṫeṗ Sḋonḋun d'eġ.—Ġilliḃeṗṫ,' mac Mailiṗ,
d'eġ.'—Tomaṡ Maġ Ṫiġeṗna[i]n, ṫaiṗeċ Tellaiġ-Dun-
ċaḋa, d'eġ.—Tuaṫal hUa³ Maille d'eġ.

(Oenġuṡ' hUa Caiṗṗṡi moṗṫuuṗ eṗṫ Nonis Maṗcii.')

Kal. Ian. [ui]ṡ. ḟ., L [ii.ᵃ], Anno Domini M.° ccc.° L°
ix.°ᵇ [-lx.° ii.°] Eoġan ḟinn hUa¹ Conċoḃuiṗ, mac ṗiġ
Connaċṫ [d'heġ].—Tomalṫaċ hUa¹ Biṗn d'ec.—Eoġan
hUa¹ Maille 7 Diaṗmaiṫ, a mac, d'ec.—Maelṗuanaiġ
O Duḃḋa d'eġ.—Inġen hUi Maille, ben Domnaill [U]i
Duḃḋa [d'ec].—Domnall, mac Ruaiḋṗi [U]i Chellaiġ,

A.D. 1358. ¹ O, A. ² —aġ, A. ³ a, B. * om. A. ¹¹ a n-eġ iṗin laim
ṗin—they died (lit.: their death [took place]) in that captivity, B, ᵍ⁻ᵍ om.,
B. ʰ⁻ʰ Placed after n-Eṗinn (with ṗi—this, for ṗin—that), B. ᴴ n. t.b.,
A; om., B.

A.D. 1359. ¹ O, A. ᵃ .ui., A, B. ᵇ 1362, B.

---

² *Cell-Athracht*[a]. — Church of [St.] Athracht: founded by St. Patrick for the patron saint (*Tripartite Life*, Part II.), who received the veil from his hand (*ib.* and the Book of Armagh, fol. 13a). It is now called Killaraght, "a parish in the bar. of Coolavin, in the south of co. Sligo, where the memory of this virgin is still held in great veneration" (O'D. iii. §19).

² *Domnall.* — Mac Murchadha (Mac Murrough). "Being sinisterly taken by the king of England's son in his house, died prisoners with him," Mageoghegan (1361).

⁴ *King's Game.*—An epidemic, the

Athracht[a]², rested in Christ.—Art Mac Murchadha, [1361] king of Leinster and Domnall³ the Swarthy, who was to be king of Leinster, were captured in treachery by the son of the king of the Saxons in his own house, and they perished with him.—Cormac Ua Mail[-Sh]echlainn the Freckled, king of Meath, died.—Donnchadh Ua Lochlainn, king of Corcumruadh, died.—Nicholas O'Finachta died.—Tomaltach Mac Neill was killed.—Sir Redmond de Burgh died.—Dubog, daughter of Aedh Mag Uidhir, wife of Cu-Connacht, son of Philip Mag Mathgamna, died this year.—The King's Game⁴ was rife⁵ in this year in Ireland. Richard Savage died thereof.—Cathal and Muircertach, two sons of Aedh, son of Eogan,⁶ died.—Redmond, son of de Burgh of the Muine, died.—Walter Stanton died.—Gilbert, son of Meyler,⁷ died.—Thomas Mag Tigerna[i]n, chief of Tellach-Dunchadha, died.—Tuathal Ua Maille died.

(Oengus¹ Ua Cairpri died on the Nones [7th] of March.) (1358)

Kalends of Jan. on [7th] feria, [2nd] of the moon, A.D. [1362] 1359¹[-62]. Eogan Ua Conchobuir the Fair, son of the king of Connacht, died.—Tomaltach Ua Birn died.—Eogan Ua Maille and his son died.—Maelruanaigh O'Dubda died.²—The daughter of Ua Maille, wife of Domnall Ua Dubhda, died.—Domnall, son of Ruaidhri

---

nature of which is unknown. The native name apparently arose from the common belief that, like the king's evil, the disease was curable by royal touch.

⁵ *Rife.*—Literally, *thickly.*

⁶ *Eogan.*—O'Conor.

⁷ *Meyler.*—Probably, as the editor of the *A. L. C.* suggests (ii. 22), Meyler Mac Goisdelbh, or Mac Costelloe, in which family Gilbert and Meyler were names frequently employed.

(1358) ¹ *Oengus, etc.*—This obit I have not found elsewhere.

[1362] ¹ *1359* = 1362 of the *A. L. C.*

² *Died.*—His wife, the daughter of Mac Donough, died this year likewise, *A. L. C.*

d'eg.—Niall Mag Samraḋa[i]n, taireċ Tellaiġ-Eaċaċ, d'eg.—Aengur' Mac-in-Oglaiċ, oircinneċ Cille-oiriḋ, quieuit in [Chrirto]ᵃ.—Caṫal óg, mac Caṫail [U]i Concobuir, in° trer la iar Samain' d'ég.—Murċaḋ' Manaċ Mac Taiḋg quieuit in [Chrirto].—Ḋicair Iméa, ioon, O ferguṙa, d'eg.—Diarmait, mac Seaain, taireċ Muinntiri-hAngaile, d'éc.—Cairḃri hUa¹ Cuinn, taireċ Muinntiri-Gillga[i]n, d'eg.—Taḋg, mac Concobuir U[i] Ḃriain, do marḃaḋ do Clainn-Cuilen.— | Pilibᵈ, mac Rouilḃ moir Meg Maṫgamna, ri Oirgiall, d'hegᵈ.

Kal. Ian. [1.ᵃ] f., L [x.iii.,ᵇ] Anno Domini M.° ccc.° lx.°[-iii.°] Muirċertaċ ruaḋ, mac Domnaill Irrair, do marḃaḋ le mac Maġnura.—Maġnur Eoganaċ hUa¹ Domnaill d'ec.—Aeḋ (ruaḋᵈ) Mag Uiḋir, ri fer-Manaċ, d'eg in* bliaḋain ri*.—Maġnur, mac Aeḋa [U]i Domnaill, aḋbur riġ Cene[oi]l-Conaill, do marḃaḋ le Maġnur, mac Caṫail [U]i Choncobuir.—Taḋg Mac Con[Sh]nama, taireċ Muinntiri-Cinaeṫa, do' lot 7 do ġaḃail' le Caṫal, mac Aeḋa Ḃreirniġ h[U]i* Concobuir' 7ˢ a éc irin laim rin*.—Caiterfina, inġen [U]i Fhergail, | ben [U]i Raiġillaiġ, d'ec.—Caṫal Mac Donnċaḋ do marḃaḋ la luċt Muiġi-Luirg.—Gaeṫ mor irin bliaḋain rinʰ dobrir tiġi 7 tempaill, dobaiṫ longa 7 artraiġi imda.

A.D. 1359. ᶜ⁻ᶜ om., B. ᵈ⁻ᵈ r. m., t. h., A; text, B.
A.D. 1360. ¹ O, A. ᵃ·ᵢᵢ., A, B. ᵇ ˣˣ·ᵘᶦᶦ·, A, B. ᶜ 1363, B. ᵈ itl., n. t. h., A; text, B. ᵉ⁻ᵉ om., A. ᶠ⁻ᶠ do marḃaḋ—was killed, B. ᵍ⁻ᵍ om., B. ʰ om., B.

ᵃ *Mac-in-oglaich.—Son of the young warrior.*—From two other entries in the *Four Masters* [1333, 1416], it may be concluded that the herenachy of Cell-oiridh (Killerry, bar. Tirerrill, co. Sligo) was hereditary in the family of Mac-in-Ogley.

ᵈ *Died.*—In Sligo, of the plague (doubtless that mentioned under the previous year), *A. L. C.*

Ua Cellaigh, died.—Niall Mag Samradha[i]n, chief of [1362] Tellach-Eathach, died.—Aengus Mac-in-oglaich,[3] herenagh of Cell-oiridh, rested in Christ.—Cathal junior, son of Cathal Ua Concobuir, died[4] the third day after November-Day.—Murchadh Mac Taidhg, the monk, rested in Christ.—The Vicar of Imaidh,[5] namely, O'Ferghusa, died.—Diarmait, son of John,[6] chief of the Muinter-hAnghaile, died.—Cormac Ua Cuinn, chief of Muinter-Gillga[i]n, died.—Tadhg, son of Concobur[7] Ua Briain, was slain by the Clann-Cuilen.—Philip, son of Ralph Mor Mag Mathgamna, king of Oirgialla, died.

Kalends of Jan. on [1st] feria, [13th] of the moon, [1363] A.D. 1360[1][-3]. Muircertach the Red, son of Domnall[2] of Irras, was slain by the son of Maghnus.[2]—Maghnus Ua Domnaill of [Tir-]Eoga[i]n[3] died.—Aedh Mag Uidhir (the Red), king of Fir-Manach, died this year.—Maghnus, son of Aedh Ua Domnaill, one who was to be king of Tir-Conaill, was slain by Maghnus, son of Cathal Ua Concobuir.—Tadhg Mac Con[Sh]nama, chief of Muinter-Cinaetha, was injured and taken prisoner by Cathal, son of Aedh Ua Conchobuir the Brefnian, and he died in that custody.—Catherine, daughter of Ua Ferghail, wife of Ua Raighillaigh, died.—Cathal Mac Donnchaidh was slain by the people of Magh-Luirg.—Great wind in that year that broke houses and churches [and] sank[4] many craft and barks.

---

[5] *Imaidh.*—The island of Omey off Connemara. See O'Donovan's note (iii. 622).

[6] *John.*—O'Farrell.

[7] *Concobur.*—Conor, son of Turlough, king of Thomond, who died [1306], *supra.*

[1363] [1] *1360*=1363 of the *A.L.C.*

[2] *Domnall, Maghnus* —O'Conor.

[3] [*Tir-*]*Eoga*[*i*]*n.*—An adjective in the original. O'Donnell was so called from having been fostered in Tyrone.

[4] *Sank.*—Literally, *drowned.*

[bιr.] Kal. Ian. [11.ᵃ] p., l. [xx.1111.ᵇ] Anno Domini M.° ccc.ᶜᶜ lx.° 1.°[-1111.°] Diarmait hUa¹ briain, ri Tuad-Muman, d'ec.—Mael[-Sh]eclainn hUa¹ Fergail, tairec Muinn- tire-hAngaile, d'éc.—Domnall, mac Ruaidri [U]i Chellaig, adbur rig hUa¹-Maine, d'ec.—Ingin baiter a burc, ben Aeda, mic Feidlimid, d'éc.—Derbail, ingen in errois [U]i Domnaill, ben Meg Uidir (idon⁴, Aeda ruaid Meg Uidir ᵈ), d'ég.—Aed hUa¹ Neill, in t-aen ri ir ferr tainic² do Let Cuinn irin aimrir n-deigenaig i n-airdrigi Coicid Ulad, d'ecc in° bliadain [ri]ᵉ.—Dom- nall Mag Uidir, tigerna Clainni-Fergaile, mortuur ert.—Gilla-na-naem O Duidaboirenn, ollam breite- man Corcumruad [U]i Loclainn, d'éc².—bran hUa¹ brain, rai timpanaig³, d'eg.—Diarmait hUa¹ Sgingin, rgelaigi mait 7 rendaid, d'eg'.—Airfric, ingen briain [U]i Raigillaig, ben briain Meg Tigernain, d'eg rect- muin⁶ re Cairc. Ocur nirr'oinded ar a mait[i]ur co haimrir a hoidedaᵉ.

Kal. Ian. [1111.ᵃ] p., l. [u.ᵇ], Anno Domini M.° ccc.ᶜ lx.° 11.°ᶜ[-u.°] Ruaidri, mac Domnaill [U]i Neill do mar- bad do Mael[-Sh]eclainn, mac i[n]¹ girr, d'aen urcur roigdi.—Tomaltac, mac Murcada² [U]i Fhergail, d'eg. —Cogad mor irin bliadain ri³ eter Clainn-Goirdelb 7 Luigni᷇g 7ᵈ innraigid do denam do Clainn-Goirdelb ar

A.D. 1361. ¹ O, A. ²₋₁₅, B. ³rem—, A. ᵃ 1111, A, B. ᵇ uιιι., A, B. This epact is not found in the Decemnovennal cycle. ᶜ 1364, B. ᵈ⁻ᵈ itl, t. h., B; om., A. ᵉᵉom., A. ᶠmortuur ert, B. ᵍᵍom., B.

A.D. 1362. ¹ a[n], B. ²-cad, A. ⁻³om., B. ᵃ u., A, B. ᵇ xιx. (obtained by adding 11 to the previous textual epact and not found in the Cycle of Nineteen), A, B. ᶜ 1365, B. ᵈᵈom., B.

[1364] ¹ *1361*=1364 of the *A. L.* C.
² *Diarmait.*—Son of Turlough, who died in [1306], *supra.* He succeeded Brian (al. [1350] *supra*) in the kingship of Thomond.

Kalends of Jan. on [2nd] feria, [24th] of the moon, [1364 Bis.] A.D. 1361¹[-4.] Diarmait ²Ua Briain, king of Thomond, died.—Mael[-Sh]echlainn Ua Ferghail, chief of Muinter-hAngaile, died.—Domnall, son of Ruaidhri Ua Cellaigh, one who was to be king of Ui-Maine, died.—The daughter of Walter de Burgh, wife of Aedh, son of Feidhlimidh,³ died.—Derbail, daughter of the bishop Ua Domnaill,⁴ wife of Mag Uidhir (namely, of Aedh Mag Uidhir the Red), died.—Aedh Ua Neill, the best king of the Half of Conn that came in the late time into the kingship of the Fifth of Ulster, died this year.—Domnall Mag Uidhir, lord of Clann-Fergaile, died.—Gilla-na-naem O'Duibhdaboirenn, chief judge of Corcumruadh of Ua Lochlainn,⁵ died.—Bran Ua Braic, an eminent timpanist, died.—Diarmait Ua Sgingin, a good historian and antiquary, died.—Aiffric, daughter of Brian Ua Raighillaigh, wife of Brian Mag Tigernain, died a week before Easter.⁶ And there was no stint to her goodness up to the time of her decease.

Kalends of Jan. on [4th] feria, [5th] of the moon, [1365] A.D. 1362¹[-5]. Ruaidhri, son of Domnall Ua Neill, was killed by Mael[-Sh]echlainn, son of the Dwarf,² with one shot of an arrow.—Tomaltach, son of Murchadh Ua Ferghail, died.—Great war in this year between the Clann-Goisdelb and the Luighni and an attack was made

---

³ *Feidhlimidh.*—O'Conor.

⁴ *Bishop Ua Domnaill.*—Thomas of Raphoe, who died in [1337], *supra*.

⁵ *Corcumruadh of Ua Lochlainn.* —The barony of Burren, so called to distinguish it from the Corcumruadh of O'Conor, bar. of Corcumroe, co. Clare. (See *Book of Rights*, p. 65, note z.) The brehon of the latter was O'Daly.

⁶ *Week before Easter.*—Sunday, March 17, Easter (XVI. F) falling on March 24.

[1365] ¹ *1362* = 1365 of the *A. L. C.*

² *Son of the Dwarf.*—According to the *A. L. C.*, he belonged to the family of Mac Cathmail (Mac Cawell, chiefs of Cenel-Feradaigh, bar. of Clogher, co. Tyrone).

Luiʒnecaiḃ[d]. Erbaiḋ anboil 7[d] oiṫ oeʒoaine oo ṫabairt ar Luiʒnecaiḃ oo'n[e] toirc rin[a]: ioon[f], reirer mac riʒ oo maiṫiḃ Muinntiri-heʒra oo marbaḋ ra Cormac hUa[d] n-eaʒra.—Aoam[s] hUa riala[i]n mortuur ert[t].—Inoroiʒiḃ[d] oo ṫenum o'Aeḋ Mac Diarmata ar Muinntir-eolu[i]r. Cinta mora 7 creca aiḃbli oo ṫenam ar eoluraċaiḃ oo'n oul rin: noċur creca ʒan cairecaiḃ na creca rin; uair oo marbaḋ eċta uairli

A 74d
anboile umporan, ra'n aerirer | tiʒi n-aiḋeḋ ˙coitcinn ir rerr oo bi i Connaċtaiḃ 'n-a aimrir, ioon, ra Cormac, mac Diarmata ruaiḋ 7 ra ḃa mac Tomaltaiʒ [U]i ḃirn. Diarmait Mac Diarmata 7 Maelruanaiʒ, mac Donnċaḋa riabaiʒ, oo ʒabail ar a creiċ cetna[d].—reiḋ- limiḋ in éiniʒ hUa[d] Concobuir, rí Corcumruaḋ, ioon[d], mac Domnaill [U]i Concobuir, rai ʒan aiṫḃi n-éiniʒ[d], o'éc in[d] bliaḋain rin[d].—ḃrian, mac Maṫa Illeʒ Tiʒerna[i]n, mac tairiʒ ra[a] mó aʒ 7 oirroercur[b], reiċem[d] coitcinn im biaḋ 7 im eallaċ[d], o'éʒ[i] im[d] reil 8anʒ 8eaa[i]n in bliaḋain rin[d], amail aoḃert:[5]

Rann[j]: ḃrian Maʒ Tiʒerna[i]n na trer,
Re [a] einec nír' coir coimer:
Relean ʒan ric an feile,
ḃuo neam criċ a ċaṫreime.

B 72b
ḃrian, mac Aeḋa Meʒ Matʒamna, oo ʒabail riʒi n-Oirʒiall | 7 cleamnur 7 caraorar o'ray oó ar 8omarliʒ, mac eoin ouiḃ Mic Domnaill, ar Conroabla

A.D. 1362. [d]O, A. [a]rob—, B. [e-e]in tan rin—*that time*, B. [f]om., A. [s-t]om., A. [h-h]lan o'aḋ 7 o'oirroercur—*full of prosperity and of pre-eminence*, B. [i]verb is placed after Tiʒernain in B. [j]om., B.

---

[3] *Cormac.*—Heir-presumptive to the lordship of Luighni (Leyney, the territory of the O'Haras, co. Sligo).

[4] *Muinter-Eoluis.*—Plural adjec-tival from of *Eolus* in the original.

[5] *Numbers.*—Literally, *deeds*; by metonymy for the slain.

[h] *Diarmait, Donnchadh.*—Mac Dermot.

by the Clann-Goisdelb on the Luighni. Excessive loss and destruction of good persons was inflicted on the Luighni on that expedition : namely, six sons of kings of the nobles of Muinter-hEghra were slain under Cormac[3] Ua Eaghra.—Adam Ua Fiala[i]n died.—An attack was made by Aedh Mac Diarmata on the Muinter-Eolu[i]s. Great wrongs and excessive preys were made on the [Muinter-]Eoluis[4] on that occasion. [But] they were not forays without retaliations, those forays; for there were slain enormous numbers[5] of nobles about them, under the best man for a general house of guests that was in Connacht in his time, to wit, under Cormac, son of Diarmait[5a] the Red and under the two sons of Tomaltach[6] Ua Birn. Diarmait Mac Diarmata and Maelruanaigh, son of Donnchadh[5a] the Swarthy, were taken prisoners on the same foray.—Feidhlimidh Ua Concobuir of the Hospitality, king of Corcumruadh,[7] that is, son of Domnall Ua Concobuir, distinguished without ebb of hospitality, died that year.—Brian, son of Matthew Mag Tigerna[i]n, the son of a chief of greatest felicity and pre-eminence, general patron respecting food and cattle, died about the feast of Saint James [July 25] that year, as [the poet] said :

Stanza[8] : Brian Mag Tigernain of the contests,
With his hospitality comparison were not just :
He practised hospitality without reward,
Heaven was the end of his battle-career.

Brian, son of Aedh Mag Mathgamna, took the kingship of Oirghialla and marriage-alliance and friendship were contracted by him with Somairle, son of John Mac

[1365]

---

[6] *Tomaltach.* — O'Donovan, by oversight, prints "Cormac" (*F. M.* iii. 629).

[7] *Corcumruadh.* — That is, the moiety co-extensive with the present barony of Corcomroe. *Cf.* [1364], note 5.

[8] *Stanza.*—The metre is *Debide.*

520   annala ulaoh.

Coiciṫ Ulaṫ, co tuc fair ingin [U]i Raiġillaiġ do Léġan 7 co tuc fan a ingin fein dó. Ferr ar a aiṫle rin co tuc cuiġi[k] i n-a teċ fein[k] é d'ol fina. Ocur mur do fail rin' an rin d'faġbail, ir e cuired fuair gur'iaḋ Brian fein a da laim tairir 7 a ġabail co doċraċ, domiaḋaċ 7 a ċoġbail amaċ—7 uaċaḋ dia[l] ṁuinntir i n-a focair—gur'craḃleḋ 7 gur'cengleḋ a ċora 7 a lama d'a ċeile 7 gur'cuireḋ a[e] loċ[e] é. Ocur ni rer a rġela o rin amaċ. Do l[e]iġeḋ ro'n tir 7 gaċ inaḋ a friċ a muinnter, do marbaḋ 7 do hairġeḋ iat. Mairġ doman 7 talam 7 uirci i n-ar'folċeḋ in t-raerclann foċeneoil, idon, aobur riġ Innri-Ġall, idon[7], mac Eoin duiḃ, mic Alaxandair. Amail adbert:

Rann' : In loċ[m] ra ar'cuireḋ[m] cenn caiċ[8],
    Somairle na fleġ rinnaiṫ,
    Eter gnai 7 glór ir ġen,
    Ór ir rin rai do roilġeḋ.

Noċor olc gan inneaċuḋ re haṫġairit in t-olc rin. Uair ro tinoil Domnall, mac Aeḋa hUi Neill 7 Toirrdelbaċ hUa[4] Neill 7 tucadar comaḋa mora 7 braṫairri 7 riċcain do clainn Aeḋa buiḋe [U]i Neill, idon, do Brian, mac Enri [U]i Neill, co n-a braiṫriḃ. Ocur tainic fór irin coimtinol cetna[n] Niall, mac Murċaḋa, mic Murċaḋa ṁoir Mheġ Maṫġamna, derbraṫair maṫar Mic Dom-

A.D. 1362. [ee] illoċ, B. [7] om., A. [8] -ġ, B. [k-k] ċuiġi fein, dia tiġ—*to himself, to his house,* B. [l] d'a (syncope for di a), A. [m-m] loċ 'n-a r' cuireḋ—*The lake in which was put,* B. [n] rin—*that,* B.

[9] *Forced him.*—Literally, put upon him.
[10] *Brian.*—Mageoghegan (1365), by a strange misapprehension, took the perpetrator to be Mac Donnell.
[11] *Wound.*—Literally, *tied.*
[12] *Bands were despatched.*—The original construction is impersonal: *it was let* [*loose*].
[13] *Innocent one.*—Literally, *head* [by synecdoche for the person] *of an innocent* [man]; a periphrasis employed to make the line heptasyllabic.

Domnaill the Black, [namely,] with the Constable of the Fifth of Ulster, so that he forced him [9] to abandon the daughter of Ua Raighillaigh and gave his own daughter to him. Shortly after that, he [Brian] [10] brought him to himself into his own house to drink wine. And when that person expected to obtain the wine, the bidding he got was that Brian himself wound [11] his two hands about him and he was seized rudely, contumeliously and carried out—and the few of his people [that were] in his company— so that his feet and hands were made fast and tied together and he was put into a lake. And tidings of him are not known from that out. Bands were despatched [12] throughout the country and wherever his people were found, they were slain and plundered. Woe the world and land and water wherein was submerged the noble, well-born offspring, to wit, one who was to be king of Insi-Gall [Hebrides], namely, the son of John the Black, son of Alexander. As [the poet] said : [1365]

Stanza [8]: This [is] the lake wherein was put an
    innocent one,[13]
  Somuirle of the sharp-pointed spears,
  Mid merriment and noise and laughter,
  For it is wine 'neath which he was submerged.

Not an evil without retribution [even] for a very short time was that evil. For Domnall, son of Aedh Ua Neill and Toirdelbach Ua Neill mustered and gave [14] large donatives and brotherhood and peace to the clan of Aedh Ua Neill the Tawny, namely, to Brian, son of Henry Ua Neill, together with his kinsmen. And there came likewise into that muster Niall, son of Murchadh, son of Murchadh Mor Mag Mathgamna; brother of the mother

---

[14] *Gave, etc.*—In order that the Clannaboy [*Clann-Aedha-buiḋhe*] and their chief, Brian O'Neill might unite with them in punishing Brian Mac Mahon.

naill 7 laiẽpiẋ Oipgiall eipiḃen.⁹ Ocuṗ ꞇangaḋuṗ ippoiḃe 1 Coiceḃ Ulaḃ ꞇo Clainn-Ḋomnaill, ṗa Coippḋelbaċ moṗ Mac n-Ḋomnaill 7 ṗa [a] mac ṗen, ṗa Alaxanḋaiṗ 7 ṗa mac Somaiṗli ṗein, iḋon, ṗa Eoin óg 7 ꞇucaḋuṗ ḋ'innṗaiẋiḃ Raẗa-ꞇulaċ iaꞇ, iḋon, longpoṗꞇ Mheg Maṫgamna 7 painic ṗabaḃ ṗompo 7 ḋo° ṗagaḋuṗ in baili° 7 ꞇucaḃ maiḋm imiṗce¹⁰ oṗṗa¹¹ 7 níṗ'hanaḃ ḋiḃ co ṗangaḋuṗ |

A 75a Loċ-Eiṗne guṗ'ꞇogbaḃ a cṗuiḃ 7 a ceṫṗa a n-ainṗeċꞇ a n-aiṗḋe le Ṗeṗaiḃ-Manaċ 7 leiṗin ṗluaẋ, guṗ'ḋibṗaigeḃ ḃṗián Mag Maṫgamna aṗꞇiṗᵇ amaċ a n-uċꞇ Muinn-ꞇiṗi-Mailmóṗḋa 7 ṗo gabaḃ a ben¹² 7 a ingen.—Cu-Connaċꞇ hUa⁴ Raiẋillaiẋ, ṗí ḃṗeiṗne, ḋo ṫul iṗna ḃṗai-ẗṗiḃ ḋ'a ḋeoin ṗein—ṗí ᵈ beoḋa, bṗiẋmuṗᵈ—7 an ṗiẋi ḋo ċaḃaiṗꞇ ḋo Ṗilibᵉ, ḋ'a ḋeṗbṗaẗaiṗ.—Eoċaiḃ, mac Coiṗṗ-ḋelbaiẋ Meg Maṫgamna, ḋo maṗbaḃ.

(An ṗ ṗeṗṗun O Congaile, iḋ eṗꞇ, ṗaiḋin, iḋon, oiṗci-ḋeaċuiṗ Roṗa-oiṗciṗ, moṗꞇu[u]ṗ eṗꞇ.)

|Cal. 1an. [u.ᵃ] ṗ., [Lᵇ x.ui.,ᵇ] Anno Ḋomini M.° ccc.° lx.° iii.°° [-ui.°] Caẗal, mac Aeḋa Ḃṗeiṗniẋ, mic Caẗail ṗuaiḃ 7 Maẋnuṗ og, a mac 7ᵈ Muiṗċeṗꞇaċ Mac [C]ail-ṗiḋocaiṗ 7 Muiṗgiṗ¹ hUa Maelaꞇuile 7 Ḋiaṗmaiḋ Mac Simoin 7 Ḋiaṗmaiḋ Mac gilla-ḃeṗaiẋ²ᵈ ḋo maṗbaḃ aᶜ ṗell,ᵉ ꞇeṗꞇioᶠ ꞇouṗ Manᵍ aṗʰ Sṗaẗ-Ṗeṗ-luiṗgⁱ le

A.D. 1362. ⁹eiṗein, B. ¹⁰-ceċ (the adj.), B ¹¹ oṗꞇa A. ¹²beam, A.
*-*ḋo ṗagbaḋ in baile ṗolam—*the place was left empty*, B. ᵖ-ᵖ aṗ an ꞇiṗ
—*from out the country*, B. ᑫ-ᑫ placed after ḋeṗbṗaẗaiṗ, B. ʳ-ʳn. ꞇ. h.,
A ; om., B.

A.D. 1363. ¹Muṗgeaṗ, A. ².Eaṗaiċ, A. ᵃ.ui., A, B. ᵇ-ᵇbl, A, B.
ᶜ1366, B. ᵈ-ᵈ partly itl., partly on c. m., t. h., A ; text, B. ᵉ-ᵉom., A.
ᶠ-ᶠ itl., t. h., B ; Man itl., t. h. (the scribe probably having forgotten to place it on text line), A. ᵍ-ᵍ itl., t. h., A. Placed after Ṗeṗaiḃ-Manaċ, B.

---

¹⁵ *Clann-Domnaill*.—The Mac Donnells of Antrim.

(1362) ¹ *The Parson, etc.*—Given at 1365 in the *Four Masters*.

[1366] ¹ *1363* = 1366 of the *A. L. C.*

² *Cathal*.—O'Conor.

of Mac Domnaill and half-king of Oirgialla was this [1366] person. And there came what was in the Fifth of Ulster of the Clann-Domnaill,[15] under Toirdelbach Mor Mac Domnaill and under his son, [namely,] under Alexander and under the son of Somairle himself, that is, under John junior and they betook themselves to attack Rath-tulach, that is, the fortress of Mag Mathgamna. And word came before them and they [the garrison] abandoned the place and defeat with loss of moveables was inflicted on them and they were not desisted from in pursuit until they reached Loch-Eirne, so that their chattel and their cattle were simultaneously seized completely by the Fir-Manach and by the [allied] host. Thus Brian Mag Mathgamna was expelled from out the country into the protection of Muinter-Mailmordha and his wife and his daughter were captured.—Cu-Connacht Ua Raighillaigh, king of Breifni, went into the Friars of his own will—a spirited, powerful king [was he]—and the kingship was given to Philip, [namely], to his brother.—Eochaidh, son of Toirdelbach Mag Mathgamna, was killed.

(The Parson [1] O'Congaile, that is, Paidin, namely, arch- (1362) deacon of Ros-orcir, died.)

Kalends of Jan. on [5th] feria, [16th] of the moon, [1366] A.D. 1363[1][-6]. Cathal, son of Aedh the Brefnian, son of Cathal[2] the Red and Maghnus junior, his son and Muircertach Mac Caelridocair and Maurice Ua Maelatuile and Diarmaid Mac Simoin and Diarmaid Mac Gilla-Beraigh[3] were killed in treachery, on the 3rd of the Ides [13th] of May,[4] on Srath-Fer-Luirg by the Fir-Manach. And

---

[3] *Gilla-Beraigh.*—See 1190, note 4, *supra*.

[4] *13th of May.*—It was the eve of Ascension Day in 1366.

Feraid-Manac 7 sreca aidbli do denum ar Clainn-
Muircertaig 7 ré do denam d'Feraid-Manac re
Muinntir-Ruairc 7 a faltana* do matam d'a ceile ar
olcaib re Clann-Muircertaig. Ocur mac Ruaidri do
gabail inaid Catail [U]i Concobuir in bliadain rin.¹

(A)

Imircí do denam le
Muinntir-Ruairc irin m-
Breifne i comdail Fer-
Manac 7 grer timcill do
denum do macaib-rig óg-
a[ib] Clainni-Muircertaig 7
do marbad uirre, tairec Dartraigi.

(B)

Catal Mag Flannčada,
| tairec Dartraigi, do
marbad le clann Muir-
certaig hUi Concobuir ar
greir oidče.
Catal Mag [Fh]lanncada
do marbad uirre, tairec Dartraigi.

Tinol¹ do Domnall hUa Neill 7 do Clainn-Domnaill,
idon, do Thoirrdelbac Mac Domnaill 7 d'Alaxandair
Mac Domnaill d'innrad Neill [U]i Neill. Ocur Mac
Cutmail do cur arsir amac doib 7 a dul rein d'innred
Neill [U]i Neill. Breit ar dered na n-imirced. Ocur
Ragnall, mac Alaxandair, oigri Clainni-Alaxandair,
do tect a hinnrid-gall fa'n am rin docum Neill [U]i
Neill. In da ceitirn do tecmail ar a ceile, idon, oirect Clainni-Domnaill. Ocur Ragnall docur dectai-
recta mar a roibe a bratair rein, idon, Toirrdelbac
7 a mac, idon, Alaxandair 7 a iaraid dó a n-onoir na
rinnrerecta 7 in braitrera gan tect 'n-a cenn. Ocur
gan aire do tabairt dó 7 nir'reced dó, act ro inn-
raigdur cum in ata ar a facadur Ragnall 7 tucadur
troid d'a ceile. Ocur do marbad mac Ragnaill ano

ᵇ faltanuy, B. ¹ om., B. ʰ om., B.

---

⁵ *An incursion, etc.*—The A entry is followed by the *Four Masters* (1366).

⁶ *Overtaken.*—The account in the *F. M.* adds that they were defeated and despoiled of their cattle by the

enormous preys were made on the Clann-Muircertaigh [1366] and peace was made by the Fir-Manach with the Muinter-Ruairc and their injuries were mutually forgiven for ill to the Clann-Muircertaigh. And the son of Ruaidhri[2] took the place of Cathal Ua Concobuir that year.

(A) An incursion[5] was made by the Muinter-Ruairc into the Breifni in the company of the Fir-Manach and a flank attack was made by

(B) Cathal Mag Flannchadha, chief of Dartraighi, was slain by the clan of Muircertach Ua Concobuir on a night attack.

the young sons of kings of the Clann-Muircertaigh and Cathal Mag [F]lannchadha, chief of Dartraighi, was slain therein.

Muster was made by Domnall Ua Neill and by the Clann-Domnaill, namely, by Toirdhelbach Mac Domnaill and by Alexander Mac Domnaill to attack Niall Ua Neill. And Mac Cathmail was put from out the country by them and that chief went to join Niall Ua Neill. The rear of the migrating forces was overtaken.[6] And[7] Ragnall, son of Alexander, that is, the heir of the Clann-Alexandair, came from Innsi-Gall about that time to Niall Ua Neill. The kerns of the two parties met with one another, that is, the [whole] sept of the Clann-Domnaill. And Raghnall sent messengers to where his own kinsman, namely, Toirdelbach and his son, to wit, Alexander, were, and he asked in honour of the seniority and of the brotherhood not to come against him. And no attention was paid to him and respite was not given to him, but they advanced up to the ford whereon they saw Raghnall and they gave

---

forces of Domnall O'Neill. But this is at variance with the tenor of the more detailed narrative of the Ulster Annals.

[7] *And, etc.*—The episode relative to the coming of the Mac Donnells is introduced to explain their junction with MacCawell on the present occasion.

7 do gonaḋ 7 do marbaḋ daine eteru. Ocus do gabaḋ Alaxandair Mac Domnaill ar in aṫ cetna. Ocus rob'ail le muinntir Raġnaill a marbaḋ 7 nír'leig Raġnall doib; uair adubert naċ biaḋ erbaiḋ a mic 7 a braṫar fair. Ocus do bi mac Caṫmail co n-a marċsluaiġ ic tabairt do ṁarċsluaiġ Domnaill [U]i Neill 7 ruc O Neill feinn orra fa'n ran sin 7 do ġaḃ Domnall dereḋ a marċsluaiġ fein 7 ruc leis iat. Ocus do gonaḋ 7 do marbaḋ moran d'a muinntir.— Caġaḋ mor eter Ġallaiḃ Connaċt 7 Clainn-Muiris d'innarba[ḋ] le Mac Uilliam 7 a n-dul ren cum Clainni-Ricaird 7 sluaiġeḋ | mor do ḋenum le Mac Uilliam 7 le hAeḋ, mac Feiḋlimṫe, ri Connaċt 7 le mac Maġnura [U]i Conċobuir 7 le hUilliam O Ceallaiġ, ri O-Maine, a n-Uaċtar Connaċt cum Clainni-Ricaird. Moran do Muimneċaiḃ d'eirġi le Clainn-Ricaird 7 beiṫ forba raiṫi ag forbairs ar a ceile doiḃ 7 nert do ġaḃail do Mac Uilliam fa ḋeoiġ. Braiġdi Clainni-Ricaird do ṫabairt do leis 7 a tiaċtain fein co beoḋa, laidir do'n turus sin¹.—Muirċertaċ, mac Raġnaill, mic Raġnaill moir Meg Raġnaill, adbur arotairiġ gan erbaiḋ, do marbaḋ a fell la tairec Muinntiri-hEolu[i]s, idon, la Mail-[Sh]eċlainn Mag Raġnaill, in' cet Luan iar Samain¹. Ocus in* tairec le'n-dernaḋ in marbaḋ, a dul fein * d'eg i·cinn da mís d'a eiri.—Huigin Triél do marbaḋ (in' bliaḋain sin¹), idon, triaṫ Fer-Tulaċ, la Clainn-Fheorair 7 fa mór in gnim ġoill" é¹ gan amurus¹.

ᵏ⁻ᵏ Maeil[-Sh]eclainn fein do dul (and Maeil[-Sh]echlainn himself met [lit. to go to] death), B. ˡ⁻ˡ itl. t. h, A.; om., B. ᵐ sin—that—added, B.

⁸ And, etc.—This sentence is a prolepsis. The incidents in question obviously took place after the battle.

⁹ Pressing upon. — Whilst Mac Donnell was engaged with the foot.

¹⁰ And many, etc.—This and the previous sentence are omitted by the Four Masters.

battle to one another. And the son of Raghnall was slain [1366] and wounded between them. And Alexander Mac Domnaill was taken prisoner at the same ford. And[8] it was the wish of the people of Raghnall to kill him: but Raghnall did not allow them; for he said that the loss of his son and kinsman should not be upon him. And Mac Cathmail with his horse-host was pressing upon[9] the horse-host of Domnall Ua Neill and O'Neill himself overtook them . . and Domnall took the rear of his own horse-host and brought them [safe] with him. And many [10] of his people were wounded and killed.—Great war [arose] between the Foreigners of Connacht and the Clann-Maurice were expelled by MacWilliam and they went to the Clann-Ricaird and a great hosting was made by Mac William and by Aedh, son of Feidhlimidh, king of Connacht and by the son of Maghnus Ua Conchobuir and by William O'Cellaigh, king of Ui-Maine, into the upper part of Connacht against the Clann-Ricaird. And many of the Momonians rose out with the Clann-Ricaird and they were the greater part of a quarter [of a year] in leaguer against one another and sway was got by Mac William at the end. The pledges of the Clann-Ricaird were brought by him with him and himself came with spirit and force from that expedition.—Muircertach, son of Raghnall, son of Raghnall Mor Mag Raghnaill, material of an arch-chief without defect, was killed in treachery by the chief of Muinter-hEolu[i]s, namely, by Mail[-Sh]echlainn Mag Raghnaill, the first Monday [11] after November-Day. And the chief by whom was done the killing, he died himself at the end of two months after that.—Huigin Tyrrell, namely, chief of Fir-Tulach, was slain (that year) by the Clann-Feorais [Birmingham] and it was without dispute a great Foreign deed.

---

[11] *First Monday.*—Nov. 2. All Saints fell on Sunday in 1366.

|Cal. 1an. [ui.ª] r., [l.ᵇ xx.uii.ᵇ], Anno Domini M.º ccc.º lx.º 1111.ºᶜ [uii.º] In t-erpuc hUa¹ Ferġail, roon, erpuc Arda-acain, rai ᵈ ġan erbaiḋ ı crabaiḋ, no a n-ḋerc, no a n-ḋeiżeinec, in Chrirto quieuit ᵈ.—Airciḋeoċain Oirġiall, roon, Malaici Maġ Uiḋir, rai ġan urḋubaiḋ n-einiġ, in ᵈ Chrirto quieuit ᵈ.—Sitriuġᵉ, mac in oircinniġ, plait coitcenn conġairec 7 cenn uaral a aicme rein, ḋ'eġ.—Catal, mac Ihair Meġ Tiġernain, irtuḋ' coitcenn do truaġaiḋ 7 do trenaiḋ, ḋ'eġ.— Imirci* mor do ḋenum la Clainn-Muircertaiġ ı Maġ-Nirri 7 toirc do ḋenum doiḃ ar luċt Muiġi-Luirġ, roon, la Taḋġ, mac Ruaiḋri [U]h Concobuir 7 la maiṫiḃ a muinntiri 7 a mortinoil: roon, la Feraġal Maġ Tiġerna[i]n, taireċ Tellaiġ-Dunċaḋa 7 la Diarmait Mhaġ Raġnaill, taireċ Muinntire-hEolu[i]r, a cointinol Ġaiḋel 7 ġalloġlaċ. Lonġport Aeḋa Mic Diarmata do lorcaḋ doiḃ. Feraġal Mac Diarmata, ri Muiġi-Luirġ 7 Aeḋ Mac Diarmata d'eirġi ra'n n-ġuaraċt rin. Gleire ġlan marcruaiġ 7 taċur do ṫabairt doiḃ ann d'a ċeile iġ Ait-tiġi-Mic-Coire 7 breirim maoma do ṫabairt ar luċt Muiġi-Luirġ 7 da rer dec do marbaḋ do maiṫiḃ aera ġraḋa Mic Diarmata 7 Aeḋ rein do lot ann. Ocur Mac Diarmata 7 Aeḋ Mac Diarmata do ġabail derriġ ar a muinntir co beoḋa, laidir o roin amaċ*.—Cu-Chonnaċt hUa¹ Raiġillaiġ, ri Breirne, mortuur ert,—roon, rġel uirriġ ıı

A.D. 1364. ¹O, A. *.uii., A, B. ᵇᵇbl., A, B. ᶜ.1111.ᶜ was put in overhead by the scribe and .lx. above that, by a more modern hand; 1367, B. ᵈᵈ mortuur ert, B. ᵉᵉ om., B. ᶠᶠ taireċ Teallaiġ-Dunċaḋa, d'heġ —chief of Tellach-Dunchadha, died, B.

[1367] ¹ *1364*=1367 of the *A. L. C.*
O'Farrell succeeded Mac Keogh (ob. [1343] *sup.*) as bishop of Ardagh. Ware (p. 152) says he was not consecrated before 1347.

² *Oirgialla.*—Clogher. According to the *A. L. C.*, the archdeacon was one of the principals in the slaying of O'Conor and his associates, mentioned in the first entry of the previous year.

Kalends of Jan. on [6th] feria, [27th] of the moon, A.D. 1364¹[-7]. The bishop, Ua Ferghail, namely, bishop of Ard-achaidh, eminent without defect in piety, or in charity, or in good hospitality, rested in Christ.—The archdeacon of Oirgialla,² namely Malachy Mag Uidhir, eminent without want of hospitality, rested in Christ.—Sitric, son of the herenagh,³ a prince of general fame and noble head of his own sept, died.—Cathal, son of Imar Mag Tigernain, general support for weak and strong, died.—A great migratory incursion⁴ was made by the Clann-Muircertaigh into Magh-Nissi, and an attack was made by them on the people of Magh-Luirg, namely, by Tadhg, son of Ruaidhri Ua Conchobuir and by the nobles of his people, together with their great muster: that is, with Fergal Mag Tigerna[i]n, chief of Tellach-Dunchada and by Diarmait Mag Raghnaill, chief of Muinter-Eolu[i]⁹, along with a muster of Gaidhil and gallowglasses. The stronghold of Aedh Mac Diarmata was burned by them. Fergal Mac Diarmata, king of Magh-Luirg and Aedh Mac Diarmata rose out in that movement. An onset and attack of cavalry exclusively was given to each other at Ait-tighi-Mic-Coise⁵ and decisive defeat was inflicted on the people of Magh-Luirg and twelve persons were killed of the favourite nobles of Mac Diarmata and Aedh himself was injured there. And Mac Diarmata and Aedh Mac Diarmata took charge of the rear of their people spiritedly and powerfully from that out.—Cu-Connacht Ua Raighillaigh, king of Breifni,

---

³ *Herenagh.* — Mag Tighernain (Mac Tiernan).

⁴ *Migratory incursion.* — Undertaken, that is, for the purpose of expelling the Mac Dermots and taking possession of their patrimony, Magh-Luirg (in bar. of Boyle, co. Roscommon).

⁵ *Ait-tighi-Mic-Coise.* — Place of the house of Mac Coise. Not identified.

mó tainíg ¹ᶠ n-ᴅereḋ na haimrири 7 ticrur co braṫ. Ocur co tairbena Ḋia a maiṫ[i]ur rein ᴅoᵉ.— | Ⲁinnriarˢ hUa Taiċliġ, tiġerna ar Leṫ rerainn Muinntir-Taiċliġ, mortuur erṫʰ.—Ḟeiḋlimiḋ hUa¹ Raiġillaiġ ar n-a ṁarbaḋ ᴅ'erġur in bliaḋain rin².—Maiᴅm mor ([Mai]ᴅm¹ Traġa [Eoṫ]aileʲ) ᴅo ṫabairt la Ḋomnall, mac Muircertaiġ 7 la Muintir-Ruairc 7 la Mac Ḋonnċaiḋ 7 la Teboiᴅ a búrc co n-a ceiternaiḋ congbala ar Taḋg, mac Maġnura. Ocur breiṫ rorra ar traiġ Eoṫaile 7 ġalloġlaċa mic Maġnura ᴅo marbaḋ ann—ᴅeiċnemur 7 reċt rċit—ra Ḋomnall, mac Somairle 7 ra Ḋomnall óg, a mac 7 raᵈ ᴅa mac Mic Suiḃne 7 ra mac in errиic [U]i Ḋuḃᴅa 7 ra Uilliam Mac Sitġi·— Toirec ᴅo ḋenum la Clainn-Muircertaiġ ar Muinntir-Ruairc 7 ben [U]i Ruairc moir ᴅo marḃaḋ ᴅo'n turur rin, iᴅon, Ḋirḃail, ingen Mailruanaiġ moir Mic Ḋiarmata. Ocurᵉ ní tainic o Una, ingin riġ Loċlan, ġnim mná buḋ móᵉ.—Toirc aile ᴅo ḋenum ᴅo Clainn-Muircertaiġ ar Ḟeraiḃ-Manaċ 7 Inir-moir ᴅ'arġain ᴅoiḃʲ 7 Loċ-mBerraiġ 7 inᵏ Senaᴅᵏ ᴅ'arġainᵉ ᴅoiḃᵉ 7 éᴅala aiḋbli ᴅo, ṫabairt ᴅoiḃ leo 7 tiaċtainˢ im[ṡ]lan ᴅoiḃ¹ ar a ṅ-aiṫle.

[ⲃir.] |cal. Ian. [ui]r., r., [Lᵃ ixᵃ], Ⲁnno Ḋomini M.° ccc.° lx.° u.°ᵇ[·uiii.°] Ⲁeḋ, mac Ḟeiḋlimṫe¹ hUi Conċoḃuir, airᴅriġ Connaċt, cenn ġoile 7 ġairciḋ Leiṫi Cuinᴅ, ᴅ'ec

² om., B. ³ toiġeċt, B. ᵉ⁻ᶠ irin aimrir n-ᴅeiġenaiġ—*in the latter time,*
B. ʰ⁻ʰ t. m., t. h., A; om., B. ¹⁻¹ l. m., t. h. (brackętted portions were
cut away in trimming the edge), B; om., A. ʲ om., A. ᵏ⁻ᵏ Senaᴅ-
Mic-Maġnura, B. ¹ om. B.
A.D. 1365. ¹·limiḋ, B. ᵃ⁻ᵃbl., A, B. ᵇ .ix. (om. by t. h.) is placed
overhead by the hand that added them in the previous year: 1368,
1369, B.

⁶ *Muircertach. Maghnus.* — O'Conor.
⁷ *Retained kerns.*—Literally, *kerns of maintenance:* retained in permanent service.

died,—namely, the greatest tale respecting a sub-king [1367] that came in the end of time and shall come to doom. And may God show his own goodness to him.—Andrew Ua Taichligh, lord over half the territory of Muinter-Taichligh, died.—Feidhlimidh Ua Raighillaigh was killed by a fall that year.—Great defeat (the Defeat of the Strand of Eothail) was inflicted by Domnall, son of Muircertach [6] and by Muinter-Ruairc and by Mac Donnchaidh and by Theobald de Burgh with their retained kerns[7] on Tadhg, son of Maghnus.[6] And they were overtaken on the Strand of Eothail and the gallowglasses of the son of Maghnus were slain there—seven score and ten—under Domnall, son of Somairle and under Domnall junior, his son and under the two sons of Mac Suibhne and under the son of the bishop Ua Dubhda[8] and under William Mac Sithigi.—A raid was made by the Clann-Muircertaigh on the Muinter-Ruairc and the wife of Ua Ruairc Mor was killed on that expedition, namely, Derbail, daughter of Mailruanaigh Mor Mac Diarmata. And there came not since Una, daughter of the king of Lochlann, a woman of greater beneficence.—Another raid was made by the Clann-Muircertaigh on the Fir-Manach and Inis-mor was pillaged by them and Loch-Berraigh and the Senad were pillaged by them and an excessive amount of valuables was carried off with them by them and they came safe therefrom afterwards.

Kalends of Jan. on [7th] feria, [9th] of the moon, [1368 Bis.] A.D. 136)[1][-8]. Aedh, son of Feidhlimidh Ua Conchobuir, arch-king of Connacht, head of the valour and

---

[8] *Bishop of Ua Dubhda.* — See [1358], note 2, *supra*.

[1368] ! *1365*=1368 of the *A. L. C.*

in° bliaḋain ṙin, iaṙ m-breiṫ buaḋa o ḋoṁan 7 o ḋeṁan°.—
Ferġal Mac Ḋiarmata, rí Muiġe-Luirg, leoṁan° uaiṙli
7 einíc̣ Erenn°, ḋ'eġ.—Cormac oġ Mac Ḋiarmata ḋ'eġ.—
Tomaltac̣, mac Ferġail Mic Ḋiarmata, tanurti Muiġi-
Luirg, ḋ'ec.—Riġe do ġabail ḋ'Aeḋ, mac Concobuir
Mic Ḋiarmata, in° bliaḋain ṙin°.—Cuiceḋ Connacṫ do
ġabail do Ruaiḋri, mac Toirrḋelbaiġ [U]í Concobuir,
in bliaḋain ri².—Ruaiḋri, mac Seonuc Meġ Eoc̣aġa[i]n,
reḋac̣° einíġ 7 eġnuma 7 reiġi ḟeile 7 ḟairrinġe na
Miḋe o baile Aṫa-cliaṫ co baile Aṫa-Luain, iar m-
breiṫ buaḋa o ḋoṁan 7 o ḋeṁon°, ḋ'ec.—Uilliam Sax-
anac̣ Mac Uilliam ḋ'ec.—Sluaiġeḋ mor do ḋenum le
Niall hUa Neill, la ríġ Coicīḋ³ Ulaḋ 7 la haḋbur
airoriġ Erenn a n-Oirġiallaiḃ 7 maiṫ in Coicīḋ uile |
ḋ'eirġi leir ḋ'forbair ar Brian Mac Mhaṫġamna 7
longport do ġabail i⁴ m-bolġan in tire ḋ'U[a] Neill⁴ 7
comaḋa mora do c̣airġrin o Brian° Maġ Maṫġamna
ḋ'Ua Neill: iḋon, leṫ n-Oirġiall do ṫabairt do Niall,
mac Murc̣aḋa, ḋo'n ríġ | do bi roime⁰ rin irtir⁰ 7
comaḋa mora a n-ic Mic Ḋomnaill uaḋa for. hUa⁴
Neill imorro° dia⁵ aentuġaḋ rin. Ocur comuirle° do
ḋenum ḋo° mac Murc̣aḋa Meġ Maṫġamna (iḋon,ᵏ
Niallʰ) 7 ḋ'Alaxandair¹ oġ Mac Ḋomnaill, do° tiġerna

² om., B. ³ .u.iḋ, A; cuiġiḋ, B. ⁴ O, A. ⁵ ḋ'a (syncope for do a), A.
ᵉᵉ om., B. ᵈᵈ doib ar lar in tire, aġ cungnum le Niall, mac Murcaḋa
Meġ Mhaṫġamna—*by them in the midst of the country, in aiding Niall,
son of Murchadh Mag Mathgamna*, B. ᵉ om., B. ᶠᶠ roime ṫrin tir—
before him in the country, B. ᵍ om., A. ʰ⁻ʰ itl., t. h., B; om., A. ¹ Alaxandair, B.

---

² *Died.*—A more detailed account is given in the *A. L. C.*

³ *Kingship.* — Of Magh-Luirg. Tomaltach Mac Dermot, whose obit forms the previous entry, had the prior claim.

⁴ *Ruaidhri.*—Of his descendants, Magheoghegan, who belonged to the same family, writes thus in the second quarter of the seventeenth century: "Tho' mine author maketh this great account of this Rowrie, that he extolleth him beyond reason, yett his issue now, and

prowess of the Half of Conn, died² this year, after [1368] gaining victory from world and from demon.—Ferghal Mac Diarmata, king of Magh-Luirg, lion of the nobleness and hospitality of Ireland, died.—Cormac Mac Diarmata junior died.—Tomaltach, son of Fergal Mac Diarmata, tanist of Magh-Luirg, died.—Kingship³ was taken by Aedh, son of Concobur Mac Diarmata, that year.—The Fifth of Connacht was taken by Ruaidhri, son of Toirdelbach Ua Concobuir, this year.—Ruaidhri,⁴ son of Johnock Mag Eochaga[i]n, hawk of valour and of prowess and of readiness of hospitality and of liberality of Meath from the town of Ath-cliath to the town of Ath-luain, after gaining victory from world and from demon, died.— William⁵ Mac William the Saxon died.—A great hosting was made by Niall Ua Neill, [namely], by the king of Ulster and one worthy to be arch-king of Ireland, into Oirghialla and the nobles of all the Fifth rose out with him for a leaguer on Brian Mac Mathgamna. And a fortified position was taken up in the midst of the territory by Ua Neill. And large donatives were proffered from Brian Mag Mathgamna to Ua Neill: to wit, half of Oirghialla to be given to Niall, son of Murchadh, [namely] to the king that was before that⁶ in the country and large donatives in payment [of the death] of Mac Domnaill⁷ from him likewise. Ua Neill indeed consented to that. But a compact was made by the son of Murchadh Mag Mathgamna (namely, Niall), and by

---

for a long time past, are of the meanest of their own name "[1368].

⁵ *William.*—The *A. L. C.* state he was the heir of the Mac Williams and died of the small pox in Inishcoe (on the border of Lough Conn, co. Mayo).

⁶ *Before that.*—Niall, it can be thus inferred, was deposed by Brian in 1365.

⁷ *Mac Domnaill.* — Who was treacherously seized and cast into a lake by Brian, [1365], *supra*.

na n-gallóglac 7¹ gluaract doib° gan ced do⁶ hUa⁶ Neill, tri coirici commora, cetradaca,ʰ d'innroigid Meg Matgamna. Ocur amur longruirt do cabairt doib air 7 eirgi do Mhag Matgamna co^k lin a ṗednac 7 a uaralcinoil 1 n-a n-agaid 7 maidm do buain arin t-sluaig doib 7 mac Murcada Meg Matgamna (idon,¹ Niall¹), oigrig Oirgiall, do marbad ann 7 Alaxandair óg, mac Toirrdelbaig Mic Domnaill, Conrtabla na n-gallóglac 7 oigri Clainni-Domnaill, do marbad ann 7 Eogan óg, mac Toirrdelbaig, mic Mael-Seclainn [U]i Domnaill, do marbad ann et alii multi.—Cu-Ulad, mac 1[n] girr, cenn aicme² a cinid rein, d'ec 7 a mac, maigirten og raidecta, d'eg ror ag tect a^m Saxanaib^m.— Piacra° O Flaind, adbur tairig Sil-Mailruain[aig], mac tairig rob' ṗerr 'n-a aimrir rein, d'eg 7 a ben, idon, rai mna gan eiliugud°. — Comorba Moedoic—7 airciDeocain na Oreiṗne e° ror°—rer lan do rat in° Spiruta Naeim° 7 do derc 7 do daennact, d'eg in bliadain rin°, ar m-breit buada o doman 7 o deṁon°.— Tomar hUa⁴ Floind, ri hUa⁴-Tuirtri, rai gan erbaid n-einig no uairli, no° oiregdacta°, d'eg in° bliadain r¹°.—

ʲ do (verbal particle), B. ᵏ ᵏ d' O, A.   ᵏ om., B : lin is thus nom. Cf. he came, 100 strong. ˡ·ˡ itl., t. h., A; om., B.   ᵐ·ᵐ o'n Roim—*from Rome*—was first written, then erased and the textual words were placed there. The original transcription can be plainly made out, B.

---

⁸ *Son of the Dwarf.*—See [1365], note 2, *supra*. The *Four Masters* (1368) erroneously state that Mac Cawell died in England. Whereupon, O'Donovan vainly sought (iii. 644) to discover what part of England he taught in.

⁹ *Successor of St. Moedhoc.*— Abbot of Drumlane, co. Cavan. (See Vol. I., p. 554.) *Mo-edh-oc* (my young Aedh) is the devotional form of the name By a fortunate mis-apprehension of the *F. M.*, who, taking them to refer to different persons, copied this and another obit which gives only the name and offices, we learn that the ecclesiastic in question was called Murray O'Farrelly (Muiredhach Ua Fairchellaigh). The herenachy was hereditary in the family. From the present entry it may be concluded that the foundation of St. Aedh had become a house of Regular Canons.

Alexander Mac Domnaill, [that is] by the lord of the [1368] gallowglasses and they went, without leave from Ua Neill, three equal, manageable battalions, to attack Mag Mathgamna. And a camp-attack was delivered by them on him and Mag Mathgamna rose out with the whole of his forces and his noble muster against them. And victory was gained from the [attacking] host by them and the son of Murchadh Mag Mathgamna (namely, Niall), heir of Oirgialla, was slain there and Alexander junior, son of Toirdelbach Mac Domnaill, Constable of the gallowglasses and heir of the Clann-Domnaill, was slain there and Eogan junior, son of Toirdelbach, son of Mail-Sechlainn Ua Domnaill, was slain there along with many others.—Cu-Uladh, son of the Dwarf,[8] family head of his own ilk, died and his son, a young master of learning, died likewise in returning from Saxon-land.—Fiachra O'Flainn, who was to be chief of Sil-Mailruanaigh, the son of a chief that was best in his own time, and his wife, namely, a superior woman without challenge, died.—The successor of [St.] Moedhoc[9]—and he was archdeacon of the Breifni likewise—a man full of the grace of the Holy Spirit and of charity and of humanity, died that year, after gaining victory from world and from demon.—Thomas Ua Floinn, king of Ui-Tuirtri, eminent without defect of generosity, or of nobleness, or of pre-eminence, died this year.—Tadhg, son of Maghnus, son of Cathal

---

[10] *Taken prisoner.*—"Was deceiptfully taken by the king of Connought in his house of Ardankilliu [*Ard-in-choilkin*, height of the little wood: in par. of Killukin, bar. and co. of Roscommon. O'D. iii. 642-3], being brought tither to the king's house by Cormack Mac Donough upon his security; of which villanus dealing that old Irish proverb grew by comparing thereof to any wicked art: *The taking of Mac Manus is no worse*" (Magcogbegan, 1368).

[11] *And—detained.*—Omitted in the other accounts, which state instead that he was delivered up to O'Conor Sligo. For his ultimate fate, see second entry of [1372], *infra*.

Tadg, mac Magnura, mic Cathail Mic Domnaill, do ġabail d'O Cončobuir i feall 'n-a longport fein 7 a čur illaim [U]í Ferġail d'a coimed. Cogaḋ mor d'eirġi a Connaċtaib trid rin eter Mac Uilliam 7 O Con-čoḃair.

Kal. Ian. [ii.ª f., l. xx.ª]. Anno Domini M.º ccc. lx.º u[i.]ºᵇ [-ix.º]. Pilib hUa¹ Raiġillaiġ do ġabail 7 do aiṫriġuḋ d'a braiṫriḃ fein 7 a cur a Cloič Loča²-huač-tair co n-dočar mor air. Ocur an riġ do ġabail do Magnur hUa¹ Raiġillaiġ 7 cagaḋ mor irin ḃreifne trid fein.—Ġeralt Caemanač, aḋḃur airoriġ Laiġen, do marbaḋ do'n Rioire duḃ,—gnim mor do ġaiḋelaiḃ Erenn uile.—Tiġernan hUa¹ Ruairc do ṫul ar creic illorg 7 in creač do ṫabairt doiḃ leo co³ beoḋa⁴ 7 Aeḋ og, mac Aeḋa [U]í Ruairc, do marbaḋ uirre d'hUa⁵ Mhaelaḋuin⁶ Luirg.—In Deġanač hUa¹ ḃard-a[i]n, rai gan erbaiḋ, mortuur ert. — Diarmait Laimderg Mac Murčaḋa, airoriġ Laiġen, do beiṫ illaim rita ag Gallaiḃ Aṫa-cliaṫ, ar n-a ġabail a fell do'n Rioire duḃ 7 a tarraing fa deoiġ doiḃ,—gnim ir mo do ronaḋ a n-dereḋ aimriri. — Matgamain Maen|muiġi hUa¹ ḃriain, ri Tuad-Muman, in t-aen Gaiḋel ir ferr 7 ir oirega do ḃi re [a] linn fein i n-Erinn, a ḋul d'eg 'n-a longport fein, iar m-buaiḋ aiṫriġe. Ocur ḃrian og hUa¹ ḃriain do ġabail a inaiḋ d'a eiri.—Maidm do ṫabairt ar Magnur hUa¹ Rai-ġillaiġ (iḋon. Maidm na Traga, ag Oilen na Tri-

A.D. 1366. ¹ O, A. ² Laċa—, A. ³ go, B. ⁴ -ġa, B. ⁵ d' O, A. ⁶ Mhaol—, B. ᵃ bl., A, B. ᵇ .u.º, A; 1370, B. ᶜ l. m., t. h., A; om., B.

[1369] ¹ *1366=1369 of the A. L. C.*
² *And.—With* in the original.
³ *Great war, etc.—*See the entries, *Defeat, etc.; A naval expedition, etc.,* under this year.

Mac Domnaill, was taken prisoner[10] by O'Conchobuir in treachery in his own stronghold and [11] put into the hands of Ua Ferghail to be detained. Great war arose in Connacht through that between Mac William and O'Conchobhair. [1368]

Kalends of Jun. [on 2nd feria, 20th of the moon], A.D. 1366[1][-9]. Philip Ua Raighillaigh was taken prisoner and deposed by his own kinsmen and he was put into the Rock of Loch-huachtair and [2] great hardship [inflicted] on him. And the kingship was taken by Maghnus Ua Raighillaigh. And great war [3] [arose] in the Breifni through that.—Gerald Caemanach,[4] material of an arch-king of Leinster, was killed by the Black Knight,[5]—a great deed for the Gaidhil of all Ireland.—Tigernan Ua Ruairc went on a foray into Lorg and the prey was brought spiritedly by them with them and Aedh junior, son of Aedh Ua Ruairc, was killed thereon by Ua Maeladu'n of Lorg.—The Dean Ua Barda[i]n,[6] a sage without defect, died.—Diarmait Red-hand Mac Murchadha, arch-king of Leinster, was in long custody with the Foreigners of Ath-cliath, having been captured in treachery by the Black Knight and he was drawn [asunder] at the end by them,—a deed the greatest that was done in the end of time.—Mathgamain Ua Briain of Maenmagh,[7] king of Thomond, the best and the most pre-eminent Gaidhel that was during his own period, died in his own stronghold, after victory of penance. And [his son] Brian Ua [1369]

---

[4] *Caemanach.*—(Mac Murrough) Kavanagh.

[5] *Black Knight.* — Apparently, one of the Dublin Anglo-Irish.

[6] *Ua Bardain.*—As the name is connected (16th entry of this year) with the Conmaicni, this individual, it may be inferred, was dean of Ardagh diocese.

[7] *Of Maenmagh.*—Mahon O'Brien was so called from having been fostered in that locality (the plain surrounding the town of Loughrea, co Galway).

noide'), ṙcě oiḋci ṗoim Luxnuṙaḋ, do na macaiḃ ṙiǵ 7 do Mhaǵ Mhaṫǵamna | 7 do Mac Caba 7 ṁoṙan do muinnṫiṙ [U]i Ṙaiǵillaiǵ do maṙbaḋ ann, ṙo ṫṙi macaiḃ Coṙmaic [U]i Ḟeṙǵail, iḋon, Seuinin 7 Mael[-Sh]eċlainn 7 Ḟeṙǵuṙ. Ocuṙ Ḟeiḋlimiḋ, mac Œḋa in cleiṫiǵ [U]i Conċobuiṙ, do maṙbaḋ ann—mac ṙiǵ ǵan eṙbaiḋ uaiṙli, no einiǵᵈ—7 Donṅ Mac [C]aṙṙuḋa do maṙbaḋ ann ṙoṙ'—en macaṁ Coiǵiḋ Connaċṫ aᵈ ṙeiṁ 7 a ṙoluṙ eǵnum 7 a ṙaiṙ eineċᵈ—7˙ Siṫṙiuǵ na Ṙṙona Macan-Mhaiǵiṙṫiṙ do maṙbaḋ ann—ṙeṙᵈ ṫiǵi aiḋeḋ coiṫcinnᵈ—eṫ alii nulṫi.—hUa¹ Maelaḋuin, ṙi Luiṙǵ, do maṙbaḋ i⁷ ṙeall do macaiḃ Neill [U]i Domnaill 7 Ṗilib Maǵ Uiḋiṙ, ṙi na ṙeṫṫ Ṫuaṫ, do ḃul, loinǵeṙ ṁoṙ, do ḋiǵail⁸ a oǵlaiċ aṙᵗ macaiḃ [U]i Domnaill 7 Niall oǵ hUa¹ Domnaill do maṙbaḋ leiṙ aṙ ṫṙoiḋ loinǵṙi aṙ Ḟinn-loċ.—Caǵaḋ ṁoṙ eṫeṙ Niall hUa¹ Neill 7 Domnall hUa¹ Neill iṙinᵉ bliaḋain ṙinᵉ.—Donnċaḋ hUa¹ Ḃiṙn, ṫaiṙeċ Ṫiṙi-Ḃṙiuin, ṁoṙṫuuṙ eṙṫ.—Ḃṙian, mac Œḋa buiḋe [U]i Neill, aḋbuṙ ṙiǵ Eṙenn d'uaiṙli 7 d'eineċ 7ʰ d'aiṙdeǵnum, do ḃul d'eǵ 'ṙa bliaḋain ṙinʰ.—Eṙṙuc Oḋa hUa¹ Neill, iḋon, eṙṙuc Oiṙǵiall, ṙai ċṙaiḃṫeċ, coinniṙcleċ, aṙᵈ m-bṙeiṫ buaḋa o doman 7 o demon,ᵈ in Chṙiṫo quieuiṫ (ṙeṫṫoᵢ Kalendaṙ. Œǵuṙṫiʲ).—Ṙicaṙd hUa¹ Ṙaiǵillaiǵ, iḋon, eṙṙuc na Ḃṙeiḟne, quieuiṫ in [Chṙiṫo]. — Œiṙċiḋeoċain na

A.D. 1866. ᵈ⁻ᵈ om., B. ⁷ᵃ B. ⁸-ailṫ, A. ⁹ om., A. ᶠ ṙoṙ—*ṙon*, B. ᵍ⁻ᵍ *in bliaḋain ṙi*—*this year*, B. ʰ⁻ʰ ṁoṙṫuuṙ eṙṫ, B. ⁱ⁻ⁱ itl., t. h., A; om., B.

⁸ *At.* — That is, opposite the Island (of Lough Ce), on the mainland. The *A. L. C.*, with less probability, place the battle at Blencup (four miles west of Cavan town).

⁹ *Kings.*—Of Oriel.

¹⁰ *Oirghialla.* — The diocese of Clogher. His successor was appointed by Gregory XI., (Avignon) April 6, 1373. (As the election of this pope did not take place until Dec. 30, 1370, *nos* in the statement of the Bull relative to the reservation made of the collation during the lifetime of Odo is official, not personal).

This was John Ocortran (O'Cor-

Briain junior took his place after him.—Defeat was in- [1369]
flicted on Maghnus Ua Raighillaigh (namely, the Defeat
of the Strand, at⁸ the Island of the Trinity), twenty
nights before Lammas, by the sons of the kings⁹ and by
Mag Mathgamna and by Mac Caba. And many of the
people of Ua Raighillaigh were slain there, under three
sons of Cormac Ua Ferghail, namely, Jenkin and Mael-
Sechlainn and Ferghus. And Feidhlimidh, son of Aedh
Ua Conchobuir of the Quill, a son of a king without lack of nobleness or generosity, was slain there. And
Donn Mac [C]anrubha, the unique youth of the Fifth of
Connacht in joyance and in brilliant prowess and in noble
hospitality, was slain there likewise. And Sitric Mac-in-
Maighistir of the nose, a man that kept a general
guest-house, was slain there. And many others [were
slain there].—Ua Maeladuin, king of Lorg, was killed in
treachery by the sons of Niall Ua Domnaill. And Philip
Mag Uidhir, king of the seven Territories,
went, [with] a large fleet, to avenge his vassal on the sons
of Ua Domnaill and Niall Ua Domnaill junior was slain by
him in a naval engagement on Finn-Loch.—Great war
[arose] between Niall Ua Neill and Domnaill Ua Neill in
that year.—Brian, son of Aedh Ua Neill the Tawny, one fit to
be a king of Ireland for nobleness, for generosity and for
distinguished prowess, died in that year.—Donnchadh
Ua Birn, chief of Tir-Briuin, died.—Bishop Odo Ua
Neill, namely, bishop of Oirghialla,¹⁰ a pious, generous
sage, rested in Christ (on the 6th of the Kalends of
August [July 27]), after gaining victory from world and
from demon.—Richard Ua Raighillaigh, that is, bishop

crain], Benedictine monk, priest
and doctor of Decretals [Canon
Law], of the monastery of St.
James, Wurtzburg. (Theiner, p.
349. From a Rescript of Clement
V., Avignon, Nov. 13, 1310, ib., p.

182, we learn that, by ancient and
approved custom, that monastery
was bound to receive religious
of whatsoever Order, provided
they were Irish by birth or
origin.)

Ureifne do⁴ dul⁴ d'eg ror, ɪoon, Uilliam, Cipcɪdeocain, ɟai aᵹmur ɟ' araile.ʲ—Brian,ᵈ mac Muircertaiᵹ [U]i Concobuir, mac riᵹ maiṫ, mortuur ert.—Seaan, mac Emaind, mic hoibeɪrd, mortuur ert.—Raᵹnull O hAinliḋe ⁊ Cormac O hAinliḋe do ḋul d'eᵹ do cluiċe in riᵹ.—Aeḋ O Birn [do ḋul d'eᵹ] do'n plaiḋ cetna.— Eoin mac Aeḋaᵹa[i]n ⁊ Ᵹillibert O Barda[i]n, da ɼaer macam cruiṫelaḋnaċa Conmaicne, do ḋul d'eᵹ 'rin bliaḋain riᵈ.— Mael-Seċlainn Mhaᵹ Maṫᵹamna, adbur riᵹ Oirᵹiall, mortuur ert.— Maidm mor do ṫabairt la riᵹ Tuaḋ-Muman, ɪoon, la Brian hUaˡ m-Briain, dú in roᵹabaḋ iarla Der-Muman, ɪoon, ᵹeroɪd ⁊ ᵹoill mora na Muman arċena. Ocur ni meinic (doᵏ ṫuitᵏ) doᵈ ḋainiḋᵈ a n-aen inaɪdm riam urdail ar' ṫoit ann ⁊ ar' ᵹabaḋ do Ᵹhallaiḋ Luimneċ do leᵹaḋ ⁊ do luaṫlorcaḋ le Tuaḋ-Muimneċaib do'n turur rin ⁊ ᵹallaḋ do Ᵹillaiḋ óᵹa[ib] in baile do Brian ⁊ do Chuilenaċaib arċena. Ocur Siḋa óᵹ, mac inᵹine h[U]i Dhuiḋiḋir, do ᵹaḋail bardaċta in baile ⁊ rell do ḋenum do Ᵹhallaiḋ Luimniᵹ ar in' laeċmiliḋ. Ocur irˡ⁰ e rin ᵹnim mic tairiᵹ ir mó do rinneḋ aᵈ n-Erinnᵈ arˡ dereḋ inᵐ domainᵐ.—Toirc loinᵹri do ḋenum la Pilib Maᵹ Uiḋir, ɪoon, ri Fer-Manaċ, co n-a macaib riᵹ oᵹa[ib] coˡˡ Loc-uaċtair ⁊

A.D. 1366. ⁹an, B. ¹⁰ar, A. ¹¹ᵹu, A. ᴶᴶom., A. ᵏ⁻ᵏitl., t. b., A; text, B. ˡre—*during*, B. ᵐ⁻ᵐaimrire—*of time*, B.

---

¹¹*Breifni*.— Kilmore diocese. O'Reilly succeeded Mac Kinawe (Mac Conshnama), who died [1355], *supra*

¹²*William*.—O'Farrelly, abbot of Drumlane (*F. M.* 1369). Very likely, brother of Murray, who died the previous year.

¹³*And so on*.—This expression has reference perhaps to the next five entries, which the compiler of B omitted.

¹⁴*Hubert*.—Most probably, de Burgh.

¹⁵*Athletic*.—Literally, *form-expert*. The *F. M.* made the original into *cruiṫealaḋnach*—expert at the harp!

of the Breifni,[11] rested in Christ,—The archdeacon of the [1369] Breifni died likewise ; namely, William,[12] the archdeacon, a felicitous sage, and so on.[13]—Brian, son of Muircertach Ua Concobuir, a good son of a king, died.—John, son of Edmond, son of Hubert,[14] died.—Raghnall O'hAinlidhe and Cormac O'hAinlidhe died of the King's Game. —Aedh O'Birn [died] of the same plague.—John Mac Aedhaga[i]n and Gilbert O'Barda[i]n, two noble, athletic[15] youths of Conmaicni, died in this year.—Mael-Sechlainn Mag Mathgamna, one fit to be king of Oirgialla, died.— Great defeat was inflicted[16] by the king of Thomond, namely, by Brian Ua Briain, wherein were captured the Earl of Desmond, that is, Gerald and the chief Foreigners of Munster likewise. And not often fell in one defeat before such a great tale of persons as fell and as were wounded of Foreigners. Limerick[17] was broken down and quickly burned by the Men of Thomond on that ex. pedition and pledgeship of young hostages of the town was made to Brian and to the Clann-Cuilen likewise. And Sida[18] junior, son of the daughter of Ua Duibidhir, assumed[19] the wardenship of the place. But treachery was practised by the Foreigners of Limerick on the heroic knight. And that was the greatest deed towards the son of a chief that was done in Ireland at the end of the world.—A naval expedition was made by Philip Mag Uidhir, namely, king of Fir-Manach, along with the young sons of kings,[20] to Loch-uachtair and the Rock of

[16] *Inflicted.*—At the Cistercian monastery of Nenay (*of the Fair*, seven miles west of Limerick. *Triumphalia*, etc., s. r. Nenay). Hence the victor is called *Brian catha an Aonaigh*, Brian of the battle of the Aonach, in the family genealogy. (O'Donoghue, *Hist. Mem.*, pp. 134, 545.)

[17] *Limerick, etc.*—At this place, a Latin hand wrote on the margin of B: *Perdicio Limericensis.*

[18] *Sida.*—Son of the chief of the Clann-Cuilen (Mac Namara). *Hist. Mem.*, p. 131-5.

[19] *Assumed.*—On behalf of Brian O'Brien.

[20] *Kings.*—Of Fermanagh.

A 76b Cloć ın loća do ġabaıl doıḃ | 7 Pılıb O Raıġıllaıġ, rí breırne, do ċabaırt aırtı 7 a ruġı rein do ċabaırt do¹² hUa¹² Raıġıllaıġ arır.—Muırġır° hUa hEoġaın, bıcaır ınnrı-caın ror loċ-hErne, mortuur ert quınto Iour Nouembrır.°

B 73b Kal. Ian. [ııı.ª r., l. ı.ª], Anno Domını M.° ccc.° lx.° uıı.°ᵇ [-lxx.°] Sıċ morᶜ, daınġén, deġċaırırı do denum do Cenıul-Eoġaın reınᵈ. Nıall hUa¹ Neıll 7 Domnall, a braċaır, anᵉ tır do roınd' daıb' atorra: braıġde² 7 ruġı o Domnall do Nıall.—Dreırım' maḋma do ċabaırt do Nıall O Neıll, do ruġ Coıcıḋ Ulaḋ, ar Brıan Mag Mhaċṁana, ar rí Oırġıall 7 moran do muınntır Meg Maċġamna do baċaḋ 7 do mıllıuḋ aır. Mac Ġıllı-Cua, raı ġan erbaıḋ, do baċaḋ aırᶠ.—Dubċablaċ, ınġen [U]ı Raıġıllaıġ ıdonᵍ, ınġean Phılıb hUı Raıġıllaıġʰ), ben ḟorta Pılıb Meg Uıdır, d'éġ.—Coġaḋⁱ mor d'eırġı írıu blıaḋaın rı eter Claınn-Muırcertaıġ 7 Muınntır-Ruaırc. O Raıġıllaıġ 7 Mag Uıdır 7 O Ferġaıl 7 O Concobuır d'eırġı do Claınn-Muırcertaıġ 7 a cur a Muınntır-Eolu[ı]r. Ocur Mag Raġnaıll d'a treġan re ronert na ruġ rın 7 a cur cuınd [l. cum] Mıc Uıllıam 7 Mag Tıġerna[ı]n leóʲ.—Indraıġıḋ urbaḋaċ do denam le claınn Aeḋa Mıc Caċṁaıl 7 ruġċaırec Cenıul-Ferabaıġ do marbaḋ doıḃ a reall, ıdon, Ġılla-Patraıġ Mac Caċṁaıl 7 a deġmac, Cu-Ulaḋ óġ 7 a ben³, ınġen Maġnura Meg Maċġamna. Murċaḋ, a derbraċaır, ıᵏ n-aᵏ ınaḋ d'a eırı.—Maġnurˡ O Raıġıllaıġ do ġabaıl

A.D. 1366. ¹²,¹² d' O. A. ᵃ⁻ᵃ 75 d, f. m., t. h., A; om., B.
A.D. 1367. ¹ O. A. ²-oı (pl.), B. ³ bean, A. ᵃ⁻ᵃ 'n-a (aphaeresis of ı), A. ᵉ⁻ᵉ bl., A, B. ᵇ 1371, B. ᶜ om., B. ᵈ Erenn—*of Ireland* (plainly a scribal mistake), A. ᶠ⁻ᶠ do roınn an tırı—*divided* (lit. *to divide*) *the country*, B. ᶠ⁻ᶠ om., B. ᵍ⁻ᵍ ıtl., t. h., A; om., B.

[1370] ¹ *1367*=1370 of the *A. L. C*.

² *Niall, Domnall, brother.*—Placed first, nominative absolute, with *by* governing *them*, in the original.

³ *Crushing defeat.* — Literally,

the Loch was captured by them and Philip Ua Raighillaigh was brought thereout and his own kingship was given to [Philip] Ua Raighillaigh again.—Maurice Ua hEogain, vicar of Inis-cain upon Loch-Erne, died on the 5th of the Ides [9th] of November. [1369]

Kalends of Jan. [on 3rd feria, 1st of the moon,] A.D. 1367[1][-70]. Great, firm, well-established peace was made by the Cenel-Eogain [amongst] themselves. The territory was divided between them by Niall[2] Ua Neill and Domnall,[2] his brother;[2] hostage and kingship [were ceded] by Domnall to Niall.—Crushing defeat[3] was inflicted by Niall O'Neill, [namely,] by the king of the Fifth of Ulster, on Brian Mag Mathgamna, [that is,] on the king of Oirgialla and many of the people of Mag Mathgamna were drowned and [many] slain[4] thereby[5]. Mac Gilli-Cua, a sage without defect, was drowned thereby.—Dubchablach, daughter of Ua Raighillaigh (namely, daughter of Philip Ua Raighillaigh), the married wife of Philip Mag Uidhir, died,—Great war arose in this year between the Clann-Muircertaigh and Muinter-Ruairc. O'Raighillaigh and Mag Uidhir and O'Ferghail and O'Concobuir rose out against the Clann-Muircertaigh and forced them into Muinter-Eolu[i]s. And Mag Raghnaill abandoned them through the excessive power of those kings and they and Mag Tigernain with them were forced to Mac William [de Burgh].—A hurtful attack was made by the sons of Aedh Mac Cathmail and the royal chief of Cenel-Feradhaigh, namely, Gilla-Patraig Mac Cathmail and his good son, Cu-Uladh junior and his wife, the daughter of Maghnus Mag Mathgamna, were killed by them in treachery. Murchadh, his brother, [succeeded] in his place after him.—Maghnus [1370]

---

crushing of defeat. For the idiom, see 1126, note 2, *supra*.

[4] *Slain.*—Literally, *destroyed.*
[5] *Thereby.*—Literally, *thereon.*

le clainn Tomair, mic Matgamna [U]i Raigillaig 7 a tabairt o'O Raigillaig 7 a cur i Cloic Loca-huactair¹.— Catair hUa¹ Concobuir, aobur rig hUa¹-failgi, aʰ toitim ar derev creice la Gallaib na Mive.

[A.D. M.° ccc.° L.° xx.° i.°] Fergal Mac Cocla[i]n o'eg illaim ag U[a] Ceinneioig.—Murcav hUa¹ Mavaga[i]n, reicem coitcenn, aʰ marbav o'en urcur roigve ar derev creice le hUr-Mumain. Ocurᶠ ir vo na gnimaib roigve ar mó avrocair a n-Erinn riam éᶠ.—Brian hUa¹ Ceinneioig, ri Ur-Mumain, vo toitim a fell le Gallaib.— Siubanᶠ cam, ingen [Mic Cartaig], ben Mic Conmara, o'eg ar m-breit buava in einic le.—Airverpuc Tuama, cenn einic Erenn, in Chrirto quieuitᶠ.—Amlaim Mac Senaig, impir rograbac na renma, o'eg von plaigʰ i Tuaim-va-gualano.—Mael-Seclainnᶠ Connaccac O Fergail o'eg.—Catal óg O Fergail o'egᶠ.—Macʲ Magnura Meg Uivir o'eg in bliavain ri : voon, brugaiv coitcenn o' Feraib Erenn, voon, Eacmarcac, mac Magnura, mic Ruaivri, mic Magnura, mic Duin moir 7ᵏ araileᵏʲ.— Artᵏ, mac Amlaim Meg Uivir, mortuur ertᵏ.

(hicʲ natur ert Carolur Magnur Mac Magnura voon, mac Gilla-Phavraig, mic Magnura, mic Airt, mic Amlaim Meg Uivir, rrivie Iour Ianuarii hoc anno.ʲ)

A.D. 1367. ᶠ⸱ᵇ, B. ᵇ ocur—and—prefixed, Λ. ⁱ bl.=5 lett•rs left in (Λ) MS. ʲ-ʲn. t. h., A; text, B. ᵏ-ᵏom.. A. ¹-ʲn. t. h., A; om., B.

ᵃ *O'Raighillaigh*. — Philip (O'Reilly), who thus got possession of the kinsman by whom he had been deposed and imprisoned the previous year.

[1371] ¹ *Fergal, etc.*—Of the following nine entries, the *A. L. C.* give the first, second (in a shorter form), third and fifth under 1371; the *F. M.* have the fourth and seventh at 1370.

Ua Ceinneidigh. - The O'Kennedy mentioned in the next entry but one.

³ *Ua Madagain.*—See Vol. I., p. 557, note 8, *supra*.

⁴ *Of Mac Carthaigh.*—Supplied from the *Four Masters.*

⁵ *Archbishop of Tuaim.* —John O'Grady (1365-71). There can be little doubt of his identity with the *Johannes Ogrado*, cleric of Killaloe diocese and Bachelor in Civil Law, who first received papal dispen-

O'Raighillaigh was taken prisoner by the sons of Thomas, [1370] son of Mathgamain O'Raighillaigh and given up to O'Raighillaigh [6] and put in the Rock of Loch-uachtair.—Cathair Ua Concobuir, one fit to be king of Ui-Failghe, fell in the rear of a foray party by the Foreigners of Meath.

[A.D. 1371.] Fergal[1] Mac Cochla[i]n died in custody [1371] with Ua Ceinneidigh.[2]—Murchadh Ua Madaga[i]n,[3] general patron, was killed with one shot of an arrow, at the rear of a foray party, by [the Men of] Ormond. And it is one of the greatest deeds of an arrow that ever occurred in Ireland. — Brian Ua Ceinneidigh, king of Ormond, fell in treachery by the Foreigners.—Joan the stooped, daughter [of Mac Carthaigh[4]], wife of Mac Conmara, died after her gaining the victory of hospitality.—The archbishop of Tuaim,[5] head of the hospitality of Ireland, rested in Christ.—Amlaim Mac Senaigh, accomplished emperor of melody, died of the plague in Tuaim-daghualann.—Mael-Sechlainn O'Ferghail the Connacian[6] died. Cathal O'Ferghail junior died.—The son of Maghnus Mag Uidhir died this year: to wit, a general entertainer to the Men of Ireland, namely, Eachmarcach, son of Maghnus, son of Ruaidhri, son of Donn Mor and so on.—Art, son of Amhlam Mag Uidhir, died.

(Here[1] was born Cathal Mor Mac Maghnusa: namely, (1367) son of Gilla-Padraig, son of Maghnus, son of Art, son of Amhlam Mag Uidhir, the 2nd of the Ides [12th] of January this year.)

---

sation in illegitimacy to the extent of promotion to priesthood and collation to a benefice with cure of souls, and subsequently, his petition being supported by the metropolitan, his own Ordinary and several more bishops of the Cashel province, on the ground (amongst others) that his part of Ireland for the most part lacked literate men, was declared by Innocent VI. (July 17, 1358) capable to accept and retain any, even episcopal, dignity. (Theiner, p. 313.)

[6] *Connacian.*—O'Farrell was so called from having been fostered in Connaught.

(1267) [1] *Here, etc.*—This item I have not found elsewhere.

A 76c [bt.]]Kal. 1an. [u.ᵃ f., l. xx.111.ᵃ], Anno Domini M.° ccc.° lx.°
uiii.°ᵇ[-lxx.° 11.°] Brian mór Mag' Mhatgamna, airpomg
Oirgiall, lam ir mó do marb Ghallaib 7 do Gaidelaib
Erenn i n-a aimrir rein in' rer rin° 7 a dul a coinne
Gall 7 gallóglac d'a muinntir rein do² fell² aᵈ n-uaigner airᵈ 7 a marbad dó 7 a dul rein ar d'a éiri.—
Feall ir gruamda 7 ir grainemla do rindeb³ a n-Erinn
riam do denum do Domnall, mac Muircertaig [U]i
Concobuir: idon, mac a brathar rein, Tadg óg, mac
Magnura, do marbad d'a lamaib rein a cairlen Sligib
7 re iᶜ laim aigi ann.—Seaan hUa⁵ Dubaga[i]n, airo-
rencaib naᵉ hErenn, ar ragbail aibnira in t-raegail
rui re rect m-bliadan 7 a eg ag Muinntir Eoin Bairti
a Rinn-nduin'.—Macᶜ Pheorair do gabail le hO Cellaig
7 le [a] macaib; Risderd, [mac] Mic Pheorair, do marbad, idon, oigri Mic Pheorair.—Uilliam óg, mac
Uilleag, cenn ruarcair Erenn d'eg in bliadain cetna'.—
Uilliam óg hUa⁵ Ceallaig, adburᵉ inreicim coitcinn ir
rerr do bí i n-Erinn', d'éc in' bliadain rí'. Ocurᶜ ní
tainic o Cormac na Loinger, mac Concobuir, anuar
mac rig bud rerr inar.ᶜ

B 73c [A.D. M.° ccc.° lxx° 111.°] | Indraigid do denum do
Ghallaib na Mide a Muinntir-Angaile 7 Ruaidri, mac
Catail [U]i Phergail, do marbad 7 a mac 7 moran d'a
muinntir 7 Donncad hUa⁵ Pergail d'a leanmain 7

A.D. 1368. ¹ At first, c was placed over M (= Mac), but subsequently
erased, B. ².³ d'fell (the elision of o arose from the infection of f), A.
³ ronad, B. ⁴ a, B. ⁵ O, A, ᵃᵃ bl., A, B. ᵇ 1372, B. ᶜᶜ om., B.
ᵈᵈ air, a n-uaigner, B. ᵉᵉ mait, mortuur ert—(arch antiquary)
excellent, died, B. ᶠᶠ om., A.

[1372] ¹ Brian, etc.—Of the six opening entries of the textual year 1368, the A. L. C. give the first, third, fifth and sixth at 1372; the second, at 1371.

² In custody.—See [1368], note 11, supra.

³ Ua Dubagain.—Well known as the author of a poem descriptive of the native tribes and territories of Ulster, Connaught and Meath. It has been edited by O'Donovan (Ir. Arch. & Celt. Soc., Dublin, 1862). A quatrain above the average from

Kalends of Jan. [on 5th feria, 23rd of the moon,] [1372 Bis
A.D. 1368[-72.] Brian[1] Mor Mac Mathgamna, arch-king
of Oirgialla, the hand that most slew of the Foreigners
and of the Gaidhil of Ireland in his own time [was] that
man and he went against the Foreigners and a gallowglass of his own people fell upon him treacherously in a
solitary place and he was slain by him and [the assassin]
himself escaped thereafter.—Treachery the most repulsive
and hateful that was ever done in Ireland was done by
Domnall, son of Muircertach Ua Conchobuir: to wit, the
son of his own kinsman, namely, Tadhg junior, son of
Magnus, was slain by his own hands in the castle of
Sligech, whilst he was in custody[2] with him therein.—
John Ua Dubaga[i]n,[3] arch-historian of Ireland, abandoned the delight of the world for the space of seven
years and died with the Community of John the Baptist
in Rinn-duin.—Mac Feorais [Birmingham] was taken
prisoner by O'Cellaigh and by his sons, and Richard,
[son] of Mac Feorais, that is, the heir of Mac Feorais, was
killed.—William junior, son of William [de Burgh],
head of the urbanity of Ireland, died the same year.—
William junior Ua Cellaigh, the best material of a general
generous patron that was in Ireland, died this year. And
there came not from Cormac of the Banishments[4],
son of Concobur [son of Ness], downwards a son of a king
that was better than he.

[A.D. 1373.] Attack[1] was made by the Foreigners of [1373]
Meath on the Muinter-Anghaile and Ruaidhri, son of
Cathal Ua Ferghail and his son and many of his people
were slain. And Donnchadh Ua Ferghail followed them

---

another poem (in *Debide*) is given
by O'Curry (*MS. Mat.*, p. 658).
See O'D., *F. M.*, iii. 655.

[4] *Of the Banishments.*—For the
origin of the name, see O'Curry,
MS. Mat., p. 260; for the chro-

nology, *Todd Lect.*, III. pp. 282,
302.

[1373] [1] *Attack, etc.*—Of the eight
remaining entries of the textual
year 1368, all, except the third and
eighth, are given (with differences

moṗan do maṗbaḋ oib leiṗ 7 en uṗċuṗ ṗoiẓoi o'a maṗbaḋ ṗein. Ocuṡ ṡo buḋ ṁaiom oo'n t-ṡluaẕ uile, aċt'
muna beiṫ in t-oṗċuṗ ṗin.—William Dalatuin 7 Seiṗ-
ṗiam na Miḋe do maṗbaḋ la Cenel-Ḟhiaċaiḋ 7 la hUa
Maelṡ[-Sh]eċlainn.—Mael-Seċlainn⁰ Connaċtaċ O Neill
o'eẓ⁰.—Aḋaṁ hUa⁶ Ciana[i]n o'eẓ in⁶ bliaḋain ṗi i n-a
cananaċ⁶, aṗ n-a ẕeṗṗaḋ do⁶ ċananċaiḋ leṗa-ẕaḋail,
aṗᵢ m-bṗeiṫ buaḋa o oeṁon 7 o ooman¹.—Ḋaṗṗouḋ,
inẕen [U]ḣ Ruaiṗc, o'eẓ.⁰—Ẕaeṫ moṗ iṗin bliaḋain ṗinᶠ,
leṗ'bṗiṗeoᶤ tiẓi 7 templa imḋa.—Coiṗṗoelbaċ⁰ ṗuaḋ
O Concoḃaiṗ do beiṫ aẕ ṗiḋal Maċaiṗe Connaċt iṗin
bliaḋain ṗin 7 a teċt tṗio imiṗceoaiḋ Mic in Ṗeṗṗu[i]n Mic Ḟheoṗaiṗ, oa maṗcaċ deẓ. Ocuṡ ẕilla o'a
ṁuinntiṗ do ṫoẕḋail ceinnbeṗti leiṗ a ceṗaiẕ. Ocuṡ
muinnteṗ Mic an Ṗeṗṗu[i]n o'a leanmuin 7 bṗeiṫ
oṗṗa do'n maṗcṡluaẕ. Ocuṡ Coiṗṗoelbaċ ṗuaḋ ṡein
do ẕaḃail oeṗiḋ aṗ a muinntiṗ. Ocuṡ niṡ'ṗeẓaḋ ooiḋ
aṗ tuṡ, aċt imuṗcṗaiẕ in maṗcṡluaiẕ do | ṫoṗtaḋ oṗṗa.
Iṡ ṡeṗḋa ṡo ṡuilnẕeḋ leoṗan in t-anṡoṗlaṁ ṗin; uaiṗ
do maṗb Coiṗṗoelbaċ ṗuaḋ oṗem oiḋ 7 ṗo maṗbaḋ blaḋ
o'a muinntiṗ ṗiun. Cumuṡc do Mac an Ṗeṗṗu[i]n
7 do Coiṗṗoelbaċ ṗuaḋ aṗ a ċeile 7⁰ Mac an Ṗeṗṗu[i]nᵏ
do toitim leiṗ¹ o'aen buille cloiḋim."' Ocuṡ⁰ ni oeṗnaḋ
iṗin aimṡiṗ ṗin maṗbaḋ iṡ cṗoḋa 7 aṗ mó noṗ [ná] in
maṗbaḋ ṗin⁰.—Maṫaᵃ, mac Oẕaiṗ Meẓ Uiḋiṗ, quieuit

A.D. 1368. ᵉ hO, A. ᶠ om., B. ʰ a-by, B. ᶤ⁻ᶤ 7 aṗaile—and so on, B.
ʲ do bṗiṡ—(that) broke, B. ᵏ Mic Ḟheoṗaiṗ—Mac Fheorais—added, B.
¹ leCoiṗṗoelbaċ ṗuaḋ hUa Concoḃuiṗ—by Toirdelbach Ua Concobair the
Red, B. This and the preceding addition were necessary to identify the
persons intended. ᵐ⁻ᵐ an bliaḋain [ṗi]—(this) year—added, B. ⁿ⁻ⁿ 76c,
f. m., t. h. (the first word is cut away), A ; text, B.

---

of detail) in the A. L. C. under 1373. The third is given at the same year by the Four Masters.

² Dalton.—The A. L. C. erroneously make him and the sheriff one person.

³ Ua Cianain.—See O'Reilly : Irish Writers, p. 102.

and many of them were slain by him and one shot of an [1373] arrow killed himself. And it had been defeat for all the host, had it not been for that shot.—William Dalton [2] and the Sheriff of Meath were killed by the Cenel-Fiachaidh and by Ua Mael[-Sh]echlainn—Mael-Sechlainn O'Neill the Connacian died.—Adam Ua Ciana[i]n [3] died this year a canon, after [4] being tonsured by the canons of Lisgabhail, on gaining victory from world and from demon.— Barrdubh,[5] daughter of Ua Ruairc, died.—Great wind in this year, whereby were broken down houses and churches numerous.—Toirdelbach O'Concobhair the Red was traversing the Plain of Connacht on foot that year and he went through the raiders, twelve horse-men [strong], of The son of the Parson Mac Feorais. And a gillie of his [O'Conor's] people raised [6] a helmet to him for annoyance. And the people of The son of the Parson followed them and they were overtaken by the horse-host. And Toirdelbach the Red himself occupied the rear of his people. And no look-out was kept by them at first, so that [7] the excessive force of the horse-host poured [unawares] on them. Most courageously was that onset borne by them; for Toirdelbach the Red slew a portion of them and some of his people were slain. [Single] combat [was given] by The son of the Parson and by Toirdelbach to each other and The son of the Parson fell by him with one stroke of a sword. And there was not done in that time a slaying that was more courageous and of greater fame than that slaying.—Matthew, son of Oscar Mag Uidhir, rested in

---

[4] *After, etc.*—The meaning is that he was formally admitted as canon a short time before his death.

[5] *Barrdubh.*—*Black[-haired] head.* Wife of Domnall Mac Tiernan, *A. L. C.*

[6] *Raised—annoyance.* — That is, saluted Birmingham derisively. Instead of *for*, the original has *in*.

[7] *So that.*—Literally, *but* (consequently).

iní Chriſtoí, decimoº quarto Kalendaſ Nouembriſᶜ 7 a derbráta[i]ſ, idon, Seaan, macᶠ Orcairí, do marbad iſin lo cetnaⁿ.

Kal. Ian. 1.ᵃ p.ˢ, [L.ᵇ x.u.ᵇ], Anno Domini M.º ccc.º lx.º ix.º[-lxx.º 1111.º] Seinicin Sadair do marbad le Mag Aengura inᵈ bliadain ſiᵈ 7ᵉ iſ dilecta in eiſri d'a eiriⁱ.— Cormac, mac micᶠ Tomaltaiġ [U]i Ferġail, do marbad. —Domnall óg hUa¹ Dočartaiġ, in mac tairiſ rob'ferr do bíᶜ 1² n-Erinn do beaġan; feičemᵉ coitcinn neoč ar mó do tinnlaic d'ečadᵇ 7 do freid d'aer elaſna Erenn 7 diċ ar mó d'a ruair in eiſri ar dered domainº, d'eg ᵖ, arᵍ m-breiċ buada o doman 7 o demonˢ.—Toirrdelbač, mac Briain Meg Tiġerna[i]n, d'eg.—Cú-coigriči og Mag Eočaga[i]n, tairec Cene[oi]l-Fhiačaig, do marbad a feall ar n-dul dó le eſruc na Miſe co hAč-Luain 7 duine do muinntir Uilliam Dalatun d'a marbad d'aen buille rleiġe. Ocur ni dernad ann ačt rin.—Tedoid a Burc, oigri Mic Uilliam, do marbad le hi-Maineˢ: nečᵉ ba mó 7 ra haille 7 crečaiſe coitcenn ar Connačtaib e rorᵉ.—Tiġernan, mac Briain Meg Thiġerna[i]n, macᵒ tairiġ beoda, laidenʳ d'eg in' bliadain ſiˢ.—Maidm la Niall hUa¹ Neill, la riġ Coicid Ulad, ar Ghallaib, dú in ro čuit in rioſere 7 Dogra na Cairrgi 7 an Sandalač 7 an Burcač 7 Uilliam Baile-dalat, cenn ainfeile Erenn. — Mael[-Sh]ečlainn,ᵘ mac Diarmata [U]i Ferġail, do dul ar coġad ar a tir rein a Muinntir-

A.D. 1369. ¹ O, A. ² a, B. ³ hlb—, B. ⁴ om., B. ⁵ bl., A, B. ⁶ 1373, B. ⁷ om., A. ⁸ om., B. ⁹ om., B. ¹⁰ co teŕc (=de beaġan, which is omitted) added, B. ¹¹ a eg—*his death (took place)*, B.

[1374] ¹ *1369.*—The ferial (1) proves that the true year is 1375. From this to the textual year 1373 (=1378), inclusive, the A.D. reckoning, the ferial notation shows, is five years in advance.

² *Bishop of Meath.* — Stephen de Valle. Appointed bishop of Limerick by Innocent VI. (Avignon, Nov. 6. 1360), having been elected by the majority of the Chapter. At the time, he was subdeacon and dean. Being but twenty-nine years old, he received

Christ on the 14th of the Kalends of November [Oct. [1373] 19] and his brother, namely, John, son of Oscar, was killed on the same day.

Kalends of Jan. on 1st feria, [15th of the moon,] A.D. [1374] 1369 [-74]. Jenkin Savage was killed by Mag Aengusa this year and orphaned is learning after him.—Cormac, grandson of Tomaltach Ua Ferghail, was killed.—Domnall Ua Dochartaigh junior, the son of a chief that was almost the best in Ireland; general patron, that bestowed most of horses and chattel to the learned folk of Ireland and the greatest loss which the erudite received at the end of the world, died, after gaining victory from world and from demon.—Toirdelbach, son of Brian Mag Tigernain, died.—Cu-coicrichi Mag Eochaga[i]n junior, chief of Cenel-Fiachaigh, was killed in treachery, after going with the bishop of Meath[2] to Ath-luain. And it was a person[3] of the people of William Dalton that killed him with one thrust of a spear. And nothing was done there but that.—Theobald de Burgh, heir of Mac William, was killed by the Ui-Maine: one that was most excellent and most beautiful and a general depredator on the Connachtmen likewise was he.—Tigernan, son of Brian Mag Tigerna[i]n, a spirited, powerful son of a chief, died this year.—Defeat [was inflicted] by Niall Ua Neill, [namely,] by the king of the Fifth of Ulster, on the Foreigners, wherein fell the Knight[4] and Bogsa of the Rock[5] and the Sandal and the de Burgh and William of Baile-dalat, head of splendid hospitality[6] of Ireland.—Mael[-Sh]echlainn, son of Diarmait Ua Ferghail, went on a war from

---

a dispensation in the impediment of age. (Theiner, p. 316.) He was translated to Meath by Urban V., Feb. 19, 1369 (ib. p. 333), and died in 1379 (Ware, ed. Harris, p. 147).

[3] *Person.*—The slayer, according to the *A. L. C.*, was hanged and quartered.

[4] *Knight.*—The *A. L. C.* state his name was Roche.

[5] *Rock.*—*Of Fergus*; i.e. Carrickfergus.

Mailmorḋa. Ocur ruaiʒ do ṫabairt do Ʒhallaiḃ orrṫa 7 Mail[-Sh]eċlainn do marbaḋ ann'.—Taḋʒ óʒ Máʒ Raʒnaill do marbaḋ d'en urċur roiʒde 7 ní rer̃· a deimin cia tuc, aċt Muinnter-Ḃirn 'ʒa ċur ar Clainn-Muircertaiʒ 7 Clann-Muircertaiʒ 'ʒa ċor oriuaran'. Caʒaḋ d'eirʒi trit rin' eter Muinntir-Eolu[i]r' 7 Muinntir-Ḃirn'.—Taḋʒ, mac Ruaiḋri h[U]i Concobuir, in' t-en mac riʒ rob' rerr eineċ 7 eʒnum i n-a aimrir rein', aᵏ eʒ la r̃eil Starain i Connaċta, iar m-breiṫ buaḋa do oman 7 o deṁan.ᵏ

Kal. Ian. ii. r̃., [L.ᵃ xx.ui.ᵃ], Anno Domini M.º ccc.º lxx.º[-lxx.º u.º] Maṫʒamain, mac Maʒnura [U]i Conċobuir, macº riʒ beoḋa, quieuit in [Christo].º—Cairlen

A 77a Rora-Comain | do ʒabail doᵈ Ruaiḋri hUa Concobuir, la riʒ Connaċt. Ocur Cairlen Baile-in-tobair do ṫabairt do Thoirrdelbaċ ruaḋ ar 7 comaḋa imḋa naċ" arimter runn'.—Serrraiʒ, mac Ʒilla-na-naem [U]i r̃erʒail,

B 73d teannaḋbur | tairiʒ na hAnʒaile, quieuitº in [Christo]ᶠ. —Macᶠ [C]arta[i]n, urriʒ Cene[oi]l-r̃hoʒartaiʒ, do marbaḋ a r̃eall d'a braṫair rein, idon, do mac Ʒille-Ṫernaind'.—Sluaiʒeḋ mor la Niall hUaⁱ Neill co Dun-da-leaṫʒlar 7 maidm mor do ṫabairt ar Ʒallaiḃ leir, du i troċair² Sar Semur Baile-aṫa-ṫid, rer inaid riʒ Saxan 7 an Buirċaċ Caimlinne do marbaḋ ann et alii

A.D. 1369. ʲ—rum, B. ¹ om., A. ʲ·ʲ Muinntir-Ḃirn 7 Muinntir-Eolu[i]r, B. ᵏ·ᵏ d'heʒ an bliadain ri—*died this year*, B.
A.D. 1370. ¹ O, A. ² torċair, B. ᵃ·ᵃ bl., A, B. ᵇ 1374, B. ᶜ·ᶜ d'heʒ —*died*, B. ᵈ *la—by*, B. ᵉ·ᵉ aili—*other*, B. ᶠ·ᶠ om., B.

⁶ *Splendid hospitality.* — *Ainfeile* in the original. Mistaking *ain* (*an*, splendid) for the negative prefix, the F. M. insert the eclipsis and aspiration (*ainbhféle*). Whereupon, O'Donovan (iv. 660) renders it "inhospitality" and annotates accordingly. This is adopted in the A. L. C., although the text has the correct form (*anfeli*). The adjective *an* does not affect the following letter.

⁷ *Mael[-Sh]echlainn, Tadhg.*—The A. L. C. erroneously state they both died a natural death.

out his own country into Muinter-Mailmordha. And an [1374] attack was delivered by the Foreigners upon them and Mail[-Sh]echlinn[7] was slain therein.—Tadhg[7] Mag Rughnaill junior was killed by one shot of an arrow. And it was not known with certainty who discharged it, but the Muinter-Birn [were] a-putting it on the Clann-Muircertaigh and the Clann-Muircertaigh a-putting it on these. War arose through that between the Muinter-Eolu[i]s and Muinter-Birn.—Tadhg, son of Ruaidhri Ua Concobuir, the one son of a king that was best of hospitality and prowess in his own time, died in Connacht on the feast day of Stephen [Dec. 26], after gaining victory from world and from demon.

Kalends of Jan. on 2nd feria, [26th of the moon,] A.D. [1375] 1370[1][-5]. Mathgamain, son of Maghnus Ua Conchobuir, a spirited son of a king, rested in Christ.—The castle of Ros-Comain was taken by Ruaidhri Ua Concobuir, [namely] by the king of Connacht. And the castle of Baile-in-tobair and many donatives that are not reckoned here were given to Toirdelbach[2] the Red in lieu.—Geoffrey, son of Gilla-na-naem Ua Ferghail, well worthy to be chief of the hAnghaile, rested in Christ.—Mac [C]artain, sub-king of Cenel-Foghartaigh, was killed in treachery by his own kinsman, namely, by the son of Gilla-Termainn [Mac Cartain].—A great hosting by Niall Ua Neill to Dun-da-lethglas and great defeat was inflicted on the Foreigners by him, wherein fell Sir James[3] of Baile-atha-thid, Deputy of the king of the Saxons. And the de Burgh of Caimlinn and many others were slain therein.

[1375] [1]*1370*.—The ferial (2) proves that the true year is 1375.
[2] *Toirdelbach.*—Turlough O'Conor.
[3] *Sir James.*—Talbot of Malahide (*Baile-atha-thid*). The Deputy at the time was William de Windsor (for the second time), 1373-6. Gilbert, *Viceroys*, pp. 234-41.

multi.—Cu-Ulaḋ Maġ Maṫġamna, ṁḋamna Oiṗġiall a eġ do cuiṡlinn.—[A.D.] 1375ᶜ. Aṗt Maġ Uiḋiṗ, mac ṗiġ lan d'eineċ 7 d'eġnum, quieuit in [Chṗiṗto].—Donnċaḋ Caemanaċ Mac Muṗċaḋa, aiṗḋṗi[s] Laiġen—7 ní tainic o ḃṗian ḃoṗuṁa anuaṡ[h] ṡeṗ iṡ mó do ḋiṫaiġ do Danuṗaiḃ anáṡ—a maṗḃaḋ do Ġallaiḃ a ṗell.—Donnċaḋ, mac Taiḋġ, mic Concoḃuiṗ in copain, do maṗḃaḋ do Mhuinntiṗ-ḃiṗn.—Toiṡc do ċuaḋaṗ clann Meġ Tiġeṗnain aṗ inḋṗoiġiḋ cum Ġall, iḋon, Caiṗḃṗi 7 Eoġan. Ocuṡ an ṡeṗ ḃṗaiṫ d'a cṗeic ṡe Ġallaiḃ 7 Ġoill do tinol i[t] n-a[d] timcell 7 coiceṗ[s] aṗ ṗiṫiṫ[s] do maṗḃaḋ ann.—Mac Ṗheóṗaiṗ, tiġeṗna ḃaile-aṫa-na-ṗiġ, d'éġ—Mac Uilliam ḃúṗc, iḋon, Emonn Alḃanaċ, cenn ġoile 7 ġaiṗciḋ na Ġalltaċta 7 impeṗ in eġnuma, d'eġ do'n ṡlun i n-a ṫiġ ṡein, aṗ' m-ḃṗeiṫ ḃuaḋa o ḋemon.¹ Ocuṡ a mac do ġaḃail a inaiḋ d'a eiṗi.—Mail[-Sh]eċlainn hUa Domnalla[i]n, aṗḋ ollam Leiṫi Cuinn, d'eġʲ iaṗ m-ḃṗeiṫ ḃuaḋa o ḋoman 7 o ḋemon¹.—Iohanneṡᵏ Maġ Uiḋiṗ, aḃḃ Cluana-Eóiṡ, moṗtuuṡ eṡt decimo ṡeṗtimo Kalendaṡ Iulii.ᵏ

(Mauṗiciuṡʲ hUa hEoġain oḃiit octauo Iouṡ Maii¹.

Noᵏ ġumaḋ aṗ in Kallainn ṡi ḃuḋ coiṗ eṡṗuc Oḋa [hUa Neill] do ḃeiṫ.ᵏ)

[ḃiṗ.] Kal. Ian. iii. ṡ. [L.ᵃ uii.ᵃ], Anno Domini M.° ccc.° Lxx. i.ᵒᵇ [-ui.°] Taḋġ hUa¹ Ruaiṗc, ṗi ḃṗeiṡne, d'eġᶜ aṗ m-

A.D. 1370. ³⁻¹ġ, A, ⁴⁻⁴ n-a (aphaeresis of i), A. ⁵⁻⁵ .xx. u., A, B. ᵍ Arabica, l. m., t. h., A; om., B. ʰ om., A. ¹⁻¹ 7 aṗaile—*and so on*, B. ʲ⁻ʲ moṗtuuṡ eṡt, B. ᵏ⁻ᵏ 76d, f. m., t. h., A; om., B. In the (A) MS. the No precedes the Iohanneṡ entry. ¹⁻¹ 77a, t. m., n. t. h., A; om., B. A.D. 1371. ¹ O, A. ᵃ⁻ᵃ bl., A., B. ᵇ 1375 overhead, B. ᶜ⁻ᶜ moṗtuuṡ eṡt, B.

---

⁴ *Foreigners.*—Literally, *Danes;* here applied to the Anglo-Irish.

⁵ *Tadhg.*—Mac Rannall (Mag Raghnaill), who died [1353], *supra.* The *A. L. C.* incorrectly represent Donough as son (instead of grandson) of Conor.

⁶ *Five and twenty.*—Including the two sons of Mac Tiernan (*A. L. C.*).

⁷ *Scotsman.*—So styled, doubtless, from long residence in Scotland.

—Cu-Uladh Mag Mathgamna, royal heir of Oirgialla, died from [the bursting of] a vein.—[A.D.] 1375. Art Mag Uidhir, a son of a king full of generosity and of prowess, rested in Christ.—Donnchadh Caemanach Mac-Murchadha, arch-king of Leinster—and there came not from Brian Boruma downwards a man that destroyed more of the Foreigners[4] than he—was killed by the Foreigners in treachery.—Donnchadh, son of Tadhg,[5] son of Concobur of the Cup, was slain by the Muinter-Birn.—The sons of Mag Tigernain, namely, Cairbri and Eogan, went on an expedition to attack the Foreigners. And a traitor sold them to the Foreigners and the Foreigners assembled around them and five and twenty[6] were slain there.—Mac Feorais, lord of the town of Ath-na-righ, died.—Mac William de Burgh, namely, Edmond the Scotsman,[7] head of courage and prowess of the Foreigners and emperor of benevolence, died of the glandular disease in his own house, after gaining victory from the demon. And his son took his place after him.—Mail-[Sh]echlainn Ua Domnalla[i]n, the greatest[8] ollam of the Half of Conn, died after gaining victory from world and from demon.—John Mag Uidhir, abbot of Cluain-Eois, died on the 17th of the Kalends of July [June 15].

(Maurice[1] Ua hEoghain died on the 8th of the Ides [6th] of June.

Or[2] it may be on this Kalend [year] it were right for [the death of] bishop Odo [Ua Neill] to be.)

Kalends of Jan. on 3rd feria, [7th of the moon], A.D. 1371[1][-6]. Tadhg Ua Ruairc, king of the Breifni, died,[2]

[1375]

(1370)

[1376 Bis.]

---

[8] *Greatest.*—Literally, high (pre-eminent). The O'Donnellans were the poets of the Connaught O'Conors.

(1370) [1] *Maurice, etc.*—This entry I have not found elsewhere.

[2] *Or, etc.*—The obit of bishop O'Neill is given at [1369], *supra*.

The suggested correction is erroneous.

[1376] [1] *1371.*—The ferial (3) proves that the true year is 1376.

[2] *Died.*—And was succeeded by his son, Tighernan (Tiernan), *A. L. C.* and *F. M.*

bpeiṫ buaḋa o ṫoman 7 o ḋemon͘.—Ḋonnċaḋ Mac Ḟiriḃiriẋ, ṗenċaiḋ ṗaiẋeċta,ᵈ ꝺ'eẋᵉ.—Nualaiṫ,ᶠ inẋen [U]i Raiẋillaiẋ, ben Tomair Mic Maṫẋamna, ꝺ'eẋ.—Cu-Ocicne O Concoḃair, mac riẋ lan ꝺ'einec 7 ꝺ'eẋnuṁ, ꝺ'eẋ.— Ruaṗcan hUa¹ hOComaill, ollam [U]i Anluain ṗe ꝺan 7° ṗer tiẋi n-aiꝺeḋ coitcinn ẋan ꝺiultaḋ ṗe ꝺreic n-ꝺuine, ꝺ'eẋ irin bliaḋain ri, iar m-bṗeiṫ buaḋa [o ꝺoman 7 o ꝺemonᵉ].—Cu-Muiẋi hUa¹ Caṫa[i]n, ri Oireċta-[U]i-Caṫa[i]n, ꝺo ẋabail ꝺo Ẋhallaiḃ a poṗt Cula-ṗatain 7 a ċur ꝺoiḃ hi² Carṗaiẋ-Ḟherẋura. Inꝺṗaiẋiḋᶠ ꝺo ḃenam ꝺo macaiḃ riẋ Oireċta-[U]i-Caṫa[i]n aṗ Ẋallaiḃ 7 Ẋoill ꝺo ċaḃairt maꝺma móir orṗa͘. Eoinᶜ hUa¹ Ruanaḋa, ollaṁ Meẋ Oenẋura, ꝺ'eẋ͘ᵉ—Mail-Seċlainn hUa¹ Mailṁena, ollam [U]i Caṫa[i], ꝺ'eẋᵉ ṗorᵉ.—Aeḋ hUa¹ Tuaṫail, ri hUa¹-Mail, ꝺo marḃaḋ ꝺo Ẋallaiḃ.— Ꝺalbaċ, mac Mail-tSeċlainn [U]i Ḃroin, cenn einiẋ 7 eẋnuṁa Laiẋen, ꝺo ẋuin ꝺ'á ṗṗor ṗein 7 a eẋ ꝺe ro cetoir.— Aeḋ, mac Seaain [U]i Ḟherẋail, ꝺ'eẋ. Roiḃeṗt h[U]a¹ Ḟerẋail, ꝺ'eẋ͘ᵉ ṗorᵉ.—Coimtinolᶠ mór le Ẋallaiḃ na Miḋe 7 ṗe Ẋallaiḃ Ulaḋ 7 le Ẋallaiḃ Laiẋen cum na hOCnẋaile 7 creaca rill ꝺo ꝺenum ꝺoiḃ aṗ O Ḟerẋail. Ꝺiẋulta mora ꝺo ꝺenum ꝺ'O Ḟerẋail orrarun ꝺo creċaiḃ 7 ꝺo loiṗc[ṫ]iḃ imḋai[ḃ]ᶠ.—Conċoḃur hUa¹ ḃeaca[i]n, rai renċura, ꝺ'éẋ͘.—Ceallaċ Mac Cruitin, ollam Tuaḋ-Muman ṗe renċur, ṗerᵒ noir ẋan imperain, ꝺ'eẋ.

(Aẋʰ ro in ḳallainn aṗ tiẋ marḃaḋ Ḃriain moir Meẋ Maṫẋamna iaṗ ṗír 7 a aꝺnucal a Máinirtir Luẋḃaiꝺ, ṫeṗtio Nonar Iuini, rcilicet, Anno Domini, 1371.ʰ)

A.D. 1371. ²a, A. ᵈ maṫ—*good*, B. ᵉ=͡. ᶠ⁻ᶠ om., B. ᵍ Before this entry one line is left vacant, A. ᵇ⁻ʰ 77a, f. m., n. t. h., A; om., B.

---

³ *Cu - Muighi.—Canis Campi.* "This name is now generally anglicised Quintin [!]. It is still very common among the family of the O'Kanes in the co. of Londonderry" (O'D. iv. 666).

⁴ *Oirecht-Ui-Cathain. — Sept of [the] Ua Cathain;* here, in a secondary sense (*cf.* 1163, note 3, *supra*), the territory occupied by them.

⁵ *Ua Ruanadha.*—See 1079, note 1, *supra*.

after gaining victory from world and from demon.— [1376]
Donnchadh Mac Firbisigh, an erudite historian, died.—Cu-Aithne O'Concobhair, a son of a king full of generosity and of prowess, died.—Ruarcan Ua hAdmail, ollam of Ua Anluain in poetry and a man of a general house of guests, without objection to the presence of anybody, died in this year, after gaining victory [from world and from demon].—Cu-muighi[3] Ua Catha[i]n, king of Oirecht-Ui-Cathain,[4] was taken prisoner by the Foreigners in the port of Cuil-rathain and put by them into Carraic-Ferghusa. An attack was made by the sons of kings of Oirecht-Ui-Cathain on the Foreigners and the Foreigners inflicted great defeat upon them—John Ua Ruanadha,[5] ollam of Mag Aenghusa, died.—Mail-Sechlainn Ua Mailmhena, ollam of Ua Catha[i]n, died likewise.—Aedh Ua Tuathail, king of Ui-Mail, was killed by Foreigners.—Dalbach, son of Mail-Sechlainn Ua Broin, head of hospitality and prowess of Leinster, was wounded by his own spur and died thereof immediately.—Aedh,[6] son of John Ua Ferghail, died. Robert Ua Ferghail died likewise.—A great muster by the Foreigners of Meath and by the Foreigners of Ulidia and by the Foreigners of Leinster against the hAnghaile and treacherous forays were made by them on O'Ferghail. Great retaliations were made by O'Ferghail on them by many preys and burnings.—Conchobur Ua Beaca[i]n, a sage of history, died.—Ceallach Mac Cruitin, ollam of Thomond in history, a man of reputation without dispute, died.

(This[1] is the Kalend [year] on which truly comes the (1371)
killing of Brian Mor Mag Mathgamna and he was buried in the Monastery of Lughbhaidh on the 3rd of the Nones [3rd] of June, namely, A.D. 1371.)

---

[6] *Aedh.*—The obit in the *F. M.* contains a eulogium of his bounty towards the bardic companies of Ireland.

(1371)[1] *This, etc.* The correction refers to the first entry of [1372], *supra*.

558

[Cal. 1an. [u.ᵃ f., L x.uııı.ᵃ], Anno Domini M.° ccc.° Lxx.° 11.°ᵇ[-uııı.°] baicep,ᶜ mac 8ap Daıbıč, d'eg.—8eſſpaıg hUa¹ flannaga[ı]n, caıpeč Claınnı-Cačaıl, d'egᵈ.— Nualaıčᵉ, ıngen Caıdg Mıc Donnčaıd, d'eg.—Coıpc do denum do Rıcapc óg ap Cuılenačaıb : ſopbaıpı da la 7 da aıdčı do denum doıb apcıp. Culenaıg do cınol ſa Aed Mac Conmapa, ıdon, mac ıngıne U[ı] Dhalaıg 7 maıdm do čabaıpc ap Claınn-Rıcaıpd ann, dú ınap'mapbad Cebord Mac Uıllıam, cenn na ceıčıpne moıpe 7 cpı meıc O n-eıdın 7 mopan aıle. Ocuſ do gabad ann bpıan O flaıčbepcaıgᶜ.—8eaan hUa¹ Roduča[ı]n, comapba Caıllín, ſaí coıččenn d'egᵈ ın° blıadaın ſı°.— | In c-eſpuc hUa¹ Ceallaıg, ıdon, eſpuc Cluana-ſepca drenuınn, d'egᶜ.—Caıplen Lıſ-aıpd-abla do denam la 8eaan hUa¹ ſepgaıl, caıpeč na hAngaıle, ın blıadaın ſı. —Cogadᶜ móp d'eıpgı ecep O Concobuıp 7 Mac Dıapmaca 7 Mag-Luıpg do ṁıllıud, ecep gopc 7 cег. Ocuſ daıne do mapbad acoppa. Ocuſ ſıd do denum d'a eıſ doıb 7 comada mopa d'ſagbaıl do Mac Dıapmaca uad hUa Concobuıp do cınn ın c-ſıda ſınᶜ.—Indſaıgıd do denum do Mac Uıllıam 7 do Mael[-8h]eċlaınn hUa Chellaıg 7 do Maınečaıb apčena ap hUa¹ Conċobuıp | co caıplen Roſa-Comaın 7 hUa¹ Concobuıp d'eıpgı 'n-a n-agaıd co n-a ſocpaıdıb 7 cſoıd do čabaıpc d'aᶠ čeıle doıbᵍ 7 maıdm do čabaıpc ap Mac Uıllıam 7 ap Maınečaıb 7 Rıſdepd a dupc, cenn ſuapcu[ı]ſ Connačc, do mapbad ann 7 Dom-

A.D. 1372. ¹O, A. ᵃᵃbl., A, B. ᵇ1376, 1377, B. ᶜom., B. ᵈmoſcuuſ eſc, B. ᵉom. (no doubt, by oversight), B. ᶠᵍdoıb d'a čeıle, B.

[1377] ¹ *1372*.—The ferial (3) of the previous year and that (6) of the following prove that the intermediate ferial is 5=A.D. 1377.

² *De Burgh*.—From the *A. L. C.*

³ *Aedh, Mathgamain.* — Halfbrothers of Sida, warden of Limerick [1369], *supra*. Their father was Loughlin Mac Namara mentioned in the *F. M.* at 1378. See also O'Donoghue, *Hist. Mem.*, p. 135.

⁴ *Successor of St. Caillin.*—That is, abbot of Fenagh, co. Leitrim. The

Kalends of Jan. [on 5th feria, 18th of the moon], A.D. [1877] 1372¹[-7]. Walter, son of Sir David [de Burgh²], died.—Geoffrey Ua Flannaga[i]n, chief of Clann-Cathail, died.—Nualaith, daughter of Tadhg Mac Donnchaidh, died.—An incursion was made by Richard [de Burgh] junior on the Clann-Cuilen: a leaguer of two days and two nights was made by them in the country. The Clann-Cuilen assembled under Aedh³ Mac Conmara, namely, the son of the daughter of Ua Dalaigh and defeat was inflicted on the Clann-Ricaird there, wherein were killed Theobald Mac William, head of the large kern-force, and three sons of O'Eidhin and many others. And Brian O'Flaithbertaigh was taken prisoner there.—John Ua Rodacha[i]n, successor of [St.] Caillin,⁴ a general sage, died this year.—The bishop Ua Ceallaigh,⁵ namely, bishop of Cluain-ferta of [St.] Brennan, died.—The castle of Lis-aird-abla⁶ was built by John Ua Ferghail, chief of the hAngbaile, this year.—Great war arose between O'Concobuir and Mac Diarmata and Magh-Luirg was destroyed, both tillage and dwelling. And people were killed between them. And peace was made after that by them and large donatives were got by Mac Diarmata from Ua Concobuir for the sake of that peace.—An attack was made by Mac William [de Burgh] and by Mael-Sechlainn Ua Cellaigh and by the Ui-Maine on Ua Conchobuir at the castle of Ros-Comain. And Ua Concobuir arose against them with his forces and battle was given to each other by them. And defeat was inflicted on Mac William and on the Ui-Maine and Richard de Burgh, head of the urbanity of Connacht, was slain there and Domnall,

---

feast of the patron was Nov. 13. The *Book of Fenagh*, falsely ascribed to St. Caillin, has been published (Dublin, 1875).

⁵ *Ua Cellaigh.*—Most probably, the Thomas O'Kelly, who, according to Ware (ed. Harris, p. 640), was bishop of Clonfert in October, 1347.

⁶ *Lis-aird-abla.*—*Fort of the height of apples.*

nall mac Catail óig [U]i Concobuip, do mapbaḋ ann 7
Taḋg og, mac mic Taiḋg [U]i Ceallaiġ 7 hUa¹ Maidnin
mop 7 Mac Dubġaill do mapbaḋ ann póp 7 mac Neill
caim 7 mopan aile.—Mael-Domnaiġ pigleċ°; paċtna,
mac Daibiċ [U]i Mhópda, d'eg.—Edubapd, pi Saxan,
d'eg ᵈ.—Donnċaḋ, mac Uilliam alaind [U]i Cepball, pi
Eile, paiᶜ n-einiġ 7 n-eġnumaᵉ, d'eg ᵈ inᵉ bliaḋain piᶜ.—
Maṫgamain Mac Conmapa, idon, mac inġine [U]i
Dhalaiġ, d'eg inᵉ bliaḋain pinᵉ.—Mainípτep Epa-puaiḋ
do lopcaḋ 'pa bliaḋain ceτnaᵉ.—Ġoppraiġ, mac Annaiġ
[U]i Raigillaiġ, do mapbaḋ do Cloind-in-ċaiċ².—Mac
Ḃpana[i]n bacaċ d'eg a cuipτ in³ Pápa 7 in deganaċ
mop, Mac Muirġipa.—Domnall ʰ hUa Ġallċobuip, idon,
mac pepġail, mic Inmanaiġ, moptuup epτ.ʰ

Kal. Ian. ui. p., [Lᵃ xx. ix.ᵃ], Anno Domini M.° ccc.°
lxx.° iii.°ᵇ [-uiii.°] Mopᵉ, inġen [U]i pepġail, ben Diapmada Meg Raġnaill, idon, τaipeċ Muinnτepi-hEolu[i]p,
pai mna ġan impepain, d'eg do bap Onġτa 7 aiṫpiġe 7 a
hadlucuḋ i Cluain-Conmaicne co honopaċ°.—Toippdel-
bac Mac Suibne, apd Conpτabla Coiciḋ Connaċτ, d'eg ᵈ

A.D. 1372. ²ċaeiċ. B. ³an, B. ⁴ pi—*this*, B. The order in B is:
Mainipτep—Maτġamain. ʰ⁻ʰ 77b, r. m. (imperfect, owing to excision
of edge), n. t. h., A ; text supplied from B.

A.D. 1373. ᵃ⁻ᵃ bl., A, B. ᵇ The third i is n. t. h., A ; 1378, B. ᶜ⁻ᶜ om.,
B. ᵈ moptuup epτ, B.

---

⁷ *Died.*—June 21, 1377.

⁸ *Clann-in-caich.* — Clan *of the
Blind* (O'Reilly ; sl. 1256, *supra*) ;
anglicised Clankee, a bar. in co.
Cavan, the patrimony of the sept.

⁹ *Mac Branain.*—Dermot, lord
of Corca-Achlann (the Mac Branan
territory in the east of co. Roscommon), A. L. C.

¹⁰ *Mac Muirghisa.*--From a Rescript of Gregory XI. (Anagni,
Aug. 29, 1377), we learn (what the
native Annals, as far as I know,
have omitted to record) that, on
the death of O'Finaghty ([1354]
supra), before the collation reserved to the Curia was made,
Charles, the archdeacon, procured
his election by the Chapter, got it
confirmed by Thomas [O'Carroll]
of Tuam, and had himself consecrated bishop of Elphin. One of
the acts for which he was excommunicated by bishop Thomas

son of Cathal Ua Concobuir junior, was slain there and [1377] Tadhg junior, grandson of Tadhg Ua Ceallaigh and Ua Mainnin Mor and Mac Dubghaill and the son of Niall [Mac Neill] the Crooked and many others were slain there likewise.—Mael-Domnaigh the vigil-keeper, [and] Fachtna, son of David Ua Mordha, died.—Edward [III.], king of the Saxons, died.[7]—Donnchadh, son of William Ua Cerbaill the handsome, king of Eili, eminent in hospitality and prowess, died this year.—Mathgamain[3] Mac Conmara, namely, the son of the daughter of Ua Dalaigh, died in that year.—The Monastery of Es-ruadh was burned in the same year.—Geoffrey, son of Annagh Ua Raighillaigh, was killed by the Clann-in-caich.[8]—Mac Brana[i]n[9] the Lame and the great Dean, Mac Muirghisa[10], died in the court of the Pope.—Domnall Ua Gallchobuir, namely, son of Eerghal, son of Inmanagh, died.

Kalends of Jan. on 6th feria, [29th of the moon,] A.D. [1378] 1373[1][-8]. Mor, daughter of Ua Ferghail, wife of Diarmait Mag Raghnaill, namely, the chief of Muinter-Eolu[i]s, an excellent woman without dispute, died a death of Unction and penance and was buried honourably in Cluain-Conmaicne.—Toirdelbach Mac Suibne, high

---

[appointed by the same pope, on the translation of Gregory to Tuam in 1372] was the confirmation of elections to dignities (Theiner, p. 363).

In the account returned by John de Cabrespino, papal Nuncio in England and Ireland, of benefices granted in the third year of Urban V. (1362-70), it is stated that the canonical election and subsequent confirmation by bishop Charles of canon Thomas Ma[c]murgoasa [the Mac Muirghisa of the text] was ratified by the Curia on Feb. 5 and confirmed (by the pope) on Feb. 14, 1365 (ib. p. 340).

The most probable explanation is that Gregory remained in the papal Court until his elevation to Tuam and tacitly acquiesced in the administration of the diocese by the bishop in possession.

From the fact of Mac Morrissey dying in Rome it may be inferred that he proceeded thither in connection with the charges mentioned in the Rescript.

[1378] [1] *1373*—The ferial (6) proves that the true year is 1378.

in⁰ bliaδain ceυnaᶜ.—Caŧalᶜ, mac Mael-τ8eċlainn (micᵉ Ϛilla-Iρa ρuaιδ⁺) [U]ι Raιξillaιξ, υo éξ.—Ϛilla-Cριrτ O Ruaιρc υ'eξᵈ.—Peaρξalᶠ O Mail-Mίaδaιξ, τaιρeċ Muinnτιρι-Ceρballa[ι]n, ρaí coιτċenn ξanᵉ υιulτaδ ρe υuine,ᵉ υ'eξᵈ.—Bριan Maξ Uιδιρ, aδbuρ ριξ Peρ-Manaċ, υo maρbaδ υoᶠ cloιnυ Αιρτ Meξ Uιδιρ.—Domnall Maξ Bρaυaιξ, τaιρeċ Teallaιξ-Ceρδaιll, ρaι coιτċenn, υ'eξᵈ inᵉ bliaδain ριnᶜ.—Vaιτeρ Mac Uιlliam Buρc υo maρbaδ le Muιnnτιρ-Maιlle ιριnᵉ bliaδain ceτnaᶜ.—Bρan hUa¹ Bρain, ρί hUa-Paela[ι]n, cenn beoδaċτa 7 eίnιξ na Laιξneċ, υ'eξ.—Maξnuρ, mac Caŧaιl óιξ [U]ι Concobuιρ, υ'eξ inᵉ bliaδain ceτna.ᶜ—| Inυ-ροιξιδᵉ υo δenum υo Maξ Raξnaιll co n-a bρaιŧριδ 7 co n-a oιρeċτaιδ 7 υo δa Cloιnυ-Αeδa 7 υ'Peρξal hUa Ruaιρc aρ Caŧal ρuaδ Maξ Raξnaιll. Caŧal υo τιnol a ceιŧιρn 7 a ċaρaυ 7 a cleamnaċ, ιυon, ρa Dιaρmaιτ Mac n-Dιaρmaτa 7 ρa Domnall n-υuδ, aρ cίnn na ρocρaιυe ριn. Maξ Raξnaιll co n-a ṁuιnnτιρ υo maŧṁaċuδ ann. Eċτa moρa υo maρbaδ aρ an maιυm ριn, ιυon, Peρξal Maξ Raξnaιll—cenn ρonuρa 7 ρaιδρίρa an ρaeρŧeρ ριn—7 Mac 8enυlaιċ 7 Mac Ϛille-υuιδ 7 moρ an aιle naċ aιρímŧeρ ρunn.—Dubċablaċ, ιnξen Meξ Raξnaιll, bean [U]ι Maιl-Mhίaδaιξ, υ'eξ.—Donnċaδ, mac Muιρceρτaιξ [U]ι Concobuιρ, υ'eξᶜ.—Uιlliam hUa¹ hUíξιnυ υ'eξ inᵉ bliaδain ceτnaᶜ.—Bριanᵉ mac Taιδξ, mιc Ruaιδρí, [U]ι Chonċobaιρ, υo maρbaδ.—8eaan hUa Pιala[ι]n, ιυon, ollam maιŧ ρe υan, υ'eξ ιn bliaδaιn ριᵉ.—Eoιn hUa Droma, bιcaιρ Cιlle-Naaιleᵍ, moρτuuρ eρτ quιnτoᵃ Iouρ Decιmbριrᶜʰ. |

A.D. 1373. ¹ O, A. ²-uιle, B.—ᵉ-itl., n. t. h., (A) MS. ᶠ The order in B is: Peρξal—Uaιτeρ—Bριan. ᵍ e—by, B.

ʰ The remainder of A 77d was left vacant by the original hand.

ᵉ *High Constable.*—This term is used to denote the chief captain of gallowglasses (O'D. iv. 670).

ᶠ *By the sons of.*—Omitted in O'Donovan's translation (iv. 673).

Constable [2] of the Fifth of Connacht, died the same year.—[1373] Cathal, son of Mael-Sechlainn (son of Gilla-Isu the Red) Ua Raighillaigh, died.—Gilla-Crist O'Ruairc died.— Ferghal O'Mail-miadhaigh, chief of Muinter-Cerballa[i]u, a generous man in general without refusal to anybody, died.—Brian Mag Uidhir, one fit to be king of Fir-Manach, was killed by the sons of[3] Art Mag Uidhir.— Domnall Mac Bradaigh, chief of the Tellach-Cerbaill, a general sage, died in that year.—Walter Mac William de Burgh was killed by the Muinter-Maille in the same year.—Bran Ua Brain, king of Ui-Faela[i]n, head of the courage and liberality of the Lagenians, died.—Maghnus, son of Cathal Ua Concobuir junior, died the same year.— Attack was made by Mag Raghnaill with his kinsmen and with his septs and by the two Clans of Aedh[4] [Ua Ferghail] and by Fergal Ua Ruairc on Cathal Mag Raghnaill the Red. Cathal mustered his kerns and his friends and his marriage-kindred, namely, under Diarmait Mac Diarmata and under Domnall[5] the Black, to make head against those forces. Mag Raighnaill with his people was defeated there. Great numbers were killed in that defeat, namely, Fergal Mag Raghnaill—head of happiness and wealth was that noble man—and Mac Sennlaich and Mac Gille-duibh and many others that are not reckoned here.—Dubchablach, daughter of Mag Raghnaill, wife of Ua Mail-Miadhaigh, died —Donnchadh, son of Muircertach Ua Concobuir, died.—William Ua hUiginn died the the same year.—Brian, son of Tadhg, son of Ruaidhri Ua Conchobair, was killed.—John Ua Fiala[i]n, namely, a good ollam in poetry, died this year.—John Ua Droma, vicar of Cell-Naaille[6], died on the 5th of the Ides [9th] of December.

---

[4] *Two Clans of Aedh.*—Namely, of Aedh (Hugh) O'Farrell, i.e. the Clann-Hugh and the Clann-Shane (for whom see [1355], note 5 *supra*).

[5] *Domnall.*—Mac Dermot.

(Laraipṗina¹, ingen Maiġirtep Tomair Mic Ghilla-Choirgle, d'heg octauo Idur Maii, 1373¹.)

Kal. Ian. [i. ḟ., l. xu.,] Anno Domini M.° ccc.° lxx· iiii.°

Kal. Ian. [ii. ḟ., l. xxui.,] Anno Domini M.° ccc.° lxx.° u.° Dubcablaiġ, ingen hUa Concobuir, mortuur ert quarto Idur Auguṙti.—Orcar, mac Airt, mic Fhlaiṫbertaiġ Meg Uidir, mortuur ert.

Kal. Ian. [iii. ḟ., l. uii.,] Anno Domini M.° ccc.° lxx· ui.° Mac Craiṫ Mag Uidir mortuur ert.

Kal. Ian. [u. ḟ., l. xuiii.,] Anno Domini M.° ccc.° lxx.° uii.° Pol hUa Fiala[i]n mortuur ert.

Kal. Ian. [ui. ḟ., l. xxix.,] Anno Domini M." ccc.° lxx· uiii.°

A.D. 1373. ¹⁻¹ t. m., n. t. h.. A ; om., B.

* *Cell-Naaile.*—*Church of* [St.] *Naile* (whose feast was Jan. 27). The parish containing the church of Kinnawley (an instance of *l* replaced by *n*) is partly in the barony of Knockninny, co. Fermanagh, and partly in the barony of Tullyhaw, co. Cavan. See O'D. *F. M.* iv. 708–9; Kelly: *Calendar of Irish Saints,* p. 62.

A.D. 1374–8. These five textual years are omitted in A. In the (B) MS., spaces are left for the respective ferials and epacts. Folio 74b is occupied by the years being placed at wide intervals.

(END OF VOL. II.)

(Lasairghina,[1] daughter of Master Thomas Mac Gilla-Coisgle, died on the 8th of the Ides [8th] of May, [A.D.] 1373.) (1373)

Kalends of Jan. [on 1st feria, 15th of the moon,] A.D. 1374. (1374)

Kalends of Jan. [on 2nd feria, 26th of the moon,] A.D. 1375. Dubchablaigh[1] daughter of Ua Concobuir, died on the 4th of the Ides [10th] of August.—Oscar, son of Art, son of Flaithbertach Mag Uidhir, died. (1375)

Kalends of Jan. [on 3rd feria, 7th of the moon,] A.D. 1376. Mac Craith Mag Uidhir died. (1376)

Kalends of Jan. [on 5th feria, 18th of the moon,] A.D. 1377. Paul Ua Fiala[i]n died. (1377)

Kalends of Jan. [on 6th feria, 29th of the moon,] A.D. 1378. (1378)

(1373) [1] *Lasairghina, etc.*—This obit I have not found elsewhere.

⁎ On the blank space left in A, a different hand wrote the following: ꝼač aon ℓei[ṡ]ꝼuꞃ an bec ꞃo, caḃꞃaḋ benḋačč aꞃ anmuin an ꝼiꞃ ꞃo ꞃcꞃaiḃ. Each one that shall read this little bit, let him bestow a blessing on the soul of the man who wrote [it].

Whereon another commented thus: Iꞃ coꞃa a caḃuiꞃč aꞃ anmain Ruaiꞃꞃi hI Ɫuinin do ꞃꞅꞃiḃ an Ɫeaḃuꞃ co maič. It is fitter to bestow it on the soul of Ruaidri O'Luinin who wrote the book well.

(1375) [1] *Dubchablaigh, etc.*—The entries under this and the two following years are taken from a source with which I am unacquainted.

(END OF VOL. II.)

27

THE BORROWER WILL BE CHARGED
AN OVERDUE FEE IF THIS BOOK IS
NOT RETURNED TO THE LIBRARY ON
OR BEFORE THE LAST DATE STAMPED
BELOW. NON-RECEIPT OF OVERDUE
NOTICES DOES NOT EXEMPT THE
BORROWER FROM OVERDUE FEES.

Harvard College Widener Library
Cambridge, MA 02138   (617) 495-2413